THE
ANNUAL REGISTER
Vol. 225

ANNUAL REGISTER ADVISORY BOARD

CHAIRMAN AND EDITOR

H. V. HODSON

ASSISTANT EDITOR

VERENA HOFFMAN

CHARLES OSBORNE
Literature Director of the Arts Council of Great Britain
NOMINATED BY
THE ARTS COUNCIL OF GREAT BRITAIN

FRANK E. CLOSE, BSc, PhD
Senior Principal Scientific Officer, Rutherford Appleton Laboratory
NOMINATED BY
THE BRITISH ASSOCIATION FOR THE ADVANCEMENT OF SCIENCE

M. R. D. FOOT
Formerly Professor of Modern History, University of Manchester
NOMINATED BY
THE ROYAL HISTORICAL SOCIETY

MICHAEL KASER
Fellow of St Antony's College, Oxford
NOMINATED BY
THE ROYAL INSTITUTE OF INTERNATIONAL AFFAIRS

THE LORD ROBBINS, CH, CB
Sometime Professor of Economics at the London School of Economics and Political Science

JAMES BISHOP
Editor, The Illustrated London News

Dramatic events in the Middle East in 1983 included a split in the Palestine Liberation Organization, resulting in the departure of its chairman, Yassir Arafat, with his armed followers, from Tripoli in Lebanon, his reconciliation with President Mubarak of Egypt and his arrival with a thousand men in North Yemen. Symbolic of that unexpected development is this picture of him kissing the Egyptian flag officially presented to him with other gifts, on his voyage through the Suez Canal.

Rex Features

THE
ANNUAL REGISTER

A Record of World Events

1983

Edited by

H. V. HODSON

Assisted by

VERENA HOFFMAN

FIRST EDITED IN 1758
BY EDMUND BURKE

Poynter Institute for Media Studies
Library

MAR 29 '89

GALE RESEARCH COMPANY
DETROIT
1984

Distributed exclusively in the United States and possessions, Canada and Mexico by Gale Research Company, Book Tower, Detroit, Michigan
© Longman Group Limited 1984
ISBN 0-8103-2033-9
Library of Congress Catalog Card Number 4-17979

PRINTED IN GREAT BRITAIN

CONTENTS

PREFACE TO 225th VOLUME   xiii
EDITORIAL

I HISTORY OF THE UNITED KINGDOM
1 Politics before the Election   7
2 Labour Meets Disaster   14
3 Post-Election Turbulence   21
4 The New Parliament   28
5 Foreign and Commonwealth Affairs   35
6 Crime and Punishment   42
7 Scotland   42
8 Wales   45
9 Northern Ireland   46

II THE AMERICAS AND THE CARIBBEAN
1 The United States of America   50
2 Canada   69
3 Latin America: Argentina 75   Bolivia 76   Brazil 77   Chile 78   Colombia 79   Ecuador 80   Paraguay 80   Peru 81   Uruguay 82   Venezuela 83   Cuba 83   The Dominican Republic and Haiti 84   Central America 85   Mexico 87   74
4 Jamaica 88   Grenada 91   The Windward and Leeward Islands 93   Trinidad and Tobago 95   Guyana 96   Barbados 96   Belize 97   The Bahamas 97   Suriname 98   88

III THE USSR AND EASTERN EUROPE
1 The USSR   100
2 German Democratic Republic 107   Poland 109   Czechoslovakia 112   Hungary 115   Romania 117   Bulgaria 119   Yugoslavia 121   Albania 123   Mongolia 124   107

IV WESTERN, CENTRAL AND SOUTHERN EUROPE
1 France 127   Federal Republic of Germany 133   Italy 138   Belgium 141   The Netherlands 143   Luxembourg 144   Republic of Ireland 145   127
2 Denmark 148   Iceland 150   Norway 151   Sweden 152   Finland 154   Austria 155   Switzerland 157   148
3 Spain 159   Portugal 163   Malta 165   Gibraltar 166   Greece 167   Cyprus 169   Turkey 172   159

V THE MIDDLE EAST AND NORTH AFRICA
1 Israel   175
2 The Arab World 179   Egypt 181   Jordan 183   Syria 184   Lebanon 186   Iraq 190   179
3 Saudi Arabia 192   Yemen Arab Republic 194   People's Democratic Republic of Yemen 195   The Arab States of the Gulf 195   192
4 Sudan 200   Libya 202   Tunisia 204   Western Sahara 206   Algeria 207   Morocco 208   200

CONTENTS

VI EQUATORIAL AFRICA

1 Ethiopia 210   Somalia 212   Djibouti 213   Kenya 213   Tanzania 215
   Uganda 217   210
2 Ghana 219   Nigeria 220   Sierra Leone 223   The Gambia 223
   Liberia 224   217
3 Senegal 225   Guinea 226   Mali and Mauritania 227   Ivory Coast 227
   Togo and Benin 228   Upper Volta 228   Niger 229   Cameroon 230
   Chad 231   Gabon 232   Central African Republic and Congo 232
   Equatorial Guinea 233   225

VII CENTRAL AND SOUTHERN AFRICA

1 Zaïre 234   Rwanda and Burundi 236   Guinea-Bissau and Cape Verde 236
   São Tome and Principe 237   Mozambique 237   Angola 239   234
2 Zambia 242   Malawi 244   Zimbabwe 246   Namibia 249   Botswana 250
   Lesotho 250   Swaziland 251   242
3 The Republic of South Africa   252

VIII SOUTH ASIA AND INDIAN OCEAN

1 Iran 256   Afghanistan 259   256
2 India 260   Pakistan 263   Bangladesh 266   Sri Lanka 268   Nepal 269   260
3 Seychelles 271   Mauritius 272   British Indian Ocean Territory 273
   Malagasy 274   Comoro State 275   271

IX SOUTH-EAST AND EAST ASIA

1 Burma 276   Thailand 277   Malaysia and Brunei 279   Singapore 281
   Indonesia 282   Philippines 283   Vietnam 285   Kampuchea 286
   Laos 287   Hong Kong 287   276
2 China 289   Taiwan 294   Japan 296   South Korea 300   North Korea 301   289

X AUSTRALASIA AND SOUTH PACIFIC

1 Australia 302   Papua New Guinea 306   302
2 New Zealand   308
3 The South Pacific   311

XI INTERNATIONAL ORGANIZATIONS

1 The United Nations and its Agencies   314
2 The Commonwealth   324
3 Defence Organizations and Developments   327
4 The European Community   340
5 Council of Europe 349   Western European Union 350   North Atlantic
   Assembly 351   European Free Trade Association 352
   Organization for Economic Cooperation and Development 353
   Nordic Council 355   Comecon 356   349
6 African Conferences and Organizations 360   South-East Asian
   Organizations 362   Caribbean Organizations 364
   Organization of American States 365   360
7 Non-Aligned Movement   365

XII RELIGION   368

CONTENTS vii

XII THE SCIENCES

1 Science, Medicine and Technology 374
2 The Environment 383

XIV THE LAW

1 International Law 388   European Community Law 389 388
2 Law in the United Kingdom 393

XV THE ARTS

1 Opera 399   Ballet 401   Theatre 403   Music 409   Cinema 413
 Television and Radio 416 399
2 Art 421   Architecture 426   Fashion 429 421
3 Literature 430

XVI SPORT 437

XVII ECONOMIC AND SOCIAL AFFAIRS

1 A World of Debt 446
2 The International Economy 448
3 Economy of the United States 451
4 Economy of the United Kingdom 453
5 Economic and Social Data 457

XVIII DOCUMENTS AND REFERENCE

Political Declaration of the Warsaw Treaty Member-States 473
Nuclear Arms: A Roman Catholic View 479
Commonwealth Heads of Government Meeting in New Delhi 480
Republic of South Africa Constitution Act 482
The UK Conservative Administration 495

OBITUARY 497

CHRONICLE OF PRINCIPAL EVENTS IN 1983 510

INDEX 520

MAPS

The Caribbean Area 90
Nato and Soviet intermediate-range nuclear missiles in Europe 328

FRONTISPIECE

Yassir Arafat kisses the Egyptian flag after his expulsion from Beirut

ABBREVIATIONS

ACP	Africa—Caribbean—Pacific
AID	Agency for International Development
ASEAN	Association of South-East Asian Nations
AR	Annual Register
AWACS	Advanced Warning and Communication Systems
CAP	Common Agricultural Policy
CARICOM	Caribbean Common Market
CBI	Confederation of British Industry
CIA	Central Intelligence Agency
COMECON	Council for Mutual Economic Assistance
ECA	Economic Commission for Africa (UN)
ECE	Economic Commission for Europe (UN)
ECOSOC	Economic and Social Council (UN)
ECOWAS	Economic Community of West African States
EEC	European Economic Community (Common Market)
EFTA	European Free Trade Association
EMS	European Monetary System
ESCAP	Economic and Social Commission for Asia and the Pacific (UN)
EURATOM	European Atomic Energy Community
FAO	Food and Agriculture Organization
GATT	General Agreement on Tariffs and Trade
GCC	Gulf Cooperation Council
GDP/GNP	Gross Domestic/National Product
IBRD	International Bank for Reconstruction and Development
ICAO	International Civil Aviation Organization
ICBM	Inter-Continental Ballistic Missile
IDA	International Development Association
ILO	International Labour Organization
IMF	International Monetary Fund
LDCs/MDCs	Less/More Developed Countries
MBFR	Mutual and Balanced Force Reductions
NATO	North Atlantic Treaty Organization
OAPEC	Organization of Arab Petroleum Exporting Countries
OAS	Organization of American States
OAU	Organization of African Unity
OECD	Organization for Economic Cooperation and Development
OPEC	Organization of Petroleum Exporting Countries
PLO	Palestine Liberation Organization
SALT	Strategic Arms Limitation Talks
SACEUR	Supreme Allied Commander Europe
START	Strategic Arms Reduction Talks
SWAPO	South-West Africa People's Organization
TUC	Trades Union Congress
UN	United Nations
UNCTAD	United Nations Conference on Trade and Development
UNDP	United Nations Development Programme
UNESCO	United Nations Educational, Scientific and Cultural Organization
UNRWA	United Nations Relief and Works Agency
VAT	Value Added Tax
WEU	Western European Union
WHO	World Health Organization

CONTRIBUTORS

Salmon A. Ali (Formerly Pakistan diplomatic service) — Pakistan

Hilary Allen, BSc (Econ), DPhil (Writer on Nordic affairs) — Nordic States and Nordic Council

Roderic Alley, PhD (School of Political Science and Public Administration, Victoria University of Wellington) — New Zealand, South Pacific

Mary Allsebrook, BA (Writer on international and UN matters) — United Nations

Ahmed al-Shahi, DPhil (Lecturer in Social Anthropology, Department of Social Studies, University of Newcastle-upon-Tyne) — Sudan

D. G. Austin (Emeritus Professor of Government, University of Manchester) — Ghana, Gibraltar, Malta

Maurice Baggott (Principal, Scottish Industrial Communications) — Scotland

R. W. Baldock, BA, PhD (Director of Academic Publishing, Weidenfeld and Nicolson; writer on African affairs) — Zimbabwe

Robin Bidwell (Secretary, Middle East Centre, University of Cambridge) — Libya, Tunisia, Western Sahara, Algeria, Morocco

James Bishop (Editor, *The Illustrated London News*) — USA

Z. J. Blazynski (Writer and broadcaster on Polish and communist affairs) — Poland

Hermann Böschenstein, DPh (Historian and editor) — Switzerland

R. M. Burrell (Lecturer in the Contemporary History of the Near and Middle East, School of Oriental and African Studies, University of London) — Saudi Arabia, Yemen

Peter Calvert, AM, MA, PhD (Professor of Comparative and International Politics, University of Southampton) — Latin America

Christopher Clapham, MA, DPhil (Senior Lecturer in Politics, University of Lancaster) — Ethiopia, Somalia, Djibouti

Richard Clogg, MA (King's College, University of London) — Greece

Sue Cockerill (Statistical Department, *The Financial Times*) — Economic and Social Data

H. N. Crossland (Free-lance journalist) — West and East Germany

Reginald Cudlipp (Director, Anglo-Japanese Economic Institute) — Japan

Jane Davis (Lecturer, Department of International Politics, The University College of Wales, Aberystwyth) — Seychelles, Mauritius, BIOT; Defence Organizations and Developments

CONTRIBUTORS

Martin Dent (Senior Lecturer, Department of Politics, University of Keele)	Nigeria
Neville C. Duncan, PhD (Senior Lecturer, Faculty of Social Sciences, University of the West Indies)	Caribbean and Caribbean Organizations
Ann Edwards (Registered Indexer of the Society of Indexers)	Index
David M. L. Farr (Professor of History and Director, Paterson Center for International Programs, Carleton University, Ottawa)	Canada
George Fodor (East European Service, BBC)	Romania
Peter Frank (Senior Lecturer in Soviet Government and Politics, University of Essex)	USSR
Christopher Gandy (Formerly UK diplomatic service; writer on Middle Eastern affairs)	Arab World, Egypt, Jordan, Syria, Lebanon, Iraq
Doug Gardner (Freelance sports journalist)	Sport
Angela Gillon (Researcher in West European affairs)	Austria
Giles Gordon (Theatre Critic, *The Spectator*)	Theatre
Richard Grant (Information Officer, North Atlantic Assembly)	North Atlantic Assembly
Edward G. Greer (Associate Professor, Drama Department, Syracuse University USA)	New York Theatre
Muriel Grindrod, OBE (Writer on Italian affairs; formerly Assistant Editor, *The Annual Register*)	Italy
Robin Hallett, MA (Writer and lecturer on African affairs)	Zaïre, Rwanda and Burundi, Guinea-Bissau and Cape Verde, São Tome and Principe, Mozambique, Angola, Zambia, Malawi
Martin Harrison (Professor of Politics, University of Keele)	France
G. A. M. Hills, BA, DLit (Writer and broadcaster on Iberian current affairs and history)	Spain, Portugal
H. V. Hodson, MA (Formerly Editor, *The Sunday Times*)	United Kingdom, Western European Union, EFTA, OECD
David Holloway (Literary Editor, *The Daily Telegraph*)	Literature
Brian Hook (Senior Lecturer in Chinese Studies, University of Leeds)	China, Taiwan
Arnold Hughes, BA (Lecturer in Political Science, Centre of West African Studies, University of Birmingham)	Sierra Leone, The Gambia, Liberia
N. March Hunnings, LLM, PhD (Editor, *Common Market Law Reports*)	European Community Law
Derek Ingram (Editor of *Commonwealth* and author and writer on the Commonwealth)	Commonwealth
George Joffe (Middle East Editor, Economist Intelligence Unit; journalist and broadcaster on North Africa and the Middle East)	Arab States of the Gulf
James Jupp, MSc (Econ), PhD (Principal Lecturer in Politics, Canberra College of Advanced Education, Australia)	Sri Lanka

CONTRIBUTORS

Michael Kaser, MA (Reader in Economics, Oxford, and Professorial Fellow of St Antony's College, Oxford) — Comecon

Peter King (Professor, Political and Administrative Studies Department, University of Papua New Guinea) — Papua New Guinea

Vladmir V. Kusin, PhD (Senior Analyst, Radio Free Europe, Munich) — Czechoslovakia

Richard Last (Television Critic, *The Daily Telegraph*) — Television and Radio

Michael Leifer, BA, PhD (Reader in International Relations, London School of Economics and Political Science) — Malaysia, Singapore, Brunei

Anton Logoreci, BSc (Econ) (Writer and broadcaster on communist affairs) — Albania

Peter Lyon, PhD (Reader in International Relations and Secretary, Institute of Commonwealth Studies, University of London) — India, Nepal, Afghanistan, Bangladesh

W. A. McKean, PhD (Fellow of St John's College, Cambridge) — Law in the United Kingdom

J. D. McLachlan (Managing Director, Marketing, FT Business Information Ltd.) — Benelux countries

Keith McLachlan, BA, PhD (Senior Lecturer in Geography with reference to the Near and Middle East, School of Oriental and African Studies, University of London) — Iran

Louis McRedmond, MA, BL (Head of Information in Radio Telefis Eireann, the Irish Broadcasting service) — Republic of Ireland

A. J. A. Mango, BA, PhD (Orientalist and writer on current affairs in Turkey and the Near East) — Turkey

George Mansell, RIBA (Architectural writer) — Architecture

Roger Manvell, PhD, DLitt (Director, British Film Academy 1947-59; Visiting Fellow, University of Sussex; University Professor and Professor of Film, Boston University) — Cinema

W. N. Medlicott, DLitt, MA, FRHistS (Stevenson Professor of International History Emeritus, University of London) — Extracts from the Annual Register 200, 150, 100, 50 years ago

Maurice Mendelson, MA, DPhil (Fellow of St John's College, Oxford) — International Law

Rodney Milnes (Deputy Editor, *Opera*) — Opera

John Newell, BSc (Editor, Science, Industry and Agriculture, BBC External Services) — Science, Medicine and Technology

Rada Nikolaev (Head of Bulgarian research section, Radio Free Europe) — Bulgaria

Thomas O'Dwyer (News director, Middle East Media Operations) — Cyprus

A. S. B. Olver, MA (Specialist in South-East Asian affairs) — South-East Asian States (except Malaysia, Brunei, Singapore); South-East Asian Organizations

CONTRIBUTORS

Geoffrey Parrinder, MA, PhD, DD (Emeritus Professor of the Comparative Study of Religions, University of London) — Religion
Anne Price (Fashion Editor, *Country Life*) — Fashion
The Hon. Terence Prittie, MBE, MA (Director, Britain and Israel) — Israel
Peter Riddell (Political Editor, *The Financial Times*) — Economic and Social Affairs
Sir John Rodgers, Bt, MA, DL, FRSA (Former President, Political Affairs Commission, Council of Europe and Vice-President of the Assembly of Western European Union) — Council of Europe
Francis Routh (Composer and author; founder/director of the Redcliffe Concerts of British Music) — Music
Alan Sanders, FIL (Soviet Regional Editor, BBC Monitoring Service) — Mongolia
Geoffrey Sawer, LLD, DLitt, BA, LLM (Emeritus Professor of Law, Australian National University) — Australia
George Schöpflin (Joint Lecturer in East European Political Institutions, London School of Economics and School of Slavonic and East European Studies, University of London) — Hungary
Gerald Shaw, MA (Chief Assistant Editor, *The Cape Times*) — Botswana, Lesotho, Swaziland, South Africa, Namibia

Richard Sim (Consultant and political analyst on Far Eastern affairs) — North and South Korea
John V. Simpson (Senior Lecturer in Economics, Queen's University of Belfast) — Northern Ireland
F. B. Singleton, MA (Formerly Chairman, Postgraduate School of Yugoslav Studies, University of Bradford) — Yugoslavia
Peter Stead (Lecturer in History, University College of Swansea) — Wales
John Thornton (Expert on European Community affairs) — European Community
Lloyd Timberlake (Editorial Director, *Earthscan*) — Environment
William Tordoff, MA, PhD (Professor of Government, University of Manchester) — Kenya, Uganda, Tanzania
Marina Vaizey, MA, (Art Critic, *The Sunday Times*) — Art
Kaye Whiteman (Editor, *West Africa*) — Senegal, Mauritania, Mali, Guinea, Ivory Coast, Upper Volta, Togo, Benin, Niger, Equatorial Guinea, Chad, Cameroon, Gabon, Congo, Central African Republic; African Conferences and Organizations

Peter Willetts, PhD (Lecturer in International Relations, The City University, London; author of *The Non-Aligned in Havana*) — Non-Aligned Movement
G. B. L. Wilson, MA (Ballet critic of *The Jewish Chronicle* and *Dancing Times*; author of the *Dictionary of Ballet*) — Ballet

PREFACE

THE Annual Register 1983 records a year of international crises. The conflict in Lebanon turned to virtual civil war, in which the multinational 'peacekeeping' forces were almost impotent but into which they were increasingly drawn. US-Soviet talks on arms limitation stagnated until crisis point was reached when the first Cruise nuclear missiles—Nato's initial answer to the multiplication of Soviet SS-20s—arrived in Europe and the USSR walked out of the Geneva talks. In this context the decisive electoral victories of Chancellor Kohl in West Germany and Mrs Thatcher in Britain, defeating oppositions hostile to the deployment of Cruise, were crucial events; but throughout the Western world the morality of possessing nuclear arms became more and more explicitly a live issue for the churches, ecological groups and others, apart from political opposition to their deployment by left-wing parties in Europe. Anxieties were heightened by the increasingly hostile confrontation of the superpowers, especially after the destruction of a South Korean airliner by Soviet aircraft and the Russian rejection of successive Western proposals for limitation of intermediate-range weapons. The Western allies were divided by European fears about United States policy in the Caribbean and Central America, heightened as they were by the invasion of Grenada.

If politically 1983 was a calamitous year, economically it saw a brightening of the horizon, as some Western economies, especially that of the US, began to revive, and inflation was checked, though the heavy debts of Latin American and Third World countries continued to menace world financial stability. Massive unemployment, however, was increasingly recognized as an economic and social problem which the best recovery of industry and trade that could be expected would leave still to be solved. And the more affluent countries became more keenly aware of the desperate poverty and misery of many millions of people, especially those affected by drought in Africa and other natural disasters.

Much of this volume, then, does not make cheerful reading. But it is the business of the Annual Register to record events, not to pass judgments on them or prognosticate their consequences. Changes in the structure of the contents have been minimal this year.

ACKNOWLEDGEMENTS

The Advisory Board again gratefully acknowledges its debt to a number of institutions for their help with sources, references, documents, figures and maps. The Board, and the bodies which nominate its members, disclaim responsibility for any opinions expressed or the accuracy of any facts recorded in this volume.

THE ANNUAL REGISTER

200 years ago

17 February 1783. *Debate on the peace treaties*. The preliminary articles of peace between Great Britain and France, and between Great Britain and Spain, were signed at Versailles on the 20th of January; and on the 27th copies of the same, and of the provisional treaty with the United States of America, were laid before both houses of parliament ... The defence of the peace was undertaken on three grounds; first, on the weak and impoverished state of this country; secondly, on the merits of the articles themselves; and lastly, on an attempt to disarm the arguments and objections on the other side of their force and effect, by throwing on the opposite party the odium of acting entirely, on this occasion, from interested motives; and of having entered into an unnatural coalition, merely for the purpose of displacing his Majesty's ministers by inducing parliament to censure the peace.

150 years ago

2 January 1833. *Occupation of the Falklands*. On the 2nd of January, his Majesty's sloop-of-war *Clio*, appeared off the Buenos Ayrean military establishment at Port Soledad, where a ship-of-war, the *Sarandi*, belonging to the republic, was likewise lying. Captain Onslow of the *Clio*, immediately went on board the *Sarandi*—informed her commander, that he had come to take possession of the Malvinas, as belonging to Great Britain ... *(This extract is taken from the account of the Falklands developments in 1833, which was reprinted in the Annual Register 1982, pp. 488-9.)*

April 1833. *Texan aspirations*. The people of the province of Texas, who had assembled a convention in their town of San Felipe, in the month of April, declared themselves independent, and adopted a constitution. They did not attempt to conceal their own opinion of their importance ... The constitution contained the following provision:- 'No bank or banking institution, nor office of discount and deposits, nor other monied corporation, nor private banking establishment, shall exist during the continuance of this constitution.'

100 years ago

1 August 1883. *Parcel Post*. The Parcel Post came into operation, the minimum charge being 3*d*. for parcels not exceeding 1 lb., and the maximum weight 7 lbs. for which one shilling was charged.

1-4 November 1883. *Defeat of Hicks Pasha*. On November 1 a treacherous guide led the Egyptian force to a rocky, wooded defile, without water, where an ambuscade had been prepared by the enemy, who were armed with rifles and artillery ... For three days the army, worn out by thirst, gallantly defended itself, but on the fourth, when the last cartridge was expended, Hicks ordered bayonets to be fixed, and put himself at the head of the force, which was speedily annihilated to a man.

50 years ago

1933. *The Nazification of Germany*. The methods of the Nazis brought about a widespread terrorisation and intimidation of the population. Spying and denunciation became rampant. The liberty of the Press was abolished, since all newspapers must choose between being subservient to the powers that be or being prohibited. The stage, the cinema, broadcasting, every artistic, scientific or literary production was in the hands of the Nazis. Non-Aryans and unpopular individuals cannot write in the papers or publish books. The moral and material condition of the Jews became increasingly hopeless during the year. An extensive emigration, mainly from among the intellectuals, Jewish and non-Jewish, and from among the political opponents of the party in power set in. An estimated figure of these emigrants from Germany was round about 60,000 at the end of 1933.

ANNUAL REGISTER

FOR THE YEAR 1983

EDITORIAL

EVENTS in 1983 involving one or other of the superpowers reminded all but the most insensitive that an incident anywhere in the world could lead to a fatal confrontation between them. Neither the military embroilment of Western powers in Lebanon, with its threat that a civil war might become a proxy battleground for major external rivals, nor the destruction of a civil airliner over Russian territorial waters nor the American invasion of Grenada could be rated a *casus belli* for the greatest powers. Yet all three incidents suggested how easily the powder-keg on which the world was sitting could be ignited by hasty or mistaken action. And all stemmed from the ingrained belief that the East-West conflict was the paramount issue in every disturbance anywhere that engaged the concern of either superpower.

* * *

When Mr Enoch Powell, MP, pronounced in September 1983 that 'who is in Beirut or who governs Beirut is a matter of the utmost indifference to the United Kingdom', he was characteristically exaggerating, but he approached the truth. While France, Italy and Britain had their own motives, the main impulse for the Western presence in Lebanon came from Washington. Secretary of State Shultz, justifying American policy in the Middle East to US Senators in October 1983, claimed that America had an abiding commitment to Israel, that the region was one of vital strategic and economic importance to the free world, and that it was an arena of competition between the United States and the Soviet Union. Commitment to Israel certainly heightened the US response to the other two interests, but those two, on inspection, appeared to be effectively one. The Middle East was no more important economically than other regions which did not attract American military intervention; strategically it was important to America because of the US-Soviet conflict, not otherwise.

Israel's national integrity, within its pre-1967 borders (but not beyond), is a common cause of every member of the United Nations. Its territorial security is primarily its own concern, and Israel has shown itself well able to defend it, with material support from the United States. On that ground, there was no more cause for its friends to intervene in

Lebanon than in any other of its neighbours. A Syrian-dominated Lebanon, however, was seen in Washington as a threat to the global balance of power because, Syria being a client of the USSR, it would import Soviet influence into the Middle East at a key point.

The excuse offered for the United States action in Grenada that the safety of American citizens was in danger was implausible; for the means employed greatly exceeded the far-from-obvious need for a rescue. President Reagan's decision was prompted primarily by fear that the marxist regime in St George's would make Grenada a military satellite of Cuba, and at one remove of the Soviet Union. The claim that this menaced America's security 'at its backdoor' hardly held water; Grenada is more distant from the United States than Russia is from England.

So again a disagreeable local development was subordinated to the proposition that advancement of the communist interest anywhere in the world must be resisted by all available means, and that effects of any incident on the superpower conflict take priority over all other considerations. Among other consequences of that American theme have been visible rifts in the Atlantic alliance, resulting from European distrust of United States judgment and American distrust of alleged European timidity, and undermining public support in Europe for nuclear armament.

* * *

How did the global antagonism of the superpowers arise? Between the two world wars, although communist Russia was wedded ideologically to the marxist doctrine of the inevitable collapse of capitalism and imperialism, and was committed to hastening that historical process, its efforts to sap the political and industrial systems of the West were peaceful, if illegitimate, and did not menace the general international order. Then, the rise of fascist dictatorships in Europe entangled the ideological conflict with the international power-structure. From 1941 to 1945 the Central Powers and Japan were the common enemy of the democratic West and the Soviet Union. Their defeat seemed to open all possibilities for a new world order. But again the scene had changed. Russia had become militarily powerful, the United States had abandoned isolationism. West and East had drawn different lessons from World War II—the liberal West, that repetition of such a disaster must be for ever prevented by a United Nations dedicated to peace; the communist East, that only military and territorial power could assure the survival of the Soviet Union and protect the gains of the revolution. While the West's internationalism was idealistic, Russia's was ideological and defensive. Where the liberal West saw one world the communist regimes saw two opposed systems.

To Soviet action in eliminating the Baltic republics, subjugating

Poland, Bulgaria, Hungary, East Germany and Czechoslovakia, the West responded by founding Nato. Later events—Khrushchev's threats to Berlin, the suppression of Hungarian revolt and 'the Prague Spring', the Brezhnev doctrine, the invasion of Afghanistan—were incidental to the territorial and defensive policy established under Stalin before 1950. American and other Western reaction was its consequence. Once the confrontation was apparent, its progress to an ever-mounting build-up of nuclear and conventional armament and to mutual menaces everywhere could hardly be stayed.

* * *

It is idle to think that the symptoms of conflict can be cured without treatment of the cause—that effective arms reduction and control can be achieved without appeasing the conflict and allaying the fears that underlie the competitive accumulation of arms; or that world peace can be secured by 'crisis management' without management of the global hostility that turns each crisis into a threat of utterly destructive war. Political disarmament is a condition precedent of genuine material disarmament. The pile-up of arms heightens the tension, but does not create it. Paradoxically, indeed, the super-armament of East and West has been the major instrument of maintaining global peace. Regional wars recur, but they are contained by mutual dread of a clash between the superpowers. In a word, deterrence has deterred. In the absence of political understanding and reconciliation, radical nuclear disarmament might actually make world war more likely.

How far, then, is the global conflict capable of being eased? On the Soviet side, the marxist dogma of the inevitability of world revolution still lurks in the ideological background, but as a practical motive it has long been suppressed by hard facts, like the persistence of dissent in East Europe, the estrangement of communist China and the failure of the demise of European empires to produce a revolutionary ex-colonial world. The governing motives of Soviet global policies lie elsewhere.

All revolutionary regimes are paranoically fearful of counter-revolution. In the Soviet case, even after two generations this dread has been prolonged by several forces. One is the introspection and secretiveness of the Russian people. Another is the immensely strong apparatus of the Soviet system, which tolerates no questioning of orthodoxy. A third is the age of the Soviet leaders. Most of the Politburo, until now, were born before the Bolshevik revolution, were reared in the ruthless, defensive stalinist era, and spent their formative years under the threats and then the mortal attack of Nazi Germany. Their outlook on the world is suspicious, hostile and defensive. To this must be added a factor too little recognized as potent in Russia, though familiar in the West, the influence of the military establishment. No nation can spend on defence up to 15 per cent of its gross product without creating a huge vested interest in the psychology of fear and enmity that alone can justify vast armaments.

Those sovietist motives reinforce an attitude historically and geopolitically Russian. The USSR is a great continental empire whose expansive impulse is not yet exhausted. Whereas the European empires have virtually disappeared, the Russian empire is intact and even expanding, and is unsteady at its fringes. Again an attitude of enmity and suspicion is engendered towards the outer world, particularly the empire's contiguous neighbours.

People in the West, with their maritime view of the world, perceive Russia's neighbours as being the Soviet-dominated countries of eastern Europe, immobile secondary powers in Central Asia, and an ambivalent communist China. But this is not how the world looks from Moscow. To the east and over the North Pole, the hostile USA itself is Russia's contiguous neighbour. To the south-east of their empire the men of Moscow see beyond a nuclear-armed China a US-oriented Japan. To the south they see a theatre of historical collision between European and Russian influence, and a Nato member, Turkey. In the West, they see as their neighbour Russia's historic foe and invader, Germany, half of it allied with American superpower. To them, Eastern Europe is a defensive glacis against a hostile West. To maintain a glacis in front of fortress Russia, to bring border areas under Russian control, and to match the maritime power of the rest of the world (which is part of the hostile enclosure that Soviet strategists see) is the natural policy of the Kremlin on geopolitical grounds.

* * *

That policy was reinforced by the American doctrine, pursued by successive Administrations after World War II, of defensive 'encirclement' of the USSR. This was an almost automatic reaction to stalinist expansionism and Khrushchevian adventurism. The Soviet counter-reaction was revealed both in the USSR's glacis-defence actions in Hungary, Czechoslovakia, Poland and Afghanistan, and in its circle-breaking efforts, which have taken two main forms: attempts to establish pro-Soviet outposts in other continents, from Cuba to Vietnam, and a vast expansion of Russian naval power deployed in all the world's oceans.

Without that Russian counter-reaction the initial American reaction of encirclement might have dwindled. The deep-rooted popular emotion in the United States against foreign involvement and spending American lives in faraway wars rose to the surface after the waste and humiliation of Vietnam. But it has been enfeebled by the evidence of Soviet penetration in every continent and ocean.

The *Weltanschauung* of the United States is in many ways the opposite of Russia's. It sees its values, interests and security menaced all over the world. Though like Russia essentially a continental power, it has pursued for a century a strategy of keeping enemies at a distance by using its openness to the oceans to project its naval (and latterly air and nuclear) power to the rim of every other continent, and to cultivate friendships and alliances with countries on the further side of America's oceanic glacis. Its forward world policy, like that of Soviet Russia, is basically nationalist and defensive.

This world conflict of opposite military and political purposes is inherently self-escalating. Each move by one side is countered by a hostile move by the other—Afghanistan by explicit American commitment in the Gulf, Russian naval presence in the Indian Ocean by the Diego Garcia base, communist infiltration in the Caribbean and Central America by American intervention in El Salvador and Grenada, American arms for Israel by Soviet arms for Syria, and so on without end. And the politic military conflict has engendered, if only to sustain popular fervour, polemical denunciations by each side of the other as being inherently vile—'empires of evil'. Such futile moral recriminations have no bearing on the issue of military confrontation. Nothing could be inherently more immoral, or destroy more human rights, than war.

* * *

The first step in appeasement of the supreme world conflict must be recognition by both sides that the posture of each is essentially defensive. That the United States and its allies have no territorial ambitions at the expense of the Soviet bloc should be unequivocably affirmed. (Germany may be reunited one day, but not by conquest.) Can the USSR affirm the like? If we are to believe the 1983 Political Declaration of the Warsaw Pact powers the answer is yes. Here is a platform of negatives on which to begin to build a positive construction.

If territorial aggression were out, subversion would remain. Once an enemy is identified, to weaken him within appears as necessary as to confront him with armed force. In the superpower conflict, subversion has been somewhat one-sided, for two reasons: the impenetrability of the Soviet system and the crusading character of communist doctrine. But not entirely so. Though capitalism is not a proselytising faith, democracy is, and will remain a creed to be spread everywhere. The perpetual rivalry of communism and open democracy for the hearts and minds of men will remain a fact of life in world affairs. So long as its means are peaceful, even if they are illegitimate, its subversive effects have to be accepted—not ignored, but countered likewise without use or threat of armed conflict.

In the long run, the outcome will be determined by the conduct of the principal exponents of the two concepts, not by their military power. It will proceed mainly in the non-aligned world: the chances of an overthrow either of the free-enterprise democratic system in the United States and other advanced countries by marxist-leninism, or of the communist system in the Soviet Union and its satellites by capitalist democracy, are equally remote. They are both unreal aims, which in any case military arms and threats can do nothing to further.

A third essential element in that negative foundation for constructive co-existence is admission of the impotence of power. The huge military might of the superpowers, and indeed the lesser might of other countries claiming an influence beyond their own borders, have availed them nothing except their own territorial security amid all the turbulence of the years since World War II. Great changes have taken place in the political, social and economic map of the world without the aid of military power and often contrary to its weight.

These negative propositions are not in themselves a sufficient base for peaceful co-existence of the superpowers, but at least they justify a truce, and they clear the ground for a positive construction. This could include East-West collaboration in coping with some of the less politico-military problems of the world—ecological decay, the law of the sea, the exploration of space, the conservation of energy, international terrorism, the hunger of the poorest peoples and regions. To attack them is the common interest of mankind, not only of any section of it labelled capitalist, communist or non-aligned. More directly, a start could be made with serious discussion of nuclear-free zones, beginning not with Europe but with the Antarctic and proceeding northwards.

The world needs some new thought—lateral thinking, in the jargon of today. It has set up a system of mutual deterrence, but it has not yet grasped the implications of that system's success.

I HISTORY OF THE UNITED KINGDOM

Chapter 1

POLITICS BEFORE THE ELECTION

IGNORING the ill omen of an exceptionally wet spring, which damaged or delayed a number of food crops after a bumper agricultural year in 1982, Mrs Thatcher called for a dissolution of Parliament nearly a year before the expiry of its five-year term; thanks chiefly to the decline of the Labour Party and to the distortions of a first-past-the-post voting system the Conservatives won an overwhelming victory at the general election on 9 June.

At the beginning of the year such an outcome seemed by no means certain. The economic signs were dismal. Sterling was weak in expectation of a fall in oil prices, and on 11 January the banks raised their base rate by a point to 11 per cent. Industrial output (excluding North Sea oil and gas) had fallen in November 1982 to the lowest figure since 1965. Between December and January the gross total of unemployment rose by 127,718 to 3,224,715, a figure which Opposition spokesmen claimed would have been at least 200,000 higher but for changes in the counting procedures; the seasonally adjusted number, excluding school-leavers, at 2,984,100, represented 12·8 per cent of the work-force.

The Government was undeterred from pursuing its established economic policy, based upon control of public expenditure in the interest of defeating inflation and creating the conditions for business to provide 'real jobs'. 'Inflation', the Prime Minister declared in a speech on 19 April, 'is a tax, and a savage and capricious one, which Governments impose without seeking or securing Parliament's approval.' The Public Expenditure White Paper published on 1 February estimated that spending in 1983-84 would be £500 million less than had been previously planned, despite major increases in the cost of law enforcement and defence, including an additional £624 million for the defence of the Falklands. In his Budget statement on 15 March the Chancellor of the Exchequer fixed the public sector borrowing requirement (PSBR) in the ensuing financial year at £8,000 million, the 1982-83 target figure of £9,500 million having been undershot by £2,000 million. 'The lesson for today,' said Sir Geoffrey Howe, 'is that it is prudent to keep planned borrowing down.'

Nevertheless he announced some reliefs of direct taxation and some improvements in social security benefits. Tax thresholds would be raised by 14 per cent, a measure taking 1,750,000 low-income people out of the income-tax range. The limit for tax relief on mortgage interest would be raised from £25,000 to £30,000 of debt. The national insurance surcharge (often denounced as 'a tax on jobs') would be cut by ½ per cent from August. Changes in the taxation on North Sea oil would cost £800 million. Child benefit was raised, and unemployment pay was relieved of the 5 per cent cut imposed in 1981—this under considerable pressure from backbench Tory MPs. The annual rise in old age pensions and other benefits from November would henceforward be based on the actual price index for May, instead of a forecast for November; this would reduce benefits in real terms when the rate of inflation rose over the intervening six months, as it was correctly forecast to do in 1983—a grievance of which the Opposition made the most. On the other side, taxes were heightened on beer, wines, spirits and tobacco, and the car licence fee raised. The Chancellor also announced that legislation would soon be introduced to enable freeports to be established, and that workers close to retirement age need no longer claim unemployment benefit, a change which would further reduce the published figures of unemployment.

Financial commentators saw it as a neutral Budget. This did not save it from passionate attack by Labour speakers in the ensuing debate. Mr Michael Foot, Leader of the Opposition, declared that it made no effort to deal with the fundamental problems of the economy. The losses the nation had suffered during the industrial collapse of the past three years, he said, were of historic proportions: there was an even deeper division in society between the rich and the poor, between the North and the South of the country. Pensioners, declared Mr Peter Shore, had been robbed and deceived.

An important part of the Government's financial policy continued to be the control of expenditure by local authorities, through cuts in central support grants for those which budgeted to spend more than maximum totals fixed by the Secretary of State. English local authorities planned to spend in 1983-84 £771 million above the Government's target, itself slightly lower than the target of 1982-83; more than half of that excess was recorded by the Greater London Council (GLC) and the closely-associated Inner London Education Authority (ILEA), and most of the rest by Labour-controlled metropolitan counties and Inner London boroughs. Contemptuous of the penalty it would suffer, the GLC on 15 February voted a £1,500 million 'municipal socialist budget' requiring a 14 per cent rise in the rate precept. One acute cause of conflict over GLC spending, however, was removed when the High Court ruled that a plan to cut London Transport fares by a quarter was not *prima facie* illegal, as had been the 1981 plan for a much larger cut (see AR 1981, pp. 34 and 405). The Government's acquiescence was signalled by an increase of £30 million in its allowance to the GLC for London Transport. More emotive were some of the other actions of Mr Ken Livingstone, the egregious Labour leader of the GLC. Mr Foot was furious with him for exciting bad publicity for the party on the eve of a critical London by-election (see p. 11) by a proposal to grant £53,000 to a protest movement called 'Troops Out', which Labour's leader told him was 'committed to policies that would cause immense suffering in Northern Ireland'. The Police Federation complained that the GLC was handing out thousands of pounds to groups seeking to undermine public confidence in the police.

On industrial relations, the Prime Minister told the House on 24 February that the Government was considering legislation to outlaw strikes in essential public services, including hospital staff. No such legislation, however, was introduced. On 11 January the Government published a Green Paper (discussion document) proposing legislation to enforce secret ballots in elections of trade union officers and before strikes, and to make the unions' political levy on behalf of the Labour Party subject to 'contracting in' instead of 'contracting out'. The TUC refused to engage in talks with the Employment Secretary on his proposals.

Two Government Bills encountered cross-bench opposition. On a Housing Bill, extending the right of tenants of publicly-owned houses and flats to buy their own homes, the House of Lords on 26 April, by a majority of 182 votes to 96, knocked out a clause granting that right to tenants of housing associations and trusts, which provided homes for the specially needy. More fundamental criticism greeted a Police and Criminal Evidence Bill, on two main grounds, that it enhanced the arbitrary powers of the police and diminished the rights of citizens who might be accused and that new powers of search and compulsory disclosure of documents would menace essential confidence. In face of strong criticism from the churches and other interests as well as the political opposition, Ministers claimed that the proposed changes in the law struck a fair balance. On 14 April the Home Secretary, Mr Whitelaw, told the House that he was introducing amendments that would exempt from disclosure the confidential personal records of the medical and certain other professions, including clergy and social workers; later he extended that privilege to the confidential records of journalists. Theatre, film, television and radio directors still protested that material vital to their private purposes might be seized. The Commission for Racial Equality was among the bodies calling for deletion of the clauses enlarging police powers to 'stop and search'.

On the nationalized industries front, a furore was provoked by the report of a committee under the chairmanship of Sir David Serpell, a member of the board of British Rail (BR), on the future of the railways. The study, published on 20 January, had been initiated by BR itself, but brought it no comfort. The Serpell verdict was that the existing state subsidy of £900 million was enough, and could indeed be reduced by about a quarter through economies. For further improvement there were various options: cutting the present 10,400 route miles of track to 9,000 would save £200 million, to 6,000 miles £400 million, and to 1,600 miles the whole subsidy. The railwaymen's unions and Labour spokesmen demanded that the report be strangled at birth. The Transport Secretary, Mr David Howell, was cautious, promising only that the Government would now reach lasting decisions on the railways' future.

The Government's theme of 'privatization' was expressed in a Bill to enable 51 per cent of the equity in British Telecommunications to be sold to the public, and in the too-successful sale of shares in Associated British Ports, the issue being 35 times over-subscribed on 11 February. The National Freight Corporation, which had been sold to its own workers (see AR 1981, p. 37), made a profit of £18·3 million on an investment of £55·5 million in the first 14 months of its independence, to the disgruntlement of employees who had failed to take up shares.

The water and sewerage industry was afflicted by a prolonged national strike, the first in its history, which began on 24 January after rejection of the employers' offer of a 7·3 per cent pay rise over 16 months, and a cut of the working week to 39 hours, on condition of job flexibility. After vain efforts by the conciliation service ACAS the parties agreed on 14 February to a committee of inquiry. This in turn became bogged down, largely in dispute as to whether the wage scales should be compared with local-authority manual workers or with skilled electricity and gas men. By a majority the committee, taking the latter view, recommended a package which in effect raised the offer of 7·3 per cent to 10·4 per cent, plus enhanced marginal benefits, including £5 a week for agreement to flexible working and a further reduction of the working week to 38 hours from April 1984. The unions, having patently won hands-down, called off the strike on 23 February. Meanwhile $7\frac{1}{2}$ million people had been directed to boil all water, 76,000 homes had been without piped water, and many districts suffered problems with sewage.

The wearing of seat-belts in the front seats of cars became compulsory on 31 January. On 18 April the Environment Secretary, Mr Tom King, announced that the Government would make it compulsory for all new cars to run on lead-free petrol by 1990, a timetable which the opposition spokesman, Mr Gerald Kaufman, described as far too leisurely, but which Mr King argued was imposed by the need to secure EEC agreement. He had succeeded Mr Michael Heseltine at the Environment Department on 6 January when the latter took over the Defence portfolio from Sir John Nott, whose political retirement had previously been announced. A combination of sabbatarianism and the interests of most large and many smaller retailers caused the defeat of a Bill to abolish restrictions on Sunday opening of shops, on a free Commons vote, by 205 to 106 on 4 February.

The internecine conflicts in the Labour Party that had been so prominent in the previous year (see AR 1982, pp. 25–27) continued into 1983. The leadership's efforts to rid the party of the far-left activist group Militant Tendency (MT) only turned the knife in a self-inflicted wound. On 26 January the party's National Executive Committee (NEC), against Mr Tony Benn's protest, decided to prepare charges against members of the editorial board of MT's newspaper *Militant*. On 23 February the NEC, after giving five members a long hearing, voted by 19 to 9 to expel them from the party. The position of MT supporters who were Labour candidates for Parliament was unresolved, and several remained at the general election—indeed the party leader appeared on the platform of one of them.

Many constituency party management committees were the bane of the national leadership (see AR 1982, p. 25). None was more irksome than that of Southwark, Bermondsey, in south London, where a by-election was pending. On 9 January it selected Mr Peter Tatchell, of whom Mr Foot had once said that he 'is not an endorsed candidate for the Labour Party and as far as I am concerned never will be', by reason of his advocacy of extra-parliamentary action to defeat a democratically elected Government (see AR 1981, p. 23). Mr Foot, however, now offered Mr Tatchell his 'full backing'. After a campaign sullied by much personal abuse, at the by-election on 24 February Labour lost the seat, its majority of 11,756 in 1979 becoming a Liberal (Lib.-SDP Alliance) majority of 9,319 over Mr Tatchell. The Liberal vote was up by over 50 per cent, the Labour vote down by 37½ per cent, the Conservative down by nearly 20 per cent. A right-wing 'Real Labour' candidate polled 2,243 votes. Besides being a personal humiliation for Mr Tatchell, an admitted homosexual, the by-election was a fearsome lesson for Labour, a triumph for the Liberal-SDP Alliance. Alliance leaders claimed it as proof of Labour's 'terminal decline'. Labour spirits were revived, however, by the by-election on 24 March at Darlington, in the industrial North-East, where they held the seat with a majority of 2,412 (against 1,052 in 1979) over the Conservatives. Although the Alliance gained from both the other parties, it polled less than 25 per cent of the total vote.

In face of reverses like Southwark, and a consistently poor showing in national opinion polls, it was not surprising that Mr Michael Foot's leadership was called into question. *The Times* led its issue of 25 February with a report that 'a majority of Labour's Shadow Cabinet now feel that Foot must go'. Mr Foot called this 'a malicious fabrication'. 'Labour leaders', he said, 'are not elected by polls or newspaper campaigns. I was elected by the party . . . I have an obligation to the people who voted for me and that is what I intend to carry out.'

Labour's champions set much store by a pact between the party's leadership and the TUC which was reached on 21 March. A Labour Government, it was agreed, would not impose norms or fixed limits on pay rises. But incomes, including state benefits, would be comprehended in annual talks between Ministers and representatives of industry, commerce and the trade unions on a 'national economic assessment'. 'The assessment process will have produced an agreed statement on the framework within which decisions will be made on investment, prices and pay.'

The national economic assessment was embodied in a Labour campaign document published on 29 March, under the title *New Hope for Britain*. Along with a new national investment bank and a Ministry of Economic Planning, it would be integral to a plan to rebuild industry. 'Within days of taking office, Labour will begin to implement an emergency programme of action, to bring about a complete change of direction for Britain.' Besides a massive increase in public investment and construction, promised expenditure included the repurchase of those parts of nationalized industry which had been sold off, increases in social benefits, more resources for the National Health Service (NHS) and for public transport and education, big increases in house-building by local authorities and the phasing-out of all health charges. The only specific source of new funds foreseen to pay for all this was an annual wealth tax. The rest, apart from any economies on defence, would presumably be found from borrowing. Reflation on that scale, it was claimed, would reduce unemployment below one million within five years. Other policies included nationalization of all ports, early abolition of the legislative powers of the House of Lords and repeal of all Tory legislation on industrial relations. Labour would immediately open discussion with Britain's European Community partners with a view to complete withdrawal from the EEC within the lifetime of a Labour Government. On nuclear arms, Labour pledged itself to cancel the programme for replacement of the Polaris force by Trident, to refuse to deploy Cruise missiles, and within five years completely to remove all nuclear bases from British soil.

The rather smudgy formula on the EEC barely concealed a capitulation of the pro-Europeans, mainly on Labour's right, to the principle of early withdrawal. On defence, the concession by the right wing to total unilateral nuclear disarmament was explicit. The embarrassment of Labour moderates on these issues was an evident handicap to the party's credibility. Nuclear arms had become the subject of much debate in the churches and of militant demonstrations. Most publicized among the latter was the continuous picketing of the air base at Greenham Common in Berkshire, where Cruise missiles were due to be sited, throughout the year by large numbers of women who camped along its outskirts and from time to time attempted to penetrate the perimeter and to stop vehicles carrying workers and supplies into the base. Arrests were made and fines imposed for various offences, but the Greenham

Common women remained defiant and won a vast deal of publicity for themselves, and more dubiously for their cause.

They were not officially sponsored by the Campaign for Nuclear Disarmament, the main anti-nuclear pressure group, but on 1 April, a bank holiday, CND organized a demonstration intended to link, arm to arm, Greenham Common with a Royal Ordnance Factory believed to be engaged on nuclear armament, 14 miles away. The organizers claimed that 100,000 people took part; the police estimate was 40,000, a more likely figure, as there were many gaps in the human chain. It was reported on 27 April that Cardinal Hume, the Roman Catholic Archbishop of Westminster, had warned Mgr Bruce Kent, a priest who was general secretary of CND, that he might have to resume under direction his pastoral duties if the movement became more political, but the Cardinal evidently did not think that condition had been fulfilled. His fellow R.C. archbishop, Derek Worlock of Liverpool, in a sermon on 30 January, had advocated an act of unilateral disarmament by Britain as 'a calculated risk in a nuclear age where risk abounds'. Leaders of the Methodist Church were also calling for unilateral policies. The Church of England's general synod in February voted down a unilateralist motion but called for a policy of 'no first use'. The anti-nuclear cause's appeal was furthered by the report of a British Medical Association (BMA) committee, published on 3 March, which declared that official estimates of casualties after a nuclear attack were too low by a factor of $2\frac{1}{2}$, and that effective planning for medical services in such an event was impossible.

Despite the evidence of a February opinion poll that two out of every three citizens were in favour both of retaining nuclear weapons and of strong conventional forces, the Government were sufficiently perturbed by the waxing anti-nuclear agitation to engage a leading advertising firm in a publicity campaign supporting their twin-track nuclear arms policy. Meeting at Chequers on 4 February, Mrs Thatcher and Chancellor Kohl had agreed on parallel programmes: the Geneva negotiations, they observed, must lead to a balance between the USSR and the USA in intermediate-range nuclear weapons—with which the Government steadfastly refused to include the British Polaris, regarding it as a strategic and independent deterrent. A strong public and parliamentary feeling, extending into all parties, emerged in favour of 'dual key' control of all Allied nuclear weapons, that is, a system whereby no American weapons on British soil could be activated without positive British ministerial consent. An opinion poll in mid-February showed 89 per cent in favour of dual key, while 30 per cent of those opposed to siting Cruise missiles in Britain would change their minds if the missiles were subject to dual key. The Defence Secretary and the Prime Minister repeatedly affirmed their faith in the existing understanding with the United States, going back to 1952, whereby 'the use of US bases in an emergency would be a matter for joint decision'. Mr Heseltine claimed that to insert a dual control system in Cruise would cost £1,000 million. A Commons resolution calling for dual-key control, signed by 30 Conservative MPs, was withdrawn under Government pressure.

On nuclear arms an unresolved difference remained between the allied Liberal and Social Democratic parties, turning on whether or not Polaris should be phased out (see AR 1982, pp. 23-24). The difference did not, however, impede the progress of the Alliance towards a united electoral front. Conflicts over seats which one of the two parties would contest while the other stood down were settled definitively, if not always amicably, the total number of constituencies being equally divided but the Liberals having the advantage in winnable seats. An emotion-raising question was who would be the Alliance's Prime Minister designate if an election enabled it to form a Government. Liberals were angry when on 28 March Mrs Shirley Williams of the SDP said bluntly that it would be Mr Roy Jenkins, 'the obvious choice', but a month later Mr Jenkins and Mr Steel, the Liberal leader, confirmed their agreement that Mr Jenkins would be the potential Prime Minister while Mr Steel would lead the Alliance's campaign in the general election that now seemed imminent.

Chapter 2

LABOUR MEETS DISASTER

ON 9 May Mrs Thatcher announced that, after taking counsel of senior Ministers, she had asked the Queen for a dissolution of Parliament on 13 May, to be followed by a general election on 9 June. Only a few days previously, she had said in a press interview that she had not made up her mind and was keeping all options open. On the one hand, the Government, enjoying an ample majority, had an uncompleted programme of legislative and administrative action, and Mrs Thatcher's reputation required her to dismiss mere party tactics in the timing of the election. On the other hand, the Conservatives' need for a second parliamentary term in which to consolidate the radical change that her leadership had sought to impose on British society ought not to be hazarded upon chances of misfortune which might injure the Government's popularity during the coming twelve months. In the end, Mrs Thatcher's freedom of choice was greatly restricted by the speculation which her silence on the matter had allowed to boil over in press and Parliament. To end it, in the interests of the economy, was her main acknowledged reason for settling on the earliest date open. Predictably, Mr Foot and other political opponents charged her with having decided to 'cut and run'.

The dissolution involved the demise of several measures still before Parliament, including the Police Bill and the Bill enabling British Telecom to be privatized. The Finance Bill was passed with the consent of the Opposition after deletion of some 50 clauses, including the raising of thresholds for higher-rate tax and the heightening of the limit on tax relief on mortgage interest; the Government promised to restore these changes after the election. The dissolution also marked the retirement of a number of distinguished elderly MPs, among them Sir Harold Wilson, twice Prime Minister, Mr Jo Grimond, the former leader of the Liberal Party, and Mr George Thomas, who had been, in Mrs Thatcher's words, 'one of our greatest Speakers'.

Although the Conservatives had held much of the popular lead over Labour that they had gained after the Falklands war (see AR 1982, p. 19)—the average of three opinion polls taken just before Mrs Thatcher's announcement showed them backed by 46 per cent of the electorate, Labour by 34 per cent, the Alliance by 18 per cent—they could by no means take electoral victory for granted. The appearance of a strong 'third force' could threaten many marginal Tory seats and a swing of opinion during the campaign was always possible. Each of the main parties entered the election campaign conscious of certain handicaps: for the Conservatives those of the depressed economy and high unemployment; for the Alliance, that of an electoral system heavily loaded against any party or combination that could not obtain about one-third of the votes overall; within the Alliance, for the SDP those of an untried constituency organization and the likelihood that many of its floor-crossing MPs would fail to hold their seats; for the Labour Party those of unimpressive leadership and of its manifest internal divisions. A further Labour disadvantage was the redrawing of constituencies by the Boundary Commission, which was reckoned to present the Conservatives with some twenty extra probable seats (see AR 1981, p. 27). On 11 February the House of Lords refused leave to appeal from the Appeal Court's rejection of an action to quash the Commission's report, which was then endorsed by Parliament.

The result of the local authority elections on 5 May in England (excluding London) and Wales was equivocal. The Conservatives and Liberals were the chief gainers in terms of seats won and lost. Labour lost control of Cardiff and Bristol but won Liverpool from the Liberals. The Conservatives won Reading from Labour but lost Chelmsford to the Liberals; significantly, they held Birmingham in the heart of the depressed West Midlands. In total votes, on a 40 per cent turnout, Labour was only 5 per cent behind the Conservatives; in Scotland, where there were no local elections, Labour counted on a commanding popular lead.

The Alliance was first in the campaigning field with a manifesto published on 12 May. Emergency action would be taken to cut unemployment by a million in two years, through capital investment in public works and special programmes for the long-term unemployed, youth training schemes and employment subsidies. Public sector pay would be settled by an assessment board. A new pay and prices commission would be empowered to restrict prices when pay rises above a norm were granted, and a counter-inflation tax would be imposed if necessary, with a statutory incomes policy in reserve. Tax relief on mortgages would be limited, and higher tax thresholds held down; the married man's allowance against income tax would be phased out. Social benefits would be raised. Nato was the cornerstone of Britain's defence policy, but it should move away from the early use of nuclear weapons against attack; Britain's Polaris should be included in the Geneva talks; a decision on Cruise should await the outcome of disarmament negotiations.

Labour's manifesto, published on 16 May, closely followed the document *New Hope for Britain* (see p. 12), laying great stress on high unemployment and its proposed cure by massive public expenditure; an immediate emergency programme would cost some £6,000 million. 'Our aim is nothing less than to bring about a fundamental and irreversible shift in the balance of wealth and power in favour of working people and their families.' Within the life of a Parliament Britain would withdraw from the EEC 'in an amicable and orderly way' and convert to a non-nuclear defence policy. Independent education would be penalized by withdrawing charitable status and charging VAT on school fees. Police policy would become the responsibility of elected authorities. A directly elected Scottish Assembly, with its own executive, would be set up. Mrs Thatcher described the policy in the manifesto as 'the most extreme that has ever been put before a British electorate'.

The Conservative manifesto was published on 18 May. In sum it promised that present policies would be continued. 'Unemployment can be checked and then reduced only by steadily and patiently rebuilding the economy so that it produces the goods and services which people want to buy, at prices they can afford.' Inflation must be brought lower still, with the ultimate goal of stable prices. On privatization, 'our aim is that British Telecom, Rolls-Royce, British Airways and substantial parts of British Steel, British Shipbuilders and British Leyland and as many as possible of Britain's airports should become private-sector companies', besides the offshore oil interests of British Gas. Taxes would be lowered on incomes and capital. Old age pensions and other long-term benefits would continue to be protected against rising prices. Church schools and independent education would be protected and parental choice of schools would be widened. 'We shall legislate to curb excessive and irresponsible rate increases.' The Greater London Council and other metropolitan councils would be abolished, as a 'wasteful and unnecessary tier' of local government. 'We shall give union members the right to hold ballots for the election of governing bodies of trade unions and to decide periodically whether their unions should have party political funds. We shall also curb the legal immunity of unions to call strikes without the prior approval of those concerned through a fair and secret ballot.' Mr Foot described the manifesto as 'just more of the same shameful, disastrous policies we have had over the last four years'.

The state of the economy, especially unemployment, appeared at first sight to be the major issue in the election. Mrs Thatcher herself said on 9 May that she thought unemployment would be 'a very important issue'. She held out no optimistic promises: asked whether unemployment would be up or down a year hence she replied that she could not tell, but she hoped that the underlying trend would start to fall. Conservative spokesmen made good use of figures showing that the economy had shown 2 per cent growth between the first quarters of 1982 and 1983, and that in May inflation was at an annual figure of only 3·7 per cent, the lowest rate of increase for 15 years. Opposition leaders protested that official forecasts showed both inflation and unemployment rising in later months of 1983. Trebled unemployment, said Dr David Owen of the SDP, was too high a price to pay for the achievement on inflation. If unemployment went on rising, warned Mr Healey, Labour's deputy leader, law and order would break down.

However, the more decisive electoral issue soon appeared to be defence policy. Despite the swelling propaganda for nuclear disarmament, the Conservatives' very efficient campaign managers soon found that in reality defence, nuclear defence in particular, was a winning card.

Mrs Thatcher and her team of Ministers explicitly avoided making the Falklands war an electoral issue, confident of the greatly enhanced prestige that it had brought them. The Opposition, however, sniped when it could against her silent redoubt. Mr Neil Kinnock demanded a full inquiry into the sinking of the *General Belgrano*. There was no evidence that such attacks made any impact on the electorate, and two other references to the Falklands war by Labour's leaders undoubtedly rebounded against them. When Mr Healey—moving, said Dr Owen, from the politics of the gutter to the politics of the abattoir—declared on 1 June that the Prime Minister 'glories in slaughter' he felt obliged to withdraw the word in favour of 'conflict'. And Mr Kinnock did Labour more harm when on 6 June, in reply to a heckler who shouted 'Mrs Thatcher has guts', he said: 'It is a pity that people had to leave theirs on Goose Green in order to prove it'. He likewise was constrained to send an explanation to the families of dead servicemen and to the Welsh Guards, who had suffered their worst casualties at Goose Green.

The Tory stance on nuclear defence was greatly assisted by the palpable divisions in the Labour Party on this vital subject. An election broadsheet, *Labour's Programme 1982*, spoke of Britain's becoming 'the first nuclear weapons state to renounce unilaterally such weapons'. This unilateral policy did not accord with the views of many leading Labour figures. Challenges at press conferences or in broadcast interviews were met by some deft side-stepping, such as Mr Foot's statement that 'of course the Government must have the power to judge the circumstances as we proceed'. Mr Heseltine, with some justice, accused the leaders of 'rewriting Labour's defence policies on the run'. Dr Owen, who for the SDP maintained a robust line on defence throughout the campaign, declared that 'Labour's defence policies make them unfit to govern'.

The Labour divisions were nakedly exposed when the former Labour Prime Minister, Mr Callaghan, said in a speech at Cardiff on 25 May: 'Our refusal to give up arms unilaterally has brought better and more realistic proposals from the Soviet Union . . . Britain and the West should not dismantle their weapons for nothing in return.' The Labour left was furious. Mr Callaghan's speech, bewailed Mr Alex Kitson, a former party chairman, could have cost Labour the election. Mr Tony Benn said on 27 May: 'No individual is going to divert the Labour Party from carrying out its policy.' That policy, he said, was 'No Trident, no Cruise, no bases, no Polaris'.

Tory campaigners found another useful target in Labour's financial and industrial plans. Speaking on 23 May Mrs Thatcher named six major electronic, pharmaceutical and construction firms as being on Labour's 'hit list' for nationalization, adding: 'Under a Labour Government there is virtually nowhere you could put your savings where they would be safe from the state.' Although quitting the EEC was a major plank in Labour's platform the policy was not vigorously pressed, whereas Tory campaigners made much of the threat that they claimed it would bring to British exports and jobs, not least in the highly Europeanized car industry. On the eve of the poll Mr Pym accused Labour of ignoring the EEC issue in their campaign because they knew it was a vote-loser.

Much Labour effort was spent on warnings of dire economic and social consequences if Mrs Thatcher were returned to power. A Conservative Government, Labour spokesmen said, would move still further to the right. Conservative promises and forecasts on public spending, unemployment, interest rates and inflation were proved false, they claimed, by confidential official documents which came into their hands during the election. Citing a 'secret' document, Mr Healey declared on 30 May that the Conservatives planned to destroy the NHS by piecemeal privatization. The document proved to be no more than a confidential circular to health authority chairmen on the need for economy in overheads. Mrs Thatcher branded Mr Healey's charge as 'a cruel, callous scare', adding 'I have no more intention of dismantling the health service than of dismantling Britain's defences.'

For the Alliance, Mr Steel led an effective electoral campaign and was a particularly convincing television personality. On the SDP side, Mr Jenkins cut a less prominent figure than Dr Owen, who also figured well on 'the box'. One trade union leader urged his members to vote tactically in order to remove the Thatcher Government, expressly by voting for Liberals where Labour's chances were weakest. This idea found no favour with his party's leaders, but there were signs that the Tories were suffering late anxieties about a swing to the Alliance.

Dr Owen claimed on 5 June that the Alliance was now the second force in British politics—the only group able to prevent a Tory landslide. A poll taken on the eve of election day, 9 June, gave the Alliance 26 per cent against Labour's 28 per cent, figures which proved very close to the actual result. The effect of the first-past-the-post system, however, was to make the numbers of seats obtained by the several groups very different from their proportions of the votes.

GENERAL ELECTION RESULTS

	May 1979			*June 1983*		
	votes '000	% of poll	Seats won	votes '000	% of poll	Seats won
Conservative	13,697	43·9	339	13,012	42·4	397
Labour	11,509	36·9	268	8,461	27·6	209
Liberal/Alliance	4,313	13·8	11	7,776	25·4	23
Scottish National	504	1·6	2	332	1·1	2
Plaid Cymru	132	0·4	2	125	0·4	2
Others*	887	2·8	13	962	3·1	17
	31,042		635	30,669		650

*Mainly Northern Irish seats (see pp. 47-48).

The turnout was 72·7 per cent, 3 per cent less than in 1979.

The SDP's leaders Mr Jenkins and Dr Owen, with four other supporters, held their seats against the odds, but their former ministerial colleagues Mr William Rodgers and Mrs Shirley Williams failed. Among other prominent political figures defeated were Mr David Ennals, Mr Albert Booth, Mr Gerry Fitt—the Independent Member for Belfast West (see p. 48)—and Mr Tony Benn, who, when his previous Bristol constituency was abolished, was obliged to fight on less favourable ground. The notorious north-south imbalance between Labour and parties to its right was somewhat redressed in England (the Darlington by-election result, for instance, was reversed), and even in Scotland Labour lost its majority of the seats (see p. 43).

Despite their winning a Commons majority of 144 over all other parties, the result was manifestly less a victory for the Conservatives than a catastrophe for the Labour Party. The numbers who voted Labour fell by 26½ per cent, to their lowest proportion of the poll since 1935. Even more telling was the count of lost deposits—that is, candidates who failed to obtain one-eighth of the votes cast. Labour notched up more lost deposits in this one election than the total it had suffered in all the general elections since World War II. It was evident that, outside its strongholds in Scotland, South Wales, other coal-mining areas and the inner cities, much of Labour's traditional working-class support had melted away. Fewer than 40 per cent of trade unionists were estimated to have voted Labour. South of a line from the Severn to the Wash the party won only 29 of the 260 seats, against 103 in 1966.

What were the reasons for this disaster? The party's campaign direction and organization were undoubtedly much weaker than those of the Conservatives. The appearance of a new moderate party could attract some blame, though if the SDP had not existed, and if the Liberals had contested all constituencies, the result might not have been far different. Mr Foot, the party leader, was unconvincing as a potential Prime Minister. But the major reasons lay much deeper. The Labour Party had wasted its energy for two years or more upon internecine disputes. The 'soft left', to which Mr Foot belonged, had proved unable either to bridge or to conceal an ever-widening split between left and right. Virtual capitulation to the left had saddled Labour with a number of policies, especially those on nuclear arms and EEC membership, in which many of its best-known figures did not believe with any conviction, and which were inherently unpopular. As for Labour's spectacular economic promises, one after another former Labour Ministers recounted after the election that people had simply not believed them. Such fringe policies, too, as ending private medicine and attacking independent education were vote-losers rather than vote-winners.

Behind all this, however, lay a deeper cause, subsequently admitted by influential party and trade union leaders. In the past twenty years the socio-economic character of the country had radically changed. The working-class, as known to Labour tradition and ideology, had declined not only in relative but in absolute numbers. More and more workers had gained middle-class incomes and adopted middle-class values. The changes were epitomized in the decline of city population and the dispersal of people to suburbs and new towns. (In Milton Keynes, for example, a new town with a large working population engaged mainly in light industry and services, the Labour candidate secured only 22·2 per cent of the votes, against 48 per cent for the winning Tory and 28·4 per cent for the SDP/Alliance candidate). Trade union leaders, elected for their industrial militancy, were politically deserted by many of their members. In short, Labour's old power base had been permanently eroded.

The second conspicuous aspect of the election figures was the huge distortion of the parliamentary outcome by the lack of any system of proportional representation. If seats won had been in direct ratio to votes cast nationally, the House of Commons would have comprised Conservatives 276, Labour 179, Alliance 165, Others 30. No one knows what would have been the result of any preferential or second-ballot system, but it would have been unlikely to return an absolute Conservative majority. The protests of Alliance spokesmen were predictably loud, but neither of the two larger parties was apt to forego a system which had served them so advantageously.

Chapter 3

POST–ELECTION TURBULENCE

MRS Thatcher's first move after her electoral victory was to reconstitute her Cabinet. The severest change was her dismissal of Mr Francis Pym, the Foreign Secretary. That Mr Pym and the Prime Minister had their differences was an open secret: he was, in terms of the colloquial epithets 'wet' and 'dry' on economic policy, too damp for Mrs Thatcher's liking; and during the election campaign he blotted his copybook by saying that rather than a Tory landslide he would prefer a majority of 50 to 100—to which Mrs Thatcher retorted 'We want as many Conservatives returned as we can possibly get', adding 'I think I could handle a landslide majority all right.' Nevertheless his dismissal from office was a shock to many Tories. In the House of Commons on 29 June he described it as an 'acutely hurtful experience'. He called on the Prime Minister to 'use her formidable talents to serve all the people of this country, not only those who can stand on their own two feet': the first priority should be an imaginative long-term approach to the problem of unemployment, so that 'the country never has to make the choice between being divided but rich and being united but poor'.

The other Cabinet changes were less dramatic, though their tenor was to favour those Ministers closest in line with Mrs Thatcher's own thinking. Mr Whitelaw, Home Secretary, was elevated to the Lords with a viscounty, but remained in the Cabinet as Lord President and still Mrs Thatcher's deputy. For the rest, it was mostly a case of reshuffling portfolios among the previous incumbents (see DOCUMENTS). Of these translations, the most important was that of Sir Geoffrey Howe to the Foreign and Commonwealth Office (FCO) and his succession as Chancellor of the Exchequer by Mr Nigel Lawson. The Secretaryships for Trade and Industry were combined, in the person of Mr Cecil Parkinson, formerly Chancellor the Duchy of Lancaster, the party chairman. Mr David Howell (Transport) and Baroness Young (Lord Privy Seal) left the Cabinet, but the latter was consoled with a Ministry of State at the FCO. Lord Hailsham, Mr Heseltine, Sir Keith Joseph, Mr Prior and Mr Tebbit retained their former offices. A newcomer to the Cabinet, as Minister of Agriculture, was Mr Michael Jopling, previously Chief Whip. Ministerial appointments outside the Cabinet appeared to favour no particular section of the party. Mr Richard Luce, who had resigned as Minister of State at the Foreign Office after Argentina had invaded the Falklands (see AR 1982, p. 8), was restored to his former post.

On 15 June, when MPs reassembled, Mr Bernard Weatherill, a Conservative member of long standing, was elected Speaker. His Labour predecessor cheerfully accepted a peerage, becoming Viscount Tonypandy. The dissolution honours list was preceded by a well-publicized argument between the Prime Minister and Mr Foot. The latter was reported to have asked for 27 Labour peerages in order to strengthen the party's relatively small representation in the House of Lords, but to have been told flatly that he could have no more than the usual Opposition quota of half-a-dozen. When the list was published he was seen to have secured seven, all but one of his nominees being in their late 50s; omitted were at least four former senior Ministers, all over 65, who might have expected elevation to the Upper House. (In the New Year honours list, published on 31 December, Mrs Thatcher, on her own initiative, elevated two of them). Peerages were also granted, among others, to Sir Harold Wilson, Mr Jo Grimond and Mr Gerry Fitt.

While the Tory team in high office remained much as before, Opposition leadership underwent sharper change. On 13 June Mr Jenkins resigned as leader of the SDP, expressing the hope, which was indeed fulfilled, that Dr David Owen would succeed him without a contest. The reason he gave was that the party should choose a leader for the next general election; at that time he might be 68, Dr Owen only 50. On the previous day Mr Foot had confirmed that he would not seek re-election as Labour's leader, thus setting in motion the cumbrous, three-month-long process of choosing his successor. The possibility of a leadership struggle in the Liberal Party loomed when on 14 June Mr Steel said that he was not committed to leading the party at the next general election, a statement interpreted as demanding his own terms for remaining, especially continuance of the Alliance with the SDP. On 7 July it was announced that Mr Steel was taking a two-months' break to recover from the effects of overwork, and it was later revealed that he was suffering from a glandular infection which took toll of his energy and spirits.

The dilemma of the Labour Party in face of its defeat was manifest: should it stick to is electorally proclaimed policies in the belief not only that they were right, but also that the electorate would come to see that they were right, or should it conclude that the electorate would continue to reject them, and that any hope of office depended upon their being changed? The choice was commonly depicted as one between a future for the party, in the words of Mr Roy Hattersley, as 'an unhappy compromise between a protest movement and a pressure group' and a future as an alternative government with a broad national base. This fundamental controversy was publicly aired in the contest for the party's leadership and deputy leadership, Mr Healey not wishing to stand again for the latter post.

The declared candidates were: for leader, Mr Neil Kinnock, Mr Roy Hattersley, Mr Peter Shore and Mr Eric Heffer; for deputy leader, Mr Hattersley, Mr Michael Meacher, Mr Denzil Davies and Mrs Gwyneth Dunwoody. A television debate between the four contenders for the leadership on 31 July revealed sharp differences in attitudes towards radical changes in party policy. Mr Kinnock, of the 'soft left', who throughout the campaign made party unity his main theme, insisted that 'the main body of our policies must not be jettisoned', though they needed refinement. Mr Heffer, of the hard left, took a similar line. The candidates of the moderate right, Mr Hattersley and Mr Shore, thought differently. Those who held no change was necessary, said Mr Hattersley, showed extraordinary complacency. Labour must distance itself from 'corrosive extremism' or a third defeat would set socialism back for the rest of the century, perhaps for ever.

These contradictory positions were elaborated in speeches and broadcast interviews. Mr Hattersley and Mr Shore were strongly against unilateral nuclear disarmament—the most unpopular policy on which Labour had ever fought an election, said Mr Hattersley; 'despairing and negative', said Mr Shore. According to Mr Kinnock, a confirmed supporter of CND, Britain's status as a nuclear power should be used for the sole purpose of securing force reductions, 'culminating in a non-nuclear defence strategy within the lifetime of a parliament'. On the EEC issue Mr Kinnock retreated a step from the policy of immediate withdrawal, Mr Hattersley was emphatically for remaining a member, Mr Shore emphatically against. Mr Hattersley and Mr Shore called for a comprehensive incomes policy to counter inflation, but Mr Kinnock saw no difficulty in avoiding inflation under Labour's economic plan and the national economic assessment. On wider electoral strategy there were also different approaches. Labour, said Mr Shore, had failed to respond to the great social changes that had taken place in Britain since the 1950s. The party, said Mr Kinnock, had lost votes to the Alliance by concentrating on policies for the poor, the unemployed and minorities: 'if we are to be of real use to the deprived and insecure, we must have the support of those in more secure social circumstances.'

When it became clear that Mr Kinnock was running far in front as leader the crucial contest appeared to be between a Kinnock-Hattersley and a Kinnock-Meacher ticket, the former signalling an attempt to hold left and right together by compromise, the latter a ratification of the party's radical move to the left. Mr Meacher described the 'dream ticket' of Kinnock - Hattersley as 'putting together two persons fundamentally opposed in their views'. Even he of the hard left, however, trimmed on nuclear disarmament, saying: 'I do not believe Labour will win an election ... unless its defence policy broadly obtains national support', which might be demonstrated by a referendum.

The actual vote, on 2 October, the eve of the Labour Party conference at Brighton, overwhelmingly endorsed the 'dream ticket'. For leader, Mr Kinnock received 71·3 per cent of the electoral college votes, and for deputy leader Mr Hattersley received 67·3 per cent. All three elements in the college—MPs, constituencies and unions—showed majorities for a result that clearly placed electoral considerations above socialist militancy.

Before the contest, Neil Kinnock had been a little-known figure outside the Labour Party. He had never held Cabinet office, and as front-bench spokesman on education he had not been conspicuous. Scots on both sides, red-haired, the son of a labourer, he was born, brought up and educated in Wales (see also p. 45), had married a Welsh girl, had represented a Welsh constituency since 1970, and had acquired much of the oratorical manner of the Welsh; his political foes called him a windbag, his friends likened him to his hero Aneurin Bevan. At 41, he was the youngest man ever to lead his party. Of the democratic left, he had incurred the enmity of the far left by his criticism of Mr Benn. His political opponents did not underrate him as an attractive public personality and a determined leader of his party. The first national opinion poll taken after his election showed the following voting intentions: Conservatives 37 per cent, Labour 32, Alliance 19, Others 2. This was a dramatic contrast with the only by-election held since 9 June, in Penrith and the Borders, Lord Whitelaw's former constituency. There, on 29 July, the Alliance increased its share of the vote by 16·7 per cent, cutting the Conservative majority from 15,421 to 552, while the Labour candidate won only 7·4 per cent of the votes.

Notwithstanding Mr Kinnock's stress on party unity the major sources of disunity could not be concealed at Brighton. On 5 October the conference voted decisively for the unconditional renunciation of all existing nuclear weapons and their elimination from British soil and British waters within the lifetime of a Labour Government. At the tail end of the debate Mr Callaghan intervened after being accused of sabotaging Labour's electoral campaign by his Cardiff speech (see p. 18). The party's established multilateralist policy, he said, had been cast aside without any attempt to convince the electorate. Mr Healey, in broadcast interviews, said that he broadly agreed with Mr Callaghan, and that Mr Kinnock should aim to expunge unconditional nuclear disarmament from party policy.

Other conference votes were less radical. By a majority of over three to one the appeals of five MT leaders against their expulsion were rejected. The conference also rejected motions for ending the sale of council houses to tenants and for binding Labour MPs to party policy on every issue. It resolved on campaigns of attack against the abolition of the Greater London Council and of defence of the NHS against the Government's economies. It gave a rapturous ovation to the man who acknowledged his responsibility for Labour's defeat, Mr Michael Foot, as if to say that not only the defects of his leadership but also the divisions over which he had presided were now to be forgotten. The delegates departed confident that they had placed Labour back in its role of alternative government.

The party's trade union component had already changed its stance. It, too, was facing a sectional decline, having lost half a million members of TUC constituent unions in 1982. The TUC's annual Congress in the first week of September approved by a card vote of 5·8 million to 4·0 million a fundamental reappraisal of the movement's political policies. By a decisive show of hands it defeated a motion refusing participation in the National Economic Development Council, and its elections to the TUC's general council gave a two-to-one majority to pragmatists who wanted, *inter alia,* to resume regular contacts with the Employment Secretary. The TUC's general secretary, Mr Len Murray, told the Congress: 'We cannot talk as if the trade union movement were some sort of alternative government . . .. We cannot just say that our policies are fine and that it is our members who are all wrong.' A divergence on policy from the Labour Party was clearly seen in a resolution on nuclear arms, overwhelmingly supported, which while condemning Trident as well as Cruise omitted any mention of unilateral disarmament or the removal of nuclear bases.

Labour's annual conference had been preceded by comparable meetings of the Council for Social Democracy (CSD) and the Liberal Assembly. For both, the prime issue was continuance of the Alliance, which each overwhelmingly supported. The two parties differed, however, on the means of cementing it. Among Liberals there was a strong call for joint selection of parliamentary candidates, which was already being practised in a number of constituencies and which would seem to lead inexorably to a merger of the two parties. This was not the programme of the SDP under Dr Owen's leadership; he evidently believed that his party had a long way to go before a merger would be to its own advantage or that of the Alliance. The CSD voted decisively on 11 September against a merger before the next general election and in favour of joint selection for the 1984 European Parliament elections only 'in exceptional circumstances'. This had to be reluctantly accepted by the Liberals. Speaking to the Liberal Assembly as an applauded guest, Dr Owen, adverting to the problem of indicating who would be Alliance Prime Minister, said: 'The proper constitutional position would be that whoever had the largest number of MPs would be called upon by the Queen to form a Government'; Mr Steel agreed. The Liberal Assembly showed its confidence in Mr Steel by voting decisively both for retaining the party leader's final authority over an election manifesto and against having a deputy leader, as desired by Mr Steel's critics, notably Mr Cyril Smith, who petulantly distanced himself from his fellow Liberal MPs.

Among other resolutions, the Liberal Assembly voted against further privatization of public services and for the opening of negotiations with Argentina. It dismayed the leadership by adopting by 395 votes to 324 a resolution affirming the long-term objective of a united Ireland and demanding the creation meanwhile of an all-Ireland Council.

On nuclear arms the Liberal Party's unilateralist policy (see AR 1982, pp. 23-4 and 26) held the field. Mr Steel hedged on the deployment of Cruise missiles by saying, in his closing speech to the Assembly, that the Liberal vote in Parliament would partly depend on the Government's contribution to the arms limitation process in the coming weeks. Dr Owen had told his own party conference (CSD) that the SDP was ready to support the Government over Cruise unless the USSR made adequate concessions in the Geneva talks. It was a profound mistake, he said, to reject Cruise simply over the absence of 'dual key' (see p. 13). Dr Owen widened the intra-Alliance split by saying on 19 October that Cruise should be deployed and thereafter the INF arms talks should concentrate on Pershing, to the introduction of which the Liberals were totally opposed. The CSD endorsed a radical social policy which would combine tax and social benefits in one system and replace all means-tested benefits by a single benefit granted according to need, the system to be partly financed by abolition of the married man's allowance against tax.

The Conservative Party conference in the second week of October was almost totally overshadowed by a personal affair concerning one of the party's most admired leaders. On 5 October solicitors acting for Mr Cecil Parkinson, Secretary of State for Trade and Industry (he had been succeeded as party chairman by Mr John Selwyn Gummer, MP, in mid-September), issued a statement acknowledging that he had had a long relationship with his former secretary, Miss Sara Keays, of such a nature that she was expecting his child; that he had wished to marry her but had now decided to stay with his wife, and was financially providing for his mistress and their child; and that they had agreed to say nothing further on the subject in public. On behalf of the Prime Minister it was at once declared that the question of Mr Parkinson's resignation did not and would not arise. The popular and indeed the more respectable press, and the broadcasting institutions, made the most of this luscious scandal. Mr Parkinson braved the conference by making the final speech in a debate on industry on 13 October, and was received with applause by the great majority of the delegates.

Late that same evening, however, Miss Keays broke the agreed silence with a long statement to *The Times*, made, she said, because 'press judgment and public opinion have been influenced by inadequate information, speculation and the Government's desire to restore Mr Parkinson's position'. 'My baby,' said Miss Keays, 'was conceived in a long-standing loving relationship which I allowed to continue because I believed in our eventual marriage.' Mr Parkinson had first offered marriage in 1979, but between May and September 1983 he changed his mind three times, back and forth.

Within hours Mr Parkinson resigned office and left the party conference, accompanied by his wife. By this time he had no other option, though some thought the whole affair smelled of hypocrisy. Whether or not in principle private conduct should affect public office, the fact remained that a course of a double deceit and inconstancy had struck down the ministerial career of a rising political star, and had tarnished the public's estimate of Mrs Thatcher's judgment. Mr Parkinson, after consulting his constituents, decided not to leave the House of Commons. His daughter by Miss Keays was born on New Year's Eve.

Meanwhile, at the Conservative conference, at least one event had achieved banner headlines against the competition of sexual scandal. Mr Leon Brittan, the new Home Secretary, responded to widespread Tory clamour for sterner defence of law and order by announcing a series of measures intensifying the punishment of violent crime. Murderers of police or prison officers, sexual or sadistic murderers of children, terrorist murderers and criminals who killed with firearms in the course of robbery would serve a minimum of 20 years in prison. Killers of security guards, post office or public transport staff could expect very long imprisonment, and there would be no parole for those sentenced to more than five years for violence or drug trafficking. The maximum sentence for carrying firearms in furtherance of crime would be raised from 14 years to life. At the other end of the scale of offences, in order to lighten the overload on prisons, studies would be made both of ways to keep minor offenders like fine defaulters or drunks out of gaol, and of day or weekend imprisonment and possible 'camp-style' prisons; and a stepped-up prison building programme would create 4,800 new places by 1991.

The Blackpool conference revealed some difference within the Cabinet as to priority for tax cuts over maintained social spending. The Chancellor of the Exchequer committed the party to a reduction of taxation, which he claimed afforded the best chance of faster growth. But in a pre-conference television interview Mr John Biffen, Leader of the House, had said that the need for tax cuts must be set alongside other responsibilities, fulfilling the Tory party's 'well-established tradition of the protective role of the state'; and at a Blackpool fringe meeting of the Tory Reform group Mr James Prior, Secretary for Northern Ireland, expressed opposition to cuts in taxation at the expense of health, education and the social services. The Prime Minister, in a characteristic closing speech which brought the conference to its feet for some eight minutes, pledged the Government's unswerving adherence to its strict financial course. Aware of widespread unease at its chiselling of the resources of the health service, she declared: 'the NHS is safe only with us because only this Government will see that it is prudently managed and financed.'

Leakage of the report of an inquiry instituted by the Young Conservatives (YC), which had concluded that 'extreme and racialist forces are at work inside the Conservative Party', prompted an announcement on 9 October that in future would-be Tory candidates would have to disclose whether they had ever belonged to another party. This followed the appearance of a candidate at the general election who had concealed his former membership of the far-right racist National Front and who came within 102 votes of winning the seat. At the Blackpool conference a motion demanding an end to all further immigration from the Indian sub-continent, the promotion of voluntary repatriation and the repeal of all race relations laws was decisively rejected, but its proponents were loudly cheered by a minority: the mover was one of the Tory MPs indicted for extremism in the YC report.

Chapter 4

THE NEW PARLIAMENT

THE new Parliament was opened in state on 22 June. The Queen's Speech reflected the promises of the Tory manifesto and the pursuit of financial and other policies launched in the previous Parliament. Among the actions foreshadowed beyond the main stream were measures to establish an independent prosecution service, to protect information held on computers and to develop cable broadcasting systems. The debate on the Speech followed predictable lines. In Mr Foot's view it combined complacency and callousness on a scale scarcely imaginable. Mrs Thatcher said that even now inflation was higher than that of Britain's competitors West Germany and Japan, and must be reduced further. The Government had a five-point strategy for job-creation: cutting production costs, encouragement of small businesses, support for new technology, training of manpower and trade union reform.

One issue which the Government decided to get out of the way quickly was that of restoring the death penalty for murder. It was supposed that the increased Conservative numbers in the Commons, and in particular the attitudes of the new Tory MPs, might produce a majority for restoration, at least for terrorist murders and murders of police and prison officers. The debate on 12 July was preceded by public agitation on both sides, in which organizations of the police and prison officers were ranged against the churches, the Bar Council and prison governors, among others. Votes were taken on a series of amendments to the general proposition, the decisive one being the first, on death for terrorist murder, which was rejected by 361 votes to 245, a majority of 116: the majority fell to 81 on murder of police officers. A 5 to 2 majority of the new Conservative members voted for hanging. The issue was thereafter regarded as dead for the present Parliament, perhaps for ever. Supporters of the death penalty called for a referendum, believing public opinion to be on their side, but on 14 July the Home Secretary, Mr Brittan, who had joined the Prime Minister in voting for restoration, told the House 'I do not believe that matters which are not of a constitutional kind are suitable for a referendum.'

The hottest and driest summer for many years was as misleading a heavenly signal of the Government's comfort in renewed office as the wet spring had been of its electoral fortune. The debate on the Queen's Speech behind them, the missing clauses of the Finance Bill restored, and the legislative programme set in motion, they were soon having to take unpleasant financial medicine. A Government proposal to increase the salaries of MPs by only 4 per cent, in line with public servants generally, against 31 per cent recommended in May by the Top Salaries Review Body, raising them to £19,000 p.a., aroused such fury among Tory MPs that a Commons defeat was possible, the Opposition being virtually unanimous for the higher rate of pay. A compromise was negotiated under which there would be five annual increments of $5\frac{1}{2}$ per cent, and from 1987 onwards MPs' pay would be linked with that of civil servants. In the small hours of 20 July the Government were defeated by 226 votes to 218 on an amendment linking salaries with those of officials earning £18,500 in 1983, not in 1987 as Ministers proposed; the main motion was carried by 237 votes to 216. Mrs Thatcher declined the large increase proposed for the Prime Minister by the Review Board, and other Ministers accepted far less than had been recommended.

The Cabinet was reported to have approved on 7 July departmental expenditure cuts totalling £500 million in 1983-84, nearly half of them in defence, and half of the rest in the health service. In addition, £500 million would be raised from the sale of assets. The Treasury's imperative demand for further economy, three months into the fiscal year, dismayed Ministers in charge of spending departments. It was revealed that excesses on programmed expenditure to a total of over £1,000 million were being incurred under EEC commitments, and nearly as much on payments determined by the volume of demand for statutory benefits. The room for quick manoeuvre was thus strictly limited.

Largely as a result of high unemployment and above-average pay rises for public employees, the share of national income taken and disbursed by the state had actually risen, despite the Tory efforts at economy and austerity, and was set to rise further in future years for demographic reasons. The pledge given to Nato to increase real spending on defence by

3 per cent p.a. in real terms, the honouring of which had been another major cause of the overall financial strain, would expire in 1985-86. After a stern battle between the Treasury and the Ministry of Defence, the Cabinet agreed to substitute in 1986 a new formula which would reduce the liability. Another well-publicized Cabinet dispute arose between Mr Peter Walker, Secretary for Energy, and the Chancellor of the Exchequer, who wanted faster repayment of capital advances by the electricity and gas industries, at the cost of higher prices. Mr Walker's persistence in seeking to hold down the cost of energy appeared to have succeeded when he announced on 19 December that electricity prices for industry would not be increased, and that those for domestic users would rise by only 2 per cent in March, the Treasury having demanded a 3 per cent rise all round.

A White Paper published on 1 August promised legislation enabling the Government to set maximum expenditure levels for every local council in England and Wales and to impose ceilings on increases in local rates. The Conservative-controlled Association of County Councils protested that the very essence of local democracy was being threatened. Rises in rates, it argued, had been due chiefly to cuts in central support grants and the Government's unrealistic allowance for pay and price inflation. Opponents of the Government's policy contended that it was irrelevant to control of public sector borrowing because local authorities could not borrow to meet current expenditure. The retort was to the effect that high rates and extravagant local spending were an evil in themselves, falling sharpest on the hard-pressed and particularly on industry and commerce, which contributed 60 per cent of total rates but had no vote. Pressure mounted on all sides for a fundamental reform of the sources of local authority finance. The Secretary of State, however, said on 30 September that the present system of rates would continue for the foreseeable future, no viable alternative having been identified.

On 20 December Mr Jenkin published his Rates Bill, empowering the Government to name (in the first instance by mid-1984) high-spending councils and to fix ceilings on their rate levels for the ensuing year, above which ratepayers would not be obliged to pay; and to assume reserve powers—to be used, said Mr Jenkin, 'only if absolutely necessary', but nevertheless a constant threat—to cap the rates of all councils in England and Wales. The director-general of the CBI described this as 'a much-needed restraint', but the outcry among local authorities was more hostile than ever. In the House of Commons, Sir Geoffrey Rippon, a previous Conservative Secretary for the Environment, called the Bill deplorable—'a classic example of elective dictatorship'. It was expected to encounter all-party and cross-bench opposition, especially in the House of Lords, but Mr Jenkin pledged his resignation if it were defeated. He had already announced that Treasury rate-support grants in 1984-85 would drop by one per cent in real terms, thus heightening the impulse for higher rates if local services were not to be cut.

Another front on which the Government fought for economy was the pay of public employees. On 15 September the Cabinet agreed to set a target maximum of 3 per cent for the overall increase in public sector pay in 1984-85, the comparable objective in the current year being $3\frac{1}{2}$ per cent. The announcement brought the expected protest from public service unions, especially those of civil servants, who felt themselves to be singled out for Mrs Thatcher's disfavour.

The Government followed the immediate cut in the NHS budget which it had made in August by declaring manpower targets for the several regions. After negotiation with the 14 regional authorities the required cuts were reported to total 4,837 employees, including some doctors and nurses. The Health Minister argued that manpower budgeting, never previously applied, was as necessary as financial control, and that even after the cuts the Government was spending more in real terms on the NHS than ever before. Nevertheless, defence of the health service was a popular and emotive cry, and the opposition parties made the most of their opportunity. Not only the more militant unions but also the Royal College of Nursing and many doctors protested that the financial and manpower cuts would lower the standard of health care. A team of businessmen invited by the Government to inquire into the management of the NHS reported in October that big changes were desirable, including the appointment of a national management board and general managers for all health authorities and hospitals. The report was welcomed by the Government: doctors approved, but nurses complained that they were being subordinated.

Following his predecessor's practice, the Chancellor of the Exchequer made an autumn financial statement to Parliament on 17 November. Public expenditure in 1984-85 would be held to the previously planned total of £126,400 million. The principal interdepartmental changes from the earlier White Paper forecasts were £278 million less for defence, £733 million less for nationalized industries, £492 million less for housing, £140 million more for education, £32 million more for health and personal social services, and £911 million more for social security. The PSBR was estimated at £8,000 million, about the same as the 1983 Budget forecast, which would probably be exceeded by £2,000 million. Mr Lawson based his figures on a forecast of 3 per cent per annum growth in output and inflation falling to $4\frac{1}{2}$ per cent by the last quarter of 1984. Despite these hopeful predictions he depressed his supporters by warning that the forecast expenditure implied some net increases in taxes in the next Budget. Mr Hattersley, in his new role as Shadow Chancellor, congratulated Mr Lawson on keeping faith with the arithmetic, but accused him of breaking faith with the electorate. The main thrust of

Opposition attack in the debate on the statement, however, was against the Government's failure to stimulate the economy by increased capital expenditure, and a few dissident Tories took the same cue.

Mr Pym again made himself the spokesman of Tory dissent. Speaking in Oxford on 30 November, he expressed his dismay at the Government's commitment to cut taxes. Unemployment, he said, was now a more serious problem than inflation; attempts to cure the problems of the next decade by applying economic measures in a social void could lead to catastrophe. An echo of such views was heard from within the Cabinet itself when Mr Peter Walker, in an end-of-year message to the Tory Reform group, of which he was president, pleaded for policies that would reduce unemployment, promote economic expansion and help the inner cities.

On 28 November it was announced that legislation would be introduced to allow opticians to advertise and non-opticians to sell spectacles. Critics were not slow to point the contrast between this policy and the Government's hostility towards a private member's Bill, sponsored by a Labour MP, Mr Austin Mitchell, ending the monopoly of solicitors in conveyancing house property. Despite pressure from Government Whips and an attempt by the Solicitor-General to mollify backbenchers with a promise of a Law Commission inquiry into simplifying conveyancing, Mr Mitchell's Bill was given a second reading on a Friday morning in December by a majority of 20; 24 Conservatives voted for the measure.

Thus the Government, despite its electoral triumph, suffered a series of mishaps from midsummer onwards—the ill public reception of its cuts in the NHS, the Parkinson affair, the widespread opposition to its policy towards local authorities, Tory misgivings over its reaction to the Grenada invasion (see pp. 39-40), rebuffs from the EEC, defeats on secondary issues in the House of Commons. It seemed to be accident-prone and was lampooned by the Opposition as a 'banana-skin Government'.

The Labour Party, however, suffered a graver blow to its cohesion late in the year, when an industrial dispute concerning a few employees in a small firm blew up into a major confrontation between unions and the law, which in turn split the trade union movement down the middle. A Mr Selim Shah had built up a prosperous business, known as the Messenger Group, producing give-away local newspapers in the north-west of England. He clashed with the National Graphical Association (NGA), the compositors' union, over the closed shop—a sacred cow for the Association—and dismissed six NGA men who took hostile action. Over four months later, Mr Shah obtained a court injunction against 'secondary picketing' (not at the pickets' place of employment) of his printing works at Warrington. The NGA defied the injunction and on 18 November was fined £50,000 for contempt of court, and another

£100,000 a week later. The union refused to pay and threatened a complete stoppage of the country's printing industry. On 25 November NGA employees of national newspapers walked out; all Fleet Street was idle for two days, and two newspapers did not reappear until 29 November. All members of the Newspaper Publishers' Association filed suits for damages, estimated at over £10 million.

So far from obeying the court, the NGA intensified its action at Warrington. Mass pickets, including many demonstrators from other areas and industries, resulted in serious violence and a number of arrests. On 30 November the High Court granted an injunction against any repetition of the Fleet Street walk-out, and the Court of Appeal confirmed an order to seize the NGA's assets, believed to total some £10 million, for payment of the fines and costs that had been imposed. Mr Shah launched another legal action, but the judge deferred the case for a week to give the parties time to reach a settlement. Talks with ACAS as intermediary came to nothing, however, and on 9 December a High Court judge imposed further fines on the NGA totalling £525,000, for 'blatant, deliberate breaches of the order and a very serious contempt of court' (see also Pt. XIV, Ch. 2).

The focus of the struggle now shifted to the TUC. On 29 November a statement from its headquarters had denounced the Employment Acts of 1980 and 1982 (see AR 1980, p. 11, and 1982, pp. 30-31) under which the court actions had been brought, as converting 'a small localized dispute involving an intransigent employer' into a major constitutional crisis; the TUC's general council would be asked to assist the NGA in carrying out 'its lawful functions'. In the early hours of 13 December the TUC's employment policy committee voted by 9 to 7 to support a 24-hour NGA strike in all national and local newspapers; but Mr Len Murray, the TUC's secretary-general, publicly repudiated the committee's decision and called for its reversal, arguing that it would put the TUC itself in legal jeopardy. The next day, after a long and stormy meeting, the general council supported him by 29 votes to 21. The intended newspaper strike was called off.

The issue for the TUC was epitomized in the instant comments of rival union leaders. The general secretary of the Civil and Public Services Association, Mr Alastair Graham, said: 'Opposition to the industrial relations legislation has to be within the law. We are not going to support unlawful action.' In the words of Mr Joe Wade, general secretary of the NGA, however, 'This is a black day not only for the NGA but for the whole trade union movement. The decision taken by the general council is that its policy is now in conformity with the 1980 and 1982 Employment Acts.' The NGA decided to continue its struggle with the Messenger Group, and to enlist the help of other unions individually, but to desist from mass picketing of the Warrington plant.

For the NGA, a particular interest was at stake. It had been fighting against the impact of new printing technology on behalf of operatives who had earned high wages, especially in Fleet Street, under the protection of closed-shop agreements. (An NGA strike, largely over pay differentials, which had shut down the *Financial Times* from 1 June to 8 August, was ended only after the TUC had threatened to disaffiliate the Association for its obduracy in jeopardizing the jobs of other newspaper workers.) If the closed shop for NGA members was defeated their monopolistic power was in jeopardy. Mr Shah took his stand on a contrary principle, the right of his workers to decide whether to join a union, the NGA or any other. Speaking on 16 December the Home Secretary described the closed shop as 'a flagrant and fundamental denial of individual liberties' and gave warning that unless the unions learnt a lesson from the NGA experience the closed shop would be in jeopardy.

On two other occasions during the year the Employment Acts were successfully invoked against unlawful industrial action: the National Union of Journalists was bidden to stop its action against a printing firm in a local newspaper dispute (see Pt. XIV, Ch. 2), and, more importantly, an injunction was served on the Union of Post Office Engineers halting a campaign of selective action against British Telecom, basically in opposition to its privatization and particularly to its link with the private communications company, Mercury.

The dilemma which split the TUC was equally a dilemma for the Labour Party. At the height of the dispute Mr Kinnock conspicuously avoided declaring in Parliament whether he stood squarely for observance or for defiance of the law. His line was to insist that the cause of all the trouble was legislation which overrode the established practice of industrial relations and imported legal enforcement into an area where it could only intensify problems. This theme was echoed both by the party's right wing, which was for observance of the law, and by its left wing, which was for defiance, calling in its aid a resolution of the 1983 party conference. Labour spokesmen also called repeatedly for the Government to intervene in the Messenger dispute; this Mrs Thatcher and the Employment Secretary steadfastly refused to do. These diversions could not conceal the reappearance of that bitter division between different elements in the Labour Party, and in its trade union affilate, which had led to its electoral defeat and which Mr Kinnock's emollient but somewhat ambiguous leadership had not greatly affected.

Before the NGA affair, opinion polls had shown the Labour Party regaining ground that it had lost to the Alliance, while support for the Conservatives held close to the election figure. The Government hoped for a more positive swing of opinion in the light of some cheerful economic signs. While Ministers and the Bank of England grumbled that wage increases were still too high, a string of settlements both in public services and in private industry—notably in engineering, where the unions accepted a 5·2 per cent rise coupled with an undertaking to consider far-reaching productivity changes—were recorded at around the rate of inflation. The latter stood at 4·6 per cent in December. The seasonally adjusted total of unemployment, at 2,944,000 in December, had fallen marginally from a peak in June. Specially encouraging was an upturn in the numbers employed in manufacturing for the first time since 1979. The car industry enjoyed a particularly strong revival. An end-of-year OECD report observed that Britain's recovery was the fastest in Europe. While production, trade, prices and employment emitted favourable signals, however, two grave economic problems for the Government remained unresolved—first, the persistence of high and locally concentrated unemployment, distinguishing ever more sharply the condition of those in work, whose real earnings rose further, thanks largely to increased overtime and bonus payments, and those dependent on social security; and secondly the obdurate resistance of public expenditure to all efforts to cut it.

Chapter 5

FOREIGN AND COMMONWEALTH AFFAIRS

WAVES from the South Atlantic continued to break on British shores. The unanimous report of the committee of five privy councillors, under the chairmanship of Lord Franks, appointed to review the way in which the responsibilities of Government in relation to the Falkland Islands and their dependencies were discharged in the period leading up to the Argentine invasion (see AR 1982, p. 20) was published on 18 January (Cmnd. 8787). The committee concluded:

We would not be justified in attaching any criticism or blame to the present Government for the Argentine Junta's decision to commit its act of unprovoked aggression.

While this verdict was greeted with hearty relief by the Government, many critics, not all *parti-pris*, thought such a sweeping exculpation was not entirely justified by the historical facts rehearsed.

At issue was conduct alleged to have encouraged the Argentine junta in believing that Britain would gladly be rid of the Falklands incubus and would not resist *force majeure*. The Conservative Government's decision in 1981 to withdraw the patrol vessel HMS *Endurance* from the South Atlantic and its failure to send a nuclear-powered submarine to the area until 29 March 1982 had been contrasted in Parliament (see AR 1982, pp. 8-9), with the previous Labour Government's reaction to a menacing Argentine attitude in 1977, when a submarine and two frigates were deployed in the area. The Franks committee, while holding that a submarine could well have been sent earlier in 1982, disposed of the major contention by recording that the 1977 naval force was deliberately covert: 'We have found no evidence that the Argentine Government knew of its existence.' Furthermore the Committee concluded that in February 1982 the negotiating circumstances were different and 'did not warrant a similar naval deployment'.

More generally, critics laid hold of the Government's earlier floating of the notion of ceding sovereignty to Argentina in return for a long leaseback (see AR 1980, p. 35) and other acts of omission or commission which could have signalled to Buenos Aires a lack of interest in the long-term status and defence of the Falklands. A different line of criticism, muffled in the Franks report, fastened on the Government's rejection of a recommendation to launch a campaign of educating opinion on the need for a settlement with Argentina, after the rebuff to the leaseback proposal. The committee found to be 'totally without foundation' the allegation by certain critics of the Foreign and Commonwealth Office that its officials pursued a policy aimed at getting rid of the Islands, irrespective of the views of Ministers. However, the history narrated showed beyond argument that the purpose of successive Governments to reach a diplomatic settlement was inevitably frustrated by the irreconcilable conflict between passionate Argentine claims to unqualified sovereignty and British pledges, however expressed, not to determine the future of the Islanders against their wishes. No Government, the committee observed, did or could contemplate a 'Fortress Falklands' policy before the invasion.

Allegations that intelligence of the Argentine decision to invade was available from various sources several days before the action on 2 April were found unproven. Nevertheless, the committee observed in critical terms that the Joint Intelligence Organization had not prepared for Ministers any fresh assessment of the Falklands situation between July 1981 and 31 March 1982, and recommended that the intelligence assessment machinery be reviewed, with the aim of strengthening its central control under the Prime Minister. This recommendation was promptly carried out when Sir Antony Duff was appointed chairman of a reconstituted Joint Intelligence Committee responsible directly to the Prime Minister.

The Franks report was debated in both Houses of Parliament on 25 and 26 January. Opposition spokesmen concentrated on the charge that, *pace* Franks, the Government had brought about the invasion by negligently failing to take steps to defend the islands and thus encouraging the Argentine adventure. Neither Mr Callaghan nor Dr Owen (Prime Minister and Foreign Secretary in 1977) contested the finding that the naval deployment had not been notified to the Argentine Government, but they argued that their hands in negotiation had been greatly strengthened by having the threat up their sleeve. Dr Owen harshly attacked Mrs Thatcher for lack of magnanimity in victory, and for proclaiming the 'paramountcy' of the Islanders' wishes, but the Prime Minister was adamant, pledging that their desire 'for a life of freedom and peace under a government of their choice will never again be imperilled'. There could be no negotiations with Argentina on a transfer of sovereignty. The policy of 'Fortesss Falklands' was attacked for its immense cost, its diversion of defence resources from higher priorities, and the absurdity of its scale in proportion to the number of the Islanders; but alternative proposals were not strongly pressed. Such ideas as surfaced included merging the Falklands in an international regime the whole South Atlantic, a new Antarctic Treaty embracing them, or United Nations trusteeship. A hostile Opposition amendment in the Commons was defeated by 292 votes to 240.

The Government's policy of no negotiation with Argentina until the latter had formally declared a cessation of hostilities, and no negotiation over a transfer of sovereignty, was unaffected either by votes of United Nations organs or by political sniping at home. Plans announced included the building of a new military and civil airport, to cost £215 million and to be ready by April 1985, and of a highway from Port Stanley to Darwin via the new airport at Mount Pleasant. Farm animals and equipment were shipped out. Mrs Thatcher herself visited the islands in January. A visit by 541 relatives of British dead in April, at government expense, led to agitation for helping other war widows to visit graves in distant lands, and for better pensions for dependents of those killed in action. A similar visit by Argentine relatives was barred. Many people questioned the action of British banks in participating in a financial rescue scheme for Argentina, and when, on 11 July, a Bill raising the limit of Treasury lending to the IMF was debated in the Commons Mr Shore, Labour's foreign affairs spokesman, moved to reject a measure which imposed no conditions on financial aid to Argentina while the state of hostilities continued. The Chief Economic Secretary to the Treasury argued that 'default by Argentina would be inimical to the whole financial system upon which Britain depended more than most'; the wrecking amendment was defeated by 212 votes to 107.

Mr Tam Dalyell, MP, the Government's most persistent critic over the Falklands, kept up his wasp-like stings, especially over the sinking of the cruiser *General Belgrano* (see AR 1982, p. 12-13). On 1 June Mr Neil Kinnock charged the Government with having sunk the ship in order to scotch an unpalatable Peruvian peace plan, and Mr Healey supported him. However, Sir Nicholas Henderson, who was ambassador in Washington at the time, wrote in *The Economist* of 11 November that when the *Belgrano* was sunk no peace plan existed. Indeed in his view the Argentine junta, having launched a military attack, were never in a position to reach a peaceful settlement.

An incomplete report of the Commons Select Committee on foreign affairs, questioning the long-term viability, of 'Fortress Falklands', was leaked during the election campaign. A Tory MP who had been a member of the committee was to the fore in the creation of a South Atlantic Committee, including businessmen and academics as well as politicians of all parties, devoted to promoting a peaceful settlement of the Anglo-Argentine dispute. Such initiatives were encouraged by an exchange of messages between Mrs Thatcher and the Argentine President in December. 'On the occasion of your inauguration,' wrote the Prime Minister, 'I wanted to let you know that, although we have many differences, we can all take pleasure in the restoration of democracy in Argentina'; in reply Sr Alfonsín recalled 'an old English saying, "where there's a will there's a way".' Mrs Thatcher's message, said the Foreign Secretary the next day, had been part of a process of gradually restoring relations with Argentina, but there were some issues, like sovereignty, which it would not be helpful to begin discussing. Mrs Thatcher was more forthright. In a Christmas message to the Islanders she said 'I am not negotiating the sovereignty of the Falkland Islands with anyone. They are British. You, the people, have the right to determine your own future. This is not negotiable.'

The Falkland Islands were not the only colonial remnant to raise issues of future sovereignty. Talks with Spain about Gibraltar (see Pt. IV, Ch. 3) and with China about Hong Kong proceeded but were not extensively reported, except when rumours of a deadlock in the latter caused a temporary collapse of the Hong Kong dollar in September (see Pt. IX, Ch. 1). It was put about in December that agreement was near on the principles of a settlement on Hong Kong.

Friction in relations with the EEC concerned, as so often before, fisheries, the agricultural policy and Britain's financial contribution. A flare-up over Danish rejection of the new EEC regime for North Sea fishing resulted in the arrest and fining of a defiant Danish ship in January, but was quickly extinguished by a compromise between the Community and Denmark. The settlement of North Sea herring quotas in December was thought advantageous to Britain. Although Mr Walker, the responsible Minister, claimed a great success when the scale of farm prices for 1983, negotiated in April, was raised by an average of only 4·2 per cent, long-standing British criticism of the whole Common Agricultural Policy (CAP) was reinforced by growing realization of the great distortion it imposed in British public finance in favour of agriculture.

The EEC budgetary problem provoked some sharp criticism of Britain's European partners, for bad faith and dragging their feet. When the European Parliament voted on 15 December to stop payment of the £457 million rebate due to Britain by agreement of the Stuttgart summit (see Pt. XI, Ch. 4) members of all parties in the Commons expressed their outrage, but Mrs Thatcher, while 'greatly disappointed', was characteristically unruffled, insisting that the rebate could still be duly paid before the end of March; if not, she added darkly, 'we shall have to take action to safeguard our position.' The total failure of the Athens summit had likewise left the Prime Minister undismayed. In her view, the approach of the date in 1984 when the Community would run out of funds would concentrate member Governments' minds wonderfully.

The destruction of a Korean civil airliner by Soviet military aircraft on 1 September outraged the British public. Mrs Thatcher called it 'an atrocity against humanity', and Mr Healey 'a political crime'. One British citizen was among those killed. The Foreign Secretary immediately summoned the Soviet ambassador and demanded of his Government an explanation, an apology, compensation for the damage and loss of life, punishment of those responsible and measures to prevent a repetition of such an attack. He got no satisfaction. The Prime Minister found it 'inexplicable that we could not get a clearer condemnation by Europe and clearer action in the wider Nato sphere'. Nevertheless, she said, the disarmament negotiations must not be halted. Flights from Britain to Moscow were temporarily suspended, until it was realized that the gesture was totally ineffective. Popular British revulsion was tempered by a suspicion that the whole truth of the affair had not been told.

During a visit to Canada and the United States Mrs Thatcher said in Washington on 29 September that the West was 'confronted by a power of great military strength, which has consistently used force against its neighbours, which wields the threat of force as a weapon of policy, and which is bent on subverting and destroying the confidence and stability of the Western world'. Such rhetoric was denounced as counter-productive by her critics, notably Mr Healey and Mr Steel. Lord Carrington, her former Foreign Secretary, had earlier criticized what he called 'megaphone diplomacy'. His appointment in December as secretary-general of Nato was gratifying to British opinion, which regardless of party held him in high respect.

The reinforcement of US troops in Lebanon with a strong naval task force, followed by American air attacks, aroused anxiety in British breasts, and the peace-keeping benefit of the British contingent there was widely questioned. Had there been, however, no multinational force in Lebanon, said the Minister of State for the Armed Forces in the Commons on 17 November, Lebanon might have ceased to be an independent state; and Mrs Thatcher was able to assure President Gemayel, during his brief visit to London in December, that British withdrawal was not Government policy.

The American invasion of Grenada on 25 October (see pp. 62-63 and 90-93) bemused the British public. Despite the menacing movements of US forces after the murder of Prime Minister Bishop, the Foreign

Secretary, Sir Geoffrey Howe, told the House of Commons on 24 October that there was no reason to think American armed intervention likely. It was revealed that Mrs Thatcher talked with President Reagan in the early hours of 25 October and attempted to dissuade him. Conservative opinion was divided, and the Opposition was merciless in its attack. None of President Reagan's stated objectives, said Mr Healey, justified the invasion of an independent state. In a Commons emergency debate on 26 October the Foreign Secretary said mildly that, while United States consultation was regrettably less than the Cabinet would have wished, the incident must not be allowed to weaken the fabric of the alliance. Mr Healey denounced his 'servility' to Washington, Mr Enoch Powell his 'credulity', Mr Julian Amery, an influential Tory backbencher, his 'weakness'. With a feeble brief, Sir Geoffrey had a very rough ride. The vote gave the Government a less-than-par majority of 125.

Ministers' attitudes became less cloudy when exposed to questioning on radio and television. In a television programme on 30 October the Foreign Secretary said that the invasion was not justified on grounds either of the danger to American citizens or of the Cuban presence. Speaking on the BBC World Service on the same day, the Prime Minister said: 'If you are going to pronounce a new law that wherever communism reigns against the will of the people the United States shall enter, then we are going to have terrible wars in the world.' British policy was influenced by the fact that Grenada was a Commonwealth country, having the Queen as its formal head of state, and that a Commonwealth heads of government conference was impending (see Pt. XI, Ch. 2).

The Turkish-Cypriot declaration of an independent state on 15 November was another affront to national sovereignty in the Commonwealth. It was immediately reprobated by the Foreign Secretary, and recognition of the would-be seceding state denied. No question of intervention arose.

The Irish Dimension

The reappointment of Mr James Prior as Secretary of State for Northern Ireland (see p. 21) signalled continued Cabinet support for his policies, notably the ailing Northern Ireland Assembly (see p. 48).

The mass break-out from the Maze prison on 25 September (see p. 47) drew calls for Mr Prior's resignation. It would have been a good opportunity for Mrs Thatcher to lose another 'wet' from her Cabinet had she wished to do so; in fact she went out of her way, during a short visit to the Province in December, to praise Mr Prior and his dedication to the welfare of Northern Ireland.

Political divisions over Northern Ireland were apparent within the Labour and Liberal parties (for the latter, see p. 26). Labour harboured a far-left faction opposed to British military presence in the Province: that was not the leadership's view (see p. 9). The party manifesto called for talks between the British and Irish Governments and representatives of the Province on how best to proceed with the unification of Ireland by consent—a toothless formula acceptable to all but the radical left.

A governmental brush with the Irish Republic occurred in May after Mr Heseltine, Secretary for Defence, speaking in Belfast, had criticized European countries like the Republic which sheltered under the regional protection of Nato without contributing to its resources, and warned that their neutrality might not be respected in time of war. There followed an outcry in the Dail, and the Irish ambassador in London delivered a formal protest; but Mr Heseltine refused to apologise or withdraw his remarks.

After Mrs Thatcher and Dr Garret FitzGerald had met in London on 7 November the latter said their friendly conversation had been concerned mainly with his exposition of the aims of the New Ireland Forum (see p. 48), which the British press and politicians had greeted with some scepticism. It was ironic that the two Governments should have been driven into a closer embrace by an anti-British outrage committed by Irishmen. At Christmas time three bombs were planted in main London shopping areas: one was defused, another caused only minor harm, but on 17 December a big explosion in a car parked beside Harrods department store in Knightsbridge killed five people, including two police officers and an American citizen, and injured 91 others, some very seriously; a third police officer later died of his wounds. The Provisional IRA admitted responsibility but had the gall to express its regret, because, it said, the action had not been authorized by its 'army council'. The appalled reaction was the same in all parties: Mr Gerald Kaufman, speaking for Labour, called the IRA 'evil men who contemptibly seek to creep away from the consequences of their inhumanity'.

Calls were heard for the banning of Sinn Fein as being a mere front for the men of mindless violence, but on 22 December the Cabinet, following a lead from Dublin, decided against such action. Fears that British people would tar all Irishmen with the same brush appeared to be unfounded. A demand, earlier in the year, for withdrawing the vote in British elections from Irish citizens resident in the United Kingdom had been overwhelmingly rejected by a Commons Select Committee. When Dr FitzGerald wrote in *The Times* of London on 23 December 'The Irish people feel this Christmas a stronger sense of shared grief and shared outrage with the British public than at any time that I can recall' his words met with sympathetic understanding. It was easy to applaud his plea to 'the British Government, political parties and the British public to join with the Irish in a commitment against the gunmen', an 'invitation' which Mrs Thatcher 'warmly welcomed', but when he added 'That can only mean joining with constitutional politicians in Ireland in a single urgent effort to create structures which will bring peace and real political progress' many British people felt they were again being invited to solve the insoluble. British morale and determination to defeat the bombers and the gunmen were indeed strengthened by the Christmas outrage. Disgust focused not on the Irish people generally or the Dublin Government but, beyond the murderers themselves, rather on those who professed democracy but backed terrorism, like Provisional Sinn Fein and American supporters of Noraid, whom Mr Prior castigated in a breakfast-time broadcast to the United States on 19 December.

Chapter 6

CRIME AND PUNISHMENT

AN inquest verdict of suicide on Sr Calvi, the Italian banker (see AR 1982, pp. 49 and 146), was quashed by the High Court, and an open verdict returned at a fresh inquest.

Two armed policemen, seeking a dangerous criminal, shot and grievously injured a wrong man, Mr Stephen Waldorf; charged with attempted murder or lesser offences, they were comprehensively acquitted, and received no disciplinary penalty beyond a ban on their using firearms in future.

Denis Andrew Nilsen was convicted on 4 November on six counts of murdering young men in his house, and sentenced to life imprisonment with a minimum of 25 years: his victims were believed to have numbered a score.

Insurers paid out £26 million after the richest haul in British criminal history, a raid on a consignment of bullion at Heathrow airport in November.

See also Pt. XIV, Ch. 2, regarding guidelines on rape sentences, contraception for under-16 girls and voluntary euthanasia.

Chapter 7

SCOTLAND

THE year left the impression of a turning-point in Scottish affairs. The decline in Scotland's heavy industries was characterized by the cancellation of an £86 million oil-rig contract from Scott Lithgow, making closure of the yards and the loss of 4,000 jobs likely, but 1983 was also the year of the computer. Led by American computer giant IBM, a spate of announcements of new electronics plants, capped by three on the final day of the year, confirmed Scotland's position as a key centre for the industry in Europe, particularly in microchips and computer manufacturing. The commercial success story of the year was that of London-Scot Sir Clive Sinclair, whose Dundee manufacturing contractor, Timex, produced its own millionth computer in December. In July the Queen opened the Japanese-owned Nippon Electric Company's semi-conductor plant at Livingston. Scottish semiconductor capacity now represented one-fifth of European chip manufacturing.

Offshore oil development broke new records, production rising by 17 per cent to a year-end rate of $2\frac{1}{2}$ million barrels a day. Record exploration figures, a spate of new development projects and firmer prices raised confidence in the future of the industry to new heights.

Nevertheless, unemployment continued to rise, to a year-end (seasonally adjusted) total of 311,500 (13·9 per cent), up 2,400 on the year, one per cent above the national average. Scotland's improving economic position was one reason for changes in regional financial incentives, which would reduce aid available for capital-intensive projects.

Politically, the general election in Scotland produced a staid contrast to the Tory landslide elsewhere. Conservatives ended with the same number of seats (21) as in 1979, Labour three less (41), while the Nationalists retained two. The Alliance doubled their seats to eight, including shock wins over two junior Ministers, Iain Sproat, in Roxburgh and Berwick, and Hamish Gray, in Ross and Cromarty. The Labour Party's showing gave Scots Labour MPs added influence nationally, consolidated by Livingston MP Robin Cook's successful management of Neil Kinnock's campaign for the party leadership. Nationalists lost support nationally, prompting a fundamental reassessment of key policies on independence, the EEC and Nato. The Conservatives had surprise wins in Aberdeen South and North Ayrshire, but failed to make significant inroads on Labour support, particularly in Glasgow, where they remained unrepresented.

Edinburgh University's 400th anniversary came at a time when the role of universities in Scotland was under intense review. The Scottish Council (Development and Industry) commissioned a special report recommending strengthening industrial links and consolidating campus science parks for new research-based industries. The first results of a long-term review—known as the Munn and Dunning proposals—of the Scottish education system, aimed at producing a curriculum and examinations to match modern needs, were being introduced in Scottish schools. They promised the most fundamental changes in the educational system for a century.

Among other anniversaries celebrated were the bicentenaries of the Glasgow Chamber of Commerce, the Royal Society of Edinburgh and the *Glasgow Herald* newspaper and the centennial of the Boys Brigade.

In October Scots were at last able to see the priceless Burrell Collection—gifted to Glasgow in 1947—when a new purpose-built gallery was opened by the Queen (see Pt. XV, Ch. 2). Glasgow overall had a good year. It made a considerable impact with an image-building campaign launched in the summer, and that image was enhanced when the CBI took its national conference north in November. Major hotel, exhibition and commercial development projects, including headquarter offices for Britoil, which became a public company during the year, added to the feeling of renewal. Another turning-point was the return of salmon to the river Clyde for the first time in well over a century, a tribute to decades of effort by the purification board, although also reflecting the decline of heavy industry.

The perennial row over finance for the Edinburgh International Festival flared again, following condemnation of the city by the outgoing festival director, John Drummond. Edinburgh's position as the financial centre of Scotland was strengthened by the founding of the first new bank for a century. The international spotlight was turned on Edinburgh University's annual defence seminar in September, which was attended by several leading Russian and US defence experts soon after the shooting-down of the South Korean airliner.

Renewed hope for the Highlands came with the establishment of an Enterprise Zone at Invergordon, but equally important was the announcement of a major new timber processing plant at Inverness to utilize maturing forestry resources.

Aviation policy in Scotland took a dramatic turn with the decision in December to allow transatlantic flights from Glasgow airport, putting the future of Prestwick airport on the line.

'Peace camps' at the Faslane and Rosyth nuclear submarine bases continued in existence, but demonstrations against nuclear arms did not reach the levels of Greenham Common (see p. 12).

Crime fell, albeit marginally, for the first time in more than a decade, but repentance of crime troubled the million members of the Church of Scotland in November when it was revealed that a murderer and an embezzler were training for the ministry. Initially greeted with reserve, the controversy rapidly gained momentum and threatened to remain an issue in the Church for some time to come.

Strikes also fell over the year. Scottish mineworkers' leaders were shocked by the decision of miners at Cardowan colliery near Glasgow to accept closure against union advice. The Scottish coalfield, however, did celebrate the opening of the first new pit for 15 years at Castlebridge near Kincardine.

Overall, Scotland showed signs of making a new start in 1984 far removed from the state of affairs envisaged by George Orwell in his novel written on the Scottish island of Jura 36 years ago.

Chapter 8

WALES

ALTHOUGH three previous Labour leaders—Ramsay MacDonald, James Callaghan and Michael Foot—had all represented South Wales constituencies while holding that office, Mr Neil Kinnock, MP for the Gwent constituency of Islwyn, became the first native South Walian to lead the Party; and with his essentially Bevanite, rhetorical and yet pragmatic and classless approach he was readily identified as a classic embodiment of the South Wales political idiom and style.

It was ironic that a Welshman should take over the party leadership after a general election in which Labour polled more badly in Wales than at any time since World War II. Labour's share of the poll was 38 per cent, against 61 per cent obtained as recently as 1966. The Conservatives increased their share only from 28 to 31 per cent but they gained three seats, so they now held 14 out of 38 Welsh seats as compared to three out of 36 in 1966. The Alliance captured 23 per cent of the vote in spite of being handicapped by an inadequate organization and by relatively inexperienced candidates. Its candidates came second in 19 seats, and the performance of the Liberals in particular suggested that the pattern of representation in Wales had become fluid.

Unemployment at 16 per cent remained an important issue in Wales, attention focusing on the black-spots of Clwyd, Pembrokeshire and Ebbw Vale. Prominent among the agencies bringing hope to Wales were the Government's Youth Training Scheme, the Welsh Development Agency (which acquired a new chief executive, Mr David Waterstone, a former diplomat) and the Welsh TUC, which announced that six new cooperative ventures had been set up under its cooperative development and training scheme.

In the day-to-day political debate in Wales the issue of jobs tended to be overtaken by two other controversies. The first was local government finance, as the Government stepped up its drive to cut public expenditure. Education authorities were asked to cut £7 million from their expenditure; in December Mr Nicholas Edwards, Secretary of State for Wales, announced that the annual rate support grant was to be increased by only 2·2 per cent and that there were to be specific targets for each council and tougher penalties for the over-spenders. Representatives of Welsh county and district councils warned that they were now faced with the choice of drastically cutting services or increasing rates by as much as 17 per cent. Mr Barry Jones, MP, the new Labour spokesman on Welsh affairs, talked of a threat to the whole concept of local government in the Principality, and as the year ended there were many references to 'Big Brother' in Whitehall.

The most frenetic debate in Wales was occasioned originally by the news that there was to be a sharp increase in the tolls charged on the Severn Bridge and then by the announcement of further restrictions on the bridge while essential repair work was carried out to strengthen a structure that was carrying a traffic load some 20 per cent in excess of what had been envisaged. Politicians and the Welsh CBI saw this new crisis at the bridge as a threat to the whole South Wales economy, and there were demands for a second bridge, a new tunnel or even a mini-barrage. But for the bridge, suggested Mr Barry Jones, Wales would be just an 'off-shore island'. Meanwhile Plaid Cymru stood aloof from the panic and argued that transport improvements throughout Wales were more important than a bridge, which had merely served to concentrate development in a small area on both sides of the Severn Estuary.

There was speculation as to whether the ITV companies would continue to subsidize S4C (the Welsh arm of Channel Four) as its viewing figures for Welsh programmes plunged to an average of 52,000. S4C officials disputed many of the figures and argued that they were holding 8 per cent of the Welsh audience, which was twice as good as Channel Four were doing nationally. It was a miserable year for Welsh sport but the welterweight Colin Jones showed considerable pluck when fighting twice for the world championship in the United States. In March he drew with Milton McCory in Reno, only to lose on a split decision in Las Vegas in August.

Chapter 9

NORTHERN IRELAND

POLITICAL disagreements on the future form of government institutions for Northern Ireland remained intractable during 1983. The political parties in the Province continued to express aims which, across the divided community, were seen as being mutually incompatible. Nevertheless, several moves which could have longer-term repercussions took place during the year.

Violence, in the form of terrorist activity organized by the Provisional IRA and the Irish National Liberation Army (INLA) continued as an expression of their goal of ending the political division of the island. Deaths caused by politically related violence and the operations of the security forces, though still significant, were fewer in 1983 than in any year since 1970. Of the 74 deaths, 18 were members of the police force and the police reserve, 15 were army personnel and 41 were civilians. The proportion of the deaths affecting the locally-recruited security forces increased sharply, partly because such police and army units had been carrying a larger part of the responsibility and also because the assassination tactics of terrorists were directed to this type of target.

The most poignant act of terrorism during the year was probably the random shooting into a religious service at a small Protestant church in the village of Darkley on 21 November. Three church members were killed and seven injured. This was the first time during the past 14 years of varying degrees of violence that people had been killed inside a church. Earlier in the year a Roman Catholic judge was assassinated as he left church, in a killing which the IRA justified, in their terms, because, as a judge, he was giving support to the institutions of British rule in Northern Ireland. Two prominent figures in the Ulster Unionist Party were also killed by terrorist action.

The processes of law, which included the special 'no jury' procedures for terrorist offences, came under critical scrutiny. A review of the special anti-terrorist legislation as it affected the legal process was launched by the Government, for completion in 1984. Many different opinions were expressed on the increased part played by 'informers'—especially so-called 'supergrasses'—in the evidence against those charged with terrorist crimes. The official view, as presented by the Chief Constable and endorsed by the Secretary of State, was that the role of informers was well accepted, with established safeguards, as a feature of the legal system. Criticism, from church and political spokesmen on both sides of the community, focused on fears that informers were given undue incentives, in terms either of guarantees of non-prosecution for their own offences or of financial assistance to move elsewhere to start a new life. During the year a large number of convictions was obtained which depended critically on the evidence of informers. In a few cases the evidence was withdrawn because the informer changed his mind during a trial, and most of the accused were then set free. In some instances, an informer might have withdrawn his evidence under personal pressure when relatives were taken hostage by para-military groups (see also Pt. XIV, Ch. 2).

In the largest gaol break in the prison history of the United Kingdom, 38 IRA convicted prisoners escaped from the Maze prison on 25 September. Half of the group were soon recaptured; the remainder eluded their pursuers.

The UK general election provided another test for the Northern Ireland political parties. None of the main national parties (Conservative, Labour, Liberal and SDP) nominated candidates in the Province. The election was essentially a double test of public opinion: how had support for the Unionist parties changed, and how far had the Social Democratic and Labour Party (SDLP), drawing on mainly Roman Catholic voters, lost support to Sinn Fein, the political expression of the aims of the IRA? The number of constituencies had been increased from 12 to 17, and the result was that the Official Unionists, led by James Molyneaux, won 11 seats, the Democratic Unionist Party, led by Rev Ian Paisley, won three, and of the remaining seats one each went to the SDLP (John Hume), Sinn Fein (Gerry Adams) and an independent Unionist (Jim Kilfedder). The distribution of seats was not in proportion to the numbers of votes cast. The Official Unionists gained 34 per cent of the votes, compared to 30 per cent for the Democratic Unionists; this represented a small swing to the former party which was overstated in the number of seats won. The SDLP received 18 per cent of the votes and Sinn Fein 13 per cent. The vote for Sinn Fein was four percentage points higher than that recorded in 1982 in the Northern Ireland Assembly elections. The Sinn Fein victory in West Belfast unseated Gerry Fitt, the sitting SDLP member, who was subsequently translated to the House of Lords. Gerry Adams refused to take his seat in the Commons.

The Northern Ireland Assembly continued to function during 1983 but in the continuing absence of the SDLP and Sinn Fein members. Strains emerged within it because of its purely consultative role. The Official Unionists seemed to be divided on the desirability of remaining in the Assembly; in the wake of the killings at Darkley and the murder of the Unionist chairman of Armagh district council, at the end of November they decided to boycott the Assembly as a protest on security issues and, indirectly, as a plea that the Assembly should be given more powers. They suggested that the Assembly might be given administrative but not legislative functions, and that this would be a method of breaking the impasse caused by the Secretary of State's demand for a wider measure of cross-community support for any devolution proposals. At the end of 1983, the Assembly was being boycotted by Sinn Fein, the SDLP and the Official Unionists. The two remaining larger parties, the Democratic Unionists and the Alliance party, comprised less than half the seats in the Assembly.

The SDLP became engaged in a new round of talks launched by the Dublin Government (see Pt. IV, Ch. 1), joining with the main political parties in the Republic to draw up proposals for political progress on the island. The first session of the New Ireland Forum took place at the end of May. By the end of the year the Forum had published two reports: one on the costs being incurred, both North and South, as a result of violence. The second was a discussion document on the economic effects of the political division of the island. Unionists in Northern Ireland refused to talk to the members of the Forum, regarding it as an interference in United Kingdom affairs. The Alliance party, who favoured power-sharing in Northern Ireland, also decided not to make any official submission to the Forum.

When the political affairs committee of the European Parliament appointed Mr Neils Haagerup to prepare a report on how the Community might contribute to the reduction of the political and economic problems of Northern Ireland the decision was condemned by the Prime Minister and the Secretary of State, Mr Prior, as being outside the Parliament's functions. The Northern Ireland Assembly voted unanimously that the exercise should be stopped. However, in December, the report was published and the Secretary of State commented that its contents were not unhelpful. The much-debated European Parliament proposal for the provision of European funds to help with redevelopment spending in Belfast finally received approval in March. The German veto of 1982 was removed after the proposal had been modified. Approximately £60 million, over three years, was to be made available.

Unemployment continued to increase and exceeded 20 per cent of the labour force all year. Further redundancies occurred in many sectors of industry, the biggest being that of Goodyear in Craigavon. The Harland and Wolff shipyard also reduced its labour force, although it received a welcome and overdue boost to its order book late in the year. The economic success story of 1983 was the performance of Shorts, manufacturers of small aeroplanes. Orders for the 36-seat passenger aircraft increased sharply. The firm reduced its losses and hoped to return to profitability in 1984. Its employment practices were scrutinized by the Fair Employment Agency, partly in response to a criticism from the United States that a defence contract should not be placed with Shorts unless it was shown that they were prepared to recruit both Roman Catholics and Protestants without religious discrimination. The Agency recorded its satisfaction with the first instalment of a programme of affirmative action being followed by the firm.

Although new industrial investment was at a low level, industrial production increased slightly, consumer spending seemed to have increased and the scale of government spending increased fractionally. This led to a reduction in the number of redundancies being experienced but was not enough to stop the rise in unemployment.

II THE AMERICAS AND THE CARIBBEAN

Chapter 1

THE UNITED STATES OF AMERICA

AFTER the gloom of the previous twelve months 1983 was a year when for most Americans things took a turn for the better. This had not been forecast—President Reagan had warned at the start of the year that economic difficulties presented a clear danger to the nation's health—but the unexpectedness of the business recovery, and its speed, no doubt contributed to the feeling of national well-being that became particularly noticeable during the last months of the year. By the time of his last press conference of 1983 the President was able to claim it had been a banner year for the American economy. Productivity had been rising fast, good business profits were being recorded, the inflation rate had remained low, and unemployment was falling. The facts that the recovery was being made from a low level, that the budget deficit was disturbingly large, and that the stimulus to the economy seemed to derive more from Keynesianism than from Reaganomics, were not generally seen to be significant. What mattered was that the trends were in the right direction, that the economy was proving more resilient than many had feared, and that the State of the Union, as the President had declared in January 1983 with what at that time seemed more hope than judgment, was indeed on the mend.

For those who looked further afield there was still much to be troubled about at the end of the year. American troops were still embroiled in the apparently hopeless task of helping to keep the peace in Lebanon, a commitment that cost more than 250 American lives during the year. Talks to reduce the number of nuclear weapons in the world had stumbled to a halt, with no promise of resumption, and a new generation of American missiles was being deployed in Europe. Relations with the Soviet Union, aggravated by the callous shooting-down of a South Korean civilian airliner and by American fears that Soviet influence and ambition contributed to the unrest that continued to plague some countries in the American hemisphere, were at a low ebb. In spite of such difficulties the United States remained determined to seek accommodation rather than confrontation. The Administration made clear that its troops would remain in Lebanon so long as they were needed, and that it would continue to work for its peace plan in the Middle East, for negotiations to reduce nuclear weapons, and for a more effective working relationship with the communist countries. At the same time it remained ready to defend its interests, as it demonstrated in 1983 by its invasion of Grenada. For many Americans, facing the worst winter they had experienced for fifty years, there was comfort to be drawn from the fact that at the end of the year American presence was making itself felt in the world.

HOME AFFAIRS. When he came before Congress on 25 January to present his second State of the Union address President Reagan was in no doubt that the state of the economy had to be the first priority. The union was strong, but the economy was troubled. 'For too many of our fellow citizens—farmers, steel and auto workers, lumbermen, black teenagers, and working mothers—this is a painful period,' the President said. 'We must all do everything in our power to bring their ordeal to an end. It has fallen to us, in our time, to undo damage that was a long time in the making, and to begin the hard but necessary task of building a better future for ourselves and our children. We have a long way to go, but thanks to the courage, patience and strength of our people America is on the mend.' He recognized nonetheless that the nation's economic problems—particularly the budget deficit, which was expected to be more than $200,000 million during the 1983 fiscal year—posed 'a clear and present danger to the health of our country.'

The President's tone was conciliatory. Faced with economic recession, unemployment at a higher level than at any time since the war, unfavourable opinion polls and some disarray in his Administration as well as the massive budget deficit, Mr Reagan was eager to enlist the support of Congress, and was ready to offer some concessions in his economic plans to secure it. 'Let us, in these next two years—men and women of both parties and every political shade—concentrate on the long-range, bipartisan responsibilities of government, not the short-term temptations of partisan politics', he said, and it was noted that he used the word 'bipartisan' more than half-a-dozen times in his address. His political problems, the *Washington Post* suggested, had changed his standing on Capitol Hill from king to commoner.

To cure the economic ills Mr Reagan proposed a four-point plan designed both to increase economic growth and to reduce the deficits. The plan comprised:

1. A selective freeze on federal spending, including a six-month delay in cost-of-living increases to elderly people receiving social payments and a one-year freeze on a broad range of domestic spending programmes and civilian and military pay and pension increases.

2. Controls on automatic cost-of-living increases in social programmes known as 'entitlement programmes' which provided food stamps for the needy and federal stipends to poor families with young children. These, the President said, were the largest single cause of the built-in deficit problem, and were the sources of a good deal of fraud and waste.

3. A slowing-down of the proposed increase in defence spending, saving about $55,000 million over the next five years. This would be secured partly from the deferment of pay increases and partly from reductions in inflation and oil costs. There would be no real cuts in weapons pogrammes, the President said, and the delay would not diminish America's ability to negotiate arms reductions nor endanger the country's security.

4. The introduction of future 'standby' tax increases, limited to no more than 1 per cent of the gross national product (GNP) to start in October 1985 and to last not more than three years. The introduction of such taxes would be dependent upon Congress's agreeing to the other points of the President's programme, and would come into operation if future deficits rose to more than 2½ per cent of GNP.

'I realise that this four-point programme is easier to describe than it will be to enact,' Mr Reagan said. 'But the looming deficits that hang over us—and over America's future—must be reduced. The path I have outlined is fair, balanced and realistic. If enacted, it will ensure a steady decline in deficits, aiming toward a balanced budget by the end of the decade. It is the only path that will lead to a strong, sustained recovery. Let us follow that path together.'

The President was right to acknowledge the difficulties his proposals were likely to run into. Congress, though anxious to respond to the appeal for a bipartisan approach to resolving economic problems, was wary of the 'standby' tax proposal, and the Democratic majority in the House of Representatives, which had been increased by 26 in the elections of November 1982, was critical of the continued increase in military spending at the expense of social programmes. The 1984 Budget, which was formally presented to Congress on 31 January, revealed that spending on defence would continue to rise by about 10 per cent in real terms while almost every other aspect of federal expenditure would be cut. Furthermore it was conceded by the Administration that budget deficits would remain high relative to GNP for the next few years, and that the best that could apparently now be hoped for, according to Mr Donald Regan, the Treasury Secretary, was that if all went as expected the budget would be 'trending towards balance' by the end of the 1980s.

This seemed a fairly feeble prospectus from an Administration that had come to office with a promise to balance the budget by 1984, and was certainly not something that Congressmen, many of whom had been campaigning on the need for a balanced budget only a few months earlier, wanted to hear. The result was that when Congress came to put together a budget of its own later in the year it bore little resemblance to the Administration's, proposing cuts in military growth, increased taxes, and more spending on domestic programmes. The resolution as passed by Congress on 23 June called for tax increases of $73,000 million and spending cuts of $12,000 million, but in spite of months of argument nothing had been finally agreed when Congress ended its session in late November

The Administration by this time was less concerned than it might have been because the economy was coming out of recession at a much faster rate than even its most optimistic economic strategists had forecast. GNP rose in real terms by more than 3·3 per cent over the year as a whole, with an increase in the fourth quarter of more than 4 per cent; unemployment fell below 9 per cent from a peak of 10·8 per cent at the end of 1982, which meant that some three million more Americans had jobs by the end of the year; the rate of inflation was holding steady at around 4 per cent; and on Wall Street the Dow Jones industrial average during the year rose well above the 1,000 mark for the first time. In such circumstances neither the President nor the Congress was disposed to fight too hard over a budget deficit that was stimulating the economy as an election year dawned.

In most other respects, too, 1983 was not a memorable year for the 98th Congress. Early in the year a successful combination of the Republican leadership in the Senate and the Democratic leadership in the House of Representatives passed legislation to rescue the social security system from its financial difficulties, but this bipartisan approach did not long survive, and on most issues, as with the budget deficits, it was the President's will that generally prevailed, though not without compromise. Funds were granted for the new weapons systems that the President had asked for, including the production and installation of the MX intercontinental missiles, and for an increased contribution of $8,400 million from the United States to the International Monetary Fund, though Congress attached to this Bill another which allocated $15,600 million for subsidizing houses for the poor, a legislative combination which one Congressman described as 'like putting earrings on a hog'. Congress also granted the President his request for military aid to El Salvador and for covert aid against the regime in Nicaragua, and agreed that the US marines could stay in Lebanon, though in going along with this Congress seemed to have secured from Mr Reagan an effective acknowledgement of the validity of the War Powers Act, whose provisions required congressional approval for the use of American forces overseas or their withdrawal after 60 days. No President had come so close to conceding the constitutionality of the Act since it had been passed ten years earlier (see AR 1973, p. 76).

Congress's own authority was limited by a decision of the Supreme Court on 23 June. By a majority of seven to two the judges ruled that the congressional device known as the legislative veto was unconstitutional. The veto, which came into operation in 1932, was a convenient device by which Congress was able to nullify federal agency regulations without passing legislation that had to be signed by the President before becoming law. But such political convenience could not justify a potential erosion of the Constitution, the Supreme Court decided. Presenting the majority opinion, Chief Justice Warren Burger argued that the legislative veto offended against the provisions of Article I of the Constitution, under which all lawmaking powers were vested in the two Houses of Congress, and which also required that any Bill or Order from Congress must go to the President for signature. A one-House veto sidestepped both these requirements, and was therefore unconstitutional. A two-House veto fulfilled the first requirement but not the second, and was thus also unconstitutional.

'There is no support in the Constitution or decisions of this court for the proposition that the cumbersomeness and delays often encountered in complying with explicit constitutional standards may be avoided by Congress,' Mr Burger wrote. 'With all the obvious flaws of delay, untidiness and potential for abuse, we have not found a better way to preserve freedom than by making the exercise of power subject to the carefully-crafted restraints spelled out in the Constitution.'

The specific case that brought this judgment involved a native of Kenya and a British subject named Jagdish Chadha who had lawfully entered the United States in 1966 on a student visa. When the visa ran out in 1972 he appealed against deportation, and after hearing his case the Immigration and Naturalization Service decided that he should be allowed to stay as a resident alien. Under federal immigration law such decisions have to be sent to Congress, which in this case vetoed the ruling and ordered Mr Chadha's deportation. The constitutionality of the legislative veto was challenged, and Mr Chadha won his case.

The full constitutional implications of the Supreme Court's ruling had not been established by the end of the year. Since all Presidents, from Franklin D. Roosevelt to Ronald Reagan, had opposed the legislative veto, which had on occasions been used by Congress to thwart executive action, the decision was at first sight assumed to mark a dramatic shift of power from Congress to the presidency. However, a strongly-argued dissenting opinion from Justice Byron White suggested that the result might not be as simple as that. Justice White pointed out that, since some kind of legislative veto existed in 196 statutes, the ruling struck down in one blow more laws than the Supreme Court had invalidated in its entire history. Congress, he said, would now be left with a hopeless choice between attempting to pass laws in exhaustive and impractical detail and abdicating its legislative responsibilities to the rulemaking of the departments and agencies. It seemed that the legislature and the executive would have to devise some other practical way of allowing the President or his appointees in the executive branch of government the freedom to act in certain general areas while reserving to the legislature the right to block particular actions, though how this was to be done had still to be worked out.

Within the Executive itself there were some signs of disarray during the year. Two of the more successful members of Mr Reagan's Cabinet, Mr Drew Lewis, the Secretary of Transport, and Mr Richard Schweiker, the Secretary of Health and Human Resources, resigned early in the year.

Both were replaced by women. Mrs Elizabeth Dole succeeded Mr Lewis and Mrs Margaret Heckler took over the Health portfolio. On 12 January Mr Eugene Rostow, director of the Arms Control and Disarmament Agency, was dismissed after congressional pressure had forced the removal of his choice as principal deputy at the agency, Mr Robert Grey. The President's nominee to succeed Mr Rostow, Mr Kenneth Adelman, a deputy delegate at the US mission in the United Nations, proved to be a controversial choice, and it was only after two months of heavy pressure from the White House that the appointment was approved by the full Senate, its foreign affairs committee having decided not to recommend it.

In March Mrs Anne Burford, the director of the Environmental Protection Agency, resigned after irregularities had been revealed in the running of the agency. She was replaced by Mr William Ruckelshaus. In October the President lost his Secretary of the Interior, Mr James Watt, a radical and forthright man whose fondness for plain speaking finally brought about his resignation when a joke about a new coal-leasing review commission consisting of 'a black, a woman, two Jews and a cripple' proved to be one joke too many for the public comfort. He declared in his letter of resignation of 9 October that his usefulness to the Administration had come to an end, a view evidently shared by the President, who appointed his National Security Adviser, Mr William Clark, to succeed him, with Mr Clark's deputy, Mr Robert McFarlane, stepping up to take over the Security post in the White House. The appointment relieved the Administration of a nagging concern about the relationship between Mr Clark, a close associate of the President, and the Secretary of State, Mr George Shultz, over the fashioning and conduct of foreign policy.

Another brief anxiety preoccupied the Administration in mid-year when Washington became agog with rumours of skulduggery in high places after it had been revealed that Mr Reagan's campaign staff, during the election of 1980, had somehow gained access to President Carter's briefing book before the televised debate between the two presidential candidates in October 1980. The White House, fearful that the affair could develop into a political scandal, called in the Justice Department and the Federal Bureau of Investigation to establish whether any illegalities had taken place. Mr Reagan declared that until the matter had been published in the press in 1983 he had not been aware that any of Mr Carter's campaign material had been in the possession of any people in his own campaign organization. In spite of some continued bickering within his Administration the President's prompt action successfuly took the heat out of the affair.

In a year when most politically-conscious Americans began to look towards the presidential campaigns for 1984 there were few electoral excitements, though on 12 April the city of Chicago, after one of the hardest-fought and dirtiest campaigns in its history, elected its first black mayor. Mr Harold Washington, a former Democratic Congressman who once spent a short term in prison for tax evasion, narrowly defeated his Republican opponent, Mr Bernard Epton, a Jewish lawyer, in a high poll in which the voting went mainly along racial lines, black citizens turning out to vote in record numbers. There were similar successes for black candidates in a number of elections held on 8 November. Mr Wilson Goode, a son of a southern share-cropper, became the first black mayor of Philadelphia, and Mr Harvey Gantt achieved similar success in Charlotte, North Carolina. Both men were Democratic candidates. But in the one Senate election, in Washington state, victory went to the Republicans, the former Governor Daniel Evans defeating Representative Mike Lowry to increase the Republican majority in the Senate to 10 (55 to 45).

By the end of the year eight Democratic hopefuls had declared themselves as candidates for their party's nomination to run for the presidency against the Republican candidate, who was presumed to be Mr Reagan (though the President had not by the end of the year officially announced his decision to stand for re-election). The eight were the former Vice-President Walter Mondale, Senator John Glenn of Ohio, Senator Alan Cranston of California, Senator Gary Hart of Colorado, Senator Fritz Hollings of South Carolina, former Senator George McGovern of South Dakota, former Governor Reubin Askew of Florida and the Rev Jesse Jackson, the black activist from Chicago. Of these the acknowledged front-runner was Mr Mondale.

During 1983 the United States continued its series of successful flights of the space shuttle. On 4 April its newest shuttle vehicle, *Challenger*, was launched on its maiden voyage from Cape Canaveral in Florida. During the course of their five-day mission in space, which comprised 80 orbits of the earth, members of the crew left the shuttle to test their space suits outside the vehicle, the first American 'walk' in space for nine years. During the voyage the crew also launched a tracking and data relay station, but it failed to go into its intended orbit. On 18 June *Challenger* was launched into space again, this time with a crew of five on board, including America's first woman astronaut, Sally Ride. During this flight the crew released another satellite, built in West Germany, three times, and three times manoeuvred their craft alongside it to recover it with a long mechanical arm. After six days in space *Challenger* was neatly glided down to land at the Edwards air force base in California, the weather in Florida being too bad for the planned return to Cape Canaveral.

The third *Challenger* flight, and the eighth of the American shuttle series, began from Cape Canaveral on 30 August, again with a crew of five and this time including the first black astronaut, Lieut.-Colonel Guion S. Bluford. In its cargo bay the shuttle carried a weather satellite for the Government of India, and in order to reach the required position above that country the shuttle had to be launched at night. This was successfully accomplished, as was the deployment of the Indian satellite, and the shuttle returned after six days in orbit for a safe landing, also at night. The final space flight of the year began on 28 November when the *Columbia* shuttle was launched from Cape Canaveral carrying with it a 17-ton European space laboratory built in West Germany for the 11-nation European Space Agency. After ten days in orbit, the mission having been extended for a day to give the six-man crew, who included a West German physicist, more time to carry out experiments in the spacelab, the *Columbia* returned safely to earth, though its landing had been slightly delayed because of a faulty computer.

There were other preoccupations for Americans back home. For many the concern was the weather, for 1983 was a year of extremes. A large part of the country was affected by a prolonged heatwave in July, when at least 150 people died. A state of emergency was declared in the city of St Louis, Missouri, and in Louisville, Kentucky, where the hospitals were crowded with people overcome by the heat, and many deaths were recorded in these states and in Illinois, Georgia, Indiana, Arkansas and New York. Severe drought affected these and other areas during the summer, but much of this was forgotten when winter came, for it proved to be one of the worst recorded in this century. By the end of December more than 270 deaths had been attributed to the bitterly cold weather. In Chicago a temperature of minus 19 degrees Fahrenheit was recorded, the lowest for 111 years. In New York several people froze to death on the streets and in the subway, and low temperatures were recorded even in the southern states of Florida and Texas, where the citrus fruit in some areas froze on the trees.

In the small town of Times Beach, Missouri, the inhabitants were afflicted by the consequences of an earlier natural disaster compounded by a man-made problem. In December 1982 the town had been flooded when the Meramec river broke its banks, and then in the early months of 1983 the residents learnt that their streets had been contaminated by a highly toxic waste, dioxin, which had been mixed with oils and sprayed on the streets in the 1970s to keep the dust down. It had now been discovered that dioxin caused cancer and other diseases in laboratory animals, and as it had not been washed away by the floods it was decided that the risk to humans was too great to allow people to continue living in the town. The federal Government therefore offered to buy out all home-owners and businesses in Times Beach and move the inhabitants away from their contaminated community.

Later in the year some 75 million Americans took the opportunity of observing the possible consequences of a much greater calamity when the film *The Day After*, which portrayed the results of the dropping of nuclear bombs on a town in Kansas, was shown on the ABC television network. The film, which offered no crumbs of comfort about the consequences of a nuclear war, inspired fierce political debate in the country about America's nuclear policy, and the Administration took it seriously enough to put the Secretary of State on television immediately after the film to say that this was not the future at all. 'The film,' Mr Shultz said, 'was a vivid and dramatic portrayal of the fact that nuclear war was simply not acceptable.' He declared that the Administration was pursuing the right policy of balance and deterrence, and of trying to reduce nuclear stockpiles.

FOREIGN AFFAIRS. The question of reducing nuclear arsenals was addressed by President Reagan at his first press conference in 1983, on 5 January, when he welcomed the suggestion of Mr Yuri Andropov, the Soviet leader, that there should be continuing talks on the subject between the US and the USSR, perhaps leading to a summit conference between the two leaders. Mr Reagan said that he was in favour in principle of attending such a meeting, provided that it was clear that it would achieve results. He was more cautious in his response to the proposal put forward by the Soviet Union and its Warsaw Pact allies at the beginning of the year that they should sign a non-aggression pact with the Nato countries agreeing that both alliances would pledge not to be the first to use any kind of military force, either nuclear or conventional. Mr Reagan said the US would consider the proposal with its allies. 'Peace with justice must always be this nation's highest priority,' he said. 'We are and will continue to be receptive to ideas which would genuinely promote peace and peaceful settlements of disputes. Our discussions with our allies will consider whether this is such a proposal.'

American scepticism was founded on the fact that the idea of a non-aggression pact was not new. It had originated at the summit of 1955 when Mr Bulganin, the Soviet Prime Minister, had put it forward as a step towards dissolving both the Nato and the Warsaw Pact alliances. It was rejected at that time partly because it was suspected of being part of a plan to try to separate West Germany from the Western alliance, and partly because the principle of non-aggression was already enshrined in the Charter of the United Nations.

American policy on nuclear arms reduction rested on the 'zero option' proposal of November 1981, which would allow the cancellation of the deployment of 572 American Pershing II and Cruise missiles in Europe, due to take place before the end of 1983, if the Soviet Union agreed to remove its SS-20 and other medium-range missiles. During 1982 several attempts to find an acceptable compromise on this formula had been made without success, but as the two sides prepared to resume the strategic arms reductions talks (START) in Geneva in February 1983 the US, concerned that it was being out-manoeuvred in the propaganda exchanges that inevitably accompanied such negotiations, was eager to indicate its readiness to be flexible. On 28 January President Reagan proposed that he should meet Mr Andropov 'to sign an agreement banning US and Soviet intermediate-range land-based nuclear missile weapons from the face of the earth'. The offer was contained in an open letter addressed to the people of Western Europe and made public by Mr George Bush, the American Vice-President, in Berlin at the start of a 12-day tour of West Germany, the Netherlands, Belgium, Switzerland, Italy, France and Britain. Though Mr Andropov was quick to reject the proposal for a summit meeting on the abolition of medium-range missiles (without totally dismissing the idea of a summit), the Americans were in optimistic mood when the Geneva talks resumed on 2 February. Mr Bush met the chief Soviet negotiators and made clear, he said, that the US was 'deadly serious' about reaching an agreement. He emphasized that the zero option was not a take-it-or-leave-it proposition, but also said that the US would accept only an 'effective and balanced' agreement, and one which did not leave the Soviet Union with a monopoly in the systems.

A new proposal for an interim agreement to reduce the number of intermediate nuclear missiles was put forward by the US negotiators in Geneva on 29 March. Announcing the new initiative, which was made in response to requests from America's Nato allies, Mr Reagan said in Washington that the plan envisaged a substantial reduction in the numbers of Pershing and Cruise missiles to be deployed in Europe if the Soviet Union agreed to reduce the number of warheads on its medium-range missiles 'to an equal number on a global basis.' The President did not give figures to indicate the balance he was prepared to accept, but it was made clear in Washington that there would have to be equality between the Soviet Union's triple-headed SS-20 missiles and the single-headed Pershing and Cruise missiles.

Within the United States the Administration did not receive wholehearted support for its stance at Geneva. In spite of the President's warning that the idea of a freeze on all nuclear weapons could destroy all hope of reaching agreements with the Soviet Union, the movement calling for such a freeze won increasing support during the early part of the year. On 3 May the country's Roman Catholic bishops voted overwhelmingly to endorse a pastoral letter calling for a halt to the testing, production and deployment of new nuclear weapons, and on the following day the idea of a nuclear freeze received the endorsement of the House of Representatives. By 278 votes to 149 on 4 May the House voted in favour of a resolution calling for an immediate US and Soviet freeze on their nuclear arsenals, though a rider was added to revoke the freeze if it was not followed by the negotiated arms reductions 'within a reasonable, specified period of time.' The Administration had opposed the resolution because it would freeze an existing margin of Soviet nuclear superiority and remove any incentive for the Russians to continue to negotiate. The resolution was not binding and was not supported in the Senate, but like the bishops' letter it reflected the growing public concern at the lack of progress in reducing nuclear weapons.

The US Government's policy of negotiating with the Soviet Union from strength was reiterated in detail by Mr George Shultz, the Secretary of State, before the Senate foreign relations committee on 15 June. Having begun to rebuild its strength, he said, America now sought to engage the Soviet leaders in a constructive dialogue to find political solutions to outstanding problems. The US did not accept endless confrontation with the Soviet Union as inevitable, but it was nonetheless clear American policy to oppose and counter Soviet activities on a global basis. 'Our policy is not based on trust, or on a Soviet change of heart,' he said. 'It is based on the expectation that, faced with demonstration of the West's renewed determination to strengthen its defences, enhance its political and economic cohesion and oppose adventurism, the Soviet Union will see restraint as its most attractive or only option.'

This tough policy did not deter the American Administration from taking steps to improve relations with the Soviet Union when this could be done without undermining the basic strategy. At the end of July a new long-term agreement was signed for the sale of American grain, providing for an increase in supplies over the next five years. The export of grain had been embargoed by President Carter in January 1980 in response to Russian intervention in Afghanistan, but the embargo was lifted by President Reagan in April 1981. On 20 August the Administration made a further move towards economic accommodation by lifting the ban, introduced in December 1981 after the imposition of martial law in Poland, on the sale of American-made pipelaying equipment for use in the construction of the natural gas-pipeline from Siberia to Western Europe. Although the sanctions had been lifted in November 1982 in deference to European objections the Soviet Union had refused to complete the purchase because the continued existence of American controls made American suppliers unreliable.

Relations between the two countries deteriorated abruptly in September when the US Government revealed that a Soviet jet fighter had shot down a South Korean Boeing 747 commercial airliner with 269 people on board. Mr Shultz, who made the announcement of what he described as 'an appalling act' at a news conference in Washington, said that Soviet aircraft had tracked the airliner for more than two-and-a-half hours after it had strayed over the Soviet island of Sakhalin before shooting it down with an air-to-air missile. There were no survivors. Among those on board was a US Congressman, Mr Lawrence McDonald of Georgia. President Reagan, who was on holiday in California at the time, cut short his stay to return to Washington to preside at a meeting of the National Security Council, demanding that the Soviet Union should give a full explanation of 'this appalling and wanton deed.' The US Government requested a meeting of the UN Security Council to investigate the incident, and to give the world an opportunity to express its revulsion.

The outrage felt in the United States led to demands for some quick and effective response, such as the suspension of the arms reduction talks at Geneva, cancellation of the new grain agreement or the reimposition of the embargo on pipeline equipment. In the event the Administration did none of these things. The President and other members of his Adminstration were vehement in their denunciation of the Soviet action, and pulled no punches at the UN, where a transcript of the exchanges between the Soviet pilot and his ground control in the minutes leading up to the shooting-down of the airliner was played, but they were cautious in their actions. The only immediate retaliatory measure was an order closing down the offices of Aeroflot, the Soviet airline, in Washington and New York. The US was also put slightly on the defensive by the Soviet claim that the airliner had been mistaken for an American spy plane; for the Administration had had to admit that there had been a US RC135 reconnaissance aircraft in the area earlier, though it was back at its base in Alaska when the South Korean Boeing was shot down.

In spite of American determination to stay in constructive communication with the Russians this incident seriously set back attempts to improve relations, and made progress at the arms reduction talks more difficult. A meeting between Mr Shultz and Mr Gromyko, the Soviet Foreign Minister, on 8 September proved abortive, and later in the month Mr Gromyko cancelled a planned visit to the United Nations in New York after the Port of New York Authority had refused permission for his aircraft to land at a civilian airport.

President Reagan went to New York on 26 September and took the opportunity of an address to the UN General Assembly to make public some suggestions he had already put forward privately to the Soviet Union for making progress in the reduction of intermediate-range nuclear weapons. He said that if the Soviet Union would agree to an equal number of warheads on a global basis, and lower than the present size of the Soviet arsenal of land-based medium-range weapons, the US would not offset the entire global missile deployment through US deployment in Europe, though it would retain the right to deploy missiles elsewhere. In addition the President said the US would agree to the Soviet request that Nato and Warsaw Pact intermediate-range bomber forces be included in the Geneva talks, and that, in the event of an overall agreement being reached, the number of Pershing II missiles to be deployed could be reduced. He added that it was now up to the Soviet Union to prove that it genuinely wanted an agreement. 'The door to an agreement is open,' he said: 'it is time for the Soviet Union to walk through it.'

Mr Reagan followed this initiative by offering, on 4 October, more flexible proposals for the strategic arms reduction talks based on a 'build-down' concept that called for the destruction of two old land-based warheads for every new one deployed. Neither of the President's suggestions was acceptable to the Russians, and at the end of October Mr

Andropov responded by suggesting that if Nato cancelled plans to deploy the Pershing and Cruise missiles in Europe the Soviet Union would reduce its number of SS-20s to 140 (100 less than its current arsenal). This was rejected by the State Department on the grounds that it would have left the Soviet Union with a monopoly of intermediate-range missiles in Europe, and in November the US resumed the diplomatic ping-pong by proposing that both the US and the Soviet Union should be limited to 420 intermediate-range warheads each. This was rejected on 14 November by the Soviet Union because it would involve some deployment of Pershing and Cruise missiles. On the same day the first Cruise missiles arrived at the US Air Force base at Greenham Common in England. A week later the first consignment of Pershing II missiles arrived in West Germany, and on 23 November the Russians walked out of the INF talks at Geneva. In December, when the START talks adjourned, they refused to agree on a date for their resumption. The US officially regretted both actions but expressed its confidence that, in time, the bargaining would be resumed.

America's concern with the activities of the Soviet Union was not confined to the frontiers of Europe in 1983. Even within its own hemisphere the US Government feared that subversive elements, directed from Cuba and supported by the Soviet Union, were working with increasing success to exploit social and economic unrest to create a revolution that would spread through the Central American republics and the Caribbean islands. For most of the year the countries of chief concern, as they had been in the previous year, were Nicaragua and El Salvador, but the most dramatic and unexpected demonstration of American sensitivity in the area came on 25 October when US forces invaded the tiny island of Grenada. The American action followed a coup in the island by a left-wing military group who seized power after murdering the Prime Minister, Mr Maurice Bishop. A total of 6,000 marines and army rangers were sent to the island, together with some representative troops and police from certain neighbouring Caribbean countries. They met unexpectedly strong resistance from some 700 Cubans who had been working on the construction of a new airport, and it was a week before the island was securely under American control.

President Reagan announced that he had ordered the invasion for three reasons: 'First, and of overriding importance, to protect innocent lives, including up to 1,000 Americans whose personal safety is, of course, my personal concern. Second, to forestall further chaos. And, third, to assist the restoration of conditions of law and order and of democratic institutions in the island of Grenada, where a brutal group of leftish thugs violently seized power.'

Mr Reagan said the invasion was justified by a treaty of mutual support signed by eastern Carribean nations, including Grenada, in 1981. Six of these countries had asked for help. It was also revealed that Britain had been invited to join in the operation but had refused, and that Mrs

Thatcher had spoken to Mr Reagan on the telephone in a vain attempt to dissuade him from the invasion. There was disappointment in Washington at the British attitude, but as the reservations of the British Government were shared by many other allies in the West the Administration was resigned to going it alone, with support only from the Caribbean countries that had asked for help, as was demonstrated at the United Nations when a Security Council resolution deploring the invasion was supported by 11 nations, with three abstentions (including Britain). The United States exercised its veto.

Within the US, opinion was initially uncertain, the press generally reflecting doubts about the justification for invasion. The *Washington Post* said that the burden of proof lay on the President to justify the immensely grave act of invading a sovereign state. 'Some Americans will rejoice that the United States has finally recaptured a seemingly lost capacity for great-power military response, that it has flashed a warning signal to Nicaragua and other sources of torment,' the paper commented; 'but this is hardly adequate reason to invade a small country.' The *New York Times* was equally critical. Even if the President's worst suspicions were confirmed, it noted, 'he will have denied the Russians and Cubans another Caribbean airfield, an auxiliary station for small-arms transfers and a modest source of new recruits for international mischief,' but at what cost? It was, the paper suggested, more than the loss of a dozen soldiers: 'simply put, the cost is loss of the moral high ground: a reverberating demonstration to the world that the United States has no more respect for laws and borders, for the codes of civilization, than the Soviet Union.'

As time passed, and as the American troops began to return home, the doubts faded, and it became evident that grass-roots opinion in America believed that the operation had been justified. In the opinion polls the President's stock rose substantially. A fact-finding team of Congressmen, many of whom had been critical before they set out for Grenada, returned from a tour of the island convinced that there had been a real threat to American citizens there, and that the circumstances justified the invasion. The *Washington Post* revised its judgment and concluded, two weeks after the invasion, that the President had made the right decision. By the end of the year the last US combat troops had been withdrawn from the island, leaving about 300 support troops, mainly engineers and military police, from a force which at the height of the operation had totalled some 6,000 men.

The Administration's frustration with the situation in other parts of Central America, and its anxiety over the influence of communism in the region, was made evident early in the year when President Reagan asked Congress for an increase of $168 million in economic aid for El Salvador, Honduras, Costa Rica and Belize, together with an additional $110 million in military assistance for El Salvador to help fight left-wing guerrillas there. 'Central America is simply too close, and the strategic stakes are too high, for us to ignore the danger of governments seizing power there with ideological and military ties to the Soviet Union.' Aware that many Congressmen feared American involvement in Vietnam style Mr Reagan repeated his assurance that he would not send American soldiers into El Salvador, nor 'Americanize the war with a lot of United States combat advisers'. On 27 April the President took the unusual step of going before a joint session of Congress to set out what some observers called 'the Reagan doctrine' for Central America. This comprised a commitment by the United States to encourage the development of democracy in the region, to provide military assistance to its countries to help them defend themselves against left-wing revolution and tyranny, to provide economic support so as to eradicate poverty and other root causes of internal unrest, and to support dialogue and negotiation among and within the countries of the region.

At the same time the President warned Congress that the security of all the Americas was at stake. 'If we cannot defend ourselves there,' he said, 'we cannot expect to prevail elsewhere. Our credibility would collapse, our alliances would crumble, and the safety of our homeland would be put in jeopardy.' He declared that the United States was not seeking the overthrow of the left-wing Sandinista Government in Nicaragua, but would not protect it 'from the anger of its own people'. The prime American interest, he said, was to ensure that the Nicaraguan Government did not infect its neighbours through the export of subversion and violence. 'Our purpose, in conformity with American and international law, is to prevent the flow of arms to El Salvador, Honduras, Guatemala and Costa Rica.'

A special envoy to Central America, Mr Richard Stone, a former Senator from Florida, was appointed, while Mr Thomas Enders, the Assistant Secretary of State for Inter-American Affairs, was removed from the post and replaced by Mr Langhorne Motley, the American ambassador in Brazil, who was thought to be more in tune with the Administration's policies for Latin America. These changes were followed on 18 July by the creation of a bipartisan national commission to advise the President on the long-term problems of Central America, with Dr Henry Kissinger, the former Secretary of State, as chairman. The commission was charged with reporting on how a 'national consensus' might be established for a policy dealing with threats to American interests in the area. At the same time large-scale military exercises were organized, involving the manoeuvres of US warships off both Central American coasts and troop exercises of some 4,000 US military personnel in Honduras, and it was announced that the United States would maintain indefinitely a naval and military presence in the area.

This show of force brought the United States into diplomatic disagreement with Mexico and with the so-called Contadora group of

Latin American nations (which included Colombia, Panama and Venezuela as well as Mexico), who sought to reach a solution to Central American problems by diplomatic negotiation and who called for the demilitarization of the area and a ban on foreign intervention. President Reagan tried to keep the door open to negotiation by praising the efforts of the Contadora Presidents, but when he met President Miguel de la Madrid of Mexico in La Paz on 14 August he made it clear that the United States would not abandon its precautionary military measures. Occasionally, he said, the United States had to roar on behalf of democracy.

Dr Kissinger and his 12-man commission began their first foray of inquiry into the area on 10 October, when they arrived in Panama before moving on to Costa Rica, El Salvador, Guatemala, Honduras and Nicaragua. During his visit to El Salvador, and after meeting President Alvaro Alfredo Magaña there, Dr Kissinger said that people should not have to choose between security and human rights, but that it was precisely those areas that were in the front line between totalitarianism and democracy. His comment was taken to refer not only to the guerrillas seeking to overthrow the government but also to the right-wing 'death squads', whose terrorist activities, denounced by the American ambassador in San Salvador as 'fascists serving the communist cause', seemed to be achieving their objective in blocking land reform, and it certainly aggravated the US Government's difficulties in winning the wholehearted approval of the American Congress and people for making such a strong commitment in so unstable an area.

Farther south in the hemisphere the United States made a determined effort to repair its relations with Argentina, damaged by its support of Britain during the Falklands war in 1982. Encouraged by the substitution of democratically-elected government for the military junta, the US Government announced on 8 December that it would be taking the necessary steps to end the five-year ban on arms supplies to Argentina. In doing so the United States risked running foul of the British Government, whose Prime Minister, Mrs Margaret Thatcher, had pointed out to President Reagan during her visit to Washington in September that Argentina had not made a formal declaration ending hostilities over the Falklands, but though the decision was regretted the British Government was to some extent reassured by American undertakings that no arms would be provided that could be used in any new attempt to attack the Falklands.

In the Middle East the United States found itself in difficulties throughout 1983. When the year began it had some 800 marines stationed in Beirut as part of an international force designed to help the Lebanese Government maintain order in the city, it had failed to persuade Israel to evacuate its forces from Lebanon, and its formula for bringing peace to the Middle East was in trouble. President Reagan's plan (see AR 1982, p.498) had called for a freeze on Jewish settlements on the occupied West Bank and the opening of Jordanian/Palestinian talks with Israel for Palestinian autonomy, but it collapsed on 10 April when King Husain of Jordan failed to reach agreement with the Palestine Liberation Organization (PLO) on the terms. Eight days later a truck full of explosives was detonated outside the US embassy in Beirut, killing 63 people including the senior Middle East expert of the CIA, Mr Robert Ames, who was on a visit from Washington, and a First Secretary, Mr Frank Johnson. Describing the bombing as 'a cowardly act', President Reagan said it would not deter his Government from pursuing its peace initiative, and instructed his Secretary of State to resume his shuttle diplomacy round the capital cities of the Middle East to try to get things moving again. Lebanon could not begin to reconstruct itself as a nation, he said, until all foreign troops had withdrawn.

The stumbling-block to withdrawal was Syria, which had 40,000 troops in eastern and northern Lebanon and refused to pull them out even when Mr Shultz secured agreement between Israel and Lebanon. Although the US Government removed its Middle East negotiator, Mr Philip Habib, from the scene because Syria regarded him as hostile to the Arabs, his successor, Mr Robert McFarlane, had no more success.

Meanwhile the situation in and around Beirut got worse. On 29 August two US marines were killed and another seven wounded when Beirut airport, around which the American contingent was encamped, was shelled. The United States joined with other countries providing peacekeeping forces—Britain, France and Italy—in refusing a request from the Lebanese Government to move into the Chouf area, but nonetheless found its troops increasingly vulnerable to attack. A powerful US naval task force was assembled off the coast of Lebanon, with some 2,000 marines held in reserve to support the force of 1,600 now in the city, and the President gave the marine commanders authority to call up air strikes against targets in the Chouf mountains. American ships were also authorized to shell Druze areas in those mountains above the city.

On 23 October 241 American servicemen were killed when a truckload of explosives was smashed by its suicide driver into the marine barracks in Beirut. The United States responded by sending replacements from the marine base in North Carolina, by sending the commandant of the marine corps to Beirut to examine ways of improving the safety of American forces there, and by emphasizing that it would keep its peacekeeping detachment in the city. President Reagan said the attack was 'a horrifying reminder of the type of enemy we face in many areas around the world today'.

In Lebanon the most notable consequence was an escalation of military activity. Four American F14 fighter aircraft were fired on by Syrian anti-aircraft guns over northern Lebanon on 10 November as a new US naval task force, led by the aircraft-carrier *Independence*, sailed into Lebanese territorial waters. On 4 December two US navy jet aircraft were shot down by Syrian gunners, and on the same day eight US marines were killed and two wounded when their positions came under heavy fire. Ships of the US sixth fleet responded with a heavy bombardment on the anti-government forces who had been firing on the marines.

In spite of this there was renewed hope in Washington as the year ended that some progress might be made towards peace in the Middle East. A visit to Washington by Mr Yitzhak Shamir, the Israeli Prime Minister, early in December led to an agreement to strengthen strategic cooperation between the two countries, though not, as the United States was at pains to emphasize, at the expense of America's ties with moderate Arab nations. Mr Shamir was followed to Washington by President Amin Gemayel of Lebanon, who said that he was hopeful that the deadlock on the withdrawal of foreign forces from Lebanon would soon be broken, and that this withdrawal would include the Syrians. But Washington's principal cause for optimism followed the withdrawal from Lebanon of Mr Yassir Arafat and 4,000 of his PLO supporters and a subsequent meeting, on 22 December, between Mr Arafat and President Mubarak of Egypt, which it was thought might lead to a revival of Mr Reagan's peace plan.

Once again the United States was in diplomatic conflict with Libya during 1983. The cause on this occasion was the neighbouring country of Chad, which the US Government said was being harrassed by Libyan-backed rebel forces. Early in August American AWACS electronic surveillance aircraft, F15 fighters and support aircraft were sent to assist Chad in overcoming the rebellion. A communique put out by the State Department said that after consultation with several Governments, including the French, 'we have moved some of our aircraft to where they could be most useful in monitoring the situation in Chad.' President Reagan authorized emergency military aid of $15 million to President Habré's government in Chad, and it was emphasized from the White House that the United States had a strong strategic interest in ensuring that Colonel Qadafi, the Libyan leader, was not able to intervene in or gain control of neighbouring countries. At the same time it was recognized in Washington that Chad was of particular concern to France, and after delivering a stern warning to Colonel Qadafi the US was ready to leave the problem to the French Government.

The United States made determined efforts to improve its relations with China during 1983, but seemed unclear at the end of the year whether it had made much progress in achieving this aim. Mr Shultz set off with high hopes at the end of January on his first visit to Peking, but when he got there the Chinese Foreign Minister, Mr Wu Xuequan, reminded him that there were many obstacles still to be overcome in Sino-American relations. These included the continuing links between the US and Taiwan, American limitations on Chinese textile exports, and China's retaliatory trade sanctions against the US. Little progress was made on these matters during Mr Shultz's visit, but agreement was reached on a proposal to revive military contacts, and the Chinese Prime Minister, Mr Zhao Ziyang, accepted an invitation to visit Washington.

In April the Chinese Government cancelled all sports and cultural exchanges with the United States for the rest of the year in protest at the Administration's decision to grant political asylum to a Chinese tennis player, Miss Hu Na, who defected while playing in America in 1982. However, this sour note did not prevent the United States from agreeing, two months later, to allow China to buy American computers and other high-technology equipment, the sale of which had previously been prohibited for security reasons. Further progress on trade was agreed at the end of July, when the two countries accepted a five-year arrangement regulating Chinese textile exports to the US. The agreement would allow a steady growth of textile exports over the five years. In September Mr Caspar Weinberger, the US Defense Secretary, went to China and agreed upon an exchange of visits by Chinese and American military personnel for the coming year. It was also announced during his visit that the Chinese Prime Minister would go to Washington in January, and that President Reagan would visit China in April.

In spite of those evident signs of a diplomatic thaw there was some concern in Washington at the end of the year because China had reacted angrily to two congressional messages which had referred to Taiwan by name as the Republic of China. A White House spokesman was quick to proclaim that the Administration recognized the People's Republic of China as the sole legitimate government of China, but not before the Chinese Communist Party leader had warned that President Reagan's visit in the coming year might have to be cancelled. It seemed that relations could be improved only by resolving the problem of Taiwan, or by agreeing to put that delicate issue on one side.

President Reagan's first visit to Asia, which took place in 1983, was relatively untroubled. The original schedule was abandoned after the assassination of the Filipino opposition leader Benigno Aquino in Manila (see Pt. IX. Ch.1), when the Philippines, Indonesia and Thailand were cut out, leaving only Japan and South Korea on the itinerary when Mr Reagan left Washington on 9 November. His intention was to reaffirm America's deep involvement in the area, and to emphasize the importance of the alliance with Japan. The trip to Japan was uneventful because trade and other differences between the two countries were left in the background by mutual consent. And in South Korea, where Mr Reagan visited the demilitarized zone between North and South Korea, the American President found, within range of enemy guns, a dramatic setting for demonstrating the American commitment to what he called 'the front line of freedom'.

On 29 December the United States formally gave notice that it proposed to withdraw from the United Nations Educational, Scientific and Cultural Organization (Unesco) at the end of 1984. The State Department said that the Administration had made this decision because it believed that Unesco had 'extraneously politicized' virtually every subject it dealt with and had 'exhibited hostility towards the basic installations of a free society, especially the free market and the free press', and because its budgetary expenditure was wasteful and unrestrained. The US, which contributed about one quarter of the agency's budget of some £250 million, was not prepared to go on, but would seek other mechanisms for providing aid for educational, scientific and cultural activities. Unesco was one of six international organizations which the US felt were falling short of the criteria required for its continued participation, the other five being the International Atomic Energy Agency, the Food and Agriculture Organization, the International Labour Organization, the United Nations Environment Programme and the International Telecommunications Union—but the Administration had decided not to withdraw from these agencies because they had made 'measurable improvements' during the year.

Chapter 2

CANADA

A SENSE of impending political change dominated public affairs in Canada in 1983. The Liberal Party, in office for all but nine months over the last 15 years, saw its national popularity plummet to an embarrassingly low point. Most recently elected in 1980, the Liberal Government of Pierre Trudeau would have to face another electoral test by early 1985. Its prospects were clouded by the uncertainty surrounding the intentions of the Prime Minister, still the most compelling political personality in Canada. When he resumed office in March 1980, Trudeau had stated that he would not lead his party into another election, but, as an election drew near, he gave no sign that he intended to step down. Now 64, Trudeau had become the focus of much of the criticism, especially in Western Canada, directed against the federal Liberals. He was seen as arrogant and insensitive, intermittent in his attention to issues, indifferent to the aspirations of regions outside central Canada and deficient in his management of the economy. It was frequently stated that Canada's Prime Minister, one of the longest serving heads of government in the Western world, enjoyed more respect abroad than he did within his country.

Demands for an early election were strenuously voiced by the opposition Progressive Conservative Party. In 1983 the Conservatives selected a new leader to replace the hapless Joe Clark, who had toppled the Trudeau Government in 1979 only to throw away his hold on office by a political miscalculation after nine months (see AR 1979, p. 71, and 1980, pp. 69-70). At a party convention in January 1983 Clark was endorsed as leader by only two-thirds of the delegates and he promptly resigned his post. He stood for the position at a second convention held in Ottawa in June, when he was faced by seven challengers, three of them former Ministers in his 1979-80 Administration. On the fourth ballot the leadership was won by Brian Mulroney, a 44-year-old Montreal lawyer and business executive who, although he had been an active party worker for years, had never stood for Parliament. The son of a millworker, born and raised in a small community on the rugged north shore of the Gulf of St Lawrence, he was fluently bilingual, experienced in labour conciliation and, until recently, president of the Iron Ore Company of Canada. He made a particular point of stressing his Quebec roots, which, he claimed, would allow him to rebuild Conservative electoral strength in the solidly Liberal province. Mulroney won a seat in Parliament, at a by-election in Nova Scotia, on 29 August. On the same day his party captured a British Columbia seat from the socialist New Democratic Party.

When Parliament began its autumn sittings on 12 September there were 147 Liberals in the 282-seat House of Commons, 103 Progressive Conservatives, 31 New Democratic Party members and one independent. Opinion polls showed the Conservatives far ahead of the Liberals, a September count giving them a 62 per cent preference among decided voters. This was the best popular showing they had enjoyed in a quarter of a century, and it gave the party a new confidence. Prime Minister Trudeau shuffled his Cabinet on 12 August, dropping five Ministers and bringing in five new faces in an effort to improve his Government's image. Three of the new Ministers came from metropolitan Toronto, the country's largest city, where many seats would be at issue.

Only one province held a general election in 1983. In British Columbia the Social Credit party, in office since 1975, was returned with a larger majority on 5 May. Premier William Bennett, emphasizing restraint in public expenditure during his campaign, saw his party's representation rise from 31 to 35 seats in the 57-seat legislature. The New Democratic Party took the remaining seats. After enacting measures to reduce the size of the provincial bureaucracy, Mr Bennett's Government successfully overcame a massive strike of public employees in November.

The first session of Canada's 32nd Parliament, the longest in the country's history, ended on 30 November after three and a half years. Parliament had sat for 591 days and passed over 150 Bills. A new session began on 7 December, the Trudeau Government announcing a miscellany of measures to stimulate job creation, foster research and public education in disarmament and promote social harmony.

Parliament passed the first amendment under Canada's 1982 constitution, guaranteeing aboriginal groups full consultation before constitutional provisions affecting their rights were enacted. The amendment emerged from a federal-provincial-native groups meeting held in March, the first of a series of such discussions to be held over the next four years. On 6 October Parliament unanimously endorsed a resolution urging the Province of Manitoba to restore language and educational rights to the 60,000 (six per cent) French-speakers in the province. These rights, contained in Manitoba's original constitution of 1870, had been suspended 93 years ago by the English-speaking majority in the legislature. The provincial Government had now decided to entrench them in the laws of Manitoba, a proposal which generated much controversy in the province. By approving the resolution the federal Parliament threw its support behind official bilingualism for Manitoba. Quebec and New Brunswick were the only other Canadian provinces formally designated as bilingual. Language rights were one of the most sensitive issues in Canada's history and there was satisfaction that Parliament had taken an unequivocal stand on the Manitoba question.

The economy showed signs of regaining its health in 1983. The inflation rate fell from 9·8 per cent in November 1982 to 4·2 per cent a year later. Negative growth rates of the 1981-82 recession were replaced by a five per cent gain in output during the first nine months of 1983. Unemployment remained disturbingly high, however. In October 11·1 per cent of the labour force was out of work. The year saw strong export sales to the United States, a market in which Canada earns $7 out of every $10 it receives from exports. Government spending, checked by unprecedented deficits, could not substantially support the economic recovery. Business investment was still hesitant, worried by lending rates which, although down by an average of two per cent from 1982, were still formidable.

In an economy displaying contradictory signs Finance Minister Marc Lalonde, presenting his first full Budget on 19 April, found little room in which to manoeuvre. He announced a record deficit of $31,300 million for the fiscal year 1983-84, about $6,000 million larger than the previous year's shortfall. The Finance Minister emphasized job creation through modest capital spending and offered tax concessions to private business.

The Canadian Government showed itself to be both a staunch supporter of the Western alliance and a believer in renewed East-West dialogue during 1983. The shooting-down of a Korean airliner on 1 September, with ten Canadians among the dead passengers, aroused indignation. The Government suspended Russian landing rights at Mirabel international airport, north of Montreal, for 60 days, thus temporarily closing Aeroflot's only remaining gateway to North

America. In an emergency debate the House of Commons passed a resolution condemning the Soviet use of military force to destroy a civilian aircraft.

On the other hand, Mr Trudeau distanced himself from the bellicose position taken by Mrs Margaret Thatcher when she visited Canada and addressed Parliament on 26 September. 'The Soviet Union is engaged in a remorseless military build-up going far beyond the needs of defence', the British Prime Minister said. 'It is time for freedom to take the offensive.' Trudeau made it plain that he felt such anti-Soviet rhetoric was unhelpful. He called on the West, in the words of the Williamsburg summit statement of 29 May, 'to devote [its] full political resources to reducing the threat of war'. 'At such a time the peoples of Nato countries expect more than familiar nostrums from their leaders', he told Mrs Thatcher. In the Commons on 4 October Trudeau described the Korean airliner affair as an 'accident', caused by a reckless pilot and a misguided ground commander. 'I do not believe it was the intention of the people in the Kremlin to shoot down innocent passengers.' The Prime Minister refused to support or condemn the United States' invasion of Grenada on 25 October, stating that he was not satisfied with Washington's explanation of the reasons for the intervention. There were indications that Canada was upset by the United States' failure to consult the largest Commonwealth state in the western hemisphere before taking action affecting another Commonwealth member in the region.

The Trudeau Government agreed to allow the United States to test unarmed Cruise missiles over northern Canada in early 1984 despite vociferous criticism from peace groups and labour unions. An umbrella agreement to permit weapons-testing of all forms except chemical, biological and nuclear weapons was signed with the United States on 10 February. On 13 June a request to test the guidance system of Cruise was received from Washington. During an emergency debate on the subject, held the next day, the Government stressed that it was Canada's duty as a member of the Nato alliance to cooperate in the tests. A New Democratic Party motion to reject the request was defeated by the combined Liberal and Conservative party members. The following day the Government announced approval of Cruise testing. The flights would begin over the Beaufort sea in the western Arctic and travel 2,600 kilometres over flat featureless terrain, similar to that found in the Soviet Union, to an air weapons range on the Alberta-Saskatchewan border. Anti-Cruise groups tried to halt the testing in the courts, claiming that the action violated the guarantees of life, liberty and security found in Canada's new Charter of Rights and Freedoms. Government lawyers argued that the test decision was a political act, not subject to review by the courts. The Federal Court of Appeal in Ottawa, on 28 November, upheld this contention.

The final months of 1983 saw a personal initiative, a so-called 'peace crusade', by Prime Minister Trudeau. Its object was to reduce the level of

East-West tensions which were remorselessly leading to an escalation of the arms race. Trudeau unveiled his plan to a Canadian audience on 27 October and communicated it to world leaders thereafter. From 8 to 11 November the Prime Minister visited six Western European states to discuss his initiative with their leaders. The key elements in his proposal were:

1. a ban on the testing and deployment of weapons placed in outer space in order to destroy another country's communication satellites,
2. a search for new ways to avoid a breakdown in the MBFR (conventional forces) talks going on in Vienna,
3. a summit meeting of the world's five nuclear states to negotiate limits on nuclear weapons, and
4. measures to strengthen the 1970 Nuclear Non-Proliferation Treaty and to link financial savings on disarmament to development needs in the Third World.

Mr Trudeau took his message to Prime Minister Yasuhiro Nakasone of Japan on 19 November and brought it before the Commonwealth heads of government meeting in New Delhi in the following week. He broke away during the Commonwealth talks to fly to China to meet Premier Zhao Ziyang. The Chinese leader showed little interest in the suggestion of a nuclear summit conference. On his return from Asia Trudeau arranged a meeting on 15 December with President Ronald Reagan of the United States, from whom he won good wishes for his initiative but no commitments to specific parts of the plan. Trudeau put the best face on Mr Reagan's response, saying that he was encouraged by the President's insistence that the United States did not want nuclear superiority over the Soviet Union but equality and balance. As the year ended Trudeau anticipated a meeting with the ailing Soviet leader Yuri Andropov as the final consultation of his two-month peace initiative. It was clear, by late December, that the Canadian leader had exerted all the influence he could muster.

Chapter 3

LATIN AMERICA

INTRODUCTION—ARGENTINA—BOLIVIA—BRAZIL—CHILE—
COLOMBIA—ECUADOR—PARAGUAY—PERU—URUGUAY—
VENEZUELA—CUBA—THE DOMINICAN REPUBLIC AND HAITI—
CENTRAL AMERICA AND PANAMA—MEXICO

FOR Latin America, 1983 was the year in which the free-spreading growth-orientated economic policies of the 1970s finally collapsed. In both big and small countries the root cause was the same, the fact that revenues from foreign trade in time of recession were no longer sufficient to meet the costs of servicing the foreign debts that had accumulated. The fact that energy-rich Mexico had been one of the first countries to reach the point of crisis, in September 1982, precipitated a much more serious reappraisal of the long-term position of Brazil. Paradoxically, the very magnitude of the debts appeared to have left the debtor countries a freedom to dispute the creditors' terms of which they did not fail to take advantage. On the other hand, Argentina's successful transition to civilian rule under a Government with strong majority support, and Brazil's further moves towards freely-operating party government, both promised well for future political stability and made the *immobilismo* of the Pinochet Administration and the *continuismo* of General Stroessner in Paraguay look increasingly isolated.

Though the debt question was equally important in Costa Rica, in the Caribbean area the year was dominated by the build-up of United States pressure against the Provisional Government of Nicaragua, which the Reagan Administration continued to blame for the civil war in El Salvador. To the presence of US military advisers in El Salvador and ill-concealed covert support for counter-revolutionary forces (*contras*) in Honduras was later added a massive series of 'exercises' by combined forces in Honduras just to the north of Nicaragua. Direct military intervention in Grenada (see pp. 90-93) was seen, not just in Nicaragua and Cuba, but throughout the area as proof that the Reagan Administration would not hesitate to intervene directly in Nicaragua itself if it thought that in so doing it could safely further its avowed policy of militant anti-communism. Conciliatory moves by both Cuba and Nicaragua and the efforts of the 'Contadora group' of countries (Mexico, Venezuela, Panama and Colombia, so-called because of their meeting on the Panamanian island of Contadora in January) to bring about a negotiated settlement were greeted by a lukewarm response in Washington.

ARGENTINA

Two major issues dominated Argentine politics in the early part of the year: the fate of the 'disappeared' and the return to civilian government promised for early 1984. With inflation in 1982 at 209 per cent and the foreign debt standing at US$37,000 million, the failure of the military government to handle the key problems of the economy was manifest, and was only emphasized by the decision to introduce from 1 June a new monetary unit, the peso argentino, equal to 10,000 of the old pesos (peso ley) introduced in 1969. Part of the reason for the failure was the desire to rearm as quickly as possible. By the beginning of the year the handing-over of the remaining 9 Super-Etendard aircraft from France, and the purchase of 10 secondhand Mirages from Peru, some 22 Dagger interceptors from Israel, Lockheed C-130 Hercules transports and Electra maritime patrol aircraft from the United States, had gone far to replace the air losses of the Falklands war. On 3 February Blohm and Voss of Hamburg handed over the 3,360-ton frigate *Almirante Brown*, powered by British Rolls-Royce gas turbine engines. (Its sister ship, *La Argentina*, arrived at Puerto Belgrano on 19 July). The granting of a US$2,180 million (equivalent) loan by the IMF in late January came just in time to keep the defence budget more or less intact, but not soon enough to prevent the annual inflation rate from doubling. Under pressure from civilians the junta finally overrode military hardliners and resolved on 25 February to call elections for 30 October.

The repeal on 15 April of the Institutional Act banning from political activity ex-President María Estela ('Isabel') Martínez de Perón and 25 other politicians and trade unionists opened the campaigning season. The same evening a massive demonstration took place in the centre of Buenos Aires demanding an explanation of the fate of the 'disappeared'. The Government responded on 28 April by releasing its own report on the 'dirty war', which, while it accepted full responsibility, offered no explanation. Human rights groups declared that they had identified some 12,000 unmarked graves in 14 cemeteries in the greater Buenos Aires area alone. But even this macabre statistic aroused less horror than the calm comment of the Government's 'Final Statement' that the missing might now be presumed dead.

In face of the furore, no civilian politician could be found to court political annihilation by agreeing to the military demand for an amnesty. The Peronists, who had dominated Argentine electoral politics for a generation, were in a particularly difficult position, since the military had attempted to strengthen their own position by claiming that the armed repression had begun under Peronist rule, and when on 23 September they proceeded to amnesty themselves the amnesty, to emphasize this claim, was made effective from 1973. The Radicals (UCR) met first and on 10 July nominated Dr Raul Alfonsín and Victor Martínez as their candidates for President and Vice-President. They were already campaigning by the time that Dr Italo Luder, the Peronist front-runner and former provisional President, was nominated in September in a divided convention with the support of the party's first vice-president Deolindo Bittel, who gained the vice-presidential nomination. With no other serious candidate in the field, the Peronists failed to recover the lost ground, and on 30 October the charismatic Dr Alfonsín scored an overall majority for the Radicals, who also gained a majority in the new Chamber of Deputies. The Peronists won control of the Senate and a number of provisional governorships, but ex-President Perón's congratulations to Dr Alfonsín were noticeably warmer than is usual from the titular leader of a defeated party to the victor.

The new Government, which was sworn in on 10 December, faced massive problems at home and abroad. They had general support for acceptance of the Papal mediation on the Beagle Channel islands dispute, on which the military Government had failed to act. Mrs Thatcher had indicated her desire for improved relations through a well-timed message of goodwill to the incoming President (see p. 38). Dr Alfonsín immediately supported congressional rejection of the military amnesty, lost no time in appointing military commanders untainted by association either with the 'dirty war' or with the Falklands debacle and initiated proceedings against members of all juntas since 1976.

BOLIVIA

On 9 January the six members of the Cabinet from the Movement of the Revolutionary Left (MIR) resigned to put pressure on the Government of President Hernán Siles Zuazo to act more decisively against the continuing power of the military and cocaine interests. Over the previous few years the combined effect of these had wrecked the Bolivian economy and left inflation running at over 300 per cent per annum. Growth of coca for export—estimated at 82,000 tons in 1982—had eroded other crops and sources of income, and the Government of President Garcia Meza had refused to meet IMF conditions for new loans, leaving the Government unable to meet the interest payments due in April on the foreign debt of US $3,000 million. On 29 and 30 March the President paid an official visit to France and accepted an offer of US $14 million (equivalent) in credits and technical assistance. This followed the decision to expel to France the Nazi war criminal Klaus Altmann, alias Klaus Barbie, who had been arrested in La Paz at the end of January and held in connection with an unpaid debt. He had previously successfully contested an extradition order in 1974 when Bolivia was under military government.

At home, however, the Government still faced severe pressure from all sides. On 4 March two died and more than 20 were injured in rioting and looting during a police strike for more pay. At the end of March Congress passed a vote of censure on Sr Zenon Barrientos, Minister for Rural Affairs, for his alleged failure to cope with the problem of rural poverty. Poverty among the rural population, exacerbated by the worst drought for a century, was soon so desperate that by July some three million peasants were on the verge of starvation and thousands had migrated into the capital, where severe shortages of essential foods led to daily queues outside the breadshops. In these circumstances the Government was fortunate to survive the year.

BRAZIL

At the beginning of the year the problem of the Brazilian national debt, then standing at US $83,800 million, had already assumed international proportions, and the Central Bank was urgently seeking a loan of US $4,400 million from its fellow central banks in order to avert total default, only technically averted by their agreement in December 1982 to an emergency bridging loan. Foreign reserves had fallen to danger level, $4,000 million, and in January foreign trade figures were even worse than expected, requiring a surplus of £600,000 in each month for the rest of the year if promised targets were to be achieved. This seemed so unlikely that in late February Professor Delfim Netto, the Minister of Planning, decided to abandon the 'crawling peg', devalue the cruzeiro by 30 per cent, raise export taxes, and ask for a 'roll over' of the bridging loan. On 25 February agreements both for the new loan and for extension of time on $4,700 million of old loans due for repayment in 1983 were signed in New York.

With March, however, politics regained primacy. On 2 March the new Congress met for the first time, and on 15 March ten opposition governors took office along with their government colleagues. The result was a further increase of pressure on the Government of President João Batista Figueiredo to accelerate liberal reforms and meet the urgent demands of the poor, particularly in the north-east where a four-year drought had made rural conditions almost insupportable. For three days in April, riots in São Paulo, suppressed by the new opposition MDB governor, raised fears of workers' revolt also in the cities. Since just under half the population were below the poverty line, the dilemma for the Government was acute. On 14 July the 65-year-old President handed over power, as he had done for 50 days in 1981 (see AR 1981, p. 80), to Vice-President Aureliano Chaves de Mendonça, and entered a clinic in the United States for further treatment for his heart condition. He did so only a fortnight after major strikes in oil refineries and car factories had shown militant anger at the IMF-inspired wage cuts, and rumours of an impending moratorium had sent gold prices sharply upwards. At this juncture the Bank for International Settlements finally refused to 'roll over' its loan after 15 July, and, after the strikes had been effectively crushed by orders of General Otavio Medeiros, the Government agreed to a strict austerity package announced by President Figueiredo immediately before his departure. It was followed on 21 July by a one-day strike in protest, but this was only partially successful.

Clear evidence that the Central Bank had been juggling with its limited funds to create an illusion of solvency caused the IMF to require a fresh examination of the situation by its own team before the February loan would actually be paid. Before it had time to report, government action to hold down interest rates had driven 25 state banks into insolvency and caused an acute cash crisis. Next, several Government deputies voted against the austerity package in Congress, forcing the Government to resort to its decree powers to meet its international obligations. In October the payment of the next tranche of the IMF loan went ahead on schedule, but at the year's end, despite some encouraging trade signs, Brazil appeared hardly to have rounded the corner toward recovery.

CHILE

Despite the approval by the IMF at the beginning of January of an aid package for Chile worth US $882.5 million, the country's economy continued to deteriorate. Unemployment stood at 25 per cent and production had fallen by 13 per cent in 1982. On 14 January, following the failure of two small banks and a finance company, the Government 'intervened' in five other banks responsible for foreign borrowing totalling $3·35 millions, including the two biggest private banks, the Banco de Chile and the Banco de Santiago. It ordered the continued payment of interest, but declared it would not guarantee any part of the loan capital. Its own position, with a foreign debt of $17,000 million, was so precarious that a run on the banks followed, and by the end of the month it had declared a 90-day moratorium on repayments totalling $2,800 million. On 14 February the Finance Minister, Sr Rolf Luders, lost his place in a Cabinet reshuffle, and Sr Carlos Caceres, former president of the Central Bank, succeeded him. His departure marked the end of the Government's moves to break the control of Sr Roberto Vial over the banking system. It also marked the final failure of the military experiment with Chicago monetarist economics.

Inevitably the failure called into question the political future of President Pinochet, not only, for the first time, among middle-class civilians but also among nationalist elements of the armed forces. On 25

March hundreds of demonstrators in the capital were dispersed, and a series of explosions cut off water supplies over a wide area. In July, a day of protest organized by the National Union Coordinating Group, preceded by the abduction of some of its leaders and the detention of the president of the banned Christian Democratic Party, Sr Gabriel Valdés, was precipitated by the arrest on 15 June of Sr Rodolfo Seguel, who had led two earlier days of protest in May and June. It was followed by much more widespread demonstrations than had been seen in Chile for ten years, and the army was called in to disperse dissidents who had breached the curfew. Two were shot and hundreds arrested. On 13 July the Supreme Court, holding that peaceful protest was not a crime, freed Sr Valdés.

Opposition leaders immediately called for further demonstrations on 11 August. On the eve of it, the President reshuffled his Cabinet and appointed as Interior Minister Sergio Onofre Jarpa, to try to bring about an opening (*abertura*) to conservative civilian leaders. But after a massive government show of force 26 were killed and over 2,000 detained. On 30 August the Military Administrator of Santiago, General Carol Urzua Ibáñez, was assassinated. Three days before 11 September, the tenth anniversary of the coup that overthrew President Allende, dozens died in fresh demonstrations and more in October.

On 18 November an open mass protest in a Santiago park, the first since 1973, called by the newly-formed Democratic Alliance, was harassed by the authorities but not prevented. At it the Radical Party leader, Sr Enrique Silva Simma, called for the resignation of President Pinochet, the establishment of a provisional Government, the dissolution of the secret police and an emergency economic plan. Though at the year's end President Pinochet still hesitated to return to democracy, it seemed unlikely that further delay would do anything but play into the hands of the unidentified group that blacked out much of greater Santiago ten days before Christmas, and on 28 December plunged more than half the country's population into darkness with explosions in Concepción, San Fernando, Concón and Viña del Mar.

COLOMBIA

Violence continued to be the theme of life in Colombia. On 26 January, after a three-month 'truce', the guerrilla movement M-19 resumed operations by kidnapping Sonia Sarmiento, daughter of the owner of the Banco de Occidente, and demanding a ransom of £15 million. Its leader, Jaime Bateman, was killed in an air crash in April, and succeeded by his former second-in-command, the 43-year-old lawyer Ivan Marino Ospina. Despite its inability to overcome the violence, which had become endemic in the country over many years, the Government of

President Belisario Betancur remained in power throughout the year with only a minor Cabinet reshuffle in August on the anniversary of its formation, and played an active role overseas in the Contadora initiative (see p. 74).

ECUADOR

In common with other oil-producing countries, Ecuador found itself hit hard by falling oil prices on the world market. In mid-March the Government of President Oswaldo Hurtado Larrea devalued the sucre by 21 per cent and introduced a wide range of austerity measures. Violent demonstrations followed in which one person died and at least fifty were wounded. The Government defended the measures as necessary to enable it to meet IMF conditions for the rescheduling of US $2,500 million of the country's $6,300 million foreign debt. On 23 March the three major unions began an indefinite strike demanding their repeal.

PARAGUAY

The Paraguayan bishops said in their New Year message to the people: 'One cannot but be concerned by the total lack of interest in the holding of elections, by the lack of faith in the country's rulers, in its politicians, and in the administration of justice.' They also criticized 'arbitrary detention, torture, lack of freedom, and the absence of personal guarantees' under which further detentions had occurred in the previous two years.

On 6 February President Alfredo Stroessner, aged 70, was re-elected to a fifth five-year term of office. Running as candidate of the Colorado Party, General Stroessner received 919,582 of the 1,021,597 votes cast, the remainder being divided between Senator Enzo Doldan of the Liberal-Radicals and Dr Fulvio Celauro of the Liberal Party. Under the constitution the Colorado Party automatically received two-thirds of the 60 seats in the Chamber of Deputies and 30 in the Senate.

President Stroessner was sworn in on 14 August for his new term and appointed three new Ministers. The stability of the regime seemed assured for the present by its success in the economic sphere, where consumer spending was based on the profits of increased smuggling across the Brazilian frontier and the bonanza expected from the production of electricity from Itaipú for sale to Brazil, though this last had yet to become a reality. The influx of Brazilian immigrants in the frontier region created a potential threat to the country's sovereignty.

PERU

The year began with a spate of incidents as security forces clashed with members of the maoist guerrilla movement Sendero Luminoso (the Shining Path). Shortly afterwards nine reporters died in mysterious circumstances, allegedly at the hands of the local villagers, close to a 'liberated zone' at Uchuraccay near Ayacucho while reporting the conflict. This followed the decision by President Fernando Belaúnde Terry in December 1982 to impose a state of emergency in the province and to send in the army and marines to reinforce the police counter-insurgency forces, the Sinchis. It was followed by a series of conflicting reports about the extent of their success or otherwise. To make matters worse, no rain fell on the highlands between November and March; the staple crop, potatoes, failed, and crop losses generally exceeded 70 per cent.

The civilian Government came under strong pressure from the trade union movement to reverse the ten-year trend in decline of living standards, and to fulfil its promises of 1980. With an external debt of US $11,000 million, it was forced to accept IMF guidelines for economic management which included devaluation, increases in the domestic price of petrol, and massive cuts in public spending, including food subsidies. On 8 March the Government requested a deferment of debt principal payments and new bank loans of $800 million. Two days later, confronted by a general strike, it proclaimed a state of emergency. In June, discontent with the free-market orthodoxy and austerity measures of the Finance Minister, Sr Carlos Rodríguez Pastor, led to the resignation of the Minister of Labour, Sr Alfonso Grados Bertorini, who despite rising inflation and unemployment had been on good terms with union leaders. The measures had led to the cancellation of the major public works projects promised by the Government as a cure for unemployment, and the private sector was squeezed into bankruptcy by a combination of high interest rates and low import tariffs. At the beginning of July, however, the Popular Christian Party (PPC), on which the Government relied for its Senate majority, decided to renew its support for a further year.

By that time it was already clear that the guerrillas had shifted their emphasis to terrorist attacks in the capital itself. Within a week of a police strike brought on by low pay, Lima was plunged into darkness by the simultaneous demolition of a series of electricity pylons. Then, on 13 July, three people were killed and 32 wounded in an attack on the headquarters of the ruling Popular Action Party (AP), apparently designed to take top leaders hostage. The President responded by calling for the restoration of the death penalty, abolished by the 1979 constitution, and stating his intention to call in foreign security advisers. Although within a month a new drive by police and armed forces in the central highlands brought two successes, the capture of 27 guerrillas and the death of some 40 more, attacks continued on AP officials. On 11 November, on the eve of the municipal elections, while a strike paralysed Ayacucho, guerrillas attacked the residence of the Honduran ambassador. The following day three policemen were killed in attacks on polling stations and party offices. In the elections themselves the Government suffered a series of crushing defeats. The candidate of the marxist United Left coalition (IU), Sr Alfonso Barrantes, who had described Sendero Luminoso as 'terrorists who have usurped the will of the people', won the mayoralty of Lima with 33 per cent of the votes cast to 27 per cent for Sr Alfredo Barnachea of APRA and 20 per cent for the PPC candidate, while the government candidate, Sr Alfonso Grados Bertorini, got only 12 per cent. In the provincial cities APRA swept the polls in a series of victories that demonstrated the continuing national appeal of the centre-left.

URUGUAY

Uruguay continued its slow return to democracy. The military Government of General Gregorio Alvarez reopened negotiations with the political parties in March, having been unable to secure popular acceptance for their own draft constitution in 1982. In the changing political climate in Brazil, they could no longer hope for support from that quarter, and in February they received a request from 85 Brazilian officers for the freeing of General Liber Seregni, former presidential candidate of the left-wing Frente Amplio (see AR 1974, p. 105), who had been held in detention for several years. The opposition Colorado party, whose leader Jorge Batlle clearly enjoyed widespread if totally unofficial support, was pressing for an early and full return to civilian government, but confronted a policy dilemma in wishing neither to bring in heavy foreign investment nor to replace dependence on Brazil with dependence on Argentina. The negotiations collapsed early in July.

At this point, left without any possibility of imposing a tame civilian Government, leaders of the armed forces met secretly on 13 and 14 July and decided in any case to hold elections in 1984 and hand over power to the civilians in March 1985. As elections in neighbouring Argentina approached, political protest became more vocal and monthly demonstrations demanding a return to civilian rule showed open defiance of the military ban on unauthorized parties. When on 17 December a radio station in Montevideo was closed by the authorities for broadcasting the proceedings of Uruguay's two traditional political parties, the Colorados and Blancos, the proprietor went on hunger strike, backed by crowds that were forcibly dispersed by police on 29 December.

VENEZUELA

Venezuela, hit both by the world recession and by the slump in the world oil market, began the year with a serious liquidity crisis which led it to seek rescheduling of its $24,300 million foreign debt, though as yet without recourse to the IMF. Increasing depletion of its foreign currency reserves, however, a further 5 per cent cut in the rate of oil production and the cuts in oil prices initiated by the British National Oil Corporation led on 20 February to the suspension of dealings in foreign currency. A week later the Finance Minister, Sr Arturo Sosa, introduced a three-tier exchange rate for the bolivar, ending 18 years of free convertibility, and making an effective devaluation of some 40 per cent. At the insistence of the president of the Central Bank, Sr Leopoldo Díaz Bruzual, who blamed them for causing the crisis, finance houses investing overseas and multinationals operating in Venezuela were both excepted from the preferential 4·3 per cent rate of repayment guaranteed to other creditors. Early in March the Minister of Planning, Sra Maritza Izaguirre, announced further measures to ban luxury imports and so cut the import bill by a quarter. Since these measures ran directly contrary to the recommendations of the IMF, and were not accompanied by any attempt to catch up with chronic arrears on both private and public sector interest repayments, Sr Sosa's request for a rescheduling of $18,000 million of public sector debt was not greeted with enthusiasm, and in July Venezuela's creditors made it clear that any rescheduling would have to be conditional on meeting regular economic performance tests.

In the latter part of the year the approaching elections submerged all other issues. At the beginning of December it looked as if ex-President Rafael Caldera, candidate of the ruling Christian Democrats (COPEI) to succeed President Luis Herrera Campins, was reducing the lead of his rival, Sr Jaime Lusinchi, 59-year-old former secretary-general of Accion Democratica (AD). But at the elections on 4 December Sr Lusinchi swept the board in the capital, the federal district of Caracas, all twenty states and both territories, to secure 53 per cent of the votes cast to 36 per cent for Dr Caldera. Contributing to the victory was not only AD's traditional support in the labour movement but also the advance agreement of the private business sector to a price and dividend freeze if wage controls were to be introduced under a new austerity package.

CUBA

Early in January Sr Humberto Pérez, head of the state planning commission, abruptly announced that the country's balance of payments estimates for the year made no allowance for the repayment of certain external debts, for which Cuba had been seeking rescheduling since September 1982. The debt crisis, caused by a combination of high energy costs and low export prices for sugar, was moderate by Latin American standards, and talks proceeded slowly. As the year wore on, security of the country in face of the bellicose and unpredictable posture of the United States became the primary concern.

In the previous two years heavy shipments of arms from the Soviet Union had extended the range and capacity of Cuba's air defence. In May large-scale manoeuvres were held to test defences against seaborne attack, and in June air-raid warnings were instituted. So great was the anxiety at repeated US allegations of Cuban military activity in the Caribbean area that on 26 July, the 30th anniversary of the Moncada uprising, President Fidel Castro Ruz offered to withdraw all 200 Cuban military advisers from Nicaragua if the US would do the same from El Salvador and Honduras. The proposal was given a cautious welcome by President Reagan. Immediately afterwards, welcoming Mr Maurice Bishop, President Castro insisted that the new international airport which Cubans were helping to build in Grenada was an entirely civil project, a claim which was subsequently to be proved true. Though the continued popularity of the regime was not in doubt, some unofficial labour unrest led to heavy sentences against dissidents, and four defence lawyers and a judge were also arrested.

The overthrow of Maurice Bishop by the Coard faction in Grenada and his subsequent death took Cuba by surprise. On 15 October the leaders of the Cuban Communist Party expressed their deep concern to the new Grenadan leadership and called for generosity toward its predecessors. On 20 October they denounced the murder of Bishop, and indicated that, although for the sake of the people of Grenada Cuban construction workers would not be withdrawn yet, they reserved the right to remove them later, and two days later informed the United States that they were willing to cooperate to avoid violence in Grenada. The United States invasion of the island on 25 October, however, met with resistance from some of the 800-odd Cubans there, and 25 were killed. In a major speech in their honour on 14 November President Castro took the opportunity to refute what he termed the '19 lies' of the Reagan Government in attempting to shift the responsibility for the invasion to Cuba (see pp. 91-93).

THE DOMINICAN REPUBLIC AND HAITI

In the DOMINICAN REPUBLIC, the Government of Dr Salvador Jorge Blanco remained in power throughout the year. Vice-President Manuel Fernández Marmol died on 20 January aged 69.

In HAITI a car bomb exploded near the presidential palace on

1 January, killing at least four people. The guerrilla group responsible, the Hector Riobe Brigade, threatened the life of the Pope before his visit in March, which came only three months after the arrest of a popular Catholic lay worker, Gerard Duclerville, for allegedly insulting the President's mother in a radio broadcast. Having been beaten almost to death, M Duclerville was released at the request of Archbishop François Ligonde, a cousin of the President's wife. Municipal elections were promised for the first time in 20 years just before the visit in January of Mr Thomas Enders, who reassured the President of US support and praised the economic policies which had long been the despair of international agencies.

Early in February Marie-France Claude, Vice-President of the opposition Christian Democratic Party, and five of its leading figures were driven into exile. Her father, M Sylvio Claude, who had escaped from house arrest the previous month, remained in hiding. At the elections held on 14 August Colonel Franck Romain, a former chief of police, was declared to have secured 98 per cent of the poll to become the new mayor of Port-au-Prince, and later a new constitution approved by the outgoing Assembly confirmed Jean-Claude Duvalier's Presidency for life and authorized him to nominate his successor.

CENTRAL AMERICA AND PANAMA

For Central America, the overwhelming fact of 1983 was the United States Government's growing offensive against 'communism' in what President Reagan now described as his country's 'back yard'.

In EL SALVADOR the civil war that had already cost the lives of some 30,000 in three years continued, the Minister of Defence, General José Guillermo Garcia, being challenged in January by the army's most successful combat leader, Lieut.-Colonel Sigifredo Ochoa Pérez. The Archbishop's office said that 5,399 civilians were murdered in 1982. The major political problem remained the ascendancy of the extreme right-wing President of the Constituent Assembly, Major Roberto d'Aubuisson, whose Republican Nationalist Alliance (ARENA) and its allies continued with the aid of the 'death squads' to block urgently-needed reforms. The Pope's tour of Central America at the beginning of March included a visit on Sunday 6 March to El Salvador, where he paid a private visit to the tomb of the murdered Archbishop Romero (see AR 1980, p. 87) and made a public appeal for peace. A week later President Reagan announced a massive increase in military aid, which was denounced by the Salvadorean bishops. In June a new major government offensive was launched, and the number of deaths due to political violence grew. Mr Richard Stone, the special US envoy, met the guerrillas in Colombia in August. Elections planned for November were postponed to March 1984 when it was found that registration could not be completed in time.

The Reagan Administration declared its intention of resuming arms sales, suspended by President Carter in 1977, to GUATEMALA a week after the Council on Hemispheric Affairs had nominated it as the country with the worst human rights record in Latin America in 1982, because of attacks by the army on Indians in the north-western departments of El Quiché and Huehuetenango, where some 2,600 had died in counter-terror campaigns since President Efraín Rios Montt had taken power in March 1982 (see AR 1982, p. 92). After the execution of six alleged 'subversives' for whom the Pope had asked clemency, the Pope's call at Quezaltenango on 7 March for the Indians to defend their rights, though non-violently, aroused deep feeling.

The deaths of a USAID employee and four other aid workers arrested in Huehuetenango led to public penitence by the President. On 28 June he was forced by senior military officers to dismiss his Protestant advisers and the head of his personal intelligence service, Lieut.-Colonel Arturo Sánchez, but on 8 August he was overthrown in a classic military coup led by the Minister of Defence, General Oscar Humberto Mejía Victores, who replaced him as head of state. Following the coup, unpopular special courts were disbanded but killings continued. The new Government did not go back on General Rios Montt's decision in January, in otherwise unsuccessful talks with Belize and Britain, to abandon four-fifths of Guatemala's traditional claim to Belize, and indeed seemed glad that British troops should remain there so long as the violence continued. It did enter talks in October designed to reactivate the Central American Defence Council (CONDECA) in an anti-communist alliance against Nicaragua.

It was in HONDURAS that the main impact of the US policy was evident. There the incursions of the US-backed Nicaraguan Democratic Force (FDN) into Nicaragua became bolder and more serious. The joint exercises held by the United States with the Honduran army in Gracias a Dios in the first week of February, openly described as 'a warning to Nicaragua and Cuba', proved to be only the prelude to the massive 'exercise', Big Pine II, which from 10 August brought 5,600 US troops into Honduras backed by three fleets carrying some 16,000 military personnel. The commander of the Honduran army, General Gustavo Alvarez, claiming that Honduras was menaced by Nicaragua, stated 'The gringos are here because we called them in.' This was followed by a statement from Sr Edgar Chamorro of the FDN that a military victory in Nicaragua was unlikely, and at the year's end the prospect for negotiation, resumed under the Contadora group's auspices in December, looked somewhat brighter.

The fact was that the Sandinista Government in NICARAGUA, defending the gains of the revolution of 1979, continued to enjoy much support, despite rationing, a shortage of foreign exchange and criticism by the Pope both for the active presence of priests in government and for harsh treatment of the Miskito Indians in the counter-insurgency campaign. Thereafter, their chief anxiety was that the August offensive of the *contras*, while a huge US task force was openly practising blockades off their coast, might give a pretext for US intervention. This anxiety became acute after the US invasion of Grenada in October, though the substantial build-up of arms from the Soviet Union and Eastern Europe in the previous years would have made the success of any direct attack dubious.

COSTA RICA was careful to maintain its traditional neutrality in the Nicaraguan situation. Domestically, its main problem was the refinancing of its US $4,000 million foreign debt, on which a further $350 million interest had accumulated since the suspension of payments in 1981. In April a preliminary agreement was signed. At the same time moves were initiated for the first time in many years to increase the strength of the national security forces, though without reintroducing an army.

PANAMA, though actively engaged in the Central American peace negotiations throughout the year, had a troubled year in internal politics, where the commander of the National Guard, General Rubén Dario Paredes, a conservative populist, had entered the arena in preparation for the elections in 1984. On 24 April a referendum endorsed the new constitution, a majority of 5 to 1 voting for a return to full civilian rule. But in August President Ricardo de la Espriella, General Paredes's nominee in 1982, came under opposition on charges of fraud, support for which by the Attorney-General, Sr Rafael Rodríguez, was followed by the latter's flight to Miami. It was agreed that the US military training base for Latin American officers in the former Canal Zone would stay open under US administration after it reverted to Panama in 1984.

MEXICO

Mexico's financial crisis, whose onset in September 1982 had shaken the world financial system and added to the problems of most of the major Latin American economies, remained critical, its outlook worsened by the British decision to cut oil prices in February. Ironically, this coincided with the Queen's visit to Acapulco and the British-financed steel complex at Lázaro Cárdenas, at which she referred to Britain's 'wish to help in the most useful way' it could. On 3 March agreement was reached with bankers in New York on a new US $5,000 million loan, but this in turn delayed talks on debt rescheduling and on 18 March the Secretariat of Finance had to ask its commercial bank creditors for a five-month extension of its original seven-month moratorium on debt repayments, to enable it to complete plans for the rescheduling of some

$20,000 million of public sector debt falling due up to 1985. The package was further complicated by the Opec decision to cut back oil production, which would have limited Mexico to 1·5 mn. b/d and cost it $1,300 million in lost revenue. In August, the Government began to pay indemnities in government bonds to stockholders of the 11 banking groups nationalized in 1982, the bonds to pay an annual interest rate of 54·74 per cent.

Criticism of the ruling Party of the Institutionalized Revolution (PRI) for incompetence and corruption in office resulted in unprecedented victories at the state and municipal elections on 3 July for the right-wing Party of National Action (PAN) in Chihuahua, Ciudad Juárez, Durango and seven smaller towns in Chihuahua. At the end of the same month, which saw a rise of 41 per cent in the price of tortillas, Senator Jorge Díaz Serrano, sometime director of the state oil corporation Pemex, was stripped of his Senatorial immunity and charged with defrauding the state of the equivalent of US $34 million. In his first annual message to Congress on 1 September, President Miguel de la Madrid Hurtado, calling for 'moral sobriety and austerity' in government, was very frank about the country's plight. 'The crisis is not over', he said. 'The only thing we can say is that the Government has the worst aspects under control.' The annual rate of inflation had been brought down from over 100 per cent to under 60 per cent in July, currency reserves were up from their critical level, and the June trade balance had been good. The Secretary of Finance, however, said in an interview that the process of recovery would not be quick. 'The trouble about a belt-tightening policy in Mexico is that many people cannot afford a belt, so they have nothing they can tighten.'

Chapter 4

THE CARIBBEAN

JAMAICA—GRENADA—THE WINDWARD & LEEWARD ISLANDS—
TRINIDAD AND TOBAGO—GUYANA—BARBADOS—
BELIZE—THE BAHAMAS—SURINAME

JAMAICA

JAMAICA ended 1983, its 21st year of independence, under a cloud of economic and political uncertainty. Foreign debt stood at about US$2,000 million, nearly 50 per cent of export earnings. The country's trade deficit rose to US$293·2 million in the first six months, 22·9 per cent higher than for the same period in 1982.

The bauxite-alumina industry recorded its lowest level of production for 20 years—7·7 million tonnes of bauxite. Bauxite-alumina, sugar and bananas accounted for 77 per cent of the value of Jamaican exports in 1982. Sugar production fell to 198,000 tonnes in 1983, and the industry had accumulated losses of over J$350 million: 11,000 sugar workers were laid off and seven factories closed, perhaps temporarily. With the development of 2,000 acres of new banana lands at a cost of J$30 million, an upsurge in banana production was anticipated in 1984, when another 4,000 acres were scheduled for production with the aid of a structural adjustment loan from the World Bank.

It was announced that J$18 million would be spent on establishing 20 garment factories with a total of 500,000 square feet of space in the next four years. The newly-established National Industry Development Corporation (NIDCO) would oversee the structural adjustment process in seven priority industrial sub-sectors. Areas of growth in the economy included the coffee industry, which had been expanding production at the rate of 14·5 per cent per year, and the tourist sector, which was expected to gross US$405·6 million in 1983. The value of exports to the Caribbean Community had increased by 12 per cent in the first three quarters of the year.

Jamaica, by running up a deficit of US$151 million at the end of March, failed to meet the criteria laid down by the IMF, which suspended the three-year US$650 million stand-by credit package. Numerous fiscal and budgetary measures were introduced, first to meet the IMF terms and then to qualify for a waiver. These included the introduction of a two-tiered, then a three-tiered exchange rate system, giving way on 3 November to a full-scale devaluation of the currency by 43 per cent (77 per cent against the US dollar). New taxes were imposed to raise J$75 million. Austerity measures were introduced in June which included a 4·6 per cent cut-back in 1983-84 budgeted spending. The IMF granted a waiver and Jamaica secured a loan of US$180 million, but now was obliged to produce a balance of payments surplus of US$125 by March 1984, and to hold its budgetary deficit to the tighter target of 10·8 per cent of GDP.

Parliament was dissolved on 25 November, and new general elections were called for 15 December, two years before they were constitutionally due. The opposition People's National Party abstained from the elections, claiming that the Government had defaulted on a 1980 agreement between the two major parties that fresh elections would not be called until new anti-electoral fraud mechanisms were put in place. The Jamaica Labour Party accordingly secured all 55 seats in the House of Assembly. The Prime Minister, Mr Edward Seaga, named a Government, and, dubiously, also the Opposition Senate members, constitutionally appointable by the Leader of the Opposition in the House of Assembly.

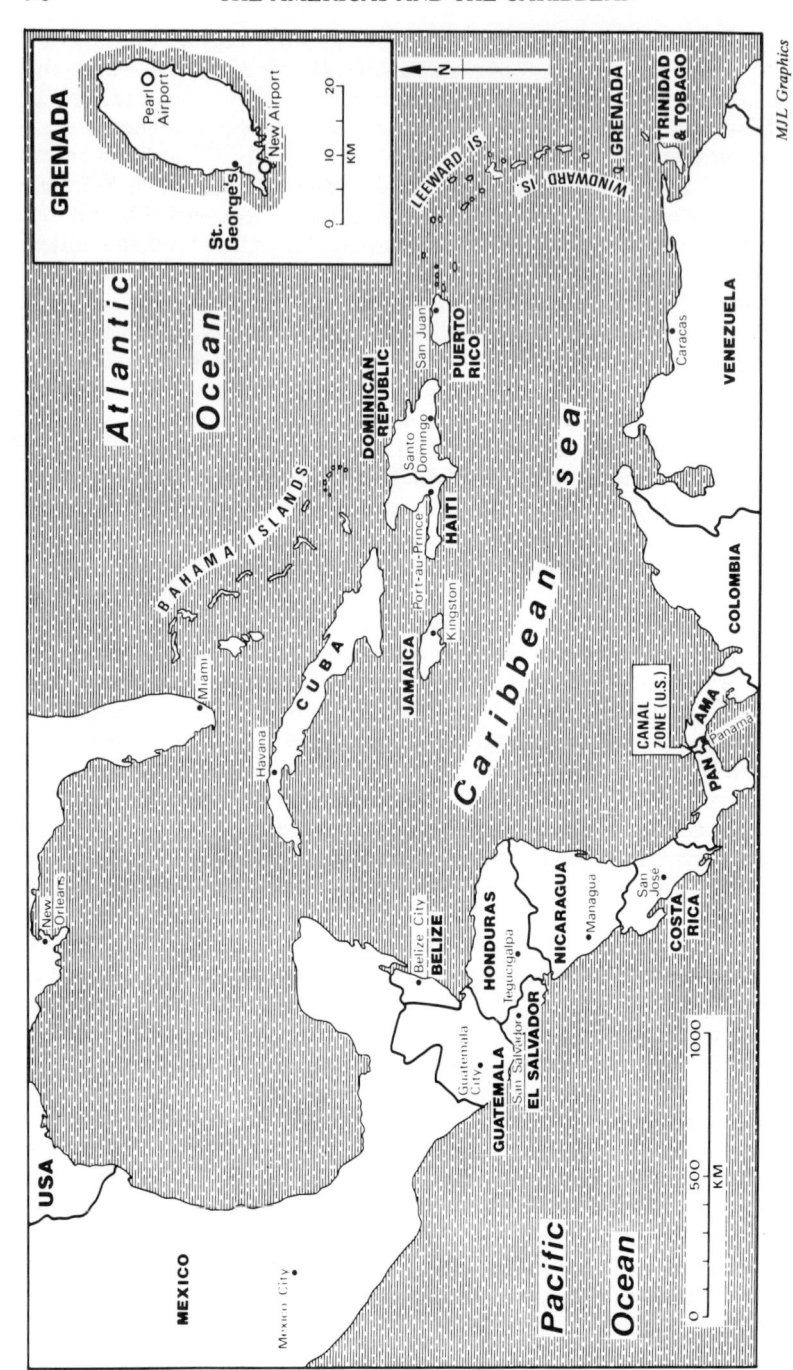

The United States' 'back yard'

GRENADA

Three and a half years of rule by the People's Revolutionary Government of Grenada came to an abrupt end on 25 October. The country was invaded by a massive force of American marines and aircraft from a US naval fleet, accompanied by token contingents from the Commonwealth Caribbean states of Barbados, Jamaica, Dominica, Antigua, St Lucia and St Vincent.

During those 3½ years, Grenada had earned commendations from the World Bank, achieved a 5·5 per cent growth rate in 1982 and received a balance of payments support loan of US $14·1 million from the IMF. An aid package worth EC $25 million had been secured from North Korea, and Hungary and Czechoslovakia had also provided material aid. The private sector remained intact, guaranteed by a government investment code. Grenada enjoyed good and improving relations with its partners in the Organization of Eastern Caribbean States (OECS) and the Caribbean Community (Caricom). The major areas of dispute continued to be the regime's failure to hold general elections and its growing militarization. In response it appointed a constitutional commission chaired by a Trinidadian lawyer, and by 1983 had freed a substantial number of detainees: only 20 persons were said to be still in detention.

Nevertheless, the opposition of the United States to Grenada was strident, implacable and concrete. It openly frustrated the country's efforts with international funding agencies. In 1981 the Administration had considered covert action in Grenada. In repeated statements, intensified in 1983, President Reagan declared that there was a Soviet-Cuban build-up in Grenada for the export of revolution and that the country constituted a serious security risk to the USA. The persistence and vehemence of the attacks, and the US Government's dismissive treatment of requests for high-level talks to improve relations, led Grenada to prepare for war. It organized a people's militia in every parish by April 1983, aiming to recruit 10,000 persons. Their potential armament was indicated by the US capture of 6,322 rifles, 5 million rounds of ammunition and 29 tons of TNT, among other weapons.

A serious split within Grenada's ruling party emerged in September/October when Prime Minister Maurice Bishop renounced his previous agreement to share leadership with the Deputy Prime Minister, Mr Bernard Coard. A rumour that Mr Coard was plotting to kill Mr Bishop was attributed by the army to Mr Bishop himself. On 12 October Mr Bishop was placed under house arrest by the military and Mr Coard was said to be ruling the country. Six Government Ministers resigned after efforts to secure a compromise on the leadership question and the release of Mr Bishop had failed. Mr Coard himself resigned on 15 October, saying he did so to scotch rumours about the murder plot.

The following day a crowd of over 3,000 freed Mr Bishop and led him triumphantly to Fort Rupert, where he persuaded the garrison to lay down their arms. A company of soldiers was sent by the military command to retake the Fort. The crowd was fired upon, several being killed and nearly 200 wounded. Mr Bishop and his colleagues surrendered to the soldiers, only to be executed soon afterwards. General Hudson Austin, commander of the armed forces, subsequently announced that a 16-man military council had been appointed to rule the country, and that a Cabinet would be named within 14 days.

Commonwealth Caribbean leaders were outraged by these events, feeling that their security was threatened, and some resolved to invade and restore 'democracy'. An emergency meeting of Caricom, held in Trinidad on 23 October, by a majority vote suspended the membership of Grenada and endorsed proposals for sanctions put by the Eastern Caribbean states. It did not, however, support an OECS decision on 21 October, strongly backed by Barbados, to invade Grenada along with friendly foreign forces. Guyana, Trinidad and Tobago, the Bahamas and Belize opposed the move.

The OECS, as well as Barbados and Jamaica, had already requested assistance from the US Government, invoking as legal justification for intervention s.8 of the treaty establishing the OECS and stating, subsequently, that they had received a request for assistance from the Governor-General of Grenada. Section 8 dealt with the need for collective action in the face of external threats to territorial sovereignty: it offfered no legal grounds for intervention in the internal affairs of a member country.

Mr J.M.G. Adams, Prime Minister of Barbados, related that in a telephone conversation the Governor-General of Grenada had said that he needed help; the latter wrote a confirming letter several days after the invasion. Prime Minister Miss Eugenia Charles of Dominica stated that the Eastern Caribbean Governments never considered asking the British Government for help at any time.

Among the reasons given by President Reagan for intervention was the receipt of an urgent request from the OECS on 21 October, following one from Prime Minister Adams of Barbados. He had already, on 21 October, diverted a flotilla headed for Beirut to Grenadan waters. Assurances from Cuba and from the military in Grenada that US citizens were safe, and international urgings against invasion, were brushed aside by the US Government and no serious effort was made to negotiate with the military regime.

It was the invasion itself, not any previous threat, which put the more than 600 American medical students in Grenada at such risk as there was. No attempt was made by the island's defenders to take them hostage, although the Grenadan forces had had advance notice of the invasion

The military reasons given for the invasion were unconvincing. The

Point Salines airport, site of a major US landing, had been designed as a tourist airport with a 9,000 ft. runway. The managers of the project, Plessey Airports, a British firm, who had a £6·6 million contract for its equipment, stated that none of the requirements for a military airport was being installed. Of the 784 Cubans in Grenada, 636 were construction and engineering workers based at the airport; 43 were armed forces personnel, 21 were translators and the remainder were diplomatic staff and technical experts in education, agriculture and fisheries.

Some Cubans at the airport offered resistance but quickly surrendered, 600 being captured on the first day of the invasion. About 70 other Cubans fought with Grenadian soldiers in the hills until 27 October. Before the capture of Mr Bernard Coard and General Hudson Austin on 29 October all fighting was virtually over. Although many targets of American firepower, such as small bridges and roads, had very little military significance in the light of the very limited action by Grenadan/Cuban armed forces, the overall damage was not extensive and by 1 November electricity and some telephone services were restored.

When the firing had ceased, by the end of October, dead were 45 Grenadans, 25 Cubans, and 18 Americans; and wounded were 337 Grenadans, 116 Americans and 59 Cubans. At the height of the battle over 6,000 US troops were engaged, and 15 US ships were in Grenadan waters. The nearly 400 troops from the Caribbean islands did not participate in the actual fighting.

On 4 November the US army handed over the prisoners to the Governor-General, who declared a state of emergency. A nine-man Interim Advisory Committee was established. General elections within one year were promised. The US Government voted $18 million in all for restoration work. The IMF suspended its loan to Grenada. A Joint Defence Force of Caribbean contingents, masterminded by Mr Adams of Barbados, would receive $15 million from the US government; it was to be headquartered in Barbados, and permanent units would be stationed in Antigua, Dominica and St Vincent, also in St Kitts-Nevis after independence.

The invasion received widespread support among the peoples of the Commonwealth Caribbean—though their governments differed—and helped to improve the popularity of the party in power in each state which intervened.

THE WINDWARD AND LEEWARD ISLANDS

ANTIGUA AND BARBUDA rejected IMF recommendations on the economy because of the hardships that would result. The IMF sought a 40 per cent reduction in the public service, a wage freeze, reduction of the working day for some departments and the abandonment of a youth employment programme. A total deficit of EC$163·1 million on its 1983-84 budget was anticipated. The West Indies Oil Company (WIOC), which was sustaining an average monthly loss of over EC$2 million on its operations, implemented a retrenchment plan. The Government had secured a commitment from Nigeria for the supply of 20,000 barrels of crude oil per day for WIOC. Brazil announced a scaling-down of the cost of its hotel and shipping complex in Antigua from US$90 million to US$55 million.

DOMINICA experienced an improved export performance, especially of bananas. Dominica's 1983-84 budget was reduced by 32·4 per cent over the previous year's. External debt had doubled in the past three years, although GDP had grown in real terms from EC$99·5 million in 1981 to EC$102·8 million in 1982. New capital totalling TT$3·489 million was to be injected into the lime industry. Additionally, the Government was seeking EC$80 million from a consortium of international lending agencies, including the World Bank, for the development of Dominica's hydroelectrical potential.

ST KITTS-NEVIS became an independent state on 19 September. The opposition St Kitts Labour Party objected strongly to the federal-type arrangement with Nevis which it claimed would give Nevis inordinate influence in the state. The Nevis Reformation Party won all five seats in the island's first Assembly in an election on 22 August.

The sugar industry, which had accumulated debts of up to EC$40 million, produced 28,000 tonnes of sugar in 1983. The St Kitts-Nevis 1983 budget amounted to EC$194 million and a wide range of tax increases was announced.

The ST LUCIA Government announced austerity measures involving an overall cut in expenditure of 20 per cent for 1983, a 10 per cent cut in ministerial salaries, and a freeze on all new appointments in the public service, among other measures. The April Budget cut nearly 10 per cent off the 1982-83 figures. Import taxes were increased, and ceilings were placed on consumer credit. A negative growth of 5 per cent in the economy was recorded for 1982, and the 1982-83 trade balance was in deficit by EC$119·5 million. Extensive crop damage caused by a tropical depression and a glut of bananas on the UK market dealt St Lucia's banana industry hard blows. A US$20 million grant from the US to assist in modernizing the island's agricultural sector was agreed on with USAID. A project costing EC$18 million to cut up 1,600 acres of land formerly owned by Geest into five-acre farms was started.

ST VINCENT AND THE GRENADINES recorded real growth of 4 per cent in the economy in 1982. According to the Opposition Leader, Mr Mitchell, a Caribbean Development Bank study found that the sugar industry had lost EC$3·6 million in 1982, and was expected to lose more than EC$6 million in 1983-85.

The People's Liberation Movement, in MONTSERRAT, led by Chief Minister Mr John Osborne, won 5 of 7 seats in the 24 February general elections.

TRINIDAD AND TOBAGO

The twin-island state celebrated its 21st anniversary of independence in August. Since 1973, when the Trinidad and Tobago economy was on the brink of collapse, an eight-year windfall in oil earnings had fuelled the economy. Heavy industry utilizing the country's energy resources was planned to become the lasting basis of growth, but a World Bank report on the Iron and Steel Company of Trinidad and Tobago had cast doubts on the success of this strategy. The company had operated on average at less than a quarter of its capacity in 1982. Losses in the fiscal year ending July 1982 had been TT$262 million, and for the eleven months ending in June 1983 were TT$220 million.

Similarly, the fertilizer manufacturers Federated Chemicals continued to record poor sales. The company had already started a retrenchment policy and closed two plants. Weak markets and high production costs were blamed. At least 5,000 workers were laid off in various industries. The 1983 sugar production amounted to 78,069 tonnes.

An anticipated substantial deficit on the 1983 Budget forced the Government to make its first entry into the eurodollar bond market through an issue of US$50 million floating-rate notes on 10 June. This deficit and the urgent need for further structural adjustment of the economy presumably caused the postponement of the presentation of the 1984 Budget from 15 December to January-February 1984. The value of Trinidad and Tobago's exports for the first six months of 1983 declined by TT$742 million from the TT$3,750 recorded for the same period in 1982. The petroleum sector accounted for 84 per cent of 1983 exports. During the year the state-owned electricity corporation was granted rate increases ranging from 113 to 233 per cent, effective from 1 January 1984.

By a 10-4 vote the Tobago House of Assembly resolved to put an end to the present union between Trinidad and Tobago, which the majority thought unjust, and to secure either its replacement with a union based on terms acceptable to the authorized representatives of the people of Tobago, or the full independence of Tobago with secure territorial boundaries. Three meetings were held with the Prime Minister on the question.

After 27 years of national and local political dominance, the ruling People's National Movement (FNM) received a shock when the results of the local government elections were known. The elections had been delayed from April to August. The PNM managed to retain control of the municipalities, but two mayors failed to retain their seats and the opposition made significant inroads in PNM strongholds. Of 120 county council seats contested, the 'coalition of opposition' parties won 66 seats to 54 won by the PNM and took control of six out of seven councils.

GUYANA

Guyana's gross external debt was estimated to be US$1,350 million in July. Unemployment exceeded 30 per cent of the work-force. The US Government stopped the flow of 'undisbursed' loans amounting to US$19 million through the USAID programme and blocked an IDB loan of US$46 million. The IMF and World Bank proposed a 66 to 100 per cent devaluation of the Guyanese dollar, continuation of the wage freeze, increased electricity rates, removal of subsidy on local consumption of sugar, and cuts of G$150-200 million in public expenditure within the framework of a general review of all government projects that were not foreign-exchange earners. It was proposed that the bauxite industry and the rice board be returned to private enterprise. These proposals were stridently rejected by the Executive President, Mr Forbes Burnham. The Government faced serious and mounting unrest from civic and political groups demanding the immediate importation of basic foods and drug items.

The Guyana bauxite industry was expected to lose G$198 million on its operations for 1983, and had a projected overdraft of G$235 million. This was due to declining production, falling sales and low productivity. The alumina plant and three bauxite mines were closed and 1,721 workers were laid off. Sugar fared badly with a 1983 output of just over 250,000 tonnes of raw sugar, a 30,000 shortfall on the official revised estimates. Rice production fell nearly 50,000 tons short of its production target because of disease and unfavourable weather conditions. A total production of 144,103 tons of rice was anticipated.

Guyana received a Can.$3·2 million grant to assist nearly 2,000 fishermen, and was seeking British assistance to get its G$61 million glass factory into production. The prospects for economic survival remained bleak.

BARBADOS

The economy grew by about 2 per cent, reflecting an increase in tourist arrivals of more than 6 per cent over the 1982 figure, increased oil production of approximately 1,400 barrels per day, and an improved performance in the construction sector. The oil bill had been steadily reduced from B$92·5 million in 1981 to around B$56 million in 1983.

The foreign exchange reserves stood at B$206·6 million in August, up B$80 million over twelve months. Up to 9 September, Barbados had drawn down about B$70 million from a B$98·6 million standby and compensatory financing facility agreement with the IMF. However, it still had a credit, on its foreign exchange account, of B$130 million in the Caribbean Multilateral Clearing Facility.

The sugar output, 85,550 tonnes, was the lowest since 1948. Inflation for the twelve months to August 1983 was down to 4·3 per cent. The Government concluded negotiations for purchase of the assets of Mobil Oil, having secured eurodollar financing of US$12 million. It received two loans of US$7 million each from USAID for an education and industrial programme and an economic adjustment programme. All the IMF tests for 1983 were passed.

The new Development Plan for 1983-84 to 1987-88 was unveiled. The Government planned to inject at least B$750 million into capital works during the period.

BELIZE

Britain announced that it wished to pull out its military garrison from Belize. This policy was ostensibly based on the assurances of a modified claim to Belizean territory coming from General Efrain Rios Montt of Guatemala. Subsequently, his former Defence Minister, General Oscar Humberto Mejia Victores, replaced him as President after a military coup. He refused to settle for an outlet to the Atlantic with guaranteed access to Belize's Southern Toledo district in exchange for recognition of Belize. Prime Minister George Price noted that the US had resumed arms supplies to the Guatemalan regime and declared that the total integrity of Belize was not up for sale (see also p. 86).

The sugar company Tate and Lyle called on the Government to buy or 'nationalize' its interests or it would pull out. About 20 to 25 per cent of the Belizean population was dependent on the industry for a livelihood. Nearly 110,000 tonnes of raw sugar was produced in 1983.

Increased duties were imposed on a wide range of consumer items. The economy grew by 2 per cent in 1982. Belize received a US$5·3 million loan from the World Bank for highway construction and drainage systems. Additionally, the Government signed the second part of a Caribbean Basin Initiative agreement for US$5 million.

THE BAHAMAS

Prime Minister Sir Lynden Pindling set up a commission of inquiry with broad powers to investigate the full spectrum of drug trafficking through the Bahamas. It would be assisted by an international team of police investigators. He was named in a US television programme as one of the high-ranking officials bribed by an international drug ring.

The Prime Minister was also annoyed with the US Government for trying so he alleged, to cajole him into liberalizing his bank secrecy laws and making information available to US government agencies. The financial sector contributed 13 per cent of GDP. By 15 November tourist arrivals were up by 18 per cent over the same period in 1982.

SURINAME

Suriname, whose military council claimed it had put down at least six coup attempts since it seized power in 1980, experienced a difficult political year. Two more coup attempts were scotched in 1983. The first was said to have occurred in January when the deputy commander of the army, Major Roy Horb, and 14 other persons were arrested. The second occurred in November when the Government arrested 25 persons who were said to have collaborated with a Netherlands-based liberation movement, led by the former President, Mr Henck Chin-A-Sen, in a plot to overthrow the Government.

There were reports that the CIA planned covert action against the regime and that Colonel Hans Valk, the former Dutch military attache in Paramaribo, had 'masterminded' the February 1980 coup along with two other Dutch officers. Embassy personnel from the US and the Netherlands were expelled from Suriname, and Suriname's embassy at The Hague was closed. On 25 October Cuba was asked to withdraw its ambassador and scale down relations between the two countries to the level of chargé d'affaires. The head of the National Security Council of Brazil, General Danilo Venturini, at short notice, flew to Suriname and offered the military commander, Desi Bouterse, and the new Prime Minister, Errol Alibux, unlimited credit, military training and purchase of half of the country's rice exports, among other proposals, in exchange for a pledge to keep the Cubans out of Suriname.

The national military council started the year by establishing anti-intervention committees in industry and business to identify, locate and fight mercenaries. The 'Unity Movement of February 25' was formed to spearhead Suriname's transformation into a socialist state and to promulgate, on 25 November, a one-party system. The fourth Cabinet since the 1980 coup was appointed. Mr Errol Alibux, a former Housing and Social Affairs Minister and a Dutch-trained sociologist, became the new Prime Minister. A strongly pro-socialist Cabinet was appointed. A four-member Policy Centre, under the chairmanship of Colonel Bouterse and including Mr Alibux, Sgt.-Major Sital and Dr Winston Caldeira, was established to oversee policy, including the budget. Plans were announced to triple the size of the army, and radical changes in the educational system were promised.

Dr Caldeira, head of the National Planning Bureau, announced that there was a 2 per cent growth in the economy in 1982, despite a 28·1 per cent fall in revenue from bauxite, which accounted for 80 per cent of foreign exchange earnings. The 1983 Budget amounted to 650 million guilders. Bridging credit of 200 million guilders was needed. The economy was described as having a small foreign debt and a very strong repayment capacity. Unemployment was between 11 and 15 per cent of the working population and national income was 1,800 million guilders. The EEC announced that it would continue its aid programme of 60 million guilders.

III THE USSR AND EASTERN EUROPE

Chapter 1

THE UNION OF SOVIET SOCIALIST REPUBLICS

THE new Soviet leadership began the year in purposeful mood, in marked contrast to the inertia that had characterized the latter part of the long Brezhnev era. By the year's end, however, there was once more uncertainty and speculation about the leader's capacity to govern: Yuri Andropov had not been seen in public, nor had a recent photograph of him appeared in the press, since 18 August when he had met a group of American Senators in the Kremlin. In the meantime, the economy (which had shown welcome signs of recovery in the first quarter of the year) appeared to be in danger of losing momentum, there was jockeying for position in the upper echelons of the political structure in anticipation of early leadership change, and Soviet-US relations were at an exceptionally low ebb. Central to these problems was the unanticipated, rapid and apparently serious decline in Andropov's health.

In the first half of the year the collective leadership remained virtually unchanged. In January the Party first secretary in Belorussia, T. Ya. Kiselev, died unexpectedly, to be succeeded by N.N. Slyunkov, who, since he was not a member of the Central Committee, could not be promoted to candidate membership of the Politburo as custom dictates. Then on 29 May, less surprisingly, 84-year-old Arvid Pel'she died, thus severing the Politburo's last link with the Revolution. His demise reduced the voting membership of the Politburo to eleven, the level at which it remained even after the two-day plenum of the Central Committee held in June.

This plenum was devoted to questions of ideology, the main speech being delivered by Konstantin Chernenko, Andropov's erstwhile rival for the General-Secretaryship. A shorter, more pungent and intelligent speech by Andropov demonstrated his command of the political structure, a command which was institutionally consolidated the next day when the USSR Supreme Soviet voted him chairman of its praesidium. Now he held simultaneously the offices of Party General Secretary, Chairman of the Defence Council (mentioned *en passant* in the Victory Day speech by Defence Minister Ustinov early in May), and President. Yet, despite his rapid consolidation of power, Andropov was apparently unable to enhance it still further by filling vacancies in the depleted Politburo.

M. S. Solomentsev was appointed chairman of the Party Control Committee, in succession to Pel'she; and G. V. Romanov, hitherto in charge of the Leningrad Party organization, was brought to Moscow to join the Central Committee secretariat, a move that greatly enhanced his chances as a possible successor to Andropov. There was one appointment to candidate membership of the Politburo: V. I. Vorotnikov was brought in and soon afterwards appointed to the post of chairman of the Council of Ministers of the RSFSR, the largest constituent republic.

Even before the June plenum there were anxiety and speculation about the state of Andropov's health. Photographs published in connection with the visit to Moscow of the Finnish President and, later, when he delivered his speech to the Supreme Soviet seated, helped to fuel rumours of a serious, debilitating illness. Following two appearances in mid-August, Andropov remained invisible, although a regular flow of statements in his name was maintained, many of which bore the imprint of his characteristic, cliché-free style.

At the end of October, Sh. R. Rashidov died suddenly. As first secretary of the Communist Party of Uzbekistan since 1959, he had joined the CPSU Politburo as a candidate member in 1961. He was replaced as first secretary, but not in the Politburo, by I. B. Usmankhodzhaev, hitherto chairman of the praesidium of the Supreme Soviet of Uzbekistan.

Failure to appear at the Kremlin reception marking the 66th anniversary of the Revolution, followed two days later by his absence from the Red Square parade, raised the question of Andropov's continuing ability to govern, a contingency that seemed even more uncertain when the autumn plenum of the Central Committee and the Supreme Soviet meeting were postponed to the last possible dates in December. Still the General Secretary failed to appear, although the personnel changes that occurred at the plenum suggested that Andropov (or at any rate his supporters) remained in control.

V. I. Vorotnikov (aged 57), since June a candidate member of the Politburo, was raised to full membership status—a meteoric rise by Soviet standards that made him (together with G. V. Romanov, aged 60, and M. S. Gorbachev, 52, the secretary responsible for agriculture) a possible successor to Andropov, whose client he undoubtedly was. M. S. Solomentsev, aged 70, was also raised to full membership of the Politburo, and although not obviously an Andropov protégé was likely to feel indebted to Andropov for his belated promotion.

The appointment of V. M. Chebrikov, head of the KGB, to candidate membership of the Politburo at the December plenum also strengthened the Andropov group's position, as did the addition of E. K. Ligachev to the Central Committee secretariat. Ligachev, formerly Party first secretary in Tomsk, assumed direction of the Party-Organizational Department of the Central Committee in April, thus facilitating

Andropov's manipulation of cadre appointments in consolidating his power base. Change came mostly in the Soviet ambassadorial corps (particularly amongst ambassadors accredited to fraternal socialist states), in the Central Committee apparatus and, towards the end of the year, among first secretaries of provincial (*oblast*) Party committees (although here progress was more modest). Thus, at the close of 1983 Andropov's personal position, for reasons of health, was delicately poised; while that of the group that put him in office plus those who more recently owed their appointments to him seemed to have the edge over the old Brezhnevite faction led by Chernenko.

The *leitmotiv* of Soviet foreign policy during 1983 was the 'struggle for peace'. In January a Soviet delegation headed by the General Secretary attended a meeting of the Warsaw Pact political consultative committee in Prague, which issued a call for peace and disarmament (see DOCUMENTS). A few days later, and with an obvious eye on the forthcoming West German general election, Andropov had talks in Moscow with Herr Vogel, no doubt in the hope that they would enhance the SPD's electoral chances: in the event, it was Herr Kohl and the Christian Democrats who were victorious in March, and it was widely held that Soviet intervention had been counterproductive.

At the end of January Andropov rejected President Reagan's offer of a meeting to discuss the possibility of a ban on all intermediate-range nuclear missiles in Europe. On 8 March, in a bout of unrestrained rhetoric before a gathering of evangelical Protestants in Florida, President Reagan described the USSR as 'the focus of evil in the modern world' and 'an evil empire', charges that caused deep and widespread offence in the Soviet Union. The American President's 'Star Wars address' of 23 March (when he envisaged the use of laser weaponry in space) seemed to be at odds with his offer a week later to reduce the number of medium-range missiles in Europe as an interim solution. This offer was rejected on 2 April by Gromyko, while on 27 April Andropov made a plea for the banning of weapons in outer space, followed a few days later by a Soviet offer to reduce the numbers of SS-20s deployed against Western Europe. At the heart of the Soviet position, however, was the demand that US Cruise and Pershing missiles should not be stationed in Europe, while Nato maintained that the introduction of these weapons was in direct response to the Soviet deployment of SS-20s in 1979. The Soviet diplomatic and propaganda effort, therefore, was aimed not only at Western Governments but also over their heads to the burgeoning 'peace movements'.

The reception of the veteran American diplomat Averell Harriman and his wife by Andropov at the beginning of June and the visit to the USSR by an American schoolgirl at the General Secretary's personal invitation were symptomatic of the range of unconventional initiatives that were taken in the first half of the year.

Contrary to usual practice, President Andropov remained at his desk in Moscow during August and towards the end of the month offered to destroy SS-20s targeted against Western Europe, on condition that new US nuclear missiles were not stationed there. But then an incident occurred that put paid to any slight possibility of an understanding being reached by the two superpowers. On 1 September a Soviet fighter plane shot down a Korean Airlines Boeing 747, killing all the 269 people on board. The fact that the Korean aircraft was in Soviet airspace and flying over a strategically sensitive area, Sakhalin, did little to mitigate the shock, and fears were further exacerbated when it became apparent that the incident had occurred as the result of decisions taken at regional level, almost certainly without reference to the political authority at the centre. The fact, too, that President Andropov remained silent and out of sight during the ensuing furore, leaving the military to brazen it out, did nothing to restore confidence.

In November the West German Bundestag's reaffirmation of the decision to allow the stationing of American nuclear missiles on its territory, the arrival of Cruise missiles in England and in Italy, and growing speculation that President Reagan would run again for office in 1984, were all setbacks for the Soviet Union which contributed no doubt to its decision to withdraw from the disarmament negotiations in Geneva on 23 November. By the end of the year the two superpowers had virtually ceased to speak to each other. However, if the USSR had failed to halt the stationing of US nuclear missiles in Western Europe, it had had some considerable success in encouraging anti-American feeling and there were signs that the emphasis was shifting to an attempt to 'de-couple' Europe from the United States.

In Eastern Europe Poland remained an embarrassment to the USSR. Although martial law was ended by General Jaruzelski on 21 July, the Polish Party remained weak and popular support for Solidarity, although lacking organizational shape, stayed strong.

Relations between the USSR and China improved somewhat in 1983, but the continuing Soviet presence in Afghanistan was a stumbling-block to further progress. In the Caribbean and in Central America the Soviet Union eschewed any temptation to become too closely involved, no doubt fearing a head-on clash with the United States, although US intervention in Grenada in October provided the Soviets with a no-cost opportunity to gain substantial propaganda advantage in that region. In similar fashion the Soviet Union was glad to leave matters in the hands of its Cuban surrogates in southern Africa, but at the same time made it clear to South Africa that it would not tolerate any overthrow of socialist Angola.

It was in the Middle East that Soviet and US interests clashed most sharply. US participation in the peacekeeping (*sic*) force in Lebanon and its growing support for Israel inevitably produced condemnation from the

Soviet Union, which was giving material and diplomatic assistance to Syria. The split in the PLO, Yassir Arafat's expulsion from Lebanon and his arrival with 4,000 PLO supporters in North Yemen were further reminders to the Soviet Union of the volatility of Middle East politics, since the USSR had begun the year as Arafat's firmest supporter.

Domestically, the main stress of the new leadership's policy was discipline. The media were full of accounts of corruption and peculation, and Ministers were told that they would be held responsible personally for shortcomings in efficiency and labour productivity. In January the militia (police) were making spot checks of people in queues, cinemas, shops and public transport to ensure that they were legitimately absent from their places of work. There were reports that buses and trucks were being stopped on the outskirts of Moscow and other major cities, and were being turned back if passes were not in order. To meet the rumbling criticism caused by the discipline campaign, shopping hours were changed so that purchases could be made outside normal working-time. Several Ministers were dismissed from their posts, while at the Party's June plenum the corrupt former Minister for the Interior, Shchelokov (a close associate of Brezhnev) and the former Party first secretary in Krasnodar (the centre of a notorious racketeering scandal) were both expelled from the Central Committee. Expectations that they would be brought to trial before the civil courts, and possibly sentenced to death, proved groundless, although the incongruity of not bringing them to justice inevitably weakened the force of the Government's strictures on discipline. Nonetheless, productivity and output in the industrial sector of the economy improved in the first quarter of the year, and, although the momentum slackened later, overall 1983 showed a marked improvement, with the growth rate at 4 per cent, against a target of 3·2 per cent and the 1982 result of 2·8 per cent. Labour productivity, up 3·5 per cent, also exceeded the planned target.

Still, in his message to the Central Committee at the end of December President Andropov made it clear that even greater effort was needed. He called for the eradication of bottlenecks in the supply system, clearer definition of the rights, responsibilities and duties of enterprise managers, and 'higher effectiveness of economic levers and stimuli of the economic mechanism in its entirety, including price formation, the credit-financial system, and the methods of evaluating the results of economic activity'. Whether this presaged the long-expected economic reform remained to be seen. The tenor of Andropov's statement certainly accorded with sentiments expressed in the so-called 'Novosibirsk document', a paper leaked to Western journalists from a Central Committee-sponsored conference held in April; but, having correctly identified the malaise, he was either too timid, or politically too weak *vis-à-vis* entrenched bureaucratic interests, to draw the necessary inferences and go for far-reaching reform. However, a limited reform on an experimental basis was announced on 25 July and was due to begin in January 1984. This envisaged giving managers more autonomy to take their own production decisions, while leaving overall planning with the centre, but initially it related only to certain industries in Byelorussia, Latvia and the Ukraine.

Once again, details of the grain harvest were not published. US Department of Agriculture estimates, in the region of 200 million tons, would suggest the best result since 1978, although still markedly below the planned average of 240 million tons for the current five-year plan. Output of meat and dairy products improved, too, according to Andropov, but no details were given in support of this claim. Since prices of basic food commodities were pegged at artifically low levels and demand was high, shortages remained widespread.

In March the Secretary responsible for agriculture, Gorbachev, demonstrated the leadership's commitment to extending so-called *kollektivnii podryad*, a form of group contract work designed to encourage small groups of peasants to take a more responsible attitude towards production by increasing their material self-interest. Essentially, it involved payment by results for work done on a contract basis.

In April there was a special meeting of the Politburo and the regional Party first secretaries on agriculture at which, following a report by Gorbachev, Andropov made what was described as 'a major speech'. In it he spoke of the need to shift the emphasis to intensification of production and to speed up the application of industrial technology to agriculture. Social services in the countryside must be improved and turnover of cadres reduced. Greater reliance upon the peasants' private plots, stated Andropov, would go far to satisfy local needs. Massive allocation of funds to agriculture would be continued, but these must be utilized more rationally. It was a realistic-sounding speech that served both to emphasize the scale of the problems of agricultural production in the USSR and to suggest a growing realization that agricultural output was deeply affected by social as well as purely economic factors.

By the end of the year gas from the Urengoi deposits in Siberia reached France via the 2,800-mile pipeline. Already in August the US had lifted its pipeline ban (in place since December 1981), yet another embargo that had proved to be more trouble than it was worth. However, the speed with which the project had been constructed gave rise to doubts about its long-term reliability. Similar haste in construction was thought to have contributed to serious problems at Atommash, the huge complex at which serial production of nuclear power stations takes place. The creation of a new State Committee for Safety in the Atomic Energy Industry in July was symptomatic of the dangers inherent in over-hasty completion of grandiose projects.

The seriousness with which the leadership viewed such bungling was exemplified in June, when, following heavy loss of life through the sinking of a Volga pleasure steamer, a commission of inquiry was set up headed by First Deputy Prime Minister G. A. Aliev. Reporting in July, the commission found that gross negligence had occurred.

The cultural scene was drear in 1983. The Central Committee's June plenum on ideology seemed to reinforce the restraints on creativity. There were no new novels, films or plays worthy of special mention. Yurii Lyubimov came to London and staged his version of Dostoevsky's *Crime and Punishment* with a British cast and at the same time unburdened himself by making a sustained attack on censorship and the lack of cultural freedom in the USSR. In Moscow, Lyubimov's Taganka theatre continued to enjoy immense popularity.

In February, the cartoonist Sysoev was arrested following several years of underground existence and was given a prison sentence for alleged distribution of pornography. His depiction of block-head bureaucracy (a salient feature of his caricature) was the more likely cause of his difficulties.

The Politburo announced its decision in September to start the planning and design of a vast Park of Victory and national war museum in Moscow. Earlier a new monument had been erected in central Moscow to commemorate the two-hundredth anniversary of the unification of Georgia and Russia. Designed by the Georgian architect Z. Tsereteli with the assistance of the Russian poet Andrei Voznessensky (himself an architect by training), it aroused much controversy and some criticism.

One of the best-known voices in the USSR was silenced in August when veteran radio announcer Yurii Levitan died. He would be remembered particularly for his reading of government statements and announcements of Soviet victories in battle during World War II.

Winter descended early in the Soviet Arctic, and ships, including ice-breakers, were locked in dense pack ice from as early as 20 October. For several weeks interest in their fate gripped the Soviet public, as the press, in a rare example of human-interest news reporting, devoted close attention to the story.

Overall, 1983 was an uncertain year for the Soviet Union. Worsening East-West relations, the general tightening-up in society and, most particularly, growing doubts about President Andropov's capacity to govern—his intrinsic ability was not in question—all contributed to a feeling that, while progress had been made in the material sphere, politically, both within the Soviet Union and in the international arena, the promise of the early part of the year had not been fulfilled.

Chapter 2

GERMAN DEMOCRATIC REPUBLIC—POLAND—
CZECHOSLOVAKIA—HUNGARY—ROMANIA—BULGARIA—
YUGOSLAVIA—ALBANIA—MONGOLIA

THE GERMAN DEMOCRATIC REPUBLIC

ECONOMICALLY, East Germany experienced a far better year than had been expected. Some 125 of the 132 state industrial concerns reached or surpassed their targets. Exports to the Soviet Union more than doubled, and there was also a considerable expansion of exports to the capitalist countries. But these successes possibly escaped the people of East Germany. There were frequent shortages of basic foods, even in East Berlin, to say nothing of consumer goods. Imports were cut back drastically, as part of the Government's strategy to restore a healthy trade balance and to prove that East Germany was creditworthy.

In May the East German leader, Herr Erich Honecker, postponed a projected visit to West Germany on the grounds that the intra-German climate had deteriorated since the death in April of a West German citizen while being interrogated at an East German border post. The East Germans protested that West German press comment about this and a similar subsequent incident—in both cases death was found to be due to heart attacks—amounted to a virulent campaign against the German Democratic Republic, and was not conducive to a successful summit. It was inconceivable that Herr Honecker would have cried off the trip to Bonn and to his native Saarland without seeking the fraternal advice of the Soviet Government. In counselling a cancellation, the Russians were more likely to have been moved by other considerations than a storm in an intra-German teacup. Herr Honecker was due in September, which was uncomfortably close to the deadline for the deployment of the first Pershing II nuclear missiles in West Germany. It was not the best time for summitry.

Yet, despite heightening tension between the power blocks over nuclear missiles deployment, the two German states took pains to protect and cultivate their relationship. Indeed there was a flurry of intra-German activity. Even so it caused great surprise when, in July, the West German Government underwrote—without attaching political strings— a DM 1,000 million bank credit to East Germany. It was even more surprising that the Bavarian Premier, Herr Franz-Josef Strauss, had put his considerable weight behind this deal. Without the Bonn Government's guarantee, a loan of this size, the largest that West German banks had granted to East Germany, would not have been possible. The banks could not have accepted the risk—after all, the credit was mainly needed to enable East Germany to meet interest charges and repayments of other debts. Herr Strauss's role, though heavily criticized at home, won him a long and cordial meeting with Herr Honecker. Subsequently, East Germany agreed to modify its border charges scheme under which Western visitors must exchange a minimum sum of money when entering East Germany or East Berlin. The regulations were eased for visitors under the age of 15.

The granting of the loan was also followed by East German assurances that the murderous automatic firing devices along the inner-German border would be dismantled. But by the end of the year only 1,800 of the 55,000 devices had in fact been removed. Such minor concessions made nonsense of the West German Government's insistence that intra-German relations should be pursued on a basis of 'strict reciprocity'. To the East German leader, the phrase 'intra-German relations' was a synonym for West German economic assistance. Herr Honecker was perfectly prepared to have Herr Kohl make East German life a little brighter, so long as West Germany stuck to realities, like continuing to acknowledge that there were two German sovereign states, belonging to different alliances.

The Soviet leader, Mr Yuri Andropov, received Herr Honecker in Moscow in May, and used the occasion to warn the West Germans of the grave consequences of allowing deployment of the nuclear missiles on their territory. Later the East German authorities urged Bonn to form an 'East-West coalition of reason' against a new round in the nuclear arms race. The East German Communist Party organ *Neues Deutschland* declared that should the missiles be deployed intra-German relations would enter an ice age.

At least 20 members of the unofficial East German peace movement were expelled to West Germany during the year. Most of them were from the university town of Jena and belonged to an organization which for many years had been a thorn in the flesh of the East German regime. Demonstrating in East Germany for peace was fine so long as it was under the official banner, which protested only against Nato's rearmament. It became offensive and sometimes dangerous when the demonstrators called for disarmament in both East and West. The Jena group, about 60 strong, was essentially pacifist, and had been campaigning not only against nuclear weapons but also against military training in schools and factories, and against the sale of war toys and games. The authorities responded for a time with a mixture of harshness and grudging tolerance. Some of the group were sent to prison, but occasionally Jena dissidents were allowed to unfurl their banners at official peace rallies, though they were usually torn down after a while by Party loyalists who, in their words, could no longer contain their anger. The wave of expulsions was the first since 1976, when the dissident poet and song-writer, Wolf

Biermann, and several other writers were banished to the West.

Both German states, but East Germany specially, celebrated the 500th anniversary of the birth of Martin Luther, the most famous German dissident of all (see also Pt. IX). Herr Honecker, a convinced marxist, placed himself at the head of the committee which prepared Luther Jubilee Year. The classic Luther sites were restored at great expense. Biographies were published, exhibitions staged and postage stamps issued. Many aspects of Luther's personality, it was discovered, were ideally suited to today's self-understanding of the German Democratic Republic as the true heir to German history and culture. Luther's extolling of hard work, of obedience to the state, of praise for military service in defence of peace, all this was now music to the ears of the East German Politburo. The Protestant church leadership reacted to the state's bid for Luther's blessing with mixed feelings, and the bishops, who formed their own jubilee committee, consented to join the state committee only as observers. World religious leaders joined the East German Protestants at a service at Luther's birthplace of Eisleben, south of Berlin. Herr Honecker, who was expected to attend the service, stayed away, and his absence was explained by his displeasure with the strongly independent line on disarmament taken by the Protestant church. Later the Government gave mild encouragement to the rehabilitation of Bismarck as a worthy son of Germany.

POLAND

General Jaruzelski attempted to reconcile the irreconcilable. Those whose liberties he trampled upon were unwilling to submit cooperatively to his order. Neither Poland's leaders nor the Polish nation—evidently reluctant to be led—were sure what to do next. The cost of preserving by force the unreformed political system was high. In political terms it deepened a profound split between the system and society; in institutional terms it fostered public hatred of the state, its agencies and its representatives; in economic terms it contributed to a major decline in production, nourishing inflation and crippling all efforts at reform. Once again the Pope's triumphant 'religious pilgrimage' to his native country dramatically narrowed the regime's options.

The tug of war between the authorities and an underground Solidarity led by the Provisional Coordinating Commission under Zbigniew Bujak continued. This and other small political parties associated with Solidarity were contemptuously described by officials as a miniscule group of 'fanatics and counter—revolutionaries'. But even peaceful demonstrations were crushed by massive security forces, always present in the streets on various anniversary days. Running street battles erupted in twenty Polish cities when tens of thousands of Poles tried to stage peaceful pro-Solidarity rallies to mark May Day. The authorities even mounted a crude display of force against an unofficial ceremony to commemorate the 40th anniversary of the 1943 Warsaw ghetto uprising.

Solidarity's programme, consistently advocating peaceful resistance, was to establish an 'underground society', a network of unofficial pressure groups, study projects and cultural or educational initiatives. While members would continue to defend working and living standards, Solidarity would help to organize a whole underground culture and to draw up reform programmes. Bujak claimed a million of the banned union's ten million members were still active, in 90 per cent of work-places, through secret factory committees.

On 12 April Lech Walesa met underground leaders in secret to coordinate their strategies and then offered to talk to the authorities if they accepted trade union pluralism. He stressed that if this approach failed he would be forced to change his tactics. A constant barrage of mockery and insults, and continuous police harassment, contrasted with the public perception of Walesa as a leader in the open and of Solidarity underground as a viable organizational entity. Jaruzelski's answer to demands for a dialogue was the Patriotic Movement of National Rebirth (see AR 1982, p. 115), officially established in May and presented as expressing the opinion of the whole of society. Significantly, it was boycotted by the Church.

The first half of the year was overshadowed by the imminent Papal visit, the result of difficult negotiations. Primate Josef Glemp twice discussed the details with Jaruzelski. The Polish episcopate appealed to the Government to lift martial law, free political prisoners and reinstate dismissed Solidarity activists. Cardinal Glemp told the authorities that peace could be assured only when the voice of the people was heard and 'understood with good will' (5 May). Earlier the bishops had asked for an amnesty and stressed the fundamental right of working people to organize themselves into unions which suited them best.

From 16 to 23 June Pope John Paul visited Warsaw, Czestochowa, Poznan, Wroclaw and Cracow, to bring guidance, as he said, for the nation at a 'particularly difficult moment in its history' and bring solace to a country that 'has suffered much and suffers ever anew'. In his first meeting with Jaruzelski the Pope hoped 'that social reforms worked out at a price of such pain in August 1980' (see AR 1980, p. 111) 'and contained in the accords reached between the Government and the striking workers would be gradually put into effect'. In seeking a second unscheduled meeting with the Pontiff Jaruzelski tried to gain some vestige of authority in the public mind. The hope was expressed that the Papal visit would contribute to a peaceful and favourable development of social life in Poland. Walesa's meeting with the Pope at the latter's insistence on 23 June signalled the Pope's recognition of society's wish for self-determination, of which Walesa emerged again as a living symbol.

Crowds totalling an estimated 14 million pressed to see the Pope and hear him. The spirit of self-identity was repeatedly demonstrated through the persistent display of posters and slogans, chants and prayers, through periodic marches of Solidarity supporters, and through 'V for Victory' signs massively displayed at each gathering. The Pope's principal message was that society has an innate and inalienable right to maintain its own identity. Genuine dialogue must be the first step leading to restored civil rights and 'social structures which correspond to the nation's requirements' and 'only then to the consensus needed by the state'. Deputy Premier Rakowski and Foreign Minister Olszowski publicly attacked the Papal pronouncements but otherwise the authorities showed considerable caution, while preventing explicitly political demonstrations in some cities.

The lifting of martial law on 21 July was accompanied by amendments to the constitution and a package of government powers which retained and even reinforced most provisions of martial law, ensuring for the authorities a wide range of powers and scope for arbitary decisions affecting the key areas of labour, youth movements, the economy and intellectual life. In August the Polish Writers' Union, the last of the cultural and artistic associations, was dissolved. The limited amnesty passed by the Sejm encompassed some political prisoners and included a pardon for underground activists who surrendered to the police. Some seventy political prisoners, including seven Solidarity leaders and five KOR members, awaiting trial in prison were excluded. Some of the 560 activists who came out of hiding were re-arrested.

In November Jaruzelski relinquished the post of Minister of Defence (filled by General Sawicki) to become chairman of the National Defence Committee and commander-in-chief. This gave him extensive prerogatives over the vitally important security area, particularly when the Sejm ensured the committee's 'capacity to fulfil the task of securing the country in conditions of war'. The key posts in the Party, the Government—central and local—and in economic adminstration remained in the hands of the military. It was their job to 'regenerate socialism'.

At the Party plenum (18 November) Jaruzelski admitted that 'the economy has become an arena of political struggle' and that the people did not believe in the Government's good intentions and ability to tackle problems. In 1982 industrial production decreased by 6 per cent, agricultural production by 4·5 per cent. National income dropped 8 per cent. The standard of living fell by 30 per cent and over one-third of the population lived below the basic poverty line. Inflation exceeded 100 per cent. Only some of the Polish foreign-currency debts were rescheduled. However, a three-year anti-inflation plan 1983-1985 envisaged a 16 per cent increase in industrial output and a 37 per cent rise of exports to the West.

In November the Government announced, subject to consultation, an increase in food prices of between 10 and 70 per cent, as from 1 January. The authorities admitted that popular response was overwhelmingly negative. Party activists in the 200 biggest plants warned the leadership that the increases would bring trouble. Jaruzelski ordered a mobilization to check 'the defence preparedness' of the army. Officers and troops reappeared in towns and villages for the first time since the lifting of martial law. The Church condemned the official policy on prices and demanded the introduction of 'proper social and political reforms that would facilitate the emergence of trust'. Walesa met underground Solidarity leaders again and they underlined an 'obligation to organize a fight in defence of the people's interests since the working people cannot agree to price increases'.

Walesa's stature rose tremendously when he received the Nobel peace prize. This struck at the legitimacy of government policies towards him and, by implication, towards Solidarity. In his acceptance speech, read out in Oslo by his wife, Walesa made a ringing assertion of the rights of independent trade unions and called for a resumed dialogue between Solidarity and the Government. He donated the prize money to the Church towards a fund being set up to help private farmers.

The situation remained tense. In a Christmas message Cardinal Glemp urged the Poles to stay calm and expressed the fear that unrest in Poland could trigger off a crisis with serious international dimensions. There was, he said, 'a basic threat to our existence' and therefore there must be a limit to 'complaints, accusations, grudges and spiteful actions'. This was regarded in Poland as directed against some Solidarity activists but the Primate also attacked the government slogan 'reconciliation', which, he said, 'has lost its full meaning, contains no programme ... Nevertheless Poland has to be saved'.

CZECHOSLOVAKIA

It was not a momentous year for Czechoslovakia. In the international field the Government spent most time and energy on pushing the Soviet 'peace line', particularly the campaign to prevent the deployment of new American missiles in Europe, with the help of the Western peace movements. Czechoslovakia played a prominent and active part in this drive. Yuri Andropov, venturing outside the Soviet Union for the first and only time in 1983, attended the Warsaw Pact summit in Prague on 4 and 5 January, from which a stern appeal against new US missiles was issued. From 21 to 26 June a large 'World Assembly for Peace and against Nuclear War' was held in Prague in the presence of several thousand delegates from many countries. On 24 October the Czechoslovak and Soviet Governments announced that 'operational-tactical missiles with an enhanced range' would be installed in Czechoslovakia (a similar announcement related to East Germany) in case the West European plans went ahead, and in later references the preparations for missile bases in the country were said to be going on 'at an accelerated pace'.

While emphatically upholding the Soviet line, officials explained that the decision had been forced on them by American bellicosity and that 'no one rejoices' over the need to have Soviet missiles in Czechoslovakia. The public apparently questioned the deployment to a larger extent than the regime expected, and even official media had to acknowledge popular unease on this matter. Reports reached the West of unofficial protests and petitions, possibly heralding the emergence of an independent peace movement, but the clampdown on information did not permit an accurate evaluation. A number of Charter 77 activists were briefly held by the police on several occasions and warned not to issue any appeals in connection with the missiles, but they succeeded in establishing contact with some factions in the West European peace movements and made it clear that they advocated 'peace worthy of man', that is, a joint promotion of peace efforts and human rights. A state that was not at peace with its own citizens, the Charter said, could not aspire to play a truly peaceful part in international life. Virtually the same platform was advocated by Cardinal František Tomášek, the senior Roman Catholic hierarch in the country.

All forms of dissent—political, cultural and religious—continued to be suppressed. Over thirty prisoners of conscience were serving gaol terms and a vicious six-year sentence was passed toward the end of the year on Jiří Wolf. Encouraged by the authorities to emigrate after an earlier imprisonment for political reasons, Wolf described conditions in prison in his application for asylum to the Austrian embassy in Prague, an act that the prosecutor qualified as betraying state secrets and calumnying the regime. In a large police raid at the end of March, many Franciscan priests and sympathizers were arrested, detained for a time, and then released. A strident suppression campaign was also directed against the so-called 'new wave' of rock music, both the performers and the fans. Human rights, religion and alienation of the younger generation were, and evidently would remain, painful thorns in the side of the authorities. The treatment of political prisoners seemed to have worsened, and there were several instances of blatant disregard for the offenders' ill health. Despite adverse circumstances, the dissident movement stood its own. Charter 77 issued over forty statements on a variety of topics and a lively *samizdat* activity continued.

It was rumoured at the year's start that the Andropov accession in the Kremlin would lead to a purge in the high echelons of the Czechoslovak Communist Party, known for its rather slavish devotion to the Brezhnev-Chernenko team, but fears subsided around the middle of the year as illness pushed Andropov out of active politics. Instead, nature struck thrice: a CPCS Praesidium member (Václav Hůla), a Central

Committee secretariat member and editor-in-chief of *Rude pravo* (Oldřich Švestka) and the chairman of the Party's control and auditing commission (Miroslav Čapka) died. None was immediately replaced, except of course that the party daily was given a new editor (Zdeněk Hoření). An undisclosed illness incapacitated the federal Prime Minister and CPCS Praesidum member, Lubomír Štrougal, for a number of months, but he bounced back in the autumn. The only personnel change worthy of note was the assignment in June of the former Interior Minister Jaromír Obzina to head a new State Commission for Scientific and Technical Advancement, possibly a removal further away from the springboard to the top party caucuses, or else a stepping-stone to the premiership should Štrougal's health falter again. As to inner Party matters, the leadership showed disquiet over a decline in the capacity for action of the Party cadre. The old guard had been retiring and the constituency of successors was seen as far less dedicated. Also, young people were becoming increasingly unwilling to join the Party and showed unmistakable signs of political indifference.

Although the leadership expressed pleasure over economic growth, said to have been over 2 per cent of the net domestic material product and under 3 per cent of industrial output, complaints persisted over lack of progress in technical modernization. More goods were produced for stock as their standards failed to attract buyers, and an increasing percentage of new investments had to be sunk into the energy base, including domestic programmes as well as projects in the Soviet Union. The ambitious programme of nuclear power plant construction again ran into delays, and no nuclear-generated electricity could be added to the existing capacity. The overall austerity campaign continued unabated, industrial inputs of fuel and raw materials being cut by decree and a 6 per cent rise in wholesale prices across-the-board ordered from 1 January 1984. Imports from Western countries were kept artificially below the level of lagging exports, for which markets were hard to find, mainly because of the low quality of goods on offer. As a result, while debt to the West, estimated at under $3,000 million, did not grow, the economy failed to acquire much-needed modern machinery and equipment. A kind of grim plodding-on performance did not promise rapid improvement, especially as no radical reform plans were broached. Supplies of food and consumer goods to the public remained roughly at the previous year's level—not bad by East European standards, but far from satisfactory.

Anti-reformism, steadfast adherence to Soviet policies and an uphill economic struggle stand out as the three dominant features in the Czechoslovak experience in 1983.

HUNGARY

The relatively gloomy economic situation which had begun to affect Hungary in the mid-1970s did not change appreciably in 1983. Official spokesmen hinted relief that at least the country had avoided the near-bankruptcy of 1982, but otherwise many sectors of the economy turned in rather poor performances. In a pessimistic speech in September, Ferenc Havasi, the Central Committee secretary in charge of economic affairs, made it clear that, unusually, agriculture had signally failed to reach its targets. The shortfall in grain production, the result of the drought in the summer, was of the order of two million tons. This would have far-reaching impact on Hungary's export performance, on its ability to continue the servicing of its foreign debt and, consequently, on imports of both producers' and consumer goods.

During the year there were several price increases, notably of fuel, fats, sugar and bread. The last was regarded as a particularly serious step, with possible political repercussions, in as much as the stability of bread prices was regarded as a significant factor in assuring popular acceptance of the situation. In the event, no serious unrest was recorded, but the general economic deterioration undoubtedly contributed to the nervousness shown by the authorities towards the undercurrent of questioning among the intelligentsia.

The prospects for 1984 looked no better. A fall in real incomes of roughly 2 per cent was expected, a development that would bear especially hard on the poorest quarter of the population, many of whom were living on or below the poverty line. There was widespread adverse criticism of the industrial sector, and the Party daily, *Népszabadság*, openly condemned overspending by public agencies. Hungarian industry exhibited the standard problems of socialist economics—low productivity, obsolete products, poor organization and a low rate of innovation and restructuring to meet new requirements. Finally in this area, considerable anxiety emerged as to whether Hungary was capable of meeting its 1984 foreign debt schedule (estimated at around $600 million). The authorities were evidently determined to avoid rescheduling if possible.

In the light of this continuing economic debacle, it was at first sight somewhat surprising that the reform debate of the previous year ended with the adoption of only very few structural changes in the running of the country. In an important speech to the Central Committee, the Party leader János Kádár made it clear that there would be no 'reform of the reform'. In other words, despite the pressures, the authorities would persist with their cautious attitude to change and there would be no question of refashioning the economic system with the thoroughness that some radical economists were advocating. Change in the political system was entirely off the agenda and the existing imbalance in the distribution of power—concentration in the hands of the Party—would not be altered. The only concrete result of the debate on political reform was the new electoral law. This provided for an obligatory minimum of two candidates for every parliamentary and local council constituency and for a national list to ensure that the top leadership would be comfortably returned to Parliament.

The deteriorating situation, coupled with the rather more open conditions of debate perceived in 1982, encouraged the more contentious section of the intelligentsia to press highly controversial ideas in public. The Party having insisted on restoring more restrictive limits on discussion, these radical critics found themselves exposed to the attacks of the Party conservatives. The Party leadership issued several warnings that, whilst honest criticism was welcome, hostile views would not be tolerated: the definition of these terms remained, of course, exclusively in the hands of the Party. However, some groups of intellectuals refused to bow tamely to the renewed restrictions and found themselves disciplined. The crusading journal *Mozgó Világ*, which had printed numerous trenchant critiques of Hungarian affairs, was singled out for particular attention and its editor was eventually sacked.

At the same time, the tighter limits on officially permitted discussion translated themselves into much harsher police repression against Hungary's small opposition movement. Official efforts to end the publication and circulation of *samizdat* (officially unsanctioned writings) resulted in the harassment of known dissidents and the closure of the so-called *samizdat* bookshop. One or two individuals were beaten by the police and others were dismissed from their jobs.

Despite these blemishes on Hungary's human rights record, the country received the accolade of being singled out for special praise by the US Vice-President, George Bush, who became the most senior American politician ever to visit Hungary. Bush also commented on the generally excellent state of US-Hungarian relations. In this connection, the Hungarian leadership had every reason to congratulate itself; for not only did Hungary bask in the warmth of US approval, but it also received the cautious endorsement of the Soviet Union. In July, Kádár led a top-level Party and state delegation to Moscow and clearly succeeded in gaining the backing of the Kremlin for Hungary's careful reform programme. Indeed, the only serious cloud over Hungary's foreign relations was the long-simmering dispute with Romania over the treatment of the large Hungarian ethnic minority in that country. Polemics in a fairly low key continued during the year.

Only three personnel changes of note took place. Péter Várkonyi, regarded as an able and personable diplomat, was promoted to Foreign Secretary (replacing Frigyes Puja) and Mátyás Szürös was appointed Central Committee secretary in charge of international affairs. Szürös, formerly ambassador to Moscow, was regarded as having close connections with the Soviet establishment. In November, the long-serving head of the trade union organization and a highly influential figure in Hungary's politics, Sándor Gáspár, stepped down, to be replaced by Lajos Méhes.

ROMANIA

For the first time in several years, there was a change for the better in Romania's financial position vis-à-vis the West. The balance of payments was turned round from a deficit of $1,500 million in 1980 to a surplus of the same amount or more, and the foreign debt figure was reduced. But this result was achieved at great cost in domestic terms. There was a draconian reduction in imports and an all-out effort to export any saleable goods, including food and agricultural produce. At the same time a sort of economic mini-reform was introduced, embodying a more authoritarian approach to the economy. Enterprises were put under far stricter financial obligations, export achievement being turned into a major indicator of their performance. The domestic price of energy and raw materials was increased to align it better with world prices, and the national currency was devalued on 1 July against a basket of convertible currencies.

Also in July, the National Assembly adopted new laws on norms for payment of salaries, introducing an 'overall piece-rate system'. It abolished the existing guarantee of 80 per cent of basic salary to be paid irrespective of the workers' actual production, and linked salaries far more closely to performance. This applied not only to factory workers, but also to administrative employees and service institutions such as foreign trade agencies, as well as ministries and state administration. Every manager and employee would be required to sign a contract with the state, whereby they assumed responsibility for discharging their obligations; if the plan was not fulfilled, employees would be in breach of contract. Only full application of this regime in 1984 would show how far the Ceauşescu Government was prepared to go in actually reducing pay to a fraction of nominal wages if production results were poor.

Meanwhile the economic crisis, which had drastically reduced living standards since 1980, continued. Drought caused by a long and hot autumn added to the already severe food shortages. It also brought about a wave of power shortages as the level of the Danube and its tributaries fell to figures unrecorded for many decades, affecting the hydroelectric industry. The Government responded with more legislation, limiting the amount of electricity each household was allowed to consume, imposing shorter heating hours and reducing television programmes. While there was grumbling, no disturbances or protests were reported. This may have been partly due to intensified surveillance of the population by the security forces and the party *apparat*.

According to 1982 figures, the Romanian Communist Party had a membership of 3·2 million, representing 31 per cent of the entire adult employed population, probably the highest proportion in any communist country. In 1983 there emerged what could be described as a specific Romanian communist ideology, a mixture of communism and nationalism aimed to give a theoretical basis to Ceauşescu's political line and the position he had adopted within the international communist movement. It took a few years to elaborate this new ideology, but in its comprehensive form it was articulated in April 1983 at a conference held in Bucharest and was subsequently expanded in several important articles by Politburo member Dumitru Popescu, the director of the Party academy. It also served to underpin the months-long campaign running up to the 65th anniversary in December of Romania's absorption of Transylvania from Hungary in 1918. This occasion was treated domestically as the major event of the year and made into a powerful demonstration of Romanian nationalism. Both in Hungary and in the Soviet Union, Romanian writings were criticized in the media, and these criticisms were in turn rejected in bellicose articles in the Romanian press. Relations between Romania and Hungary reached their lowest point since World War II.

Relations with the rest of the Warsaw Pact deteriorated as well and seemed to be heading towards a conflict over the Geneva disarmament negotiations. Throughout 1983 Ceauşescu criticized with increasing openness the Soviet intention of deploying nuclear weapons in East Germany, Czechoslovakia and elsewhere. Simultaneous criticism of the US missile deployments sought to create the impression of objective neutrality. Ceauşescu wrote letters to the US and Soviet Presidents, with pleas to postpone the planned deployments and proposals for a compromise. In public, the Warsaw Pact ignored these activities, and reaction behind the closed doors of the many Pact meetings in which Romania took part during the year remained unknown. But no Romanian representatives went to the latest such meeting, in December, a conference in Moscow of party secretaries in charge of ideology and foreign affairs—an indication that positions were becoming difficult to reconcile.

Relations with the US went through a crisis early in the year when President Reagan announced that Romania's most-favoured-nation trade status would be withdrawn if a law requiring would-be emigrants to repay in hard currency the cost of their education was not repealed. Ceauşescu protested and in March accused the US of interference in the country's internal affairs, but he later relented and gave assurances that the law would not be applied. In June, the m-f-n status was extended for another year. Relations with the West improved in the second half of

1983, particularly as the result of Romania's role in the final stage of the Madrid conference, where a Romanian initiative led to the acceptance by the Soviet bloc of some Western amendments to the final document on human rights (see Pt. XI, Ch. 3) and thus to the successful conclusion of the conference. Subsequently US Vice-President Bush visited Romania and relations with Washington improved. The Romanian stand on missiles, however, made no great impact on the West. The only Nato government which showed some interest was West Germany. The Greek Prime Minister Papandreou, who tried to play in the Western alliance a role similar to that played by Ceauşescu in the Warsaw Pact, went to Bucharest in December and the two leaders agreed on joint actions in 1984.

BULGARIA

Alexander Lilov, long considered one of the likely candidates for Todor Zhivkov's succession, disappeared in 1983 from the political scene. On 28 September, soon after his 50th birthday, he was released from his posts of a Communist Party (BCP) Politburo member and Central Committee secretary in charge of ideological matters, allegedly 'at his own request', because of 'transfer to another job'. This turned out to be the relatively insignificant post of director of an ideological institute. His demotion was generally believed to have been due to political reasons, connected with his support for the relatively liberal and nationalistic cultural policy bequeathed by the late Lyudmila Zhivkova, who died in 1981.

A congress of the Committee on Culture, held in May, was also marked by the conflict between the Lyudmila Zhivkova line and a more dogmatic approach, although the issue was not openly discussed. The proponents of the harder line, which enjoyed the favour of the Kremlin, seemed to gain the upper hand. Toward the end of the year, however, some publications indicated that Mrs Zhivkova and the ideas she stood for would not be allowed to be forgotten. Unorthodox works of literature and the arts appeared as in preceding years, contrasting with the criteria set in official speeches and articles.

After his bout of illness in 1982, Todor Zhivkov appeared again to be firm in the saddle. Lilov's eviction was the only visible dark spot on the calm surface of the Bulgarian political scene, in respect of the highest leadership. At a lower level, however, unusual disclosures were made about rumblings of indiscipline in a municipal party committee. On 16 September the Party daily *Rabotnichesko Delo* reported an almost open revolt of BCP members in Zlatitsa against Party and state acts which had merged their town with neighbouring Pirdop to form a new town named Srednogorie. It may have been more than a coincidence that Zlatitsa was the birthplace of BCP stalinist leader Valko Chervenkov, who died in 1980. The case was a rare public admission of developments which reduced the credibility of the professed 'monolithic unity' of the Party.

A decision was taken in late April to devote to the problem of quality a national Party conference in March 1984, and Zhivkov spoke on this subject in Varna on 30 May. After that, quality of production, and quality of work in all spheres of life, became the main topic of the mass media. The issue emerged as extremely important for two reasons: the negative effect poor quality had both on the national economy and on the general mood of the people, and complaints by Bulgaria's trade partners in Comecon and increasing difficulties in selling Bulgarian products on international markets.

Other developments aimed at appeasing possible popular discontent included a decision of 14 February on the standard of living, a decree of 18 July on public services and guidelines of 2 December on legal and administrative services. A law on plebiscites was voted on 30 March, but was not applied and seemed to have served the main purpose of displaying increased 'socialist democracy'. The low birth-rate and inadequate health services remained topical issues in the social sphere.

The national economy continued to develop at modest but relatively stable rates. Agriculture suffered great losses because of drought throughout the winter and spring and rainfalls during the harvest season. Food supplies, however, remained among the best in Eastern Europe. Some price increases were announced in May. An attempt to solve the persisting housing shortage was made by a decree in August, laying on enterprises and organizations the task of participating with funds and labour in the construction of housing.

Propaganda about the international situation was dominated even more than in past years by a campaign against 'the militaristic course' of the USA, contrasted with the 'peace-loving policy' of the Soviet Union and the socialist states. Bulgaria's own contribution to the latter, the propagandist suggestion of a nuclear-free zone in the Balkans, was pointed out on every suitable occasion.

Apart from official visits by Zhivkov to Turkey in June and to India in December, high-level exchanges were restricted to some East European countries and were particularly lively with the two neighbours who were the greatest advocates of nuclear-free Balkans, Papandreou's Greece and Ceauşescu's Romania. Relations with Yugoslavia, strained by the perennial Macedonian problem, remained frosty,

Year-long Italian investigations of the 'Bulgarian connection' in the assassination attempt on the Pope were completed in December, but the findings were not announced.

YUGOSLAVIA

In an effort to provide a breathing-space which would enable the economic stabilization programme announced in 1982 (see AR 1982, p. 127) to produce results, the Government applied to the IMF and to its Western creditors for an easing of the burden of foreign debt repayment. Temporary relief was granted during the first quarter while a long-term debt restructuring programme was worked out.

The chief Yugoslav negotiator, Janko Smole, publicly criticized banks in Macedonia, Kosovo, Montenegro and Vojvodina for financial irresponsibility in running up foreign debts without consultation with the federal authorities, and then expecting the Government and the National Bank to help them with the repayments. The Western negotiators insisted that the federal Government must take responsibility for the servicing of foreign debts, but this raised constitutional difficulties for the Yugoslavs, whose banking system had become decentralized during the previous decade. A compromise formula was agreed on 25 March and a $4,000 million relief package was announced in which the IMF, the World Bank, several Western governments and a consortium of European and North American banks participated.

Anxious to show their support for non-aligned Yugoslavia, both the Soviet Union and China also offered help. The Soviet Premier, Mr Tikhonov, visited Belgrade while the IMF negotiations were in progress, to offer a barter agreement which would enable Yugoslavia to buy 20 per cent more Soviet oil on favourable terms. In May Hu Yaobang arrived in Belgrade, bearing the offer of a $120 million short-term loan, and ended his visit by signing a trade agreement involving large Chinese purchases of ships and machinery. Later in May Mrs Planinć ended her first year in office as Prime Minister by visiting EEC headquarters in Brussels to seek long-term aid for the restructuring of Yugoslav industry. In her address to bankers at the Mansion House on 17 November during her visit to Britain, she indicated that further help would be necessary in addition to the amounts already granted in 1983.

The austerity programme created some hardship and inconvenience on the domestic market. Inflation continued to rise, reaching 50 per cent by the year-end. The value of the dinar declined steadily, its exchange rate against the £ falling by 80 per cent. This massive devaluation had an effect on foreign trade, stimulating exports to hard-currency areas and damping down imports. In December it was announced that price rises in energy, rail fares, tobacco, iron and steel would add three per cent to the cost of living, but a six-month price freeze would be imposed on other goods. The energy situation was made worse by a prolonged drought, which cut back hydroelectric output and caused power cuts in all major cities during the autumn. Unemployment came near to the one million mark as industry ran well below capacity.

Echoes of the 1981 disturbances in Kosovo rumbled on as scores of Albanians in Macedonia and Kosovo, accused of fomenting nationalist dissension, were brought before the courts. One of the charges involved the dissemination of tapes recorded from Tirana radio. Sentences of up to 10 years were handed down. In April Mahmut Bakalli, who had been deposed as chairman of the Kosovo League of Communists after the 1981 disturbances, was expelled from membership of the League. Action was also taken in other republics against alleged nationalists, the accused including Bosnian Muslims and Serbs.

On the other hand a wide-ranging, open debate, touching issues which had been previously taboo, gathered momentum in academic circles, in the quality press and even in the forums of the League of Communists (LCY). At one level there were criticisms of the Government's mishandling of the economy, pleas by LCY leaders for unity and pleas of *mea culpa* from state and party leaders because of their failure to implement agreed policies. The Federal Secretary for Finance, Jože Florijančić, was the only senior figure to resign over the economic crisis. There were warnings from the army of the need to increase the military budget—which took 75 per cent of federal expenditure—in order to safeguard both external and internal defence. The Defence Minister, Admiral Mamula, strongly denied any intention that the army should act independently of the political leadership. 'We are a people's army rather than a *Putsch* army', he declared.

At the academic level an examination of the behaviour of the communists in the immediate post-war period in eliminating the democratic parties, and in assuming absolute power, was used as the basis for a discussion about the possibilities of creating a multi-party democracy, albeit on socialist lines. This view was particularly associated with the Belgrade University Institute for Social Science, which was created to accommodate the *Praxis* group of marxist humanists.

The ranks of the ex-partisans who formed the inner corps of the state and party leadership were thinned by the deaths of several prominent members, including Vladimir Bakarić, whose death at the age of 71 in February created a vacancy in the Federal Assembly. He was succeeded by Mika Špiljak (aged 66), another Croat, who in May duly took the post of President which should have gone to Bakarić. In October Mitja Ribičič (aged 64), of Slovenia, was replaced as President of the LCY Presidium by Dragoslav Marković (63 years), a leading Serbian communist.

The large crowds attending the funeral in September of Aleksandar Ranković, the former Vice-President and head of internal security until his dismissal in 1966, provided an embarassing reminder to the authorities of the strength of Serbian national feelings.

In continuing Tito's non-aligned foreign policy the new leaders supported the initiative of the N+N group in helping to reach an agreed resolution at the Madrid conference on European security, and in promoting the concept of a Balkan nuclear-free zone.

ALBANIA

An intense undercover campaign of purges of Party leaders and government officials continued throughout the year. It had been set in motion after the suicide of the former Prime Minister Mehmet Shehu in December 1981 (see AR 1981, p. 131), involving a large number of people who had been closely associated with him. No hard information about the purges was provided by official sources, which confined themselves to political vilification of the main victims. The Yugoslav official news agency, citing statements made to the Greek press by recent defectors from Albania, reported in November that at least five former prominent politicians, military figures and officials had been executed and many others imprisoned. Among those believed to have lost their lives were the former Minister of Defence Kadri Hasbiu and the former Minister of the Interior Feçor Shehu; those said to have been given prison sentences included Mehmet Shehu's widow and their two sons.

As in earlier similar political convulsions, alleged external and internal perils facing both the communist regime and the country became the grim theme of official propaganda. This was a constant refrain of speeches by Enver Hoxha, the Party leader, and Ramiz Alia, the nominal head of state, as well as numerous articles in the press. The heated polemics between Albania and Yugoslavia, prompted by the Albanian riots of Kosovo in 1981 (see AR 1981, pp. 127-8), continued almost unabated. They were conveniently linked to the wider campaign about alleged dangers threatening the country. Albanian official sources criticized the heavy prison sentences given during the year to many young Yugoslav citizens of Albanian origin charged with various political offences. Yugoslavia, for its part, regarded such Albanian attacks on its policies as unwarranted interference in its own affairs.

In 1979 Albania and Yugoslavia had concluded an agreement to build by the end of 1983 a railway link of 70 km between Titograd in Montenegro and the northern Albanian town of Shkodër. But the link was not completed in time. The Albanians maintained that, whilst they had built their own part of the track of some 50 km, Yugoslavia had failed to construct its shorter section because it was displeased with Albanian criticisms. Yugoslav sources, on the other hand, ascribed the non-fulfilment to their country's serious economic difficulties. After failing to create a link with the European railway system via Yugoslavia, Albania signed in October an agreement with Italy to establish a regular ferry service between the Albanian port of Durrës and Trieste. This service, which began operating in December, was intended to provide Albanian exports with an access to the markets of Italy and central Europe.

Albanian political leaders had always claimed that, because of its adequate mineral and other resources as well as its wise socialist policies, their country was practically immune from the dire effects of the world economic recession. However, a new, more realistic note was struck in July, when a Communist Party newspaper admitted for the first time that Albania, like other countries, was also suffering from its consequences. The paper stated that because of worldwide inflation the country had to pay constantly increasing prices for all the goods, particularly the industrial equipment, that it imported from abroad. Consequently, greater efforts were required to seek fresh international markets for its minerals and farm products and to improve the quality of its exports. The paper was only telling the plain truth, given the painful fact that the country had had no foreign economic aid of any kind since its break with China in 1978. Albania and China signed in October a protocol on the exchange of goods and payments, the first agreement of any kind concluded between the two countries for over five years.

Enver Hoxha's 75th birthday was celebrated on 16 October amidst an official campaign of adulation unsurpassed since Stalin's political apotheosis in the Soviet Union at the height of his career.

In a broadcast at the beginning of November, Vatican radio referred to 'the very grave and systematic persecution of religion' in Albania and said that Pope John Paul II had called upon Catholics throughout the world to pray for religious freedom there during November.

MONGOLIA

Congratulating Yuri Andropov on his election as General Secretary of the Soviet Communist Party after Leonid Brezhnev's death in November 1982, the General Secretary of the Mongolian People's Revolutionary Party (MPRP), President Yumjaagiyn Tsedenbal of the MPR, pledged that Mongolia would 'continue tirelessly to strengthen the unbreakable ties of fraternal friendship and cooperation' with the Soviet Union. When Tsedenbal visited Moscow in December, he had a meeting with Andropov, and they resolved to continue developing Mongolian-Soviet relations on the basis of 'unbreakable friendship, selfless mutual aid and firm ideological unity'.

A new Soviet ambassador to Mongolia was appointed in February—54-year-old Sergey Pavlov, a former first secretary of the Youth League and chairman of the State Committee for Sport. He replaced 70-year-old Aleksandr Smirnov, who had been stationed in Ulan Bator for almost ten years.

In April, the Mongolian party and government newspaper *Unen* accused China of trying, at the Sino-Soviet talks in Moscow, to obtain the withdrawal of Soviet military units from the MPR 'as a precondition for normalization of PRC-USSR relations'. The stationing of Soviet troops in Mongolia was a 'purely domestic affair of the MPR government', *Unen* said, and the Chinese leaders were seeking to 'solve issues directly affecting the interests of the Mongolian people behind their back'.

In June, the PRC Foreign Ministry presented a *note verbale* to the Mongolian ambassador in Peking, Puntsagiyn Shagdarsuren, complaining that the Mongolian authorities had ordered 1,764 Chinese nationals living in Ulan Bator to move to farms in the provinces. The Mongolian trade union newspaper *Hodolmor* denied Chinese claims that these people were being forced to settle in the Gobi, but said that they were 'avoiding socially useful work'. Expulsion from the MPR had been ordered only of individual Chinese citizens who 'systematically break the laws' of the country.

In August, the MPR Foreign Minister, Mangalyn Dugersuren, said that Mongolia was 'not anti-Chinese', but it was 'critical of the foreign policy of the current Peking leaders': China had long been trying to destroy the independence of Mongolia and annexe it. Dugersuren sharply rejected 'lying claims by Western and Chinese propaganda' that Chinese residents had been forced out of Mongolia. 'About 5,000 are living in Mongolia,' he added, 'although only two or three hundred of them are working.'

The MPR Defence Minister, Colonel-General Jamsrangiyn Yondon, paid official visits to Hanoi, Phnom Penh and Vientiane in October, and while in Vietnam signed an agreement on inter-army cooperation. 'The peoples and armies of Vietnam and Mongolia have the same enemies, the Peking expansionists,' he remarked. The new Chinese ambassador to Mongolia, Li Juqing, former deputy director of a Foreign Ministry department, presented his credentials to President Tsedenbal at the end of November. Tsedenbal told him that the MPR firmly pursued a policy of normalizing relations with the PRC.

One of the MPR's most senior leaders, Sampiliyn Jalan-aajav, was dismissed in July from his posts of Secretary of the MPRP Central Committee (held since 1971) and member of the party Politburo (since 1973), and in December he was also removed from membership of the Central Committee. A session of the People's Great Hural (national assembly) then approved an undated decree dismissing Jalan-aajav from his post of deputy chairman of the Hural Presidium (MPR Vice-President). The MPRP Central Committee promoted Bugyn Dejid, chairman of the Party Control Committee, to full membership of the party Politburo, and elected Tserendashiyn Namsray, head of the MPRP's general department and a member of the Hural Presidium, to the party Secretariat.

The Mongolian-Soviet copper and molybdenum mining and concentrating combine at Erdenet attained its rated annual capacity of 16 million tonnes of ore, and was accounting for over 30 per cent of the value of Mongolia's exports. In Ulan Bator, No. 2 house-building combine, a gift from the Soviet Union, was handed over to the MPR; its annual production capacity of 140,000 sq. m. was to double the scale of house-building in the country. A lorry trailer works went into production, and the first turbine of No. 4 heat and power station, under construction in the Mongolian capital, began feeding the grid, helping to reduce the power shortage.

The grain harvest in 1983 was a new record at around 780,000 tonnes, but livestock surviving from birth during the year numbered only 8,100,000, the lowest figure for six years.

IV WESTERN, CENTRAL AND SOUTHERN EUROPE

Chapter 1

FRANCE—FEDERAL REPUBLIC OF GERMANY—ITALY—
BELGIUM—THE NETHERLANDS—LUXEMBOURG—REPUBLIC OF
IRELAND

FRANCE

THROUGHOUT the year the Government struggled with varying fortune to maintain its social reforms in the face of persistent economy problems, falling support in the polls and a resurgence of opposition in parliament and on the streets. At the New Year President Mitterrand pointed to economic 'rigour' as the way to recovery, and in February Prime Minister Pierre Mauroy bravely declared that 'the big problems are now behind us'. But within days the optimism was punctured by alarming trade figures and a resumption of rapid inflation.

Action had to bow to the exigencies of the political calendar, namely the approaching municipal elections in March. Increasingly reflecting national moods rather than purely local considerations, these went badly for the left, which lost 31 of the towns with over 30,000 inhabitants that it had won in 1977. The opposition won a striking victory in Paris, which was seen as a disavowal of the Government over its clumsy reform of the capital in 1982, and which strengthened the hand of the ebullient mayor of Paris, Jacques Chirac, in his contention for the 1988 presidential election—for which jockeying was already under way.

The election results raised speculation about M Mauroy's future as Prime Minister. However, he was appointed to head a new Government in which the political balance was unchanged, though ten ministries were moved out of the Cabinet, now one of the smallest in the Fifth Republic. The most important casualty was M Jean-Pierre Chévènement, the Industry Minister, while the chief beneficiary of the shuffle was seen as M Jacques Delors, who was now Minister for the Economy, Finance and the Budget.

Certainly the austerity programme announced once the elections were safely over represented a victory for his views over calls for alternative strategies involving reflation or protectionism. He aimed to cut internal demand by 2 per cent, to eliminate the trade deficit and to reduce inflation, even at the cost of increasing unemployment by some 100,000. The programme included the third devaluation in eighteen months (10 per cent against the Deutschmark), cuts in subsidies to the nationalized industries, economies in social security, higher public service charges, increased taxes on cigarettes, liquor and petroleum products and a compulsory state loan for many income-tax payers. The greatest public outcry was directed at the limiting of foreign travel expenditure to under £200 per head. Presenting his new Government's programme in Parliament, M Mauroy blamed the measures on the economic mess they had inherited in 1981. Despite rumblings of discontent from some Socialists and token resistance from the Communists, the Assembly approved the new Government by 323 votes to 155 and authorized it, by 325 votes to 159, to take further economic measures by decree.

Although M Chévènement attacked the austerity programme for betraying socialist principles, the Government's support held firm then and throughout the year, despite the greater assertiveness of an opposition fired by success in the municipal elections and in the senatorial elections in September. Although the Socialists' Communist partners showed signs of restiveness over foreign and industrial policy, the two parties' alliance was formally continued at a summit meeting in December—if only because, for the moment, it was in neither's interest to break it. Earlier, at the end of October, the Socialists' party congress had ended in a rosy glow of unity, thanks to intensive preparation by the leadership, timely small concessions to the left and appeals to party loyalty.

But, if the Government's survival was never in danger, its effectiveness was. As so often in France, the most awkward opposition was found on the streets. In the first half of the year hospital doctors struck for six weeks against proposals to reorganize the hospital system, securing a postponement until the autumn, when there were further demonstrations against the Government's Bill; medical students went on strike, and there were demonstrations by small-businessmen, pharmacists, travel agents and, inevitably, farmers aggrieved by low prices. In June many policemen, in turn, demonstrated in Paris over the murder of two of their number and against the liberal policies of the Justice Minister. The director-general of the national police and the Paris prefect of police left their posts and the leaders of two police unions were dismissed from the force. Though fears of a repetition of the upheavals of May 1968 proved unfounded M Mauroy accused the opposition of encouraging illegal activity.

More gravely, violence continued in Corsica, where the senior local-government official in Upper Corsica was assassinated, apparently in retaliation for the alleged murder of a nationalist leader by government undercover agents. International terrorism again left an ugly mark, notably when Armenian extremists killed six people and injured 48 in a bomb attack against Turkish Airlines at Orly in September. And on New Year's eve an Arab group killed four people and injured fifty with bombs at a Marseilles station and on an inter-city express.

However, the chief preoccupation remained the economy. The main aim of the 1984 Budget was to restrict the budget deficit to 3 per cent of GNP (roughly £10,000 million). While this target could be attained only by window-dressing, the 6·5 per cent increase in planned expenditure was the smallest in fifteen years and represented a standstill in real terms. Sectors receiving real increases were industrial innovation, civil research and support to employment. The one-per-cent special levy on income tax introduced in 1982 was retained for a further year, and surtax rates were increased sharply—sparking further demonstrations in November by white-collar workers and small-businessmen over what they saw as punitive tax increases directed against the middle class. President Mitterrand acknowledged that with public expenditure now rising to 45·5 per cent of GNP the limit of what could be considered supportable had been reached.

Not that the burden of harder times was falling exclusively on the middle class. As the year progressed the implications of the austerity programme became clearer in industry. The Communist chairman of the coal board resigned in November in protest against a cut in state aid which would reduce production and cut the work-force by at least 6,000. Even after drastic surgery another 25-30,000 jobs were in danger in the steel industry. And France's largest private company, the Peugeot group, was in difficulties. At the end of the year a bitter strike followed the company's decision to cut the mainly immigrant work-force at the Poissy plant. Unemployment rose by 2·9 per cent to about 2,225,000. For the first time since 1980 disposable incomes and domestic consumption fell slightly. Prices went up by 9·4 per cent, rather more than the Government had hoped. However, the fall in industrial investment slowed and both industrial production and GNP marginally increased. Following the March measures the trade deficit fell sharply, and over the full year it was down to almost half the 1982 level, though a sharp rise in the foreign debt implied heavy burdens for the future. All in all, while the economy seemed to be recovering, progress was still precarious.

But the economy was not the sole concern. For the first time immigration emerged as a prominent political issue. Although the number of immigrants had mounted to around 4·2 million, many of them concentrated in a few urban areas and in the poorest jobs, the ensuing tensions had rarely been articulated by the mainstream political leaders. However, the extreme-right National Front, led by M Jean-Marie Le Pen, had no such inhibitions. It worried the main parties with a series of relatively strong showings in local and parliamentary by-elections in the autumn—even in areas with few immigrants.

The Government attempted to promote a number of reforms, often against considerable opposition. Its major measures in 1983 included hospital reorganization, further steps towards decentralization, measures to democratize the public service, to equalize job opportunities for women and to change the career structure of university staffs. No issue was more delicate than a proposal by the Education Minister, M Alain Savary, aimed at drawing the state and church school systems closer together, which earned him abuse from *laics*, who alleged that he had ratted on election promises, and complaints from the clericals of back-door nationalization. Negotiations dragged sourly on. Another controversial measure that came before Parliament in the autumn was a Bill aimed at preventing undue concentration of newspaper ownership; it was widely understood to be directed at the spreading press empire of M Robert Hersant, whose papers took a strongly anti-government line. The Government also announced three new television networks, one a pay-TV system, another an access network open mainly to a range of associations and institutions, and the third offering a selection of francophone programmes by satellite. Plans were also pressed forward to introduce cable TV into a number of major cities.

FOREIGN AFFAIRS AND DEFENCE. Foreign policy activity focused mainly on Europe, Africa and the Middle East. In Europe emphasis was laid on French membership of the Western alliance. President Mitterrand's speech to the Bundestag in January, marking the 20th anniversary of the Franco-German Treaty of Cooperation, called for greater determination and solidarity among Nato members. Then and at the Atlantic Council in Paris in June (the first held there since 1966) he backed introduction of Pershing missiles elsewhere in Western Europe and emphasized France's readiness to meet all its responsibilities within the alliance. The establishment of a new Rapid Action Force geared defence planning more closely to cooperation with France's allies—though the Defence Minister, M Charles Hernu, reiterated in July that there was no question of France's rejoining the Nato command structure.

However, Franco-German relations did not run altogether smoothly. Despite an outward show of harmony at the twice-yearly summits there was little substantive agreement. The French were displeased at the continuing imbalance in trade and lack of German support for their criticism of American economic policies. France also found little backing for its ideas on the Middle East or its proposal at the Williamsburg talks of a world monetary conference. After the expensive failure at Versailles early in his term Williamsburg confirmed M Mitterrand's scepticism about international summitry. Williamsburg also did nothing to improve relations with the United States: American restiveness at France's independent line on defence and its criticism of American policy in Central America (President Mitterrand characterized the Grenada intervention as 'illegal') were matched by French irritation at US economic policies on interest rates and the dollar.

Relations with the other superpower were much worse. M Claude Cheysson's trip to Moscow in February led to blunt speaking over Poland, Afghanistan and human rights, and he told Mr Gromyko that France had no intention of joining the Soviet-American talks on medium-range missiles in Geneva, or of allowing its missiles to be included in the tally of Western strength. The fact that he returned from Moscow with little hope of movement on any of the outstanding issues strengthened President Mitterrand's resolve in expelling 47 Soviet diplomats, journalists and commercial staff for espionage in April. The USSR refrained from retaliation, but relations between the two countries became exceptionally chilly. Only at the end of the year were there signs of attempts to revive them.

On coming to power the Socialists had hopes both of preserving the Third World from superpower rivalries and of avoiding being the policeman of Africa. The President visited francophone Africa in January and June in the hope of 'dedramatizing' relations and of developing a more coherent policy towards the African continent. But he was unable to avoid involvement in the Chad imbroglio (see Pt. VI, Ch. 3). The dispatch of troops there was finally agreed in August, and numbers rose rapidly to nearly 2,000—France's most substantial involvement in Africa since the Algerian war, costing a sobering £85 million per year. But, while the French presence helped stabilize the battle-lines, it was not available to help the Chad Government reconquer the north, and the stalemate persisted. Despite intensive French efforts the 10th Franco-African summit at Vittel in October broke up without reaching agreement on the issue. In December France withdrew from the contact group of five Western countries dealing with the Namibian problem because it was 'powerless to fulfil its mandate'. More agreeably, in October a three-day visit to France by President Chadli of Algeria was hailed as a final reconciliation between the two nations. During the year France, exceptionally, enjoyed good relations with all three countries of the Maghreb. However, the resurgence of tension over the treatment of immigrants in France threatened this new-found harmony.

France also found itself with a thankless role in Lebanon. After attacks on the French units in the peace-keeping force early in the year they were reinforced in February. In November, 59 French troops died in a terrorist bomb attack in Beirut and the force suffered further casualties in a similar episode in December. Although public opinion had remained remarkably phlegmatic over such losses in playing so uncertain a role, at the end of the year the President announced a reduction in the French contingent. One reason why the French were singled out for attacks might have been their agreement in February to supply Iraq with 29 more Mirage F-1 fighter-bombers and, later, to lend Iraq five Super Etendard naval attack aircraft, thus courting the hostility of Iran, several of whose diplomats were expelled from France in December for alleged complicity in terrorist activity.

The five-year military programme law was unveiled in April. Its main emphases were on modernizing and extending the nuclear forces and on restoring France as part of a coordinated Western defence system—while retaining her 'absolute autonomy of decision'. Costed at £72,000 million, the programme provided for a seventh nuclear-missile submarine equipped with MIRVs having a range of 2,250 miles, and a tactical strike force which would become operational in 1992 with Hades missiles having a 250-mile range, capable of delivering either H- or N-bombs. A Rapid Action Force of some 47,000 men would be equipped with helicopters, light tanks and anti-tank weapons, which would be capable of intervening anywhere within the 'three circles' of French defence planning (whether France or Western Europe, where it would be matched against Soviet mobile mechanized forces, or in the Middle East or Africa). Although the navy was to receive a new aircraft-carrier, the opposition and some serving officers criticized the programme for sacrificing the conventional forces to the nuclear effort. They were to lose 35,000 men. The Government, however, considered deterrence illusory without a strong nuclear base. M Cheysson pledged at the Atlantic Council that the defence effort would be maintained despite economic difficulties.

Although a 'Festival of Peace' attracted 250,000 to Vincennes in June, and there were demonstrations for European nuclear disarmament to coincide with those in other countries in November, public support for nuclear weapons appeared more solid in France than in other West European countries in 1983.

OVERSEAS DEPARTMENTS AND TERRITORIES. The year's major development was the establishment of regional councils in the four overseas departments as part of the Government's decentralization programme. The aim, said President Mitterrand, was to bind the departments still more closely into the national family while allowing them to express their distinctive identities. In the regional elections to the new councils in February the Government parties made a strong showing, but, although they won a majority of votes in Guadeloupe, Martinique, Guayane and Reunion, only in Martinique was this translated into a majority of seats. Although the 'independentists' polled badly in all three Caribbean departments this did not prevent the extremist wing from pursuing its aims violently. In May there were sixteen bomb attacks in one night across the three departments and in Paris, while in November a further night of bombing in Guadeloupe badly damaged the prefecture at Basse-Terre.

The other trouble spots were in the Pacific. In New Caledonia tensions between predominantly European and Melanesian groups led to the death of two policemen in an ambush in January. Government proposals for the political future of the island were severely criticized by advocates of independence. The Minister for Overseas Departments and Territories, M Georges Lemoine, faced a demonstration by over 30,000 people when he arrived at Noumea in May for talks on the island's future. From a conference of the main political forces which he called in Paris in July there emerged a commitment by the Government to self-determination for the island. In November it was announced that this would take the form of a referendum in 1989.

THE FEDERAL REPUBLIC OF GERMANY

INTERNAL AFFAIRS. A federal election was held on 6 March to resolve the situation caused by the break-up in September 1982 of the centre-left coalition of Social Democrats and Free Democrats (see AR 1982, p. 139). Herr Helmut Kohl, the Christian Democrat leader who had succeeded the Social Democrat Herr Helmut Schmidt as Federal Chancellor on a Bundestag vote, was decisively confirmed in office at the election. His party, the Christian Democratic Union (CDU), and its Bavarian sister party, the Christian Social Union (CSU), polled 48·8 per cent of the total vote, compared with 44·5 per cent at the previous federal election in 1980. Their liberal coalition partner, the Free Democratic Party (FDP), whose popularity had waned since its defection from the Schmidt Government, polled 6·9 per cent (against 10·6 per cent), while the Green Party, by polling 5·6 per cent, succeeded in winning Bundestag seats for the first time. The Social Democratic Party's (SPD) 38·2 per cent share of the poll was its lowest since 1961. The result was a 58-seat majority for Herr Kohl's centre-right coalition.

In the campaign Herr Kohl used similar arguments to those which had won Konrad Adenauer an absolute majority 25 years previously. Hard hit by the recession, the Germans voted for the economic upturn promised by Herr Kohl's Government, but in doing so they also expressed their consent to a further tightening of the belt, their support for the Western alliance and for a no-nonsense attitude towards the Soviet Union.

But it was not back to the 1950s in Bonn—and not just because Germany and the world had changed since then. The political establishment was shaken by the arrival of 27 Green Party representatives in the Federal Parliament. Some Greens favoured at least a loose collaboration with the sadly depleted Social Democrats, and some left-wing Social Democrats wanted to join the Greens in the fight against missiles. The SPD's Chancellor candidate, Herr Hans-Jochen Vogel, had swung the party on a leftish course in the hope of mopping up Green voters. But in the closing stages of the campaign he began to look as if he had realized his mistake. He was like a lawyer struggling with a brief in which he did not really believe. He was unclear on missiles and never came completely clean about parliamentary cooperation with the Greens. The architect of Herr Vogel's strategy was the SPD chairman, Herr Willy Brandt, who claimed to detect, in those nervous weeks after the collapse of the Schmidt coalition, a majority of voters to the left of the Christian Democrats.

What frightened voters most was the spectre of a red/green coalition, dominated by Social Democrats like Herr Egon Bahr, for whom *Ostpolitik* appeared to take precedence over Germany's commitment to the Western alliance. So they voted in droves for the safe if unexciting alternative personified by Herr Kohl. His success was overwhelming. Research institutes found that 1·5 million people who voted for the SPD in 1980 (or perhaps for Herr Helmut Schmidt) supported the CDU/CSU this time. Even in North Rhine Westphalia, which includes the Ruhr industrial area, the CDU became the strongest party. Moreover the CDU Minister of State in the Foreign Ministry, Herr Alois Mertes, polled more than 69 per cent of direct votes in his constituency of Bitburg, which was earmarked for a nuclear missile base. The Social Democrats managed to attract support from 37 per cent of first-time voters, but 32 per cent voted for the CDU/CSU. Some 23 per cent of young voters backed the Greens, but the party also gained support from many bourgeois ecologists as well as from a lot of people who wished a plague on all the 'established' parties.

Not since the 1950s had German voters been faced with such clear options as faced them in this year's election. Thirty years ago the argument was about rearmament, Nato membership and Germany's place in the world. Although issues of quite such magnitude were not at stake in 1983, there were striking similarities between the political debate then and the positions adopted by the main political parties in the 1983 election. Voters were able to choose between a coalition which advocated unswerving loyalty to the Atlantic alliance and a Social Democratic Party which was increasingly questioning some of the fundamental assumptions on which German foreign policy had been based since the formation of the Federal Republic.

As he set about putting together a new Government and drafting its programme, Herr Kohl discovered that his Bavarian political relatives were much more tiresome than his Free Democrat associates. The Bavarian CSU, led by Herr Franz-Josef Strauss, the Bavarian Premier, firmly reminded the Chancellor of the role Bavaria played in the Union's election victory. The CSU, which fielded candidates only within the state borders, had a 10·6 per cent share of the Union's total vote. So, before the coalition bargaining started, the CSU made known its 'natural and unanimous conviction' that Herr Strauss, as chairman of the second largest coalition party, had a claim to 'cooperate and to exercise joint responsibility' in the federal Cabinet. His duties, it was added, should be commensurate with the weight of the party and with Herr Strauss's 35 years' service in federal politics.

Ideally, Herr Strauss wanted to be Foreign Minister and Vice-Chancellor, but would have accepted the Finance Ministry as second choice. Neither post was available. The retention of the Foreign Ministry by the Free Democrat leader, Herr Hans-Dietrich Genscher, was virtually a condition of liberal membership of the coalition. Nor could Herr Gerhard Stoltenberg be budged from Finance. A Christian Democrat, he was persuaded to give up the premiership of Schleswig Holstein in 1982 to assist Herr Kohl in Bonn. However, the CSU was given five posts in the Cabinet instead of four, thus achieving its strongest presence since the chancellorship of Herr Ludwig Erhard in the mid-1960s. The most controversial appointment was that of Herr Friedrich Zimmermann, a right-wing CSU member, who became Minister of the Interior. He replaced Herr Gerhart Baum of the FDP, which had to be content with three posts.

The new Government fulfilled its promise to change the course of policy by prescribing a stiff dose of law and order. Herr Zimmermann set about the task of keeping down the foreign population—more than 4·8 million—of sharpening the law on demonstrations, and generally of equipping the state with the means of keeping a closer watch on its citizens. A scheme was introduced to tempt certain categories of non-EEC foreigners to return home with the offer of a modest financial handshake. Herr Zimmermann was also planning to lower the age-limit for the entry of non-EEC minors from 16 to six. His argument was that young children would have a much better chance of becoming integrated in German society than older ones who arrived without a word of German and mostly without educational qualifications.

A Government Bill to tighten the demonstration law provided for the arrest not only of violent demonstrators, but also of passive ones who refused to leave a demonstration which had become violent. In Herr Zimmermann's words, 'If the police say to a demonstrator "please go away" and he doesn't do so, he is not a normal citizen.' It was intended that the Bill should become law early in 1984, which would be too late for the wave of autumn demonstrations against missile deployment. But the Minister hoped that the mere declaration of intent would have a sobering effect. It was also agreed that a new plastic, forgery-proof identity card which could be read at ease by computers should be introduced in 1984. A plan for a new identity card was hatched in 1976 at the height of the terrorist campaign, and was revived ostensibly to assist the police in combating crime.

The Germans were asked to tighten their belts again in order to aid the promised economic recovery. The Government approved a Budget for 1984 in which savings of DM 6,500 million (£1,620 million) were made, most of it in social welfare spending and public sector pay. In recent years state borrowing had been increasing at a rapid rate, caused by falling tax revenues due to the recession and by bigger bills for social welfare. There was not much sign of a lasting recovery, and certainly not of the kind that would help solve the country's biggest domestic problem, unemployment. The unemployment total was expected to stay at well over two million for a long time. The Budget provided for a slight reduction in unemployment benefit for recipients without children, and for a temporary freeze of public sector pay.

Demonstrations by the peace movement against nuclear missiles deployment reached a climax in the autumn, but in the event caused less trouble than the Government had feared. An 'action' week was held in October, involving a blockade of many bases. Between Stuttgart and Neu-Ulm some 200,000 peopled formed a human chain 67 miles long, and in Bonn another chain linked the embassies of the five nuclear powers, the United States, the Soviet Union, Britain, France and China. A rally in Bonn attended by 200,000 people was addressed by Herr Willy Brandt, who expressed 'bitter disappointment' that no political will for agreement had been shown at the Geneva arms control talks between the Soviet Union and the US. Herr Brandt's participation in the rally was criticized by the Government, which claimed that the Social Democrats had finally abandoned a common security policy.

This claim was justified. At a special conference in November the SPD voted overwhelmingly against deployment, although the former Chancellor, Herr Schmidt, stood firm by the Nato twin-track decision. On 22 November the SPD joined the Greens in opposing the missiles when the issue was put to the vote in the Bundestag, but the Government parties had a comfortable majority.

FOREIGN AFFAIRS. The Soviet Government interfered in the federal election campaign with a lack of subtlety unprecedented even by Russian standards. Thanks to the Russians, the campaign was dubbed the 'missiles election' and, apart from choosing the central issue, the Soviet leadership came out unequivocally in favour of a Social Democrat victory. The Soviet leader, Mr Andropov, expressed his preference for the Social Democrats during a meeting with Herr Vogel in Moscow on 11 January. A week later the Soviet Foreign Minister, Mr Andrei Gromyko, visited Bonn and attempted to whip up anti-American sentiments in the West German electorate. He publicly accused the United States of baulking progress in the Geneva talks. And he dismissed as 'unserious' President Reagan's 'zero-option' under which the West would forego deployment of American missiles if the Soviet Union scrapped its missile arsenal directed against Western Europe.

The Americans were equally concerned to influence the German voters. The US Vice-President Mr George Bush was in Germany at the end of January on the first leg of a West European tour to drum up support for American policy on missiles, and generally to remind the allies of the benefits of alliance membership. This message seemed especially apposite in West Berlin, where Mr Bush made the major speech of his German trip and where he looked sadly over the wall that put detente into perspective. It was clear that the US Government wanted Herr Kohl to stay Chancellor.

Herr Kohl visited Mr Andropov at the beginning of July, but their talks brought no shift of position by either side on the missiles issue. The Chancellor emphasized, however, that while maintaining closer relations with the US his Government wished also to remain on good terms with the Soviet Union and its allies. Subsequently, the Chancellor's tone became tougher, and as the Geneva talks became bogged down he went so far as to accuse the Soviet Union of threatening to launch a nuclear war limited to Central and Western Europe. There was no other way to explain, he said, why the Soviet Union was trying to secure a monopoly of land-based medium-range missiles in Europe.

The Chancellor was bold enough to raise with Mr Andropov a matter which for many years had been taboo—the question of German reunification. Predictably, it fell on deaf ears. It had become fashionable since the change of Government from centre-left to centre-right to revive the legal claim that Germany continued to exist within its 1937 frontiers. Herr Heinrich Windelen, the Minister of Intra-German Affairs, declared that public discussion about the German question had been reopened, and that he had asked the education ministers of the Länder to ensure that the subject was given more attention in schools. During the election campaign, Herr Friedrich Zimmermann said that the Eastern treaties and the intra-German accord of 1972 (see AR 1972, pp. 512-513) did not prejudice a peace settlement for Germany as a whole and were not a substitute for such a settlement. Moreover, Herr Zimmermann did not limit the German question to the two German states, but maintained that it must include the future of the former German territories beyond the Oder-Neisse line.

The US invasion of Grenada was sharply criticized by members of the Bundestag, and Government speakers did not hide their dismay at the damage this crisis could cause to East-West relations. Herr Genscher said the American move had also political and psychological consequences for West Germany. He expressed his Government's anger that it had not been consulted beforehand, and said that, had it been consulted, it would have advised against the invasion. The German Government, he added, had been reinforced in its conviction that military solutions should be avoided.

The Chancellor told the Bundestag on 7 December that he was deeply disappointed by the outcome of the Athens EEC summit. There was no reasonable alternative to the European Community, he added, either for West Germany or for its European partners. Europe must unite, the Chancellor declared. Differences in economic interests must not cause this political imperative to fade into the background.

ITALY

The stop-gap coalition Government formed in November 1982 under the veteran Christian Democrat statesman Amintore Fanfani soon ran into difficulties, especially from its Socialist partners, and on 22 April the Socialist Party leader Bettino Craxi announced their withdrawal. Fanfani, faced with the defection of the largest of his three coalition partners, resigned on 29 April. So President Pertini, who had hoped to avert an election before the statutory date of 1984, dissolved Parliament and fixed the general election for 26-27 June.

Apart from the Socialists, who had high hopes of improving their position, no one really wanted this election. The Christian Democrats, still the country's largest party after 36 years of predominance, were undergoing a drastic reorganization under their uncompromising secretary Ciriaco De Mita, whose austerity programme was proving unpopular. The Communist leader Enrico Berlinguer, at his party's congress (2-6 March), while reiterating criticism of Soviet policies towards Afghanistan and Poland, put forward a 'democratic alternative' policy for ousting the Christian Democrats, but won no response from the Socialists, whose cooperation was essential. Serious policy differences existed between the two left-wing parties, notably about the location of Cruise missiles in Sicily, which the Socialists supported, whereas the Communists, though accepting Italy's continued membership of Nato, were campaigning against the missiles. The country itself seemed apathetic about the election, and little change was anticipated.

It was consequently a shock for everyone, party leaders, commentators and the electorate alike, when on 28 June the election results proved to be little short of what the press termed a 'political earthquake'. The most striking feature was the spectacular drop in the Christian Democrat poll, from their previous 38·3 per cent of the total to 32·9 per cent; the gap between them and the Communists, still the second largest party, had narrowed to 3 per cent. Far from Christian Democrat votes going straight over to the Communists, however, the Communist poll itself fell slightly, from 30·4 to 29·9 per cent: apart from abstentions by the disillusioned, they went mainly to the smaller centre parties, the Republicans, Social Democrats and Liberals, who together took 12·1 per cent of the total vote as compared with their previous 8·7 per cent. The small Republican party in particular (led by the former Prime Minister Giovanni Spadolini) went up from 3 to 5·1 per cent. But the Socialists, who had hoped to secure as much as 15 per cent of the total, in fact went up only from 9·8 to 11·4 per cent. Finally, the extreme right-wing Movimento Sociale Italiano (MSI) unexpectedly improved its position, going up from 5·5 to 6·8 per cent of the total, the increase being mainly from Christian Democrats scared by De Mita's austerity programme.

The Socialists' relative failure was attributed in part to a recent series of damaging corruption scandals in Liguria and Piedmont. The Christian Democrats' much more serious setback could also date back to a history of alleged corruption, added to general disillusionment with a party so long in power. But Craxi, aged 49, had vigorously reformed the Socialist Party ever since he became its secretary in 1976, changing it from an outdated faction-ridden group to an efficiently-managed organization in which he had the majority behind him. Despite its electoral disappointment it was still the most significant of the smaller centre parties and essential to the formation of any coalition. The Christian Democrats, realizing their weakened position, made it clear that they would join a five-party coalition provided there were no alliance with the Communists. In the circumstances President Pertini (himself a Socialist), though hitherto not particularly sympathetic towards Craxi's ambitions, decided on 21 July that Craxi should be given the chance to become Italy's first Socialist Prime Minister.

Craxi eventually managed to secure support for a five-party coalition, including the Republicans, who had held aloof from Fanfani's Government and now insisted on stiffer economic policies. Its composition—16 Christian Democrats, six Socialists, three Republicans, three Social Democrats and two Liberals—reflected the price that Craxi had had to pay for the Premiership. He surrendered the Ministries of Defence and Finance, previously held by Socialists, to two Republicans, respectively ex-Premier Giovanni Spadolini and the prominent critic of previous economic policies Bruno Visentini. Another important change was at Foreign Affairs, still in Christian Democrat hands but now taken over by another former Prime Minister, Giulio Andreotti, from Emilio Colombo who had very capably held that office for several years. The programme which Craxi announced on 9 August included stiff policies for economic recovery, modernization of the country's institutions and Italy's continued support for EEC and Nato. It secured a vote of confidence (261-243) on 12 August.

The outlook facing the new Government was bleak, with a serious economic situation, inflation running at 16-17 per cent and continuing problems of law and order. Terrorism had at least been brought to some extent under control—indeed at the end of November crimes attributed to terrorism were lower by 30 per cent than in 1982. The main scene of internal violence had shifted from the north and centre to the south and Sicily, and to involvement with drug-trade gangs, the Mafia and its Neapolitan counterpart the Camorra. Many of the terrorist leaders, both of left and right, were now in prison as the result of effective action by anti-terrorist squads, often acting on information from 'repenting' suspects hoping thus to secure shorter prison sentences. On 24 January, in the biggest anti-terrorist trial in Italian legal history, 32 out of 65 Red Brigaders were given life sentences for 17 murders and four kidnappings committed in 1977-80. The murders included that of the statesman Aldo Moro in 1978, and among those imprisoned for life were Mario Moretti, said to have directed his kidnapping, and Prospero Gallinari, who perpetrated his murder. On 23 April 83 members of Prima Linea (Front Line, the other main left-wing terrorist gang) were sentenced to prison terms of up to 30 years. On 7 March the trial opened in Rome of 71 persons arrested in 1979 on charges of involvement with the extreme Padua group known as Autonomists. The accused included their leading spirit, Professor Antonio Negri, who though in prison was elected a Radical Party Deputy in the June election, thereby raising the question of his parliamentary immunity. On 21 September the Chamber voted to strip him of immunity and authorized his rearrest, but next day Negri escaped to France.

In Sicily, by now a centre of the international arms-and-drug traffic, the assistant public prosecutor in Trapani was murdered by the Mafia. In March and June large-scale sweeps by carabinieri in south and central Italy brought the arrest of some 1,700 suspects from the Mafia, Camorra and drug-crime world.

On the economic side, the Government's main problems were to bring down inflation and reduce the public sector spending deficit and labour costs. The latter had appeared to be brought under control by an agreement on 22 January between Government, industry and the trade unions which slowed down the impact of the *scala mobile* system of automatically indexed wage bonuses. But later in the year the private industry confederation claimed that the agreement had not had the desired effect and sought to reopen the issue. When Craxi took office the budget deficit had reached 90,000,000 million lire, around 17 per cent of GDP. On 30 September the Government presented a stiff Budget for 1984, aiming to cut the public sector deficit by 40,000,000 million lire and introduce spending cuts which, for the first time, would affect pensions and social security. The foreign trade and balance of payments positions improved slightly, but industrial production fell, and unemployment was still running at about 9 per cent of the labour force.

Repercussions of the collapse, in June 1982, of the Milan-based Catholic Banco Ambrosiano (see AR 1982, p. 146) continued. The main unsettled question was the extent of the involvement of the Vatican Bank, the Istituto per le Opere di Religione, on which the report of an Italo-Vatican commission set up in December 1982 was still awaited. The family of the Banco Ambrosiano's head Roberto Calvi persisted in claiming that he had been murdered (see p. 42).

The 100th anniversary of Mussolini's birth on 29 July made relatively little impact. On 18 March the exiled former King, Umberto II, died in Geneva, aged 78 (see OBITUARY). He had wished to see Italy again before his death, and a special session of Parliament on 9 March had debated the possible repeal of the constitutional ban on his return, but the necessary procedures had not been completed.

Foreign affairs played a considerable part in the latter half of the year. Craxi himself made a tour of West European capitals in mid-September, and in mid-October paid a five-day visit to the USA, where in talks with President Reagan he reaffirmed Italy's commitment to the installation of Cruise missiles at Comiso, in West Sicily, if no agreement on missiles were reached at Geneva. Parliament approved their installation on 16 November, and on 27 November the first contingent of 16 missiles (out of an eventual 112) arrived at the Italian-US base of Sigonella, near Catania. Demonstrations against their instalment took place then at Comiso, and again on 4 December. Some 500,000 people demonstrated against them in Rome on 22 October. Late in December the Defence Minister and President Pertini said that the Italian contingent of 2,100 men in the peacekeeping force in Lebanon should be gradually withdrawn; 249 left for Italy on 28 December,

BELGIUM

Given the severe economic recession, accompanied by extremely high unemployment running at over 11 per cent of the economically-active population, and continuing antagonism between the two language communities, there seemed little chance that Mr Wilfried Martens, the Prime Minister, would be able to press forward with the austerity policies that were still economically and politically necessary at the beginning of the year. Thus, at the end of January, he inevitably was obliged to seek an extension of the special authority given him in 1982 (see AR 1982, p. 147) in order to push through his policies without the need for constant referral to parliament for approval. Most immediately, the deepening crisis in the steel industry, of which Mr Martens had taken personal control, had reached a point where reaching a viable economic solution was impracticable within the normal parliamentary process. The Prime Minister, taking advantage of the large measure of popular support he personally enjoyed across the normal political and cultural borders, was able to persuade members of parliament to grant him a further period of the special powers, without which his Government could easily have fallen.

The specific areas where the Prime Minister employed this authority included limiting growth in public spending, balancing the social security accounts, which were previously running into catastrophic deficit, and implementing a job-creation programme that involved a cut in the working hours of people in employment in order to open up employment for others.

Even as Mr Martens was making his approach to parliament in January, the fragility of the coalition was made particularly apparent when a sudden flare-up in the hitherto relatively quiescent linguistic issue almost brought down his Administration. Though affecting only 6,000 people, a dispute over the acceptability of the newly-elected mayor of the Fourons district quickly assumed national status. Transferred though they had been from Wallonia to Flanders in 1963 as part of a local arrangement to straighten out the language frontier, the majority of the population still regarded themselves as part of the French-speaking community. Their new mayor, who, it was claimed, did not speak enough Flemish to qualify legally as a mayor in Flanders, was declared unacceptable by the Flemish wing of the Christian Social Party, whose members threatened to withdraw from the national coalition Government; this would inevitably have led to its collapse. In the event a temporary solution was adopted, involving the administrative transfer of the Fourons, situated close to the Dutch border, to Brabant, an officially bilingual area 100 miles away. And thus the coalition survived and the processes of central government were resumed.

The Belgian franc was revalued by 1·5 per cent within the currency grid when the European Monetary System (EMS) was restructured in mid-March. The bigger revaluations of the Deutschmark and guilder nevertheless still made Belgian goods relatively more competitive in these important markets, which together took 35 per cent of total Belgian exports. The restructuring of EMS rates also had the effect of relieving pressure on the Belgian franc, enabling the central bank's discount rate to be cut from 14 per cent to 11 per cent. This was an important move in the context of the Government's efforts to get the economy out of recession. Further movements in this key interest rate left it at 10 per cent at the year end.

The deepening crisis in the steel industry was the subject of continuing debate, accompanied by plan and counter-plan, throughout 1983, even though none denied that the situation had reached the point at which fundamental decisions on the industry's future could be delayed no longer. That very large reductions were necessary in the steel industry's capacity and consequently in its labour force was clear to all. However, the Government faced a dilemma in that, whatever solution was adopted, one or other, very possibly both, of the linguistic regions would be bound to raise serious objections. The Walloons, in whose region most of the steel plant was located, resisted major capacity cuts, while the Flemish objected to either funding a closures programme or to continuing state subsidies. Despite these objections, the Government put forward a plan involving closing at least two of the crude steel plants and of at least 20 per cent of rolling capacity, with implied job losses of 8,000. The authorities stated that before the plan was implemented the consent and commitment of the work-force would be required: by the end of the year this had not been forthcoming.

The economy as a whole continued to emerge from recession as 1983 progressed. By the third quarter business sales and output were growing strongly, though investment was still running below the previous year's level in real terms. Consumer spending, too, had fallen, largely because of a decline in real incomes made more acute by the continuing high level of unemployment, though by the end of the year the number of jobless was stabilizing.

NETHERLANDS

The new centre-right Government, led by the head of the Christian Democrats, Mr Ruud Lubbers, looked precarious at the beginning of the year. Although it had a majority of six in the Lower House, there was always present a substantial risk that some Christian Democrat members would vote with the opposition if the Prime Minister's policies became strongly coloured by the right-wing Liberal Party, the Christian Democrats' partner in the coalition. However, a general swing to the right in opinion poll results was effective in dissuading the left-wing element in the Christian Democrat Party from causing the Government to fall.

During the summer Mr Lubbers prepared an austerity budget, aimed at drastically curbing public sector borrowing and spending, and in effect reducing personal spending power. Public employees' pay, social security benefits and spending on health services were among the main victims of the austerity package.

Trade unions took the view that job preservation rather than wage increases should be their main objective, given the extremely problematic economic environment. Most collective labour agreements provided for shortening the working week by between 5 and 10 per cent, often with the sacrifice of indexation of wages to the cost-of-living index. As well as protecting existing jobs, these measures allowed for creation of new jobs for young people, a process assisted by a cut in statutory minimum wages for this category from 1 July. The Christian Democrat Party developed this policy, also endorsed by the Labour Party, by proposing a cut in the average working week from 40 hours to 32 hours by 1990, with the aim of opening up more jobs in an effort to reduce the appallingly high level of unemployment.

For the year as a whole, industrial production showed no real growth compared with 1982, and investment was depressed. Though wages continued to rise slowly, the growth in the number of unemployed, and a rise in the savings ratio as consumers' confidence diminished, contributed to a 3 per cent decline in the volume of personal consumption. As a result of these developments and of the weak trend in investment, gross national product showed virtually no real growth during the year.

The country became embroiled in controversy over the issue of whether Cruise and Pershing II missiles should be deployed in the Netherlands. The coalition parties stood by their readiness to allow the missiles into the country, but the Labour Party and other left-wing parties were vehement in their opposition. Public opinion polls showed a majority favouring installation of Cruise missiles, though opposition was increasing.

In the closing months of the year, strikes by public sector workers resisting wage cuts occurred on a large scale but the Government continued to look capable of riding out the political storm.

LUXEMBOURG

For the Grand Duchy 1983 was a grim year. In an atmosphere of uncertainty and stagnation, the Minister of Finance brought in a budget which assumed zero growth for the year. Though the budget estimates revealed only a small borrowing requirement, the Government found itself having to incur substantially increased social expenditure as unemployment rose in the steel industry. A measure of the severity of the economy's problems was provided by the industrial output index, which in the first quarter was over 10 per cent lower than a year earlier. The steepening deterioration in the steel industry, where a 30 per cent contraction in the value of exports produced a 27 per cent fall in steel output, was the dominant factor in the overall decline.

At the end of June a rescue plan for the steel industry was put forward, to be carried out in conjunction with Belgium's similar programme. Tax rates were increased to provide funding for the restructuring plan, which involved plant closures and manning cuts.

Early in the year Parliament formally approved the renewal of the monetary agreement with Belgium, though the Socialist and Communist opposition parties voted against the measure. In its new form, the agreement gave the Luxembourg Monetary Institute various watchdog responsibilities over policy on exchange reserves and currency management, but its powers remained far less than those of a conventional central bank, to the concern of the more nationalist members of parliament.

Luxembourg adopted an aggressive attitude towards the development of television and telecommunications by satellite, seeking to consolidate its position as continental Europe's largest commercial broadcasting service. Discussions took place with France and Germany to secure cooperation in these ventures.

THE REPUBLIC OF IRELAND

The new coalition Government formed under Dr Garret FitzGerald the previous December (see AR 1982, p. 152) had majority support in the Dail. This promised a degree of political stability unknown since 1979. Attention could now be focused on the parlous state of the economy. At some IR £1,100 million the budget deficit had reached its highest level ever. So had unemployment at 179,000, or 13 per cent of the work-force. Public borrowing, public spending, inflation and income increases had all to be severely checked.

The Government set about the task with more determination than imagination. It soon became evident that the Labour Party, the smaller partner in the coalition with Dr FitzGerald's Fine Gael, could not endorse the range of expenditure cutbacks and tax increases felt necessary by Finance Minister Alan Dukes. Mr Dukes had to tolerate a deficit target of IR £900 million for the year instead of the IR £750 million to which he had hoped to confine it. Contrary to its first intentions, the Government conceded a pay increase for the public service and drew back from several other austerity proposals, such as imposing a charge for the school buses on which so many pupils depended in rural Ireland. Together with a controversial income-cum-property tax on expensive houses, these indications of left-wing restraint on economic orthodoxy enabled the Tanaiste (Deputy Prime Minister) and leader of the Labour Party, Mr Dick Spring, to claim that Labour was an effective force in government. Both as Taoiseach (Prime Minister) and as leader of Fine Gael, Dr FitzGerald could assert at the same time that the Government had grasped the nettle and taken the stringent measures needed by raising more taxes, curtailing the cost to the state of health and education services, forcing state corporations to prune their activities and reducing the scale of public borrowing. By the year's end, the economic indices were all showing signs of improvement, with inflation falling, industrial production and exports expanding, a maximum budget deficit of IR £980 million likely and the growth in unemployment slowing down.

These solid achievements were purchased at a high political price. Economic reform fell short of the objectives adopted by the Government but the burden on the citizen exceeded what many expected. High VAT and other taxes exacerbated the effects of international recession. Living costs went up while real income remained static or actually fell. Factory closures and company receiverships inevitably followed, while the tourist trade suffered from Ireland's new reputation as a highly expensive country to visit. The popularity of the Government plummetted. At a Dublin by-election in November not only did the Fianna Fail opposition hold its seat with a higher percentage of the poll but Labour lost votes to the Workers' Party, a socialist group with a background in revolutionary politics, and even to Sinn Fein, the political wing of the IRA. Labour suffered a further blow when its former leader, Mr Frank Cluskey, resigned his Cabinet post as Trade Minister because he disapproved of a Government decision to allow a private-enterprise gas company to benefit substantially from a natural-gas find exploited by the state. The potential harm to the Govenment of ideological tensions between Fine Gael and Labour was ameliorated by an amicable working arrangement between Dr FitzGerald and Mr Spring, who often appeared to have more affinity of view with one another than with the extremes among their own followers.

Fianna Fail was prevented from taking full advantage of the Govenment's difficulties by the persistence of internal divisions over the party's leadership by the former Taoiseach, Mr Charles Haughey. Early in the year a major crisis followed the disclosure that the telephones of two newspaper political commentators had been improperly 'tapped' in 1982 at the instigation of Mr Sean Doherty, Minister for Justice in Mr Haughey's Administration. These and other revelations forced the commissioner of the national police force to resign and Mr Doherty to leave the Fianna Fail parliamentary party. An attempt—the third in twelve months—to remove Mr Haughey as party leader failed but the animosities engendered did not quickly disappear.

Relations between the Republic and the United Kingdom had become strained in the aftermath of Mr Haughey's refusal to support the British position during the Falklands war in 1982. Neither Dublin nor London rushed to mend these fences when Dr FitzGerald resumed office. Although the Taoiseach rejected his predecessor's view on the Falklands he had been critical of what he believed to be British misconceptions regarding Northern Ireland (especially over the hunger strikes of 1981) and British inaction generally in pursuing a political initiative on the Irish question. Dr FitzGerald himself took an important step in that direction by setting up the Forum for a New Ireland. Membership of this body was open to all political parties represented in the Dail or in the Northern Ireland Assembly who were committed to advancing their policies by non-violent means. It was intended that the various aspirations and ideals for which the parties spoke would be examined in detail, common ground established if possible and a blueprint outlined which would show the essential elements to be incorporated in future governmental structures.

The idea seemed to be stillborn when only the SDLP agreed to participate from the North (see p. 48). With Fianna Fail, Fine Gael and Labour also present, however, the Forum encompassed virtually the whole Irish nationalist tradition. When a wide variety of Unionists, the major churches and many other groups and individuals consented to make oral and written submissions to the Forum, and to be questioned at its sittings in Dublin Castle, it became clear that Irish nationalists were open to hearing every possible point of view on the future destiny of the island. Interim reports on the cost of violence and on the economic circumstances of the two parts of the country proved to be serious studies which policy-makers could scarcely ignore. By the time the Taoiseach visited Mrs Thatcher at Chequers in November (see p. 41) there were signs that the British Government recognized the worth of the experiment.

The Republic meanwhile underwent its share of the murderous violence which plagued Northern Ireland and reached London in the pre-Christmas bombings (see p. 41). A number of bank robberies took place as well as 'shoot-outs' between the security forces and subversives. A police recruit and a soldier were killed in December while rescuing the kidnapped director of a supermarket chain. Such generally condemned incidents did little injury to efforts aimed at developing North-South cooperation.

Some observers alleged that more damage was done by a time-consuming campaign and referendum to write into the Republic's constitution an amendment prohibiting abortion. Since abortion was already banned by statute law, since the *obiter dicta* of the Supreme Court suggested that any measure to legalize it would be found to be unconstitutional, and since only a very small lobby favoured the introduction of abortion, the referendum was widely judged unnecessary. A wrangle over the wording of the amendment left Dr FitzGerald first supporting the step and then opposing it, thus injuring his prestige with his party and the public. The Catholic bishops, by recommending the proposal despite Protestant resistance, confirmed the suspicion of Northern Unionists that the Roman Church dictated civil law in the Republic. The amendment was eventually carried by 36 per cent of the electorate, a large majority of those who voted. Nearly 50 per cent of the voters stayed away from the polls. Commentators read this as a rebuke to the bishops—and to the Fianna Fail party, which had also approved the amendment.

A more immediate social evil than the possible but improbable legalization of abortion was drug addiction. Several investigations exposed an alarming traffic in hard drugs, as many as ten per cent of young people in the deprived parts of inner-city Dublin being addicted to heroin. Some of the distributors were successfully prosecuted and imprisoned but the problem had not noticeably abated by the end of the year. Serious crimes in 1983 included the theft of the stallion Shergar, probably the most valuable racehorse in the world, from a stud farm in County Kildare. The horse was not recovered (see also Pt. XVI).

The failure of the EEC summit meeting in Athens (see Pt. XI, Ch. 4) was not an unmitigated disaster for the Republic. It meant that the threatened levy on milk production would be delayed, if not altogether rescinded. The Taoiseach travelled to every EEC capital to put the case that Irish farmers should not be penalized by application of the levy since they were not responsible for excess dairy production within the Community. There was some hope that this intensive lobbying would eventually result in concessions for the Irish. It was less certain that a commercially-viable oil find would be confirmed, although predictions were favourable when drilling in the sea off the west Waterford coast was suspended for the winter.

President Patrick Hillery took office in December for a second seven-year term as head of state. A distinguished journalist, Mr Michael Mills, became the Republic's first Ombudsman, and runner Eamon Coghlan won the 5,000-metre world championship in Helsinki. Well-known Irish people who died during the year included the former Finance Minister, Mr George Colley, the former Minister for External Affairs, Mr Frank Aiken, and the social reformer, Bishop Peter Birch of Ossory.

Chapter 2

DENMARK—ICELAND—NORWAY—SWEDEN—
FINLAND—AUSTRIA—SWITZERLAND

DENMARK

THE budget-cutting programme of Mr Poul Schlüter's non-socialist coalition of Conservatives, Liberals, Centre Democrats and Christian People's Party produced a striking improvement in Denmark's economy in 1983. The 1983 budget deficit, earlier forecast to be DKr 80,000 million, was reduced to DKr 62,000 million, inflation fell from 10 per cent to 6 per cent; interest rates fell sharply; the current account deficit was halved from DKr 19,000 million in 1982 to DKr 9,000 million; and in February two-year wage agreements providing for wage increases in line with the Government's 4-per-cent a year target were reached for both the public and private sectors. Moreover, despite the Government's austerity programme public opinion polls showed a steady rise in support for the Conservative Prime Minister and his party. Serious problems still remained, both for the economy and for the Government's survival. The economy was burdened by foreign debts amounting to 33 per cent of GDP, public spending was still absorbing about 60 per cent of GDP, the budget deficit amounted to 12 per cent of GDP, and unemployment had risen to 10 per cent.

The minority Government's political problem was its dependence on the votes of the Radical Party and the anti-tax Progress Party. The Radicals broadly supported the Government's economic policy but joined with the three socialist parties to inflict on Mr Schlüter's

Government a series of defeats on foreign and defence policy. After forcing in December 1982 a suspension of Denmark's contributions to the Nato infrastructure programme for receiving Cruise and Pershing missiles in Western Europe, these four parties in March defeated a Government proposal to prolong trade sanctions against the USSR and in May passed a Folketing resolution calling on Nato to prolong the INF negotiations beyond the December 1983 deadline even if no agreement had been reached and not to deploy new missiles while the talks continued. In September the Radicals' congress decided to oppose deployment of new missiles in Western Europe by all democratic means. On 1 December they joined the socialist parties in passing a Folketing resolution forcing the Government to refuse to take any responsibility for Nato's missile deployment and to state this position in a reservation to the communique from the Nato Council's December meeting. Mr Schlüter accepted these foreign policy defeats, arguing that his Government would resign only if the Folketing rejected its economic programme.

It was the Progress Party, the other party on whose votes Mr Schlüter depended, which finally in December caused the Government's resignation. On 22 June the Supreme Court sentenced its leader, Mr Glistrup, to 3 years' imprisonment for tax fraud. At the end of June the Folketing voted by 128 votes to 22 to expel him. During the two months until his imprisonment on 31 August, Mr Glistrup urged his party's representatives to oppose the Government's economic policy unless it introduced large income tax cuts. Two representatives resigned from the party to become Government-supporting Independents, and when on 9 September the party voted for the Government's reduction in grants to local government it seemed that the decision had gone in favour of supporting the Government in office. On 24 October the Government reached agreement with the Radicals and Progressives on budget cuts of DKr 7,800 million for 1984, reducing the deficit to DKr 59,000 million. But then on 15 December the Progressives joined with the socialist parties in voting against the 1984 Finance Bill, defeating it by 93 votes to 77. The Government was thus defeated by a coalition of Progressives demanding bigger budget cuts and socialists demanding higher government expenditure. Mr Schlüter immediately resigned and called an election for 10 January 1984.

Greenland's election on 12 April gave 12 seats to the ruling anti-EEC Siumut Party under Mr Jonathan Motzfeld and 12 also to the pro-EEC Atassut Party. Siumut remained in office, relying on support from the Eskimo Inuit Party, which entered the Landsting with 10 per cent of the votes and 2 seats. Negotiations over terms for Greenland's withdrawal from the European Community continued. The EEC offered Greenland overseas territory status entitling it to financial aid and duty-free access for its exports. But disagreement continued over Community fishing rights in Greenland waters.

ICELAND

On 7 January the committee set up in 1978 to consider constitutional reforms delivered its recommendations. Although these failed to obtain sufficient support in the Allting, the party leaders did agree on an electoral reform Bill (not applicable to the forthcoming election) which the Allting passed early in March. Among other measures this lowered the voting age from 20 to 18 years and increased the number of Allting representatives from 60 to 63. On 15 February the Prime Minister, Mr Gunnar Thoroddsen, announced that elections would be held by 23 April, and on 28 February, with the Independence Party abstaining, the Provisional Law of August 1982 finally passed the Allting. By now Mr Thoroddsen's coalition was deeply divided, particularly over its policy towards the company Swiss Aluminium. The economic situation was also extremely serious, with inflation approaching 130 per cent, foreign debts amounting to 48 per cent of GNP and a balance of payments deficit amounting to 10 per cent of GNP. On 14 March Mr Thoroddsen recessed the Allting and elections took place on 23 April. Mr Thoroddsen himself, who died five months later (see OBITUARY), did not seek re-election. The results were as follows (changes from 1979 in brackets):

	% of votes	seats
Independence Party	38·7 (+3·3)	23 (+2)
Progress Party	18·5 (−6·4)	14 (−3)
People's Alliance	17·3 (−2·4)	10 (−1)
Social Democrats	11·7 (−5·7)	6 (−4)
Social Democratic League	7·3 (+7·3)	4 (+4)
Women's List	5·5 (+5·5)	3 (+3)
Others	1·0	
	100·0	60

The election was a success for the Independents and for two new groups, the Social Democratic League and the Women's List. On 26 May a coalition of Independents and Progressives took office, with Progress Party leader Steingrímur Hermannsson as Prime Minister and Independence Party leader Geir Hallgrímsson as Foreign Minister, and holding 37 of the Allting's 60 seats. On 27 May the new Government, acting quickly to control inflation, issued a Provisional Law discontinuing the indexing of wages to price rises. A 22 per cent wage rise due on 1 June was reduced to 8 per cent, and a 4 per cent rise was decreed for 1 October irrespective of price increases between June and October. All wage agreements were extended to 1 February 1984 and the inclusion of index-linking provisions in wage agreements was declared illegal until June 1985. Simultaneously the krona was devalued by 14·6 per cent.

By late summer the inflation rate was falling rapidly. Real wages had also fallen sharply. By October inflation was about 45 per cent and the Government's aim was 30 per cent by the end of the year. The unions protested strongly against the ban on collective bargaining and demanded that the Allting reject the Provisional Law when it met in October. The Government lifted the ban on new wage agreements before February 1984, but its majority ensured the passage of its other measures through the Allting in December.

NORWAY

Since taking office in October 1981 the minority Conservative Government of Prime Minister Kåre Willoch had been dependent in the Storting on the votes of the Centre Party and Christian People's Party. At the Centre Party's congress in March a large majority favoured a coalition with the Conservatives. The Christians at their congress in April also voted to give their leaders a mandate to negotiate the formation of a coalition should a parliamentary situation arise which was judged to make one necessary. Soon afterwards two political obstacles to a coalition were removed. On 19 April the Storting accepted by 80 to 27 a Government recommendation to retain Norway's liberal abortion law. Although the anti-abortion Christians could not have joined a Government proposing such a policy to Parliament, once the vote was over and the matter settled so decisively they were prepared to do so. April also produced a compromise between the Conservatives and the Centrists and Christians on modifying the highly contentious Establishment Law regulating the procedure for acquiring agricultural property.

When, therefore, in May the Centre's leader, Mr Jakobsen, proposed the opening of coalition negotiations, events moved quickly. Formal negotiations began on 2 June and agreement was reached within a week. The new three-party Government—the aim of many non-socialist politicians ever since the collapse of the last non-socialist majority Government in 1971—contained 18 members (11 Conservatives, 4 Christians and 3 Centrists) and held 79 of the 155 seats.

The local elections on 11 and 12 September were a sharp setback for the Conservatives. Gains were made by Labour and the Progress Party. The results, showing changes from the 1979 local elections and the 1981 Storting election, were as follows:

	Poll 1983 %	Change from 1979 %	Change from 1981 %
Labour	38·9	+2·9	+1·7
Conservatives	26·4	−3·5	−5·3
Christian People's Party	8·8	−1·4	−0·6
Centre	7·2	−1·4	+0·6
Socialist Left	5·3	+0·9	+0·4
Progress	6·3	+3·8	+1·8
Liberals	4·4	−0·9	+0·5
Others	2·6	−1·4	+1·0

Commentators attributed the Conservatives' losses to rising unemployment (3·7 per cent by November) and the party's failure to implement its electoral promises to make significant cuts in personal taxation and public expenditure. There were two main reasons for this failure: the Conservatives' dependence on the votes of the Centre and Christian parties, which were both committed to relatively high public expenditure, and the rapid rise in unemployment since 1981, to which the Conservative Government had reacted in the traditional manner of holding up public spending.

The issue of siting Cruise and Pershing missiles in Western Europe continued to divide the Storting. The opposition Labour Party advocated halting preparations for receiving the missiles and continuing negotiations in Geneva beyond the December 1983 deadline. Three times (in March, May and November) the party forced the issue to a vote in the Storting. Supported by the Liberals and Socialist Left (both opposed to missiles on any terms) and by some Christians and Centrists, the Labour Party each time lost by only one vote. The close votes demonstrated the unprecedented division over defence policy within Norway's large pro-Nato majority.

SWEDEN

The minority Social Democratic Government under Prime Minister Olof Palme held firm to its policy of export-led growth (boosted by the 16 per cent devaluation of October 1982) combined with low wage settlements to curb inflation, and cuts in public expenditure to contain Sweden's massive central government deficit. The Budget for 1983-84 announced on 10 January cut the deficit from SKr 91,800 million in 1982-83 to SKr 90,200 million; merely servicing the debt would cost SKr 11,000 million more in 1983-84 than in the previous year. In March the annual wage negotiations ended in wage rises of around 7 per cent in both the public and private sectors, which with inflation at around 9 per cent implied a cut in real incomes. However, the 1983 wage negotiations also saw the collapse of centralized bargaining between the blue-collar LO and the employers' organization. In August the LO's chairman announced that his organization would not participate in centralized negotiations in 1984, signalling perhaps the end of the wage-bargaining system which had characterized Swedish industrial relations since 1938.

By summer the Government's policy was producing some encouraging results: exports were rising fast and the trade account had moved from deficit to a surplus. The trend continued for the rest of the year. By November the value of exports had increased by 26 per cent since devaluation. As imports had risen by only 10 per cent the trade balance showed a surplus of SKr 10,000 million compared with a SKr 5,700 million deficit in 1982. The overall current account was held in deficit by heavy interest charges on Sweden's SKr 201,000 million of foreign debts, but the deficit had dropped from SKr 22,000 million to SKr 7,200 million. Severe structural problems remained in the huge foreign debt and central budget deficit, high inflation and rising unemployment, officially at 4 per cent but closer to 8 per cent when the effect of job-creation and training schemes was discounted. In October the Government announced SKr 2,000 million of further such job-creation measures. Also in October the Government announced further measures aimed at stabilizing the 1984 budget deficit at the 1983 level. These included SKr 2,000 million of tax increases and SKr 5,000 million of expenditure cuts, including the abolition of some food subsidies, increases in health charges, a curb on rises in welfare benefits and a freeze on development aid.

On 13 October the Government published its Bill to introduce wage-earner funds. This came a week after an estimated 80-100,000 members of Sweden's business community had demonstrated against the funds during the state opening of the Riksdag. Public opinion polls showed that the funds were opposed by not only the non-socialist parties and business community but over 50 per cent of the electorate and even by a majority of the Social Democrats' own voters. On 21 December the Bill passed the Riksdag by a majority of six, with the Communists abstaining and the non-socialist parties pledged to repeal it when they returned to office. The legislation, intended to give trade unions a growing share in industrial ownership, would create five investment funds, on whose boards union representatives would dominate, financed by a 0·2 per cent increase in payroll tax and a new 20 per cent tax on real company profits (profits after inflation and after an allowance of 6 per cent of the wage bill). The funds would invest their money in the shares of Swedish companies.

By late autumn the Government's support in the public opinion polls had fallen sharply despite the successes for its economic policy. This was generally attributed to its domestic austerity programme, rising unemployment and the breach of its promise to raise pensions in line with the cost of living. Mr Palme's own standing in the country and within his own party was also weakened in November by his handling of the resignation of his Minister of Justice, Mr Ove Rainer, in a scandal over Mr Rainer's tax affairs.

FINLAND

Mr Kalevi Sorsa's coalition of Social Democrats, Centrists and Swedish People's Party, formed on 31 December 1982 after the People's Democratic League had left the previous four-party coalition, remained in office until the election on 20 and 21 March. Public opinion polls predicted large gains for the Conservatives and large losses for the People's Democrats, whose badly-split Communist Party component was fielding two rival lists in the important Lapland electoral district. The prediction of League losses proved correct, but the Conservatives' victory failed to materialize. Instead the result was a victory for the Social Democrats, whose two coalition partners also made small gains (the Liberals, now fused with the Centre Party, lost their four seats but the Centre Party itself gained one), and especially for the populist Rural Party, which succeeded in harvesting much of the protest vote against the political establishment. 'Greens' also entered the Eduskunta for the first time. The election result was as follows (changes from 1979 in brackets):

	% of votes	seats
Social Democrats	26·7 (+2·7)	57 (+ 5)
People's Democrats	14·0 (−4·0)	27 (− 8)
Conservatives	22·2 (+0·5)	44 (− 2)
Centre-Liberals	17·8 (−3·2)	38 (− 3)
Swedish People's Party	4·6 (+0·4)	11 (+ 1)
Rural Party	9·7 (+5·1)	17 (+11)
Christian Party	3·0 (−1·8)	3 (− 7)
Constitutional Party	0·4 (−0·8)	1 (+ 1)
Greens	1·5 (+1·5)	2 (+ 2)
Others	0·1	
	100·0	200

The election produced a majority for neither the traditional non-socialist parties (Conservatives, Centre and Swedish) nor the two left-wing parties, while the three centre-left coalition parties had only a tiny six-seat majority. The People's Democrats were considered too deeply divided to be included in a Government, and the Social Democrats did not want to coalesce with the Conservatives. Long and difficult coalition negotiations were predicted. Instead Mr Sorsa, entrusted by President Koivisto on 25 April with forming a Government, produced his fourth coalition in a relatively speedy and wholly unexpected manner by extending the previous three-party coalition to include the Rural Party, thereby giving his Government a 23-seat majority in the Eduskunta. In the new Government, which took office on 6 May, the Social Democrats had eight seats and the non-socialists nine (Centre 5, Swedish 2 and Rural 2). Its programme emphasized cutting the budget deficit, reducing inflation (10 per cent) and unemployment (7 per cent), and improving industry's competitive conditions. The four parties also agreed on limited constitutional reforms designed to introduce an element of direct election into presidential elections and to enable economic enabling laws to be passed by a two-thirds instead of five-sixths majority,

After the Communist Party's election defeat its rival wings made up their differences sufficiently to form a single parliamentary group. Potentially more significant for the future of the left was the first congress in May of socialists belonging to the People's Democratic League. In June 1982 the League's socialists had decided to create their own separate organization within the League. The May congress decided to set up an executive committee, agreed on programme guidelines for the new organization, and demanded equality between socialists and communists within the League.

On 24 September the Government presented its Budget for 1984. Based on the assumption of nominal wage increases of 8 per cent from April 1984 (compared with 10 per cent in 1983) and hopes of stronger demand in Western export markets, the Budget aimed at reducing inflation to 6 per cent and lowering unemployment, especially among young people. An agreement with the Conservatives on 24 November ensured the Budget's passage through the Eduskunta.

On 13 May the long and eminent career of Centre Party politician Ahti Karjalainen ended when President Koivisto dismissed him from his post as Governor of the Bank of Finland. Mr Rolf Kullberg was appointed as his successor on 27 May.

On 28 October the Eduskunta voted unanimously to extend the Treaty of Friendship, Cooperation and Mutual Assistance with the USSR beyond its expiry date of 1990.

AUSTRIA

At the general election on 24 April the ruling Socialist Party (SPÖ) lost its absolute majority, relinquishing four seats to the People's Party (ÖVP) and another to the Freedom Party (FPÖ). Nonetheless, with 90 seats to the ÖVP's 81 and the FPÖ's 12, the SPÖ remained the largest party in Parliament and, after a short period of negotiation, an SPÖ-FPÖ coalition Government was sworn in by President Rudolf Kirchschläger on 24 May. Immediately after the election Dr Bruno Kreisky, Federal Chancellor since 1970, announced that he would not stand again for this post. His successor as Federal Chancellor was Dr Fred Sinowatz, previously Vice-Chancellor and federal Education Minister. Herr Norbert Steger, leader of the FPÖ, became Vice-Chancellor and Minister of Commerce, his party receiving in addition the Ministries of Defence and Justice and three junior ministerial posts. In addition to Herrn Sinowatz and Steger, the new Government team included the following: Minister of Foreign Affairs, Erwin Lanc (SPÖ); of Finance, Herbert Salcher (SPÖ); of Internal Affairs, Karl Blecha (SPÖ); of Justice, Harald Ofner (FPÖ); and of Defence, Friedhelm Frischenschläger (FPÖ).

Although Dr Kreisky maintained his active interest in international affairs, particularly in the problems of the Middle East and the Third World, his departure from national politics was universally acknowledged as the end of an era. He made his farewell speech to Parliament in September and resigned the SPÖ party chairmanship at the party congress in October, being succeeded in this function also by Dr Sinowatz. Neither his departure nor the move to coalition government produced any changes in Austrian foreign policy. Significantly, the two major visits of the year were to East European countries. President Kirchschläger became the first Western head of state to visit East Germany, from 11 to 14 October, and Chancellor Sinowatz's first official visit was to Hungary, from 15 to 17 November. The most important foreign guest of the year was undoubtedly Pope John Paul II, who visited Austria from 10 to 13 September.

Throughout 1983 the new Government was mainly preoccupied by the economy. The 1983 Budget in particular threatened to result in a much larger deficit than planned. In attempting to deal with this problem, the Government was constrained partly by the reduction in planned rises in personal taxation agreed for the sake of FPÖ participation in the coalition; partly by the commitment to full employment and improved social benefits which remained the SPÖ's key economic aim. The extensive package of austerity measures announced in September sought accordingly to safeguard employment and to encourage small and medium-sized industrial enterprises, but was primarily aimed at increasing revenue and decreasing expenditure; and further measures intended to reduce the budget deficit were contained in the draft 1984 Budget presented to Parliament on 19 October. In that month the annual rate of inflation stood at 3·6 per cent, with 4 per cent of the work-force unemployed, while for the second quarter of 1983 GDP had shown a real growth rate of only 1·5 per cent over the same quarter of the preceding year. Although by December forecasters were predicting a slight upturn in the economy, the immediate prospect was for a perceptible fall in the standard of living of the average Austrian consumer.

Although the coalition's first few months in office were otherwise relatively untroubled, there were some signs of stormier waters ahead. The position of the former Vice-Chancellor and Finance Minister, Dr Hannes Androsch (see AR 1980, p. 159, and 1981, p. 164), still divided the SPÖ, and tension was developing between the FPÖ's liberal and nationalist wings. The environmentalist parties had failed to win a parliamentary seat at the general election, but they still presented a potential threat. More immediately, the ÖVP had gained votes and its leader Dr Alois Mock had increased in standing. This trend was confirmed in the provincial elections held in Lower Austria on 16 October, when the ÖVP unexpectedly added three seats to its existing majority, in spite of allegations of financial corruption in the local party. By the end of the year, however, this affair had become an embarrassment to the ÖVP nationally, because of the refusal of the provincial Governor, Herr Siegfried Ludwig, to relinquish his parliamentary immunity and submit to judicial investigation.

SWITZERLAND

While the economic situation of Switzerland slowly improved and the inflation rate subsided to less than 2 per cent, politically the year came to a stormy and unforeseen end. The so-called 'magic formula' for the composition of the Federal Council, namely, two Socialists, two Liberal-Radicals, two Christian Democrats and one representative of the People's Party (formely Farmers' Party), that had been established at the end of 1959 was shattered after the election of the Government in December 1983. The Socialists announced that they would consider whether to leave the seven-member Government, and therefore assume the role of an opposition, at an extraordinary party congress in February 1984.

After ten years in high office two Federal Councillors, Vice-President Willy Ritschard, a Socialist, and the Liberal-Radical Georges-André Chevallaz, announced their resignation with effect from the end of the year. Some weeks later Mr Ritschard collapsed and died. At once the party leader, Helmut Hubacher, MP, declared that the time had come, twelve years after the introduction of women's political rights, to elect a woman. The parliamentary party, somewhat reluctantly, proposed Mrs Lilian Uchtenhagen, since 1971 a member of the National Council (People's Chamber), for election as Federal Councillor. To succeed Mr Chevallaz the Liberal-Radicals nominated Jean-Pascal Delamuraz, former mayor of Lausanne, a member of the Vaud cantonal government and of the National Council.

On 7 December the Federal Assembly, comprising 200 members of the People's Chamber and 46 of the Council of States, elected Mr Delamuraz, but Mrs Uchtenhagen was rejected by 124 votes to 96 in favour of the Socialist Otto Stich, for 20 years a member of Parliament and manager of the Swiss Cooperative. The result provoked a tremendous uproar in the Socialist Party, mainly among the women members. Mr Stich accepted his appointment and took over the Treasury, Mr Delamuraz the Department of Defence. Mr Leon Schlumpf, since 1980 head of the Department of Transport and Energy, was unanimously elected Swiss President for 1984 and Mr Kurt Furgler, head of the Department of Economics, Vice-President. Within the Socialist Party there existed a generation conflict, the younger members longing for opposition, the elder statesmen and the trade unions resisting the loss of influence on government policy. Relations between the left-wing party and its centre and right-wing partners had suffered in face of Socialist opposition to nuclear power stations and national defence policy.

The Swiss electorate was called to the polls, as it must be every fourth year, to elect the National Council by proportional representation, which traditionally prevents any landslide, and the Council of States (cantons) by the majority system. A quite lively campaign failed to arouse the electorate: only 49 per cent of the citizens went to the polls. In the National Council the Socialists, with 51 seats, had lost two, as had the Christian Democrats, with 44 seats, while the Liberal-Radicals raised their numbers by three to 54. The old Communist Party fell back from three seats to one, but a new and very active left-wing group won those they lost. In the Council of States the Socialists lost three seats to the Liberal-Radicals, who scored 28·3 per cent of the poll, by far the highest figure of the four governmental parties. The slogan 'more freedom, less state' had proved successful.

On 27 February a referendum was called on a new distribution of the taxes on petrol, which yielded about 2,300 million Swiss francs per year to finance the network of national (dual-highway) roads. Their capital cost, roughly Fr. 30,000 million, had been almost covered. A constitutional rule to allot Fr. 500 million to the Federal State and Fr. 1,800 million to improving and extending the network as well as for secondary roads was adopted by 680,000 votes to 610,000; the opposition came mainly from the 'Greens', fighting against new and better roads. On the same day a majority approved new regulations for the economic use of electrical energy, but the draft failed because the majority of the 23 cantons said No. Only 32·4 of the voters went to the polls.

Six weeks after the general election the people and the cantons adopted new regulations for Swiss citizenship. Hitherto, if a Swiss man married an alien the wife automatically got Swiss citizenship, whereas if a Swiss woman married an alien her husband got Swiss citizenship only after a long procedure. The new regulation established equality of the sexes. But on the same day a clear majority (793,000 to 644,600) refused facilities for about 300,000 foreign young people brought up in Switzerland to become Swiss. The reaction against foreigners was unmistakeable. The number of coloured refugees (Tamils) increased.

The economic situation of Switzerland slowly but steadily improved. The extremely hot summer, after a wretched spring, brought records for for the tourist industry and for the production of wine.

Chapter 3

SPAIN—PORTUGAL—MALTA—GIBRALTAR—
GREECE—CYPRUS—TURKEY

SPAIN

THE million Spanish workers paid out of public funds received a shock at the start of 1983. On 19 January the Government began its promised reform of the administration with orders that as from 24 January they should start work at 8am, remain at work for the full seven hours a day, and not absent themselves except on official holidays. Subsequently it ruled illegal the receipt of more than one salary out of public funds. The practice of receiving more than one full-time salary had been widespread among professional men. Of the 202 recently-elected Socialist congressmen some 50 were still receiving their pay as university professors and 30 as state lawyers. The Prime Minister, Felipe González, proudly announced that for the first time in history Spanish Government Ministers would have a salary as Ministers 'and no other'.

By appointing to the Ministries of Economy and Finance, Industry and Agriculture men whose interpretation of socialism was not strictly marxist, González had allayed most of the fears of financiers and industrialists. On 23 February the Cabinet issued a decree-law expropriating Spain's biggest holding company, Rumasa. Rumasa had control of over 200 trade and industrial concerns, among them construction firms, hotels, vineyards, wine shops and department stores. It had over 50,000 employees, and in 1982 an estimated turnover of US $2,700 million, a sum equal to 1·8 per cent of Spain's GDP. Rumasa also controlled 18 banks with 1,200 branches. The 'unorthodoxy' of a commercial enterprise owning banks disturbed Spain's major private bankers and the Bank of Spain, and the expropriation pleased them. The Government assured the country that this was not a case of nationalization: Rumasa's companies would be returned to the private sector once the 'irregularities' in Rumasa's commercial conduct had been straightened out. According to the Government, Rumasa owed $600 million in taxes and another $1 million in unpaid social security contributions; furthermore, the Government had reason to suspect that in the near future Rumasa would not be able to service the debts it had incurred in acquiring control over so many enterprises.

The large Socialist majority in the Congress endorsed the Government's action on 3 March, at the end of a two-day debate. The Opposition challenged the legality of the use of a decree-law in this case, overriding the constitutional rights to private property and enterprise. The Government, in defence, cited the constitutional provision for legislation by degree in an instance of 'extraordinary and urgent necessity'. The issue was put to the Constitutional Court, which in December decided, by its chairman's casting vote, that the Government had been justified, finding that Rumasa's situation had called for immediate action, and that the decree as such did not infringe any of the rights enshrined in the constitution. Other courts would have to determine the future of Rumasa's companies and banks and establish what compensation, if any, should be paid to shareholders affected by the decree.

With its large overall majority in the Congress, the Government had no difficulty in fulfilling several of its election promises. The working week was reduced to 40 hours, and the minimum number of paid holidays increased to 30 days. A start was made towards the nationalization of the electricity grid system (but not the generating concerns), and the dismemberment of the oil and petrol marketing monopoly CAMPSA.

The Government faced the reality that the country had steel-manufacturing and shipbuilding capacity for which no use could be foreseen in the immediate future. In July it received Congress approval for the 'rationalization' of the two industries. The consequent closure of steel works and shipbuilding yards angered the communist-dominated Workers' Committees (*Comisiones Obreras*), but met with only mild reaction from the socialist UGT. Both labour organizations, however, had readily agreed in February with the employers' federations on keeping wage rises within a band of 9·5 to 12·5 per cent, and the number of workdays lost through strikes was unprecedently low. There was an 8 per cent increase in exports. The inflation rate was reduced to 12 per cent, although the strength of the dollar forced a further rise in the price of fuel.

Earlier proposals to amalgamate the Civil Guard and National Police (see AR 1982, p. 167) were abandoned. On 7 September the Cabinet reaffirmed the *status quo*. The 62,000-strong Civil Guard, though responsible for police work in the smaller towns and rural districts, and 'in peacetime under orders from the Minister of the Interior', was to retain its military 'internal organization, discipline and defence role'. Its officers were to remain on the Army List and would aspire to promotion to the highest army ranks and appointments. On the other hand, officers in the National Police had their military titles replaced by those more normal in civilian police forces, and the 47,000-strong body was amalgamated with the 8,700-strong plain-clothes *Cuerpo General de Policiá* as a civilian force.

The Minister of Defence, Narcis Serra, and the joint chiefs of staff committee cooperated during the year in planning a reform of the army. The period of compulsory service was cut by three months to 12, to reduce the standing army fom 255,000 to 165,000 men by 1987. Over the same period the officer corps was to be reduced by 25 per cent. Promotion to field and general rank was to be by virtue of aptitude rather than seniority, and at an increasingly younger age. Private political sympathies were not to be a bar to promotion. On the Minister's recommendation, provision was made in the Budget for an increase in defence spending from 2 per cent to 3·3 per cent of GDP. Orders were placed for the Franco-German ground-to-air missile, the shadow of Gibraltar standing in the way of its British rival. Spain's arms manufacturing capacity was to be amplified.

There was agreement also on two more fundamental changes. First, the country was to be divided into five instead of nine military regional commands; the operational units of the reformed and 'smaller but more mobile and efficient force', as Serra called it, were to be distributed among the regional commands and a central reserve with the object of defending Spain against foreign aggressors, and not, as they had been, against its 'internal enemies'. Secondly, the joint chiefs of staff committee was redefined as 'an advisory body to the Prime Minister and Minister of Defence' instead of 'a link in the chain of command'. The new wording implied the armed services' recognition of the supremacy of the civil power.

In April the Supreme Court gave its verdict on the previous Government's appeal against the leniency of the sentences on some of those convicted of taking part in the February 1981 attempt at a coup, and on their counter-appeal (see AR 1982, p. 165). The court not only upheld the 30-year sentences on Tejero and Milans del Bosch, but also increased Armada's from six years to 30, as having been equally responsible. Dismissing the original court-martial's findings that Torres and four other senior officers had been guilty only of conspiracy and not of rebellion, it increased their sentences to 12 and 10 years, sentences carrying the extra penalty of dismissal from the army. In July the colonels who had plotted to imprison the King and seize Madrid on the eve of the 1982 election (see AR 1982, p. 168) were tried without fuss, convicted and sentenced to terms of 15 and 12 years.

ETA terrorist activity continued sporadically throughout the year. Herri Batasuna, the Basque party which shared ETA's separatist extreme left objectives, embarked in July on action calculated to embarrass both the central and the autonomous Basque Governments; its adherents took down the Spanish flag from one after another town hall in Euskadi. The

Central Government, afraid of army reaction to this 'insult to the flag', ordered its police to enforce the law that the Basque flag should not fly on its own. They used a degree of force which alienated even the moderate Basque Nationalist Party. This 'war of the flags' was reaching a crisis point when, on 26 August, disastrous floods befell Euskadi. On 19 October an army captain whom ETA had kidnapped was found murdered. In the face of strong army reaction the central Government asked all parties to hold rallies and demonstrations to reaffirm popular support for democracy. The response was widespread. In Bilbao the demonstrators marched under the Basque flag alone, but without police intervention.

On 10 August the Constitutional Court had ruled unconstitutional 14 of the 38 Articles of the LOAPA—Organic Law on the Harmonization of the Autonomic Process (see AR 1982, p. 166). The findings pleased the Basques, but the central Government had introduced an Education Bill which, in Basque opinion, proposed fresh infringements of their hard-won Statute of Autonomy. The central Government rejected all Basque amendments to the Bill.

The Constitutional Court was now to be asked to rule on another law approved by the Socialist majority in the Congress. In February the Government had tabled an Abortion Bill. Catholics and a substantial body of doctors campaigned against it to no effect, and the Bill had been passed by 186 votes to 109. Its opponents had thereupon referred it to the Court, since the constitution affirmed the right to life of everyone. In November, the Minister of Education demanded the withdrawal from all schools of a catechism in which abortion was explicitly equated with murder. The ban was withdrawn only after strong representations. In practice the Government was also breaking its promise to provide religious education in state schools for the children of parents who demanded it. The Education Bill's provisions appeared, furthermore, to deny the constitutional right of parents to send their children to schools of their choice, for it stipulated that a teacher's religious beliefs were not to be a bar to appointment in any school.

In international affairs, the Government had an uneven record. It negotiated a four-year fishing agreement with Morocco at the cost of lending it $500 million. The status of Gibraltar continued to hamper friendly and even commercial relations with the UK. Spain endorsed the Argentine resolution on the Falklands at the UN; it would not buy British-made weapons for its armed services. González in vain asked President Mitterrand to deny ETA terrorists sanctuary in France and to withdraw his objections to Spain's entry into the EEC. His most popular action was to condemn US intervention in Grenada and Central America. His own party pressed him to hold the promised referendum on whether Spain should remain in Nato, but this he postponed *sine die*.

PORTUGAL

President Eanes gave Vitor Pereira Crespo till 15 January (see AR 1982, p. 170) to nominate his Government. The President did not approve Crespo's choice and asked the Council of State to determine whether he was bound to accept it. The Council divided equally for and against. Eanes therefore announced that he would call a general election, but first Francisco Pinto Balsemão, recalled to head a caretaker Government, would have to pilot a provisional budget for 1983 through the Assembly. He did so on 5 February and Eanes chose 25 April, the ninth anniversary of the Revolution, as election day, to the delight of the left and the chagrin of the rest.

The Balsemão Government had failed to improve the country's economy during 1982. In the face of trade union agitation it had not enforced its proposed 16 per cent limit on public sector wage increases. Home production had remained stagnant; there had been a record demand for imported goods. Portugal had had to import 74 per cent of its food requirements. The visible trade deficit had exceeded $5,000 million; the total foreign debt had risen to $12,000 million. Many of the loans were short-term and due for repayment or renegotiation during 1983.

The Democratic Alliance of Social Democrats (PSD), Centre Democrats (CDS) and Monarchists (PPM) had proved a failure. Its component parties decided to contest the elections separately. At hastily-arranged congresses, the CDS chose Francisco Lucas Pires as leader in succession to Freitas do Amaral who had resigned over the nomination of Crespo as Premier (see AR 1982, p. 170), and the PSD appointed a triumvirate to take it through the election after Balsemão had renounced his leadership on 8 February.

Mario Soares, as leader of the Socialist Party (PSP), promised 'a hundred measures in 100 days' if the electorate gave the Socialists an overall majority in the Assembly. He did not belittle the seriousness of the economic situation: there would have to be negotiations with the IMF and foreign banks for further loans, and severe cuts in and rigid control of government spending; the escudo would have to be devalued again.

The PSP received 36·3 per cent of the votes cast, giving it 100 of the Assembly's 250 seats; the PSD received 27 per cent (76 seats), the CDS 12·4 per cent (30 seats), the communist PCP and PDM 18·2 per cent (44 seats). The PPM and various radical republican parties polled percentages too small to entitle them to a single seat.

Soares was accordingly invited by President Eanes to form a Government. With none too happy memories of trying to govern without an overall majority in the Assembly during 1976 and 1977, he sought an alliance with the PSD. After five weeks of hard bargaining, he reached an agreement with the PSD triumvirate on 4 June. Priority had to be given to the drafting of a plan to reduce the foreign debt over the next two or three years. Home production was to be encouraged to its maximum, and the adverse balance of payments righted. The process of allowing private enterprise to compete with the state-controlled industrial concerns was to be resumed—the Bills to that end introduced by Balsemão had not completed their passage through the Assembly when it had been dissolved. The laws on the dismissal of workers and on strikes and picketing were to be revised. Corruption in the civil service and private enterprise was to be fought. The armed forces were to be modernized. Portugal was to remain in Nato and keep up the pressure for admission to the EEC.

Soares allocated seven of the 17 portfolios in his Cabinet to the PSD. He chose Carlos Mota Pinto, the senior member of the PSD triumvirate, as his Minister of Defence and Deputy Prime Minister. The new Government, the fifteenth since the 1975 revolution, took office on 9 June and its programme was approved in the Assembly by all except its Communist members.

The new Finance Minister, Ernani Lopes, professionally an economist and previously Portugal's ambassador to the EEC, set about his task with vigour.

In June he devalued the currency by 12 per cent, and to discourage unproductive borrowing raised interest rates to 30 per cent. The foreign debt now stood at over $14,200 million—58 per cent of the nation's GDP. He paid off a loan of $400 million by selling 34 tonnes of gold, and, offering gold as security, raised new loans totalling $600 million. In August the IMF granted Portugal a standby loan of $480 million, committing Portugal to austerity. Lopes persuaded the Government into authorizing severe reductions in subsidies on fertilizers, sugar, bread and milk, and high rises in the prices of petrol and public transport. In October he presented a daringly tough Budget, which was approved by the Assembly with opposition again only from the Communists. Wage rises in the public sector were to be kept well below inflation rate. Tax evasion and smuggling were to be severely punished.

Soares, too, showed unprecedented energy. By the end of the year most of what he had promised was in the process of fulfilment. The communists had warned him of a 'hot autumn' if he went ahead with his proposed labour legislation. Undaunted, he had introduced a law enabling the many enterprises—public and private— which were in severe economic difficulties to lay off surplus workers for up to two years, during which time they would be paid 60 per cent of their wages either by the company or, if the company could not afford it, by the state. Public response to communist calls for demonstrations and strikes was limited. Soares' popularity increased. He was in fact firmly carrying out what the previous Government had promised and left unfulfilled.

MALTA

In a troubled year the principal domestic issues were the continuing dispute over television broadcasting and new legislation on Church property. The Nationalist opposition re-entered Parliament in March but continued its boycott campaign of products advertised on the state-controlled television (see AR 1982, p. 171) until 30 December. The Government counter-attacked by exerting pressure on businessmen to advrtise and by threatening to control imports.

In July the Government introduced legislation giving it the right to appropriate Church property which was not clearly documented or which had been held for more than ten years. The Church was given until 15 October to respond; Archbishop Joseph Merciece pronounced the law 'unacceptable' and sought satisfaction in the courts. Dr Mifsud Bonnici, Mintoff's designated successor, argued that 'a good part of the property was acquired on the pretext that the Church could go on saying Masses for the repose of souls indefinitely. We consider that a person enters heaven under his own steam.' Mgr Philip Calleja, in charge of the Church's finances, accused the Government of a 'systematic campaign against the Church', and on 8 September there was a further quarrel over the holding of an open-air Mass in Valletta during the International Marian Congress in Malta.

Party animosities turned to violence on the night of 25-26 November when more than 100 police ransacked the Nationalist Party headquarters and press offices in search of 'cordless telephones'. Dr Fenech Adami and the party's general secretary, Louis Galea, protested, but secured no redress.

From 1 January Malta was a member of the UN Security Council. In March the European Parliament accused the Government of infringing civil liberties in Malta, and the combative style of Mintoff's Labour Administration was maintained not only against the old adversary, Britain, but European governments in general. Early in March the Government demanded that Britain should pay the cost of removal of shipwrecks and unexploded bombs in the Grand Harbour and round the island of Filfla; on 29 July, Malta's delegate to the European Security Conference in Madrid, Evarist Saliba, refused to sign the final document on the grounds that it did not deal adequately with the problem of arms reductions in the Mediterranean (see Pt. XI, Ch. 3).

Anthony Price, a British army deserter, was arrested in Malta on 13 April and accused of plotting to assassinate Mintoff. The trial began on 5 August but Price was released from prison and deported in September.

GIBRALTAR

It was a year of stalemate—argument without action, a familiar feature of the triangular relationship between Gibraltar, Spain and Britain. The sticking-point, as always, was the question of sovereignty *versus* the wishes of the people of Gibraltar, although a new problem emerged, that of interpretation of the April 1980 Lisbon agreement (see AR 1980, p. 171). Spain had opened the border to pedestrians in December 1982, but that was all. On 16 March talks concerning the agreement took place in London between the Spanish Foreign Minister, Sr Fernando Morán, Mr Francis Pym (then Foreign Secretary) and Mrs Thatcher. In July, Sr Morán called for a reciprocal gesture by London to match the concession to pedestrians, whereupon Her Majesty's Government stressed the need to lift all remaining restrictions on the frontier under the terms of the agreement.

In April, the week-long customary naval exercises were held by Britain in the Atlantic, and HMS *Invincible* entered Gibraltar at the head of a small flotilla. The newly-elected Socialist Government under Sr Felipe González twice protested to the British ambassador in Madrid. Dockworkers on the Rock also protested by going on strike, not against the naval visit—indeed, they sent a note of apology to the men on the ships—but against the decision by London to close down the naval dockyard facilities in Gibraltar.

An announcement in London on 27 July spelled out the terms of closure. A saving of £10 million to the Defence Ministry would be offset against payment of £28 million to compensate for the estimated loss of 1,000 jobs. The UK Government would also help over the privatization of the dockyard, which, it was hoped, would find commercial employment. Sir Joshua Hassan, who began the year by visiting London at the start of a vigorous campaign to stress the urgency of the problem of unemployment, was reluctantly prepared to explore the possibility; Mr Joe Bassano, for the Opposition and for the Transport and General Workers Union, was decidedly opposed.

As the year drew to a close, it brought nearer the date in 1986 when Spain would be a full member of Nato and of the EEC. Yet the deadlock continued. In July, Sr Morán had pointed to the anomaly of one member of the European Community maintaining a colony on the territory of another. Mrs Thatcher spoke of the need to end all restrictions on the border before Spain was admitted to the EEC. On 16 December the Spanish Government announced that Gibraltarians would be able to make more than one visit a day to Spain during the Christmas period. And that was that.

GREECE

The most important developments affecting Greece in 1983 were the agreement with the American Administration over the future of the US bases in the country; the Greek presidency of the EEC during the second half of the year; and the unilateral declaration of an independent Turkish republic in northern Cyprus.

The signing of the bases agreement on 8 September ended a long period of uncertainty over the future of US military installations (two bases near Athens, two on Crete and minor installations elsewhere in Greece), whose status had first been called into question by Constantine Karamanlis after the fall of the military dictatorship in 1974. While in opposition Andreas Papandreou's Pasok had called for the outright removal of the bases and had bitterly criticized New Democracy for negotiating over their future. Once in power, however, Pasok resumed the negotiations that had been broken off by the Government of George Rallis shortly before the 1981 elections. The final terms provided for the bases to remain *in situ* until 1988, when either side could give notice of closure. If the Greek side requested closure then the US would have 17 months in which to close down its operations. The Greek Government gained the right to restrict the use of the bases in times of emergency in order to safeguard 'vital national security interests', while Washington undertook that the existing military balance between Greece and Turkey would be maintained. For 1983-84, for instance, credits for military equipment amounting to $500 million were proposed for Greece, against $715 million for Turkey. The extraterritorial status of US military personnel, which had been the subject of much controversy, was not abolished. While the settlement clearly provided that the bases agreement was 'terminable', it was not, as the Government claimed, an agreement for their removal. Much would depend on the political complexion of the Government in office in 1988.

Greece's tenure of the EEC presidency provoked considerable controversy when on 12 September the Foreign Minister Yannis Haralambopoulos, at a meeting of EEC Foreign Ministers in Athens, exercised his presidential powers very substantially to tone down criticism of the Soviet Union over the shooting-down of the South Korean airliner. Mr Haralambopoulos's call for the 'normalization' of relations with the Polish military junta and his reiteration of Mr Papandreou's earlier call for a six-month delay in the siting of Cruise and Pershing missiles in Europe further aroused the wrath of his European colleagues. There was little disposition, however, to blame the Greek presidency for the fiasco of the Athens summit in December, while the Greek Government made no effort to exploit the presidency to further its aim of renegotiating the terms of Greece's accession to the EEC.

The unilateral declaration by Mr Rauf Denktash of an independent 'Turkish Republic of North Cyprus' on 15 November (see p. 171) provoked outrage in Greece. Mr Papandreou refused to consider participation in tripartite talks with the other guarantors of the 1960 constitutional settlement in Cyprus, Britain and Turkey, insisting that negotiations with Turkey were inappropriate while the Turkish army was in occupation of Northern Cyprus. The open disagreement that emerged between Mr Papandreou and Mr Spyros Kyprianou, the Cypriot President, over the best way of handling the crisis forced President Karamanlis to act as mediator between Athens and Nicosia.

A meeting at Strasbourg on 26 April between Mr Haralambopoulos and his Turkish opposite number, Mr Ilter Turkmen, at which both sides agreed to refrain from provocative action, had held out some hope for improved relations with Turkey. In September, however, Greece boycotted the Nato exercise 'Display Determination 83', lest participation be interpreted as acquiescence in the Turkish claim that the island of Lemnos should be demilitarized. Subsequently Greece complained of infringements of its air space by both Turkish and US aircraft.

In late February the first official visit to Greece by a Soviet Prime Minister took place but the final communique offered no support for the Greek position in the Aegean dispute with Turkey. In late April Greece called off a proposed visit by the US Assistant Secretary of State for European affairs, Mr Richard Burt, after he had criticized Greek foreign policy while on a visit to Ankara. In early June Mr David Kimche, the secretary-general of the Israeli Foreign Ministry, was invited to Athens in an apparent effort to improve relations with Israel in the wake of Mr Papandreou's outspoken support for Mr Yassir Arafat and the PLO.

In June the Government announced plans for the convening of a Balkan summit meeting in 1984 to discuss, *inter alia*, a nuclear-free zone in the Balkans. Relations with Yugoslavia took a turn for the worse when the Yugoslav Prime Minister, Mrs Milka Planinć, during an official visit in late October, urged her Greek hosts to accept as an 'historic reality' the existence of a Slav minority in Greece and to regard it as a bridge between the two countries. The official Greek response was not made public but Mrs Planinć's remarks were known to have caused considerable disquiet in Athens.

On 27 February rumours of an attempted coup by army units in the north of Greece were denied by the Government, although Pasok and Greek Communist Party (KKE) militants throughout the country were placed on alert. On 20 March Mr George Athanassiadis, the publisher of the right-wing newspaper *Vradyni*, and on 15 November Captain George Tsantes, a naval attache at the US military aid mission, were assassinated, apparently by extreme left-wing terrorist groups.

The severity of the economic problems facing Greece showed no sign of diminution. The drachma was devalued by 15 per cent in January and continued to fall against the dollar and other hard currencies throughout the year. Unemployment remained at approximately 10 per cent and strikes, directed against the tough wage-freeze imposed at the end of 1983, took place among public transport workers, taxi-drivers, hospital employees and school teachers. Further industrial unrest was occasioned by the introduction in May of legislation severely limiting the right of public sector unions to strike. The reaction to this legislation was, however, muted by the fact that it was backed by the Pasok-controlled General Confederation of Greek Workers.

There was some indication that 'big business' was being made the scapegoat for the Government's continuing economic difficulties. In September, only a few days after Mr Papandreou appeared to be holding out an olive branch to industrialists in a speech at the Thessaloniki trade fair, the Government suddenly announced that it had evidence of serious malpractices on the part of thirteen directors of the AGET/Iraklis cement company, one of the largest and most successful industrial enterprises in the country. The original board resigned, to be replaced by a board nominated by the state-owned National Bank of Greece. At the same time the pro-Government press launched a witch-hunt to uncover the names of the many businessmen alleged to have illegal bank accounts in Switzerland. At a huge rally in October, held to mark Pasok's first two years in power, Mr Papandreou announced an end to the wage-freeze and the restoration of index-linking of wages. Shortly before Christmas wage increases for 1984 were announced in excess of the rate of inflation.

In May, the Greek Cabinet decided to make a formal claim for the return of the Elgin marbles and on 13 October an official request was lodged with the British Foreign Office.

CYPRUS

The year saw a depressing deterioration in relations between the Greek and Turkish Cypriot communities, still living without contact in their separate sectors of the island, divided by the Turkish invasion of 1974. Attempts to pursue the goal of a united federal republic steadily petered out, a promising United Nations initiative ran aground and the worsening situation collapsed into a dangerous crisis which made world headlines.

The talks between the two communities under the auspices of the UN were suspended early in the year to allow the Greek Cypriots to concentrate on a presidential election campaign. Although the Turkish Cypriot minority—some 20 per cent of the population—had withdrawn from the Republic's political processes, the presidency and government elected by the Greek Cypriots were internationally recognized as legal in fact and in law. The presidential election brought no surprises. Cyprus is a vigorous multi-party democracy, but national voting patterns change slowly. The incumbent President, Spyros Kyprianou, in making an alliance with the AKEL (Communist Party) combined the 20 per cent vote of his own Democratic Party with AKEL's 34 per cent. He was opposed by Glafkos Clerides, whose Democratic Rally right-wing party commanded about 34 per cent of the electorate, and by Dr Vassos Lyssarides, leader of the EDEK Socialist Party.

In a bitterly-contested election campaign personalities and policies on the handling of the Cyprus problem virtually wiped out economic and social issues. Mr Kyprianou won with 56·5 per cent of the valid vote. Mr Clerides got 34 per cent and Dr Lyssarides 9·5 per cent. Voting was compulsory and keen public interest assured virtually a 100 per cent turn-out. Fears of a communist takeover proved groundless. The AKEL party was committed both to democracy and to free enterprise, and only on foreign policy issues urged adherence to a Moscow line. Mr Kyprianou, himself centre-right, made no changes to his existing Cabinet and did not offer AKEL any ministries.

With the election victory secured, the Government turned to a vigorous international campaign seeking support for moves to solve the division on the island. This 'internationalization' of the Cyprus problem enraged Mr Denktash. Greek Cypriots, supported by Athens, saw the Cyprus problem as one of invasion and occupation by Turkey and therefore the concern of the international community. Turkish Cypriots said it was purely an internal, intercommunal problem. Thus when the Government went to the UN General Assembly in May and won an astounding measure of support for a tough resolution calling for the immediate withdrawal of Turkish troops, Turkish Cypriots were infuriated. An angry Mr Denktash told the London *Times* that he would end the Cyprus problem by declaring independence. Back in Cyprus he announced that he was cancelling the intercommunal talks scheduled for the end of that month. Having secured maximum international press coverage he thus rendered the Government's victory in the UN pyrrhic.

The General Assembly resolution asked the Secretary-General, Sr Perez de Cuellar, to take a special interest in Cyprus. In August he produced a two-page document submitting tight negotiating alternatives to the two communities for their views. Among the possibilities proposed were Turkish concession on territory, a rotating presidency and a power-sharing federal system. A row among Greek Cypriots over how to handle the proposals resulted in the resignation of Foreign Minister Nicos Rolandis, who urged their acceptance. Eventually, Mr Kyprianou accepted 'the UN involvement and the method of approach' but effectively stalled on accepting the proposals as a negotiating position. Seizing advantage of Greek Cypriot divisions, Mr Denktash brushed the

UN initiative aside and demanded a summit meeting with the President, thus taking the initiative once more. He again threatened independence if the meeting was not arranged.

While the Secretary-General was arranging the requested meeting, to which Mr Kyprianou tacitly agreed, Mr Denktash, on 15 November, astounded the Government, the diplomatic corps and the United Nations by suddenly closing the Nicosia border crossing-point, calling an emergency session of his own Turkish Cypriot Assembly and declaring an independent 'Turkish Republic of North Cyprus'. Tension rose to fever-point and there were immediate fears of open war, but the Government, though shocked and furious, immediately declared that there was no military option, and that the assault on the Turkish Cypriot move would be diplomatic.

Turkey, while protesting that Denktash had taken even Ankara by surprise, immediately recognized the new state and was alone in so doing. International condemnation was loud, and the Government swiftly won a Security Council resolution calling for a reversal of the move in the North. This was quickly followed by a successful effort to have exports from North Cyprus barred from concessions under the Cyprus-EEC association agreement. The year ended with the island plunged in gloom about the future. But already there were signs that the United States and other Western powers, shocked at the imminence of another dangerous clash in the turbulent Middle East, were at last stirring themselves for an all-out offensive on the Cyprus problem.

The island's proximity to the Middle East crisis brought it into the news several times. For the second year running Larnaca town witnessed a major evacuation of Palestinian guerrillas when Yassir Arafat's forces were sent through there on their way out of Tripoli, Lebanon. In June, two Lebanese hijackers were gaoled after surrendering a Libyan airliner and its passengers to Cypriot authorities at Larnaca airport. During the Tripoli seige, 12 hijackers brought a Romanian ship into Limassol and also surrendered.

Economically, despite a continuing air of prosperity, the year was uneven, according to early analyses. Tourism and invisibles were still the most vigorous sectors. Tourism brought in 223,812 visitors in the first six months, up nearly four per cent, and foreign exchange reserves rose by almost one-third to $588 million. Industry and trade continued to pose big problems, and a drive to achieve an early customs union with the European Community was aimed at improving export performance, which was declining because Cyprus was no longer a low-cost labour country. The trade deficit in 1983 would probably be $750 million, compared with $628 million in 1982. At the end of the year the Government announced a $28 million indirect-taxation package aimed at cutting consumer spending on imported luxuries.

TURKEY

Turkey returned to parliamentary rule under new laws and with new institutions devised by the armed forces, but martial law remained in force throughout the country. Old political parties were not allowed to re-form, and their leading members were banned from politics—242 for ten years, and 481 for five. But new political parties were allowed to register, provided they had 30 founding members, all of whom had to be approved individually by the ruling military National Security Council (NSC). Under a new electoral law, promulgated on 13 June, all parliamentary candidates likewise had to be approved by the NSC.

The military made wide use of their discretionary powers. On 31 May they banned the new Great Turkey Party, accusing it of being a continuation of the old dissolved Justice Party. The two founders of the GTP, the former Prime Minister and leader of the JP, Süleyman Demirel, and twelve other prominent politicians of the JP and its centre-left rival, the Republican People's Party (formerly led by Bülent Ecevit), were exiled to a military base at Çanakkale, on the Dardanelles, whence they were released on 30 September. While the GTP remained permanently banned, two other parties were prevented by repeated disqualifications from completing the requisite panel of founding members by 25 August, the deadline for electoral registration. The two were the Right Path Party (believed to be an alias for the GTP and, therefore, for the JP), and the Party of Social Democracy (SODEP), which sought to group all those supporters of the old Republican People's Party who were prepared to work under the new dispensation. However, soon after the deadline the two parties were allowed to complete their panels of founders, thus acquiring the right to enter the local elections due next year. Professor Erdal Inönü, physicist son of the famous statesman Ismet Inönü, banned as a founder of SODEP, was nevertheless elected leader of the new party after the deadline for parliamentary elections. Of the 475 independent parliamentary candidates 438 were disqualified; permitted political parties also lost some candidates, but they were able to substitute others.

Three parties remained in the field for the elections on 6 November. The first was the Nationalist Democracy Party (NDP), formed by retired General Turgut Sunalp on 16 May, as soon as registration of new political parties began. Since the NSC Prime Minister, retired Admiral Bülent Ulusu, and some of his Ministers, as well as certain members of the nominated Consultative Assembly, entered the elections under the banner of the NDP, it was naturally regarded as the generals' favourite party. Ulusu's former private secretary, Necdet Calp, formed the second permitted party, the Populist Party, which sought to replace the Republican People's Party as the guardian of civil service interests.

The third party allowed to contest the elections was the Motherland

Party (MP), led by Turgut Özal, an engineer and liberal economist, who had been chief economic adviser of the JP Prime Minister, Süleyman Demirel, when the latter applied drastic free-market remedies to cure the economic crisis in January 1980. After the military coup of 12 September that year, Turget Özal was recruited by the NSC as Deputy Prime Minister in charge of the economy and presided over a remarkable recovery until his resignation in June 1982 in the wake of the collapse of the Kastelli finance house (see AR 1982, p. 180). Özal campaigned for economic liberalization, including selective privatization.

The campaign was confined largely to a few polite television appearances, and to well-ordered but ill-attended public meetings. On the eve of the election, Kenan Evren, President of the Republic and of the NSC (who had shed his third title of chief of the general staff when he retired from the army on 1 July), urged a vote for an Administration that would continue the policies of the NSC, and warned the people against the politician who had 'falsely' claimed exclusive credit for the successful economic recovery programme (in other words, Turgut Özal). Voters took the contrary course. Özal's Motherland Party came first with 45 per cent of the poll and gained an absolute majority of 211 out of 400 seats in the new single-chamber Parliament, elected for a term of five years. Necdet Calp's Populist Party was second with 30 per cent of the poll and 117 seats, and General Sunalp's NDP third with 23 per cent and 71 seats.

Bülent Ulusu resigned as Prime Minister when the new Parliament met on 24 November, and the NSC transformed itself into an advisory Presidential Council (its members retiring from the armed forces) on 6 December, when Parliament elected its Speaker (Necmettin Karaduman of the MP, and not Bülent Ususu, as had been widely predicted) and other officers. On 3 December the armed forces acquired a new head, General Necdet Urug, who was appointed the new chief of general staff. Özal was asked by President Evren to form the new Government, and his Ministers took office on 13 December. All were drawn from Motherland Party members of parliament, except for two outside specialists, one being the new Foreign Minister, Vahit Halefoglu, formerly ambassador in Moscow. The number of ministries was reduced, and an inner Cabinet formed of Ministers without departmental responsibilities. On 26 December the new Government was confirmed in office when Parliament endorsed its programme by 213 votes to 115. It promised liberal economic policies, a conservative foreign policy and the gradual relaxation of martial law when circumstances allowed it.

The transfer of legislative power to an elected but individually vetted Parliament, and of executive power to Turgut Özal's team, completed a process which had included the promulgation of new laws on higher education, labour relations, security courts and martial law. Universities were purged early in the year, when over 200 teachers were dismissed or resigned.

There were periodic security operations to hunt down suspected terrorists. According to official figures, between the proclamation of martial law and 31 May 1983 military courts had passed 33,000 sentences, including 173 death sentences, 25 of which were carried out. On 14 November, members of the executive of the Turkish Peace Association were given prison sentences of five to eight years. Among many trials still in progress at the end of the year were those of members of the executive of the marxist union confederation, DISK, and of Alpaslan Türkeş, leader of the dissolved extreme right-wing Nationalist Action Party.

It was in the interregnum between the parliamentary elections and the formation of the Özal Government that the NSC took its most important foreign policy decision of the year, when it decided on 15 November to grant immediate recognition to the Turkish Republic of Northern Cyprus proclaimed by the Turkish Cypriot Assembly on the island. This strained relations with the United Kingdom and Greece, the other two guarantor powers of Cypriot independence, and with other Western countries. While brushing aside protests, both the outgoing and the new Turkish Governments stated that a federal solution of the Cyprus problem remained possible.

In May, three Turkish soldiers were killed by raiders from Iraq. With the permission of the Iraqi authorities, Turkey then mounted a limited security operation across the border. The effect of the Gulf war on border security in the Kurdish areas preoccupied Turkey throughout the year. Another preoccupation was the threat posed to Turkish diplomats by Armenian terrorists: the Turkish ambassador in Belgrade was killed in March, and there were attacks in Paris, Brussels and Lisbon, where resolute action by the Portuguese authorities resulted in the death of the assailants and led to a lull in the campaign.

The economy continued to grow, although at a lower rate than in the previous year, while inflation rose again above 30 per cent and the balance of trade worsened. The contract for construction of a second bridge across the Bosphorus was awarded to the British firm (Freeman, Fox and Partners) which had designed the first bridge, completed in 1973.

At the end of October an earthquake devastated a mountainous area on the borders of the provinces of Erzurum and Kars in eastern Turkey, killing more than a thousand people.

V THE MIDDLE EAST AND NORTH AFRICA

Chapter 1

ISRAEL

SAVE when full-scale wars were fought, Israel never had a more tempestuous year than 1983. Hostilities in Lebanon grumbled on. The financial crisis was the worst in Israel's history. Prime Minister Menachem Begin resigned and there were difficult negotiations on the consolidation of the existing coalition Government under his successor, Yitzhak Shamir. There was periodic trouble in the West Bank and Jerusalem, and stirrings of protest in Israel itself against the settlements policy.

The financial crisis overshadowed all else. In January the Tel Aviv stock market crashed, many share prices falling by up to 40 per cent, and in the autumn came a fresh wave of selling, especially of over-priced bank shares. Inflation was rampant, Israel's foreign debt soared, and in May three no-confidence motions in the Parliament (Knesset) were narrowly defeated. In October the Minister of Finance, Yoram Aridor, resigned and was replaced by Yigal Cohen-Orgad.

The Bank of Israel had explained that Aridor's policies, consisting of reducing the prices of consumer goods to gain popularity for his Government, printing more and more money and making no serious attempt to curb government spending, were a classical recipe for disaster. His successor announced an austerity package in November, cutting public expenditure by 12 per cent and private by 5 per cent, levying taxes on pensions and charging fees for 300,000 out of 380,000 schoolchildren, and proposing a cut-back of spending on West Bank settlements. But on 30 December the Cabinet was unable to agree on these measures, and opposition to Cohen-Orgad's plans to reduce spending in the West Bank was particularly strong.

There was no improvement in the situation at the end of the year. During 1983 the trade deficit reached $4,100 million and the total foreign debt $23,100 million, while inflation was running at just under 200 per cent annually. Periodic devaluations of the shekel resulted in a continuing flight into dollars and other foreign currencies.

Immediate austerity measures included the doubling of the travel tax to roughly $100 per person per trip, cuts in overtime pay, minor reductions in civil service staffs by a phasing-out programme, and reductions in expense allowances. Plans to link the shekel with the dollar had to be dropped. A by-product of the financial crisis was a rash of strikes, the most damaging being that of the doctors, from mid-March until the end of June. Government threats of fines and imprisonment for doctors who refused to work led to many going on hunger-strike. The Government eventually agreed to a new salary-scale which represented a 60 per cent pay increase. In December came a threat from Israel's seven universities to close down unless given adequate budgets.

The national airline, El Al, was temporarily grounded by a strike against redundancy notices. Teachers went on strike in May for better pay, and on 16 October there was a partial but nation-wide strike against the austerity measures. In December postal workers struck over a proposed 12 per cent wage cut. Particularly disturbing for the Government was the report of the National Insurance Institute, on 27 January, that over 300,000 Israelis were living below the poverty line.

The war in Lebanon went on throughout 1983. The inquiry into the September 1982 massacres of Palestinian refugees in Beirut ended on 8 February with the recommendation that Defence Minister Ariel Sharon should resign or be dismissed, and with the censuring of chief of staff Raphael Eitan and three other officers of high rank as well as, in discreet terms, Prime Minister Begin. At least this official Israeli inquiry forced Sharon to resign his Defence office, and Israeli justice was vindicated by an admirably full and non-partisan report.

On 6 May an Israeli-Lebanese security pact was signed, and later ratified by both Governments, providing for total Israeli withdrawal from Lebanon, if Syrian and PLO forces did likewise. Syria refused to withdraw, and Arafat's Fatah quitted its remaining northern base at Tripoli only on 20 December, after a split in the PLO and a 'PLO civil war' in which Arafat was defeated. The Israeli-Lebanese pact came under attack in the outside world, ostensibly for hardening Syria's attitude and for complicating the position of the Gemayel Government in Beirut. Israel was also criticized for shelling PLO positions up to the last moment before withdrawal.

Israel was again under attack for announcing a partial withdrawal—as evidence of good faith, and in order to save casualties—to the line of the Awali river. This withdrawal was completed on September 4.

On 24 November six Israeli prisoners of the PLO were exchanged for 4,500 Palestinians and Lebanese, many of them convicted of terrorist crimes. Israel's Defence Minister, Moshe Arens, denied that this was a sign of weakness. Israel's reasons were that Arafat was going to be forced out of Tripoli and that his PLO had ceased to be an effective fighting force.

Israeli forces in Lebanon were constantly harassed. After one year of occupation of southern Lebanon, Israeli losses in dead and wounded reached 500 and 2,750 in July. On 4 November a suicide raid took place on the Israeli command-post in Tyre, on the pattern of the attacks on

American and French positions in Beirut; 29 Israelis were killed. These and other military incidents triggered sporadic fighting between Israeli and Syrian units both on land and in the air, and on 8 November Syria called up all its military reserves and all Israeli reservists were put on temporary alert.

By the end of 1983 Israel had lost 562 soldiers killed since the invasion of Lebanon began. The PLO, even after leaving Lebanon, left no doubt of its intentions, and on 28 December Arafat promised future PLO military action against Israel. One positive achievement was the evacuation, under Israeli protection, of nearly 15,000 Lebanese Christians, besieged in the Chouf mountains, who would probably have been massacred after surrender.

There was growing opposition in Israel to the continuing occupation of Lebanon, mainly by members of the 'Peace Now' movement. One of them was killed at a demonstration in February outside the Prime Minister's office in Jerusalem, and over 10,000 attended his funeral in Haifa. There were renewed calls for the resignation of Begin and his Government, and over 100,000 people attended a mass rally in June in Tel Aviv, when officers and soldiers returned their service ribbons of the Lebanon campaign. These and other events depressed the Prime Minster and on 30 August he confirmed rumours that he would resign.

Mr Begin had been deeply affected by the death of his wife, late in 1982. He stayed on in office, completely out of the public eye and allegedly a very sick man, until mid-September, when his designated successor, Yitzhak Shamir, announced his ability to form a new Government with the existing coalition parties. Shamir was confirmed in office only on 10 October, after going through the motions of trying to form a 'national' coalition at the prompting of a small group of his supporters. Apart from changing his Finance Minister, Shamir chose much the same team as before. His Government carried out a bridging action but had solved no problems when 1983 ended; indeed, public opinion polls showed the Labour Opposition ahead of the main Government party, Likud.

The Begin Government was shaken by the election on 22 March of Chaim Herzog, the Labour Party's candidate, as President. He won by 61 votes to 57 in the Knesset, after seven Government supporters changed sides. Herzog owed much to his moderation, experience and recognition abroad. He paid a visit to the USA later in the year and on 16 November explained Israel's aims and interests in a powerful speech to the UN General Assembly.

There was chronic trouble in the West Bank. Plans were published for building 57 new settlements and increasing overall Jewish population in the area from under 25,000 to over 100,000, a policy which caused unrest in refugee camps and schools and universities, led to frequent demonstrations and minor acts of violence, and provoked brawls between settlers and Palestinian Arabs. Support in Israel itself for the settlements policy declined and there were impressive demonstrations against it. A number of Arabs were killed by members of a self-proclaimed Israeli 'terror against terror' group. One curious event was the supposed 'mass-poisoning' of hundreds of Arab school-girls. This matter was never fully cleared-up, but investigations indicated mass-hysteria encouraged by young Arab ringleaders.

There were some disturbing events in Jerusalem. In March Jewish militants tried to occupy the Temple Mount area of the Old City. In July there were armed clashes and an internal Israeli quarrel, between archaeologists and religious sects, over excavations in the ancient city of David. On 16 October Mayor Teddy Kollek was assaulted by a mob of ultra-orthodox Jews, but later in the month he was confirmed in office in 'no-change' municipal elections, and a record 12,000 Jerusalem Arabs went to the polls, almost all to vote for him.

Then on 6 December four Israelis were killed and over 40 wounded in a bomb explosion in a Jerusalem bus. The PLO claimed responsibility. Two more Israelis died later of their wounds, but the outside world took remarkably little interest in the event (see p. 180).

Israel's external relations ran an uneven course. In the United Nations efforts to impose economic sanctions upon Israel, and to oust her from the International Atomic Agency and the International Labour Organization, failed. Relations with Egypt cooled perceptibly, but the EEC agreed to unfreeze economic aid for Israel while the USA granted a record increase of military aid, amounting to $1,700 million. This followed a successful visit to Washington in late November by Prime Minister Shamir. Indicative of Third World behaviour was the arrest in Zimbabwe of Bishop Muzorewa for allegedly saying that his country should follow Zaïre's example and reopen diplomatic relations with Israel.

Relations with Britain were uncertain. Annoyance was caused by talks between the British Foreign Office and the PLO. Controversy over the appointment of a new ambassador to London ended with that of Manchester-born Yehuda Avner. Israel was gratified by the action of Mrs Thatcher, in concert with Australian Prime Minister Bob Hawke, in blocking a pro-Arab declaration at the Commonwealth conference in Delhi in November, and by the stern gaol sentences on the three Arabs who tried to murder ambassador Shlomo Argov in London in June 1982.

Israel's population increased by 67,000 to 4,055,000 during 1982, and Jewish immigration increased slightly in 1983. But immigration from the Soviet Union fell to a record low—about 1,300 against over 51,000 in 1979. A fall of 25 per cent in total Jewish population outside Israel during the next 25 years was forecast by the Institute of Jewish Affairs.

Chapter 2

THE ARAB WORLD—EGYPT—JORDAN—SYRIA—LEBANON—IRAQ

THE ARAB WORLD

ANY hopes of peace which survived the fighting of 1982 were further dashed in 1983. Lebanese consolidation proved illusory. Syria and Israel still held most of the country, while armed minorities disputed the rest with the nominal Government. Encouraged by Israel, which harped on the supposed hostile designs of a Soviet-dominated Syria, and imagining it needed Israel's help in frustrating them, the US subordinated all else to superpower rivalry. It negotiated an Israeli-Lebanese agreement which rewarded Israeli aggression, was unacceptable to Syria and so could not achieve the US object of clearing Lebanon of all non-Lebanese forces. Syria reacted by encouraging armed opposition to the Lebanese Government and this led the US to reactivate the strategic cooperation agreement with Israel.

Meanwhile the PLO, instead of staying in Tunis to cultivate the political field where alone it could recoup 1982's military defeats, returned in strength to Lebanon under Syrian auspices and there fell apart. Yassir Arafat had to abandon his rapprochement with Jordan and leave the Levant to the hard-liners, portending renewed terrorism against Israel and loss of the PLO's solid political gains. But Arafat's reconciliation with Egypt lit up the year's last days. The Arabs were still deeply divided also by the Gulf war, Syria and Libya backing Iran and the rest Iraq.

Already in 1982 Arafat had failed to exploit President Reagan's offer to prevent, in effect, Israel's absorbing the occupied territories. Now on 17 January 1983 the minority PLO factions, meeting in Libya, refused 'all formulas permitting Jordan the right to represent the Palestinian people'. The Palestine National Council (PNC), meeting in Algiers on 14-25 February, condemned the Reagan plan and gave only grudging support to the Fez alternative (see AR 1982, p. 499); the hawks downed the doves, one of whom, Isam Sartawi, resigned in protest and was assassinated in Portugal on 10 April by the Syrian-backed gunmen of Abu Nidal. The doves had hoped to join King Husain in rescuing the occupied territories by associating them with Jordan. This plan failed in early April when a Husain-Arafat understanding was disowned by PLO radicals. On 10 April the Jordan Government announced that it and the PLO could not proceed with the agreed plan. Syria and Israel were delighted.

It had been earlier reported that Syria was organizing an anti-Arafat movement to condemn his preference for political over military action.

He had also unwisely promoted officers accused of cowardice in the 1982 fighting. In mid-May, after the failure of his talks with Husain, a rebellion against him began inside the dominant Fatah group. Syria was partly or wholly responsible, as was shown when the rebels were allowed to seize PLO premises in Damascus. On 22 June Arafat publicly attacked the Syrian Government, which expelled him on 24 June. Moving first to Tunis and then restlessly touring the Third World and communist countries (though not the Soviet Union, whose support for him was cooling) he reached Lebanese Tripoli on 16 September. All efforts—Arab, Soviet, Cuban and others—to reconcile him and the rebels had failed.

Here, despite being under siege, he scored or was credited with a notable success. The 1982 fighting had left a handful of Israeli prisoners in Palestinian hands. Negotiations for their release had been slowly proceeding; now Arafat's wing of the PLO secured a deal whereby on 24 November six Israelis were released in exchange for 1,000 Palestinian and 3,500 Lebanese detainees. Unfortunately for Arafat, this was followed by a sanguinary gaffe when on 6 December several Israeli civilians were killed by a bomb in Jerusalem which some PLO sources claimed was theirs, thus forfeiting sympathy and undermining the Israeli peace movement.

When the siege of Arafat's forces started they held two refugee camps outside Tripoli but they were soon driven from each in turn into the town itself. This Sunni centre had already seen violence between Shia supporters of Syria and their fundamentalist Sunni opponents and now seemed threatened by Syrian and anti-Arafat Palestinians and by Israeli bombardments, presumably intended to satisfy Israeli public opinion and demonstrate Israeli power. A meeting of Arab and non-aligned representatives in Damascus on 23-24 November negotiated a ceasefire, and Arafat with 4,000 of his men left Tripoli on 20 December in Greek ships under the UN flag, French naval protection and the baleful watch of Israeli aircraft.

Arafat's escape had been a blow in the eye for Israel and Syria. It had been achieved against protests by Israeli hawks but with the approval of the US Government, who had told the Israelis to pipe down. The Syrians had not, after all, brought the Palestinian movement under their entire control; Arafat's moderates, widely supported on the West Bank, and the marxists under Habbash and Hawatmeh rejected the Syrian line. The Gulf states, the Palestinians' paymasters, seemed behind Arafat.

Sailing south he was warmly received by President Mubarak on 23 December, to general surprise, Israeli fury and muted disapproval from some of his supporters. With his usual mobility he then hurried to Tunis via North Yemen, leaving there 1,000 of his men, the others having gone direct to North Africa.

Arafat had saved something from the wreckage, but the Palestinian position had deteriorated. Israel's colonization of the occupied territories, meeting only verbal opposition from the US (which vetoed an otherwise unanimous Security Council resolution of 2 August declaring it illegal) was proceeding apace, and Israel's new Prime Minister Yitzhak Shamir, was no less intransigent than Begin and had more US support.

EGYPT

Egypt remained close to the USA, on whose money it so much depended, but did not let this dictate its foreign policy and resisted American pressure to return its ambassador to Israel: 'this fuss', said President Husni Mubarak, 'is considered a direct intervention in Egypt's sovereignty'. Contact with the Soviet bloc increased. Rapprochement with the Arabs advanced, and Mubarak ended the year embracing Yassir Arafat. More fundamental than politics, however, was Egypt's struggle to stay financially afloat in an adverse climate.

In foreign affairs Egypt, like America's other Middle Eastern friends, wanted above all to see the US Government acting with greater determination against Israeli expansionism. Mubarak, who visited Washington in January and September (also the UN General Assembly, London and other European and Asian capitals, including Peking), and his foreign affairs team spoke persistently in this sense, though initially supporting the controversial Lebanese-Israeli agreement. The Government resisted US wishes for permanent rights to a base at Ras Banas and its construction by American firms instead of Egyptian. In February, after reported Libyan-Sudanese tension, four AWACS aircraft and the battleship *Nimitz* were sent to Egypt, which denied having invited them. Egypt condemned the US-Israeli military agreements of 29 November and the US had to organize a visit of mollification, followed by a special trip to Washington by Egypt's Foreign Minister. US aid to Egypt exceeded $2,000 million, over half being for defence.

Relations with Israel remained chilly and Egypt insisted that, before its ambassador could return there, Israel must evacuate Lebanon, halt Jewish colonization of occupied territory and return the Taba enclave which it had kept when evacuating Sinai. Egypt's rapprochement with the Arabs heightened its reluctance to take risks for Israel's sake, though it reiterated its loyalty to the Camp David agreements. The oil glut produced one piquant reversal of roles; now it was Egypt which insisted on Israel's taking all the oil it had contracted for as part of Camp David.

Arab-Egyptian reconciliation included several visits by Iraqi Ministers to Cairo and the signature with them of an economic cooperation agreement on 16 August. Egypt was supplying Iraq with Soviet arms and much-needed manpower; over one million Egyptians were now working in Iraq and 15,000 reported to be fighting there. In

April Jordan revived a lapsed trade protocol and in December signed an important new one; there, too, there was a large Egyptian community. Mubarak met King Husain and other Arab leaders at the February Non-Aligned summit in Delhi. The Foreign Minister visited Morocco, the first such visit since 1979. Egypt came out on Yassir Arafat's side in his dispute with Syria and the Palestinian radicals; when he escaped from Lebanon in December, Arafat's first visit was to Mubarak, who wanted to help build a Husain-Arafat axis.

Nothing brought Syria or Libya any closer, the latter being strongly opposed by Egypt in its policies towards Chad and Sudan. Integration with Sudan reached another stage—the opening by Mubarak of an Egyptian-Sudanese assembly, the Nile Valley parliament. Its first session (25-31 May) confirmed that integration was to be primarily strategic and political and was to develop only gradually.

With the Soviet bloc rapprochement was less dramatic. Soviet engineers returned to work on the High Dam and cultural and trade agreements were signed. To diversify its arms sources Egypt bought 200 Soviet tanks from Romania.

At home, in the drive against corruption, on 12 February Sadat's brother Ismet was condemned with his sons to imprisonment and sequestration, but released on 1 August. On 13 March two Ministers were dismissed in this connection; other scandals concerned US aid and the flight of a noted swindler. On 29 October the New Wafd party won their appeal to the Supreme Court for government recognition. Although the Coptic patriarch Shenouda remained exiled, Mubarak said on 28 October that he would be reinstated 'when the time came'. At Mubarak's suggestion, Parliament voted to allow representation to parties with 8 per cent of the popular vote, down from the 10 per cent originally proposed. The senate elections on 4 October gave the Government party their expected victory on a less than 50 per cent poll.

Despite these signs of political relaxation, there were recurrent arrests of communists, Libyan agents and fundamentalist militants. On 2 October the Interior Minister listed thirteen attempts in twelve months to unseat the Government; Parliament on that occasion agreed to extend the state of emergency for another year, but abolished or modified Sadat's laws against demonstrators and rumour-mongers.

The economy remained unsatisfactory, with the budget and the balance of foreign payments in serious deficit. Defence expenditure stayed high, nor was it politically possible to reduce food subsidies sufficiently to persuade the IMF to release its stand-by credit. The payments deficit reflected high imports, especially of food (Egypt being now one of the world's biggest eaters and importers of wheat) and declining or stationary foreign earnings. The oil glut reduced Egypt's exports and Canal revenues. Over three million Egyptian emigrants were believed to remit barely half of their $7,000 million earnings. However, at year's end the current account deficit was falling slightly, as remittances responded to better exchange management. Egypt owed up to $20,000 million abroad, costing a quarter of its export proceeds to service. Inflation was over 20 per cent. And the swollen and inefficient bureaucracy—over 11 million strong—still burdened the budget and strangled development in red tape; a new General Motors plant, opened on 3 May, had required seven years' negotiations.

JORDAN

King Husain's position was uncomfortable; he was friend to the US, which disregarded his advice; neighbour to Syria, vindictive and unscrupulous, and to Israel, arrogantly expansionist; and ally to a losing Iraq. To make matters worse, the US identified itself increasingly with Israel.

He was hoping to exploit the Reagan plan (see AR 1982, p. 498) by allying himself with moderate Palestinians to prevent, before it was too late, Israel's absorbing what remained of Palestine; only with Palestinian consent could he 'enter the peace process', as the Americans and Israelis called it. Yassir Arafat visited Amman in January, February and late March and was nearing agreement with Husain on somehow linking the West Bank to Jordan, but then retreated after opposition to him inside the PLO. Washington tried vainly to lure Husain into the peace process by promising that it would then 'do its best' to halt Jewish settlement in occupied territory. On 10 April Jordan announced that talks with Arafat had failed, the PLO having tried to modify an agreement already reached. Husain believed that Arafat had preferred failure to dividing the Palestinian movement.

In a message to President Reagan on 12 April Husain attributed the breakdown partly to the Americans' failure to recognize the PLO and criticized them for weakness—only doing their second-best in practice—towards Israel. Next day a Congressional sub-committee proposed to make further military aid to Jordan conditional on its recognizing and negotiating with Israel. However, Jordanian contact with the US on defence seemed to continue; on 12 October Israel radio publicized a US scheme to turn two Jordanian battalions into a 'rapid deployment force'.

Husain's dialogue with Arafat continued. One of the latter's closest counsellors saw the King on 3 May. On 22 June, answering a message from Arafat, the Jordanian Government denounced attempts to 'overthrow democracy inside the PLO and subvert its independence', meaning Syria's anti-Arafat campaign. On 26 August Husain, interviewed by a newspaper, blamed the American veto of a Security Council resolution condemning Jewish settlement of the West Bank and invited Arafat to renew their meetings. On 14 October Arafat spoke to a journalist of visiting Amman soon; another had already reported him as saying that a Palestinian-Jordanian dialogue on confederal ties between Jordan and a liberated West Bank was inevitable. Arafat himself was now besieged in Tripoli, but two of his senior colleagues saw the Jordan Prime Minister on 19 October.

By then a new measure was preparing which emphasized Jordan's role in Palestine—a meeting of the half-Palestinian Parliament which had not met since 1974, when Husain had renounced any claim to speak for the Palestinians. Officials spoke later of reconvening the Parliament simply to authorize the establishment of a new one, half elected from the East Bank and half being West Bankers, coopted or appointed. On 21 November Husain described Jordan as 'the defence line of the Palestinian land and people'. Egypt was busy promoting an Arafat-Husain meeting after Arafat's meeting with Mubarak (see p. 180).

Meanwhile Jordan had become a target for renewed terrorism. In May American buildings in Amman were attacked; by end-November there had been six bombings in Amman (including an attempt on the British embassy) and attacks, some fatal, on Jordanians in Athens, Rome, Delhi and later Madrid. All were ascribed by Jordan to the terrorist Abu Nidal, now based in Damascus.

As usual, Husain paid many visits abroad, spending September in the Far East. Particular interest attached to his visit to London on 17 March, heading an Arab League delegation which had been delayed by the Prime Minister's reluctance to admit a member of the PLO as part of it.

Jordan's economy, though healthier than those of most Middle Eastern states, had a worrying payments deficit, due to the failure of the Arabs, other than the Saudis and Kuwaitis, to meet their 1979 aid commitments. Iraq, formerly a generous aid donor and investor, was now borrowing from Jordan to maintain trade between them. The austere draft budget for 1984 proposed expenditure only a fraction up on 1983, despite 12 per cent inflation. Petrol prices were raised and income tax made to yield more.

According to the latest census Amman's population was over half the East Bank's total of 2·4 million.

SYRIA

Despite hopes that, once Israel agreed to leave Lebanon, Syria would follow, and notwithstanding a Lebanese-Israeli agreement on evacuation, Syria's forces remained in Lebanon, where they later clashed with America's. President Hafiz al Asad was out to humiliate PLO chairman Yassir Arafat, whose enemies he encouraged, until Arafat was expelled from Syria and Lebanon. Internally things seemed calmer, but Asad's illness in November put his continued dominance temporarily in doubt. The USSR strengthened its influence and re-equipped the armed forces, but Syria's cooperation with anti-Soviet Iran suggested that it was not quite the Soviet satellite Israel painted it to America.

Hostility to the Lebanese-Israeli agreement became the determinant of Syrian policy. Israel's success in forcing on Lebanon both sovereignty concessions and a new foreign policy seemed to Syria to threaten Lebanon's independence and Arab links and to impose a Camp David-style separate peace without solving the problems of Syria and Palestine. Syria also resented being omitted from the negotiations and the apparent US assumption that it would accept a *fait accompli*. Damascus further demanded the departure from Lebanon of 'the new crusaders', the US and France, denounced the 'Falangist hegemony' and called for Lebanon's expulsion from the Arab League.

US and Saudi efforts to persuade Syria nevertheless to evacuate Lebanon included President Reagan's 17 April message to Asad saying that Israel should exchange territory—the Golan—for peace. But Asad steadfastly rejected all such persuasions, reportedly asking the Saudis for $10,000 million as his price for evacuation. American and Saudi persistence in contacts with Damascus, and the disorders in Lebanon following Israel's partial withdrawal in September, brought Syrian acquiescence in intra-Lebanese agreement on a ceasefire and a national reconciliation conference. But the Shia suicide attacks of 23 October on the multinational force in Beirut reinforced US suspicions of, and hostility to, Syria, increased Israel's leverage in Washington and set Syrian and US forces firing at each other. Nothing suggested that Syria had organized the outrage (indeed on 22 July it had successfully liberated an American victim of Iranian terrorism, the president of the American University of Beirut, who had been abducted to Iran), but Syria had allowed the Iranians responsible into Lebanon. Already in May Syrian batteries had attacked US reconnaissance planes; now the Americans in attacking these batteries lost two aircraft, one pilot becoming a Syrian prisoner, and US warships shelled Syrian positions.

Besides combating a separate peace for Lebanon, Syria was as anxious as Israel that President Reagan's scenario for Israeli-Palestinian recognition and negotiations should fail, particularly as it starred King Husain of Jordan, whom Asad bitterly opposed. There were elements in Arafat's entourage ready for negotiation, and Syria was intriguing against him even before his talks with King Husain collapsed (see p. 183) and his Syrian-supported opponents rebelled against him. On 24 June Arafat was expelled from Damascus and later besieged, with Syrian backing, in Tripoli. However, again like Israel, Syria let him escape once it became clear that other Governments, Arab and Western, favoured his doing so.

At home less was heard of opposition to the Baath regime from the Muslim Brotherhood and other critics of alleged Alawite predominance.

(Two key regime figures, the Foreign and Defence Ministers, were, incidentally, Sunnis, not Alawites, and in December an Alawite pressure group under a brother of Asad's was reported to have been dissolved). But on 13 November Asad was compelled by alleged appendicitis to cancel what might have been a historic visit to Beirut. Later something graver was suggested and his duties were assumed by a directorate, in order to forestall, it was suspected, a takeover by his ambitious brother Rifa'at. Finally it was established that Asad had had a heart attack but was recovering. The powerful Alawite Information Minister, Ahmad Iskander, died on 28 December.

Syria's economy fared ill. Its support of Iran against Iraq and opposition to Arafat discouraged aid from the Gulf; indeed the Kuwaiti parliament voted to end it, as did the US Congress. Syria's rejection of Arab pleas to reopen the pipeline from Iraq cost it Gulf sympathy and transit revenue (Iran was supplying Syria's refineries). Soviet arms and technical assistance—some said there were now 9,000 Russians present—did not necessarily mean Soviet cash, and Libya's offer to replace Saudi subsidies was weakened by Colonel Qadafi's known preference for promising over paying. Meanwhile defence was costing more and more—an estimated $2,700 million, or 57 per cent of total current expenditure. Food imports were increasing and currency reserves were reported to be 75 per cent down from 1981.

LEBANON

Lebanon did not recover in 1983. Neither Israel nor Syria evacuated its territory, and a partial Israeli withdrawal aggravated the sectarian fighting. Syria fomented these conflicts, which forced the multinational force (MNF) from its supposed impartiality. Its involvement deepened after Iranian-inspired outrages. Lebanon suffered also from inter-Palestinian feuds (see p. 180).

As the year opened, east and north Lebanon were occupied by Syria, south and centre by Israel, with only Beirut and its environs in Lebanese hands. Nowhere was there effective central control; everywhere irregular forces were active. In greater Beirut the Maronite militia was still quasi-independent of the government; so was the Shia militia Amal. Syria's zone held Druze, Palestinian, Shia, anti-Syrian fundamentalist and, ominously, Iranian Shia forces. All the irregulars depended, to varying extents, on the occupying powers. Israel reportedly helped both Falangists and Druze in the Chouf (pronounced Shouf, the traditional transliteration being French) mountains, besides encouraging some guerrilla forces in the south and fighting others. The UN interim force remained in south Lebanon, and in Beirut the MNF was supposed by its mere presence to keep the peace until the Lebanese army, now being successfully trained and re-equipped by the US, could take over.

The Lebanese and Israeli Governments were negotiating, with US help, Israel's terms for evacuation. People had assumed that Syrian forces would leave directly after Israel's, but this was improbable without unconditional Israeli withdrawal. Although the Israelis' demands for concessions incompatible with Lebanese sovereignty were severely pruned under US pressure, they would not admit, by withdrawing unconditionally, that their invasion had been mistaken. Besides security against guerrilla operations they wanted to force the Lebanese Government towards a peace treaty, which the Syrians would certainly resist. Thus, inducing them to accept the agreement and withdraw their forces would be a formidable task anyhow, and they could not be expected to rubber-stamp an agreement reached without consulting them at all. Yet such appeared the US assumption.

By the Lebanese-Israeli agreement signed on 17 May Lebanon's obligations to Israel were to outrank its existing ones (meaning those to the Arab League and the PLO) and a joint committee was to develop Israeli-Lebanese trade and communications; in short, it was all but a peace treaty and thus unacceptable to Syria. Lebanon's Foreign Minister took the text to Damascus but would not let the Syrians see it; and when Philip Habib, the US emissary, proposed to come and explain matters he was warned off as 'an enemy to the Arabs'. Regular US-Syrian contacts continued but never induced Syria to accept the agreement.

In Lebanon there now arose, with Syrian incitement, in opposition to the agreement, a coalition (officially inaugurated on 23 July) under the hereditary Druze chieftain Walid Jumblatt, with one Sunni and one pro-Syrian Maronite colleague, to which Shia and Nasserist leaders soon acceded. Thus Syria's alienation had grave implications for internal security, especially in the Chouf, which dangerously overhung Beirut and was traditionally the Druze heartland, dominated by Druze chieftains and militias, though with many Christian and some Sunni inhabitants. In July 1982 Israel had allowed the Falange into the Chouf, which had produced intense Druze-Christian conflict. The crisis widened and deepened on 17 August when Israel's Defence Minister came to visit, not the Government, but the Falange commanders; this enraged Beirut's Muslims, Sunni and Shia alike.

The Israelis, unable to control the Chouf and suffering more casualties than during the invasion itself, had long been planning to leave it, though not the adjoining Beqa'a valley. The US urged Israel to delay till the Lebanese army could control the area. Reluctantly Israel waited, but tension still rose; the Druze refused replacement of Israeli by Lebanese troops, let alone the Falange, and used their strategic position to shell Beirut. Extra trouble began when the army clashed with Amal in south Beirut, with its many Shia refugees.

On 28 August the airport was forced to close. On 4 September the last Israelis left the Chouf, rejoining their comrades behind elaborate fortifications along the Awali river covering Sidon. On 6 September the Druze took Bhamdoun, a strategic Chouf village, and were soon struggling with the Falange and the Lebanese army for Souq al Gharb in the foothills.

President Amin Gemayel (pronounced Jimayyil) now invoked the MNF. This and the death by gunfire of MNF soldiers involved the force in sectarian fighting, reprisals and deterrent shellings, which continued amid frantic shuttle diplomacy, Lebanese, Saudi and American. On 24 September the US battleship *New Jersey* arrived with more marines. The next day brought agreement on a ceasefire and a 'national reconciliation conference' to include representatives of the four main communities, Maronite, Shia, Druze and Sunni. The conference, which eventually met in Geneva on 31 October and lasted three weeks, faced three problems—revision of the 1943 conventions on power-sharing in Lebanon, the country's relation to the Arab world and the future of the agreement with Israel, which Lebanon had not ratified. No agreement was reached on the first topic; on the second, the meeting agreed that 'Lebanon was an Arab country'. This almost decided the third topic, since the 17 May agreement had been meant to distance Lebanon from the Arabs. The agreement would surely now have to be suspended or modified if reconciliation was to proceed and the Syrians persuaded to leave if it were not, the Geneva meeting would have failed.

The ceasefire proved no more effective than its countless predecessors, and the dangers were aggravated by terrorism by the Iranian-led Shias in Baalbek. On 18 April a bomb had destroyed the US embassy, killing 87 people. The Geneva conference had not begun when, on 23 October, the same organization made simultaneous suicide attacks, using lorry-bombs, on US and French forces in Beirut, killing 239 and 58 people respectively. On 4 November a similar attack on Israel's Tyre headquarters killed 29 Israelis and 32 Lebanese and Palestinian detainees. These attacks produced demands for reprisals, the Israelis losing no time in bombing various guerrilla forces, while the French made a precision attack at Baalbek. The Americans threatened, without taking, reprisals but toughened towards Syria, which they blamed for the attacks.

Besides thus reinforcing the US conviction that Syria and behind it the USSR were causing all the trouble, these events pulled the MNF further into the fighting. The US maintained their right to defend their forces and, like Israel, to make unrestricted aerial reconnaissance. This climaxed on 3-4 December; Syrian guns, having been bombed by Israelis, fired on US reconnaissance aircraft; American planes then attacked the Syrians, losing two pilots; shelling of the US detachment followed, whereupon the *New Jersey* shelled Syrian batteries.

One extraordinary story was the siege of Deir al Qamar. This

Christian township in the southern Chouf became the refuge of thousands of Christians fleeing the Druze occupation. Negotiations to evacuate them stuck for weeks until on 15 December Israeli forces from the Beqa'a were allowed to escort them out.

Hardly less bewildering than the continual bloody flux in Lebanon was the worldwide *va-et-vient* of politicians trying to stem it. Emissaries, official and unofficial, American, French, Saudi, Druze, darted about. The key men were Americans—the Vice-President, the Secretary of State and three assorted trouble-shooters—and Saudis, one a royal prince, one a Lebanese-born business man. Gemayel himself went twice to Washington. His first visit in July was to press the accelerator—or indeed the starter—for the evacuation, while the Americans wanted him first to organize national reconciliation, which meant redistributing power from his own Christian minority to the Muslim majority. At his second meeting with President Reagan in early December Gemayel, on behalf of the Geneva conference, urged the freezing of the Israeli-Lebanese agreement, or its modification, to render it acceptable to Syria and the Lebanese opposition. This Reagan refused, offering money instead.

The intensified fighting had endangered and embarrassed the MNF (American, French and Italian with, since February, a dash of British) and the governments providing it. The MNF had not been sent to fight nor was it organized for doing so (no headquarters, unified command or uniform rules of engagement), and its mere presence could not keep things quiet. Through bad luck and wrong decisions it had become involved in fighting and exposed to terrorist attack; self-defence, its undoubted right, only increased its involvement. By year's end this dangerous situation and resulting apprehensions in the parent countries had brought pressure for its withdrawal. For their part the Israeli occupiers had been so frequently attacked and incurred such casualties that their further withdrawal or even evacuation seemed possible even before that of Syria. On 29 December there was an effective general strike against them in Sidon and they retaliated by virtually shutting off their zone from Lebanon proper.

Lebanon had been the centre of the Middle East's most serious crisis since 1973, while the superpowers glared at each other from behind their respective Israeli and Syrian protégés. For the Lebanese themselves, besides heavy loss of civilian life, the turbulence threatened economic ruin. The national debt had risen by 40 per cent in twelve months; the trade deficit had seriously widened; the currency was at its lowest ever; and material damage in Beirut and Tripoli was huge.

IRAQ

The war continued. Iran failed to break the stalemate militarily but refused any realistic peace negotiations, despite international appeals. A war of attrition favoured Iran: its finances were sound, Iraq's embarrassed. President Saddam Husain, whose removal was Iran's main object, showed no readiness to abdicate and threatened an air offensive on Iran's oil industry; the risks this implied for Gulf oil installations and navigation did not materialize. Iraq's habitual secretiveness shrouded both battlefield and internal developments.

In January Algeria was attempting mediation but found Iran still adamant. A new Iranian offensive on 7 February proved indecisive. Iraq's reprisals on Iranian naval and oil targets achieved only a big oil seepage into the Gulf. On 8 February Iraq invoked the Security Council, whose ceasefire call was rejected by Iran on 23 February, as was Iraq's 10 March proposal, at the Delhi Non-Aligned summit, for arbitration. The Gulf Cooperation Council's suggested fund for repairing war damage was equally unsuccessful. Another Iranian offensive on 10 April achieved no more than its predecessors, nor did Iraq's fresh appeal on 12 April to the Security Council. Even a limited ceasefire to permit sealing the oil leak proved unattainable.

The war's human consequences, including possibly up to 500,000 deaths, attracted international publicity, the UN sending a mission to investigate damage and casualties, and the Red Cross accusing both governments of violating human rights and maltreating prisoners of war. Iraq's proposals to outlaw attacks on civilian targets and to cease fire during Ramadan were both immediately rejected as ploys to give Iraq military advantage.

On 22 July Iran attacked afresh in northern Kurdistan, and again on 19 October, this time further south, about 100 miles east of the Kirkuk oilfields, surrounding the Iraqi border town of Panjwin. Iran threatened but withheld a further offensive. Heavy casualties included many from long-range missile attacks on Iranian towns.

The potential dangers to oil supplies prompted further efforts for a ceasefire. The French, especially, were delicately placed, having promised Iraq five Super Etendard aircraft which, armed with Exocet missiles, would seriously threaten Iran. Keeping the whereabouts of the aircraft mysterious, the French secured passage of a Security Council resolution calling for a ceasefire and a guarantee by both sides to leave Gulf shipping alone. On 21 October Iran rejected this and a GCC attempt a week later could not revive it.

The world feared that, if Iran would not end the war, Iraq might use its French and Soviet missiles for an all-out attack on Iran's oil industry and exports. Iran had already said that it would then block the Hormuz Strait, a threat which prompted the US Government on 26 July to declare its determination to keep the strait open. An Iraqi Exocet sank a Greek cargo ship on 21 November, but further major attacks did not follow; stern warnings from Japan apparently helped prevent Iraq from raiding the Japanese-built petrochemical complex at Bandar Khomeini. December saw the military positions of both sides little changed since January.

However, Iraq's economy was shakier than before, with rising defence bills (about $1,000 million each month) and less money from oil exports to pay them. Iranian action had stopped oil shipments in 1980 and Syria would not reopen the main Mediterranean pipeline, closed since April 1982. The smaller Turkish line was working beyond its stated capacity, soon to be enlarged, and in December Iraqis and Saudis were reported to have agreed to connect Iraq's southern oilfields to the existing Saudi line to the Red Sea. Meanwhile Kuwait and Saudi Arabia were shipping 300,000 barrels per day on Iraq's account. The Gulf states having, however, reduced or stopped their cash payments to Iraq, reserves had fallen possibly to $2,000 million (from $31,000 million in 1980). Shortage of money was not yet discernibly affecting the war effort, but Iraq halted its ambitious development programmes and embarrassed foreign companies by withholding payment and demanding further credit. Even consumer imports were affected and immigrant Filippino workmen were part-paid in promissory notes. Manpower was becoming scarce; it was reported that 15,000 Egyptian immigrants and troops seconded from Sudan were fighting for Iraq.

Faced by enemies on either side, Iraq needed friends. It had led the pack against Egypt in 1979; now their relations improved (see p. 181). Courting moderate Arab support, Iraq expelled the Palestinian murderer Abu Nidal and backed Yassir Arafat against the extremists. Outside the Arab world, France and the USSR supported Iraq—both, doubtless with some embarrassment, protecting previous investments. Donald Rumsfeld, President Reagan's Middle East envoy, reached Baghdad on 19 December, the first senior American visitor for years.

Internally, recurrent reports of bombings suggested increasing activity by the Shia group *Al Da'wa*, backed from Teheran and avenging Baath maltreatment of leading religious families. The Kurds needed conciliating, to economize garrisons, protect the Turkish pipeline and encourage them against Iran, and on 5 August elections were held for Kurdish local councils; nevertheless Kurdish exemption from conscription, though granted, was soon withdrawn.

The greatest potential threat, however, lay inside the army and party and was to Saddam himself, his person being the main obstacle to ending the disastrous war he had begun. On 21 October a British newspaper reported a movement against him inside the army; this was immediately denied.

Chapter 3

SAUDI ARABIA—YEMEN ARAB REPUBLIC—PEOPLE'S DEMOCRATIC
REPUBLIC OF YEMEN—THE ARAB STATES OF THE GULF

SAUDI ARABIA

IN 1983 Saudi Arabia was again made aware that prosperity cannot purchase tranquility. The lesson was reinforced by the reluctant realization that petroleum-producing states were not immune to the laws of economics, and that income from oil was not predestined to go on rising forever. The major sources of external concern were the continuation of the Iran-Iraq war, the turmoil in Lebanon, and the associated bitter struggle between Yassir Arafat and the Government of Syria. At home both the decline in oil income and the existence of concealed but real differences of opinion within the royal family caused disquiet.

The failure of all attempts to end hostilities between Iran and Iraq was deeply regretted by a Government which found the cost of providing financial support for Baghdad increasingly burdensome. In April an oil slick from damaged Iranian wells threatened to pollute a stretch of the coastline near Al Khobar, and water desalinization plants there had to be closed for a time. When Iraq (see p. 000) received Super Etendard aircraft and Exocet missiles from France in the summer, and said it might use them against the vital Iranian oil port on Kharg island, Teheran stated that any such attempt would lead to Iranian forces closing the Straits of Hormuz to all shipping. This caused great consternation in Saudi Arabia and among the other members of the Gulf Cooperation Council (GCC), all of whom were believed to have impressed upon Baghdad the need for moderation.

In early November King Fahd flew to Qatar for a meeting of the GCC held in conditions of unprecedented security. There were several reports that a terrorist group had planned an attempt on the life of the monarch there. The bomb attacks in Kuwait on 12 December made the Government even more nervous, and additional internal security measures were introduced.

Several senior princes made repeated journeys to Arab capital cities as the Government continued with its diplomatic efforts to reach an agreement between the warring factions in Lebanon, and to resolve the differences between Yassir Arafat and the Syrian Government. There were reports of internal family differences on this matter; Crown Prince Abdullah and the Foreign Minister, Prince Saud, were said to favour a more pro-Syrian policy than did the King, who wished to maintain a close association with Washington. The possibility of warmer relations between Riyadh and Damascus caused dismay to other Arab Governments, particularly that of Jordan. The abrupt, and most unusual, dismissal of the Minister of Information, Abdo Yamani, on 24 April, and his replacement by the Saudi ambassador in Lebanon, General Ali Hassan al Shaer, were seen by some diplomats as a sign of the deep divisions within the royal family over foreign policy.

Diplomatic relations with the UK began the year on a sour note when it was made clear that a proposed visit by the Foreign Secretary, Mr Francis Pym, would not be welcome. The reason for this was Mrs Thatcher's refusal to receive an Arab League delegation in London which included a representative of the PLO (see AR 1982, p. 49). The consequences of this rift between London and Riyadh were not, however, as serious as those in 1980, and by the end of the year better relations prevailed.

As in previous years Saudi Arabia took a prominent role in the discussions of Opec. At its lengthy meeting in London in March the organization set target-levels of output in order to defend the new price of $29 per barrel for Saudi Arabian 'marker' crude.The country again agreed to act as the swing producer, regulating its output so that overall target production levels would not be exceeded. Not surprisingly this led to later accusations that some members were producing more than their quotas, thus depressing Saudi Arabia's income even further. In the first and second quarters of the year Saudi Arabia had a trade deficit, but in the third quarter the balance of payments was favourable. The Saudi rial was slightly devalued against the US dollar in March and twice again in August.

The fall in oil prices and the drop in output prompted the introduction in April of an 'austerity' Budget for 1983-84. This anticipated a deficit of some $10,000 million, a small sum in relation to total Saudi reserves. Some observers believed that the deficit would turn out to be greater because oil sales would not generate the target income of $54,000 million. The Government decided that it would not abandon any of the projects included in the 1980-85 development plan; but retrenchment would be effected by extending the construction period of some schemes. Again there were differences of opinion within the family, some older members taking the view that the country should abandon some of its more ambitious plans and learn to live on a reduced income. It was notable, however, that no one was prepared publicly to recommend any cut in the size of the military budget.

Projects which had been begun in earlier years continued to come to fruition, the most spectacular being the opening in December of the King Khalid international airport at Riyadh—the largest airport in the world, with a total surface area of some 90 square miles, having already cost over

$3,000 million. It was also announced that the domestic agricultural sector was now able to meet the country's demand for wheat; not publicized was the fact that the home-produced crop cost at least six times as much as imported wheat.

The annual pilgrimage to Mecca and Medina in September was believed to have been attended by a record number of over 2·5 million Muslims, of whom approximately one million came from abroad. As in previous years there were violent clashes between the security forces and some Iranian pilgrims who sought noisily to publicize the virtues of the Khomeini regime.

YEMEN ARAB REPUBLIC

During the year most of the Government's attention was taken up with economic matters. The major earthquake which had hit the province of Dhammar on 13 December 1982 caused even more damage than was at first feared, and the cost of the repair programme would obviously weigh very heavily on an economy already under great strain. Over 400,000 people had been made homeless, 25,000 houses were totally destroyed and nearly 20,000 others had sustained serious damage. An emergency reconstruction programme costing $112 million was begun and immediate financial aid was provided by Saudi Arabia and several Western states. A later detailed study raised the total bill for reconstruction by an additional $900 million. Consequently major changes had to be made in the proposed 1982-86 development programme. The YAR continued to rely on massive subsidies from Saudi Arabia, but as that state's oil revenues declined there were signs that Riyadh might not provide as much assistance as it had in previous years. The Government sought aid from other Arab oil-producers and it endeavoured to increase revenues by imposing still heavier import duties on cars, while some luxury imports were banned.

In May President Ali Abdullah Saleh announced his resignation, but he was promptly re-elected as head of state for a further five-year term by the People's Consultative Assembly. Economic considerations were believed to have influenced the Cabinet changes made by the President in November. Mr Abdul Karim al Iryani, who had been Prime Minister since October 1980, was made chairman of the supreme council in charge of reconstruction in the earthquake areas, and his place was taken by Mr Abdul Aziz Abdul Ghani, his predecessor as Prime Minister. Other ministerial changes concerned the departments of Foreign Affairs, the Interior, Finance and Industry, and Economy. The President's reported aim was to retain military control over internal security, while endeavouring to reinvigorate those departments most concerned with economic development.

The many difficulties facing the Government were in no way diminished by the arrival, in late December, of Yassir Arafat and over 1,000 of his supporters evacuated from Lebanon (see p. 180). Arafat was said to be considering establishing a Palestinian government in exile, possibly with Sanaa as its first location. (On relations with PDRY see the following section.)

PEOPLE'S DEMOCRATIC REPUBLIC OF YEMEN

Compared with previous years 1983 was a relatively calm one with no major political upheavals. In January an aircraft was hijacked on a flight from Aden to Kuwait and forced to fly to Djibouti by three disaffected Palestinians, whose sole request was to be granted Djibouti passports in order to be free to travel (see Pt. VI, Ch. 1).

The economy continued to fare badly and the effects of the severe flooding of March 1982 were still being felt (see AR 1982, p. 204). While the Government retained its close links with Moscow and the Eastern bloc, there were signs that aid from the West would be welcomed and European firms began to be involved in several development projects. In August the Iranian Foreign Minister, Mr Ali Akbar Velayati, visited the PDRY and the two Governments signed a memorandum concerning economic and cultural cooperation. It was later reported that Iranian crude oil would be processed at the little-used refinery in Aden, and the products then re-exported to Iran.

In that same month the President, Ali Nasser Muhammad, went to Sanaa to meet his YAR (North Yemen) counterpart, Ali Abdullah Saleh, and together they opened the first meeting of the Supreme Yemeni Council, a body created to foster the unification of the two countries. External observers, however, had difficulty in discovering any evidence of progress towards that goal. In October the PDRY and Oman signed an agreement in Kuwait to exchange ambassadors, and to seek a settlement of their border dispute. This improvement in relations between two formerly hostile neighbours was welcomed by the other states of the peninsula, but on ideological matters Aden and Muscat remained poles apart.

THE ARAB STATES OF THE GULF

THE Arab states of the Gulf saw their political and economic futures dominated by the ongoing war between Iraq and Iran and by the continuing crisis in the world energy market. At the same time, internal affairs had a marked impact, as the consequences of the collapse of the unofficial stock-market in Kuwait in 1982 spread throughout the region.

Other states moved to prevent similar problems and turned increasingly to their banking and finance centres as a source of revenue at a time of an uncertain future for Opec oil sales. In addition, the Gulf Cooperation Council (GCC)—originally set up to support mutual defence interests in the Gulf—moved on in 1983 towards economic integration of its members as well.

The Opec agreement on production quotas, marker crude prices and differentials which came out of the March ministerial meeting in London had a profound effect on the Gulf states. All the states involved, except OMAN, which was not a member of Opec, had to make considerable sacrifices. KUWAIT, for instance, which was given a quota of 1.05 million barrels a day (b/d) in London—a level which, although well above the 700,000 b/d it had been producing in January, was still only half of its production level in January 1981—was still forced to constrain output. Although the Opec output level of 17.5 mn. b/d had been exceeded by July, Kuwait steadfastly refused to exceed its quota and, according to Oil Minister Shaikh Ali Khalifa, had even turned away some customers. The UNITED ARAB EMIRATES, on the other hand, which had made a considerable sacrifice at London by agreeing to drop their quota demand from 1.6 mn. b/d to 1.1 mn. b/d, like Saudi Arabia, did exceed their quota in July by some 100,000 b/d (some reports suggested that the true figure was double this). Shaikh Otaiba, the UAE Oil Minister, made it clear that the UAE would expect priority consideration when production quota limits were raised.

The UAE's demand for special consideration arose from the massive investment in ABU DHABI's new Upper Zakum field, which was expected to come onstream with a production of some 200,000 b/d, but which was now limited to under 50,000 b/d. In fact, Abu Dhabi's contribution to the UAE quota was set at 800,000 b/d, while DUBAI saw its quota cut from about 360,000 to 300,000 b/d, BAHREIN'S situation was less serious, since its oil output had been declining as its fields approached exhaustion. Nonetheless, output now limited to 42,000 b/d was scarcely sufficient to pay for the development on which the country hoped to base its non-oil future. QATAR also found the Opec quotas to be worrying. Although its high-priced crude had been a poor seller on world markets at the start of the year, with sales falling to as little as 171,000 b/d, output rose to the Opec limit of 300,000 b/d by mid-year, and the Oil and Finance Minister, Shaikh Abdel-Aziz Bin Khalifah al-Thani, claimed that a level of 425,000 b/d was essential if Qatar's development plans were to be sustained after November. In part, Qatar's increased production was disposed of through oil barter deals, but the country also had to turn to its financial reserves to maintain its development plans.

Only OMAN, given its non-Opec status, seemed to have escaped the general economic gloom. Oil production levels rose from 336,000 b/d at the end of 1982 to more than 400,000 b/d by August 1983, and the country enjoyed one of the most buoyant economies in the region, despite the falls in crude prices. Revenues rose to 1981 levels—although an $851 million deficit on current account was still expected for the year overall. Elsewhere in the region, falls in oil revenues were reflected in budget cutbacks and austerity programmes. KUWAIT anticipated a 4 per cent fall in oil revenues to K$3,268 million in fiscal 1983-84, and a 5·3 per cent fall in overall state revenues to K$3,137 million. The situation in the UAE was even more alarming. In August, the UAE federal Budget showed that, although oil revenues were expected to fall by 40 per cent, expenditure was to be held at 18 per cent below 1982 levels and a record deficit was forecast, 141 per cent up on the 1982 level of Dh2,283 mn. Cuts announced in the QATAR Budget in mid-April were even greater, with total expenditure down 31 per cent on 1982/83 levels. Oil revenues, accounting for 80 per cent of total revenue, had fallen by just under 20 per cent on a year-on-year basis. In BAHREIN, however, the considerable diversification away from oil meant that the state was able to avoid the worst effects of the fall in crude prices, current spending being maintained at 1982 levels and capital spending—which, under the 1982-88 capital budget plan should have peaked in 1983 at just under $700 million—being unaffected.

One way in which the Gulf states had tried to diversify was to develop their financial sectors. Most active in this respect was KUWAIT, whose investment earnings were equivalent to half the state's oil earnings in 1981/82, a proportion which almost certainly increased in 1982-83. During 1983 the Kuwait Petroleum Company bought distribution networks from Gulf Oil in Belgium, the Netherlands, Luxembourg, Sweden and Denmark. This acquisition also gave it two small refineries in Europe and, in conjunction with the purchase of Santa Fe International in 1981, meant that Kuwait now had a fully-integrated, multinational petroleum operation—the first of the Middle East oil producers to achieve this.

Other aspects of financial operations in the Gulf states were not so successful. In Kuwait, business confidence was sapped throughout 1983 by the consequences of the Souk al-Manakh unofficial stock-market crash in September 1982 (see AR 1982, p. 206), when outstanding debts totalled a staggering $94,000 million. Although the Kuwaiti Government arranged for a $500 million aid fund to help those owed up to $2 million, two to three hundred investors were not covered by this aid and there was a clear determination to prosecute the major figures responsible, the 'magnificent nine', who had incurred two-thirds of the overall debt. Further aid of $500 million was expected to be provided by the government and the net uncovered debt would eventually be only $25 million. Several resignations included those of the Finance Minister, Mr al-Hamad, in September and the governor of the central bank, Mr Hussein, in October. Meanwhile, the formal end of the crisis was signalled in August, when the National Assembly passed a Bill limiting liability on Souk al-Manakh debts.

One way in which Kuwait hoped to overcome the effect of the Souk al-Manakh fiasco was to resuscitate the official stock market created in 1982 and to reopen the international bond market. Other states in the Gulf had similar ideas. The UAE contemplated creating a similar exchange, but in the event the federal Government decided that enactment of a company law should have priority. At the same time, it was felt necessary to introduce some control over the activities of banks in the Emirates, particularly those which lent major sums to shareholders. In November, the UAE central bank moved in on one family bank and took over the chairman's assets, as a warning to other banks to diversify their activities. The move was much resented among the banking community, but was clearly felt necessary to prevent scandals like that which had so poisoned the business atmosphere in Kuwait.

Other states used similar techniques to increase non-oil revenue. BAHREIN drew up plans to open a stock exchange in 1984, seeing this as a way of augmenting the already significant earnings from the offshore banking sector, now involving 75 units, holding $40,000 million worth of dollars and $10,000 million worth of other currencies. The commercial banking sector which doubled in 1983 to four units was ideally placed to take advantage of the new stock exchange. An $80 million bond issue in November, organized by the Bahrein Monetary Authority to fund governmental projects, was over-subscribed.

However, all these activities were overshadowed by the major political factor affecting the Gulf states throughout 1983. The Iran-Iraq war was entering its fourth year with no resolution in sight. The Gulf states were affected in three different ways. First, they had to support Iraq economically, with financial aid and counterpart oil sales, making good the deficiencies in Iraq's own oil exports; secondly, they had to contend with the uncertainties engendered in the Gulf by the war—including the dangers associated with a massive oil slick from Iran's offshore fields at Nowruz after bomb damage which threatened desalination and power plants in the Gulf states; and, finally, they had to cope with domestic problems resulting from the war. In the result, all the Gulf states took an increasingly reluctant attitude towards support for Iraq, while, at the same time, looking towards the Gulf Cooperation Council (GCC) for mutual support and defence.

KUWAIT was the state most strongly affected by the war. In January, Kuwait had to respond to an Iraqi request for additional financial aid of $7,000 million on top of the $25,000 million already provided. Although the transfer of the main centre of land-based military activities to Kurdistan during the year calmed Kuwaiti fears of Iranian threats to its territory should Iran break through Iraqi lines around Basra, the renewed threat to Iranian oil exports posed by the delivery to Iraq of Super

Etendard bombers equipped with Exocet missiles, together with Iran's hints that the Straits of Hormuz would be closed if the planes were used, rekindled anxieties in Kuwait. In addition, car bomb attacks on the French and American embassies in Kuwait, in late December, reminded the Kuwait Government of the domestic threat posed by its large Shia minority and encouraged it to take a more cautious stance over the war. Despite the moderating role that QATAR had tried to play between Iran and Iraq, the Qatari Government had to face an attempted coup timed to take place during the GCC summit held in Doha in early November. BAHREIN was able to avoid direct involvement in the war, although the island was still claimed by Iran, while OMAN, with its coastline along the Arabian sea and its responsibility for the Straits of Hormuz, beefed up its defence forces during 1983. Not only were arms being purchased from Britain, France and the United States, with particular emphasis on modern fighter aircraft, but the air bases at Seeb and Thumrait were also to be improved and the naval base at Wudam expanded. In addition, Oman secured her western flank by opening full diplomatic relations with South Yemen in October, thus bringing fifteen years of hostility to an end.

The Gulf states also expressed their anxieties over the Arab-Israeli conflict and the associated crisis within the PLO during 1983, through the GCC summits held in Saudi Arabia in August and in Doha in November. The GCC states—Saudi Arabia, Kuwait, Qatar, Bahrein, the UAE and Oman—carried out joint naval and land-based military exercises for the first time in October. The Council also attempted to mediate between the opposed factions of the PLO in Lebanon. The organization, which celebrated its second birthday in May, introduced its 'Unified Economic Agreement' in March. The agreement covered intra-GCC trade and provided for uniform customs tariffs for goods from third countries. Further aspects of the agreement were brought into effect during the year and, despite reservations on the part of the UAE, the GCC secretary-general, Abdullah Bishara, justly claimed in March that the GCC was now a 'confederal endeavour'. Further moves were planned for the future, including joint electricity tariffs and further integration of military forces.

Various Gulf state leaders made visits to major capitals during the year. In July, Shaikh Isa bin Sulman al-Khalifah visited Washington and London, apparently to discuss further US military supplies, a visit which generated considerable Iranian hostility. Earlier, Sultan Qabous of Oman had visited the United States, where he had talks with President Reagan on the Arab-Israeli situation and the problems in the Gulf. It was reported that they also discussed the supply of advanced fighter aircraft to Oman. Sultan Qabous later visited Egypt, Jordan and the UK. Kuwait, however, found itself in disagreement with the United States over the appointment of a new US ambassador. In August, Kuwait rejected the nomination of Mr Brandon Grove because he had been stationed in Jerusalem. Washington refused to reconsider the nomination and the post remained vacant.

Several Gulf states decided to reduce their expatriate populations during the year. KUWAIT, which had introduced strict new regulations at the end of 1982, saw thousands of Arab and Asian workers leave suddenly in early 1983, creating a temporary labour shortage. Nonetheless, Ministry of Planning forecasts, published later, estimated that by 1985 the non-Kuwaiti population could grow to 1,228,000, out of a total population of 1,910,000. Non-Kuwaitis represented 78 per cent of the labour force in 1980, a percentage that had certainly increased. Similar moves took place in the UAE, after figures showed that the proportion of UAE nationals in the population of the Emirates had fallen in 1981 to 26·7 per cent. Stringent new provisions introduced at the beginning of the year to control the growth of expatriate labour reduced it significantly. Nevertheless, the Ministry of Labour and Social Affairs expected that the proportion of UAE nationals in the population would continue to drop towards only 9 per cent by 1990.

Despite the disappointing economic climate, the Gulf did see some hopeful signs on the non-oil front during 1983. The new Omani copper-smelting complex exported its first cargo of refined copper in October, and fairly successful reports were issued from the Bahrein aluminium-smelting unit and the shipyards and ports in both Bahrein and Qatar. Kuwait continued development of the all-important Southern Gas Project, while Qatar decided to proceed with the North Gas Field development. Indeed, Gulf states could feel relatively satisfied with their demonstrated ability to diversify away from exclusive reliance on oil revenues during 1983.

Chapter 4

SUDAN—LIBYA—TUNISIA—WESTERN SAHARA—
ALGERIA—MOROCCO

SUDAN

THE year was characterized by political turbulence and a worsening economic situation. Reports that southern Sudanese troops were to be moved to the north and the decision of President Nimairi to divide the Southern Region into three regions, both in contravention of the Addis Ababa agreement of 1972, led to a number of armed incidents. In an attack on a railway station in the province of Bahr al-Ghazal 18 people were killed. Army and police deserters and civilians joined the Anyanya II, an organization formed to speak for southern Sudanese opposing Nimairi's regime. The gravest incident was the mutiny by a company of the army in the south which left 70 mutineers and eight government troops dead. An attack by rebels in Aweil in Bahr al-Ghazal killed 18 civilians. The Southern Sudanese Liberation Front, whose aim was an independent southern state, held five Western aid workers hostage but they were released by the Sudanese army and during the operation nineteen people were killed. Later eleven hostages were taken by the rebels but they were released. The Government claimed that the army killed 480 rebels who laid siege to the town of Nasir. It attributed the troubles in the Southern Region to foreign intervention, mainly by Libya and Ethiopia. Opposition by some southern Sudanese politicians to the President's policies and actions led to their imprisonment. Despite the amnesty offered by President Nimairi to the rebels, it was reported that about 25,000 southerners crossed to neighbouring Ethiopia.

The north was equally fraught with political discontent. The army remained loyal to Nimairi but a close political alliance was formed with the Muslim Brothers, to the displeasure of the ruling party (Sudan Socialist Union) and other banned political forces. Dr Hassan al-Turabi, leader of the Muslim Brothers, was appointed an assistant to President Nimairi for foreign affairs. The Sudan official news agency reported that 56 people had been arrested and accused of planning subversion and sabotage. The authorities uncovered 70 tons of weapons and explosives and accused Libya of supporting subversion. Six military officers were arrested on charges of plotting a coup. To rally support from the Muslim north and from conservative Arab countries President Nimairi introduced the *Sharī'ah* (Islamic laws). He accordingly freed 13,000 prisoners, banned the selling and consumption of alcohol, and approved the implementation of strict Islamic penalties. The non-Muslim southerners protested. Some prominent northerners, including the leader of the Mahdists, al-Sadiq al-Mahdi, were imprisoned for opposing the policies of the regime.

The rising disenchantment with the regime's political and economic performance increased President Nimairi's isolation, obliging him to rely on the support of Egypt, the USA and Saudi Arabia. The integration of Sudan with Egypt became of vital political and military importance to President Nimairi. President Mubarak of Egypt attended the first meeting of the Higher Council for Integration, which approved the formation of institutions and departments related to this integration. It was assumed that American manoeuvres around Libya were prompted by reports that Libya was planning to dismantle President Nimairi's regime. The US sent four AWACS aircraft to Egypt to monitor Libya's border with Sudan. President Nimairi visited the US and some European countries to ask for arms and financial support. Like Libya, Ethiopia was accused of fomenting troubles in Sudan: it denied reports that Ethiopia had amassed troops on Sudan's border.

President Nimairi was re-elected for a third six-year term as President and was also elected to the presidency of the Sudan Socialist Union. He appointed eleven councillors to advise him on domestic and international affairs. In endemic reshuffles, he appointed five Ministers, including two from the south: Abel Alier (the previous Vice-President of the Republic) as Minister of Construction and Work, and Miss Mary Bissiouni as minister of state in the Ministry of Internal Affairs.

Under increasing pressure from the International Monetary Fund (IMF) and other creditors for an austerity programme, the income tax threshold was increased by 25 per cent and the bank interest rate was raised by three per cent. Oil explorations continued and Chevron Oil Company (Sudan) discovered oil in the Unity Field. Chevron and the Government signed an agreement for the export of crude oil and the allocation of production, due to start in 1985, between the two parties. Despite a sizeable international debt, spiralling inflation and lack of foreign exchange, Sudan continued to receive aid and loans, which amounted to nearly $2,500 million, for agricultural, industrial and communication projects, and more significantly for balance of payments support.

LIBYA

The ceaseless activity of Colonel Qadafi ensured that his country was rarely absent from the headlines. Although he made some startling changes of direction in foreign policy, his quarrel with the USA remained a constant feature. In February the Americans announced that he was planning an attack upon the Sudan and that they were sending AWACS aircraft to Egypt to watch the situation and moving the fleet into position. Both Egypt and Sudan denied asking for help and the incident fizzled out amidst suspicions that the Americans had attempted to trick the Colonel into an adventure or to humiliate him. Secretary of State Shultz commented: 'at least for the moment Qadafi is back in his box, where he belongs'. Verbal warfare continued: Qadafi threatened to bomb American bases in Europe and called upon the Red Indians to rise, while President Reagan called him 'the most dangerous man in the world'.

Qadafi increased his activity in the Americans' 'back-yard', promising that 'all our forces are at the disposal of the Sandinista Front in Nicaragua'. In April four Libyan aircraft, supposedly carrying medical supplies for Colombia, were detained in Brazil and found to contain 200 tons of arms. After much acrimony they were returned in June. In August the Prime Minister of St Lucia accused the Libyans of luring young men with promises of scholarships but instead training them as terrorists.

After the American invasion of Grenada 16 Libyan agents found there were expelled.

Qadafi also clashed with the Americans in Africa. In June he intervened actively in the Chadian civil war (see Pt. VI, Ch. 3), sending a reported 1,500 troops and 3,000 mercenaries of the 'Islamic Legion' to support Oueddeye. Libyan aircraft bombed towns amidst American charges of 'flagrant and unprovoked aggression'. Otherwise in Africa Qadafi suffered setbacks. His constant meddling in their internal affairs led the Liberians and others to renew ties with Israel. At the OAU summit in Addis Ababa (see Pt. XI, Ch. 6) the Colonel was isolated and virtually humiliated and rapidly took his leave.

Disputes with Egypt and Sudan continued noisily, and Qadafi watched with alarm the growing links between the other North African states. Fearing exclusion, he salvaged what he could by setting up a joint investment corporation with Tunisia and welcoming its Prime Minister with half his Cabinet for a joint ministerial meeting. More dramatically, he pocketed his pride and went to visit King Hassan: however frequently the Colonel had reshuffled the pack of friends and enemies, Morocco had remained one of the few constant targets. The King and the Colonel announced their resolve to end everything capable of harming relations.

Equally dramatically, having denounced them as 'pigs', Qadafi made his peace with the Saudis. He also visited Jordan and tried to hasten Yemeni unity. He demanded a boycott of Lebanon after the signature of its treaty with Israel and backed with arms and money the attempt of the Druze to overthrow President Gemayel—whom he later welcomed in Tripoli. Libyan troops gave active support to the Palestinian dissidents in their attack upon Yassir Arafat, whom he accused of plotting against his life in conjunction with the CIA. Arafat vowed to tear out the Colonel's tongue. Qadafi also found time to rebuke the Ayatollah Khomeini for cruelty to communists.

He also continued to threaten 'stray dogs'—his exiled opponents—with murder and to protect his agents by ignoring international practice. In April eight West Germans and in October 37 Frenchmen were held as hostages to secure the release of Libyans accused of terrorism. In each case the European Government, fearing for the safety of its citizens and for its economic interests, gave way.

Qadafi remained convinced that he was an inspired prophet with a message which he should spare no expense in spreading. In April about a thousand people from all over the world, mostly described as 'researchers', were assembled for an 8-day congress to discuss the Colonel's *Green Book*. They handsomely repaid his hospitality by congratulating him upon 'solving problems that had baffled Plato and Aristotle'. He constantly complained of misrepresentation in Western media: a newspaper report that the missing race-horse Shergar had been seen in Tripoli showed that he had a point.

There were the usual unverifiable rumours of attempted coups and executions, including those of Islamic fundamentalists. In May an official paper carried an astonishing article by a cousin of the Colonel accusing the army of 'Hashish and Frivolity', pornography and black marketeering. Qadafi issued a rather formal disavowal but repeated his call for the replacement of regular troops by the people in arms. Even at primary school military instruction was given and there was a growing reliance on mercenaries.

Oil production fluctuated and early in the year Qadafi visited Sofia and Bucharest with projects of barter, but later sales improved and it was stated that Libya had replaced Britain as the second principal source of EEC oil imports. Even so, economists forecast that the shortfall of revenue could lead to a crisis and pointed to Libya's enormous debts, particularly to Russia and France. Government salaries and benefits were cut and some projects, such as workers' housing, had to be abandoned. Work progressed, however, on the largest scheme of all—a 2,000-km pipeline from wells in the desert to move annually twice as much water as would fill Lake Como to irrigate the coastal plains. It was estimated that oil would run out in 20 years, so plans to live from agriculture were clearly wise, although many doubted whether the expenditure on the pipeline would ever be recovered.

A new feature of Libyan life was the celebration of 'Vengeance Day' with demands for reparations for the Italian occupation. The day chosen was the anniversary of a student demonstration, apparently unnoticed at the time, which had been led by the youthful Qadafi.

TUNISIA

The Government faced problems from many directions. Islamic fundamentalists and militant leftists were active, liberals protested against political stagnation, growing numbers of young unemployed showed angry frustration and the southern provinces resented what they saw as undue favouring of the north. In January there were arrests of Islamic fundamentalists, some of them military officers, and a plan to infiltrate the army was feared. Sentences of between 6 and 8 years imprisonment were imposed. In the same month 12 members of the (legal) Communist Party were arrested and later gaoled for between 2 and 10 years.

Also in January there was an unprecedently fierce debate upon the Budget in the Chamber of Deputies—taxation levels had not been changed for ten years. The opportunity was taken to voice demands for multi-party democracy, political amnesty and the restraint of torture by the police. In June, the Prime Minister, Muhammad Mzali, insisting that social considerations took precedence over financial orthodoxy, dismissed his rigidly conservative Finance Minister, Mansur Moalla.

To woo the liberals Mzali for the first time brought ladies—one his own wife—into the Cabinet and, more importantly, in November, two political organizations, previously recognized merely as 'movements', were given the full status of parties. Apart from the small Communist Party, only the official PSD had been allowed to exist, and in its quarter-century of power it had become inextricably linked with the apparatus of government at every level. The strongest proponent of the single-party state, the hard-line former secretary-general Muhammad Sayah, was sent abroad as ambassador to The Hague. Opinion in Tunis regarded this as a real step towards democracy and gave much of the credit to Mme Bourguiba, who had called strongly for reform (see AR 1982, p. 215).

Financial difficulties grew and the trade deficit, $725 million in 1982, rose by 11 per cent in the first half of 1983. There was great dissatisfaction among the business classes, which complained of increasing bankruptcies because prices were held down to prevent pay demands. Faced with this, Mzali announced in October a doubling of the price of bread, to become effective in the new year. At the end of December this led to violent riots, which started amongst the unemployed of the south and rapidly spread throughout the country. After at least 15 people had been killed when tanks fired on the demonstrators, the Government gave way and repealed the price increase.

Perhaps the presence of the PLO headquarters caused Tunis to take a firmer line than in the past on the Palestine question. President Mitterrand's visit in October was regarded as a disappointment because of his caution on the issue and the following month the US Secretary of State admitted that he had had 'an earful' of criticism. The main event in foreign policy was the establishment of close links with Algeria, a Treaty of Brotherhood and Concord being signed after a visit by President Chadli in March. All outstanding differences were settled and joint ventures established in frontier areas. When Bourguiba returned the visit in May he was accorded a welcome more enthusiastic than anyone since Nasser. There was heady talk of Maghreb unity, which the Algerian Foreign Minister said in Tunis was the principal objective of Arab nationalists. There was an obvious need for coordination to face the cross-frontier problem posed by Islamic fundamentalists and for a joint negotiating stance towards the EEC. Mzali, however, cautioned that a summit or a common market would be premature but said that a start could be made with a customs union. Steps were taken to reassure Colonel Qadafi, who feared that there were plans to exclude him, but relations with Libya remained cool.

The announcement in *The Times* of the engagement of 'King Rechad al-Mahdi of Tunisia' to a young lady from Hampshire appeared to pass without comment from his 'subjects'.

WESTERN SAHARA

Talk of a Greater Maghreb caused both hope and alarm in Polisario leaders; while a solution of the Saharan problem might be found within the framework of a federation, Polisario's allies seemed more likely to sacrifice it in the interests of overall agreement. The meeting of the Moroccan King and the Algerian President (see p. 205) did not weaken Algerian support for Polisario; for President Chadli insisted that North African unity could not be purchased at its expense and that he could not negotiate on its behalf, although subsequently he sponsored a solution combining Moroccan sovereignty with local autonomy. However, Polisario's other principal ally, Colonel Qadafi, visiting Rabat, said that he had done all he could for it and effectively washed his hands of the movement. Moroccan complaints that he was supplying the guerrillas ceased, and he received pro-Moroccan Saharan chieftains. The Russians, anxious to secure fishing rights off the Saharan coast, tacitly recognized its Moroccan status by sending a football team to Al Ayoun. Hopes reposed in the new Spanish Socialist Government were disappointed, and President Mitterrand's visit to Rabat brought Polisario no comfort.

In February its leaders were adamant that they would attend the long-delayed OAU summit, but at the meeting at Addis Ababa such pressure was exercised, even by the Algerians, that while maintaining its full membership Polisario 'voluntarily and temporarily' absented itself. The summit called for direct negotiations, thus accepting Polisario as an equal partner to the dispute, and for a referendum before the end of the year. Although Polisario claimed that talks had taken place with Moroccan leaders, at a September meeting of the OAU committee set up to implement the decisions the Moroccans refused direct discussions.

Several Moroccan Ministers visited the area to campaign in the referendum, but the King declared that whatever its result he would not 'hand over our Sahara on a silver platter to a gang of mercenaries'. He also ruled out the possibility of a Saharan 'mini-state'. Although he continued to express readiness to let the referendum take place nothing had happened by the deadline of 31 December.

Fighting during the year was spasmodic and in January Hassan said that his troops were bored as Polisario was so ineffective. In March Polisario claimed a victory and there was more fighting in July and August. In November and December, expecting attacks as the deadline approached, the Moroccans left the 'Wall' and launched large-scale sweeps, using up to 25,000 men. Their weakness in the air, however, prevented decisive victory.

ALGERIA

President Chadli continued his policy of reversing the alliances formed by his predecessor. Under Boumédienne the closest friends of Algeria had been Russia and Libya but by the end of 1983 relations with those powers were less significant than those with the West and with Algeria's other immediate neighbours. US Vice-President Bush, visiting in September, could speak of 'growing friendship' and, despite the difficulties of switching arms suppliers, Algeria replaced its Russian transport aircraft with American ones and bought £300 million worth of mainly naval equipment from Britain. In November, accompanied by Mme Chadli, the President paid a state visit to France, with which relations had been difficult after a series of racialist attacks on Muslims. The appearance of the two Presidents, hand in hand, struck an emotional response in Algeria: Chadli called on his people to end all resentment and Mitterrand declared that henceforth the two nations should be brothers. Relations with Spain were good, and King Juan Carlos paid a state visit.

Enunciating a policy of 'positive good neighbourliness', Chadli settled older frontier disputes with Mali, Niger and Mauritania, and in February held a dramatic meeting with King Hassan. Chadli hoped that the Saharan problem could be settled within the framework of a Greater Maghreb, and this possibility looked even closer in May when, after signing a Treaty of Brotherhood and Concord, Bourguiba came to Algiers (see p. 205). The two Presidents were joined by Ould Haidallah, the Mauritanian leader, and there were rumours that King Hassan might also arrive. Qadafi, extremely resentful that unity appeared to be coming under leadership other than his own, claimed that Algeria was already committed to unity with Libya and hinted that force might be used to ensure it: he was told that he could join the Treaty if he wished.

Domestically, attention focused on preparation for the fifth congress of the sole party, the FLN. This was the first regular congress since the death of Boumédienne and its meetings in December showed further breaks with his policies. Agriculture was given definite priority over industrialization, and in the encouragement of the private sector avowals of socialism seemed little more than lip-service. Close associates of Boumédienne were dropped, including his Director-General of National Security and the party chief Yahyawi, who had once been regarded as a possible President. Boumédienne's Foreign Minister was accused of embezzlement and another of his advisers on foreign affairs dropped from the Central Committee.

There were worries about the increased activity of the Islamic fundamentalists, who demanded an Islamic Republic, replacement of the consitution by the *Sharī'ah* and the abolition of cinemas, alcohol and female education above primary level. From exile the former President

Ahmad Ben Bella was believed to be spurring them on, and in October one of his former Ministers was arrested for threatening state security and other associates were accused of smuggling arms.

The continuing difficulties of the oil market—a price cut in March cost Algeria dear—was compensated by the increasing sale of gas, which now provided 70 per cent of all revenues from hydrocarbons. Since service of the debt absorbed 27 per cent of import revenues there was little to spare, and growth slowed down.

MOROCCO

Morocco had a year of active domestic politics. In January there were rumours that the King had invited the socialist leader, Abderrahim Bouabid, to form a Government—perhaps to provide a scapegoat if things went wrong. In the same month the Prime Minister, Maati Bouabid, formed a new party which called for a new atmosphere rather than specific new policies. In the local elections in June this fledgeling Union Constitutionelle emerged as the single largest party, just surpassing the historic Istiqlal, which complained bitterly that the results were the most fraudulent ever recorded. The actual campaign had, however, been fairly fought: 57,120 candidates stood for 15,480 seats, the leaders of the six parties which contested 10 per cent of the seats were given broadcasting time, and a local Pasha was dismissed for not giving the opposition a fair chance. The Government coalition won 58 per cent of the seats.

In June the King postponed parliamentary elections, due in September, in order not to clash with the referendum on the Sahara; but in November, to prepare for them, he appointed the politically neutral and generally respected Karim Lamrani, director of the state phosphate monopoly, to preside over a Cabinet which included both Abderrahim and Maati Bouabid and the other four principal party leaders as Ministers without Portfolio.

The skilful diplomacy of the King in making apparent concessions which in the event meant nothing won another year for Morocco to consolidate its position in the Western Sahara. The war, however, was reported to be costing $800 million annually and causing frustration in the army. Early in the year there were rumours of arrests of officers, which sharpened interest in the announcement that General Ahmad Dlimi, one of the King's closest associates who had combined command in the Sahara with headship of the intelligence services, had died in a car accident: a French journalist was expelled for reporting that he had been murdered.

After 'honest broking' by Saudi Arabia and France, the King and the Algerian President met in February in a tent on the frontier. Although they did not agree about the Sahara, there was a marked improvement in relations; direct air and rail links were reopened after seven years and plans were announced for detailed cooperation in other matters. The reconciliation with Libya was still more remarkable. After 15 years of unremitting hostility, Qadafi came to Rabat and announced that there was no further dispute and that henceforth 'permanent fraternal relations' prevailed. Each agreed not to meddle with what concerned the other—Chad and the Sahara.

The King tried to arrange another Arab summit to repeat his triumph of the previous year (see AR 1982, pp. 219–20) and he welcomed the first visit of an Egyptian Foreign Minister since Camp David. He received Israeli peace advocates and tried to arrange for them to meet Palestinian leaders. Behind the scenes he tried to reconcile Syria and the USA.

All senior American officials visiting the Arab world included Morocco in their itineraries, and the visit of President Mitterrand, postponed from the previous October to January, was a deliberate attempt to regain influence lost by France. He expressed no objection to supplying nuclear power plants to help irrigation—the King's favourite dream was of a great green belt along the Atlantic coast made fertile by desalination plants. Fears that the Spanish Socialist Government might prove a difficult neighbour were dissipated when Sr González chose Morocco for his first foreign visit and accords were made over fishing grounds.

Apart from the ending of a drought which had lasted in some areas for ten years, Morocco saw no improvement in its economic position. There was a slump in exports, partly due to increased protectionism by the EEC, a rise in the cost of imports following the hardening of the dollar—which also made the servicing of the debt, estimated at $10,000 million, more onerous—and a reduction in aid from the Gulf states. The IMF demanded a massive devaluation and the end of all food subsidies, but when the Government raised prices it caused unrest. In July an austerity Budget imposed new taxes and cut 19,000 projected new jobs. In October leading Western creditors rescheduled some of the debt and the IMF provided a standby credit. Perhaps the decision to call upon Britain's National Coal Board for development advice might ease Morocco's problems.

VI EQUATORIAL AFRICA

Chapter 1

ETHIOPIA—SOMALIA—DJIBOUTI—KENYA—TANZANIA—UGANDA

ETHIOPIA

THE second congress of the embryo communist party COPWE opened on 3 January with a six-hour speech by its Chairman, Mengistu Haile-Maryam. He revealed that COPWE had offices in about half of Ethiopia's hundred provinces and included 450 'basic organizations', a quarter of them in the army. Despite vigorous attempts to recruit workers and peasants, these accounted for only a quarter of the membership, the remaining three-quarters coming from the bureaucracy, army and intelligentsia. The seven-man executive was drawn entirely from the ruling Provisional Military Administrative Council (PMAC), though the 90-man Central Committee included civilians; six members of the previous Central Committee were expelled from the party. Party cadres were being trained in the Soviet Union and other socialist states. In March, the PMAC established an Institute for the Study of Ethiopian Nationalities, whose brief was to classify Ethiopia's various national groups, and to draw up an administrative structure for autonomous regions within a marxist-leninist system.

There were no major upheavals in government during the year, but a Cabinet reshuffle in April saw the Foreign Minister Feleke Gedle-Giyorgis switched to Information, and replaced by Colonel Goshu Wolde, who had previously been at Education; Captain Fikre-Selassie Wogderess took over as Secretary-General of the PMAC. Compulsory military service of thirty months' duration was introduced in May for all men aged between 16 and 30. Some 1,200 prisoners, over a hundred of them labelled 'political', were released on the ninth anniversary of the revolution in September.

Once again, drought, famine and the tangled politics of relief received wide publicity. Signs of a severe famine became evident early in the year, especially in the Tigre and Wollo regions, which had suffered badly in 1973–74. Relief aid was shipped to Ethiopia from Western sources, including the European Community and a wide variety of charitable agencies, and widespread allegations were made that much of this aid was being diverted to commercial sale, to supply the Ethiopian army or even to send to the Soviet Union in payment for arms. Some evidence was produced to support these claims, and the European Parliament placed a temporary ban on famine relief to Ethiopia, but a Community delegation to Ethiopia in June found no evidence to confirm the charges, which were also denied by relief agency officials. The famine was exacerbated, and relief impeded, by continued fighting in much of the affected area between government troops and Tigre People's Liberation Front (TPLF) guerrillas, who in April kidnapped ten relief workers, four of them British, from the Tigrean town of Korem; they were later released unharmed in the Sudan. The well-known Ethiopian relief administrator, Mr Shimelis Adugna, was dismissed in April, apparently after criticizing the failure of Soviet bloc countries to provide relief. As late as August, more than a million people were reported by a visiting US Congressional mission to be still needing food relief.

The security position in northern Ethiopia was little changed. Fighting was reported in April between government and Eritrean People's Liberation Front (EPLF) forces around the EPLF's citadel of Nakfa in the extreme north, but at a lower level of intensity than in previous years. Thereafter there was a lull in the fighting in Eritrea, and the Ethiopians concentrated on economic rehabilitation in the main towns, especially the capital, Asmara. Secret negotiations took place in Rome between the EPLF and the Ethiopian Government in February and March, but nothing emerged from them.

As the level of fighting against the Ethiopians diminished, long-standing rivalries among the Eritrean groups reasserted themselves. The three main factions of the non-communist Eritrean Liberation Front (ELF) met in Jeddah, Saudi Arabia, in January, and agreed to unite their forces, which had been driven from Eritrea by the EPLF in 1980–81. A pitched battle between ELF and EPLF guerrillas took place in November in south-western Eritrea as the ELF sought to re-establish itself in the territory. Further fighting took place in Tigre, especially in the area close to the Sudanese border in the first half of the year; Ethiopian aircraft were accused of using napalm during one attack in April, and the TPLF claimed to have killed over 4,000 Ethiopian troops. In contrast, very little disturbance was reported from southern Ethiopia.

Despite the evident inadequacy of food supplies, exportable coffee production increased in 1982-83 to 1,883,000 bags, the highest for some years. Cuban aid was used to construct roads in the main coffee-producing region of Kaffa. Economic relations with the Soviet bloc were nonetheless strained. In his Revolution Day speech in September, Colonel Mengistu drew attention to the poor rate of economic growth, and singled out the state sector, in which Soviet aid was concentrated, for special criticism. The chairman of the Soviet State Planning Committee visited Ethiopia in March to discuss aid for the prospective Ethiopian ten-year plan, but an Ethiopian request for $7,200 million aid for it was turned down at the October Comecon meeting in

Berlin. Earlier in the year, a decree had been issued to encourage Western investment in collaboration with the Ethiopian government, as yet without result; problems still remained over compensation for Western companies nationalized in 1975. It was reported in December that many of the 12,000 Cuban troops stationed in Ethiopia since 1978 were preparing to leave, both because they were no longer needed and to improve relations with the West.

Relations with the Sudan deteriorated sharply in November when the Khartoum Government accused Ethiopia of massing troops on the border, a charge dismissed by the Ethiopians as a publicity device during President Nimairi's tour of Western capitals; no fighting took place. Relations with Somalia were strained but fairly quiet, and the crew of a small Ethiopian naval vessel defected to the Somali port of Berbera in September. Colonel Mengistu became Chairman of the OAU following the Addis Ababa summit meeting in June.

SOMALIA

General Mohamed Siyad Barre retained power in the face of opposition to his Government, especially from the northern region, and strengthened his ties with the United States. On 2 January, opposition Somali National Movement guerrillas attacked the main prison in the region, near Berbera, releasing 724 prisoners, including eleven political leaders gaoled the previous year. Another opposition group, the Somali Democratic Salvation Front, also claimed a successful attack on government forces in the north in February. President Siyad immediately toured the region, promising an amnesty for 'crimes against the state' to anyone surrendering within a month, but riots broke out in the northern capital of Hargeisa the following month after a ban on the use of the popular narcotic plant qat. Further rioting was reported in August. Conditions in the camps housing some 700,000 Somali refugees from Ethiopia were said by a UN High Commission for Refugees (UNHCR) spokesman in December to have improved markedly; this followed strained relations between the Government and the UNHCR in May, when the local director was asked to leave and two officials were deported after charges that refugees were being forcibly recruited into the army and scholarships meant for refugees diverted to the children of high officials.

President Reagan's roving ambassador, General Vernon Walters, visited Mogadishu in February. US military credits to Somalia increased by fifty per cent on the 1982 level, and the United States also supplied most of a $1,200 million economic loan announced in November. About 2,800 American troops took part in joint exercises with the Somalis in August. In January, it was announced that an Italian consortium was to build a $62 million cement plant, funded mostly from Italian aid, at Bardera in the southern region. Further aid came from the European Community, China and Arab states, and at $400 million accounted for some forty per cent of GNP.

DJIBOUTI

Two events during the year indicated closer relations with Djibouti's principal neighbour, Ethiopia. Djibouti received a $6.4 million World Bank loan to improve the highway network with Ethiopia. In February, the Government reached an agreement with Ethiopia, under the auspices of the UNHCR, for the voluntary repatriation of some of the 30,000 refugees living in Djibouti; the first group of 171 refugees returned in September, being resettled and provided with agricultural equipment, and others followed later in the year. Three Palestinian hijackers who forced a South Yemeni Boeing 707 airliner to land at Djibouti in January surrendered in exchange for being allowed to leave for a country of their choice.

KENYA

Following the coup attempt in August 1982 (see AR 1982, pp. 224-6), the Government was preoccupied with security, though the release from prison of over 500 ex-servicer1en and 61 students early in the year and the lifting in June of the house order against the former police commissioner were signs of its increasing confidence. Courts-martial imposed prison sentences of up to 25 years on over 900 members of the disbanded Kenyan Air Force (officially reinstituted in December as the '82 Air Force'), including its former commander; seven were sentenced to death, though none was executed. Sedition laws were vigorously applied against students and others, and Nairobi University, though reopened temporarily in February for a 10-week examination period, was closed until October. In March Mr Raila Odinga (son of former Vice-President Oginga Odinga, who was himself under house arrest until October), along with a journalist and a university professor, were detained without trial after being cleared of treason charges by a Nairobi court. The Government reacted angrily the next month to mild criticism by Mr David Steel, the British Liberal Party leader, of its handling of dissidents: nine others, including university lecturers, were held in preventive detention.

Relations with Britain deteriorated in May when President Daniel Arap Moi accused foreign powers of plotting to replace him with an unnamed 'traitor' and the influential *Weekly Review* hinted that Britain and Israel might be involved. Mr Moi's accusation sparked off intense political in-fighting in the Cabinet, Mr Charles Njonjo, the Constitutional Affairs Minister, being widely identified as the internal conspirator. At the end of June the President suspended Mr Njonjo until a three-man judicial inquiry had reported. In July the ex-Minister resigned from Parliament and was suspended from the Kenya African National Union (KANU), the ruling party.

Presidential and parliamentary elections were called by the President in September, a year ahead of schedule, to 'cleanse the system' and wipe out corruption and disloyalty in his administration. Mr Moi was nominated by KANU as its sole presidential candidate and, together with Mr Mwai Kibaki, the Vice-President, was re-elected for another five-year term. In the parliamentary elections five candidates, including the President and Vice-President, were declared elected unopposed; 153 seats were hotly contested by some 760 KANU candidates, with up to 15 candidates contesting the same seat. KANU, the only legalized party, stressed rural development in its election manifesto; at constituency level the emphasis was on local issues. Violent clashes occurred between supporters of rival candidates and at least three people died. Turn-out of the 7.19 million registered electorate was poor—less than 50 per cent in most constituencies. A number of Ministers—including those for Agriculture, Lands and Physical Planning, and Labour—and junior Ministers were defeated, as well as a score or more backbenchers. Mr Philip Leakey, Assistant Minister of Environment and Natural Resources and the only white candidate, was returned for a Nairobi seat. The President appointed people whom he could trust, including fellow Kalenjin, to sensitive posts such as the directorship of personnel management and the Ministry of Foreign Affairs, and brought other key departments under the control of his own office. For the first time in Kenya's history, a member of the Somali ethnic group was given a Cabinet post, while another—Major-General Mahmoud Mohammed—commanded the new air force.

Relations with Tanzania and Uganda improved considerably. In November the three state Presidents, meeting in Arusha, northern Tanzania, agreed to the recommendations on the division of the assets and liabilities of the former East African Community made by Dr Viktor Umbricht, the Swiss mediator appointed by the World Bank. When the Community broke up in 1977 Kenya had inherited the biggest share of assets and Uganda the smallest, so substantial compensatory payments were therefore due to Uganda. The border between Kenya and Tanzania, closed since 1977, was reopened. The United Nations expressed concern that, prior to this agreement, 30 political refugees had been exchanged between the two countries.

In November Queen Elizabeth paid a five-day state visit and in December the Presidents of Tanzania and Uganda attended the celebrations to mark the twentieth anniversary of independence. Seven thousand petty criminals were released from prison, perhaps to underline President Moi's claim that Kenya was 'standing on a solid rock of political stability'. This seemed an extravagant claim in view of the gross inequality of income, the rapidly rising population (the growth rate was among the highest in the world) and mounting fiscal problems as the Government vainly tried to maintain both its recurrent expenditure and its development programme: all expenditure except on salaries had to be frozen for a four-month period. Against World Bank advice, the Government retained price controls on maize and beef. Fortunately, the world market for tea became unexpectedly buoyant, while tourism—the most important source of foreign exchange earnings after refined petroleum products and coffee—was not seriously damaged by armed attacks on tourists and the murder in June of a British businessman. Nevertheless, Kenya's debt service ratio continued to rise and its reliance on the West increased, particularly on the United States which was providing $100 million aid a year, one-third of it military. In November Kenya voted against the UN resolution condemning America's invasion of Grenada. Israel established more business interests in Kenya and links with Saudi Arabia and other conservative Arab states were strengthened.

TANZANIA

The sharp decline in exports and foreign exchange revenues over the past four years, leading to acute shortages of basic commodities, high inflation and increased black-marketeering and corruption, were the backdrop to a plot to assassinate President Julius Nyerere and overthrow his Government uncovered early in January. The Government played down the incident and claimed that Zambian newspaper reports that more than 600 soldiers and 1,000 civilians had been arrested were grossly exaggerated. It admitted to the arrest of 30 soldiers and civilians: the group was said to include a former adviser to the President and three senior army officers, but the People's Defence Force was not itself involved. In June, following the escape from prison of two of those awaiting trial—a businessman and an airline pilot—the court charges against the rest were dropped, but they were held in preventive detention.

In February, President Nyerere reshuffled his Cabinet. Mr Edward Sokoine, who had resigned as Prime Minister in November 1980 because of ill-health, was reinstated and Mr Cleopa Msuya, his immediate predecessor, was moved to the Ministry of Finance. The former Finance Minister—the Asian-born Mr Amir Jamal—became Minister without Portfolio, while the former Defence Minister, who was himself replaced by the ex-Minister for Home Affairs, was assigned to special duties (assumed to relate to state security) in the President's office. The former

Ministers for Trade and Justice were dropped and three Ministers without Portfolio were appointed to handle liaison between the Government and Chama cha Mapinduzi (CCM), the ruling party, and to coordinate Tanzania's role in the implementation of a new international economic order.

In his budget speech in June Mr Msuya said that the country's exports—85 per cent agricultural—and foreign aid would account for only 50 per cent of necessary imports and debt servicing requirements, and that Shs. 5,000 million a year for three to five years was needed from external sources to fill the gap and rehabilitate the economy. The protracted negotiations with the IMF and World Bank continued—some Shs. 2,500 million a year for three years was being sought. The Government went some way to satisfy IMF prescriptions by agreeing in principle to the progressive reduction over three years of the subsidy on maize meal (other subsidies on foodstuffs were removed early in 1980) and in June it devalued the shilling by 20 per cent, bringing its value to Shs. 12.2 to the US dollar. However, a much heavier devaluation and substantially increased incentives for producers were called for by the Fund. The Government questioned the relevance of the traditional financial and fiscal devices favoured by the IMF to the Tanzanian situation, but had little room to manoeuvre given the desperate state of the economy and its wish to conclude bilateral agreements with the US and other donor countries which awaited the outcome of the negotiations with the IMF.

The Government's own initiatives included moves to step up agricultural production: cooperatives were reinstituted and restrictions on private farming eased, and members of the Asian community were allowed to launch large-scale agricultural projects. (The future of the high-technology Tanzania-Canada wheat project, begun in November 1970 and centred on Arusha in northern Tanzania, was threatened by severe erosion.) The Government also cracked down on 'economic saboteurs'—mainly private traders accused of hoarding and racketeering on a large scale. On the industrial front, a large paper plant at Sao Hill was due to be completed by early 1985 and preparations were made to exploit natural gas from Songo Songo and elsewhere on the coast.

In July Tanzania agreed to pay Lonrho, the British-based multinational company, Shs. 121·5 million in compensation for assets nationalized five years earlier; the agreement opened the way for Lonrho to resume its business activities in Tanzania. In November the *Observer* (London) alleged that Tanzania, which spent over 50 per cent of its export earnings on oil imports, had been secretly trading in oil with South Africa. The Government denied the allegation but, following an inquiry, admitted that in October a British-registered tanker had, without its knowledge, off-loaded at Dar es Salaam 30,000 tons of oil from South Africa; forged documents had shown the oil to have originated in

Singapore. The Energy Minister and the head of the state oil corporation announced that they were suing the newspaper for libel.

In February the central committee of CCM recommended changes in Tanzania's 1977 constitution to define the division of power between the President, the Prime Minister and the National Assembly. This prompted a number of senior Zanzibari civil servants to call for the rotation of the Union presidency between the mainland and the islands, among other constitutional changes. A number of Zanzibaris alleged that mainland civil servants and army personnel received preferential treatment at the expense of islanders and that Zanzibar's foreign exchange reserves were depleted by the Union government's access to them. Mr Aboud Jumbe, the President of Zanzibar and Vice-President of Tanzania, refrained from public comment, preferring to settle the issue quietly.

UGANDA

Uganda continued to face serious security problems. In February government forces mounted counter-insurgency operations to destroy the guerrilla bases of the National Resistance Army (led by Mr Yoweri Museveni, a former Minister of Defence) in the area to the north of Kampala inhabited by Baganda, who had voted heavily for the Democratic Party (DP) in the December 1980 general election. Some 100,000 villagers fled in fear of their lives: some went to Kampala, but the great majority took refuge in overcrowded and insanitary 'banana leaf' camps, supposedly under army protection.

The sad plight of the refugees, of whom many were killed (including at least 40 at the hands of guerrillas in Kikyusa village, Luwero district, in May) evoked international concern. In September, under pressure from foreign embassies and relief agencies (including the International Red Cross, whose 1982 expulsion order was revoked) an embarrassed Government announced that it was assuming full responsibility for coordinating the distribution of relief food. A special administrator was appointed within the Prime Minister's office and, as well as coordination, was entrusted with making plans to resettle the displaced people. The Government also undertook to provide security escorts for relief workers; however, two members of the Ugandan Red Cross were killed in late November and many aid officials and nurses complained of daily harassment by the military at roadblocks and in the camps. President Obote accused the foreign press of distorted reporting and invited a small team of Cuban experts to help the Ministry of Information and Broadcasting to improve Uganda's image abroad.

The continuing indiscipline and lawless behaviour of many soldiers led the Government in July to ask for a six-month extension to the stay of the 40-member Commonwealth military team, which was training the army at Jinja, 50 miles east of Kampala. The capital itself, and the area surrounding it, were the scene of a number of ugly incidents; politicians belonging to both the government and opposition parties were assassinated. On the other hand, there was a renewed bustle of activity in the streets of the capital, indicating a partial return to normality. President Milton Obote committed his Government to a policy of national reconciliation, but did not respond to the repeated pleas of the head of Uganda's Roman Catholic community to hold talks with the guerrilla groups. Two to three hundred Ugandan Asian families, including members of the Madhvani family with its extensive business interests, returned to Uganda and, under the terms of the 1982 Expropriated Properties Act, began negotiations with the Government for compensation for their assets seized by President Idi Amin in 1972 (see AR 1972, p. 234). Ugandan Asians resident in Britain were dissatisfied with the British Government's policy of not pressing their claims for compensation but merely offering to serve as a channel of communication with Uganda.

The modest signs of economic recovery in 1982, when inflation fell to approximately 30 per cent and GDP rose by 6·1 per cent, continued, and there was increased optimism in business and diplomatic circles. President Obote announced a revised two-year recovery programme, placing emphasis on stepping up agricultural output, curbing inessential imports and promoting investment schemes. Good relations were maintained with the IMF and the World Bank, and IMF prescriptions for reviving the economy continued to be followed; these included a heavy devaluation of the Uganda shilling, sharp increases in producer prices for export crops, tax reforms and the lifting of price controls, and tight curbs on government spending. Mr Malcolm Rifkind, Minister of State at the Foreign and Commonwealth Office, visited Uganda in July and announced that Britain would release a further £4 million; Britain also made £200,000 available for the relief of refugees in the Luwero triangle. The US, Italy, the EEC and UNDP promised assistance.

In March Mr Yoweri Kyesmira, a former Minister of Industry and a member of the DP, was charged with treason. The DP, which eschewed violence, boycotted the special elections in November to eight vacant National Assembly seats on security grounds. All the seats went to the ruling party: the Uganda People's Congress was unopposed in six of the seats and easily won the other two from the tiny Conservative Party. In December Major-General David Oyite-Ojok, the army commander and head of the Coffee Marketing Board, and the director of Uganda's small air force were killed in a helicopter crash.

Chapter 2

GHANA—NIGERIA—SIERRA LEONE—THE GAMBIA—LIBERIA

GHANA

THE dramatic event of the year came on 19 June when an attempted coup d'état was once again defeated in Accra. It was a further consequence of the November 1982 coup (see AR 1982, p. 230) since this renewed bid to overthrow Flight-Lieut. Rawlings and the Provisional National Defence Council was led by those under Sergeant Malik and Lieut. Korah who had earlier escaped to the neighbouring republic of Togo. They succeeded in releasing some 52 military intelligence officers and other servicemen from prisons in Accra and Nsawam, including Lieut.-Colonel Ekow Dennis and assistant police superintendent William Oduro. Shortly before 11 am on 19 June the rebels were able to broadcast over Accra radio that the PNDC had been overthrown by 'revolutionary fighters with the support of the suffering masses'; Rawlings, the rebels said, was 'a naive dictator, a preacher of virtue and doer of vice, heavily supported by the people of his team like Kojo Tsikata "the murderer" '. By 12.45 pm Captain Courage Kwashigah had regained control of the radio station and, later that evening, Flight-Lieut. Rawlings proclaimed that 'the objectives which we declared for the revolution on 31 December 1981 will be upheld'. It had been a two-hour coup, though none the less serious for that. There had been fighting between rival factions within the army. The revolution within the revolution had been thwarted, but many of those held for trial under the PNDC were now back in Togo or the Ivory Coast.

The Government struggled against disaffection throughout the year. When students protested against the April Budget, all three universities were closed. In August, 69 foreign service officers were dismissed because of 'financial irregularities, misuse of diplomatic bags, gross inefficiency, indiscipline and desertion of posts'. The Government also warned that smugglers who resisted arrest would be shot. Between 26 July and 2 August judgments were handed down relating to the November 1982 and June 1983 coups of the 47 on trial, all but three abroad. One member—Lance-Corporal Nkrabea Poku Ware—of the five-man tribunal under Mr Addo Aikins was absent when judgment was given, having fled into exile in the Ivory Coast. Among those sentenced to life imprisonment *in absentia* was Captain William Ampomah Nketia. His brother-in-law, the former head of the Cocoa Marketing Board, Andrew Kwame Pianim—the only civilian on trial—was given an 18-year sentence. Three were acquitted. On 18 August, Joshua Amartey Kwei and Johnny Dzandu—and on 31 August Michael Senya—were executed by firing squad after being found guilty, by a Special Investigation Board under Mr Justice Azu Crabbe, of involvement in the murder of the three judges and a retired army officer in June 1982 (see AR 1982, p. 230). Lieut. Kenneth Korah was sentenced, *in absentia*, to life imprisonment for his part in the November 1982 coup and to death for his role in the June attempt. In September, Dr Hilla Limann, the former President, and Dr de Graft Johnson, former Vice-President, were released from custody on bail.

Evidence of the destitute state of the economy came with the April Budget, described by Kwesi Botchway, Finance and Planning Minister, as a 'bitter pill' and opposed by those who most felt its effects—farmers, trade unionists, students and the urban poor. The Budget was delayed by arguments over the extent of the basic reforms needed, including those put forward by the IMF and World Bank. Rawlings added his own stern note of rebuke. Higher taxes and lower subsidies were needed to 'mop up the excess cedis of the privileged': hence the tenfold increase in the cost of airline tickets to Lagos and London. The basis of the new Four-Year Plan was said to be the encouragement of agriculture, although the Budget added to farmers' grievances by raising the price of petrol, diesel and kerosene fuel and of farm cutlasses. Botchway warned on 22 December that cocoa production was likely to fall to 150,000 tonnes in 1983-4 compared with 170,000 tonnes in 1982-3. The bush fires which raged through the country in April and May devastated a large acreage of cocoa and timber, a disaster made worse by deteriorating roads and inadequate transport; the only bright feature was the sharp increase in world cocoa prices—to £1,985.50 a tonne at the end of December. In the industrial sector, redundancies took their toll as the shortage of foreign exchange slowed imports: some 64 per cent of Ghanaian industry was dependent on imported raw materials. Unemployment increased, worsened by the return of the 1·2 million Ghanaians expelled (on a bare fortnight's notice) from Nigeria on 17 January.

In April, Rawlings flew to Libya to take part in a symposium on socialism; he spent 24 hours in Mali early in November, and on 17 December paid his first official visit to the Ivory Coast for talks with President Houphouet-Boigny.

NIGERIA

The events of 1983 led up to a dramatic climax on 31 December when a civilian constitutional and democratic government was overthrown by a military coup, launched by senior officers of the army. The coup was bloodless apart from the death of Brigadier Bako, shot by the presidential guard while seeking to arrest the President; otherwise, there was no resistance. President Shehu Shagari himself, who was generally thought to have been honest but weak, was treated with some respect and detained in a comfortable house in Lagos. The general rejoicing with which the coup was greeted indicated that the civilian government had failed to meet the needs of Nigeria. The new head of state, Major-General Muhammed Buhari, commander of the Third Armoured Division, was Commissioner for Petroleum in the last Military Government. The new army chief of staff, Major-General Ibrahim Babangida, was generally reckoned to have been one of the leading spirits behind the coup.

General Buhari ascribed the coup to the indiscipline and corruption rampant under the civilian regime, to their mismanagement of the economy, resulting in acute shortages and a level of foreign debt ($15,000 million) which had reduced Nigeria to the status of a 'beggar nation'. He also declared that the election held in August 1983 had been 'anything but free and fair'. General Babangida declared that more than $1,500 million had been embezzled by five or six leading figures under the Shagari regime.

The military coup's suspension of Nigerian's elective legislatures would at least effect a budgetary economy. The total cost of running the federal and 19 state legislatures took over 5 per cent of the total 1983 federal and state budget of 5,000 million naira. This ultra-expensive structure had a very low legislative output, and contributed little to the efficient running of Nigeria. The Open Universities Bill, for instance, rejected by the Senate for unexplained reasons in 1981, was passed in 1983 in almost exactly the same terms. Some 70 per cent of the legislators lost their seats through party primary elections or general elections in August, depriving the two federal Houses of much-needed legislative experience.

The major reason for the failure of the regime, however, was its continuing poor economic performance (see AR 1982, p. 231). Oil production averaged 1·3 million barrels per day (the Opec quota), but fell as low as 700,000 barrels in March. At a price of $29 a barrel, this brought the government a revenue only about half that which it enjoyed when it came to power. President Shagari reacted by cutting imports by 40 per cent. This resulted in very severe shortages of essentials, exacerbated by widespread hoarding by merchants, and in a drastic fall in economic activity. Many factories closed down, creating severe unemployment. Nigeria's short-term debt rose to $2,000 million and remained a problem despite refinancing arrangements agreed with a consortium of bankers. Nigeria approached the IMF for a $2,000 million loan, but was reluctant to accept the IMF condition of a substantial devaluation.

The economic crisis resulted in a failure to pay civil servants and teachers in state governments for several months, and in a closing-down of primary schools through strikes. Nigerian students abroad were stranded by total lack of funds. The Shagari Government eventually provided emergency finance to remedy both those situations, but the coexistence of acute suffering of lower-paid staff and conspicuous consumption by political notables—among all parties—created a level of discontent which made the coup acceptable.

Local government elections, already three years overdue and often promised, were again postponed, but federal and state elections were held in August. The Federal Electoral Commission had decided that the order of elections should be reversed from that of 1979, to allow the presidential election to take place first. Shehu Shagari won 12 million votes out of $25\frac{1}{2}$ million, and easily obtained the required quarter of the votes in two-thirds of the states. The opposition parties failed to agree upon one candidate. Shagari had taken great care to improve his relations with his main opponent, Chief Awolowo (see AR 1982, p. 232), and before the election all party leaders issued a joint statement asking their supporters to remain peaceful. Despite this, there was a considerable level of violence in Ondo, Oyo, Niger, Benue and Annambra states, where all the parties complained of massive rigging, and some two hundred people were killed in inter-party fighting. The chairman of the Federal Electoral Commission, Justice Ovie-Whiskey, proved too weak to prevent a very high level of rigging in a number of places, through rendering of false returns from the counts at polling stations, substitute voting for other people on the register and intimidation of polling agents. All parties rigged the election where they were able, but even without rigging Shehu Shagari would probably have won a comfortable majority.

In the gubernatorial elections, a bandwagon effect gave Shagari's party, the NPN, 12 out of 19 states. They lost Kwara state, however, owing to a quarrel between the two leading NPN figures in the state, the governor and the leader of the senate: UPN won four states, NPP two, and PRP one. The elections were followed by a spate of electoral petitions, which resulted in the reversal of the NPN victory in the election for governor of Ondo state. After his inauguration for a second term on 1 October, President Shagari, in an attempt to instil dedication into government, announced a new smaller Cabinet of 35 members, having dropped all but seven of his previous Ministers.

Earlier in the year, the Internal Affairs Minister caused considerable embarrassment to Nigerian foreign policy, and to the cause of Pan-Africanism, by expelling 2·2 million Ghanaian residents in Nigeria, who did not have proper papers. Their mass exodus, depicted on television screens all over the world, caused grave problems for Ghana (see p. 220). Thousands were reported to have returned illegally to Nigeria by the end of the year.

1983 saw the deaths of Alhaji Aminu Kano, the doyen of Nigerian radical politicians, Dr Kenneth Dike, Nigeria's leading historian (see

OBITUARY), and in November of 65 people in an air crash in Enugu. In December, General Yakubu Gowon made his first visit home to Nigeria since his overthrow in 1975, and met an enthusiastic reception.

SIERRA LEONE

The economy remained in the doldrums throughout the year. While demand for the country's exports remained depressed there was little chance of an economic recovery. Agriculture was helped by improved producer prices but the vital mineral sector languished. Rutile showed some improvement and the Marampa iron-ore mine was reopened, but bauxite production fell and diamond exports, though up in volume, dropped some 40 per cent in value. As in previous years, several domestic factors also contributed to economic difficulties: smuggling, mismanagement and corruption. Finance Minister Salia Jusu-Sheriff continued his efforts to impose financial restraints and fiscal discipline and was rewarded in December with a one-year IMF loan of some US$53 million to help alleviate a chronic foreign exchange shortage which was hampering industrial recovery and causing widespread shortages of consumer goods. Two of the three commissions of inquiry into civil service financial scandals (the 'vouchergate' affair) submitted their findings to the Government and firm action was promised against miscreants.

It was a quiet year politically, except for the Pujehun district, where persistent violence provoked by political rivalries occurred: several thousand people fled to neighbouring Liberia and the army was dispatched to restore order. Once again President Siaka Stevens scotched rumours of his imminent resignation when he announced that he would remain in office until the present crisis had subsided.

Financial necessity led to the closure of six foreign missions but, intriguingly, relations were established with Iran. The Mano River Union celebrated its tenth anniversary, though relations with Liberia cooled in the early part of the year because of an unfounded press report in Freetown that the Liberian head of state had murdered his wife.

THE GAMBIA

There was a measure of economic recovery during the year, largely the result of better weather conditions and a revival in tourism, but uncertain rainfall in the summer planting season compelled President Jawara to call for international assistance. The agricultural recovery was most evident in the all-important groundnut sector: an excellent harvest of some 128,000 tonnes was reported. Unfortunately poor world demand

and a commitment to high prices to local producers proved costly to the Government. With some 45,000 visitors in 1982/83, The Gambia recorded its highest-ever level of tourism. Other agricultural products fared less well than groundnuts and the country faced a chronic balance of payments deficit and shortage of foreign exchange. The Budget was balanced at about 136 million dalasi, thanks to 16 million dalasi additional taxes and duties.

The 1983 census revealed that the population was now 695,886, compared with 494,499 in 1973; most worrying for the Government was the 161 per cent growth in the population of the townships surrounding the capital, Banjul. Youth unemployment and the drift from the land continued to preoccupy the Administration.

There were two parliamentary by-elections during the year in which the ruling People's Progressive Party (PPP) recovered seats lost to Independents the previous year. Party strength in Parliament was now PPP 30; NCP (National Convention Party) 3; Independents 3. The NCP refused to contest the local-government Area Council elections in May but the one Independent who stood (in Sandu East ward) won by a large majority. There were few leadership changes in 1983: the Minister for Local Government resigned on health grounds and the Speaker of the House of Representatives was forced to resign because of improper behaviour.

Although all those held after the 1981 abortive insurrection had been released, sentenced or put on trial by the summer, the apparently voluntary return of three rebels from Cuba in the autumn led to fresh arrests: 11 civilians and military or police personnel were detained and several senior police officers dismissed following the revelations of the returnees. An anti-corruption drive was linked to the creation of a three-man Assets Evaluation Commission. A senior civil servant and a chief inspector of police were gaoled for peculation.

Relations with Senegal remained cordial: two meetings of the Confederal Council of Ministers took place and defence and security protocols were ratified. Preliminary work on economic and monetary union was announced.

LIBERIA

The economic situation remained critical as recovery measures ran foul of depressed world markets for Liberian exports and persistent resistance to financial discipline at home. An emergency donors' conference was summoned to try and reschedule the country's alarming foreign debts of some US$1,200 million: head of state Samuel Doe appealed for half this amount to be written-off in order to encourage economic recovery. As usual the United States provided most foreign assistance—some $32 million in 1983.

Hopes of a positive move toward civilian rule were raised by the publication and deliberation of a draft revised constitution during the year. The Constitutional Advisory Assembly, like the steering body, was dominated by members of the former ruling party, the True Whig Party (TWP)—a cause of concern to those expecting more fundamental political changes. The continuing dependence of the People's Redemption Council (PRC) on ex-TWP supporters (see AR 1981, p. 237, and AR 1982, p. 235) was also seen at government level, where remaining civilian radicals such as Baccus Matthews and Henry Fahnbulleh were ousted from office. A purge of radicals in the educational system was also instigated.

Another power struggle, perhaps related to the ideological division, came to a head in October-November with the dismissal of General Thomas Quiwonkpa, a senior army officer and PRC member and former staunch ally of General Doe. A few weeks later he was accused of plotting the overthrow of the Government and of exploiting Nimba ethnic grievances against the PRC. The Soviet Union and Ghana were implicated in the November plot and their heads-of-mission expelled. The rightward stance in external relations was accentuated by the recognition of Israel in August and closer identification with the Reagan Administration.

Chapter 3

SENEGAL—GUINEA—MALI AND MAURITANIA—IVORY COAST—
TOGO AND BENIN—UPPER VOLTA—NIGER—CAMEROON—CHAD—
GABON—CENTRAL AFRICAN REPUBLIC AND PEOPLE'S REPUBLIC
OF THE CONGO—EQUATORIAL GUINEA

SENEGAL

IN ONE of Africa's few multi-party democracies, the 28 February elections were keenly awaited. The President, Abdou Diouf, who had followed the long term of office of Leopold Sédar Senghor in 1981, was standing in his first election, and it was also the first election since the early 1960s in which the number of parties that could stand was unrestricted. Some commentators had even believed that the result, at least in the elections for the National Assembly, might be genuinely in doubt. As it turned out, the President and the ruling party, the Parti Socialiste (PS), were returned comfortably, but not without accusations of election-rigging from all the opposition parties. The elections were followed by a government reshuffle which was said to demonstrate the President's desire to control the 'barons' of the PS.

In the elections the President had obtained 913,569 votes (83·55 per cent of a total vote of 1,097,398, or 58·11 per cent of the electorate), while his nearest rival, Maître Abdoulaye Wade, of the Parti Démocratique Sénégalaise (PDS), obtained 160,809 votes (14·17 per cent). In the National Assembly the PS won 111 seats with 79·92 per cent of the poll, the PDS 8 seats with 13·98 per cent, and the Rassemblement Nationale Démocratique (RND) of Cheikh Anta Diop one seat with 2·62 per cent. Because of the electoral fraud, some of which was confirmed by independent observers, the opposition parties decided to boycott the National Assembly, a boycott which was rescinded later in the year following an appeal from the President for national unity because of the grave economic situation facing the country. There was some talk of 'national consensus' and Maître Wade said he would support a common programme, but by the end of the year there was no sign of any such development.

Of the gravity of the economic situation there was no doubt, an increasingly difficult budgetary situation being compounded by drought, and some areas suffering poor rainfall for the first time since Diouf had come to power. The end of the year saw an aggravation of the regional problem in Casamance, when violent incidents took place as the trial began of 27 separatists who had held a demonstration twelve months earlier. Three gendarmes and four others were killed when a meeting of the Mouvement des Forces Démocratiques de la Casamance (MFDC) became out of control, after the gendarmes had penetrated a sacred grove. The MFDC leader, Abbé Diamacoune Senghor, and several others received gaol sentences of several years, and at least twenty more deaths followed another still more violent demonstration at the regional capital of Ziguinchor.

GUINEA

The most dramatic event of the year came late in December when two earthquakes left a death toll of at least 300 people, with as many as 1,500 injured and many more left homeless. The first quake, the first serious one in West Africa in living memory, measured 6·3 on the Richter scale and destroyed the towns of Koumbia and Gaoual in the northern part of the country. The second shock came three days later. Substantial relief effort was offered, mainly from Western Europe, the USA, Arab and neighbouring African countries.

Internally, although the economic situation remained serious, the increasing export of minerals improved Guinea's foreign exchange position, and President Sekou Touré's new leaning to the West expressed itself in his willingness to permit more capitalist activity, above all in the field of the 'privatization of commerce', where substantial steps were taken early in the year. In December the President berated traders for hoarding money, and threatened a devaluation of the national currency, the syli, unless deposits were made in official banks.

The increasingly important role of foreign policy was seen in the hosting of the summit of the Economic Community of West African States in May, even if the prize for which the President had been working for some time, the hosting of the 20th-anniversary summit of the Organization of African Unity, eluded him because of the delays of the previous year (see AR 1982, p. 368-9). It was still hoped to host the 20th summit in the 21st year of the OAU's existence, and there had been considerable expenditure on the construction of a lavish OAU village of 57 villas. Guinean foreign policy was pitched firmly in the 'moderate' camp as far as the OAU was concerned, although, like Abdou Diouf of Senegal, Sekou Touré was ready to distance himself somewhat from his Moroccan friends for the sake of the organization (see also Pt. XI, Ch. 6).

MALI AND MAURITANIA

These two West African Sahelian countries, whose northern parts cover large areas of the Western Sahara, were both suffering from cumulative effects of drought and desertification, which sapped permanently at their economic base. Both continued to be governed by military regimes, and, although Mali had a political party imposed from above, political freedoms in either country continued to seem marginal in face of the struggle to survive. Both continued to be subjected to pressures from powerful northern neighbours, especially Algeria and Libya, and Mauritania to be unavoidably drawn into the Western Sahara conflict.

IVORY COAST

It was a troubled year for the country, as aggravated economic problems expressed themselves in social tensions, breaking into the open in a teachers' strike in April. This began with a strike of secondary school teachers which threatened to escalate to higher education and other sectors until President Houphouet-Boigny, combining firm action with concessions, defused the crisis. Some teachers were sacked, but so, too, were the Ministers of Secondary and Primary Education, Paul Akoto Yao and Pascal N'guessan Dikebie. A new unified Ministry was created, to be headed by Dr Balla Keita.

The crisis was marked by one of the most extraordinary actions of

Houphouet-Boigny's long and varied political career, a lengthy speech to a party meeting at which he felt obliged to reply to charges made against him in tracts distributed by striking teachers, and to justify his considerable wealth accumulation. The admission of his vast fortune, and the fact that an important portion was kept outside the country, were seen by many as wholly outweighing any benefits he might have brought to the Ivoirian people. There was even speculation that his political flair was failing. However, after an extended four-month holiday during which he visited the US, the UK and other countries, he made a triumphant return to Abidjan, and set about taking measures to face basic problems such as the crime wave and the power shortage. The shadow of the succession to *le vieux* still hung over Ivoirian political life, and, in spite of promises, still seemed no nearer a solution.

TOGO AND BENIN

Both of these small buffer states, strips of land sandwiched between Ghana and Nigeria, continued to survive as best they could, although inevitably affected by the turbulences shaking their larger neighbours. At the beginning of the year both were momentarily in the spotlight as they acted as transit territory for the vast wave of Ghanaian illegal immigrants expelled from Nigeria. The People's Republic of Benin, in particular, also received a substantial group of their own citizens who had to be resettled, and it was President Kérékou who visited Nigeria on behalf of the countries of the Council of the Entente (Benin, Togo, Ivory Coast, Niger and Upper Volta) and secured $1 million assistance for the expelled. Like others, their reaction was muted, because of the continued need to live with their giant neighbour.

Togo was also increasingly sensitive during the year to 'plot phobia' and in November alleged destabilization attempts from an undisclosed source centred on northern Togo.

UPPER VOLTA

A dramatic year reached its climax in the 'revolution' of 4 August, which finally brought the charismatic Captain Thomas Sankara to undivided power. The year began with Sankara emerging, after his appointment as Prime Minister, as the strong man behind the coup of the previous November (see AR 1982, p. 238), although the head of state, Commandant Jean-Baptiste Ouédraogo, tried to exercise real power.

After a period of jockeying for power, which included a visit by Sankara to Libya, and a return visit by Colonel Qadafi to Upper Volta in which Sankara received all the limelight, Ouédraogo sacked Sankara on

17 May and arrested him with several of his associates in the army. This was seen by some as a pre-emptive coup, engineered with discreet backing from both France and the Ivory Coast. Ouédraogo, however, was not apparently strong enough within the army for the move to be fully successful, as a group of officers loyal to Sankara held out at the commando base at Pô on the Ghana border. Sankara was arrested and released three times in less than two months, and a complex series of negotiations between Ouagadougou and Pô attempted to arrive at a new *modus vivendi*, but finally Sankara, perhaps reinforced with external arms, marched on the capital.

The coup involved bloodshed, including the death of the army commander General Gabriel Somé and some twenty others, but the arrival of Sankara in power seemed genuinely popular, and was followed by a honeymoon period in which revolutionary rhetoric flowed and new structures were established, such as a National Revolutionary Council and in both towns and villages Committees for the Defence of the Revolution (CDRs), similar to Ghana's People's Defence Committees. Popular Tribunals also echoed the Ghanaian experience. The problems of staging a revolution were clearly only beginning, as Upper Volta could not be divorced from its unfortunate geographical context as one of the poorest countries in Africa, beset by drought and famine, with a desperate need to get on with its neighbours and to be on the receiving end of international aid, most of which was from Western sources. This did not prevent a deterioration of relations with Ivory Coast in particular, where 1·5 million Voltaics were living and working.

NIGER

The dramatic event of the year was an attempted coup at the beginning of October. It was announced on 6 October that in the absence of the head of state, Colonel Seyni Kountché, at the Franco-African summit in Vittel a 'group of armed men' had tried to seize power but had been foiled by the army and that order had been re-established. The brain behind the coup attempt was said to have been the *marabout* (holy man) advising President Kountché, an army lieutenant called Oumarou Adamou, better known by the soubriquet of 'Bonkano', who was believed by many in Niger to be one of the most powerful men in the country because of his influence over the head of state. Bonkano's reasons for turning on his patron were obscure, but he seemed to have been fooled by his apparent power into thinking it would be easy to capture real power. He involved two other key soldiers, Lieut. Idrissa Amadou, commander of the presidential guard, and Major Amadou Seydou, commander of the Niamey battalion, in his plans. They were among those subsequently arrested.

The coup attempt was followed by a major shake-up of the Government, several key figures being dismissed. The Prime Minister, Mamane Oumarou, who had been appointed only in January, was made full-time chairman of the 'Development Society', the pet project of the regime to involve all levels of society in discussion of the development process. The new Prime Minister was Hamid Algabid, former acting Finance Minister.

CAMEROON

The shadow of Ahmadou Ahidjo, who resigned as President of the Republic towards the end of 1982, hung over much of 1983. For, if his departure seemed at the time to have happened in good order, with a quiet transition to his successor, Paul Biya, complications emerged during the following year. All seemed well at its start, with Ahidjo using the position he had retained, that of chairman of the Cameroon National Union (UNC), the ruling party, to eliminate difficult elements that regretted his departure. By the middle of the year, however, it looked as if Ahidjo was beginning to regret his resignation, and was contriving to use the party as a power-base to be built up for a possible comeback. Parliamentary elections in May, it was said, confirmed a single list of largely pro-Ahidjo candidates, and a Government reshuffle in June (on the eve of a visit by the French President) was designed to remove some of the remaining Ministers close to the former President.

The row did not come into the open until August, when President Biya announced the arrest of two pro-Ahidjo army officers, claiming that they were plotting a coup. He also dismissed the Prime Minister, Bello Bouba Maigari, and the Defence Minister, both northerners and closely linked with Ahidjo. The new Prime Minister, Luc Ayang, was also a northerner, but from one of the Christian minority ethnic groups, whereas Ahidjo had represented the Muslim Peulhs who had hitherto dominated Cameroonian politics. Biya had preceded these moves with a series of measures designed to encourage the loyalty of the army, and, in spite of a series of bitter attacks from Ahidjo, now in France, quietly went ahead with plans to hold a UNC party congress. A number of spontaneous anti-Ahidjo demonstrations took place in Cameroon (where the ex-President had been feared and respected rather than loved), and at the end of August Ahidjo resigned as chairman of the party. The Congress was held two weeks later and elected Biya as chairman. Expectations that the new less repressive atmosphere might lead to an introduction of multi-partyism proved to be premature, in spite of an expectant recrudescence of opposition parties in exile. Towards the end of the year there were signs of agitation in the anglophone areas of the western part of southern Cameroon.

CHAD

The early part of the year was quiet, despite the existence of a government in exile centred on Libya and based on many of the members of the former Transitional Government of National Unity (GUNT), overthrown in June 1982. Apart from the loss in February by Ndjamena Government troops of the oasis of Gouro, warfare was mainly of the verbal variety; 'Radio Bardai', with its powerful transmitter, claimed to be broadcasting from a far northern oasis said to be in the hands of GUNT troops. Ironically, units of the Chad army were involved in military action over possession of a small number of islands on Lake Chad in April and May with units of the Nigerian army.

The key which unlocked the launching of serious military action in 1983 was the snub delivered to Colonel Qadafi and the GUNT by the successful holding of the OAU summit in Addis Ababa in June. Not only was Qadafi defeated over the Sahara issue, and denied the hosting of the 19th summit and thus becoming OAU chairman, but the Chad delegation from the Ndjamena Government of Hissène Habré (led by Foreign Minister Idriss Miskine) was seated without any objections (see Pt. XI, Ch. 6). In Addis Ababa it was felt that this would mean a new outbreak of Libyan-encouraged fighting, and on 23 June, just two weeks after the OAU summit ended, an attack was launched by troops loyal to Goukouny Oueddeye, former GUNT President, on the key northern centre of Faya-Largeau, which was captured a day later, and a surprise attack on eastern Chad towns, including Abèché.

Not surprisingly both the French and the Americans riposted by sending increased arms to the Habré Government, and the French, while avoiding the actual sending of troops, supplied technicians and advisers to help bolster Habré's flagging army. Egypt and Sudan also supplied assistance, while President Mobutu of Zaïre announced the sending of 2,000 troops. These were not to be engaged in combat, but were to guard installations in the capital as a morale-boosting exercise. With this backing, Habré troops recaptured Abèché, partly because Goukouny had over-extended his supply-lines, and then moved back on Faya-Largeau, which was recaptured on 30 July. At this stage the international escalation became very serious; for, just as renewed Libyan support became available to Goukouny and a counter-attack on Faya was launched, the US announced the sending of AWACS surveillance planes to be stationed in neighbouring Sudan as well as more military hardware, and made other warning signs to Colonel Qadafi. It seems to have been the threat to Faya, and fear that if the French did not intervene the US would, that prompted President Mitterrand's decision on 5 August to commit French troops in order to prevent the new advance. The arrival of the first 500 was too late to prevent Goukouny retaking Faya with Libyan air support, but with the posting to Ndjamena of Jaguar fighter bombers, and the positioning of French troops (destined to rise in number to 3,000) along the fifteenth parallel, by the end of August a complete stalemate set in, Chad being *de facto* partitioned. Few military attempts were made to disturb this stalemate, although President Habré showed periodic signs of restlessness. Qadafi and Goukouny could be said to have got more than they had hoped for, and the French, although they could claim to have kept the peace and saved Ndjamena, were not in a satisfactory position. Hence they were in the forefront of those seeking for a peace agreement that could involve Chadian national reconciliation, but by the end of the year this had not progressed very far.

GABON

A visit by President Mitterrand in January illustrated the tense state of Franco-Gabonese relations, a tension that dominated the year. President Bongo took his visitor by surprise by criticizing members of the French community in Gabon, and by calling for French assistance in providing a nuclear reactor, in his speech at a public banquet. The question of the gaol sentences on members of the opposition group MORENA, which had earlier been a subject of Franco-Gabonese controversy, was also raised. Although the visit ended amicably enough the 'incident' was evidence of French nervousness about France's interests in this rich country, which seemed keen on diversifying its international friends. The same fears cropped up later in the year, when President Bongo was displeased with the publication in Paris of a book on Franco-Gabonese relations called *Affaires Africaines,* and banned all mention of France by Gabonese media. The displeasure took several weeks and high-level missions to be assuaged.

CENTRAL AFRICAN REPUBLIC AND PEOPLE'S REPUBLIC OF THE CONGO

Both countries had quiet years, although in the Central African Republic there was continued nervousness about troubles in neighbouring Chad, and French troops based there were among those deployed to Chad. The departure of the former Emperor Bokassa from Ivory Coast, after what seemed to have been a plan to return to Bangui in an aircraft full of mercenaries, caused some temporary anxiety at the end of the year. In the Congo, President Sassou Nguesso continued to balance dextrously between East and West, conserving his especially good relations with Paris, in spite of opposing the French on Chad.

EQUATORIAL GUINEA

Less than four years after the coup in which he overthrew President Francisco Macias Nguema, President Obiang Nguema himself escaped an attempted coup in May. Several dozen officers and NCOs, reported to be led by Lieut. Pablo Obama Eyang, were arrested. One of the rebels, a sergeant, sought asylum in the Spanish embassy, and this led to renewed tension in Equatorial Guinea's relations with its former colonizing power. Spain complained of misuse of Spanish aid and rampant corruption, and the Equatorial Guinea regime disliked the way in which opposition groups were freely permitted to operate in Spain. Several of these which had joined forces in Madrid a few weeks before the attempted coup made a statement attributing it to 'the insulting state of misery in which the country's 300,000 inhabitants live'. The struggle for power, it said, was within the President's ruling group.

There were continued reports of friction between France and Spain over the approaches being made by the Malabo regime to France, which was in turn influenced by the need for stability in the two neighbouring states, Cameroon and Gabon. Hence the bid by Equatorial Guinea to join the Union Douanière et Economique d'Afrique Centrale (UDEAC), the Central African francophone economic grouping, which was finally accepted at that organization's end-of-year summit. Equatorial Guinea also applied to join the franc zone.

VII CENTRAL AND SOUTHERN AFRICA

Chapter 1

ZAÏRE—RWANDA AND BURUNDI—GUINEA-BISSAU AND CAPE VERDE—SÃO TOME AND PRINCIPE—MOZAMBIQUE—ANGOLA

ZAÏRE

'THERE will be no more political prisoners in Zaïre' President Mobutu Sese Seko declared in May at a ceremony marked also by his announcement of his self-promotion to the rank of Marshal. Two months earlier, Amnesty International had published a report drawing attention to the use of detention without trial in Zaïre and to the ill-treatment of political detainees, whose number was put at about two hundred. The report was promptly dismissed by an official Zaïrean spokesman as 'low-grade tittle-tattle'.

Among those released from detention under the May amnesty were the thirteen parliamentary deputies who had first come to prominence in 1980 when they presented a highly critical address to the President (see AR 1981, p. 246). Punished first by being sent into internal exile, they had been sentenced in 1982 to fifteen years' imprisonment. On their release they formed themselves into the Democratic Union for Social Progress. On 13 August several members of the 'thirteen' were among a group of sixty opponents of President Mobutu who were badly beaten up by Mobutu supporters after attending a meeting with members of the US House of Representatives African Affairs sub-committee, then on a visit to Kinshasa. Their offence was said to have been compounded by the fact that they came to the meeting wearing European-style suits, not the tie-less jackets designed by the President as the appropriate dress for the Zaïrean elite.

The incident occurred at a peculiarly unpropitious moment for the President, who had just returned from a six-day visit to the United States where he had been given a cordial reception by President Reagan and other members of the Administration. It was hoped that the visit would serve to lessen the profound suspicion with which President Mobutu had come to be regarded by influential Congressmen, a suspicion which led Congress for the second year running to cut the $12 million requested by President Reagan for military aid to Zaïre in financial year 1984 to $4 million.

President Mobutu could console himself, however, with the

staunchness of two other backers, the People's Republic of China and Israel. In January the Chinese Premier Zhao Ziyang visited Kinshasa in the course of an African tour accompanied by 64 high officials. The visit came after ten years of bilateral cooperation between China and Zaïre, under which the Chinese provided military advisers, agricultural experts and credits for the purchase of military equipment.

In the same month the Israeli Defence Minister Ariel Sharon came to Zaïre to discuss military cooperation. He made a point of visiting Shaba province, where the Kamanyola brigade was entrusted with the task of defending this vital province against external attack. It was agreed that Israeli officers would come to 'recruit, equip and retrain' the troops of this brigade. Other Israeli officers were attached to the Zaïrean navy on Lake Tanganyika and to the presidential guard.

With a foreign debt running at over $4,000 million, Zaïre remained beset by grave financial problems. Since 1967 the country's exchange rate had been fixed at 6·06 zaïres to the dollar. In mid-September the Government announced a massive devaluation, bringing the dollar exchange rate down to 29·9 zaïres. President Mobutu described the devaluation as 'a bitter pill we have no alternative but to swallow': it was in fact one of the preconditions set by the IMF before agreeing to advance a loan for $350 million. Devaluation brought the exchange rate in line with the black market rate, to the discomforture of those Zaïrean entrepreneurs who had been able to obtain dollars cheaply and sell imported goods at exorbitant prices. But ordinary people were even more seriously affected by the sharp increase in prices. In Kinshasa the price of cassava, the basic foodstuff for most Zaïreans, rose by 150 per cent in two weeks, largely as a result of the sudden escalation of transport costs through a fourfold increase in the price of petrol. To counter the inevitable discontent President Mobutu called for 'revolutionary discipline' and urged all citizens to seek out agitators. Armed plain-clothes policemen combed the capital searching for weapons. In mid-October the situation could be described by an experienced diplomat as presenting President Mobutu with 'the greatest challenge since the Shaba invasions of 1977 and 1978'. A month later thirteen dissident parliamentarians were reported to have been rearrested. As with previous much-vaunted measures against corruption, the political 'reforms' introduced by President Mobutu with his May amnesty could be seen as no more than a 'publicity stunt for Western consumption'.

Given the strict censorship and the restrictions on travel, there was an absence of hard news about conditions in other parts of the country. Amnesty International's 1983 report noted that civilians arrested in Lubumbashi in 1982 had been killed by the military security service.

In the course of the year President Mobutu sent 2,000 Zaïrean troops and several aircraft to Chad to assist the Government of Hissène Habŕe in his struggle with the Libyan-backed forces of Goukouny Oueddeye.

RWANDA AND BURUNDI

At elections held in Rwanda in December President Juvenal Habyalimana, the only presidential candidate, was returned for a third five-year term of office. During the year Rwandan authorities launched a series of police raids in the capital ostensibly designed to round up women regarded as prostitutes and vagabonds and send them to a rural re-education centre. Many of the girls arrested appeared to have been victimized for their association with Europeans, and European residents in Kigali accused the Rwandan Government of 'racism'.

President Jean-Baptiste Bagaza of Burundi paid a working visit to Paris in June. A substantial increase in French aid was announced, including funds for the installation of a television station. Michel Micombero, President of Burundi from 1966 to 1976, died in exile in Mogadishu, Somalia, on 16 July (see OBITUARY).

GUINEA-BISSAU AND CAPE VERDE

Drought had been a perennial affliction of the islands of the Cape Verde archipelago. 1983 was a particularly bad year. In December the Government of Cape Verde was forced to issue a special appeal for international aid. Even in years of reasonable rainfall the islands had been able to produce only 40 per cent of their total food requirements, while cash crops and fishing paid for no more than 5 per cent of the required imports. In the years since independence the islands had achieved solvency partly through the remittances of emigrants—600,000 Cape Verdians, double the present population of the islands, were living in North America, Western Europe and West Africa—partly through an exceptionally high volume of international aid. The country's first five-year development plan involved investments to the value of $450 million. A conference of donor nations held during the year came up with pledges of about $350 million in aid. Eastern bloc countries were significantly absent from the conference, preferring to conclude only bilateral agreements. The Soviet Union, Cuba and East Germany provided the training and equipment needed by the police and the military, but the Government of President Aristide Pereira continued to follow a steadfastly non-aligned foreign policy, and the President made a point of stressing at the second congress of the ruling African Party for the Independence of Cape Verde (PAICV) that no foreign bases would be allowed in the islands.

Apart from a ministerial shake-up by President Vieira in September, Guinea-Bissau had a politically uneventful year. The Government launched a project for the exploration of off-shore oil deposits with the aid of a $13 million loan from the World Bank.

SÃO TOME AND PRINCIPE

In an otherwise uneventful year São Tome featured in Amnesty International's report for 1983, where attention was drawn to the continuing imprisonment of five people convicted in 1977 and 1979 by the Special Tribunal for Counter-Revolutionary Acts. The longest sentence—17 years' imprisonment—was imposed on Angelo Salvaterra, one of whose offences was to have published an article in a Portuguese newspaper advocating the secession of Principe.

MOZAMBIQUE

'The year of general struggle against the armed bandits'—President Samora Machel's words emphasized the overwhelming preoccupation of the Frelimo Government during 1983 with the guerrilla war waged by the Mozambique National Resistance (MNR), which clearly enjoyed—despite repeated denials from Pretoria—substantial support from South Africa. By 1983 the war had spread to every province except Cabo Delgado in the far north. MNR tactics were clearly designed to disrupt every aspect of the country's economy. Rebel operations continued to dislocate main roads and railways, 'making half the country', according to an experienced Western correspondent, 'like medieval Europe in the days of the highwaymen, where travel meant risking life and limb'. The guerrillas also destroyed many cotton gins, tea factories and sawmills. Attacks on grain stores involved the loss, according to official estimates, of 30,000 tonnes of grain. Development schemes provided frequent targets. In three years 50 foreign technical experts had been taken as hostages by the rebels, the most spectacular incident occurring in August when an attack on a mine in Zambezia left two Soviet experts dead and 24 as hostages in MNR hands. Mounting insecurity led some foreign Governments to require their nationals to withdraw from certain areas. The country's grave economic difficulties were further compounded by natural disasters, the central and southern provinces being ravaged by the worst drought in fifty years. To meet the loss of almost an entire grain crop the Government launched an international appeal for 235,000 tonnes of food aid.

In military terms it was impossible to produce an exact balance-sheet of the progress of the war. An offensive launched by MNR in late December 1982 from bases in the Kruger National Park on the South African side of the frontier petered out, partly in face of vigorous counter-measures by the Mozambique army, partly because the rebels had to operate in an area particularly badly affected both by drought and by cholera. In April and May, however, MNR organized a sweep through

Zambezia, agriculturally the country's most productive province, meeting virtually no resistance.

Total MNR forces were estimated to number 10,000, but the rebels operated in small mobile bands and made no attempt to establish a well-organized liberated zone. In April Orlando Cristina, regarded as the most prominent member of MNR with special responsibility for organizing the movement's links with the outside world, was murdered on his farm in the Transvaal, whether by a Frelimo agent or as the result of some internal feud was uncertain. The movement's lack of a coherent political programme was brought out in an interview given to an American journalist by the MNR's president and supreme military commander, Afonso Dhlakama, in which he readily admitted that he 'did not know how to rule' and defined his objectives in the 'vaguest terms' as involving 'elections, real democracy and a mixed economy'.

The Frelimo Government's evident military weakness was seen as being derived in part from the type of training provided by the Soviet military mission, which sought to transform Frelimo's original guerrilla detachments into a conventional standing army with much emphasis on heavy equipment. In May President Machel became more directly involved in revitalizing the army by 'assuming the direction' of the Defence Ministry. Former combatants who had proved their worth in the pre-independence guerrilla campaign were urged to rejoin the army.

Relations with South Africa remained tense throughout the year. On 5 May a meeting was held at the South African border town of Komartipoort between the Mozambique Security Minister and the South African Foreign Minister. The presence of members of African National Congress (ANC) in Mozambique was a major item for discussion. On 23 May the South African air force attacked a factory in a suburb of Maputo, killing six civilians. The South African allegation that the factory was being used to harbour ANC guerrillas was not confirmed by independent eye-witnesses. The raid was justified as a retaliation for the ANC's action in planting a bomb in central Pretoria on 20 May. On 17 October a South African spokesman claimed that South African commandos were responsible for planting bombs in an ANC office in central Maputo. The explosion caused no serious injuries.

As it became increasingly clear that Mozambique was not strong enough to stand up to South African hostility without external support, President Machel set about establishing closer relations with Western countries, partly in the hope that their Governments might exert pressure on Pretoria. A rapprochement with Washington marked the end of a period of frigid relations dating back to 1981 when Mozambique expelled four US diplomats on the grounds that they were CIA agents and President Machel vigorously criticized President Reagan. By the end of 1983 a US ambassador was back at Maputo, food aid had been resumed and President Machel could speak appreciatively of the 'frank and open dialogue' between the two Governments. In October Machel paid his first visit to Western Europe, being cordially received in Portugal, the Netherlands, Belgium, Britain, France and Yugoslavia. Apart from seeking political support against South Africa, President Machel showed himself anxious to encourage Western investment in Mozambique and to procure military aid. Closer ties with the West were also emphasized by Mozambique's decision to join the group of African, Caribbean and Pacific states associated with the EEC in the Lomé convention. Close ties with Eastern bloc countries were maintained through a presidential visit to the Soviet Union and East Germany in March. To both East and West President Machel emphasized that his policy was one of positive non-alignment: he had no intention of becoming 'the Sadat of Southern Africa'.

Frelimo held its fourth congress in Maputo in April, preceded by a country-wide series of meetings at local level. Both these and the congress itself were remarkable for the frankness with which delegates criticized the Government for its failures and shortcomings. Within the party there was a clear divide between the ideologues and the pragmatists, the former asserting that large state farms and heavy industry were essential foundations for socialism, the latter looking sceptically at 'big projects' and urging the need for greater attention to peasant cooperatives and family farms. The congress finally reached agreement that priority should be given over the next three years to smaller development projects.

The composition of the Politburo, the party's most powerful body, remained virtually unchanged, but the central committee was increased in size from 55 to 128 members. The old committee had been dominated by high party officials: the new committee, elected by the congress, included a substantial number of peasants and workers. The Government reshuffle announced by the President on 28 May was the most far-reaching since 1975: it was interpreted as marking a further decline in the influence of the ideologues. By identifying himself with the criticisms levelled against party officials President Machel clearly increased his standing in popular esteem.

ANGOLA

There was no let-up during 1983 in the massive difficulties with which the MPLA government in Luanda had been confronted ever since Angola achieved independence in November 1975. An unusually forthright survey of the Angolan situation published in Havana in August spoke of danger to the very 'independence and sovereignty of the heroic African country'. On the other hand, for Unita, the MPLA's most formidable opponent, the year was marked by substantial advances and some well-publicized military victories. Despite considerable diplomatic activity, which brought Angolan government representatives into contact with South Africa, the United States and the United Nations, the year ended as gloomily as it had begun, with no end in sight to the civil war, itself much aggravated by South African incursions into southern Angola.

In the absence of reliable statistics, it was impossible to obtain an overall view of the economy. But some light was thrown on one important activity, diamond mining, located near the border with Zaïre and Zambia, as a result of a scandal over smuggling. After oil, diamonds had been the country's greatest foreign-exchange earner. The state diamond company, Diamag, was estimated to have lost a third of its annual production, worth £100 million, by smuggling. The Government called in British mining police to help counter the smugglers. Since senior MPLA officials were said to have been involved the scandal had considerable political implications. Younger army officers were reported to have seen the scandal as yet further evidence of a lack of direction and decisiveness by President dos Santos and his closest advisers, and to have discussed the feasibility of a coup. At the end of July the emergency powers granted the President in the previous December (see AR 1982, p. 251) were extended under a new law which authorized the setting-up of special military councils in the most seriously affected areas. The powers granted to these councils came close to martial law.

Within the MPLA Government there were continued reports of a rift between old-guard ideologues, mostly intellectuals of *mestizo* (mixed-race) origin, and the younger black nationalists. In January thirty of the more radical members of the MPLA were suspended and detained: four weeks later most of them were readmitted to the party.

The exploits of Unita were far better publicized in the Western press than the activities of the MPLA Government. Among those who visited Unita guerrilla forces were four Euro-MPs. Much publicity was given to the release of the wives and children of a group of Czech technicians taken prisoner by Unita after an attack on an industrial site on the Benguela railway. The men were held hostage in the hope that they could be exchanged for Unita activists in government hands. Other foreign contract workers and missionaries were taken hostage later in the year. The most favourable estimates of Unita's position spoke of its having succeeded, in the six months ending March 1983, in doubling the area under its control, about 100,000 square miles lying between the Benguela railway and the Namibian border. North of the railway lay what Unita described as its 'zone of influence', with guerrilla forces operating to within 100 miles of Luanda. Unita's most spectacular success was the capture of Cangamba, a town 300 miles north of the Namibian border, garrisoned by 2,800 MPLA soldiers. The fact that Unita was able to deploy 6,000 troops organized up to a battalion level to attack the town clearly indicated how much its military potential had expanded. Other achievements that it claimed were the destruction of the Lomaum dam, the country's second largest (a feat which MPLA spokesmen ascribed to sabotage by South African commandos) and the occupation of Calulo, a town 100 miles south of Luanda.

On 6 December the South African defence force launched its largest incursion into Angola since August 1981 (see AR 1981, p. 250). MPLA spokesmen put the size of the South African force at 10,000. Officially, the operation was designed to disrupt Swapo plans to launch a guerrilla offensive into Namibia, but there was clearly some confrontation between South African and Angolan forces. Throughout the year the South Africans were reported to have occupied the greater part of Cuene province, and its capital, Njie, to have been developed into 'a large and sophisticated military base'. According to MPLA sources, South African military aircraft played a vital role in Unita's victory at Cangamba in August.

In northern Angola, according to a French journalist, the first Western correspondent to visit the area for several years, a small-scale guerrilla war still continued, in spite of the overwhelming defeat of the FNLA in 1975-76 and the withdrawal of support to that movement by neighbouring Zaïre. Guerrilla activity took the form of regular attacks on road convoys, military posts and coffee plantations.

The presence of an estimated 20,000 Cuban soldiers in Angola continued to be a matter for international debate. The US Government, concerned to find a solution to the problem of Namibia and vividly aware of the gains that would accrue to the Reagan Administration through a diminution of Cuban influence in Africa, advocated a policy of 'linkage' whereby the holding of UN-supervised elections in Namibia and the eventual South African withdrawal from that disputed territory would be accompanied by the simultaneous withdrawal of the Cuban forces from Angola. The MPLA Government was not prepared to accept that the Namibian and Angolan situations should be linked in this manner. But in negotiations with the South African Foreign Minister, held in Cape Verde in December 1982, proposals had been put forward that Cuban troops should be withdrawn 150 miles north of the Angolan frontier in return for a total South African evacuation of Angolan territory. At the second round of talks held in February it became clear that the South African Government, paying special attention to the views of its military, was not prepared to accept this tentative solution and the talks broke down. In December, a few days after the latest South African invasion and immediately before a Security Council debate on Angola, the South African Foreign Minister, in a letter to the UN Secretary-General, put forward proposals for a ceasefire in Angola from 31 January.

Contacts between the MPLA Government and Western countries were marked by a visit in February to Britain by the Angolan Foreign Minister and to the United States in March by the Interior Minister, for discussion with Secretary of State George Shultz. A proposal put forward by the Nigerian President, Shehu Shagari, in November that the Cubans in Angola be replaced by a multinational force was dismissed by the MPLA Government, which drew attention to the ineffectiveness of the Pan-African force sent to Chad. The MPLA Government could be seen, as the year ended, to be faced with a 'Catch-22' predicament. To secure the withdrawal of the South Africans it would have to accept the parallel withdrawal of the Cubans. But since they played a vital role in stiffening the MPLA's armed forces their withdrawal would render it increasingly difficult for the MPLA to counter the military advances of Unita.

Chapter 2

ZAMBIA—MALAWI—ZIMBABWE—NAMIBIA—BOTSWANA—
LESOTHO—SWAZILAND

ZAMBIA

FOR President Kenneth Kaunda the year brought two particularly gratifying events: a state visit to Britain in March and a substantial triumph in the presidential election in October.

The state visit to Britain, the first of its kind since Zambia achieved independence in 1964, was seen as a politically symbolic event, marking the end of a long period of tension in Anglo-Zambian relations caused by Britain's inability to deal effectively, for close on a decade and a half, with the Rhodesian rebellion. From London President Kaunda went on to Paris and Washington for 'working visits'. In all three capitals Zambia's economic difficulties and the problem of Namibia were the main items of discussion.

In the election held on 27 October Mr Kaunda, the only candidate, was re-elected for a fifth term as President. Voters were presented with two symbols on their ballot papers: an eagle against which those in favour of Mr Kaunda were required to place their mark, and a 'rather depressed-looking' frog for those who wished to record a dissentient vote. Mr Kaunda received 93 per cent of the votes in a 63 per cent poll, compared with 81 per cent of the votes in a 67 per cent poll in the last presidential election in 1978. Given the substantial grounds for discontent provided by the country's economic difficulties, this vote was seen as a remarkable gesture of continued confidence in a man who had dominated Zambian political life for more than twenty years without ever reverting to the forms of repression found in so many other African countries.

The election was the only significant political event of the year. Despite rumblings of discontent from the leaders of the powerful mining trade unions there was no serious confrontation between unions and government as there had been in 1981.

In January the long-drawn-out treason trial of those accused of involvement in the attempted coup of October 1980 (see AR 1980, p. 254) ended with death sentences on seven of the accused, including Valentine Musakanya, former Governor of the Bank of Zambia, and Edward Shamwana, a prominent Lusaka lawyer. A white lawyer, Pierre Ampfield, was named as a leading conspirator: he had escaped to South Africa in 1980. By the end of the year the sentences had been neither commuted nor carried out.

No serious incidents disturbed Zambia's relations with its neighbours. The Government studiously refrained from giving any hint of support to Joshua Nkomo after the latter's decision to leave Zimbabwe in March. 'Whatever the past was', declared the government-controlled *Times of Zambia* in a reference to the support that Nkomo and his party Zapu had received from Zambia during the guerrilla war in Rhodesia, 'the Government of Prime Minister Robert Mugabe is the one Zambia deals with, not individuals outside that Government—dissidents or not dissidents.'

Compared with other countries of Southern Africa, especially Angola, Mozambique and Zimbabwe, Zambia enjoyed a remarkably peaceful year. But the country was still gravely affected by economic difficulties that showed little sign of getting less burdensome. Central to Zambia's financial and economic problems was the depressed state of the copper market. Copper and cobalt provided 95 per cent of the country's foreign exchange earnings. Ten years earlier the government could draw half its revenue from the taxes and royalties paid by the mining companies. But, with the price of copper at its lowest level for fifty years, the mining companies were no longer able to run their operations at a profit and so could make no contribution to government revenue. At the same time the servicing of a foreign debt reckoned to have reached £1,700 million by the end of 1982 was the equivalent of 47·6 per cent of foreign earnings. In these circumstances there was a steady rise in arrears in payments to overseas suppliers and delays in the remittance of profits and dividends. External aid, especially from the IMF, was seen as the only short-term means of coping with this situation. In the course of the year the IMF provided £200 million in stand-by loans on condition that the Government introduced a new range of austerity measures, including a devaluation of the kwacha, cuts in food subsidies, a ten per cent ceiling to wage increases and an end to price controls on most commodities.

Among the symptoms of the country's malaise was a high rate of alcoholism. A recent WHO report estimated that Zambia led every other country in Africa in the consumption of beer per head. Men drank 'to forget their problems', one of the most pressing of which was unemployment. According to a Zambian trade unionist forty per cent of the work-force was jobless. Yet, in spite of high unemployment, average incomes in urban areas were reckoned to be as much as fifteen times as high as those of people living in rural areas: hence a steadily escalating drift to the towns.

In August the Vatican announced that Mgr Emmanuel Milungo had resigned as Archbishop of Lusaka and accepted a minor post in the Vatican. The archbishop, whose faith-healing powers had aroused much controversy, had been summoned to Rome in 1982 and held in seclusion (see AR 1982, p. 252). The case was seen as illustrating what one Vatican official described as 'some irreconcilable contrasts between Africa's Western-trained, traditionalist and mostly white clergy and a growing number of black priests who insist that local tribal customs and beliefs have a place in African Catholicism'.

MALAWI

After nineteen years of highly autocratic rule by the Life-President, Dr H. Kamuzu Banda, years notable for a degree of political stability and economic progress that sharply distinguished Malawi from its immediate neighbours, the country showed signs during 1983 of an unusual amount of political turmoil. For many years no foreign correspondents had been allowed to reside in Malawi. Recently much of the political news about the country had come from exiles residing in Zambia or Zimbabwe. To counter these reports the Government decided on the exceptional measure of allowing foreign correspondents to visit Malawi at the time of the general elections in June. 'If this experiment goes wrong', an official warned the journalists, 'it may be difficult for foreign journalists to come here in future'.

A fundamental cause of the new sense of unease was the President's age. Though officially stated to have been born 'about 1906', it was generally thought that Dr Banda was now in his mid-eighties. The President made a point of displaying his physical vigour by taking part in tribal dancing on state occasions, but against this must be put persistent rumours of gradually failing powers. Speculation about his eventual successor concentrated on two names: Cecilia Kadzamire, for many years Dr Banda's 'life-companion' and Malawi's 'official hostess', and her uncle, John Tembo, the governor of the Reserve Bank. According to Malawi's constitution the successor to the Life-President must be chosen by a full convention of the Malawi Congress Party, while a triumvirate of the party's general secretary and two Cabinet Ministers would exercise presidential powers until the choice had been made.

Three events, occurring within a few weeks of each other in the second quarter of the year, were the cause of particular concern. The first was the discovery on 28 March, at a busy crossroads in the Zimbabwean capital, Harare, of the body of one of the regime's most outspoken opponents, Dr Attati Mpakati, with a bullet wound in his head. Dr Mpakati was the leader of the militant Socialist League of Malawi (Lesoma): in 1979 he had been the target of a parcel-bomb attack for which Dr Banda openly admitted responsibility (see AR 1979, p. 253). Two Malawians living in Zimbabwe were later charged by a Harare prosecutor with involvement in a 'political assassination plot', but the Malawi Government vigorously denied any responsibility for Dr Mpakati's murder.

On 5 May the long-drawn-out trial of Orton and Vera Chirwa held in a 'traditional' court ended with death sentences on the two defendants. Orton Chirwa, the most prominent member of the Malawi Freedom Movement, was arrested with his wife in mysterious circumstances in December 1981 (see AR 1982, p. 254). Charged with high treason for involvement in a plot to assassinate the President, the Chirwas' trial attracted widespread attention. Elders of the Church of Scotland called on their fellow-Elder, Dr Banda, to exercise his prerogative of mercy. In December it was announced that the Chirwas' appeal to a higher traditional court had been dismissed.

On 19 May the deaths occurred of four prominent members of the Malawi Congress Party, among them the party's secretary-general, Dick Matenje. According to official sources their deaths were the result of a road accident in southern Malawi, but there was a strong suspicion that the four men had been shot by the police and that their deaths were connected with a succession dispute in which they had clashed with members of the Tembo-Kadzamire faction.

On 29 June the country held its second general election since independence, the last election having been in 1979. The President exercised his right to veto candidates, all of whom had to be members of the Malawi Congress Party, proficient in English, and acceptable under the terms of a 'social desirability' test. No suitable candidates could be found for 5 of the 101 constituencies; 21 candidates were returned unopposed; in the remaining constituencies voters could choose among two to five candidates, but no canvassing was allowed on the grounds that this would encourage bribery and corruption. Despite calls from opposition groups based in neighbouring countries to boycott the election, a 'healthy turnout' was reported.

In September Dr Banda opened the Kamuzu international airport at Lilongwe, built at a cost of £70 million and the largest single project ever undertaken in Malawi. Criticism of Dr Banda for indulging in such prestige projects was tempered in the minds of many outside observers by the fact that the Malawian peasantry evidently enjoyed a better life than the rural population of the country's neighbours. Indeed, while so many African countries had to import basic foodstuffs, Malawi was not only able to provide enough maize to feed its own population but also had sufficient over to sell to its neighbours.

ZIMBABWE

The early months of the year were marked by continuing rivalry between the supporters of Mr Joshua Nkomo's Zimbabwe African People's Union, or PF (Zapu), and those of the ruling party, the Zimbabwe African National Union, or Zanu (PF), led by the Prime Minister, Mr Robert Mugabe.

In Matabeleland and elsewhere in western Zimbabwe armed dissidents, many of them former Zipra soldiers (see AR 1981, p. 256), made sporadic attacks on farms and villages, plainly intending to undermine the Government internally and embarrass it internationally. In January, in response to mounting violence, the Government deployed the North Korean-trained 'Fifth Brigade' against the insurgents. Mr Nkomo described the Brigade as 'a tribal and political army come to wipe out the Ndebele' and, as civilian casualties rose to a reported 1,000 killed, criticism was levelled at unnecessary brutality on the part of the security forces. Western journalists reported evidence of arbitrary killing and, at the end of March, the Zimbabwe Roman Catholic bishops' conference issued a pastoral letter accusing the Government of unleashing a 'reign of terror'. The Prime Minister declared that the Fifth Brigade would remain in Matabeleland until all dissidents had been eliminated. By September, however, the Brigade had been substantially withdrawn and a committee of inquiry established to investigate alleged atrocities. At the same time press restrictions were imposed, providing for the censorship of reports on the security situation.

Mr Nkomo himself was prevented from leaving Zimbabwe on 19 February to attend a World Peace Council in Prague. But, on 8 March, following an incident in which his home in Bulawayo was searched by security forces and his chauffeur shot dead, he fled to Botswana. While his wife and other members of his family were briefly held in detention, Mr Nkomo flew to Johannesburg and thence to London on 12 March. After five months of voluntary exile he returned to Zimbabwe on 16 August to contest—successfully—a Government motion depriving him of his seat in the House of Assembly on grounds of absenteeism.

Government sensitivity to criticism was highlighted in other ways during the year. In February and March several leading Zapu officials, including three members of its central committee and two MPs, were detained. In April two former members of Zipra, Mr Dumiso Dabengwa and Lieut.-General Lookout Masuku, were acquitted in the High Court of charges of treason and the illegal possession of arms. They, with four other Zapu members, were immediately redetained, however, under the emergency powers legislation, which remained in force throughout 1983.

By far the most heavily-reported instance of Government unease was the trial of six white Zimbabwe Air Force (ZAF) officers accused of aiding and abetting unnamed South African agents in the sabotage of 13 Zimbabwean aircraft at the Thornhill air base near Gweru on 25 July 1982. After a trial lasting 44 days Mr Justice Enoch Dumbutshena, Zimbabwe's first black judge, sitting with two assessors, ruled on 31 August that the officers were not guilty. He pointed to a defective prosecution case which hinged on confessions extracted from the six defendants by police interrogators using electric shock torture, confessions which were inadmissible as evidence. The six ZAF officers were, however, rearrested immediately after their acquittal, an action that provoked international criticism and suggestions in Britain that aid to Zimbabwe should be suspended. On 9 September Mr Mugabe, travelling in Ireland, accused the British Government of meddling in his country's internal affairs primarily because the ZAF officers were 'Mrs Thatcher's kith and kin': four held dual British and Zimbabwean nationality.

The Zimbabwe Government, unhappy at the outcome of the Thornhill case, placed a full-page advertisement in the London *Observer* on 9 October, affirming its belief in the officers' guilt and attributing their acquittal to 'technical reasons' based on 'inherited law'. Two of the officers, Air Vice-Marshal Hugh Slatter, the former chief of staff, and Air Commodore Philip Pile were released and deported to England on 9 September. The remaining four officers followed by the end of the year.

The factors that had damaged the economy in 1982 and precipitated a 20 per cent devaluation of the Zimbabwean dollar on 8 December that year (see AR 1982, p. 257) continued to impede progress in 1983. The lasting impact of the world recession, low prices for the country's exports on world markets and the harsh effects of the 1982-83 drought ensured a further decline in economic growth. In March the IMF approved an 18-month standby facility for Zimbabwe totalling US$324 million. But within the country austerity marked financial policy for the year. In February fuel prices rose by 40 per cent after sabotage of the Beira-Maputo pipeline had caused a severe petrol shortage. On 28 July the Budget, presented by the Minister of Finance, Economic Planning and Development, Dr Bernard Chidzero, was notably tough. Sales tax on consumer goods rose from 16 to 18 per cent and on luxuries from 19 to 23 per cent. Half a million low-paid workers were hit hard by the introduction of a 2 per cent income tax on a minimum wage which, despite inflation running at 17 per cent, had not risen for 18 months. By the end of the year Zimbabweans were ranked among the world's most heavily taxed citizens. The Budget also provided for a reduction in food subsidies which caused an instant rise of 31 per cent in staple food prices. Following drought and poor harvests Zimbabwe became in 1983, for the first time, an importer of basic foodstuffs like wheat.

The maintenance levels of aid and the drive for new export markets made foreign relations an area of considerable importance. The Prime

Minister both travelled widely abroad and welcomed to Harare major world leaders, including, in January, the Chinese Premier Zhao Ziyang. Differences in relations with the US which threatened the continuity of American aid for Zimbabwe were apparently repaired by Mr Mugabe's meeting with President Reagan in Washington in September. The Government's anti-dissident campaign in Matabeleland seriously disturbed relations with the neighbouring state of Botswana. The charge that a camp for 3,000 Zimbabwean refugees at Dukwe in northern Botswana was being used as a dissident training centre was rejected by the Botswana Government (see p. 250). In August Mr Mugabe met President Quett Masire of Botswana to improve relations between their countries.

South African remained both Zimbabwe's major trading partner and its most conspicuous political opponent. In January the Minister of State (Security), Mr Emmerson Munangagwa, accused the South African Government of infiltrating 'bandits' into Matabeleland to encourage dissident unrest, and of establishing camps on the Transvaal border to train a brigade of Zimbabwean rebels. Both charges were refuted by South Africa. On 2 November, Bishop Abel Muzorewa, President of the United African National Council and former Prime Minister of Rhodesia-Zimbabwe (see AR 1979, p. 225), was arrested as part of 'Operation Chinyavada'—an inquiry into subversive elements connected with South Africa. Mr Mugabe accused the bishop of 'clandestine activities' aimed at the destabilization of the state.

Another former Rhodesian Prime Minister, Mr Ian Smith, now leader of the white opposition Republican Front (RF) party, was granted a British passport in April to travel to South Africa for medical treatment; his Zimbabwean passport had been withdrawn by the Government in December 1982. During the year his party suffered its first electoral defeat since 1962 when an independent candidate won the Bulawayo South seat in a by-election in April. By the end of the year the RF held only 9 of the 20 white seats in the House of Assembly, revealing the growing white view that cooperation, not opposition, was the preferable tactic.

In his end-of-year message the Prime Minister stressed that, although lack of foreign exchange had constrained the economy in 1983, outstanding progress had been made domestically in education, health and transport programmes, the provision of houses, the building of dams and the improvement of communication systems throughout the country. While foreign aid was an essential priority, Zimbabwe would not mortgage its personality for it, Mr Mugabe said, nor turn its actions into 'the guided dancing steps of a manipulated puppet state'.

NAMIBIA

Scepticism about the prospects of a Namibian peace settlement intensifed during the year. Further rounds of diplomacy aimed at implementing a ceasefire and elections in the territory made little headway. No agreement was reached on a date for the ceasefire, although the mechanics of establishing it and organizing UN-supervised elections had been pretty well settled among the parties. In apparent disillusion with the lack of progress the French Government announced during the year that it had decided to suspend its membership of the Western 'contact group', comprising also the USA, Britain, Canada and West Germany. South Africa insisted that the people of Namibia should be free to elect a government in democratic fashion without the interference of armed insurgency or the intimidating presence of foreign troops in neighbouring Angola. Supported by the US, South Africa declined to proceed with implementing Resolution 435 until the Cuban troops in Angola were withdrawn from the region.

At intervals the South African defence force (SADF) carried out incursions into Angola described as pre-emptive raids against Swapo bases. It also appeared to military observers that Dr Jonas Savimbi's Unita rebels, still operating in southern Angola, received substantial assistance from South Africa, apparently as a means of putting pressure on the MPLA Government of Angola to desist from harbouring Swapo guerrillas and allowing them to use Angolan territory as a springboard for infiltrating into Namibia. It also appeared to some observers that the survival in strength of Unita, which appeared to be launching a major offensive in mid-1983, was becoming a major stumbling-block in the path of a settlement. As long as the MPLA regime in Luanda felt threatened by Unita, so long would it insist on retaining the services of its Cuban protectors. On this analysis, South African support for Unita was a major card in Pretoria's hand and was protracting the negotiations.

As the year ended, South Africa had offered to withdraw South African forces from Angola on condition that Swapo ceased its insurgency and infiltration from Angola. At the same time Pretoria launched a major strike 250 km into Angolan territory, and bombed targets which it identified as Swapo bases. The purpose of the action, as announced by the SADF, was to thwart the annual wet-weather incursion of Angola-based Swapo guerrillas into Namibia. Although South Africa's offer of a truce evoked a conditional counter-offer from Angola, a Namibian settlement seemed as remote as ever.

In Namibian domestic politics the most significant development was the holding of a conference of a broad spectrum of Namibian political parties but excluding Swapo, the moderate Christian Democratic Alliance and the Namibia Independence Party. The conference pressed for the soonest possible implementation of an internationally-approved independence settlement.

BOTSWANA

Botswana's situation as a haven for political refugees in Southern Africa once again weighed heavily on its external relations. It found itself playing host to 3,000 refugees, from Zimbabwe, South Africa, Namibia, Mozambique, Angola and Malawi. Tough control measures were introduced, requiring all unemployed refugees to be settled in a camp at Dukwe, 600 km north of Gaborone. Zimbabwe alleged that Dukwe was a dissident training camp rather than a place of refuge for exiles. A meeting took place between Mr Robert Mugabe, Prime Minister of Zimbabwe, and the Botswana Foreign Minister, Mr Archie Mogwe, to 'clear the air' and contacts continued at ministerial level. Later it appeared that Botswana was returning dissidents who had fled across the border from Zimbabwe. In November Botswana protested to Zimbabwe after a clash between its forces and intruding Zimbabwean troops. Zimbabwe denied any involvement in the clash, alleging that South Africa was deliberately using anti-government dissidents dressed in Zimbabwean uniforms to sour relations between Botswana and Zimbabwe.

Two South Africans were shot dead by a Botswana anti-poaching patrol in October. The Botswana authorities said the men had been chasing elephant across the border into the Caprivi strip and had ignored a challenge and warning shots. In December it was disclosed that large-scale commercial poaching for ivory was taking place on the Botswana-Caprivi border.

LESOTHO

There were signs of an easing in relations between South Africa and Lesotho in late 1983 as officials of the two countries held renewed discussions on security problems. Lesotho sought an undertaking that South Africa would refrain from allowing the guerrilla group, the Lesotho Liberation Army (LLA), from using South African territory as a base for attacks on Lesotho. South Africa, in turn, sought assurances that Lesotho would not be used by guerrillas of the African National Congress (ANC) as a route for infiltration of its territory.

Earlier, relations were at a very low ebb as bomb blasts and other acts of sabotage by the LLA continued to cause damage and casualties. Lesotho insisted that the LLA campaign enjoyed the backing of Pretoria. In August the Prime Minister, Chief Leabua Jonathan, narrowly escaped death when a vehicle packed with explosives was detonated minutes after his car had passed by.

In September a group of 22 South African exiles, members of or sympathisers with the ANC, were reported to have left Lesotho. In November it was reported that members of the LLA had been arrested in South Africa after a protest by Lesotho that Lesotho police had been fired upon from South African soil. This was believed to have been the first time that South Africa had responded to a Lesotho complaint of this nature. As the year ended, however, it appeared that relations between the two countries were on the mend. In December, when the Lesotho Government informed Pretoria that it believed an anti-Jonathan coup was being planned by mercenaries in the Republic, South Africa undertook to cooperate with the Lesotho intelligence services in their investigation.

SWAZILAND

It was officially confirmed that the 16-year-old Prince Makhosetive, at school in England, had been named the Umtfwama, or heir-apparent. His mother, the Princess Novombi, appeared to be firmly in power as Queen Regent, although there was some suggestion that her predecessor, the Queen Regent Dzeliwe, who was appointed after the death of the King Sobhuza II, had been removed unconstitutionally. The former Prime Minister, Prince Mabandla, was in exile in South Africa. In August the Swazi High Court decided against giving judgment in the dispute over the deposition of Queen Regent Dzeliwe.

The Swaziland security authorities were active in monitoring the activities of guerrillas of the African National Congress. In January a group of 17 ANC members who had been detailed in 'protective custody' in a Swaziland refugee camp opted to move to Mozambique. Others who stayed in the camp said they feared an attack by the South African defence force. In May it was reported that Swaziland police had closed an ANC military training base 20 km from Mbabane and had arrested three alleged members of the ANC.

Incidents of harassment of the press caused some concern. The editor of *The Times of Swaziland*, Mr James Dlamini, was arrested and later realeased on condition that he report to the police daily. It appeared that Mr Dlamini had refused to reveal his sources for a report in his newspaper. Mr Simon Ngwenya, the *Rand Daily Mail's* correspondent in Swaziland, was also detained and subsequently released. He was told he would again be detained if he wrote reports that disturbed the Swazi people. In December eleven people, including members of the royal family, were charged with high treason in connection with an alleged coup plot and were committed for trial in the High Court.

Chapter 3

THE REPUBLIC OF SOUTH AFRICA

In 1983 the Botha Government enacted its long-promised constitutional reforms, receiving the support of 66 per cent of the white electorate, who voted at a referendum to extend limited franchise rights to the coloured (mixed race) and Indian minority groups while maintaining the exclusion of blacks from rights of South African citizenship.

The referendum victory was a triumph for the Prime Minister, Mr P.W. Botha, who routed both his rightest Afrikaner opponents and the liberal Progressive Federal Party (PFP) opposition. The rightist parties had urged the electorate to vote 'No' on the grounds that the constitution made dangerous concessions to so-called 'non-whites'. The PFP opposed it on the opposite grounds that the constitutional proposals were sham reform and did not get to the root of the country's problems.

Mr Botha's constitution was regarded with mixed feelings and was rejected by some of its supposed beneficiaries (see AR 1982, p. 261). The enactment of the Constitution Act (see DOCUMENTS) in August led to the formation of a militant new extra-parliamentary grouping, the United Democratic Front, in which more than 500 community, trade union and other organizations joined forces to oppose the constitution, particularly the exclusion of the black majority from the franchise. The UDF campaign gained considerable support among the black, coloured and Indian groups but appeared to have had little effect on the referendum, in which only whites were entitled to vote. The UDF, with patrons who included Dr Allan Boesak, a charismatic church leader with a large following in the coloured community, was regarded in some quarters as the internal wing of the underground African National Congress (ANC) and seemed destined to play an important role in South African politics. Another body formed largely in response to the new constitutional proposals was the National Forum, like the UDF a loose anti-apartheid alliance, but one which excluded white liberals and radicals, being firmly rooted in the 'black consciousness' tradition associated with the late Steve Biko and the late Pan-Africanist Congress leader Robert Sobukwe. Both the UDF and NF resolved to have nothing to do with the new constitution.

One significant anti-apartheid group, the Labour Party, opted to work within the new system. In the new structure there were to be separate coloured and Indian chambers with a dominant white chamber in a single tricameral South African Parliament. The Labour Party commanded a large following in the coloured community and its decision to take part caused a major breach in the long-established Black Alliance, headed by Chief Gatsha Buthelezi, leader of the Inkatha movement, which strongly opposed the new constitution. Although rejecting the constitution as inadequate, the Labour Party decided to contest the elections for the coloured chamber and to use this platform to fight for the extension of equal rights to all South Africans, including blacks. Elections for the coloured and Indian chambers were due to be held in the course of 1984. A movement to boycott the elections, sponsored by the UDF, seemed likely and it remained to be seen whether the new constitution would achieve a measure of legitimacy in the coloured and Indian communities.

Opposition to it in these communities stemmed from a conviction that the new parliamentary structure, apart from excluding blacks, would entrench and institutionalize the apartheid system, and require retention of the intensely unpopular Group Areas Act, which provided for racially segregated zoning of residential areas. There was also objection to the provisions which gave the coloured and Indian chambers a subsidiary position, rendering them unable to repeal apartheid legislation unless the white chamber concurred in the amending legislation, and giving sweeping powers to a restructured executive Government which was to be dominated by a strong executive President. The Progressive Federal Party, the official Opposition in the current Westminster-style system in South Africa, pointed out that its role and status would be much reduced in the new three-chamber house; henceforth it would be merely the minority party in one chamber of a tricameral legislature which would itself be in a weak position vis-à-vis a powerful executive.

In spite of the widespread opposition to the constitution and the conviction in some quarters that it would not work, there was considerable optimism in the business establishment about the future. This was rooted in a belief that the current measures were not the final word but merely the beginning of a process of reform which would gather momentum and in time extend the franchise even further, bringing in black urban-dwellers. It was said in some Government quarters that constitutional development would also move in the direction of a South African confederation, linking together a South African nation of whites, coloured people, Indians and urban Africans with a number of other nations of Southern Africa, including the nominally independent 'Bantustans', the impoverished rural states which had been carved out of South African territory by the Pretoria government as a *quid pro quo* for the blacks' deprivation of South African citizenship.

Throughout 1983, however, the majority of black leaders seemed unimpressed by the prospect of political advancement within the apartheid system. The campaign of sabotage and urban insurgency mounted by the ANC took a new and ominous turn when a devastating car bomb ripped through two buildings in the centre of Pretoria, killing 19 people and injuring about 200. Until the Pretoria blast, ANC bombings had appeared to be planned as sabotage or token attacks on military targets rather than terrorism likely to endanger the civilian population. While the Pretoria bomb appeared to have been set close to the headquarters building of the South African air force, most of the victims were civilian pedestrians. The question arose whether a major shift had taken place in ANC tactics. Other targets hit by plastic explosives and limpet mines during the year included government offices and court buildings in various parts of the country and petrol storage tanks in the Northern Transvaal town of Warmbaths, which were destroyed on the night before a political rally was due to be addressed in the town by Mr P. W. Botha. Later in the year, when Mr Botha was due to address a gathering in the Pietermaritzburg city hall, security police arrested a black man in the vicinity and confiscated an explosive device. It was claimed that a plot on Mr Botha's life had been foiled but the matter had yet to come to court.

The security police maintained an intensive campaign against the ANC throughout the year, using detention powers and bringing people to trial in a number of cases. Of six ANC members facing the death sentence for treason three were reprieved and the others—Thelle Mogoerane, Jerry Mosololi and Marcus Motaung—were executed. They had been found guilty of taking part in armed attacks on police stations and sabotaging power and railway lines. Oscar Mpetha, veteran trade unionist and former ANC leader, was sentenced to five years' imprisonment on charges arising from an outbreak of violence near the Crossroads squatter camp near Cape Town in 1980 in which two white passers-by were killed. Nine young men who were convicted with Mr Mpetha were sentenced to periods of up to 20 years in prison. In November, a young Afrikaner, Carl Niehaus, was sentenced to 15 years' imprisonment and his fiancée, Johanna Lourens, to four years' imprisonment on charges of high treason. Speaking in the dock after his conviction Niehaus said he believed that violence and even the death of innocents were options which were necessary and understandable in the ANC fight to overthrow apartheid.

The South African defence force (SADF) carried the fight against the ANC across the country's borders into neighbouring territories such as Mozambique and Lesotho. At regular intervals throughout the year there were accusations, which were consistently denied, that Pretoria was engaging in covert 'destabilization' of its neighbours, promoting sabotage and rebellion. Pretoria insisted that it would carry out pre-emptive military strikes against ANC targets whenever this was deemed necessary. It was widely believed outside South Africa that covert support was given by Pretoria to the anti-Machel MNR (Mozambique Resistance Movement) rebels in Mozambique and in Lesotho to guerrillas of the Lesotho Liberation Army. In addition, Zimbabwe accused South Africa of broadcasting subversive propaganda aimed at encouraging Ndebele dissidents against the Mugabe Government. The object of such actions, it was asserted, was to bring pressure to bear on these countries to desist from aiding or harbouring the ANC or providing contiguous land bases from which the ANC could launch cross-border attacks on South Africa. As the year progressed it appeared that Western nations, including the United States, Britain and Portugal, were encouraging a rapprochement between South Africa and its neighbours, believing that the Soviet Union would be the sole beneficiary of protracted unrest in the region. Although there were continuing contacts at diplomatic level there was no indication by the year's end that an accord was at hand. Pretoria was insisting on the whole-hearted cooperation of neighbour states in its campaign against the ANC, a tall order in the light of their anti-colonial history.

Meanwhile the defence budget rose to R3,093 million and South Africa emerged as the strongest and most efficient military power in Africa. At one point it seemed that each major ANC bombing would henceforth be answered with an air strike or other show of armed might against targets in the neighbouring states. An air raid on the Mozambique capital of Maputo on 23 May was widely seen as retaliation for the Pretoria bomb atrocity. Mozambique officials said that 15 houses and a jam factory in a suburb were destroyed, and five people killed and 26 injured. The SADF said that six ANC targets, including logistic headquarters, had been hit and an anti-aircraft missile system neutralized. Later, sources close to the SADF indicated that the jam factory had been hit in error and five of the six targets had been hit.

The South African economy suffered a severe blow in 1983 from the worst drought of the century. The loss of agricultural exports caused an estimated foreign exchange loss of R1,000 million. Starvation and huge stock losses followed in some rural areas. Operation Hunger, a project administered by the South African Institute of Race Relations, was spending R175,000 a month to help feed more than a half a million people in stricken areas. Summer rains brought some relief in the second half of the year but large parts of the country were still in the grip of the worst drought in memory. The economy was already in recession, and estimates of unemployment varied between 500,000 and 3,000,000, with thousands of new job-seekers entering the market every month. There seemed to have been less labour unrest in 1983 than in the previous year, when 394 strikes and work stoppages took place, involving 141,571 employees.

On 29 December the former commanding officer of Simonstown naval dockyard, Commodore Dieter Gerhardt, and his wife were convicted on charges of spying for the Soviet Union for twenty years. They were sentenced on 31 December to life imprisonment.

VIII SOUTH ASIA AND INDIAN OCEAN

Chapter 1

IRAN—AFGHANISTAN

IRAN

THE bitter blood-letting in Iran's border conflict with Iraq continued unabated. Iran made no progress in the southern sectors of the war front but gradually advanced in the central and northern sectors. Major Iranian attacks were launched in February in the Maisan area, east of Al Amarah, and in mid-April against Iraqi positions around Fakkeh. July brought the opening of a new front in the north around the heights of Haj Omran, where short but expensive campaigns were initiated by Iranian forces. These were followed in October by a drive into the Penjwin salient area, where small numbers of troops on both sides fought for supremacy in the heights overlooking Penjwin town. The land fighting ultimately brought small dividends to the Iranians, though at disproportionate costs in men and equipment. In effect, Iranian advances gave some strategic gains in the high peaks of the borderlands and took the fighting ever nearer to crucial Iraqi communications and oilfield areas, though the main purpose of the confrontations appeared to be maintain pressure on the Iraqi Government and to give the Iranian people apparent victories.

Iranian successes on the battlefield were offset considerably by a changing balance of power in the air war. Iranian capabilities, in numbers of aircraft and reliable personnel in the air force, diminished while Iraqi air power grew. Iran found it difficult to maintain its land attacks without adequate air support and was increasingly unable to defend its towns against Iraqi air raids. Strategic bombing of Iranian civilian military targets behind the main battle-lines became more frequent, with devastating effect in loss of life. Iraqi air supremacy in the Gulf was less obviously established. Iranian vessels moving to the ports at the head of the Gulf were regularly sunk but Iran's life-line in the form of military and civilian imports was not entirely disrupted.

Iran's position was made worse during 1983 by the threat that France would deliver to Iraq five Super Etendard aircraft and their accompanying armament. Specifically designed for use in naval warfare and armed with sophisticated missile systems, these aircraft were seen as direct threats to the security of Iranian oil export facilities at Kharg Island. The Iranian diplomatic campaign to persuade the French not to deliver the aircraft included threats that the Gulf would be closed to all shipping, that Iran would exclude all ships carrying materials to Iraq and that Western interests would be systematically damaged. The campaign failed and Iraq eventually took delivery of the aircraft.

Iran's war aims hardened even further during 1983. Minimum conditions for a peace were defined as the removal of the Ba'ath regime in Baghdad, the payment of reparations, satisfactory settlement of the border dispute and guarantees for the security and freedom of the Shia community in Iraq. The Iraqi Government was willing to negotiate on all conditions of a material kind, but clearly not on the nature of the Iraqi leadership. Peace negotiations made no headway, despite essays in mediation by the Islamic Conference, the UN and the Non-Aligned Movement. The high costs of the conflict to Iran and increasing popular disillusionment with the war and its objectives were insufficient to disturb the Government and particularly Ayatollah Khomeini in pursuit of their war aims.

Iran was almost entirely isolated from the world community. Only Syria remained entirely loyal to its Iranian alliance. Libya, which had strongly supported Iran after the revolution of 1979, affronted the Iranian hierarchy in 1983 with its criticism of the Government's purge of the Tudeh (communist) party. On the same issue the USSR was severely offended, especially after the expulsion of Russian diplomats from Teheran. The USA, however, remained the principal target for the regime's dislike, and, despite some reopening of trade through third parties, the clear American stand against Iranian threats to control navigation in the Gulf ensured that confrontation remained. The Arab states of the Gulf were overtly neutral in the Irano-Iraqi conflict but were committed to financing the Iraqi war effort and intimidated by Iranian threats against their oil facilities.

Domestic politics were concerned above all with the removal of the last elements of organizations that were not clearly affiliated to the religious front. Tudeh was ruthlessly put down despite its close cooperation with the regime, and the remnants of the opposition parties such as the Mujaheddin were virtually eliminated as forces in the land. Army advances in the west enabled the central government to impose greater control on the Kurds, whose claims to regional autonomy were all but extinguished. Factional infighting culminated in a major Cabinet reshuffle in August and an attack on the privileges of the bazaar merchants, formerly close supporters of the regime. Even so, the revolutionary Islamic wing was unable to put through radical reforms—including nationalization of trade, land reform and a new labour law—in the face of opposition from the Islamic conservatives in the Majlis and in the Council of Guardians of the Constitution.

Economic distress was widespread as massive unemployment persisted. Failure of public utilities such as electricity and water supplies were common and were met with some street disturbances in the major towns. The economic problems arising from the war and from the loss of men in the fighting prompted growing criticism of the regime among those classes that had formerly been the strongest supporters of the revolution.

Economic policies were always secondary to the claims of the war effort. A new plan for the period 1983–88 was designed to rehabilitate the economy and restore its steady growth, but in view of the shortage of resources its implementation was not seriously attempted. Agriculture in particular continued to decline in the face of uncertainties about land ownership and the poor state of its infrastructure. Movement of people to the towns tended to accelerate, while food imports grew apace to an estimated $4,000 million during the year. Attempts to restart the major heavy industries that had languished since the revolution met with little success. The Bandar Khomeini petrochemical plant, the biggest individual project, remained the centre of attention, the Japanese being wooed to resume a role in its completion, but only promises of future help were obtained. Elsewhere, some smaller industrial units were reactivated in response to growing domestic demand, stimulated by government spending on services or on war-related activities.

Levels of oil output were stabilized at some 2·4 to 2·6 million b/d in response to the Opec quota system devised in March. Iran overstepped its quotas more or less consistently but never seriously damaged the Opec arrangement. Oil revenues were comparatively buoyant at an estimated $24,000 million, making possible high levels of imports and a rise in the country's foreign exchange reserves to approximately $6,000 million. Rates of growth were high in the oil and services sector, giving an overall economic expansion of some 9 per cent over the year. Non-oil sectors such as industry and agriculture, however, were poor performers.

Inflation was a severe problem. Rates of over 20 per cent were experienced, the towns, especially Teheran, being the worst affected. There were shortages of basic foodstuffs from time to time and other consumer goods were in short supply. A black market flourished in high-grade foods and luxury goods despite government attempts to punish profiteers.

Foreign trade was buoyant as the improved foreign exchange position was translated into overseas purchases of war materials and basic commodities for the civilian sector. Some official preference was given to imports from Islamic and Third World countries, but, except where barter arrangements were in operation, the main OECD nations were the principal beneficiaries of increased Iranian purchases. War materials were bought, often at a premium, through allies, including North Korea and Syria, and through international dealers in supplies of Western origin.

AFGHANISTAN

Throughout this the fourth year of their occupation of Afghanistan, the Soviet forces were nowhere near to establishing a conspicuously Afghan regime capable of exercising governmental authority throughout the country and yet acceptable to Moscow. Indeed, resistance to the Soviet-client Government of President Babrak Karmal continued across a wide front.

Much of the fighting during 1983 followed familiar patterns: guerrilla attacks on convoys, military posts and installations. These provoked retaliatory counter-attacks by helicopter gunships, rockets and flame-throwing tanks. Fighting continued intermittently in nearly all 29 provinces. Karmal maintained that the 'limited contingent' of Soviet troops (increased from about 90,000 in 1982 to 105,000 in 1983) was not engaged in combat. During 1983, however, contrary to previous practice, Soviet media began occasionally to mention Russian participation in military operations and to admit, without giving precise figures, some Soviet casualties. Desertions from the Afghan army, according to estimates by outside observers, had cut its total manpower strength from 80,000 four years before to about 30,000, forcing Soviet troops into a more active role.

In late December the Soviet-backed Government claimed spectacular victories in three battles with guerrillas in two provinces in the country's mountainous north-eastern extremities bordering the Soviet Union.

Several foreign observers said that in the last quarter of 1983 there had been a perceptible reduction in the number of purely terrorist assassinations of civil servants, policemen and party functionaries in Kabul and the major urban centres, although for the preceding three years much of the Mujahedeen activity in the winter months had been confined to terrorism, assassinations and explosions.

The Government's People's Democratic Party of Afghanistan (PDPA) continued to be plagued by the tensions, sometimes leading to violence, between its Parcham (flag) and Khalq (masses) factions. It claimed a membership of 90,000 but comprised mainly middle-class urban dwellers rather than peasants and workers. It sought, without conspicuous success, to enrol young people from the tribes—though an estimated 10,000 young Afghans were studying or training in the Soviet Union and Eastern Europe, and many Afghan children were being sent in the summer to Soviet Young Pioneer camps.

Presumably as part of its search for international acceptability, during the 7th Non-Aligned summit meeting (see Pt. XI. Ch. 7) Afghanistan entered into agreements with Laos, Nicaragua and Grenada (each then vested with a pro-Soviet Government) to establish full diplomatic relations. In July Karmal visited Mongolia and signed a treaty of friendship and cooperation.

Efforts to reach some agreed international settlement on Afghanistan made no major progress. This was particularly true of the talks conducted in Geneva by a UN negotiator who met separately with delegates from Pakistan and from the Karmal regime. The draft under discussion was based on four main points: withdrawal of the Soviet troops, cessation of aid to the guerrillas, repatriation of refugees and international guarantees that the settlement would be observed (see also p. 264).

Chapter 2

INDIA—PAKISTAN—BANGLADESH—SRI LANKA—NEPAL

INDIA

THE electoral ups and downs of the ruling Congress Party and the absence of any credible nationwide alternative to the rule of Congress (I)—'I' stands for 'Indira'—were repeatedly evident in 1983. The rather contradictory swings of electoral fortune were propelled by strong assertions of regional and ethnic identities which in consequence immediately heightened tensions in centre-state relations. The *Times of India* adopted the conveniently ambiguous formula that 1983 was 'The Year of Mrs Gandhi, but...'.

In three state legislature elections, held on 5 January, the Congress (I) was defeated in the southern states of Andhra Pradesh and Karnataka. Both had been strong power-bases for Congress (I), held even when the party lost power at the centre. In Andhra Pradesh the nine-month-old Telugu Desam Party—founded by the major local film star turned politician, N. T. Rama Rao—won by a landslide. Both the other two southern states—Tamil Nadu and Kerala—had rejected Congress earlier. In the north-eastern state of Tripura on 5 January the Marxist Communist Party of India (CPI-M), which had held office since 1978, won another five-year term in alliance with other left-wing groups.

Mrs Gandhi reorganized her governmental team in January and early February, and changes were also made in the top posts of her ruling party in the light of the recent state elections. At her request all members of the Council of Ministers submitted their resignations. The new Council of Ministers consisted of 17 full members (two of them new) and 28 Ministers of State (six of them being new appointments).

Within weeks of the electoral defeats in Andhra and Karnataka, Congress (I) candidates won landslide victories in the elections for the

Delhi metropolitan council and municipal corporation, both previously controlled by the Janata Party. The Congress (I) campaign was led personally by Mrs Gandhi and her son Rajiv. Congress (I) had thus gained political control of the country's capital city by the time the Non-Aligned summit opened in New Delhi in March (see Pt. XI, Ch. 7). In November the Commonwealth heads of government meeting also took place in New Delhi. As host to the Non-Aligned summit India took the chairmanship of the movement for the next three years.

In June the Congress tried to dislodge the governing National Conference Party from power in the strategically important northern state of Jammu and Kashmir, but in effect heightened electoral polarization along ethnic and religious lines. In the Jammu flatlands, with its Hindu majorities, the Congress gained seats, sweeping away the apparently well-entrenched Hindu communalist BJP. In the Kashmir valley, with its predominantly Muslim population, the ascendancy of the National Conference—now led by Shaikh Abdullah's son, Dr Farooq Abdullah (see AR 1982, p. 272)—continued. All in all, the aftermath was a worsening of the state's relations with the Union government. Dr Abdullah was sworn in as Chief Minister on 12 June.

Continuing ethnic and religious conflict exploded into violence when state elections were held in Assam in February. The legislature, elected in 1977, had finished its term and the state had been placed under presidential rule because of the continued violence in protest against the presence of further influx of illegal immigrants, many of them Muslims and mainly from Bangladesh. Under the constitution presidential rule could be imposed for no more than one year, but the elections only exacerbated the problem, provoking carnage on a scale comparable with the post-partition holocaust of 1947. By the end of the year, however, the situation had gradually and unevenly calmed as the election fever subsided. The costs had been very high. Entire communities had been destroyed. More than 300,000 people had been driven into refugee camps and the death toll was estimated to be over 5,000.

In the Punjab the extremists among those Sikhs agitating for greater autonomy or independence not only made it virtually impossible for the moderates to reach an agreement with the Union Government, but also perpetrated many acts of violence. Presidential rule was imposed on 6 October because prolonged deadlock seemed to help extremists and cause Sikh-Hindu relations to become still more suspicious and envenomed. Mrs Gandhi repeatedly asserted that 'hostile external forces' were at work in the state, but she refused to be more specific or to offer the public any evidence to support this charge.

Ethnic insurgencies in the north-eastern states of Nagaland, Mizoram and Manipur were relatively quiescent during 1983. However, the clashes between Tamils and Sinhalese in Sri Lanka (see p. 268) cast shadows over politics in India's Tamil-speaking state of Tamil Nadu, complicating relations between Madras and New Delhi as well as those between India and Sri Lanka. Indian Tamil sympathy for Sri Lankan Tamils found expression in massive demonstrations of support and gave urgency to India's repeated efforts to encourage genuine Tamil-Sinhalese dialogue in Sri Lanka.

Besides the Non-Aligned and Commonwealth conferences, it was another active and on the whole rather successful year in India's foreign policy. Relations with the Soviet Union, though remaining cordial overall, had an acrimonious edge because of a continuing large trade imbalance in India's favour. Moscow rather abruptly cut its import orders for 1983, whilst pressing that India should buy more Soviet goods. But by the end of the year, with the USSR offering to supply a number of weapons to India on very favourable credit terms, following an exchange of expert missions, official cordialities had been restored. By contrast, US arms supplies to Pakistan continued to be the main irritant in New Delhi's dealings with Washington. Early in the year France signed an agreement with India to supply enriched uranium fuel for the US-built Tarapur nuclear plant—though the question of spares supply remained unresolved.

India and Pakistan, acting on the agreement they had concluded in November 1982, set up in March a joint commission to promote their bilateral cooperation. India's relations with China continued to improve slowly and circumspectly at the official level, and more pronouncedly at the unofficial level. Inter-governmental talks in Peking and New Delhi mostly focused on the border dispute.

India had prickly relationships with Bangladesh, Nepal and Sri Lanka, arising from the apprehension felt by each neighbour. Even so, the Foreign Ministers of India, Pakistan, Bangladesh, Sri Lanka, Nepal, Bhutan and Maldives met in New Delhi in early May to set up the South Asian Regional Cooperation Forum.

The estrangement between Mrs Maneka Gandhi, widow of Sanjay Gandhi, and her mother-in-law, Mrs Indira Gandhi (see AR 1982, p. 272), became more markedly political during the year. Maneka Gandhi was loosely associated with the multifarious oppositions to Congress (I), especially in Uttar Pradesh, where she declared an intention of helping to contest many parliamentary seats and personally to oppose her brother-in-law, Rajiv Gandhi, in the constituency he took over after Sanjay's death. By the end of the year Rajiv was the party chief, second only to his mother in all but formal title.

During 1983 a number of opposition parties loosely assembled in two mutually suspicious coalitions, shaped more by personalities than by ideology. One was led by the Janata Party (core remnant of the 1977-79 governing coalition) and the other principally consisted of the Lok Dal (the party of the well-to-do farmers of north-west India) and Bharatiya

Janata (basically Hindu communalist). The Communist parties were clearly sympathetic to the Janata-led group.

In its annual report on India's economy, released in June, the World Bank commended the performance of the previous year but suggested higher taxation for the more affluent farmers, price increases for power and coal and a higher rate of domestic savings. The report also noted, however, that, despite its low per-capita income, India had a high rate of taxation, which had increased from 12·4 per cent of GNP in 1970-71 to 16·5 per cent in 1981-82. The Aid-India Consortium, meeting in Paris in June, unanimously endorsed India's strategy of 'adjustment with growth and social justice', but its pledged aid, totalling 3,300 million Special Drawing Rights, actually meant a reduction of 5 to 6 per cent in real terms. Oil from India's own resources played a growing role in the economy, now supplying about 50 per cent of the home market's needs.

Indo-British trade levelled off in value terms and fell in real terms in 1983, after four years of boom. Britain remained by far the biggest single national aid donor to India. In 1983 it maintained bilateral advances at the 1982 level of £110 million, while increasingly using the £66 million set aside to secure specific contracts.

The value of the rupee against a weighted basket of currencies was adjusted from time to time. Overall the rupee declined relative to the US dollar. This was not entirely due to the latter's growing strength. Ever since India received an IMF loan of 5,000 million Special Drawing Rights in 1981, as part of India's commitment the rupee had been deliberately devalued in small instalments against the US dollar. Relative to most other major currencies the rupee generally maintained its position during 1983.

In September India, which had sent two expeditions to Antarctica, and had staked a claim to the region's resources, became a signatory of the Antarctica treaty; in December a third such expedition set sail.

The final results of the census carried out in March 1981 showed the country's total population to have been 685,200,000.

India's victory in the World Cup one-day cricket matches (see Pt. XVI) was watched avidly on television for the first time in Delhi and prompted widespread celebrations.

Mr G. D. Birla, 'the grand old man' of Indian industry, died in London on 11 June, aged 89 (see OBITUARY).

PAKISTAN

The favourable signs of an improvement in relations between Pakistan and India, evident during the earlier part of 1983, suffered a setback during the second half of the year. President Zia-ul-Haq's efforts towards reconciliation resulted in the first meeting of the Indo-Pakistan

Joint Commission in June. The meeting agreed to set up four sub-commissions to promote improved cooperation in trade, agriculture, industrial production, scientific collaboration, education and culture. As a follow-up on economic collaboration three Indian trade delegations visited Pakistan in one month.

During the second half of the year, however, Indian opposition to Pakistan's acquisition of F-16 aircraft from USA, and to US-Pakistan relations in general, was stepped up. This was followed by the Indian Prime Minister's statements in support of the Movement for the Restoration of Democracy (MRD), a group of opposition parties in Pakistan. Predictably this about-turn in New Delhi created surprise and resentment in Islamabad, where it was seen as interference in Pakistan's internal affairs. The situation was further aggravated later by the convening in New Delhi of a 'Sindhi Moot,' opened by Mrs Gandhi and sponsored by her Congress (I) party, at which an Indian member of Parliament called for the integration of Pakistan's province of Sind into India.

Despite the acceptance of massive ($3,200 million) military and economic aid from the USA President Zia made it clear that Pakistan would not compromise its non-aligned status by providing bases or other facilities to the United States. 'There is no scope for the Rapid Deployment Force (RDF) activities in and around Pakistan', he told the press. The visit to Pakistan of the US Secretary of State, Mr George Shultz, in July and of Defense Secretary Weinberger in October helped to clear the lingering misunderstandings that might have existed on the subject.

The second round of Geneva talks, held under UN auspices to seek a workable settlement of the Afghanistan issue, ended on a note of optimism. It was reported that 95 per cent of a draft concerning the creation of a 'consultative machinery' had been finalized. But the question of international guarantees could not be settled, and the next round of talks proved disappointing. However, it was made known in Islamabad that Pakistan would not give up its efforts to achieve a political settlement of the Afghan issue. Throughout the year it continued, as before, to display restraint in the face of increasing air and ground-space violations carried out by the Soviet forces of occupation. Of some 60 air-space violations between January and September the most serious occurred on September 19 near Parachinar, when two civilians were killed.

By the end of the year there were 2·8 million Afghan refugees in Pakistan and they were coming in at the rate of 8 to 10 thousand per month. They were being housed in 330 camps. Pakistan was catering to their educational need, had opened vocational training centres for them, and looked after their lievestock, estimated to number three million head.

Relief assistance in 1983 was costing $550 million, of which Pakistan met 48 per cent, the remainder coming from external sources.

President Zia-ul-Haq continued his efforts to develop closer understanding and expanded economic relations with other friendly countries. He undertook visits to Japan, Turkey and Nepal, while Foreign Minister Yaqub Khan visited Saudi Arabia, Jordan, Iraq, France, Britain, the USA, USSR and China. Joint economic commissions were set up with Nepal, Japan, Malaysia and Italy during the year. At a meeting of the Pak-China economic body held in April, three protocols were signed on trade, economic cooperation and collaboration in science and technology. Trade between the two countries rose by 10 to 15 per cent over the 1982-83 fiscal year. The opening of the Khunjerab Pass (located at the terminus of the Karakoram Highway between Pakistan and China) for regular trade and travel was expected to further facilitate the flow of trade.

Economic ties with Japan received a boost from President Zia's visit in July. By the end of the year 34 Japanese enterprises were actively operating in Pakistan; Japan had become, over the past six years, Pakistan's largest trading partner. The head of the Pakistan Planning Commission stated that the total two-way trade amounted to $2,000 million. The joint economic commission which was set up would henceforth plan and recommend future projects.

At a seminar held in London on 'Investment Opportunities in Pakistan' Lord Jellicoe, speaking on behalf of British participants, said that Pakistan's 'track record' towards foreign investments was very encouraging and that its Government had followed a healthy policy on incentives to foreign investors.

President Zia-ul-Haq announced a framework for the transfer of power to the people in his Independence Day broadcast on August 14. Elections would be held in two phases—first the provincial elections, then the elections to the National Assembly. They would be based on adult franchise and the whole process would be completed by March 1985. Elections to local bodies were sucessfully held in September. However, in spite of the announcment, the MRD intensified its campaign, particularly in Sind. The number of persons killed in Sind was, according to official estimates, about 50, though the opposition gave higher figures.

The anti-government protests did not spread to other areas of Pakistan. Differences within the MRD and lack of broad-based support led to the decline of the movement. There was also widespread popular support for General Zia's Islamization process, support strengthened also by a relatively strong economic performance.

Economic growth had exceeded 6 per cent in each of the years General Zia had been in power, compared to 3·5 per cent under the previous regime. Agriculture expanded at a rate of 4 to 5 per cent.

Production of wheat reached 12 million tons in 1982, and it was forecast that Pakistan could start exporting wheat by 1984. Cotton production jumped to over 4·4 million bales, a record. Manufacturing grew by 12 per cent and industry generally by 9 per cent. Inflation was contained at 6·7 per cent in 1982-83, from 10·7 per cent in the preceding year. World Bank figures placed Pakistan's 1981 per capita GNP at US $300 per annum, the highest in the sub-continent. The IMF also expressed full satisfaction over Pakistan's economic performance.

Exports climbed to $2,500 million, registering a growth percentage of 9·4 in the year ending June 1983. Exports of manufactured goods rose to nearly 55 per cent of total exports. National savings totalled 13 per cent of GNP in 1983. Remittances from Pakistanis abroad, amounting presently to $2,900 million dollars per year, were expected to rise at an annual rate of 10 per cent to $4,600 million.

In the 6th Five-Year Plan, industrial investment was to be focused mainly on private enterprise, with the Government relaxing controls and offering incentives. The Finance Minister, in his Budget speech, made clear the Government's intention 'to progressively dismantle the systems of control, regulation and rationing'. A little later, the head of the Planning Commission said: 'Pakistan in the 6th Plan is going to offer to the international community one of the most dynamic societies in the developing world'.

BANGLADESH

On 8 March 1983 *The Times* of London carried a despatch from Dhaka by its South Asian correspondent, Trevor Fishlock, reporting that 'the regime of General H. M. Ershad, ruler of Bangladesh, has the odour of failure. The military government that was meant to energize enervates. Instead of the promised panacea there is incoherence, and not for the first time soldiers are finding that an army is easier to run than a complex society'. This was a sombre but appropriate comment for this country almost exactly a year after General Ershad had assumed power.

Countrywide riots began at the Dhaka University campus in mid-February and left about a dozen people dead and many others injured. Ostensibly the riots were provoked by the Government's new education policy. Even after the Government modified its policy, however, in deference to student sensitivities, the unrest continued.

In mid-July General Ershad, the Chief Martial Law Administrator, carried out a major Cabinet reshuffle, his first since the March 1982 coup. The Interior Minister was demoted to a newly-created smaller Ministry, the Establishment and Reorganization Department, and was replaced by one of General Ershad's closest confidants, Mr Mahabbat Jan Chowdhury, hitherto Minister of Public Works. The latter portfolio was taken by Major-General Mohammed Abdul Munim, while the key Foreign, Finance and Food portfolios in the 14-member Cabinet remained unchanged and General Ershad himself retained the Defence Ministry. This meant that there were four army generals, three air vice-marshals and a rear-admiral in the martial law Cabinet. The reshuffle followed a general decline in law and order and rumours of differences within the Cabinet on how to deal with the situation.

Bangladesh's taka was pegged to the US dollar in January 1983 at a rate of 24·50. Alongside the official rate, however, open-market transactions in foreign currencies were conducted by commercial banks, with the help of remittances sent home by expatriate Bangladeshi workers, under a scheme whereby the workers' families received a premium of about 5 per cent over official exchange rates for all currencies, depending on supply and demand. The US dollar fetched the highest premium in late August when it traded at a rate of 26·80. About US $650 million was expected to be remitted by overseas workers in the year. The commercial banks used the foreign exchange thus earned to finance about half of the country's imports. Some 60 per cent of the workers' remittances were being spent on importing machinery and industrial raw materials, 25 per cent on importing finished goods, and 15 per cent on meeting workers' travel expenses.

Bangladesh continued to play an active role in international affairs, within the UN and its allied agencies and in the Non-Aligned Movement, the Commonwealth, the Islamic Conference and the newly-emerging seven-nation South Asian Regional Cooperation (SARC) grouping which was formally launched in August 1983 (see p. 262). Dhaka was proposed as the venue for SARC's first summit meeting in 1984. In December the Government expelled 12 Soviet officers for activity inconsistent with their diplomatic status.

Bangladesh's bilateral relations with a number of neighbouring countries—notably Nepal, Burma, Bhutan, Sri Lanka and the Maldives—further improved during 1983. A number of high-level delegations, including trade groups, were exchanged with these countries. Bilateral cooperation agreements were signed, including some establishing joint industrial ventures. Dhaka's relations with its neighbours were thus demonstrably good, despite some disputes with the largest of them all, India, especially regarding their common boundaries, the use of riverine waters and the emigration of Bangladeshis into Assam.

General Ershad returned to Dhaka without waiting for the conclusion of the Commonwealth heads of government meeting (see Pt. XI, Ch. 2) in order to attend to pressing problems at home. He had revised his earlier timetable for transferring some power back to civilian hands by announcing presidential elections for May 1984 (with himself as a candidate), and parliamentary elections in the following November.

However skilfully General Ershad might seem to conduct foreign relations, nonetheless his and his country's future hinged much more on the management, or mismanagement, of its volatile and unsettled domestic system.

SRI LANKA

Communal tensions between Sinhalese and Tamils burst into open conflict in July, doing great damage to Sri Lanka's international reputation, to the tourist industry and to democratic institutions.

Tamil militancy had been growing for some years, as various youth groups (collectively known as Tamil Tigers) took the initiative from the more constitutionalist Tamil United Liberation Front (TULF) (see AR 1981, p. 279, and 1982, pp. 277-278, and earlier volumes). The Elephant Pass army camp was attacked on 4 March and the Gurunagar camp on 31 May. Three United National Party (UNP) organizers were killed on 23 April and servicemen were killed on 18 and 19 May and 7 June. After attacks on buses, trains and post offices the violence escalated, thirteen soldiers being killed in an ambush on 23 July. The public funeral of the soldiers sparked off widespread rioting in Colombo and the massacre of 54 Tamil prisoners in Welikada gaol by Sinhalese inmates on 26 and 27 July. Emergency powers were used to impose a curfew in Colombo and elsewhere, curfew-breakers were threatened with shooting, strict censorship was imposed and the international airport closed. President J. R. Jayawardene warned on 29 July that those advocating separatism would lose their civil rights, a threat implemented as the sixth amendment to the constitution on 9 August. By 30 July, when the Pettah market in Colombo was set alight, over 35,000 people were homeless in seventeen refugee camps in Colombo and Kandy.

Indian involvement was marked by the visit of the Indian Foreign Minister, P. V. Narasimha Rao, on 29 July and by a meeting between Mrs Indira Gandhi and a delegation from the South Indian state of Tamil Nadu in New Delhi two days later. A protest strike was called by the Tamil Nadu government on 3 August. On 26 August an official Indian envoy, Gopala Parathasarathy, arrived to attempt reconciliation and there were talks between President Jayawardene and Mrs Gandhi in Delhi on 22 November and at the Commonwealth heads of government retreat in Goa in the same week. Some of the TULF leaders, including the Leader of the Opposition, Appapillai Amirthalingam, took up residence in India while an international agitation by overseas Tamils was launched in the United States, Britain and elsewhere.

President Jayawardene tried to call 'harmony talks' but these were frustrated by the absence of the TULF and by the reluctance of the Sri Lanka Freedom Party (SLFP) to attend while its leader, Mrs Sirimavo Bandaranaike, was deprived of her civil rights (see AR 1980, p. 282). A boycott of Parliament by the TULF led to its members' losing their seats on 4 November. The Government accused three marxist parties, the Communists, the Nava Samasamaja Party (NSSP) and the Janatha Vimukhthi Peramuna (JVP) of organizing the Colombo riots and they were proscribed in August. The Communists were exonerated in October but a ban on their newspaper, *Aththa*, remained. An official total of 402 killed between 23 July and 17 August was regarded by critics (as on previous occasions) as an underestimate.

Political life was restricted by the emergency and by the unseating of the TULF parliamentarians. The UNP maintained its dominance, although there were signs that the SLFP was recovering and building links with the fragmented left. In municipal elections in May the UNP retained Colombo, Kandy, Galle and Negombo but lost Ratnapura to the SLFP. The TULF retained control of councils in the north and east, including Jaffna and Trincomalee. A 'mini-election' was held at the same time, arising from the resignation of UNP members requested by the President (see AR 1982, p. 278). The UNP retained 14 parliamentary seats with 379,069 votes (48 per cent), the SLFP won three with 275,511 votes (35 per cent) and the Mahajana Eksath Peramuna won one with 27,054 votes (3 per cent). Other contestants were the Communists with 35,037 votes, the Independents with 28,796, the NSSP with 23,168, the JVP with 15,625 and the Lanka Samasamaja Party (LSSP) with 6,013. The left parties were mostly allied with the SLFP but the JVP contested alone and lost the lead over the left which had been recorded in the presidential election of 1982. Rifts within the SLFP continued (see AR 1981, p. 280, and 1982, p. 278) and in October its headquarters were transferred to Mrs Bandaranaike's home. Her son, Anura, became Leader of the Opposition on 8 November, replacing Mr Amirthalingam who had forfeited his seat along with his TULF colleagues.

Deaths during the year removed several prominent politicians. They included Leslie Goonewardena, a founder and former general-secretary of the LSSP, Sirisena B. Herat, Minister of Food, and Hector Kobbekaduwa, the SLFP presidential candidate for 1982. The prominent businessman and newspaper owner, Upali Wijewardene, disappeared off Malaysia in a private plane on 14 February.

NEPAL

The Prime Minister, Mr Surya Bahadur Thapa, made an 18-day trip to the United States, Britain, India, Pakistan and Bangladesh in early February. Shortly afterwards President Zia-ul-Haq of Pakistan visited Nepal and the two countries expressed an identity of views on Cambodia, Afghanistan and South Asian cooperation.

In 1983, for the first time in the 23-year history of Nepal's party-less panchayat (council) system, the members of the National Panchayat exercised their right to oust an elected Prime Minister, and in so doing brought to the surface of public discussion controversies which had been simmering about whether or not the country should have open competitive politics along party lines and about the parlous state of the national economy.

The Government of Mr Thapa, who had been elected for a five-year term in 1981, was dissolved after suffering a heavy defeat on a motion of no-confidence in the Rashtriya Panchayat (National Assembly) on 11 July, the day after 22 of the 35 members of his Council of Ministers had submitted their resignations. On the following day, Mr Lokendra Bahadur Chand, hitherto the Speaker of the Assembly, became the country's new Prime Minister. The no-confidence motion had accused Mr Thapa of not fulfilling his responsibilities honestly, alleging that the fundamental principles of the non-party panchayat system had not been observed, that corruption had become rampant, that the food-grain crisis had not been resolved, and that economic indiscipline had reached a climax. A week before he was ousted, Thapa had addressed the Rashtriya Panchayat for more than three hours, denying the allegations, particularly the charge that he had encouraged party feelings in the party-less system.

Less than a month after Chand had formed his Government, a move was made to table another no-confidence motion, this time regarding the proposed purchase of an aircraft for Royal Nepal Airlines, amidst allegations that Chand had encouraged 'groupism' in the Rashtriya Panchayat. Although it gained some support, the motion was rejected on the ground that it was against a clause of the constitution. To shield Chand from difficulties King Birendra prorogued the House before members could discuss in detail the modified budget for 1983-84.

With a stagnant economy and a fall of gross domestic product in fiscal year 1982-83, the new Government inherited severe problems. Almost all industries in Nepal were running below 50 per cent of planned production capacity because of such factors as the non-availability of raw materials or spare parts or frequent labour troubles. Assessing the first three years of the sixth five-year plan (1980-85), Chand admitted that only 40 per cent of development targets and 29 per cent of irrigation projects had been fulfilled.

The change of Government did not fundamentally affect the country's basic foreign policy, nor diminish the King's prominent role in the conduct of its most important aspects. King Birendra's address to the seventh Non-Aligned summit in New Delhi was a vigorous reaffirmation of his country's non-alignment. In addition to stressing the need to establish a new international economic order and to promote North-South cooperation he reiterated the desirability of making Nepal a zone of peace. Following the state visit of President Mitterrand to

Kathmandu in May, the French decision to endorse Nepal's peace zone proposal—increasing to 36 the number of countries affirming support—was acclaimed locally as a major foreign policy success. Italy, Spain, Malta and the United Arab Emirates, in addition, expressed their support during King Birendra's visits to them in September. Nepal's dependence on oil imports and its desire to improve its relations within the Arab world were reflected in the King's unofficial visits to Egypt, Saudi Arabia, Oman and the UAE while en route to Spain for a state visit.

Nepal's other foreign policy priority in 1983 seemed to be the promotion of South Asian cooperation, both by multilateral regionalism and by improving bilateral links with neighbours.

Chapter 3

SEYCHELLES—MAURITIUS—BRITISH INDIAN OCEAN TERRITORY—
MALAGASY—COMORO STATE

SEYCHELLES

THE Government of President René faced a variety of security and economic problems in 1983. At the Non-Aligned Movement's summit meeting in March, the President voiced his concern over the growing militarization of the Indian Ocean and appealed for the region to be created a zone of peace. Reverberations of the failed 1981 coup attempt (see AR 1981, pp. 282–3, and 1982, pp. 280–1) persisted. Speculation over the fate of the six white mercenaries, four of whom had been sentenced to death for their part in the attempted coup, ended in July when the six were released in an act of presidential clemency and flown to Johannesburg. However, the spectre of external intervention re-emerged in December when the South African Government announced that it had forestalled a further attempt to organize a mercenary force intending to overthrow the René Government. This reminder of the Seychelle islands' vulnerability was particularly timely in the wake of the Commonwealth heads of government decision to study the security problems of micro-states (see DOCUMENTS).

The recent history of anti-government plots was reflected in enhanced domestic security arrangements, notably the doubling of the army's strength over a four-year period. Yet it was reported in August that foreign troops continued to play a major role; while Tanzanian troops (see AR 1982, p. 281) were estimated to number about one-third of their original strength, they were being replaced, according to reports, by North Korean military advisers.

The Government was particularly security-conscious in the run-up to the National Assembly elections in August, when the sole official political party—the governing People's Progressive Party—was returned to power unopposed. Pragmatism and a balanced approach to non-alignment emerged as the hall-marks of the Government's foreign policy. Reports circulating in July suggested that President René's Government was on the point of concluding an agreement whereby British and US naval vessels would be permitted to dock in the Seychelles. Formerly the refusal to declare the nuclear or non-nuclear status of their weapons had resulted in the barring of Western warships from Seychelles waters, in contrast to the facilities enjoyed by ships of the Soviet navy.

Fading economic prospects prompted a reappraisal of the socialist Government's plans to diversify the economy and reduce dependence on tourism and foreign aid. The demands of social programmes and increased wages placed the economy under considerable strain. Also the Government's ability to attract foreign investment suffered from its policy of intervention in the economy, particularly its compulsory land purchase programme, and from the climate of political uncertainty. In August the Government signalled its desire to extend its foreign economic relations when the Chinese Minister for Foreign Trade, Mrs Chen Muhua, held talks in Victoria on economic and technical cooperation between the two countries.

Recognition of the crucial importance of the tourist industry to the Seychelles' economy led to a major government-sponsored promotional campaign directed at Western industrial nations. But an estimated 17 per cent increase in the number of tourists during the first half of the year was not matched by a comparable increase in revenue. The relatively high-technology projects aiming to utilize the country's ocean resources remained long-term developments and did little to compensate for the sharp drop in the production and value of copra, the Seychelles' immediate asset and main export.

MAURITIUS

For the first seven months of the year Mauritians experienced a period of political uncertainty. Disagreement within the Government over measures to rectify the ailing economy and the postponement of many of the 1982 election manifesto promises—including the redistribution of wealth, the raising of living standards and improvements in welfare services—in order to comply with IMF and World Bank conditions for financial assistance ultimately led to a political crisis.

The left-wing coalition Government was thrown into turmoil when eleven of the nineteen Cabinet Ministers, including the Foreign Minister, Mr Jean Claude de l'Estrac, and the influential Finance Minister, Mr Paul

Bérenger, resigned in March, expressing their lack of confidence in the Prime Minister, Mr Aneerood Jugnauth. Although able to form a new Cabinet within a week Premier Jugnauth subsequently split from the Mouvement Militant Mauritien (MMM), of which he had been President since 1973, and formed a new party, the Mouvement Socialiste Militant (MSM).

Seeking a new parliamentary majority Mr Jugnauth dissolved Parliament in June and called a general election—the second in fourteen months and only the third in the independent history of this multiracial, culturally diffuse and multi-party democracy. Along with fellow defectors from the MMM the Prime Minister entered into an election alliance with the Labour Party and the Mauritian Social Democrat Party (PMSD). One condition of the alliance was that the former Labour Premier, Sir Seewoosagur Ramgoolam, should become the island's first non-executive President once the status of Mauritius was changed to that of a republic within the Commonwealth.

In the general election of 21 August the three-party socialist alliance of Mr Jugnauth decisively defeated the MMM led by Mr Bérenger. Although the alliance won 41 of the 62 seats it received only 52 per cent of the votes, leaving the MMM the strongest single party in terms of popular support, but without its founder, its chairman and its secretary-general, who lost their seats. Mr Bérenger was subsequently admitted to the Legislative Assembly under the country's 'best loser' electoral system.

Among the more immediately compelling economic problems facing the new coalition Government were the economic stringencies required by the IMF and World Bank, the mounting national debt—compounded by the loss-making sugar industry and the decline in the once lucrative tourist trade—and unemployment estimated at 25 per cent of the working population. The new Government was similarly constrained in foreign policy. Despite its continued stand over Diego Garcia and the Chagos islands (see p. 274), and its commitment to non-alignment and the establishment of an Indian Ocean zone of peace, there was little evidence that it would embark on policies likely to disrupt the flow of tourists, many of whom were from South Africa.

BRITISH INDIAN OCEAN TERRITORY

In February, during his two-day official visit to India, the Prime Minister of Mauritius declared his intention to make the US base on Diego Garcia and the Mauritian claim to the island a major issue at the forthcoming New Delhi summit of the Non-Aligned Movement (see Pt. XI, Ch. 7). Mr Jugnauth insisted that the Mauritian ban on warships of the American and Soviet navies would continue despite the resulting loss of much-needed foreign exchange.

The strategic sensitivity of the Chagos archipelago was evident in July when 36 Mauritian coconut-fibre pickers landed illegally on Peros Banhos, 130 miles north of Diego Garcia. The British Government denied there were any plans to involve a naval vessel in the incident, and the expulsion of the merchants was left to the British military commander on Diego Garcia acting in his civilian capacity as deputy commissioner.

The United States continued to consolidate its base and communications facilities on Diego Garcia. It was estimated to have invested about $1,000 million in extending runways to handle B52 bombers, improving deep-water port facilities and building storage facilities for equipment in readiness for use by a Rapid Deployment Force. A fully-equipped RDF unit was reported to be stationed at the base.

MALAGASY

The principal political event of the year was the parliamentary election held at the end of August. More than 500 candidates from seven political parties had campaigned for the 137 seats over a short electoral period. Reports said that the public had become wearied by ten months of polls for members of decentralized collectives (village committees for the regional assemblies). All parties were considered to be on the left politically, and were members of the National Front for the Defence of the Revolution. There was little doubt that the Avant-Garde of the Malagasy Revolution (AREMA) of the President, Didier Ratsiraka, would obtain a large majority, and so it proved. AREMA obtained a vote of 2,253,957 (64·83 per cent of the electorate) which gave it 117 seats. The nearest rival groups obtained 11 per cent and 10 per cent of the poll and even fewer seats. Most conspicuous was the decline of the National Movement for the Independence of Malagasy (MONIMA) of the veteran politician Monja Joana, who had recently been freed from house arrest. In the elections of 1982 he had obtained 20 per cent of the poll.

The country continued to suffer from serious economic problems, and in spite of the elections a certain atmosphere of insecurity continued to prevail, as they were immediately followed by the third treason trial of the year, in which a businessman was accused of preparing a commando to overthrow the government. At the two earlier trials different groups of army officers, also charged with seeking to overthrow the government, had been arraigned.

COMORO STATE

It was a quiet year, with a Government reshuffle in February and a general amnesty announced on the eighth anniversary of independence in May. The President, Ahmed Abdallah Abderamane, made a forceful appeal (on the fifth anniversary of his election) for the return of the island of Mayotte to the Comoro Islands. He recalled that President Mitterrand was committed to this (Mayotte, following a referendum in 1975, was still under French rule), although 'chronic colonialists' continued to work against it.

IX SOUTH-EAST AND EAST ASIA

Chapter 1

BURMA—THAILAND—MALAYSIA AND BRUNEI—
SINGAPORE—INDONESIA—PHILIPPINES—VIETNAM—
KAMPUCHEA—LAOS—HONG KONG

BURMA

THE army continued to campaign against armed groups in the hill areas around Burma proper. Burmese Communist Party (BCP) forces were under pressure in the eastern Shan states, while further south offensives were launched against the Karen National Union (KNU) established along the Thai border. Between these areas Burmese and Thai troops fought with drug smugglers and various minority forces. The BCP had for years been based along the borders with China and Laos. After 1977 China reduced support for the BCP, which therefore had to show greater tactical flexibility in relation to minority armies which attracted greater popular support than it did. It approached several groups, including the most effective, the Kachin Independence Organization in the north and the KNU. In February the KNU attempted a raid into the Pegu Yoma hills in central Burma, and BCP political organizers seem later to have infiltrated this area.

Several influential men, mostly from the intelligence services, were dismissed from May onwards. They included especially Tin Oo, who had been regarded as the probable successor to Ne Win, and Bo Ni, the Home and Religious Affairs Minister. Both were charged with misusing relatively small amounts of state funds and sentenced to life imprisonment. The real reason for the dismissal of Tin Oo and his associates was perhaps that, as with previous apparent successors to Ne Win, he had become too visibly influential.

On 9 October four South Korean Ministers and other South Koreans and Burmese attending a ceremony were killed by a bomb. The South Korean President escaped injury only because of a traffic delay. Police later killed one North Korean army officer and captured two others, who in November were convicted of the bombing. Burma had hitherto had good relations with North Korea, but on 4 November the Government announced that it had been 'firmly established that the explosion was the work of saboteurs sent by North Korea' and that it was withdrawing recognition of North Korea. It was popularly supposed that if Tin Oo and his colleagues had still been controlling security the explosion would have been prevented.

Concern over growing trade deficits, a 19 per cent debt service ratio and declining foreign exchange reserves led to a decision to cut investment programmes, although foreign concessional aid was accepted for the modernization of basic industry, transport and communications, including Rangoon port. Efforts to raise oil production continued and a substantial offshore gas discovery was reported.

THAILAND

Fighting between Vietnamese forces and Cambodian resistance groups again spilled into Thai territory and drove Cambodian civilians into Thailand. There were clashes between Thai and Vietnamese troops and a Vietnamese claim to be entitled to pursue Cambodian guerrillas into Thailand. In November the Thai military reported Vietnamese preparations for a further dry-season offensive. They also expressed concern at increasing Soviet strength in the region and sought more advanced American weapons.

The Chinese army chief of staff arrived in Bangkok on 28 January; he promised support against any assault on Thailand by the Vietnamese. The Japanese Prime Minister also pledged continuing support during a visit in May. The Thai Foreign Minister spoke in May of showing greater flexibility towards the Indochinese states, largely in response to domestic suggestions, notably by a Deputy Premier and a former Prime Minister. This encouraged the Vietnamese to probe what was seen as a potential split within the Thai political consensus and within Asean. The Thais, however, stood by UN resolutions requiring withdrawal of all foreign forces from Kampuchea and restoration of the Cambodian people's right to self-determination, and in July the Chinese Foreign Minister found the Thais as suspicious as ever of Vietnamese intentions.

The army successfully persuaded further groups of armed guerrillas, mainly from the Communist Party of Thailand, and their dependents to return to civilian life. It was claimed that armed guerrillas, including Muslim separatist and Communist Party of Malaya supporters, had declined from 12,000 in 1978 to 3,000 in November 1983. Another 5,000 communist guerrillas and dependents surrendered in northern Thailand in December. Initially there were bureaucratic problems in finding land and jobs for those returning, but efforts were made to resolve these. Security forces also harried drug smugglers in frontier areas.

In January parliamentary elctions were called for June. Three transitional constitutional clauses were to lapse on 21 April. These provided for constituencies with individual candidates instead of larger provincial party-list constituencies, for civil and military officials to be eligible to serve in the Cabinet, and for important issues to be jointly voted on by the appointed Senate and the elected Lower House. These transitional provisions militated against the consolidation of large parties and strengthened the position of the Upper House, dominated by the military and civil servants. Some politicians and military men, especially the army commander-in-chief, General Arthit Kamlang-ek, wished to extend the transitional provisions. A special session of Parliament was convened in February to discuss proposals to stick to small constituencies, to prolong the Senate's transitional powers, and to allow officials and officers to hold Cabinet office. Despite vigorous lobbying the proposed amendments were rejected on 16 March by 10 votes in a joint session; nearly 200 members of both Houses abstained.

The Prime Minister was then persuaded into advising a dissolution which resulted in the elections' being held on 18 April, when the smaller constituency system still applied. Constitutional change became an electoral issue which seemed to benefit parties that had voted against amendment. The three largest, the Social Action (SAP), Chart Thai and Democrat (DP) parties, all of which had so voted, secured just over two-thirds of the seats. It was widely assumed that Arthit—who became armed forces supreme commander in the autumn, as well as army commander-in-chief—and others who favoured a more central political role for the army would nevertheless press again for constitutional change. Public response, however, was unenthusiastic and the issue was not formally raised again during the year.

General Prem Tinsulanond, who had not stood for election and belonged to no party, was expected to continue as Prime Minister. On 26 April, however, he announced that he would retire, and Chart Thai thereupon claimed that it should form the new Government. Prem, however, then accepted nomination, was reappointed and formed a coalition of SAP, DP and the fourth and fifth largest parties. Chart Thai was excluded, but the Defence, Foreign, Finance and Interior Ministers were all unchanged from the previous coalition. In his policy speech Prem spoke of taking 'every step possible to create confidence and faith in the parliamentary system', but also remarked that the armed forces would play an important role in 'the democratic system under the monarchy'.

Growth was estimated at 5·8 per cent in real terms, against 4·5 per cent in 1982, and inflation at 4 per cent, against 5·4 per cent. Agriculture, manufacturing and building did better than in 1982. Exports, however, fell in value, while imports, especially capital goods, raw materials and machinery, increased after declining in 1982; the trade deficit, which was unusually low in 1982, rose sharply. Reserves and credit rating were satisfactory, but increasing foreign debt caused concern and some capital-intensive projects were held back; interest rates were raised and credit was restricted. Structural adjustment remained a principal purpose of economic planning and tax reforms were introduced, together with

MALAYSIA AND BRUNEI

Apprehension over the possible political role of the next King of Malaysia prompted the Government to rush a package of constitutional amendments through the federal Parliament in August. The most far-reaching measures provided that any Bill would become law automatically 15 days after it had been presented to the King for his assent (with corresponding application at the states level) and transferred to the Prime Minister the formal right of the King to proclaim a state of emergency. Other provisions included the abolition of civil appeals to the Privy Council and an increase in the number of federal parliamentary seats from 154 to 176.

A major constitutional crisis occurred when the King (the Sultan of Pahang) refused his assent to the package of amendments and received unanimous support for his stand from all the other hereditary Sultans, from whose ranks he had been elected for a single five-year term. The crisis served to expose and widen factional divisions within the United Malays National Organization (UMNO), the dominant party within the ruling National Front coalition. It also opened up the issue of the political position of and succession to Prime Minister, Dr Mahathir Mohamad.

On 20 November, proposals were put to the Sultans which provided the basis for a compromise. On 15 December, during the indisposition of the King who had suffered a stroke in September, his deputy signed the Constitution (Amendment) Bill on the understanding that a special session of Parliament would be called in January 1984 to introduce a new Bill incorporating a formula restoring the right of the King to proclaim a state of emergency on the advice of the Prime Minister. The right of the King to refuse assent to any federal Bill would not be restored but the states' rulers would retain such a right in principle.

In March, after a trial lasting 75 days, the High Court sentenced Datuk Mokhtar Hashim, federal Minister of Culture, Youth and Sports, to death for the murder of Datuk Taha Talik, the speaker of the Negri Sembilan state assembly in April 1982. His death sentence was confirmed by the federal Court of Appeal in July. Datuk Mokhtar resigned from his parliamentary seat at the beginning of August and filed for a royal pardon. In March, Datuk Lee San-choon, president of the Malayan Chinese Association (MCA) and federal Minister of Transport, announced his retirement from all political offices at the age of 48. He was succeeded in party office by Datuk Neo Yee-pan, who had become deputy-president of the MCA in August 1982. In April, Datuk Mohammad Nasir, the head of Kelantan-based party Berjasa and a coalition partner in the National Front Government, announced his resignation from the post of Minister in the Prime Minister's Department. In June, as a consequence of these resignations, Prime Minister Dr Mahathir Mohamad announced a minor Cabinet reshuffle, in which Anwar Ibrahim was elevated from junior office to the portfolio of Culture, Youth and Sports.

The clandestine radio station 'Voice of the People of Malaya' announced that from 11 December it would call itself 'Voice of the People of Malaysia'. On that day it reported a merger between the marxist-leninist Communist Party of Malaya and the Revolutionary Wing of the Communist Party of Malaya into a single party, the Communist Party of Malaysia. It broadcast a statement by the Party's Central Committee that the Communist Party of Malaya led by Chin Peng no longer had the right to represent all communists and revolutionaries in Malaysia, including peninsula Malaysia and North Kalimantan.

In March, while on a visit to London, Prime Minister Dr Mahathir indicated a willingness to revise his Government's 'buy British last' policy in the light of tangible changes in attitude and policy by the British Government. Later in the month, he informed the federal Parliament that Britain had adopted a more positive attitude towards Malaysia, particularly in trade and education. In early April, he withdrew his directive to government departments which required all contracts with British firms to be scrutinized by the Prime Minister's office to see whether or not there was an alternative to purchasing from Britain.

It was announced in September that in the previous June Malaysian security forces had occupied Terumbu Layang Layang, an uninhabited coral atoll in the South China Sea off the coast of Sabah. The atoll, located 40 miles to the south-east of the Vietnamese-occupied island of Amboyna Cay, is part of the Spratly archipelago. Malaysia had been in dispute with Vietnam, China and the Philippines over the sovereignty of both islands, which fall within its declared 200-mile exclusive maritime zone.

After a visit by the King of Malaysia in February, the Prime Minister and Foreign Minister Tan Sri Ghazalie Shafie paid a two-day official visit to Brunei in March. Talks centred on foreign relations and defence in the light of Brunei's impending independence. Offers were made to train Brunei officials and it was agreed to conduct talks on border arrangements to facilitate travel between the two states.

At midnight on 31 December, the Sultanate of Brunei became fully independent with the transfer of power in external affairs from Britain. Negotiations between the Governments of Brunei and Britain over the terms on which a Gurkha battalion and British service personnel on loan should continue to be deployed in the Sultanate were beset by disagreement. Before they were concluded satisfactorily in September, the Brunei Government dismissed Britain's Crown Agents as manager of its multi-billion-pound investment portfolio in favour of the American banks Morgan Guaranty and Citibank.

SINGAPORE

At a National Day rally in August, Prime Minister Lee Kuan-yew provoked public controversy when he sought to encourage women graduates to marry their intellectual equals. He claimed that uneducated women in Singapore produced twice as many children as their educated counterparts and that unless the trend were reversed the country would lose its talent pool and its economy would falter. At the end of the month, deputy Prime Minister Dr Goh Keng-swee disclosed that the Government intended to provide a computerized matchmaking service to help women graduates find appropriate marital partners and so produce better-educated children for the good of the state.

On 16 September Mr Lee Kuan-yew celebrated his sixtieth birthday. The previous April, a candidate for political succession, trade-union leader Lim Chee-onn, had been relieved of his post. He resigned as Minister without Portfolio in July. Finance Minister Hon Sui-sen died of a heart attack in October. He was succeeded by Trade and Industry Minister Anthony Tan, who retained his existing portfolio.

In August, Singapore's sole opposition member of Parliament, J. B. Jeyaratnam, and Wong Hong-toy, president of his Workers' Party, pleaded not guilty to charges of making a false declaration in connection with party accounts and also of fraudulently transferring party funds. They were released on bail pending resumption of the case at the end of December. In October, Mr Jeyaratnam and two other officials of his bankrupt party were fined S$1,500 for collecting funds without a licence; S$500 short of the designated sum whereby he would automatically forfeit his parliamentary seat.

Three arrests made during police raids on Christmas Day broke up a ring engaged in smuggling advanced microchips, stolen from an American firm in Malaysia, through Singapore and then through India to countries in Eastern Europe and the Soviet Union.

INDONESIA

On 8 March the People's Consultative Assembly, consisting of Parliament and representatives of functional groups, unanimously re-elected General Suharto for a fourth presidential term; General Umar Wirahadikusumah became Vice-President. Several senior men retired, and new appointments included Ali Wardhana as economic coordinating Minister, Admiral Sudomo as Minister for manpower, and General Benny Murdani, whose career had included intelligence and security appointments and active service in West Irian and East Timor, as commander of the armed forces.

Golkar, the official party with two-thirds of elected MPs, had hitherto been inactive between elections. It was now given a more powerful general chairman, a more independent-minded executive board, individual membership instead of membership through organizations and a cadre system. There was controversy among Muslim groups over the President's wish to see the state ideology, Pancasila, adopted by all political and social groups as their ideological foundation. Some pressure was brought on Nahdlatul Ulama (NU), the former Islamic scholars' party, to give a lead to other Muslim organizations which had accepted Islamic tenets as their guiding principles. Despite rank-and-file resistance, in December a form of words was found, making a distinction between man's relationships with God and with man, which was expected to satisfy both the President and the NU.

In February the UN Human Rights Commission called, by 16 votes to 14 with 10 abstentions, for 'free and full exercise of the right to self-determination' in East Timor. For some months the Indonesian authorities concentrated on economic development and on persuading Fretelin supporters to return to civilian life. A Group of Australian MPs, visiting without military escort 14 centres which Fretelin claimed to hold or to be suffering from famine, were impressed by the signs of development, the crops and the absence of soldiers; they had one chance meeting with Fretelin, four armed men met by the roadside.

Subsequently, however, civil guards, formerly members of Fretelin, killed some 15 unarmed members of an army engineering corps. Fretelin was also said to have burnt down several villages, and the army then resorted to what it called a 'limited military operation'. Both outgoing and incoming Australian Governments seemed anxious to improve relations with Indonesia, despite public reaction in Australia to issues such as East Timor. President Suharto still thought it premature to normalize diplomatic relations with China and he put unity with Asean before further attempts to reach an accommodation with Vietnam.

Measures were taken to reduce the trade deficit caused by lower demand and prices for oil and other export commodities. Economic growth, down to 2·25 per cent in 1982, recovered a little to 3·5 per cent. The Budget proposed to freeze public sector wages again, to end subsidies on rice, cooking oil, flour, sugar and salt from 1 April and to cut oil subsidies—over half of which were on paraffin for cooking—by a quarter. Large industrial projects with a high import content were held back.

On 30 March the rupiah was devalued by 27·6 per cent against the US dollar. Despite devaluation and greatly-reduced subsidies the consumer price index rose only by 13 per cent, estimates of the current account deficit for 1983-84 fell sharply and by the end of October the international reserves, which had been almost halved in 1982-83, had recovered half the loss. In June the aid consortium pledged more assistance than had been expected. In December Parliament passed new laws which began a comprehensive reform and simplification of the tax system to improve collection and reduce dependence on oil revenues.

PHILIPPINES

The Catholic bishops' conference withdrew in January from the church-military liaison committee and in February issued a pastoral letter criticizing corruption, militarization, control of the press, violations of rights and other abuses of power. Detention of priests, prominent Catholic laymen, opposition politicians and journalists continued. Powers of indefinite detention under Presidential Commitment Orders (PCOs) were increasingly criticized, as was a tendency compulsorily to 'relocate' into restricted 'strategic hamlets' people who were adversely affected by the development of logging, plantation, hydroelectric and other large-scale public and private projects. A Church survey found that many people attributed growing poverty to 'state corruption, immorality and over-centralization of power'. In March Cardinal Sin called for the release of all political prisoners and proposed an advisory council of representatives of the regime, the opposition, the Church and private business to work for 'national survival'.

On 5 August President Marcos announced the abolition of PCOs, but retained equally formidable powers of detention. It also emerged that in 1981 Marcos had signed a decree providing the death penalty for uttering seditious words or libels, for organizing a rally aimed at destabilizing the Government and for taking part as publishers in 'sustained propaganda assaults' on the Government. Marcos, who was thought to be subject to recurring bouts of illness, came under pressure to provide for an orderly succession. He was reluctant and initially said that power, until a new President could be elected, would pass to the Executive Committee, with the incumbent Prime Minister as its Chairman. Later there was talk of reviving an elected Vice-Presidency. Marcos did, however, propose constitutional amendments, subject to a plebiscite in January 1984, to permit elections to be held on a provincial, instead of regional, basis, which was expected to lessen official advantages.

During July the best-known opposition politician, Benigno Aquino, made clear his intention of returning to the Philippines, despite a refusal to issue him with a passport, a statement from General Fabian Ver, the armed forces chief of staff in direct charge of both the presidential and aviation security commands, that Aquino would not be allowed to leave the aircraft in which he arrived, and several warnings from the regime, including Mrs Marcos in person, that he might be killed if he returned home. He returned on 21 August, was taken off the plane by soldiers and killed. Another man, Rolando Galman, was also shot dead. The regime claimed that Galman had shot Aquino and was linked to a communist conspiracy. Little popular credence was given to this claim (see OBITUARY).

Aquino's murder had a catalytic effect on popular feeling. Huge crowds visited the Aquino home and turned out for the lying-in-state and the burial. Thereafter frequent, often large and almost always peaceful demonstrations were held in Manila, including especially the financial district of Makati, and in the provinces, despite efforts to prevent them. The regime appeared nonplussed by the popular reaction and a commission of enquiry collapsed in face of widespread scepticism about its impartiality. In October a new and less suspect board of enquiry was formed to report to the National Assembly and the public rather than the President; it was still hearing evidence by the New Year.

Repression of popular manifestations of opposition after 21 August was hampered by the fear that too brutal a reaction would lead to a collapse of foreign offical and investor confidence. As it was, in October the US President found an excuse to postpone a brief visit. On 1 June the USA agreed to a new five-year bases agreement which would provide the Philippines with US$900 million in grants and credits for economic and military purposes, as against $500 million in the previous five-year period, and in July the aid consortium agreed on somewhat more support than the US $1,200 million a year provided previously. It was already clear, however, that a further IMF standby credit would be needed for 1984 and that severe measures would be required to improve the balance of payments and reduce the budget deficit.

The Aquino murder then started an outflow of funds both domestic and foreign and greatly damaged Philippine credit. It was also found that the international reserves had been overstated by around US $600 million. During October the corrected reserve figure fell below one month's import bills and the Government had to ask for a 90-day moratorium on repayments of foreign debt. By 5 October the peso was officially 34·5 per cent below its US dollar value on 1 January, and by December inflation was expected to be 28 per cent and 1983 real economic growth 1·5 per cent, negative growth being forecast for 1984.

VIETNAM

Better farming weather and more market-oriented economic policies introduced over the preceding three years had by 1983 improved the economy, despite strains created by tension along the Chinese border, which eased a little, and by the occupation of Kampuchea. Grain output had fallen by 1978 to below 13 million tons: 1982 grain production, mainly rice, was 16·59 million tons and the 1983 harvest appeared slightly higher, bringing output close to a low self-sufficiency level, despite shortages of fertilizers and pesticides. Grain supplies procured for distribution as rations to cadres, troops and other government employees, which had increased by over 50 per cent in 1982, rose again by almost 30 per cent. Also after 1980 the use of economic incentives sharply increased the output of small industries and handicrafts, of export products such as sea-food and of agricultural side-crops, notably vegetables. Larger state-run industries, however, lagged behind, and there were acute shortages of energy and transport, rising foreign debts despite inadequate investment levels, virtually no foreign reserves and a rapidly growing population.

The reforms still met intense disapproval within the party both on ideological grounds and because cadres, being on fixed salaries, did not gain from the system unless they were corrupt, but did suffer from its side-effects; these included price rises, because supplies of goods, although greater, were still short of demand. Many senior cadres were also afraid of losing control of the system; one official journal stated that the free market handled 70 per cent of goods in circulation. Cadres also disapproved of income disparities, burgeoning service industries and the greater influence given to the consumer, which encouraged even state industries to produce goods not in official plans. As had repeatedly happened in China from the 1950s onwards, once pragmatic methods had revived the economy cadres wished to revert to ideologically purer policies. During 1983, in the hope of reducing the worrying side-effects, some steps were taken to restrict private trade and independent initiatives by local bodies, both directly and by new taxes which discouraged some activities and encouraged others. In particular Saigon, regarded as a source of corrupting influences, and its party leadership were sharply criticized for pursuing independent and alarmingly liberal policies.

In December, while recognizing the dangers for party doctrine and control, it was decided that the new policies were too effective to be abandoned. The state-run economy, especially centrally-controlled industry, was severely criticized, and the party Secretary-General stated that failure to provide incentives 'will certainly lead to bureaucratic subsidy-based management and will inevitably hamper production'. Wider economic relations with non-communist countries were proposed, while a treaty with the USSR signed in November envisaged increased trade. In practice, exports increased much less than planned, partly because of the dampening effects of tighter central control.

KAMPUCHEA (CAMBODIA)

As the year opened, sharp fighting was in progress between the Vietnamese and the non-communist KPNLF near the border. The KPNLF temporarily ejected the Vietnamese from some village bases and the Vietnamese briefly overran a KPNLF-controlled refugee camp, whose civilian occupants retired into Thai territory. Despite shortages of ammunition and anti-tank weapons the KPNLF performed better than expected. The Vietnamese also temporarily overran positions held by Khmer Rouge and Sihanoukist guerrillas. During the wet season Khmer Rouge and KPNLF guerrillas and some independent armed bands again inflicted casualties on the Vietnamese and Soviet advisers in widespread small-scale attacks and disrupted traffic on a number of main roads around the Tonle Sap and between Phnom Penh and the coast. Even the extreme south-easterly Svay Rieng province was troubled with guerrillas. By November the Vietnamese were moving tanks and large troop units towards the Thai frontier, apparently for a further dry-season offensive.

Pol Pot was said to be again in active control of the Khmer Rouge, so strengthening the one reputable argument for Vietnamese occupation. Vietnamese advisers still controlled all levels of administration, and an influx of Vietnamese, and stress on the teaching of Vietnamese, suggested a deliberate process of colonization. Many incomers, however, were former residents in Kampuchea. The Heng Samrin regime did not permit dissent, but was nevertheless less demanding than the Khmer Rouge or the regime in Vietnam. Until March the Vietnamese maintained a relatively benevolent attitude to Kampuchean civilians, but they then adopted a harsher attitude. There were reports of purges of Heng Samrin officials in western provinces, of arrests and beatings of villagers accused of helping the KPNLF, of Vietnamese looting of farm animals and food supplies and of whole villages fleeing to KPNLF camps.

Drought up to late July, three typhoons in October and a lack of work animals, equipment, fertilizers and pesticides seemed likely to leave a shortage of 250,000 tons of rice and increased malnutrition and disease, especially amongst children. Although officially back in production many government factories seemed not to be operating, but private sector markets, shops and service industries revived.

LAOS

The 1980 decision to allow private trading continued to stimulate the economy. Markets were better supplied than in Vietnam and Kampuchea and the Government drew back from a proposal to take majority holdings in private restaurants. The 1982 paddy harvest had improved to 1·1 million tons and a similar result seemed likely in 1983 despite less favourable weather. Since 1980 many farming cooperatives had been disbanded. Although the Government claimed that there had subsequently been some voluntary formation of cooperatives, most of those remaining seemed to be notional rather than real cooperatives, which tended to require official subsidies to survive. The Government secured less than 8 per cent of the harvest through taxes and procurement, since procurement prices were far below market prices and it could not supply consumer goods at comparably low prices. Transport and security problems prevented it from bringing rice from southern Laos to Vientiane and it had to import 30,000 tons of rice from Thailand for government officials and employees.

Lack of security also inhibited exploitation of mineral and forest resources for export. In 1982 electricity earnings sharply increased thanks to higher tariffs for sales to Thailand, which took nine-tenths of Nam Ngum output, although some of this was reimported by way of the Thai transmission system. Other exports were tin, timber, coffee and farm produce. Most imports, including smuggled goods, came from or through Thailand, and the Laotian Government was anxious to secure a wider spread of official trading-points between the two countries. Laos also wished for better relations with China and was more relaxed about foreigners than Vietnam or Kampuchea; Chinese, Vietnamese, Thai, Indian and French residents were permitted to carry on private businesses and the Chinese ran a school. The conduct of the Vietnamese, however, was not always appreciated and in July Vietnamese residents had to be urged to cooperate with the Lao people, while Laos, as well as Kampuchea, resisted Vietnam's wish to coordinate economic development plans through a joint commission.

HONG KONG

Confidence was severely shaken by anxiety over the political future and by statements by some Chinese officials which suggested ignorance of Hong Kong's society and economy and of why local people wished to retain a status quo that guaranteed, free of bureaucratic meddling, their existing legal system, independent judiciary, free press, freedom to travel abroad and other rights. Delegations representing local Chinese visited

Peking and expressed concern at reported Chinese proposals for the future. Opinion polls conducted by both the Hong Kong Government and Peking representatives conveyed the same message. Sino-British talks, in which the Governor took part from July onwards, were held at intervals in Peking, accompanied by leaks from Chinese sources of what were said to be Chinese official proposals or intentions. Some of these may have reflected differing views among Chinese officials on ways of recovering suzerainty over Hong Kong without, in the process, destroying the territory's prosperity and all hope of persuading Taiwan towards reunification. These reported proposals created alarm in Hong Kong, assuaged occasionally by more encouraging statements from senior Chinese officials.

Weakness and erratic movements of stock-market prices and local dollar exchange rates reflected this alarm, as did indications that people with the entrepreneurial, professional, technical and managerial talent responsible for Hong Kong's economic success were prepared to depart should the outcome of the Sino-British talks prove unacceptable. Substantial deposits switched from Hong Kong dollar into US dollar accounts, and capital departed or was held back by reluctance to reinvest even in thriving export industries. Prime rate went from $11\frac{1}{2}$ to 13 per cent on 9 September, but on 24 September, after a worrying *People's Daily* article and a curt statement on the latest talks, the HK dollar was down to HK$ 9·55 to US$ 1, a loss of a third of its US dollar value in nine months. Official support and a prime rate of 16 per cent improved the exchange rate, but it continued to fluctuate sharply on every Chinese statement. On 15 October it was announced that notes would be traded between commercial banks, the two note-issuing banks and the Exchange Fund at HK$7·80 to US$1. Most transactions were left free, but arbitrage thereafter kept the free-market rate close to the fixed rate even after prime rate had been reduced to $13\frac{1}{2}$ per cent on 2 November.

None of this prevented the usual swift response by manufacturers to the first signs of an improvement in the international economy. Exports in 1982 had fallen by 3 per cent in volume, the first decline for years. Early in 1983 volume rose again. Against twelve months earlier, domestic export earnings were 20 per cent up in the second quarter, 30 per cent up in the third quarter and well over 40 per cent up in the three months September to November. Re-exports also rose rapidly. The growth rate of imports, including more producer goods, was rather less than that of overall exports. Invisible earnings seemed buoyant and the current account appeared likely to be roughly balanced. Consumer prices, closely tied to international prices and comparative currency values, were nearly 12 per cent higher in November than a year earlier, but were expected to decline sharply. Unemployment rose to 5·5 per cent in March and then fell below 4 per cent as export order-books improved. Real wages were also rising by the summer.

The collapse of an overheated property market had on previous occasions caused difficulties for some banks. This time the situation was exacerbated by political worries. Some minor banks and deposit-taking companies (DTCs) ceased business, licensing requirements for DTCs were stiffened and, unusually, the Government felt compelled to take over a medium-sized private bank in difficulties, which would normally have been allowed to fall. The building industry was depressed, although in December the property market showed some signs of reviving. Major investments were in government housing, road and rail transport and higher educational and training facilities and in private expansion of electricity generating capacity, the telephone system and the container port. Double-tracking and electrification of the railway was completed and the railway corporation was authorized to build a light rail system serving the western New Territories. Proposals for a new airport were deferred, but agreement was reached on a joint venture to build a nuclear power station in Guangdong province to supply Hong Kong.

Chapter 2

CHINA—TAIWAN—JAPAN—SOUTH KOREA—NORTH KOREA

CHINA

THE general basis for China's conduct of both internal and external affairs was the unavoidable quest for economic reconstruction. At times this was conspicuous in both word and deed, as with economic and directly related matters. On other occasions it was less so, as with issues within the Communist Party of China (CPC), in education and cultural policies, law and order, population policy, military affairs and aspects of foreign relations. However, beneath the rhetoric, no matter in which area of activity, the Government's clear and consistent aim was to sustain economic growth and effect modernization while maintaining the leadership of the CPC and ideological correctness.

The main example of economic success was in agriculture. Grain production reached 335 million tons in 1982, a new record and an increase of 8·7 per cent on 1981. This was achieved, in terms of incentive through the popularity of systems of contracted responsibility with payments linked to output, and in terms of conflicting interest in spite of diversification and the increased number of households engaged in specialized work. The need to increase grain production as the arable area was squeezed by the challenge of cash cropping and building requirements was one of many problems to emerge.

Of the total population of 1,015,410,000 in 1982, 51.9 per cent were described as working people, of whom 73·72 per cent were engaged in agriculture. The new agricultural policies which had brought relative prosperity to the rural areas had enabled each member of the rural population to produce, on average, marketable farm and sideline produce worth 130 yuan, 90 per cent more than in 1978. Ten per cent of rural households were classified as specialized or semi-specialized and they were able to offer 70 per cent of their output for sale. The gross value of agricultural output was 11 per cent higher in 1982 than in 1981. Structural changes being implemented included the separation of government and administration from communes management, with the establishment of township people's government, to be completed by the end of 1984; the building of commodity grain bases in 50 counties; and the creation of economic zones based on Shanghai for the lower Yangze, Chongqing for the upper Yangze and Guangzhou for the Pearl River delta.

The industrial and commercial sectors, besides suffering the frustration of unsuccessful efforts to improve management and efficiency, were the main forum for the planning *versus* market forces debate. Its outcome was that the former must prevail but could be tempered by the coexistence of mandatory planning with guidance planning through the application of economic levers such as price, tax and credit policies, once the infra-structure was in position. Among unresolved problems was the imbalance between agriculture, the growth of which should increase slightly, light and consumer goods industry, whose growth should increase, and heavy industry, the growth of which should be restricted. Others were the need to raise the educational standard and professional competence of cadres, the danger of over-extending capital construction, the risk of inflation, insufficient funds for investment, over 85 per cent of national income being absorbed in higher wages, bonuses and procurement prices; the failure of commerce to keep pace with commodity production; the inherited unconditional life employment system linked to a rather egalitarian distribution policy, which it was hoped to adjust by the introduction of contract employment for new employees; and rampant economic crime.

Even so, the key indicators were an increase in industrial output of 7 per cent in 1982, with more than average growth in coal, rolled steel, cement and cotton cloth, and less than average in oil, natural gas (minus 6·4 per cent), electricity, pig-iron, steel and cotton yarn. Sectoral increases included light industry 5·7 per cent, heavy industry 9·9 per cent, machine building 15·2 per cent, building materials 14·1 per cent. To control capital construction the authorities established a 55,000 million yuan ceiling for 1983, rising to 60,000 million yuan for 1984. As part of the incentive system an income tax at 55 per cent was imposed on medium and large state enterprises as a substitute for the system of remitting profits to the state. On smaller enterprises an eight-grade progressive tax was levied.

The frequent ominous references to the intolerable level of economic crime—912,000 cases involving 71,000 CPC members awaited investigation, while 8,500 members had already been expelled—coupled with warnings about the danger of bourgeois corrosion aroused fears that China might be preparing the ground for renewing restrictions on foreign trade. The leadership, however, reaffirmed the indispensable link between trade, notably high technology imports, and modernization, choosing to apply well-tried indigenous measures to cope with the problems. The value of exports in 1982 was US$21,600 million (up 3·5 per cent) and imports US$17,000 million (no change), including trade valued at US$8,860 million with Japan, US$5,240 million with the EEC and US$5,195 million with the USA. The trend showed an increase in the proportion of manufactured goods in exports and a decrease in the proportion in imports. The scope of the policies was illustrated by the substantial foreign interest, including US, British and French companies, in the offshore oil industries, the wish to absorb more foreign capital for domestic construction, the opening of more ports to foreign shipping, the promotion of joint ventures (which numbered 48 with an investment of US$223 million) and the concern to create a more attractive business environment for foreign companies and joint ventures. Noteworthy developments in 1983 were a World Bank loan of US$2,400 million, loans of US$2,000 million and yen 69,000 million from Japan, the establishment of the China Petrochemical Corporation, absorbing 39 major enterprises, the Bank of China joint-venture leasing company formed with Société Général and the Bank of East Asia, the decision to establish a nuclear-powered generating station in the Yangtze valley and another at Daya bay, near Hong Kong, and France's agreement to supply four nuclear reactors to China.

The need for unified and ideologically sound leadership over all aspects of economic reconstruction was emphasized at the second plenum of the twelfth CPC Central Committee in October. The CPC faced difficulties from leftist and rightist influences, from 'cultural contamination' and 'spiritual pollution' caused by increased foreign influence, from ineffective organization and deficiencies in workstyle. It was decided to launch a two-stage rectification campaign to correct a rightist tendency of weakness and laxity. The first stage, in the winter of 1983, would be aimed at the consolidation of main party organs at the central and provincial levels and in the military. The following winter all remaining organs of the Party would be consolidated. Methods included criticism and self-criticism and the study of documents, notably the *Selected Works* of Deng Xiaoping and articles by Mao Zedong on party organization. An ideological campaign was waged against spiritual pollution, said to be a result of the spread of decadent ideologies of the bourgeoisie and exploiting classes, and of distrust regarding socialism, communism and the leadership of the CPC, which nurtured capitalism, feudalism, individualism, commercialism and claims of alienation in a socialist society: all must be repelled with political influence.

As the campaign got under way, China celebrated the 90th anniversary of Mao Zedong's birth, *inter alia* reaffirming his aim to create a socialist society that was characteristically Chinese and noting his recognition that economic construction was the focus of national work. Deng Xiaoping was also credited with having shifted the focus of work to economic construction, eliminated dogmatism and the personality cult while upholding the value of Mao Zedong's thought, restored the importance of intellectuals and built modern armed forces. Spiritual pollution was also seen in the pursuit of foreign culture, which, together with the legacy of the Cultural Revolution, had led to the depreciation of Chinese tradition, the lauding of Western modernist schools, including sexual liberation, and neglect of the principle that art and literature should serve the people. The elimination of spiritual pollution, it was claimed, was an emancipation of the mind, and not a binding of the spirit. Actual resistance was attributed to leftist ideology and factionalism in Guangxi and Hunan, and remnants of leftist influence in the military academies and schools. The case for political rectification was accompanied by a much publicized and vigorous law and order campaign in China's urban areas, during which many convicted criminals were executed.

Social control was also a feature of China's demographic planning. It was intended, by persuasion—aspects of which drew criticism outside China—to promote the one-child family (save for national minorities who could have two-child families) in order to prevent the population including Taiwan from exceeding 1,200 million by the year 2000.

Concern was expressed that the rate of natural increase, at present 14·49 per 1,000 and tending to become static, could rise again when young women in the 15-19 age-group, constituting a quarter of all women of child-bearing age, married. The population profile was 33·6 per cent aged 0-14, 51·3 per cent aged 15-49 and 15·1 per cent aged 50 or more. Enrolment in universities and colleges totalled 1,154,000, in secondary schools—where the emphasis was being shifted to vocational education—over 47 million, and in primary schools 140 million, 93 per cent of all primary-school-age children. In 1983, 3,000 students had been sent abroad and 5,300 foreign students had gone to China. About 25 per cent of the population was illiterate or semi-literate.

The discussion, determination and execution of policy were conducted according to the party and state constitutions. The most important meetings were the sixth National People's Congress (NPC), 6-21 June, attended by 2,978 deputies, and the second plenum (see p. 291 above). The NPC elected Li Xianian as President of the PRC,

Ulanhu, a Mongol, as Vice-President, Peng Zhen as Chairman of the Standing Committee of the NPC following Ye Jianying's retirement, Zhao Ziyang as Premier and Deng Xiaoping as Chairman of the Central Military Commission. Ling Yun, a veteran policeman, was appointed head of the newly-formed Ministry of State Security, whose authority, it was surmised, might extend to the new People's Armed Police; and Liu Fuzhi, formerly Minister of Justice, replaced Zhao Cangbi as Minister of Public Security controlling the civilian police. In March the NPC Standing Commission commuted the death penalties of Jiang Qing and Zhang Chunqiao to life imprisonment with permanent loss of political rights. At the sixth National Committee of the Chinese People's Political Consultative Conference Deng Yingchao was elected Chairwoman. Among the deaths reported were those of Qiao Guanhua, a former Foreign Minister, Sun Yefang the economist, Tan Zhenlin and Liao Chungzhi, both leading political figures.

Foreign policy was based on the principles of no toleration of interference or pressure from outside, no attachment to any external power and the pursuit of a long-term strategy, rather than expediency or opportunism. Most attention was focused on Sino-US and Sino-Japanese relations. Condemnation of arms sales to Taiwan, a US Senate Foreign Relations Committee resolution, a US Congress decision affecting Taiwan and Pan American Airways' resumption of flights to Taiwan were the background to visits to China by Secretary of State Shultz, Defense Secretary Caspar Weinberger and Secretary of Commerce Malcolm Baldrige, and that of Foreign Minister Wu Xueqian to Washington, where he confirmed plans for an exchange of visits between Premier Zhao Ziyang and the American President in 1984. Agreement on textile imports to the US and the liberalizing of technology transfers to China were more substantial indications of the state of relations that had appeared soured by problems over Taiwan and the defection of the Chinese tennis star Hu Na. Relations with Japan were cordial and productive. In the background to visits by Vice-Premier Yao Yilin, Minister of Finance Wang Bingqian, Party General Secretary Hu Yaobang and Wu Xueqian were substantial Japanese financing of China's technological imports and development and continued purchases of raw materials. Talks on the normalization of Sino-Soviet relations continued throughout the year but did not yield any substantive results, the impediments for China being the Soviet military presence on its border, the occupation of Afghanistan and Soviet support for Vietnam in Kampuchea. After a period of uncertainty, the Sino-British talks on the future of Hong Kong (see p. 288) appeared to be making progress, with references to an autonomous Hong Kong maintaining its capitalist system for 50 years following its reversion to China.

Other significant events included visits by the Presidents of the Seychelles, Rwanda, Egypt, France, Zimbabwe, São Tome and Principe,

Gabon and Botswana, King Husain of Jordan, the Vice-President and Foreign Minister of Iraq, the Prime Ministers of Mauritius, Canada and Romania, the Ministers of Foreign Affairs of New Zealand, Belgium, Chad, Sierra Leone, Mozambique, Iran, Australia and Spain; the Vice-Chancellor and Minister of Trade and Industry of Austria, the Minister of External Trade of Cuba, delegations from the Yugoslav Federal Assembly and the African National Congress, Prince Sihanouk and leaders of the Kampuchean coalition Government, and the Archbishop of Canterbury. Hu Yaobang visited Romania and Yugoslavia, Zhao Ziyang Australia and New Zealand, Qian Qichen Hungary, Poland and East Germany, Wu Xueqian Canada and Turkey, Chen Muhua France and Britain. Diplomatic relations were established with Angola, Antigua and Barbuda, Ivory Coast and Lesotho. China also appeared to be repairing relations with Albania, was negotiating with India on the border dispute and successfully negotiated with South Korea over the release of a hijacked CAAC airliner. The CPC received delegations from the Italian, French and Spanish Communist Parties. China played an active role in the United Nations, whose 38th General Assembly was addressed by Wu Xueqian, championing Third World and Non-Aligned causes, received support for various projects from UN bodies and applied to join the International Atomic Energy Agency.

TAIWAN

The main trend in 1983 was the recovery from economic recession, the main event the elections to the Legislative Yuan, while attempts by the People's Republic of China (PRC) to initiate a process leading eventually to administrative reunification of the island province with the mainland dominated foreign affairs throughout.

Evidence of the recovery was provided by impressive statistics. Gross national product was estimated at US$49,800 million, economic growth at 7·14 per cent, per-capita income at US$2,444, an increase of 4·36 per cent, while the rate of inflation in wholesale prices fell by 0·97 per cent and in retail prices rose by 1·81 per cent. The basis for these achievements was the unexpected acceleration of Taiwan's foreign trade in the third quarter of the year. Total trade in January-November amounted to US$41,100 million, an increase of 9·8 per cent on 1982; exports reached US$22,800 million and imports US$18,200 million, increases of 13·2 per cent and 5·8 per cent respectively compared to 1982.

To some extent the healthy statistics masked underlying problems for the economy. Although the improvement in the US economy induced a similar effect in Taiwan it also demonstrated the continuing need for the diversification of markets, no simple matter for a territory that remained, in a formal sense, diplomatically isolated. The huge trading surplus with the US, which reached US$6,100 million over the January-November period, was a source of protectionist sentiment and led to the despatch, in September, of a buying mission to the USA, which placed orders for US$600 million of agricultural and industrial products. At the same time, efforts were made to reduce the deficit of US$2,800 million with Japan. The lack of formal diplomatic channels through which to pursue claims against defaulters was said to inhibit the diversification of trade.

Another sobering economic development was that, while the stock market rose dramatically, a number of companies failed through unsuccessful investment in the property market, weak accounting procedures and financial misappropriations.

This adverse experience did not affect the establishment of the International Investment Trust (IIT), through which foreign investors gained indirect access to the stock market. The IIT, together with preparations for developing an offshore banking centre, was also expected to assist Taiwan's financial sector in raising its professional standards, and to compensate for Taiwan's absence from such organizations as the World Bank and the IMF.

The improved economic conditions and internal stability were advantages to the ruling Nationalist Party (KMT) in the elections for 71 local seats in the Legislative Yuan, the original mainland membership of which had been reduced by attrition from 760 to 274, whose average age was 77. The triennial supplementary elections, held on 3 December, were a victory for the KMT, whose 62 successful candidates got 70.54 per cent of a 63 per cent poll. Endorsed *tangwai* (outside the Party) candidates won six seats with 19 per cent of the votes, the remaining three seats going to unaffiliated candidates. In addition, 27 supplementary vacancies for overseas Chinese were filled by presidential appointment. The KMT's sweeping success was attributed to efficient organization aimed against splitting the vote and to a factionalized opposition. The more moderate opposition faction under veteran legislator Kang Ning-hsiang, who lost his seat, was eclipsed by the radical 'New Generation', regarded as dominated by associates of the *Formosa* magazine dissidents imprisoned after the 1979 Kaohsiung riots. The elections also introduced a proportionally significant, active, well-qualified, Taiwan-orientated group of younger members to the Legislative Yuan.

Other events to capture attention included defections from the mainland, the bombing of two newspaper offices, improved facilities for trading with Europe and better communications with the resumption of Pan Am flights to Taipei and the opening of a direct service to Europe by CAL and KLM. Two Chinese military aviators defected to Taiwan from the mainland, the first flying a Mig 21 to South Korea on 7 August and the other, in a Mig 17, on 14 November. The bombings, which injured 12 people, took place in the buildings of the *Central Daily News* and the *United Daily News*, both official papers, on 26 April. It was alleged that members of the World United Formosans for Independence, based in the US, whose aim is an independent Taiwan, were responsible. On 12 December Taiwan law enforcement officials announced the arrest of an alleged accessory and released the names of three suspects living abroad.

Aware that Taiwan's survival in its existing form depended on its relationship with the US, the PRC continued to concentrate its efforts at promoting reunification on key components of that link, such as arms sales, while offering terms to the KMT leadership. While Taiwan's leaders argued that adequate defence necessitated a qualitative advantage in armaments to match the PRC's quantitative advantage, the US appeared to establish a benchmark for future declining sales by selling US $530 million of missiles, spare parts and tank equipment. The package, together with the liberalization of US technology transfers to the PRC, gave the impression that in the triangular relationship the US Administration was gradually reducing some of its commitments to Taiwan. According to the latest proposals for reunification revealed by Deng Xiaoping, Taiwan would retain the right to buy arms abroad, be free to export wherever necessary to sustain economic growth, to make its own legal decisions, to fly its own flag and to issue passports and visas, while the PRC would not send civil or military personnel to Taiwan. The only limitations on autonomy would be the designation China-Taipei—as already agreed for the 1984 Olympic Games—or China-Taiwan, and the PRC's role as sole spokesman for foreign relations in international organizations. The KMT leadership, which viewed the Sino-British talks over the future of Hong Kong with concern, publicly rejected the proposals.

JAPAN

Japan's zodiac designated 1983 as the Year of the Wild Boar, but national history, while recording a surprising general election upset, was more likely to remember it as the Year of the Tanaka, a powerful, hard-shelled political animal of remarkable resilience, adept at operating from the shadows even when badly wounded. Sometimes it was likened by ambitious rivals to an albatross, following the ship of state with sustained, effortless flight and fatal to shoot at.

The Tanaka, *alias* The Kingmaker or The Shogun, was Mr Kakuei Tanaka, a former Prime Minister of Japan and long-time member of its House of Representatives, who was due at last to learn his fate after a seven-year trial. He had always denied but was found guilty in October of receiving a Yen 500 million bribe in the Lockheed Aircraft pay-off affair (see AR 1976, pp. 297–302) and was sentenced to four years' imprisonment.

From the moment, early in the year, when the prosecution demanded a five-year sentence, Mr Tanaka had been given a rough ride by the

Opposition in the Diet and by the media, which seemed to have been conducting a parallel trial ever since his brief arrest in 1976. This was chiefly because of his continuing influence on the political scene, certainly on the political scene-shifters.

Though he saved the ruling Liberal Democratic Party (LDP) from some embarrassment when first accused of bribery by resigning his membership and serving as an Independent member of the House, he remained the moving spirit behind the Tanaka faction, the strongest element in the faction-ridden LDP. Without his support no politician, however capable or incapable, had any chance of becoming president of the LDP, coupled with the Premiership. And any Cabinet was sure to have its quota of Tanaka men in pivotal positions.

Like others recently before him, Mr Yasuhiro Nakasone, heading a faction numbered fourth in strength among the LDP pillars (Nos. 2 and 3 were led by former Prime Ministers Suzuki and Fukuda), was beholden to Mr Tanaka in achieving the country's top elective office in November 1982. It was not long before the media discovered that by borrowing the first two letters of Mr Tanaka's name they could lumber Mr Nakasone's Cabinet with a 'Tanakasone' label.

Oblivious of the fact that Mr Nakasone was busy on other matters, such as fence-mending over trade with the USA and cultivating a 'Ron-Yasu' relationship with President Reagan, the Opposition parties, united as rarely ever before, wanted a motion urging Tanaka to resign his seat put before the House at a plenary session. This was on the strength of that five-year sentence demand, before he had been found guilty.

In possession of an overall majority, the LDP could have taken the chance of rejecting the motion on a vote. But that would have needed almost all its 286 members to be of the same mind—and they were not. Not everybody belonged to the Tanaka group, after all, and what about those 'political ethics' the people and the press kept talking about? Substantial LDP abstentions from voting could have given the Opposition victory and perhaps brought down the Government. That had happened before.

The LDP was driven to emphasize that Mr Tanaka was to be deemed innocent until proved guilty, or words to that effect, and the Diet's spring session mercifully came to an end, launching Japan on a long, very hot summer which kept the Opposition and the public on the boil. When the House resumed in the autumn, the imminence of the Tanaka verdict overshadowed the Government's legislative plans. The Court's pronouncement led to a new Opposition tactic: they would not attend Diet proceedings unless Tanaka resigned. So for more than a month Japan became virtually a one-party state, with urgent business bogged down.

Mr Tanaka was in no mood to 'do the decent thing' and go, even after a man-to-man talk with Mr Nakasone, who tried in vain to end the Diet deadlock. The famous Japanese capacity for compromise was nowhere to be seen: the Opposition would call off their boycott only if the House was dissolved and the electorate given the chance to decide. By this time the Tanaka faction also favoured an election; if their chief were re-elected by his constituency then the furore might die down.

It seemed that only Prime Minister Nakasone wanted the House to run its full four-year course until the following June; perhaps time would prove a great healer. Finally he lost the argument and called the election for 18 December, no doubt trusting that the LDP would do as well as it had done in the Upper House election six months before.

In the run-up, the speculation was that the LDP would lose a few seats but still enjoy an overall majority. The electors, however, decided that 250 seats were all the LDP deserved (a loss of 36), making it six short of a majority in the 511-seat House. The Socialists advanced from 107 to 112 seats, the Komeito (Clean Government) Party from 33 to 58, and the Democratic Socialists from 32 to 38. Only the Communists among the Opposition shed seats—down from 29 to 26.

The New Liberal Club—'conservatives at heart' like the LDP, they had broken away over the Lockheed scandal in 1976—lost four of their 12 seats. But rarely have eight Independent MPs been so cherished: they were immediately recruited as LDP members (plus one other Independent) and to cement the new partnership their leader Mr Seiichi Tagawa was given the Home Affairs portfolio in the new Cabinet. Now the LDP roll was 259.

Mr Tanaka's local electorate rallied behind him to the tune of 220,000 votes, the most he had ever had in 36 years of representing the same constituency in Parliament. So The Kingmaker remained to haunt the new House—and his first appeal against conviction would not even begin to be heard until mid-1985. He looked good for a few elections yet.

For a time Mr Nakasone's own future seemed to be in doubt. The loss of 36 seats instead of a tolerable few was not a strong base from which to argue for continued leadership. But party unity was: this was no time for recriminations, in any case against whom? The party elders got together and decided to back him on condition that he reshuffled the top posts in the party and Cabinet in a way that would lessen Mr Tanaka's influence on party management and government—and the price became plain in a Nakasone statement.

'I fully recognize', it read, 'my responsibility for the election result, which makes me unworthy to continue as president of the LDP. I deeply apologize to party members for having lost many seats. I think the major cause of the defeat was that I failed to solve or put an end to the so-called Tanaka issue and dissatisfied the nation with my posture towards political ethics. Therefore I will (i) eliminate all so-called political influences from Mr Tanaka; (ii) enhance political ethics, drastically tackle party reform, and establish a clean party; and (iii) deal fairly between party workers and party management to establish unity.

'All party elders and members deeply regret the circumstances surrounding our country today. Taking note of the significant situation inside and outside Japan, I wish to make a fresh start. I am resolved to tackle courageously the harsh ordeal that we face.'

So compromise had come back to the Japan scene. Somebody had taken responsibility for the election debacle and the nation could forge ahead. Mr Nakasone, now leading a bare-majority party, bade farewell to all his Cabinet except two (three members had been defeated, anyhow). Mr Shintaro Abe remained as Foreign Minister and Mr Noboru Takeshita as Finance Minister; themselves aspiring Prime Ministers, they must have learned quite a few lessons about the scary business of running a Government. The Tanaka faction, which lost fewer seats than the other LDP factions, got six Cabinet seats but no top party posts, and the rest their due meed.

Mr Nakasone, making his fresh start, probably agreed with Shakespeare that 'sweet are the uses of adversity'. He had won himself a year's grace before having to seek re-election as party president plus-Premier in November 1984. Before the election upset he had been piling up a useful record, particularly in the foreign field. Individual in style, he had become the best-known Japanese political name overseas since 'Old Man Yoshida' was Prime Minister immediately after World War II. There was a file of glad-hand front-page pictures to prove it.

He appeared to get along famously with President Reagan, both away and at home (his visit to Washington, Reagan's to Tokyo). He had fruitful forays to South Korea and the Asean nations, and had welcomed to Japan Chancellor Kohl of West Germany and Mr Hu Yaobong, general secretary of the Chinese Communist Party. He had booked a trip to China in return.

He had made his mark at the Williamsburg summit and could look forward confidently to meeting his counterparts on equal terms at the 1984 London summit. Japan was not going to be just an economic power any longer; it appeared determined to take its appropriate place among the world's nations with an independent, positive foreign policy.

True, both the USA and the EEC kept up their huffing and puffing and threats to blow Japan's house down over its exports, but what could Japan do if the world wanted more and more of its quality consumer products? The country already had 30 to 40 per cent of its exports under voluntary restraint or direct restrictive measures; it promised further steps to open up its market to imports (while advising foreigners to 'employ the proper strategy to penetrate the market; our distribution system, business practices and company behaviour are not hampering imports'). The Japanese Government hoped to eliminate or reduce import tariffs on about 1,200 industrial products in fiscal year 1984, but meanwhile pressed for negotiations to start on a new round of GATT.

The message always came through clearly: away with protectionism! Mr Nakasone could take satisfaction on the home front in the fact that Japan's economy had at last 'placed itself on a path of recovery', to which accelerating Gross National Product provided evidence. An all-time-high unemployment rate of 2.81 per cent in September came as a shock, but the figure was falling by the year's end.

Fresh-start Nakasone had a message of hope for budding Premiers at a press conference as the New Year dawned: 'I am not attached to the Prime Ministership. I will be ready to step down whenever I have accomplished my work.' They could make what they liked of that.

SOUTH KOREA

The year was scarred by two grievous blows: on the night of 31 August/1 September a South Korean airliner was shot down by a Soviet fighter plane; and on 9 October 17 South Koreans were murdered in a Rangoon bomb blast almost certainly perpetrated by North Koreans. Both incidents, by confirming traditional anti-communist fears, helped to slow down a cautious liberalization policy and did nothing to enhance President Chun's prestige.

The first atrocity occurred when a South Korean Boeing 747 airliner strayed over the Soviet island of Sakhalin. All 269 passengers and crew were killed. The incident led to international protests against an unacceptable use of armed force against a civilian airliner. The reasons for the airliner's detour over Soviet territory were never definitively established. The most likely suggested explanation was that the Korean pilot had deliberately shortened his route from Alaska to Seoul in order to save some six tonnes of fuel. The USSR alleged that the airliner had been surveying Soviet military installations. Although this was most improbable the United States conceded that a USAF RC-135 reconnaissance aircraft had conducted a spying mission during the night of the shooting, a fact which might have contributed to Soviet nervousness.

Among the 17 South Koreans killed in the bomb attack in Rangoon, Burma, were four of South Korea's most able Cabinet Ministers. President Chun himself missed the carnage only because of a traffic delay. Although the North Koreans quickly denied responsibility, two North Koreans were later tried for the crime in Rangoon. These attacks evoked a heightened sense of insecurity only partly assuaged by President Reagan's visit to the Demilitarized Zone in November and his strongly reaffirmed commitment to the country's defence.

The year had begun with the Government still continuing its cautious liberalization policy, signalled by the decision of 22 December 1982 to suspend the 20-year prison sentence on Kim Dae Jung, a prominent opposition leader. On 25 February 250 opposition politicians banned from political activity since November 1980 were released from their ban. Additionally, on 15 March President Chun commuted two death sentences imposed on the arsonists of the US cultural centre in Pusan to life imprisonment. The most effective opposition leader was Kim Young Sam, formerly leader of the banned New Democracy Party, under house arrest since June 1982. On 16 May 1983 he released to the foreign press a number of political demands: the holding of direct presidential elections, the release of political prisoners, the lifting of bans on opposition figures and the reinstatement of freedom of speech and assembly. He conducted a hunger strike in support of these demands from 18 May to 9 June, when he was persuaded to desist by members of his family. Several supporters were arrested during the strike and there were accompanying student protests at Yonsei and Seoul Universities.

Dissent was, however, a marginal factor; and the country's remarkable economic vigour of recent times continued to be a stabilizing influence despite the worldwide recession. GNP growth rate for 1983 was believed to be over seven per cent, thanks mainly to the high level of government spending on public works and to an increase in mining and manufacturing. The economic effort was sustained by the IMF when on 8 July it announced its approval for a two-year loan worth US$613 million in support of the Government's economic programme, which was designed to sustain growth while cutting the rate of inflation.

NORTH KOREA

President Kim Il Sung's son, Kim Chong Il, although not holding an official government position, continued to be eulogized throughout the year; and there was repeated emphasis on his role as likely successor to his father. Indeed Kim Chong Il had already taken over a number of presidential functions. A number of North Korean politicians, however, were believed to oppose the assumed succession.

Changes were made in 1983 to the nine-member secretariat of the ruling Korean Workers' Party Central Committee. Kim Hwan and Yun Ki Pok left, to become respectively Deputy Prime Minister and Chairman of Pyongyang. They were replaced by Chae Hui Chong and An Sung Hak. One of the three Vice-Presidents, Kang Yang Uk, died in January and was replaced by Yim Chun Chu on 7 April.

North Korea was widely believed to have carried out the Rangoon bomb attack of 9 October which killed 17 South Koreans, including four Cabinet Ministers. This was unlikely, however, to represent a fresh departure in policy. North Korea had a long history of involvement in terrorism, kidnapping and narcotics smuggling. It was also known to have planned attacks on President Chun in the past.

X AUSTRALASIA AND SOUTH PACIFIC

Chapter 1

AUSTRALIA—PAPUA NEW GUINEA

AUSTRALIA

THE previous year's political trend to the left continued in 1983. From March on, Australian Labor Party (ALP) Governments were in power federally and in the states of New South Wales, Victoria, South Australia and Western Australia. Tasmania and Queensland continued strongly against that trend. The ALP leaders and Ministries were all of the moderate centre and right in their image and main policies, but under pressure from more radical groups within their party they were obliged to make concessions which led to disputes with upper Houses and offered the Liberal and National (formerly Country) Parties a basis for rebuilding their strength after the disarray of 1982-3.

On 3 February the federal Prime Minister, Mr Malcolm Fraser, obtained from the Governor-General an order for the dissolution of both Houses and a general election for their full membership to be held on 5 March; the ALP-AD (Australian Democrat) majority in the Senate had provided the grounds for this by rejecting 13 of the Government's fiscal measures in terms triggering the double-dissolution provisions of s.57 of the constitution on which Mr Fraser had acted when he first entered office at the head of the Liberal-National coalition in 1975.

Mr Fraser's decision upon an early election was criticized, but he had a choice of evils. Constitutionally, he was justified; the High Court of Australia had held in 1974-75 that inter-House disagreements validated a s.57 dissolution even if (as in this case) their political occasion had become stale. An election for the Representatives had to occur by the end of the year, but this could not better his position in the Senate; a double dissolution was not constitutionally permitted beyond August, and there was no reason to be confident that drought, international economic depression and other factors telling against him would become any better by then.

More immediately, he had reason to believe that notwithstanding the leadership history of the ALP in 1982 (see AR 1982, p. 317) a fresh attempt at installing Mr R. G. (Bob) Hawke as ALP parliamentary leader and prospective Prime Minister must soon occur; opinion polls continued to show that he would make an exceptionally popular national leader, but while Mr Bill Hayden remained at Labor's head the result would be less certain. In the event, by coincidence Mr Hayden resigned the ALP leadership, and announced that Mr Hawke would be elected unopposed to succeed him, on 8 February, the day on which Mr Fraser obtained the dissolution.

The election campaign was interrupted by disastrous bush fires in South Australia and Victoria, causing much loss of property and life. A general election for the Western Australian parliament, previously scheduled, took place on 19 February, at which Labor was returned, after nine years in opposition, with a majority of 8 in the Assembly and increased representation but not a majority in the gerrymandered upper house; 8 Ministers lost their seats. In the short federal campaign, Mr Fraser was continuously on the defensive. Mr Hawke proved even better on the hustings than expected; he surprised his opponents, and reassured the 'salariat', which held the balance of electoral strength, by promising not confrontation but consultation, cooperation with all major social groups and the promotion of 'mateship'. His more detailed promises included tax reforms, a more carefully considered national health scheme than that of 1975, and another attempt at a prices and incomes policy. The result was a sweeping Labor victory, with a majority of 25 in the 125-seat Representatives and 30 of the 64 Senate seats, where the Australian Democrats (5) and one Independent held as previously a balance of power, the Liberal-National coalition having 28 seats.

Mr Hawke was duly elected Prime Minister by the Labor caucus and given a Ministry of 27 members; in a surprise decision reflecting his emphasis on the workable, he decided to continue the Menzies-initiated British system of a Cabinet of 13, with 14 Ministers not in Cabinet—a system previously spurned by Labor on democratic grounds.

Mr Hawke launched his cooperation policy at a conference held through a week in April in Canberra, attended by representatives of the federal parties, the state governments and oppositions, organizations of employers and trade unions and some social service groups, with observers from many other groups. They hammered out an agreement to tackle unemployment and inflation simultaneously, by moderate stimulation of the economy accompanied by a prices and incomes policy in which unions undertook to observe restraint in wage claims and pursue them in the arbitration tribunals, and employers accepted a tribunal to monitor and in serious cases prevent excessive price rises and profit rates. Reasonable profit rates were acknowledged to be necessary in order to maintain employment. Tax avoidance was condemned. An Economic Planning Advisory Council was formed from the membership and later authorized by legislation to study specific problems.

This agreement was derided by some prominent spokesmen of the Labor left and the Liberal-National right, and from time to time individual unions continued to maintain existing or launch new claims at odds both with the 'summit agreement' and with an earlier 'accord' between the Hawke Government and the Australian Council of Trade Unions (ACTU) which also called for union restraint. However, the 'accord' and 'summit' together either achieved something or successfully predicted and encouraged a trend, assisted by the statutory and Conciliation and Arbitration Commission freeze of public service and award wage rates introduced under Mr Fraser. In September the Commission authorized a general rise of 4·3 per cent in award wage rates. But average wage rates rose by only 5·5 per cent over the year, well below the inflation rate of about 9·2 per cent, and time lost in industrial disputes steadily declined. Business profits rose, and in November-December there was a mild stock-exchange boom; the ACTU began to complain that no progress had been made on a prices and profits surveillance authority. Unemployment reached a peak of 10·7 per cent of the full-time work-force in March, then slowly dropped to 9·2 per cent in November.

The Hawke Government also had some good fortune. It became apparent in April that the Fraser budget estimates for 1982-3 would not be realized, and that the deficit was likely to exceed $8,000 million rather than the $4,500 million officially forecast on the eve of the election. This enabled Mr Hawke both to abuse his predecessors for deceit and to use the actual size of the deficit as an excuse for deferring promised tax cuts and as providing already the modest stimulation promised at the 'summit'. Accordingly his first official Budget, opened 23 August, raised some basic social service benefits but disappointed the more prosperous wage and salary earners whose incomes had been brought into the highest tax ranges by inflation over the Fraser years. Much of the financial policy of the new Government was introduced by stages through the year, often with beginning dates in the following year—for example, retrospective chasing of tax-avoiders, and imposing means tests on persons over 70 for pensions they had enjoyed since 1978.

The drought broke in July, and, although subsequent prolonged rains caused some crop losses, reasonable export prices for a much-increased output caused farm incomes to rise. Hence, notwithstanding the continued poor prices and reduced volume of mineral exports, the balance of payments remained in net credit for the year. In December, following an inrush of speculative funds attracted by rumours of a revaluation, the Government 'floated' the dollar—the first time since World War II that market forces had been allowed to determine its value. Substantial oil reserves continued to be found, especially off the northern coasts. The small recovery of the US economy in 1983 made a disproportionate contribution to that of Australia.

On a visit to the USA in June, Mr Hawke told an American audience that he would not regard himself as bound by party ideology if it was contrary to the wishes of the Australian people. In practice, he sought compromise solutions. An outstanding example concerned uranium mining; party policy favoured the complete phasing out of the industry, and the left wanted this to happen rapidly. In September, after much negotiation, the Government announced that the two operating mines in the Northern Territory would be allowed to work out their contracts, and that the giant new development at Roxby Downs in South Australia—involving many metal ores including very large uranium deposits—would go ahead. The latter decision, in a state with declining industries and high unemployment, was vital to the survival of its Labor Government. The Northern Territory decision offended many interests, white and Aboriginal, and a protest general election for the Territory Assembly in December resulted in a Labor rout—19 National members to 6 ALP. On the Tasmanian hydroelectric dams issue, however, the Hawke Government reversed its predecessor's policy (see AR 1982, p. 317), and pleased the environmental left, by legislating and taking High Court action which put an end to the dams project. A majority High Court decision in July validating federal intervention under the external affairs head of federal powers (giving effect to the World Heritage Convention) and the trading corporations head caused considerable anxiety among state-righters.

Mr Hawke said that he did not regard the question of monarchism versus republicanism, much agitated among left-wing groups, as having much significance, but his Government took small steps in the republican direction: the oath of allegiance to the Queen was removed from naturalization ceremonies, and pictures of the Queen taken down in the few government buildings where they remained. The trend was unaffected by the visit of the Prince and Princess of Wales, despite their personal popularity. The citizenship legislation was amended to remove the 'British subject' status which since 1948 had coexisted with that of 'Australian citizen'. The latter would now become the chief basis for voting and other civic rights, but British immigrants who had not been naturalized as Australian citizens would continue to enjoy rights for which they were already registered. Britain's HMS *Invincible* was denied docking for repairs in December because it might carry atomic weapons.

A more complex left-right dispute began in May when it was announced that a Russian diplomat had been expelled, on the advice of the Australian Security Investigation Organization (ASIO), on the ground that he was a member of the KGB and had been trying to enlist the services of an 'agent of influence'. The 'agent' was a former executive secretary of the ALP's federal organization who had set up in business as a public relations expert in Canberra. A Minister, Mr M. Young, who had leaked some details to acquaintances before the official announcement, was required by the Prime Minister to resign. The public-relations man was denied access to Ministers and officials. These events caused deep offence to the Labor left, since both the Minister and the ex-secretary were in good standing with the left; most leftists regarded ASIO with suspicion or contempt, and considered that a desire for friendly relations with a Russian diplomat, even if KGB, was no ground for criticism, much less destruction of the person's livelihood. The Government appointed a respected judge as a Royal Commission to investigate the whole affair, and his report confirmed the substantial accuracy of the ASIO material and approved the Government's consequential action; it left undetermined the question whether Mr Young might have breached official secrets legislation, but accepted the view of the Law Officers that a conviction would have been unlikely. Measures to register and control public-relations agents were promised.

In foreign affairs, the new Minister, Mr Hayden, similarly pursued a path to the left of his predecessor but to the right of his party. The Anzus alliance was defended and supported; aid to Vietnam, demanded by the left, was delayed in deference to Asean sensitivities, but risks were taken with Asean friendship in the development of policy on Kampuchea. There were gestures of friendship towards the Arab countries: the Arab League was allowed to establish an information office in Australia—as were the African National Congress and Swapo—but the PLO was not so favoured, since it declined to accept the legitimate existence of Israel.

Contrasting with the national political trend, Queensland went in the opposite direction at a snap state election on 22 October, called in consequence of the collapse of the coalition between the Liberals and Nationals. The Liberals were decimated, and the ALP gained 7 seats, but the Nationals, gaining 6 for a total of 43 in a House of 82, were able for the first time to form a Government on their own.

PAPUA NEW GUINEA

For Mr Michael Somare's Pangu Party Government, 1983 was the first full year in office following its big win in the 1982 elections. Despite a rather lacklustre economic performance, and a strong comeback by its most formidable political rival—the ex-Deputy Prime Minister and National Party leader Mr Iambakey Okuk—Pangu finished the year with unprecedented parliamentary support.

Pangu had already failed by mid-year to achieve its major economic reform—retrenchment in the public service. Too many and too large 'golden handshakes' were taken by senior bureaucrats, who frequently found re-employment in other public service jobs, and 12·5 million Kina (£10 million) was spent to little effect. In June, however, Pangu won its campaign for reducing the cuts in economic aid provided by the five-year aid agreement with Australia, which runs to 1986. Instead of insisting on aid cuts amounting to 5 per cent per annum, the new ALP Government of Bob Hawke finally gave PNG a generous package including most of what it wanted—an aid cut of only a 1 per cent in 1982-83, rising to 3 per cent in 1985-86. A higher rate of decline would be introduced only if Conzinc Rio Tinto Australia's Bougainville mine returned to strong profitability. Australian aid, at K225·9 million, furnished close to 30 per cent of PNG's 1984 budget revenue; and a large number of small projects earmarked for extinction were saved.

The charismatic Mr Okuk returned to Parliament after a by-election triumph in July, and at once resumed the leadership of the National Party and the Opposition, both vacated by ex-General Ted Diro. A galvanized Opposition moved quickly towards a vote of no-confidence with an appeal to Mr Okuk's Highland following inside the Pangu Party, an attempt to build a trans-party Papuan bloc, an offer of Ministries to Pangu's coalition ally, the United Party—and no serious policy alternatives whatsoever. A few defections from Pangu did not prevent a fiasco in Parliament in November when the no-confidence motion was actually withdrawn for lack of support; the Papuan 'bloc' split wide open; majority party leader and former Prime Minister Sir Julius Chan (People's Progress Party) failed to attend Parliament; and Mr Diro led his Papuan following out of the Opposition by supporting the Government, which also enjoyed full United Party support in a vote of confidence which was passed by 70 to 0 in a parliament of 110.

A new or revamped coalition of Pangu with Mr Diro's PNG Independent Group thus became a distinct possibility, as did a rethinking of the Opposition's historic commitment to regular votes of no-confidence at any price.

In foreign policy the prime concern was once again Papua New Guinea's border with Indonesia. An Indonesian strategic border road which violated PNG territory in the Western Province in three places was discovered in April, but within a few months the offending sections were closed as a result of prickly but patient diplomacy. More seriously, Defence Minister Epel Tito was forced to resign—or rather transfer portfolios—following his suggestion on Australian radio that Indonesia would invade PNG within 10 to 20 years. Having firmly disowned its Defence Minister on this extremely sensitive issue, which was stirred up by press speculation about Indonesia's long-term intentions in planning massive Javanese transmigration into Irian Jaya, the Pangu Government moved at year's end to silence questioning voices within the Department of Foreign Affairs. All responsibility for coordination of border intelligence was transferred to more conservative care in the Prime Minister's Department, and responsibility for administration of border development programmes moved to the Department of Provincial Affairs.

Chapter 2

NEW ZEALAND

CIRCUMSTANCES were dominated by the Government's decision to maintain its comprehensive freeze on prices, remuneration, charges and rents. Introduced in June 1982 for twelve months, the freeze was extended at least until February 1984, undoubtedly because of its unexpected success in curbing inflation from 1982 levels of 16 per cent to 5 per cent by late 1983. If the price for this reduction was continuing recession, the Government saw direct political advantage in claiming that its policies were not just lowering previously high levels of inflation, but ending expectation of their return.

Despite a March devaluation of 8 per cent against the Australian dollar, and some tax relief to lower-paid workers in a July Budget, internal demand for goods, services and retailing remained sluggish, and unemployment reached 8 per cent of the work-force. Positive indicators included some upturn in the building industry, expanding production and sales in horticulture and fishing, and improved export receipts for timber, alumina and manufactures—particularly to Asean markets. Returns for traditional primary exports (dairy products, meat and wool) increased through greater volumes, not better prices, while domestic recession lowered imports, so that the balance of payments deficit, NZ$ 1,429 million for the year to September 1983, was falling.

A dominant economic feature remained in the country's high level of indebtedness. Total external debt was estimated at NZ$ 14,300 million, the servicing of which took a quarter of all foreign exchange earnings. The budgeted internal deficit (before borrowing) reached a record NZ$ 3,200 million, permitting public spending to rise by 13 per cent and constituting a key obstacle in the Government's attempt to lower interest rates. During the second quarter, the Government actively entered the money market through a special stock issue called Kiss—the Kiwi Saving Stock. To the chagrin of financial institutions competing for funds under conditions of retrenchment, Kiss accrued more than $1,400 million at 15 per cent interest. When interest rates fell in July, Prime Minister Muldoon maintained they were not falling quickly enough and immediately lowered government stock rates to 8 per cent. He then stunned bankers by warning them in a speech that, unless financial institutions lowered their rates voluntarily, he would feel obliged to regulate them directly.

After this attempt to 'talk down' interest rates, the Government then acted by introducing contentious and confusing legislation designed to limit to 11 per cent interest payable on first mortgages, and 14 per cent on second. Evasion of these regulations developed, liquidity suffered, and doctrinal disarray embarrassed the Government when three of its back-benchers of a more market, private enterprise persuasion crossed the floor of Parliament to vote with the Labour Opposition, which claimed such regulations were unworkable.

Although no major strikes occurred, the year was extremely unsettled in the field of industrial relations. Frequent stoppages marred the Marsden Point oil refinery expansion project, escalating its costs and incurring demarcation difficulties. In contrast to its centralized regulation of financial activity, the Government emphasized individual rights and freedoms by legislating for voluntary unionism. Amid claims that the Bill was being rushed through Parliament without adequate opportunity for scrutiny by interested parties in committee, the measure was strongly attacked by the Federation of Labour, Combined State Unions, the Labour Party, key employers in major industries and some Government backbenchers. Passed by a single vote in Parliament, voluntary unionism effectively prohibited the following: industrial awards or agreements requiring compulsory union membership; agreements providing for the preference in employment of union members; discrimination on the grounds of union or non-union membership; any 'undue influence' on a worker to become, remain, or cease to belong to a union; strikes and lockouts over union membership; and restrictions on union fees or subscriptions.

A sister clause that would have permitted employers to pay lower than adult rates of remuneration to workers under 18 was defeated, when backbenchers Minogue and Marilyn Waring crossed the floor to vote with the Opposition. This reverse was the first parliamentary defeat of an important Government measure in the post-1945 era.

Further controversy surrounded the passage of the Government's State Services Conditions of Employment legislation. Opponents attacked a provision that state pay should be based on levels necessary to recruit and retain workers, claiming that this would necessarily advantage the Government as employer and drive down pay rates under conditions of unemployment and recession. Links between state and private pay scales were weakened, the period of review was changed from one to two years, and powers were included to invoke monetary penalties against anyone involved in strike actions in the state electricity system. The last provision was directly occasioned by an October confrontation with state electricity workers who, having exhausted negotiating remedies, gave notice of selective stoppages to advance their claims. The Government responded by threatening not just to deregister their parent Public Service Association, but to invoke the draconian provisions of the Public Safety Conservation Act permitting the Government extremely wide emergency powers, including the use of the military to man essential services.

Political tensions within the Government caucus, over the conflict between private enterprise doctrine and actual Government practice in regulating the economy, were given sharper focus by the emergence and rapid growth of the New Zealand Party under the leadership of Mr Bob Jones, a property millionaire. This emphasized a much less regulated economy, a floating exchange rate, reduced and simplified taxation, increased spending on education and a drastic reduction in defence outlays. Mr Jones left little doubt that his aim was to see the National Party defeated at the 1984 general election and have Mr Muldoon ousted as its leader.

Within the Labour Party, a February change saw two 40-year-old lawyers emerge at the top when Mr David Lange succeeded Sir Wallace Rowling as leader, with Mr Geoffrey Palmer as his new deputy. At its September annual conference, the party agreed to review its commitment to the Anzus treaty if elected. Shortly afterwards, the party encountered difficulties when two of its South Island MPs, Messrs Kirk and McDonnell, failed to win party renomination for election in 1984 and subsequently resigned from the party, to continue in Parliament as Independents.

In its foreign relations, the Government complicated the new Closer Economic Relations Agreement with Australia by denying the commencement of some Australian financial and investment activities in New Zealand, in response to restrictions on the operation of New Zealand-based banks in Australia which were regarded as unreasonable.

Throughout the year, and before a variety of forums including the Belgrade Unctad Conference, the UN General Assembly and the Commonwealth heads of government meeting in New Delhi, Prime Minister Muldoon reiterated his call for a second Bretton Woods conference to critically assess the international trade and payments system. In doing so he was critical of GATT, continuing trade protectionism, insufficient flexibility by the IMF in its handling of so-called conditionality, and lack of progress in the North-South dialogue. At the UN, New Zealand called for a ban on the production of fissionable materials for weapons and an end to nuclear weapons testing in all environments, but abstained on a General Assembly vote which deplored the invasion of Grenada and called for the withdrawal of all foreign troops. Also at the UN, New Zealand resisted Third World criticisms of the Antarctic Treaty, and was instrumental in formulating and promoting a draft minerals regime for a Treaty Consultative Parties meeting held in Bonn.

Within New Zealand, protest over nuclear weapons and nuclear ship visits intensified. Scientists opposed to nuclear weapons criticized an October visit by an Australian and New Zealand inspection team to France's Muroroa atoll nuclear testing site, as not having sufficient opportunity to appraise the relevant effects of blast and radiation on the environment concerned. In May, Mr Muldoon said that in Paris President Mitterrand had indicated to him a time-period when nuclear testing in the Pacific would cease, but this was denied by the French Foreign Minister, M Cheysson, when he visited Wellington in November.

In August, Chief Ombudsman Laking published a detailed report on his investigations into complaints against the police arising from the 1981 Springbok rugby football tour (see AR 1981, p. 318). Of 118 complaints fully investigated, 75 were sustained, a key finding of the report being that the police had 'a responsibility to make a frank disclosure of how they acted on each complaint and what they found, and to give the complainant an opportunity to comment'.

For the Maori community, a major development was a finding by the Waitangi Tribunal (established in 1975 to investigate the validity of claims under the aegis of the original 1840 Treaty of Waitangi between Maori chiefs and the British Crown) that fishing-beds on the Taranaki coast were unprotected from pollution. In particular, it was claimed, the planned waste-disposal for the Motonui petrol plant failed to meet local needs. Initially ignoring this finding, the Government then introduced special legislation permitting the use of an alternative site at Waitara, pending the planning and construction of a permanent, if more expensive, waste-disposal arrangement for the Motonui synthetic petrol plant.

The year also saw the death of former long-serving Prime Minister Sir Keith Holyoake (see OBITUARY), the visits to New Zealand in April of the Prince and Princess of Wales and of Chinese Premier Zhao Ziyang, and the Parliamentary Press Gallery's first New Zealand Communicator Award to the Coalition for Open Government.

Chapter 3

THE SOUTH PACIFIC

AT its August meeting held in Canberra, the South Pacific Forum (SPF) encountered difficulties over the future financing of the SPF shipping line. When Australia refused to assist in funding the A$3·5 million needed to salvage the insolvent line it was agreed to request the European Community to divert funds from its South Pacific regional assistance programme to keep the line afloat. This was acceptable to the EC programme administration, although not before the Solomon Islands had earlier withdrawn from participation in the line's activities.

The August Forum meeting also agreed to upgrade and install Islands telecommunications facilities, called for the transfer of control of New Caledonia's domestic affairs to 'appropriate authorities' as soon as possible, referred an Australian proposal for a South Pacific nuclear weapons-free zone (but one permitting continued nuclear ship visits) for further study, and agreed to assess the legal, financial, and political implications of a merger between the Forum and the South Pacific Commission.

The future political development of NEW CALEDONIA was discussed in France at a July meeting of French authorities and local factions concerned. This accepted the principle of recognizing Melanesian custom in future institutional arrangements, yet within a wider framework of the French constitution. In November, French Secretary of State Lemoine visited New Caledonia and presented proposals for a transition to self-rule, with a referendum on definitive status which could include independence. The local Independence Front insisted that any such referendum be restricted to citizens with at least one parent born in the territory. France also proposed the local election of an Executive Chief Minister for French Polynesia, in face of growing resentment against economic dominance by expatriate interests.

FIJI suffered from prolonged drought, a serious decline in output from the key sugar industry, and a devastating hurricane which did particular damage to tourist facilities. The Government reversed a 1980 decision banning nuclear-powered and nuclear-armed ships from entering its ports and waters. Judge White's lengthy Royal Commission of inquiry into allegations of misconduct in the 1982 general election (see AR 1982, p. 324) saw the ruling Alliance Party admit that it could not produce evidence to substantiate its earlier claims that the opposition National Federation Party had agreed to grant special facilities to the Soviet Union if it won the 1982 election.

In WESTERN SAMOA, chronic economic difficulties were partly eased by a total 16 per cent devaluation of the currency over February and March, the granting in June by the IMF of special compensatory, standby and drawing-rights facilities, and new credit arrangements for the West Samoan Trust Estates Corporation from the World Bank and Asian Development Bank. In September, the island of Savaii sustained a major setback when over 4,000 hectares of Western Samoa's best arable and forest lands were devastated by fire.

In a January election in KIRIBATI, two Cabinet Ministers lost their seats, as Mr Tabai was returned as President for a third and final term. In VANUATU, a November election saw Father Walter Lini returned as Prime Minister, his Vanuaaku Party winning 24 of the 39 seats in the Legislative Assembly. In July, Vanuatu established full diplomatic relations with Cuba following contact at the Non-Aligned conference in New Delhi.

After criticisms in the South Pacific for delay, the United States finally ratified treaties with Kiribati, the Cook Islands, Tuvalu and Tokelau, this constituting formal abandonment by the Americans of nineteenth-century-based claims to individual islands within the four groups mentioned.

In the COOK ISLANDS, two elections were held. In March, Sir Thomas Davis and his Democratic Party lost office to the Cook Islands Party led by Mr Geoffrey Henry. Mr Henry neglected to fulfil a constitutional requirement, previously regarded as a formality, that he first formally win confidence by vote in the legislature. A subsequent death and defection so reduced Mr Henry's support that a court ruling that he resign and seek reappointment through the legislature led to the fall of his Government, the dissolution of Parliament and another election. In a closely-fought contest, Sir Thomas Davis and his Democratic Party were returned to office in November by a narrow victory of 13 seats to 11.

XI INTERNATIONAL ORGANIZATIONS

Chapter 1

THE UNITED NATIONS AND ITS AGENCIES

IN a year when reasons to use force prevailed over the forces of reason, nationalist short-sightedness and antipathies deadlocked the UN, particularly the Security Council. It continually passed political predicaments to the Secretary-General. In his annual report Sr Perez de Cuellar reminded the Council of its primary obligation for collective action to achieve security and the peaceful resolution of disputes. The Council did meet privately to consider how to improve its effectiveness.

The destitution and indebtedness of the Third World deepened, while industrialized countries tried first-aid and blocked UN efforts towards long-term cures. The rich nations argued that their own recovery would trickle down to the poor ones.

The 37th General Assembly session reconvened momentarily in May to consider the problem of Cyprus. Its 38th session opened on 20 September, electing as its president Jorge Illueca, Vice-President of Panama, who, addressing the Assembly, highlighted the plight of the Third World and the collapse of the North-South dialogue. A number of top-level statesmen attended, Mrs Indira Gandhi having urged them to treat the session as a forum for world opinion. In the general debate a large majority of the 150 speakers concentrated on disarmament, the economic crisis and strengthening the UN.

The Assembly admitted the 158th UN member—St Kitts-Nevis. It voted Egypt, India, Peru, Ukraine and Upper Volta to the Security Council from 1 January 1984, replacing Guyana, Jordan, Poland, Togo and Zaïre, to join with the five permanent members and those with a year more to serve—Malta, Netherlands, Nicaragua, Pakistan and Zimbabwe. When the Assembly suspended its session on 20 December it had considered all its 146-item agenda except six, but they included two left over from 1982—the implementation of UN resolutions and global economic negotiations.

POLITICAL

MIDDLE EAST. The Secretary-General remained convinced that the UN should play a crucial role in resolving the problems of the Middle East and of the need for an international conference. Instead, the Reagan Administration attempted to tackle them.

In Lebanon the UN alleviated suffering through its hard-pressed Palestinian relief agency UNRWA, the Coordinator of Assistance for the Reconstruction and Development of Lebanon and the UN Interim Force in Lebanon (Unifil). In September the UN appealed for six-weeks' supplies to help 150,000 people in Lebanon. Unifil was engaged in protecting and assisting the local population in an area of southern Lebanon and preventing unauthorized local armed groups from operating. Israel considered Unifil had outlived its usefulness, while Lebanon wanted its mandate extended to all the country. The mandate was renewed three times during 1983 until 19 April 1984. Also the mandate of the UN Disengagement Observer Force on the Golan Heights was extended twice until 31 May 1984. In September Syria turned down a proposal for additional UN observers to monitor a ceasefire between the Druze, Phalangists and the Lebanese army.

Upon the outbreak of PLO factional strife in Lebanon during November the Security Council called for an immediate ceasefire, the settlement of differences by peaceful means, and respect for the territorial integrity of Lebanon. After consultation with the Council Sr Perez de Cuellar authorized use of the UN flag as 'symbolic protection' on ships evacuating the PLO from shattered Tripoli for humanitarian reasons.

In February and May the Security Council considered the situation in the occupied Arab territories, particularly Israeli settlements on the West Bank. On 2 August the US vetoed a resolution which declared Israel's settlement policy invalid and condemned the killing of three Arab students. From 28 August to 7 September a UN world conference on Palestine was held in Geneva. Over a hundred countries attended but not the US or Israel, and the UK only sent an observer. Extremism did not materialize as feared. The meeting called for a Middle East peace conference, to include the PLO, asserted the right of all states in the region to exist within secure boundaries, and that of the Palestinians to establish their independent state.

The General Assembly endorsed this declaration by 124 votes to 4 with 15 abstentions, including the UK. It also called for the isolation of Israel in all fields, deemed that the November agreements between the US and Israel would jeopardize a comprehensive settlement and reaffirmed the need for an international conference under UN auspices.

NAMIBIA. Another year of stalling by South Africa blocked the UN plan for the independence of Namibia. Again it insisted on the American idea of linking this with the withdrawal of Cuban troops from Angola, although that was not part of the original plan and was opposed by neighbouring states and the UN. In February Sr Perez de Cuellar visited five front-line states—Angola, Mozambique, Tanzania, Zambia and Zimbabwe—as well as Kenya and Uganda, and reiterated that the withdrawal of Cuban troops could not be a condition for Namibian independence.

A UN international conference on Namibia was held in Paris from 25 to 29 April to mobilize world opinion. Attended by 136 governments, it rejected linkage, called on four Contact Group members—Canada, the UK, US and West Germany— to dissociate themselves from linkage, as France had already done. It urged the Security Council to consider imposing comprehensive sanctions against South Africa to enforce the UN plan and called on states to prohibit corporations from dealing in Namibian uranium.

On 31 May the Security Council unanimously condemned South Africa for its illegal occupation of Namibia and mandated Sr Perez de Cuellar to seek a ceasefire and the implementation of Namibia's independence. Leading a strong team, the Secretary-General visited South Africa, Namibia and Angola from 22 to 26 August. He made progress, apparently establishing UN impartiality regarding elections which had been questioned by South Africa, but he did not budge Pretoria on linkage. He discussed the electoral system and resolved problems of the composition and status of the UN Transitional Assistance Group.

The Secretary-General reported his findings to the Security Council, which met from 20 to 28 October and agreed that Namibia's independence 'cannot be held hostage to the resolution of issues that are alien' to the UN plan, i.e. linkage, and asked South Africa to inform the Secretary-General of its electoral preference—proportional representation or a constituency system. The US abstained instead of casting a veto as South Africa had hoped. Sr Perez de Cuellar was to report by the end of December for the Council to act. The Foreign Minister of South Africa wrote that the choice of electoral system 'should not cause unnecessary problems', but the Council need not wait to know that his Government would not forego linkage. In December the Assembly condemned efforts to establish linkage and called for comprehensive mandatory sanctions by the Council. There were no votes against, South Africa having been ostracized from the Assembly years before, but the UK, US and others abstained. France then withdrew from the Contact Group, considering it powerless.

Early in December South Africa launched attacks reaching some 150 miles into Angola, allegedly to forestall Swapo raids. It offered a month's disengagement from Angola, commencing 31 January, provided Angola ensured that its forces, Swapo and the Cubans did not take advantage of the withdrawal. After Angola rejected the proposal the Security Council demanded an unconditional withdrawal, declaring Angola entitled to redress. The Secretary-General duly reported to the Council that, in his talks with South Africa, he had made no progress on the implementation of the UN independence plan.

AFGHANISTAN. The UN continued its efforts to resolve the four-year-old conflict in Afghanistan. The Secretary-General's special representative, Sr Diego Cordovez, visited Iran, Pakistan and Afghanistan from 21 January to 7 February, when he tackled time-frames for a settlement comprising the withdrawal of troops, non-interference, guarantees of non-intervention and the return of refugees (see p. 260).

At the invitation of Mr Yuri Andropov the Secretary-General visited Moscow on 27 March, where he received strong support for the UN efforts. Sr Diego Cordovez met the Foreign Ministers of Afghanistan and Pakistan separately in April, keeping Iran's UN representative in Geneva informed. Substantial progress was reported towards a draft settlement. Talks were reconvened in June, to be followed by preliminary consultations by Cordovez with the US and USSR as possible guarantors.

As the international climate deteriorated Sr Perez de Cuellar reported to the Assembly his concern at the slow pace of negotiations. On 23 November the Assembly again called for withdrawal of foreign troops, preservation of Afghanistan's territorial integrity and non-alignment, reaffirmed the right of Afghans to determine their own form of political and social system and asked the Secretary-General to continue his efforts. The Assembly also urged states to provide humanitarian relief to the many refugees (some three million in Pakistan) in coordination with the UN High Commissioner for Refugees (UNHCR). One of the stumbling-blocks to a settlement was the status of these refugees and conditions for their return.

IRAN—IRAQ. The Secretary-General was in constant touch with both Governments involved in the Gulf war, hoping for a timely moment to act, while Prime Minister Olof Palme of Sweden agreed to continue efforts to resolve the dispute. A Security Council statement of 21 February again called for an immediate ceasefire and withdrawal to recognized international boundaries with a view to a peaceful settlement, and requested the Secretary-General to continue his efforts. At Iran's request, and after consultations with Iraq, Sr Perez de Cuellar sent a UN team at the end of May to assess war damage to civilian areas in both countries. The team reported to the Council that damage had been heavy on both sides but particularly in Iran.

France inspired and the Council adopted a resolution on 31 October calling for an end to attacks on civilian targets and to hostilities in the Gulf area, and for the Secretary-General to consult on methods of verification, possibly including UN observers. The resolution was intended to ensure free navigation of the Gulf and the uninterrupted flow of oil supplies. Iran dissociated itself from the resolution; it had previously warned the

General Assembly that 'any misguided adventure' by foreigners against its vital interests would result in its closing the Hormuz Straits.

CENTRAL AMERICA AND GRENADA. As a member of the Security Council Nicaragua was especially able to voice in the Council its fears of American aggression, although a likely US veto inhibited action. The Council considered Nicaragua's complaints in March, May and September. On 19 May it unanimously urged the Contadora group (Colombia, Mexico, Panama and Venezuela) to find solutions to the problems of Central America and asked the Secretary-General to keep the Council informed, while reaffirming the right of all countries in the area to freedom from interference.

The Contadora group gave Sr Perez de Cuellar an outline for peace with 21 political undertakings as a basis for negotiations, endorsed in September by Costa Rica, El Salvador, Guatemala, Honduras and Nicaragua. On 11 November the General Assembly, by consensus, condemned aggressive acts in Central America and urged the Contadora group to persevere in its peace efforts.

In March, at the request of Grenada, the Secretary-General instructed an aide to speak to the American ambassador about its fears of US military action. American troops landed there on 25 October. A Security Council draft resolution deplored the armed intervention as flagrantly violating international law and called for the immediate withdrawal of foreign troops, but was vetoed by the US, while the UK abstained. (See also pp. 90-93)

The General Assembly adopted a similar resolution by 108 votes to 9, with 27 abstentions, which also called for free elections and asked the Secretary-General for an assessment of the situation within 72 hours. A small UN team visited Grenada and reported back on 5 November that virtually no political machinery existed for governmental functions. The Governor-General considered six to 12 months necessary for general elections, but most foreign military personnel could be withdrawn shortly. The Governor-General hoped for economic aid and felt that airport construction was a key to tourism, vital to the island.

CYPRUS. The General Assembly met on 10 May to deal with Cyprus, an issue left over from 1982. A very large majority reaffirmed support for the territorial integrity and non-alignment of Cyprus, the withdrawal of occupation forces, its demilitarization and the Secretary-General's personal involvement in the problem. It called for constructive communal negotiations to reach agreement, respect for human rights including freedom of movement and of settlement, and measures for the return of refugees, and recommended that the Security Council should examine a time-frame for implementation of UN Cyprus resolutions. The UK and US were among those abstaining.

In response to the Assembly's attitude the Turkish Cypriot leader

Rauf Denktash cancelled a meeting with the Secretary-General and discontinued the intercommunal talks. However, after meeting him on 4 July the Secretary-General sounded both communities on whether they would accept certain 'indicators' on territorial delimitation, legislative, executive and presidential representation. The Cypriot President reluctantly agreed, Denktash was opposed and wanted to meet President Spyros Kyprianou. The Secretary-General started preparations for a summit of the community leaders in the New Year.

Mr Denktash made a unilateral declaration of Turkish Cypriot independence on 15 November, although claiming it 'will not hinder, but will facilitate the establishment of a genuine federation', and asking the Secretary-General to continue his good offices. Turkey alone recognized the would-be republic. The Security Council met and adopted a UK resolution deploring the secession and calling for the withdrawal of the declaration as 'legally invalid'.

The UN Force's mandate in Cyprus was renewed twice until 15 June 1984. Voluntary contributions being insufficient, its role of holding the ring and supervising ceasefire lines operated at a serious deficit.

OTHER DISPUTES The Security Council was called on several occasions to consider contention in North Africa. In February Libya complained of American surveillance by AWACS and the aircraft-carrier *Nimitz,* allegedly there to discourage Libyan action against Sudan. Many times Chad complained to the Council against Libyan intrusions in support of Mr Goukouny Oueddeye against President Hissène Habré. On 6 April the Council's President called for due respect of Chad's territorial integrity. In August both Libya and Chad complained to the Council, the first against US manoeuvres in Egypt, the second about Libyan air strikes, which the Council considered at numerous meetings.

The Russian shooting-down of a South Korean plane early on 1 September over militarily sensitive Sakhalin was mercilessly aired by the US. A Security Council draft resolution, deploring the destruction and recognizing the right to compensation, was vetoed by the USSR. The UN's International Civil Aviation Organization (ICAO) called for an inquiry, which the Soviet Union boycotted. It reported that the plane was probably off course because of navigational error, but again called on the USSR to cooperate in the investigation before the report was considered. The ICAO agreed to hold an extraordinary assembly in April 1984 on the use of force against civil aircraft to prevent such a tragedy recurring.

Little progress was made on other disputes. The Assembly again called on Argentina and the UK to negotiate on sovereignty, which the latter refused to do.

The Assembly did not rule on who should represent Kampuchea, but reiterated that a settlement must include withdrawal of foreign forces and the right to self-determination and non-interference, adding an appeal for aid to Kampucheans.

The UN mission to assess Lesotho's need for assistance after the South African raid in December 1982 reported on ten projects to strengthen the country. The Security Council commended Lesotho for its opposition to apartheid and generosity towards refugees from South Africa. Sr Perez de Cuellar sent an envoy to discuss measures for handling the refugee situation, exacerbated by pressure from South Africa. In September the UN helped the voluntary evacuation of a few of the South African refugees whom that country wanted expelled.

GLOBAL ISSUES

DISARMAMENT. A dismal year for disarmament ended with the suspension of five sets of negotiations outside the UN, while world military expenditure neared $800,000 million a year. In letters to the superpowers the Assembly's President urged them to stop expanding nuclear confrontation, and 'to sit around the Security Council's table determined to put a stop to this madness'.

Negotiations continued in the UN Committee on Disarmament and the Disarmament Commission, but with little progress even in the most promising field of chemical weapons. The Committee of 40 countries worked on seven items. Sweden presented a draft comprehensive test ban treaty, but the Reagan Administration suspended negotiations with the USSR and UK, claiming tests were needed for development purposes. The Disarmament Commission of all UN members considered general policy and confidence-building, including a report on 'Common Security' by an independent commission headed by Olof Palme.

In December the 38th General Assembly adopted over 60 resolutions on disarmament, many similar to past ones—including a freeze on nuclear weapons, no-first-use of such weapons, the outlawing of arms in space, a ban on chemical weapons, an end to all nuclear tests and the establishment of nuclear-free zones. There were new proposals for studies by the Secretary-General on the naval arms race and the Antarctic Treaty of 1959, which had demilitarized the area, frozen all claims to sovereignty and isolated it from commercial exploitation, and which might be reviewed in 1991.

A review conference on the 1972 treaty against weapons of mass destruction on the seabed was held in September, to which the UK, US and USSR were parties. It confirmed that the terms had been faithfully observed, but stressed the need for negotiations to prevent an arms race in other weapons on the ocean floor.

ENVIRONMENT. The UN Economic Commission for Europe elaborated a Convention on Long-Range Transboundary Air Pollution, particularly to curtail acid rain, which came into force on 16 March between 32 European states, the USSR, US and Canada.

Under the auspices of the UN Environment Programme (UNEP) 17 Caribbean countries and the European Community negotiated the umbrella Cartagena Convention for the protection, development and management of the marine environment. It was accompanied by a protocol drafted by the International Maritime Organization (IMO) on cooperation in combating oil spills. Unfortunately the shattered Iranian wells went uncapped despite the anti-pollution agreement of the Gulf states negotiated under UNEP auspices in 1978. The eight parties to the agreement met, but with two of them at war cooperation proved impossible.

THE SEA. Pending the coming into force of the Law of the Sea Convention its preparatory commission considered the framework for the International Sea-bed Authority and International Tribunal, and rules and regulations for exploration and exploitation. On 4 July the IMO opened a World Maritime University in Sweden for training senior personnel from developing countries in maritime administration. In October the vitally important IMO International Convention for the Prevention of Pollution from Ships came into force, imposing stricter requirements for tankers. Under IMO auspices a convention was agreed on 17 February for a two-year suspension of dumping of all high-level radioactive wastes at sea and providing conditions for the dumping of other such wastes. The US, Netherlands, Switzerland, South Africa and Japan voted against, as did the UK, which accounted for some 90 per cent of such dumping. The moratorium was not mandatory, but was to allow time for research into the effects of such waste.

ECONOMIC

MONETARY MATTERS. There was only a patchwork response to demands for a fundamental reform of the monetary system. The debt crisis was translated into a development crisis, but also threatened the liquidity of the International Monetary Fund (IMF) itself. In February it was agreed to increase the IMF's lending resources by 47·5 per cent to $90,000 million for the growing queue of borrowers, particularly in Latin America. But owing to US Congressional delays the IMF had to freeze its operations in September, restarting them in December after the US approval of its quota increase.

The World Bank was also faced with American closefistedness towards its International Development Association for concessionary loans to poorer countries, especially in the Sub-Sahara and the Far East. The Bank sought $16,000 million for its three-year lending programme;

32 of the 33 contributing countries agreed to $12,000 million but the US insisted on $9,000 million, subject to further consideration.

DEVELOPMENT. Protectionism and high interest rates took their toll of the world economy. Consideration of global negotiations on international economic cooperation for development was again deferred from 1982 to 1984 in the General Assembly. At the Williamsburg summit on 28 May the Secretary-General called on the leaders of industrialized countries to benefit the economies of developing countries, but they assumed that their own recovery would stimulate recovery elsewhere.

They maintained that view at the VIth UN Conference on Trade and Development (Unctad) from 6 June to 3 July, although a compromise was struck that paid lip-service to interdependence, the need for changes in the international order and a denial that the trickle-down effect was sufficient. The US dissociated itself from this consensus statement and the UK, West Germany, Japan and others expressed reservations. The hopes of Third World countries for substantial progress on monetary reform, less protectionism, more liberal trade policies, more aid and debt relief were dashed. Unctad's Secretary-General summed up the conference as showing that recognition of the reality of interdependence 'was not equally matched by a recognition of its implications'.

The operational activities of the UN Development Programme (UNDP) had to be curtailed because of falling pledges and unfavourable exchange rates. In 1983 UNDP informed beneficiary governments of a cut of 55 per cent in the target sums they were originally due to receive for programmes and projects.

ECONOMIC AND SOCIAL. As was customary, the Economic and Social Council (ECOSOC) devoted its spring session in May to social and humanitarian problems. It adopted 96 resolutions and decisions on such subjects as racism, the protection of disadvantaged groups, drug abuse, crime prevention, the transportation of dangerous goods and proposals received from its Commission on Human Rights.

The summer session in July concentrated on economic matters—disaster preparedness and assistance to specific countries in Africa and Latin America, food relief without political pressure, natural resources, transnational roles, regional cooperation and the revitalization of ECOSOC's own work.

SOCIAL

HUMAN RIGHTS. Concern for human rights kept broadening across national boundaries and extending to claims to the right to life, livelihood and development.

The regular session of the Commission on Human Rights, 31 January to 11 March, continued work on many general issues including mass exoduses, arbitrary executions, torture and disappearances. Specifically it considered practices against human rights in a dozen countries, most of them already on its books. It concluded the case against Bolivia in view of the restoration of the constitutional system. With Guatemala's agreement it appointed Viscount Colville of Culross to study human rights there. Iran offered to receive a special envoy to investigate such rights, but cancelled the invitation because of the Commission's critical resolution and failure to investigate the whereabouts of 9,405 Iranians who had disappeared after the Iraqi invasion. The Commission was also concerned at the arbitrary detention of Palestinians and Lebanese by the Israelis, and in August its minorities subcommittee considered Sri Lanka's policy towards the Tamils.

The Secretary-General's special representative reported to the Commission on the situation in Poland, although he was unable to visit the country since the Polish Government had refused to cooperate. He concluded that the Government had eliminated most of the 'rigours of life' under martial law, but hoped for greater normalization. The Commission called for the report to be updated. In 1983, unlike the preceding year, the Polish Government would not invite a commission of the International Labour Organization (ILO) to investigate its observance of ILO conventions. However, the Organization set up such a commission, whereupon Poland boycotted the ILO conference.

RACISM. A world conference on racism was held in August to review past efforts in the first decade to combat racism (1973-83) and the implementation of UN decisions. Attended by representatives of 115 states it divided sharply on South Africa and Israel, but adopted resolutions condemning all cooperation with South Africa, calling on the Security Council for mandatory sanctions against it, and regretting racial discrimination against Palestinians. It suggested educational and protective laws and a programme of action against racism. Later the General Assembly endorsed this programme and declared a second decade to combat racism. It also approved a number of resolutions on aspects of apartheid similar to those of the conference and condemned South Africa's invasion of neighbouring states.

HUMANITARIAN. One of the most urgent humanitarian problems to confront the UN was mounting food deficits due to natural and man-made disasters. Africa was receiving 50 per cent of all cereal aid compared with 5 to 6 per cent in the late 1960s. Twenty-two African countries faced critical food shortages. On 19 October the Director-General of the Food and Agriculture Organization (FAO) summoned a meeting to deal with the crisis and consider the recommendation of its task force that 700,000 tons of additional food aid were needed immediately, but he received a disappointing response. At the FAO conference in November he had more satisfaction from 20 donor countries and the European Community. According to an FAO report almost 700 million people in rural areas of developing countries lived in abject poverty. The conference called on governments to consider improving land tenure arrangements.

There was no new large-scale refugee flow to add to the 10 million refugees throughout the world. The UNHCR's aim was not just relief but also to promote solutions, especially voluntary repatriation. Such repatriation in Indochina and from Djibouti helped the proportion of the programme towards that end to rise again after a low point of 26 per cent in 1981. In addition to shielding refugees from attacks new problems emerged—protection for those seeking asylum, such as Turks in West Germany, and provision for illegal workers expelled to their own country (not strictly refugees), such as Ghanaians from Nigeria.

WHO continued its work on primary health care and breast-feeding and against aggressive marketing of tobacco and pharmaceuticals. It also considered the abuse of alcohol and assessed the effects of nuclear bombs on health. A report was issued on the latter subject and the WHO Assembly concluded that health services could not prepare to deal systematically with the results of an explosion from even a single one-megaton bomb.

UNESCO. See p. 69 for US notice of withdrawal.

Chapter 2

THE COMMONWEALTH

A SEQUENCE in the television version of Queen Elizabeth's Christmas Day broadcast to the Commonwealth showed her sitting on a lawn in New Delhi talking with the Indian Prime Minister, Mrs Indira Gandhi. It seemed an apt climax to a year in which India had been the centre of Commonwealth activity.

For the first time, from November 23 to 29, a Commonwealth heads of government meeting (CHOGM) had been held in India. It was the largest gathering ever, with 42 countries represented: the absentees were Grenada, which had just suffered its coup followed by the American landings, and Vanuatu; four small countries—Maldives, Nauru, St Vincent and Tuvalu—categorized as Special Members, do not attend heads of government meetings.

The Delhi gathering concerned itself mainly with the Caribbean situation following the Grenada crisis; the deadlock in the North-South dialogue; ways and means of persuading the superpowers to reduce international tensions; the problem of Cyprus arising from the declaration of independence only days earlier by the Turkish administration in the north of the island; and the Southern African situation, particularly in relation to Namibia.

During the traditional weekend retreat, which took place in Goa, the leaders published the Goa Declaration on International Security, calling on the Soviet Union and the United States to 'summon up the political vision of a world in which their nationals can live in peace' (see DOCUMENTS). The leaders also issued a communique and the New Delhi Statement on Economic Action, announcing the setting-up of a Commonwealth consultative group to explore further the proposals made in three Commonwealth study group reports on North-South issues—*Protectionism; Threat to International Order* and *The North-South Dialogue: Making it Work,* both published in 1982, and *Towards a New Bretton Woods.*

The last-named was the product of several months work in 1983 by a group of experts from nine countries, who included Professor Gerald K. Helleiner (chairman) from Canada, Sir Jeremy Morse from Britain and Dr I. G. Patel from India. It proposed a series of immediate, near-future and long-term measures for the evolution of the world's financial and trading system and was published in time for consideration by the annual meeting of Commonwealth Finance Ministers, held this time in Port of Spain, Trinidad. In the view of many economic experts in and beyond the Commonwealth the three reports constituted the most formidable body of practical documentation on the whole complex subject of North-South economic relations so far compiled. In New Delhi, while some countries, notably Britain, did not share New Zealand enthusiasm for a new Bretton Woods conference (see p. 310), there was general acceptance of the need for changes to be made in the world's financial institutions, such as the World Bank and IMF.

The Commonwealth consultative group was to comprise representatives, up to Finance Minister level, of Governments of Britain, Canada, Fiji, India, New Zealand, Tanzania, Trinidad and Tobago, and Zimbabwe, together with the Commonwealth Secretary-General.

On Grenada, the differing perceptions of the American role among the Caribbean countries themselves and between some African and some Caribbean countries were aired in New Delhi, but the consensus was on the need to look forward, and offers of help for reconstruction were made. It was agreed that the Commonwealth should embark on a major study of the needs of small states, especially in relation to security.

Other decisions of the Delhi meeting included rejection of linkage between the independence of Namibia and the withdrawal of Cuban troops from Angola; the setting-up of a five-nation action group on Cyprus to secure compliance with UN Security Council Resolution 541 of 18 November; reaffirmation of the Gleneagles Agreement on sporting contacts with South Africa; and establishment of a higher education unit in the Secretariat to increase educational opportunities for Commonwealth citizens. New study groups would also investigate increased scientific cooperation and member countries' experience in managing technological change.

Two other Delhi decisions were to raise the budget of the Commonwealth Foundation, of which Justice Ulric Cross, of Trinidad and Tobago, had become the new chairman in 1983, to £1·46 million for 1984/6 and to hold the next CHOGM in 1985 in the Bahamas.

Commonwealth Day, 14 March 1983, was marked by the issue of a special series of stamps by every member country. Each donated 20,000 sets to make up a special album sold to the public to raise extra cash for the Commonwealth Fund for Technical Cooperation, whose total budget was raised in June to £19·93 million. The operation was a great success and the New Delhi summit decided that a second album should be launched on Commonwealth Day 1988.

Mr Shridath Ramphal's term of office as Commonwealth Secretary-General, due to expire in 1985, was renewed by Commonwealth leaders in New Delhi for a third period of five years till 1990.

Two important Commonwealth legal meetings were held in 1983—the Law Ministers conference in Colombo in mid-February and the Seventh Commonwealth Law Conference in Hong Kong, which brought together no fewer than 2,000 lawyers. Health Ministers met in Ottawa in October.

Heads of government of the Commonwealth Caribbean and Canada held in St Lucia their first summit meeting since 1966, but another regional gathering, the fourth Asia and Pacific regional heads of government meeting, due to take place in Papua New Guinea in 1984, was postponed.

St Kitts-Nevis tooks its place as the 48th member of the Commonwealth on attaining its independence on 18 September.

In February the Queen visited Jamaica, the Cayman Islands and Canada, and in November she went to Kenya and Bangladesh on her way to India, where she met all the leaders attending the Commonwealth summit. It was her first visit to India since 1961. In her Commonwealth Day message the Queen spoke of the ways in which the Commonwealth helped tackle problems of poverty, under-nourishment and under-employment. At Christmas she again dwelt on poverty and said the world would not begin to close the gap between rich and poor 'until we hear less about nationalism and more about interdependence'.

Chapter 3

DEFENCE ORGANIZATIONS AND DEVELOPMENTS

THE GLOBAL SCENE. Demonstrations of military prowess became commonplace in 1983. The extended reach of the superpowers through arms supplies and power-projection forces not only augmented their capacity for military intervention in distant countries, but also encouraged competitive meddling and accentuated the risk of direct confrontation. The US Administration confirmed previous trends by adopting an openly activist posture to counter perceived Soviet advances both in Europe (see NATO and ARMS CONTROL below) and in the Third World. Globally, the US profile was notably more visible than that of the Soviet Union.

Washington's continuing commitment to the security of the north-west Pacific was signalled by a series of military manoeuvres during the year. A major US-South Korean military exercise in March was followed in April by the US Pacific Fleet's 'Operation Fleetex 83'. Having dashed Seoul's hopes of closer security ties, Tokyo became increasingly receptive to American overtures encouraging Japan to extend its defence commitments and participate in US global strategy. US-Japanese military cooperation noticeably strengthened after Premier Nakasone's Washington visit in January (see p. 299). In September a major joint naval exercise tested the Japanese navy's ability to deny the Soviet Far Eastern Fleet access to the Pacific in time of war. This shift towards a more offensive policy and integration of Japan into American operations caused a significant deterioration in Soviet-Japanese relations, already strained by alleged Soviet espionage activities in Japan, the build-up of SS-20 missiles in Siberia, Soviet militarization of the disputed Kurile Islands and the Korean airliner tragedy. However, despite further cajoling from American leaders, including President Reagan during his state visit, domestic constraints suggested that Japan's ambitious maritime defence plans were premature.

Fears of nascent Japanese militarism, tension in the Korean peninsula and in Sino-Soviet relations dominated a Sino-Japanese summit in Tokyo in November notable for its cooperative atmosphere. In contrast, uncertainty and suspicion prevailed in the great-power triangular relationship as China attempted to pursue an evenhanded policy towards the superpowers. Despite the continuing problem over Taiwan there was promise of closer military links between Peking and Washington towards the end of the year. To balance this improvement in Sino-US relations Peking sought progress in its normalization talks with Moscow.

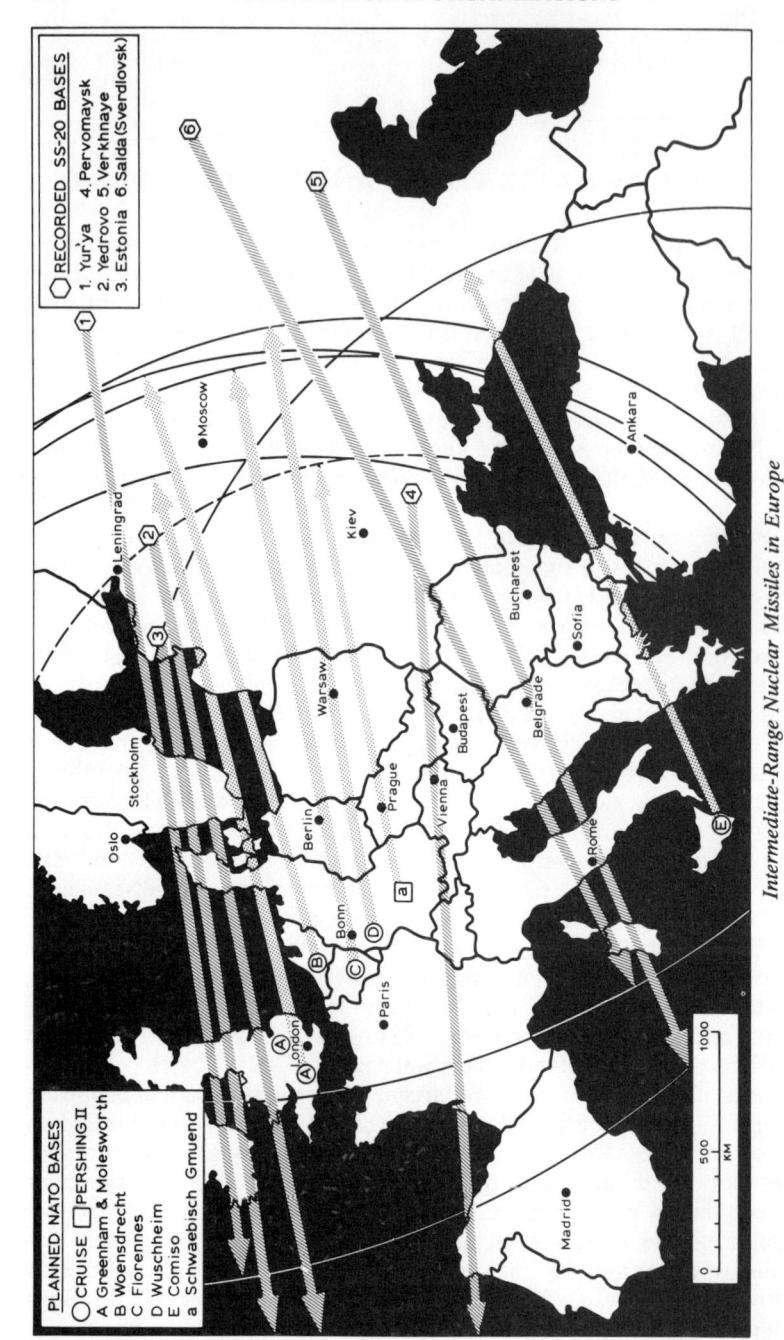

Intermediate-Range Nuclear Missiles in Europe

The maximum ranges indicated are respectively Cruise 2,500 km, Pershing II 1,800 km, SS-20 4,000 km: Soviet authorities claim that Pershing II has a range of 2,500 km. The SS-20 sites have not been confirmed; those east of the Urals have been omitted. (Based on information from the International Institute for Strategic Studies and *Jane's Weapon Systems*.)

DEFENCE ORGANIZATIONS AND DEVELOPMENTS

Washington's commitment to responding forcibly to challenges in Third World areas resulted in an unprecedented military build-up which threatened to over-extend its armed forces and provoked much criticism from Moscow, particularly in relation to the Indian Ocean and the Far East where an increase in Soviet naval activity was reported.

The Middle East enhanced its reputation for sucking in and spitting out major powers. In attempting to exclude Soviet influence from the region the US became steadily embroiled in the Israeli-Palestinian conflict and the Lebanese quagmire. The hard-won tripartite agreement on Israeli troop withdrawals from Lebanon proved but a momentary success for Washington. As US 'peacekeeping' forces became combatants and the Sixth Fleet, monitored closely by the Soviet navy, indulged in gunboat diplomacy in support of the Lebanese Government, the threat of war between Israel and Syria waxed more often than waned.

The expansion of Moscow's military support for Damascus and the escalating US involvement against Syrian positions in Lebanon induced fears of direct superpower confrontation. The US regional military profile sharpened further by December with the American-Israeli strategic cooperation accord, greater focus on Jordan as a link in Washington's Rapid Deployment Force (RDF) programme, and additional military aid to Egypt.

Further westward the US and France assumed less than coordinated roles in the fighting in Chad. The supply of American military aid, and the despatch of two AWACS planes to bolster the besieged Habré Government, brought Washington into confrontation with Colonel Qadafi in August. Against a background of Libyan threats to attack the Sixth Fleet the US proceeded with a series of joint RDF manoeuvres with Egypt (Brightstar '83) and later with Somalia and Sudan.

This show of force in north-east Africa was directly related to the defence of US interests in the Gulf—a perennial concern which had surfaced in January in a Pentagon directive committing the US to defend Saudi Arabia and other Gulf states in the event of an attack by the USSR. Simultaneously, the resumption of Soviet arms supplies to Iraq disclosed a subtle shift in its officially neutral stance on the Gulf war. In September, a periodic eruption in the Iran-Iraq conflict reached international boiling-point when Iran threatened to cut the West's oil lifeline by blocking the Strait of Hormuz if French Super-Etendard jets were delivered to Iraq. Washington responded by despatching an emergency task force to reinforce its already substantial naval presence in the Arabian Sea. The crisis receded later in November, having occasioned one of the heaviest Western naval concentrations in the north-west quadrant of the Indian Ocean.

Gunboat diplomacy and a dearth of dialogue were continuing characteristics of US policy in Central America and the Caribbean. The absence of blatant external intervention in its so-called backyard did not deter Washington from military exertions aimed at defeating leftist insurgency. The naval task force exercises off the Pacific and Caribbean coasts of Central America in July and August, amid rumours of a possible US blockade of Nicaragua, raised fears that the US was on the brink of armed intervention. Despite a flurry of attempted peace-making by regional states the Pentagon pursued its plans for a six-month series of exercises in Honduras, where pressure mounted for the establishment of a permanent US military base. The revival of the Central American Defence Council underlined the Administration's penchant for a military approach to the region's problems—an approach which was dramatically manifested in the Caribbean by the US-led invasion of Grenada in October.

An almost compulsive tendency towards military confrontation at the expense of political dialogue only made conflicts in strategically sensitive areas still more combustible. 1983 presented states with many opportunities to flex their military muscle; where such temptations proved irresistible, regional stability, and consequently world order, were undermined.

THE NORTH ATLANTIC TREATY ORGANIZATION. The accumulation of grievances among member states in 1983 threatened a fundamental change in the future direction and strategy of the alliance. Lingering controversy over the 'dual track' decision of 1979, and the burgeoning peace movement in Europe, made deployment of Cruise and Pershing II missiles less a symbol of Nato's military virility than a test of its collective political will. Anti-Americanism in Western Europe and economic protectionism joined the range of issues straining US-West European relations.

Familiar differences over expenditure were caught up in a growing debate over alliance strategy. Nato's reliance on nuclear weapons was criticized by a Brookings Institution publication, and in May the European allies openly opposed the campaign of General Rogers (Saceur) to increase conventional arms spending. Already critical of some European allies, such as Denmark and West Germany, for failing to meet their military spending targets, Washington sought to raise the level of annual increase from 3 to 4 per cent in real terms.

By December the focus had shifted from financial targets to new programmes of military hardware and emerging technologies. The weapons programme for 1984 was designed to update and increase stocks of existing weapons. A £2,000 million deal to improve Nato air defences in central Europe was also announced at the December Defence Ministers' meeting.

The US Administration remained committed to its ambitious military spending programme. The 5 per cent real increase in its defence budget covered items such as the B-1 bomber, chemical weapons production and the MX missile. For the first time the budget placed a formal ceiling on the number of troops in Western Europe. Although President Reagan's controversial 'star wars' defence system claimed to render nuclear weapons obsolete, it was subsequently revealed that the US planned to produce a further 17,000 nuclear weapons in the coming decade whilst retiring only 6,000 old weapons.

Although Spanish participation in Nato's integrated defence structure remained 'frozen', France was evidently prepared to extend its commitment to European defence, but not to the point of reintegrating its armed forces into the alliance's military command structure. In addition, there were fears that Britain's Fortress Falklands policy would weaken its naval contribution to Nato.

The alliance staged a major display of military strength in March, demonstrating its commitment to the defence of its strategically sensitive northern flank. Over 10,000 troops and naval forces from five countries took part in winter exercises in Arctic Norway, and a Nato fleet visited Greenland in August. The two-month-long annual 'Autumn Forge' series of manoeuvres was estimated to involve 250,000 allied troops, including members of the French armed forces. Extra-regional commitments caused 10,000 US troops to be withdrawn from a major US-Spanish exercise, 'Crisex-83'.

The Geneva negotiations on intermediate nuclear forces (INF) dominated Nato assemblies throughout the year. Although the eleven Defence Ministers attending the Lisbon meeting of the Nuclear Planning Group (NPG) on 22-23 March publicly reaffirmed their support for the US 'zero option' plan, there were growing doubts among some European allies about its viability as a negotiating strategy.

The US Defense Secretary faced growing disarray among the allies at the meeting of the Military Committee in June. Secretary Weinberger's concern over reports of Dutch reluctance to site its assignment of 48 Cruise missiles turned to anger at the Danish Parliament's decision to force its Government to revoke Denmark's financial commitment to the Nato deployment plan. The US feared this would undermine its negotiating position and reduce the credibility of the 'dual track' policy. The Defence Ministers were also asked to prepare contingency plans to cover the withdrawal of US forces to deal with crises elsewhere.

The historic Nato Council meeting on 9 and 10 June was consumed by arms control developments. The Foreign Ministers were clearly apprehensive about the impact of the peace movement and there was little hope of agreement at Geneva. Progress in arms control continued to be linked to Soviet actions in Poland and Afghanistan. Although the Foreign Ministers firmly endorsed the decision to deploy US missiles in Western Europe by the end of the year if the Geneva talks failed, the hoped-for united Nato front dissolved in the face of continuing Greek reservations about the 'dual track' decision and the increasingly doubtful position of the Danish, Spanish and Dutch Governments.

The nuclear debate obscured other challenges to the political and strategic coherence of the alliance in 1983. Potentially disintegrative forces hovered over both wings of the southern flank, where attention focused on the future of US base facilities. On 7 March talks resumed in Athens, where Greece, pursuing its role as Nato's Balkan maverick, was demanding compensation in exchange for Washington's continued use of bases on its territory. The negotiations were punctuated by a series of crises, but a five-year agreement was eventually signed on 8 September which provided for US military and economic aid to Greece along with Washington's pledge to maintain the balance of power in the region. The Turkish Cypriot UDI on 15 November renewed tension in the Aegean.

In the western Mediterranean the Spanish Socialist Government's commitment to the alliance remained in question. A disputed bilateral base agreement with the US was salvaged in February, but closer Spanish integration within Nato remained conditional on the result of a future referendum. Nato concern to improve the defence of Gibraltar became a significant factor in the debate over Spain's contribution to the security of the southern flank.

The US was also involved in protracted renegotiation of its Azores base agreement with Portugal. As with Greece, the new agreement signed on 13 December included substantial US military assistance to Lisbon but imposed greater restrictions on the American presence.

The allies' determination to begin the installation of Cruise and Pershing missiles was apparent at the meeting of the NPG in Canada on 27-28 October. After considering a recommendation of the High Level Group of military experts to reduce Nato's nuclear stockpile, the Defence Ministers announced a cut of 1,400 short-range nuclear warheads and the removal of such warheads on a one-for-one basis with the introduction of Cruise and Pershing II.

The first Cruise missiles arrived in Britain on 14 November. The Bundestag's endorsement of the deployment scheme on 22 November heralded both the arrival of parts of Pershing II missiles in West Germany on 23 November and the departure of the Soviet delegation from the Geneva INF talks.

East-West relations preoccupied the Nato Council meeting in Brussels on 8 and 9 December. News of the abrupt suspension of the START negotiations (see ARMS CONTROL) was greeted with equanimity by the Foreign Ministers, who subsequently authorized the publication of Nato's account of the INF talks. They formally announced the appointment of Lord Carrington to succeed Dr Luns as Nato's Secretary-General in June 1984. At West Germany's suggestion the Council agreed to a separate statement—the Declaration of Brussels—pledging Nato's commitment to seek genuine detente at the forthcoming Stockholm conference (see CSCE) and calling on the Soviet bloc to work for a balanced and constructive relationship based on moderation and reciprocity.

Although the final communique emphasized the 'spirit of cohesion and solidarity' within the alliance, the end of a momentous year brought evident apprehension over possible Soviet counter-measures and the likely consequences for future East-West relations.

THE WARSAW TREATY ORGANIZATION. The military power and political activity of the Warsaw Pact was much in evidence during 1983. Proposed missile deployments in Europe preoccupied the alliance, heightening its international profile and frequently determining the level of intra-bloc cohesion.

In December Western defence analysts estimated that the Soviet Union had deployed 369 SS-20 missiles. The new SS-21, SS-22 and SS-23 shorter-range missiles awaited deployment within the bloc, and Moscow also threatened to increase the number of nuclear submarines operating off the US coast if the Geneva INF talks failed. A Pentagon assessment of Soviet military power disclosed the flight-testing of both a new generation of long-range Cruise missiles and the Blackjack strategic bomber, and the appearance of the PT-80 main battle tank. The strengthening of Soviet anti-missile defences and the development of new mobile ICBMs and a satellite-based submarine detection system were also reported.

Revised CIA estimates noted a decline both in Soviet defence spending between 1976 and 1983 to a 2 per cent annual growth, and in the production of new major weapons. According to *The Military Balance 1983-84,* published by the International Institute for Strategic Studies, economic constraints threatened to hasten weapons obsolescence, whilst demographic trends promised future manpower problems.

The importance of military coordination within the alliance was emphasized by Defence Ministers, meeting in Prague between 11 and 13 January to discuss the Joint Armed Forces (JAF). Encouraged by Marshal Kulikov's extensive tour of Eastern Europe in February this theme subsequently materialized in a series of manoeuvres designed to enhance military preparedness and improve command and control mechanisms between the national armed forces.

Major joint military exercises included 'Danube-83', held in Hungary in January, and 'Soyuz-83' in East Germany, Poland, Czechoslovakia and the southern Baltic between 30 May and 9 June. The commander-in-chief presided over a meeting of the military council of the JAF in Bucharest in April which reviewed developments in command and communications structures. Demonstrations of Soviet military strength continued into autumn. Between 29 June and 4 July Defence Minister Marshal Ustinov supervised exercises of Soviet ground, air and naval forces in the Baltic and Byelorussia regions. In September four task groups of the Northern Fleet exercised in the North Atlantic.

Under vigorous Soviet leadership, the Political Consultative Committee, at its first meeting for nearly three years, launched a major peace offensive at the Prague summit on 4 and 5 January (see DOCUMENTS). The Soviet bloc offered to sign a non-aggression treaty with Nato based on a mutual pledge of no-first-use of nuclear or conventional weapons. The Pact proposed a radical reduction of medium-range missiles in Europe as an alternative to the US 'zero option', and condemned Nato deployment plans for Cruise and Pershing II missiles. These themes were reiterated throughout 1983 in a bid to keep the initiative in the East-West nuclear debate (see ARMS CONTROL below).

In June, indications of Soviet concern over the political cohesion of the Eastern bloc coincided with Mr Andropov's accession to the presidency amid persistent rumours of his poor health, a growing frustration with Nato arms negotiators, and the Papal visit to Poland. The continuing Polish problems prompted the Soviet leader to warn others against following the same path towards 'bourgeois reformism'. Soviet political and military leaders were evidently concerned about the loyalty and commitment of their allies. On the eve of a meeting of top Party leaders in June, *Pravda* warned of the need to close ranks against 'imperialist propaganda'. Nevertheless, the shortened and inconclusive summit on 28 June failed to endorse Moscow's proposal to station further Soviet missiles in Eastern Europe if Nato proceeded with its deployment plan. Western reports suggested that Romania's President Ceauşescu had once again broken ranks and thwarted a more aggressive supranational approach. Ceauşescu's deviationist line re-emerged in October when he opposed Soviet missile deployments in East Germany and Czechoslovakia, and again in November when he urged Moscow to drop its demands for the inclusion of the British and French nuclear deterrents in the Geneva talks. The Kremlin's unease and sensitivity over Eastern Europe resurfaced in August with direct verbal attacks against the Pope and the Polish Catholic Church, and its accusation of a Western campaign against Czechoslovakia on the 15th anniversary of the 'Prague Spring'.

Warsaw Pact leaders engaged in a flurry of summitry during October. A meeting of Foreign Ministers at Sofia on 13 and 14 October and an extraordinary meeting of the Defence Ministers' Committee in East Berlin on 20 October preceded the disclosure of Soviet preparations to deploy operational tactical nuclear weapons in East Germany and Czechoslovak territory. Significantly, the Pact's Military Council was convened at Lvov just four days later, and in Sofia in early December Defence Ministers, at the first high-level meeting since the breakdown of the Geneva negotiations, unanimously endorsed Soviet military measures to counter the deployment of US missiles.

Against a background of mounting East-West tensions, and deprived of dynamic leadership from Moscow, the Warsaw allies entered uncharted waters at the close of a politically frustrating year.

MUTUAL AND BALANCED FORCE REDUCTIONS. The Vienna negotiations on the reduction of conventional forces in central Europe resumed at the end of January. The 19 delegations assembled to face the familiar deadlock over mutually acceptable data on existing force levels and verification measures (see AR 1982, pp. 345-6). Despite this, some commentators were hopeful of progress in the wake of the Prague Declaration's call for a non-aggression pact and the reduction of forces and armaments in central Europe 'on the basis of reciprocity'.

This optimism was misplaced. The opening of the 29th round of talks witnessed a string of Warsaw Pact objections to the Western proposals of July 1982. The talks seemed doomed to return to their customary stalemate, although Nato's four-stage reduction plan had been intended to remove the Warsaw Pact's principal objection to earlier Western proposals—namely, that these did not require an immediate reduction in the West German army. In return for its concession Nato hoped for progress on the perennial stumbling-blocks of Warsaw Pact troop strengths and effective verification measures.

The Eastern bloc countered with new proposals based on the Prague Declaration on 17 February. This called for each side to determine the size of its own troop reductions without prior agreement on existing forces. A political commitment to freeze troop levels pending an agreement on major reductions would follow initial withdrawals of 20,000 Soviet and 13,000 US troops. When the Warsaw Pact presented Nato with a draft agreement in June Western diplomats agreed to consider the plan even though it lacked an agreed data base and adequate verification measures.

The talks stumbled on in the shadow of the INF negotiations. On 15 December, following the collapse of the Geneva discussions, the force reduction talks were adjourned, the Warsaw Pact failing to specify a date for their resumption.

ARMS CONTROL NEGOTIATIONS. For nuclear arms negotiations, 1983 was seen as the make-or-break year. The discussions between the superpowers in Geneva—START and INF—remained separate despite pressure to merge them later in the year.

The START discussions resumed on 2 February against a background of disarray in the US negotiating team and the Kremlin's rejection of President Reagan's call for a summit with Mr Andropov. However, *Pravda's* disclosure of the Soviet negotiating position, coupled with the Prague initiative, encouraged the West to anticipate a more positive approach by Moscow. The Soviet draft treaty tabled in March briefly raised hopes that the gap between the opening proposals could be narrowed, but deadlock ensued.

Congressional pressure for a new US negotiating position and greater flexibility at the START talks prompted the Reagan Administration to abandon its former proposal that each side be limited to 850 strategic missiles. On 8 June, the US tabled a proposal to reduce each nation's warheads to a maximum of 5,000. The offer was hastily dismissed by the Soviet news agency TASS as 'mere words'. But by the end of the month signs of a more flexible Soviet attitude on limits for land and submarine-launched missile systems and air-launched cruise-type missiles encouraged the US to table a draft treaty relaxing its limits on missiles and offering an alternative approach to the problem of reducing 'throw-weight'.

US negotiators were optimistic that a preliminary accord was in sight as they prepared to resume negotiations on 6 October, armed with their new 'build down' plan. However, agreement continued to be conditional on progress in the INF talks, and this optimism was short-lived. Moscow rejected the proposals as evidence of US intentions to achieve military superiority over the Soviet Union. The talks subsequently showed little promise of a breakthrough. When the winter session ended on 8 December Moscow signalled its displeasure at the deployment of Cruise and Pershing by declining to set a date for the resumption of the START talks.

Nato remained determined to instal its 572 US missiles in Western Europe by the end of 1983 unless a satisfactory agreement was reached with the Soviet Union at Geneva. This injected a greater sense of urgency into the INF talks, which resumed on 27 January and which became both a determinant and a barometer of East-West relations throughout the year.

The revelation in January that Washington and Moscow had repudiated an informal agreement reached between their chief negotiators in the summer of 1982 (the so-called 'walk in the woods' formula), caused embarrassment in Washington and uneasiness among its West European allies, who began to press for an interim agreement.

As proposals and counter-proposals came thick and fast the Soviet Union set the pace through the Prague initiative and the subsequent reiteration of Mr Andropov's 1982 offer to reduce the number of SS-20 missiles to 162—the total of British and French missiles—provided Nato refrained from installing US missiles. The US commitment to its 'zero option' policy (see AR 1982, p. 347) was modified in President Reagan's offer of 30 March to seek an interim agreement limiting the deployment of intermediate-range missiles to the extent that the Soviet Union agreed to dismantle its SS-20s. This new initiative was warmly welcomed by Nato's Special Consultative Group.

Moscow's rejection of the proposal on 4 April was followed a month later by a revised version of the earlier Andropov plan. On 3 May the Soviet leader offered to cut Soviet intermediate nuclear warheads to the level of warheads deployed by Britain and France, subject to the usual condition. The Western refusal to include the British and French deterrent forces, while seeking to reduce Soviet Far Eastern missiles, did not augur well when talks resumed on 17 May amid mutual recriminations over the lack of progress.

A further refinement of the Soviet proposal emerged at the end of August when President Andropov declared his willingness to 'liquidate' all but the 162 missiles deployed in European Russia. Despite the crisis over the South Korean airliner incident the US responded by instructing its negotiators to abandon the former demand for 'global equality' in the number of medium-range forces and to show greater flexibility on bombers and individual weapons systems. In return Washington required a Soviet freeze on SS-20s deployed in Asia. The plan, fully endorsed by Nato's Special Consultative Group, raised Western hopes for constructive progress which proved to be premature.

In what was held to be the toughest statement from Moscow since the collapse of detente in 1979, President Andropov condemned US arms control proposals, virtually ruled out any agreement with the Reagan Administration and embarked on a staunch defence of the Soviet action over the airliner disaster. This unusually hardline statement on 28 September drove another nail into the coffin of East-West relations. Concern grew that the Soviet Union, having given up hope of an agreement, was preparing to pull out of the INF talks and mount an intensified campaign in a final effort to dissuade West European Governments from accepting US missiles. As prospects for agreement faded Moscow warned that Western deployment would force the Soviet Union to increase its conventional and nuclear capabilities and take 'corresponding counter-measures against US territory'. A barrage of warnings preceded the tabling of an eleventh-hour Soviet proposal on 26 October offering to cut its medium-range missiles in Europe to 140 and freeze deployment of SS-20s in the Far East. Although these were perceived by the US as part of a public relations exercise to reinforce West European opposition to US missiles and to exploit divisions within Nato over the US-led invasion of Grenada, they extracted further counter-proposals from Washington in its attempt to regain the initiative. This last-minute effort to break the deadlock proposed a global ceiling of 420 intermediate-range warheads on each side, but was promptly rejected by Moscow, as the first Cruise missiles began to arrive in Britain. The talks limped on until the Bundestag's historic vote (see NATO above). On 23 November the Soviet delegation implemented its threat and walked out of the talks without setting any date for their resumption.

The subsequent suspension of the START negotiations challenged Washington's initial view that the breakdown of the INF dialogue was a temporary hiccup. Thus grimly ended a year of tortuous and fruitless negotiations in the four main arms control areas—strategic nuclear, intermediate nuclear, conventional and chemical.

THE MADRID CONFERENCE (CSCE). The seventh round of the review Conference on Security and Cooperation in Europe (CSCE) resumed in Madrid on 8 February, some 27 months after delegates of the 35 participating states first assembled. The meeting opened with a call by Spain for 'genuine dialogue' to overcome the East-West tensions and disputes over human rights which had stymied the 'Helsinki process' and reduced the conference to an arena of sterile and often acrimonious posturing. Warsaw Pact concessions on at least some of the West's human rights amendments remained a prerequisite for Western cooperation in a new European disarmament conference.

On 10 February the conference set up several groups to draft acceptable texts, each for a specific section of a final document. Then on 15 March the neutral and Non-Aligned countries sponsored a 'third and final attempt' to agree on a concluding document. After a three-week recess the conference reconvened on 19 April amid Western objections to the omission of certain of its human rights demands in the compromise draft proposal, and reports of differences among the Western states.

Efforts to break the deadlock intensified. Speculation about a possible breakthrough gained momentum in May when a message from Mr Andropov, reported to accept the draft proposal, elicited a favourable response from an EEC spokesman. But, although Western human rights amendments became much less wide-ranging than those originally demanded by the United States, the Soviet delegation consistently refused to discuss them, and deadlock ensued once more.

On 17 June the Spanish Prime Minister, Sr González, revealed his effort to end the impasse. Based on the revised version of the March draft proposal, the Spanish compromise urged acceptance of a Swiss invitation to attend a meeting of experts on the human contacts provisions of the Helsinki Final Act; proposed a solution to the dispute over the wording of the text relating to the implementation of the Final Act; and urged agreement on the convening of a disarmament conference to be held from January 1984 in Stockholm to discuss confidence-building measures (CBMs) designed to avoid a war in Europe. The Spanish proposal omitted two of the four Western amendments.

Initial reactions were mixed. Western delegates were cautiously optimistic that the compromise could bring the conference to a successful conclusion. But the Soviet delegation maintained that the Western amendments remained unacceptable to Moscow. Then on 1 July, in the wake of a Warsaw Pact summit, the Soviet Union unexpectedly reversed its position, indicating it was prepared to compromise on human rights undertakings and negotiate the final details of a concluding document within the framework of the Spanish compromise plan. Even so, this penultimate stage proved anything but a smooth passage for the Madrid negotiators.

The specialist conference on human contacts planned for 1986 remained a major sticking-point. Its status in the final document caused serious misgivings in Washington, occasioned a Swiss compromise formula and further delayed the signing of the Madrid accord. However, provisional agreement on a compromise declaration was reached on 15 July by all the participants except Malta, which demanded that more attention be paid to Mediterranean security issues in the final text.

On 21 July delegates reached a tentative agreement to hold the formal concluding session between 7 and 9 September, with the Foreign Ministers of the participating states in attendance. However, the revival of the long-standing Maltese proposal for a follow-up meeting on Mediterranean security blocked the required unanimity. Maltese intransigence evoked anger and hostility and succeded in uniting the other 34 participants as no other issue had done in Madrid. As Foreign Ministers began to arrive in the Spanish capital on 6 September an alternative plan to salvage the conference called for agreement among the 34 to abide by the terms of the declaration, including its proposal for follow-up conferences.

The Soviet destruction of the South Korean airliner threatened to jeopardize the review conference at the eleventh hour. Rhetorically at least, East-West relations reached a new low-point as the Soviet Union found itself diplomatically isolated at a critical juncture in the effort to revive detente. Denunciation of the USSR overshadowed the climax of the Madrid review conference, which ended formally on 9 September. While the concluding document underlined the commitment to detente there was little visible evidence of that particular process in Madrid, despite the strenuous efforts of the Spanish Government to retrieve the 'spirit of Helsinki'.

The Concluding Document endorsed by the Foreign Ministers committed participating states to various obligations and provided for a number of new commitments beyond the Helsinki Final Act. Governments were urged to:

make further efforts to increase security, develop cooperation and enhance mutual understanding in Europe;
undertake concrete action 'to restore trust and confidence between the participating states';
ensure continuous implementation of the Helsinki Final Act;
pursue the solution of outstanding problems through peaceful means;
recognize their duty 'to refrain from the threat or use of force in their mutual relations';
acknowledge the 'universal significance of human rights and fundamental freedoms';
recognize the right of every state 'to be or not to be a party to treaties of alliance, and also the right to neutrality';
promote favourable conditions for trade and industrial cooperation;
encourage freer and wider dissemination of printed material from other countries;and
improve working conditions for foreign journalists, including personal contact with sources.

Advances over Helsinki included:

agreement to ensure the freedom of the individual to profess and practice religion in line with the dictates of his own conscience;
agreement to ensure the rights of workers freely to establish and join trade unions, and the right of unions to freely carry out their activities in compliance with national laws;
the granting of exit permits on the basis of family ties, marriage and the reunification of families, normally within six months after application;
agreement to refrain from penalizing would-be emigrants in terms of jobs, housing and social benefit;
assured freedom of access to foreign embassies, with due regard to security requirements;
an undertaking to work for militarily significant, politically binding and verifiable confidence and security-building measures (CSBMs) to reduce the risk of military confrontation anywhere in Europe.

Agreement on a Conference on Disarmament in Europe (CDE), to begin in Stockholm on 17 January 1984 after a preparatory meeting in Helsinki in October, was potentially the most significant result of the Madrid review conference. The CDE had a precise mandate for the negotiation of CSBMs from the Atlantic to the Urals and its first phase was clearly linked to future CSCE review conferences, beginning with Vienna in 1986.

Other specialist conferences scheduled in the Concluding Document included a meeting in Athens in March 1984 concerning the settlement of disputes; an experts' conference in Ottawa in May 1984 to discuss respect for human rights; a meeting of experts on human contacts in Berne in April 1986; a seminar on economic, social and cultural cooperation in Venice commencing in October 1984; and a 'cultural forum' planned for Budapest in October 1985.

The first fruits of the Madrid meeting materialized in October at the Helsinki preparatory meeting, where delegates of the 35 'Helsinki' states were empowered to draw up the agenda and timetable for the first stage of the Stockholm CDE. Malta again threatened to disrupt proceedings by attempting to involve non-participating Mediterranean countries. However, by mid-November delegates had successfully completed their assigned task, underlining their apparent determination to retain the CSCE arena as a channel of communication between East and West.

Chapter 4

THE EUROPEAN COMMUNITY

THE very survival of the European Community as such had by year-end become the subject of respectable questioning. 1983 was the bleakest year in the Community's history. Leaders of the EEC's ten member states left Athens after their summit debacle on 4-6 December with no plans for averting the Community's imminent financial bankruptcy, and unable to agree on the type of Community they wished to belong to, even supposing funds were there to finance it. The options facing the ten were either to radically revamp the Community, or to allow a gradual rundown in the closeness of their mutual relations.

At the heart of this predicament was, as ever, the Community's agricultural policy (CAP) and the related refusal of the Thatcher Government to sanction increases in Community financing for as long as the UK's budget contribution was not settled on a long-term basis. For Britain's EEC partners, this meant two uncomfortable courses of action: subscribing in advance to a hefty rebate to the UK, and/or agreeing upon a drastic overhaul of EEC expenditure. For as long as Community spending remained focused on agriculture, Britain, with its relatively small farm sector, was bound to stay an unacceptably large net contributor to the budget. Yet in Athens the Ten agreed upon no course of action at all. Britain got no long-term settlement, the Community got no new funds, the CAP continued unreconstructed and, with neither new money nor major and immediate reform, was judged certain to push the Community into defaulting on payments by the latter half of 1984. In these circumstances, no agreement was reached at Athens either on the type of new policies needed by the EEC, nor on the date of accession of Spain and Portugal, whose applications to join the Community had been made back in 1977.

Partly explaining the paralysis of the Community's decision-making process was the obsession of member Governments with economic stringency. This concern was not limited to right-of-centre Governments, as in West Germany and Britain where elections in March and June respectively strengthened the positions of Chancellor Kohl and Prime Minister Thatcher. The Mitterrand Administration in France also found itself forced into a policy of economic rigour following the devaluation of the French franc on 21 March. In Italy, general elections on 26 June yielded the first Socialist-led Government since the war, but at the core of Prime Minister Craxi's policy was a cut-back in public expenditure. The same dose of medicine was prescribed by the centre-right coalitions in Belgium and the Netherlands. In the light of this national preoccupation with money-saving, the Community's failure to launch new policies, to attract new funding, to settle the UK's claims or even to reform its expensive CAP—financially rewarding to a majority of the Ten—was not surprising.

The Community's economic performance remained poor. The slightness of recovery in 1983—an increase in real growth estimated at around 0·5 per cent—made no impact on unemployment, which by year-end was well over 12 million for the Community as a whole. This was in sharp contrast with the USA and Japan, the Community's major trade competitors. Constant but largely ineffectual complaints were directed against high American interest rates—sucking away much-needed capital from an investment-starved Community—and others were sparked by the EEC's multi-billion dollar deficit with Japan.

In this unpromising situation, the Community's main institutions functioned with gathering inefficiency. The European Commission, supposed to be the motor of European integration, allowed itself to be sidelined from the negotiations on Community reform, the central issue of 1983. The Commission's tacit abdication, coupled with the Council's total failure to grapple with an array of vital problems, left a power vacuum which the European Parliament, despite its Cinderella constitutional status, sought manfully to exploit. It increased its nuisance-value dramatically when, on 20 December—for the second year running—it blocked the budget relief agreed by the European Council in June for Britain and West Germany.

The Community's three traditional summit meetings, or European Councils, were held in Brussels on 21-22 March, in Stuttgart on 17-19 June, and in Athens on 4-6 December.

EXTERNAL RELATIONS. The call to reverse protectionism made by the industrialized world's economic summit, held in Williamsburg (USA) on 28-31 May and attended by Commision President Gaston Thorn, met with only limited success. Tensions remained acute throughout the year between the EEC and both the USA and Japan.

With Japan, the Community faced a familiar problem—a trade deficit running at an annual rate of around $12,000 million. It sought to tackle this by pressing Japan both to moderate its exports to the Community and to open up its market to more European exports. In mid-February, Commission vice-presidents Etienne Davignon and Wilhelm Haferkamp brought back from Tokyo a deal restricting imports of Japanese video units to the Common Market in 1983 to 4·55 million, contingent on EEC producers' selling 1·2 million units to their own market. This arrangement was renewed more restrictively when on 18 November Davignon negotiated a level of 3·95 million units for 1984.

In February, Tokyo also undertook to moderate exports of ten key products (ranging from cars and hi-fis through machine tools to colour TV tubes), an undertaking which was renewed in November. On 28 November the EEC Council decided to double the import tariff on laser-operated turntables, a product whose inventor Philips (Holland) was beaten to the European market by Japancse competition. Meanwhile, the Nakasone Government showed more responsiveness than its predecessors to European pressure to liberalize import procedures and, on 21 October, it took measures to stimulate Japan's intake of foreign goods.

The Community's economic relations with the USA were conducted with reciprocal yet controlled truculence—as befitted the management of some $90,000 million of mutual trade in a climate of latent protectionism. Less than six weeks after Williamsburg, the Reagan Administration announced on 5 July restrictions on imports of special steels. Taking strong exception to this, the EEC claimed the American move threatened $150 million of annual trade, and promised retaliatory action if the Americans did not offer trade compensation. By the end of 1983 this had not happened, and the areas where the Commision was considering retaliation included chemicals and plastics. The Community also feared that the bilateral trade arrangement reached in October 1982 for the steel sector as a whole (see AR 1982, p. 351) would be undermined by renewed complaints made by individual American companies against imports of European carbon steel. Relations continued strained on trade in farm products, too. American attacks were aimed mainly at the Community's attempts to stabilize fast-increasing imports of US cereal substitutes, and at its 29 July proposal to tax vegetable oils and fats, including 1·7 million tonnes of imports from the US. Meanwhile, the Community complained on 26 January at the subsidized sale of one million tonnes of American wheatflour to Egypt—regarded by the EEC as its traditional market—and again on 4 August at US sales of dairy products to the same purchaser.

Two other developments in 1983, both raising European hackles at the extraterritorial pretensions of American law, further chilled the transatlantic climate. A Bill before Congress sought to strengthen the Export Administration Act to enable the government to exclude from the US market foreign firms not complying with trade restrictions dictated by Washington. Community concern was also aroused when on 5 December the US Supreme Court rejected an appeal by Shell Petroleum against 'unitary taxation', the practice whereby some states of the USA taxed companies on worldwide profits. On neither of these issues did the EEC receive satisfaction.

Luxembourg staged the formal opening on 6 October of negotiations between the EEC and the African, Caribbean and Pacific (ACP) countries for renewal of the Lomé Convention. An attempt to relaunch the Euro-Arab dialogue, whose general commission had not met since 1978, ended in abrupt and total failure in Athens on 14 December. Relations between the EEC and the Andean Pact (Ecuador, Colombia, Bolivia, Peru and Venezuela) progressed, with a five-year economic cooperation accord signed in Bogota on 17 December. The trade restraint measures which the Community had imposed against the USSR for its role in Poland were lifted at the end of 1983. Following a lengthy transitional period for sensitive imports, the Community's industrial trade with the Efta countries was freed of virtually all restrictions from 1 January 1984 (see p. 352).

Meanwhile, there was no shortage of tests for the Ten's efforts at foreign policy coordination outside the Community framework proper. On strife-torn Central America, a statement issued by the Stuttgart summit on 19 June spoke of the Ten's 'deep concern', while on 28 November West German Foreign Minister Hans-Dietrich Genscher called for a cooperation agreement between the Community and the Central American Common Market. On 10 September the Greek president of the Ten's Foreign Ministers stymied an attempt by his European partners to condemn the Soviet destruction of a South Korean airliner (see p. 60), and only strong pressure brought the Athens Government to revise its position in a statement it made to the UN on behalf of EEC countries on 27 September. The Middle East remained a constant focus of European attention. On 9 November the Ten, in a statement on Lebanon, reaffirmed the right of the Palestinians to self-determination 'with all that implies'. On 16 November they rejected the declaration of independence made by the Turkish Cypriots and stressed that the only Cypriot Government they recognized was that of Mr Kyprianou.

BUDGET REFORM AND THE INSTITUTIONS. The Council of Ministers, which had in recent years developed decision-avoidance into a refined diplomatic art, found itself confronted with the omissions of the past: where to find new funds for a budget already within a hair's breadth of exhaustion in 1983; how to rein in an agricultural policy (CAP) which, though largely responsible for this state of affairs, was in the vested interest of many of the Ten; in which areas to develop new policies; and, last but not least, how to ensure that unacceptably high net contributions to the budget should be avoided in the long term.

On 10 February the Parliament belatedly approved the 1982 refunds due to Britain and West Germany, respectively 850 MECU* and 210 MECU, which it had blocked the previous December (see AR 1982, p. 353). The European Council in Stuttgart agreed on 19 June that Britain's 1983 refund should be 750 MECU, to be paid out of the Community's 1984 budget. Once again, however, the Parliament demurred. On 20 December its President, Piet Dankert, duly adopted the 1984 budget, set at 25,361 MECU, but froze the British and West German refunds in protest at the Ten's failure to reach a long-term budget reform at the Athens summit.

The 1984 budget was marginally higher than total expenditure in 1983, which, including two supplementary budgets adopted during the year, just exceeded 25,000 MECU. The Community was thus nudged tantalizingly nearer the exhaustion of its income—derived from customs duties, farm import taxes and up to 1 per cent of the Community's VAT base. The Commission warned the Council repeatedly that it could not

---

* One MECU (million European currency units) equalled £587,000.

guarantee the sufficiency of funds in 1984 unless the proposed reform of the CAP, which continued to absorb two-thirds of the budget, was agreed and swiftly implemented. During the last two months of the year the Commission was forced to suspend advance payments for certain farm products.

By year-end, the cause of agricultural reform, for which Commission proposals had been tabled on 29 July (see p. 346), had suffered a sharp rebuff. The Ten's talks on this in Athens ended in deadlock. Meanwhile, Mrs Thatcher made it clear that the starting-point was a long-term solution to Britain's EEC budget deficit, running annually at around 2,000 MECU. In these circumstances, marked by acrimonious exchanges between Britain and France, negotiations on new sources of Community income—for which the Commission had on 5 May proposed a raising of the Community's 1 per cent VAT ceiling—were also doomed.

The exceptional procedures set in train by the June European Council in Stuttgart, whereby a series of monthly 'Special Councils' was to pave the way for an agreed package at Athens in December, not only failed but did so with often spectacular absurdity. With at times no fewer than 30 senior Ministers seated around the same table, negotiations on massively complex issues were reduced to the simple juxtaposition of conflicting national positions, each of which could vary when voiced by a different Minister from the same delegation. The proposals from which this extraordinary diplomatic jamboree sought to glean a solution were myriad: overshadowing those of the Commission were proposals submitted direct by virtually every member state on one or more of the inter-related issues.

This process condemned the Council to a paralysis which the Commission surveyed with impotence from a back-row seat. President Thorn's tardy condemnation of the Special Councils—*after* the Athens failure—could not hide the Commission's earlier aquiescence in its own marginalization. Since the Parliament's limited role in Community reform largely depended on scrutiny of Commission initiatives and action, loss of Commission authority implied its own diminishing impact. The Parliament found itself locked out of a procedure to which the Commission held a key that it had failed to use. Prospects for the Commission's regaining its lost authority in 1984, the last year of its mandate, appeared dim.

The Parliament's determination to make the most of its limited powers pushed it to focus on policy areas beyond the boundaries set by the Treaty of Rome. On 16 November it adopted a resolution backing the deployment by Nato of intermediate-range nuclear missiles in Europe. This not only openly broached defence as a legitimate concern for the EEC but also cocked a snook at the Greek Government, which in September had sought unsuccessfully to use its presidency to persuade the Council to support a postponement of missile deployment.

The effectiveness of the Bonn Government's presidency in the first six months of the year was limited by its preoccupation until March with electoral matters. Preparations for the Stuttgart summit in June suffered as a result.

One of the last acts of the Ten's Foreign Ministers in 1983 was to fix 1 January 1985 as the date by which Greenland was to withdraw from the Community. No compensating decision on the date of Community enlargement to include Spain and Portugal was possible in 1983, despite the revision of the Community's regulations for fruit and vegetables and olive oil, which was completed on 18 October. The whole process remained stalled because of the Community's central disagreements.

AGRICULTURE AND FISHERIES. The farm price package agreed by the Council on 17 May made an average 4·2 per cent increase in ECU terms, or 6·9 per cent when expressed in relation to the weighted average of national currencies—i.e., taking account of adjustments to monetary compensatory amounts (MCAs). These rises kept European farm incomes roughly in line with inflation. During the negotiations, the Germans successfully withstood pressure from France, Italy and Ireland urging the elimination of MCAs, whose application to strong currency countries like that of the Federal Republic effectively provided farmers there with a hefty export subsidy, while protecting their domestic market by a corresponding import tax.

The price negotiations in May also prefigured that key issue of CAP reform, the need for greater discipline, particularly in the dairy and cereals sector. An abatement of respectively 3 per cent and 1 per cent in the price rises agreed for dairy and cereal products was applied for the first time in the 1983-84 marketing year. But its impact, at least in the dairy sector, was nil, as milk producers strove to increase their output to compensate for the price abatement. By year-end, the Community's subsidized dairy surplus stood at no less than 800,000 tonnes of butter and around one million tonnes of skimmed milk powder. Spending on the dairy sector continued to run at around 40 per cent of all agriculture expenditure, or some 25 per cent of the entire Community budget.

Recognition of the need for a major CAP reform was reflected in the comprehensive review ordered by the Stuttgart summit for completion before the Athens Council. The immediacy of this need was starkly underlined when the Council, on 22 July, was forced to approve an extra 1,760 MECU to finance run-away farm spending. On 29 July the Commission tabled new proposals for CAP reform which neither of the two British Commissioners—Christopher Tugendhat and Ivor Richard—felt were radical enough. Key measures proposed included a super-levy to curb dairy output, reduction of the gap between EEC cereal prices and the lower ones on the world market, a tax on vegetable oils and fats and the dismantlement of MCAs. Some progress was made by the

Council on this package. However, by year-end no decision had been taken on any of the individual proposals, let alone on the whole package. The farm reform dossier was itself only one component of a matrix of major issues, concessions on any one of which by member Governments depended on simultaneous gains in others.

Following the deadlock at Athens, the Commission warned that the 16,500 MECU earmarked for agriculture in the 1984 budget would be sufficient only if the whole of its 29 July proposals were agreed and implemented in time for the 1984-85 price campaign. The alternative was a further supplementary budget in 1984 for which funds could well be unavailable.

The Common Fisheries Policy (CFP), meanwhile, came into existence at last. On 25 January the Ten agreed the levels of total allowable catches (TACs) and their share-out between member states for all species except herring. Yet this single point of discord blocked implementation of the policy until, on 14 December, the Ten solved the herring problem and then belatedly completed their accord on 1983 TAC and quota levels. Ministers decided that these 1983 levels would be used as a provisional basis for TACs and quotas until 31 January 1984, by which time they hoped to agree the 1984 proposals which the Commission had tabled in December. Agreement between the Ten on the CFP also unblocked the EEC's fish arrangements with Norway and Canada.

INDUSTRY, FINANCE AND EMPLOYMENT. Despite political recognition by the Commission and the European Council (at Stuttgart) of the need to develop policies to meet new Europe-wide challenges like information technology, telecommunications, investment and youth unemployment, progress during 1983 was modest.

On 5 November the Council agreed the 1,400 MECU European Strategic Programme for Research and Information Technology (the ESPRIT programme) but, despite a further meeting on 13 December, failed to take a final decision because of British and German reluctance after the Athens debacle. Ministers did then approve 700 MECU for the Community's Joint Research Centre, including the JET thermonuclear fusion reactor at Culham (UK), which had become operational on 25 June.

The main focus of EEC industrial policy, however, remained the ailing steel sector. On 29 June the Commission took its long-awaited decisions on member states' support to steelmaking, and the Council heard Vicomte Davignon confirm the targeted removal of 35 million tonnes of excess capacity by 1985. Davignon also announced at the end of June the prolongation of the mandatory steel quota system to the end of 1984, in an attempt to correct short-term imbalances in supply and demand. However, market conditions deteriorated sharply in the second half of the year.

The highpoint of economic and monetary policy was the European currency realignment decided in Brussels on 21 March. This, the seventh adjustment in the European Monetary System (EMS) since its inception in March 1979 (see AR 1978, pp. 498, 501), saw the French franc drop 8 per cent against the Deutschmark. The full readjustment in so-called bilateral pivot rates was as follows: Deutschmark + 5·5 per cent, Dutch guilder + 3·5 per cent, Danish krona + 2·5 per cent, Belgian and Luxembourg francs + 1·5 per cent, French franc and Italian lira − 2·5 per cent, and Irish punt − 3·5 per cent. This realignment, not affecting the pound sterling or the Greek drachma which were outside the EMS, completely upstaged the 21-22 March European Council. It also was a severe blow to the policies of the Socialist Administration in France and marked a return to a strategy of economic rigour which, moreover, was the condition of the 4,000 MECU loan granted to France by its EEC partners on 16 May.

Elsewhere, economic policy was characterized by attempts to consolidate the fabric of the Common Market in the face of continued protectionism, and to nurture supply-side growth in a Community where investment, at only 18·8 per cent of GDP in 1983, had dropped to its lowest-ever level. No less than six 'internal market' Councils were held in 1983, the last one agreeing in principle, on 25 November, to 15 new product norms to bolster intra-Community trade. Meanwhile, on investment, the Council on 15 April adopted a Commission proposal to increase by 3,000 MECU the so called 'New Community Instrument' for financing energy, industry and infrastructure investment in the Ten. Yet these measures had only marginal impact on the European economy at large.

In social policy, the Community's unemployment problem was highlighted on 27-28 April by a special session of the European Parliament devoted to it, but a resolution on youth employment adopted on 8 December by the Council was weak to the point of being vacuous. Ministers on 17 October did adopt new rules for the Community's social fund to enable it to tackle more directly the problems of the young unemployed. But by year-end over one in four of the active population under 25 was on the dole, while the Community's overall jobless total was 12·3 million, 11 per cent of the work-force. For business, main developments were the approval by the Commission on 15 June of the Vredeling proposal on worker rights in multinational companies, and in early August of its draft for the fifth company law directive on worker participation in company affairs. In addition, a directive standardizing the rules for financial reporting by company groups was adopted into Community law on 13 June.

Chapter 5

COUNCIL OF EUROPE—WESTERN EUROPEAN UNION—NORTH ATLANTIC ASSEMBLY—EUROPEAN FREE TRADE ASSOCIATION—ORGANIZATION FOR ECONOMIC COOPERATION AND DEVELOPMENT—NORDIC COUNCIL—COMECON

COUNCIL OF EUROPE

IN 1983, a rich year politically for the Council of Europe, it reaffirmed the need for vigilance over human rights and democratic standards in its member countries and throughout the world. The situation in Turkey continued to preoccupy the Committee of Ministers and the Parliamentary Assembly. In Resolution 803 of 30 September 1983 the Assembly declared 'that under the present conditions and on the basis of information now available, the Parliament which will be elected in Turkey on 6 November will not be able to be considered as representing the Turkish people in a democratic manner, and could not therefore validly constitute a delegation to participate in the work of the Parliamentary Assembly of the Council of Europe.' The Committee of Ministers listened on 28 April and 24 November to statements by the Turkish Minister of Foreign Affairs on the progress achieved in restoring democracy to Turkey. Both the Committee of Ministers and the Parliamentary Assembly deplored the Turkish-Cypriot declaration of independence, though they did not hold the Greek Cypriots entirely blameless. On 6 December the European Commission of Human Rights declared admissible the applications brought against Turkey by Denmark, France, the Netherlands, Norway and Sweden, without prejudging whether Turkey had violated the European Convention on Human Rights as the applicant Governments alleged.

The situation in Lebanon and the Middle East was a recurrent item on the Assembly's agenda. It urged the relevant member states, on 30 September, 'not to contemplate any withdrawal from the Lebanon of any elements of the multinational force until reliable measures have been taken to ensure the physical protection of Palestinian and other refugees remaining in that country'.

On 9 December the Committee of Ministers welcomed Argentina's return to democratic rule, expressing the hope that those values which are the very essence of the Council of Europe would come to prevail throughout that region.

The Strasbourg conference on parliamentary democracy from 4 to 6

October was attended by parliamentarians from 28 European and other states (including Australia, New Zealand, Japan, Canada and the USA), who examined means of strengthening and up-dating the system of pluralist democracy. The Council of Europe's members claimed to represent a majority of the world's minority of democracies. Its role in the unification of Europe was clarified by statements in the Solemn Declaration on European Union adopted by the European Community in June 1983, which referred to the achievements of the Council of Europe and its cooperation with the European Communities. The Community reaffirmed its full support for the Council of Europe's activities in the cultural field and in the harmonization of national legislation. Nevertheless, the Council's Secretary-General, on 24 November, again called on Foreign Ministers for a 'homogeneous European policy' for all member States, involving a collective effort by the Community and the Council to attain European unity, their common goal.

WESTERN EUROPEAN UNION

True as ever to its role as the only European body empowered to discuss defence issues, WEU gave much of its attention in 1983 to defence and disarmament. It pursued once again the cause of coordinated European procurement of European arms, which involved closer cooperation in military science and technology, and with little dissent backed the dual-track policy on arms control, including deployment of Cruise and Pershing II weapons on European soil failing agreement at Geneva on withdrawal of Soviet intermediate-range weapons.

The June meeting of the WEU Assembly heard two notable speeches on defence. M Claude Cheysson, France's Foreign Minister, speaking as chairman-in-office of the WEU Council, said that France was anxious to correct by negotiation the imbalance between East and West bloc forces created by Soviet rearmament; but in face of the vast capabilities of the superpowers the nuclear forces of France and the UK were the guarantee and condition of their independence. Believing that nuclear weapons were weapons for peace because they rendered war unthinkable, France insisted on having its own and was the sole judge and sole master on this issue. While the idea that conventional forces must be strengthened—a theme much favoured by Assembly members—was excellent it must not give the false impression that, at the present stage, the deterrent could be sought in non-nuclear forces.

The military imperative, General Bernard Rogers, Supreme Allied Commander Europe (Saceur), told the Assembly, was to be capable of implementing Nato's strategy of flexible response. If conventional war came, the West would be unable to sustain itself in manpower and military supplies for long, which would mean moving fairly quickly to nuclear escalation. To develop an adequate conventional deterrent meant first bringing forces already committed up to Allied Command standards; they must also be technologically modernized. Answering American critics who held it was time to leave the security of Europe to the Europeans, General Rogers said that a free and independent Western Europe was a vital American interest, and its contributions to its own defence were under-estimated. Presenting a report on burden-sharing in the alliance, the British rapporteur recalled that Europe provided 90 per cent of the ground forces and the armoured divisions defending Europe and 80 per cent of the combat aircraft and tanks. A big effort of information on this issue was needed. Addressing the November Assembly, Dr Joseph Luns, Secretary-General of Nato, also stressed Western Europe's enormous contribution to the civilian infrastructure of the alliance.

Such observations were well received by a body which considered itself the authentic voice of Western Europe as a whole. The two 1983 Assemblies displayed a strong demand for more concerted and unified political action by Europe in world affairs. They reflected the Union's interest in extra-European affairs in a variety of ways: they passed 'recommendations' advocating closer European collaboration with communist China, promoting the Law of the Sea Convention, calling for collaboration with Japan in high technology applied to military requirements, prescribing rules governing trade and other economic relations with the USSR which might assist Soviet war power, and backing French intervention in Chad.

Sr Alfredo De Poi (Christian Democrat, Italy) was elected President of the Assembly on 6 June.

THE NORTH ATLANTIC ASSEMBLY

During its 1983 autumn session held at The Hague in October, the North Atlantic Assembly (NAA)—a forum where 184 elected representatives from the Nato countries meet regularly to discuss issues relevant to the Atlantic alliance—adopted a recommendation calling upon the North Atlantic Council to intensify consultations within the alliance on ways to promote more effective and equitable armaments cooperation. Turkey, having no parliament, was not represented at the NAA's 1983 sessions; on the other hand, the Australian and Japanese parliaments sent observers. The autumn session also adopted two resolutions of particular importance, one urging member Governments to remain firm in the commitment to begin deployment of the 572 Pershing II and Cruise missiles, should no agreement be reached in Geneva, the other calling upon Nato Governments to support a unilateral

reduction in the total number of short-range nuclear warheads in Europe.
The debates on these resolutions were organized largely under the impetus of the Special Committee on Nuclear Weapons in Europe, founded in 1980 by the NAA to monitor implementation of Nato's 1979 dual-track decision and to consider nuclear issues in depth. Mr Olof Palme, Prime Minister of Sweden, addressed the Assembly on nuclear-free zones; Dr Manfred Wörner, West German Minister of Defence, discussed the more general issue of European security; and Mr Paul Nitze, chief US negotiator at the Geneva INF talks, briefed the members on those negotiations.

In order to provide a link between the inter-governmental structure of Nato and the member countries' national legislatures, the NAA's five committees and their eight sub-committees met regularly through the year with officials from Nato governments, officers of the armed forces and corporate executives. The sub-committees dealt with the following subjects: defence cooperation, conventional defence in Europe, the southern region, out-of-area challenges to the security of the alliance, East-West economic relations, the free flow of information and people, the successor generation and East-West technology transfer.

EUROPEAN FREE TRADE ASSOCIATION

The last tariff cuts scheduled in the free-trade agreements signed in 1972 between the Efta countries and the European Communities came into force at the end of 1983, freeing all industrial goods and some processed foodstuffs from import duties. This consummation, said Mr Per Kleppe, Efta's Secretary-General, 'marks the final achievement of Efta's efforts since 1960 to bring about a large European free trade system'. The final liberation concerned mainly paper and paper products, most industrial goods having been freed in 1977. Finland would keep certain import duties for a further year, and Portugal, by special leave, was allowed longer protection for infant and vulnerable industries.

The Efta Councils, meeting at ministerial level in Oporto on 24-25 November, expressed satisfaction with the smooth implementation of the Efta-EEC agreements, and their readiness to strengthen and expand cooperation with the Community. A joint meeting of Efta parliamentarians and members of the European Parliament, held in Geneva on 1-2 December, gave particular attention to the growing cooperation of the two groups in technological and scientific research, stressing that Europe's future in this field could be best assured by a pooling of resources.

Efta countries, with joint growth of just under one per cent in 1983, shared in the incipient revival of the European economy, and with their high international dependence—exports averaging 37 per cent of

GDP—looked for further advance from recovery in world trade. Unemployment remained a grave worry, though running on average at less than half the rate in the European Community. Ministers at the Efta Council meeting in Bergen in June called for internationally coordinated policies to sustain recovery without inflation and to reduce unemployment.

Two new loans totalling US$1·53 million were approved in September by the steering committee of the Efta Industrial Development Fund for Portugal. In June all Efta countries and Yugoslavia signed a declaration on action to strengthen economic cooperation between them and to manifest Efta's continuing interest in Yugoslavia's economic development.

ORGANIZATION FOR ECONOMIC COOPERATION AND DEVELOPMENT

At its ministerial level meeting on 9-10 May, the OECD Council agreed on a medium-term approach to sustaining and broadening the economic recovery which it saw to be under way. Member Governments would take advantage of the emerging room for growth to promote higher employment, reduce inflation, reverse protectionist trends, work to resolve international debt problems and provide more effective help to the poorer developing countries. The Council observed that collective bargaining should take account of the need to promote job-creating productive investment and higher employment without inflation. Monetary policies should allow for sustainable economic growth but should not accommodate any resurgence of inflationary wage claims, and together with a necessary reduction in budget deficits should enable interest rates to ease, so promoting world economic recovery. Thus, overall, while recognizing that conditions varied among its member countries, the OECD Council endorsed the anti-inflationary polices of most of its member Governments, while implictly rebuking the United States for its high budget deficits and consequent high interest rates.

However, the Organization was far from complacent about the present state of the Western economy, especially the dismal level of unemployment. An OECD report, *The Employment Outlook*, published on 16 September stated the problem thus:

'20,000 extra jobs will be required every day during the last five years of this decade if OECD unemployment is to be cut to its 1979 level of 19 million. The labour force is likely to grow by some 18 to 20 million people over the five years 1984-89, and 1984 unemployment is projected to be 34¾ million—so up to 20 million jobs need to be created just to keep unemployment from rising, and over 15 million extra jobs are needed to get unemployment down to 19 million.'

As the report observed, it did not seem likely that the current economic recovery would make inroads into unemployment for some time.

In partnership with sound macro-economic policies, the report suggested, labour market policies could reduce both structural and cyclical unemployment, by helping the labour force to adjust to rapid structural economic change, by reversing the rise in real labour costs relative to productivity, by anticipating economic upturn through marginal employment subsidies and job creation schemes, by work-sharing—provided it implied income-sharing—and by translating recovery 'into more output and jobs rather than into higher wages and prices'.

High youth unemployment was causing 'widespread discontent among the young leading to growing frustration and apathy'. Long-term unemployment was more serious in European countries than in North America. Total adult unemployment ranged from 9·9 per cent of the work-force in Spain and 9·0 per cent in the UK to 2·1 per cent in Japan and 1·5 per cent in Norway.

The OECD's *Economic Outlook No. 34*, published on 16 December, projected that in Europe unemployment would steadily edge upward from 18 million (10 per cent) at the start of 1983 to 20 million (12 per cent) by mid-1985. In the US, however, the rate might fall below 8 per cent by 1985. Other aspects of the economic situation were more favourable. Inflation had come down sharply—in the three largest economies, the United States, Japan and Germany, down to 3 per cent or lower. However, rates remained close to or above 10 per cent in a number of OECD countries. Real GNP for OECD as a whole had risen by $2\frac{1}{4}$ per cent in 1983; but while the US recorded a $3\frac{1}{2}$ per cent increase the growth in Europe had been a bare 1 per cent.

In this context, a high-level meeting of the Organization's Development Assistance Committee on 28-29 November made a number of recommendations for increasing the effectiveness of cooperation among member countries in development aid policies. It also adopted a statement of 'guiding principles to aid agencies for supporting the role of women in development'.

The governing board of the (OECD) International Energy Agency met at ministerial level in May in Paris. The assembled Ministers welcomed the relief provided to the world economy by the fall in energy prices and growing efficiency in energy use and production. However, they recognized that conditions could change in the future, and expressed concern that lower oil prices and uncertainty about future oil market developments could slow down investment in energy efficiency, hydrocarbon development and alternative energy sources. The easing of the oil market was no reason to change the agreed objectives of energy policies—oil substitution, energy conservation and energy research and development.

NORDIC COUNCIL

The 31st session of the Nordic Council was held in Oslo between 21 and 25 February 1983. An innovation in its proceedings was the holding of the budget debate in plenary session. Among the 34 recommendations for action by the Council of Ministers the most important was that from 1984 the self-governing territories of Greenland, the Faeroe Islands and Åland be granted separate representation within the Danish and Finnish delegations, their representatives to be chosen by the territories' own representative institutions. In order to accommodate the change, the Nordic Council's membership would be increased from 78 to 87. Its concern for environmental issues was demonstrated in a number of recommendations: that the Nordic Governments accept a revised programme for cooperation on environmental protection, intensify research into energy and environmental questions, seek to persuade other governments and international organizations to adopt uniform methods of collecting information on this subject, intensify their efforts to persuade other governments and international organizations to cut down sulphur pollution and pay regard to environmental questions in energy policy formulation, reach an inter-Nordic agreement on sulphur pollution in the Nordic area, and actively support efforts to preserve the Arctic environment.

Other important recommendations were that the Governments intensify their work on simplifying administrative and taxation regulations in order to encourage inter-Nordic regional cooperation, double the Nordic Investment Bank's own resources, adopt an action programme for housing and building, pursue further measures to encourage Nordic energy cooperation, and draw up proposals for a Nordic action programme for data technology and a Nordic plan for economic development and full employment.

Speakers in the general debate were again preoccupied with economic issues. Norway's Prime Minister, Kåre Willoch, was one of many who looked to a realistic and expanded Nordic cooperation to help in resolving the five countries' problems; he particularly welcomed the economic committee's unanimous recommendations for an action programme for economic development and full employment. The recommendations were also welcomed by Denmark's former Prime Minister, Anker Jørgensen. Both he and Mr Gunnar Berge, finance spokesman of Norway's Labour Party, called on the Nordic governments to coordinate their international efforts to persuade other countries to pursue expansive economic policies.

Sweden's Finance Minister, Kjell-Olof Feldt, defended Sweden's 16 per cent devaluation in October 1982 as a necessary step in Sweden's economic recovery and went on to propose improved consultation procedures in financial and currency matters. Ib Setter, Denmark's

Industry Minister, accused the Council's members of actions which undermined respect for Nordic cooperation; national politicians, he said, took decisions which weakened this cooperation, yet they continued to meet in the Council and its committees and extol Nordic cooperation. Denmark's Prime Minister, Mr Schlüter, posed the question whether the five countries still retained the structural flexibility to adapt to the enormous economic problems facing them. Would other countries look to them as a model for their own efforts or regard them as societies in decline?

The remarks of Sweden's Prime Minister Olof Palme in praise of the 'peace movement' against nuclear weapons, and also those of Sweden's former Foreign Minister Ola Ullsten on the possibilities of a Nordic nuclear-free zone, provoked some sharp replies from other speakers. Mr Schlüter counselled realism about the influence which proposals such as that for a Nordic nuclear-free zone could exert on the superpowers, while another member of Denmark's Government, Mr Arne Melchior, maintained that the greatest peace movement since World War II in Western Europe consisted of those people who had supported Nato.

On 30 November the so-called High Level Committee set up to propose measures to make the work of the Nordic Council and Council Ministers more effective delivered its report. The recommendations included strengthening the Nordic Council's Presidium and the role of the national Ministers for Nordic Cooperation, creating a common budget for Nordic matters instead of the present two, and giving higher priority in the Council's work to the main issues in Nordic cooperation.

COMECON

The leadership change in the Soviet Union was reflected in Comecon by divergence from its traditional schedules, by preparations for a summit meeting and by the replacement of its Executive Secretary. There had been no session of the Executive Committee in the second half of 1982: the 104th meeting had taken place during the annual Council in June (see AR 1982, p. 367), and that normally held in the autumn was cancelled (but had partially been replaced by a convocation of the permanent representatives in Moscow on 21-22 September 1982). The usual new year session (18-20 January in Moscow) was thus the 105th Executive. It patently took up one of Andropov's early priorities, the overhaul of the railways (the Soviet Minister having been dismissed amid sharp criticism soon after the leadership change): the communique said that the Committee 'stressed that one of the main tasks is a further strengthening of the material and technical base of transport, using the latest achievements of science and technology'. It was considered necessary, the communique added, 'to take additional measures to assure the uninterrupted movement of inter-member and transit freight, including the enlargement of the capacity of frontier transhipment points, the effective utilization of all modes of transport and the coordination of all current and long-term plans for transport'.

More fundamental to Andropov's new pressures was the need for a Comecon summit. He had met the East European Party leaders that month in Prague in the framework of the Warsaw Treaty Organization (see p. 353) and it was leaked that, with leaders from the three non-European member-states, they would reassemble as Comecon in May. A preparatory conference was soon held (8-9 February in Moscow), at which the permanent representatives (who all rank as Deputy Premiers) were joined by a Politburo member or a Central Committee Secretary from each member-state. One step below a full summit, the meeting was tersely reported. The complete text of its communique read: 'Questions were discussed concerning the further improvement and deepening of members' economic and scientific-technical collaboration. The meeting proceeded in an atmosphere of friendship and comradely mutual understanding'.

In the event, the summer passed without either a summit or the ordinary Council (which in recent years had taken place in June or July) and even in late August sources close to the Secretariat were saying that there was still no decision whether the October meeting would be a summit or the normal annual session. The Executive meeting of 5-6 September (the 107th) determined on the latter, which was duly held (the XXXVII, 16-18 October) in Berlin. It marked a certain new stage by accepting the retirement of Nikolai Faddeev, Executive Secretary since June 1958 and only the second in Comecon's history (Aleksandr Pavlov had been the first), and appointing Vyacheslav Sitkov, a Russian like his predecessors.

There was also an innovation in the session's issue of a wholly political statement in parallel with the usual communique on economic matters. The heads of government of Comecon members, 'having assembled to discuss current tasks of mutual economic cooperation, find it necessary in the present tense international situation to express the concern of their states with the danger of the further drastic intensification of the arms race, especially the nuclear arms race'. Adding their voice to that of their Foreign Ministers, who had just met in Sofia (13-14 October) and their Defence Ministers in Berlin (20 October) on Warsaw Treaty matters, they condemned Nato's planned deployment of new medium-range missiles with four economic arguments—that more arms spending would divert resources to the detriment of living standards, that such outlay would exacerbate inflation, that it would diminish assistance to the Third World and that the aggravation of tension reduced hopes of agreeing a new international economic order.

In the key-note speech to the session the Soviet Premier, Nikolai

Tikhonov, adverted to European stationing of the Pershing and Cruise missiles in regretting that the USSR would be compelled to take counter-measures to restore the military-strategic balance, but he was more concerned with the US 'use of international trade for putting political pressure on socialist countries'. He judged it 'expedient for member countries to agree on practical proposals aimed at the joint production of machinery and materials subject to Western embargoes'. Quoting data on Soviet deliveries of raw materials and energy in the first three years of the current quinquennial trade agreements, he called for 'no delay' in partners' paying for them 'with machinery, chemicals and consumer goods of better quality and more speedily than hitherto' and warned that in future 'our actual potentialities will largely depend on the ability of member countries to supply the products which are of importance for the Soviet Union'.

Despite some misgivings from the Romanian Premier, Constantin Dascalescu, the session approved more coordination among national science and research establishments, enhanced urgency for energy and raw material savings and a modernization programme for food and agriculture. In the latter field a report by the chairman of the USSR Gosplan on behalf of Comecon's Commission on Cooperation in Planning showed how badly farming had fared during the current five-year plans (1981-85). Even in Hungary, with an efficient marriage of private incentives with cooperative institutions, a drought-striken 1983 harvest (as the Hungarian Premier, György Lázár, observed) was cumulating on other economic difficulties, such as adverse terms of trade and inadequate liquidity in convertible currencies.

The balance of payments was in all Comecon Governments' minds. At the end of November the secretariat of the UN Economic Commission for Europe (ECE) published its estimate of the out-turn of East-West trade. In 1982, for the first time since the 1960s, East Europe and the USSR as a group had run a visible surplus with the developed market economies, and the same surplus ($900 million in each year) was expected in 1983. To achieve this remarkable turn-round (the cumulative trade deficit 1970 to 1981 had been $45,000 million), both in 1982 and in 1983 East Europe had cut its imports from the industrial West in all commodity groups, though the USSR imported more equipment, mainly for its major gas pipelines. Most Comecon members also exported more to the West; in particular, the USSR had to sell more oil to offset the price decline following Opec's decision in March.

The surpluses had been achieved—given the low rates of aggregate growth—at the expense of diminishing domestic availabilities. Such slimming could not go on for ever, and some Comecon Governments seriously considered joining the IMF (Poland's application was still barred by the United States but Hungary, Romania and Vietnam were already members). A general Comecon participation would enhance creditworthiness as well as provide at least standby lending. A paper by a faculty member of the Hungarian College of Finance and Accountancy (Maria Brüll, *Jahrbuch der Wirtschaft Osteuropas,* 1983) pointed out that if the other socialist countries joined they would need to be assured of at least 15·1 per cent of the quota (the existing socialist members aggregated 6 per cent) in order to enjoy the same rights of veto as other world groups, since the IMF required members with 85 per cent of the quota to concur on important issues.

Not a word was made public, however, about the Western intergovernmental finance institutions at either of the Council meetings of the International Bank for Economic Cooperation (the 57th in April, the 58th in October, both in Moscow). The later meeting celebrated IBEC's twentieth anniversary. Most of its settlements (95 per cent) were for members' mutual trade, and information was again deliberately withheld on how much of that was merely accountancy and short-term credit for bilateral trade. Comecon's aim to multilateralize payments among members in its 1971 *Complex Programme* (see AR 1971, pp. 367-8) was no nearer attainment. But it had to be reported that IBEC borrowing in convertible currency had been obliged, in the present international climate, to be reduced (from a peak of 2,600 million transferable roubles at the end of the 1970s). Commemorating its own twentieth anniversary, Comecon's Currency and Finance Commission (41st session in June in Varna) did hark back to the *Complex Programme*, claiming that it was still working towards its realization.

Comecon's Executive held one other session during the year—the 106th meeting on 28-30 June in Moscow. It reviewed progress under the 1982 agreement on cooperation on industrial robotics and looked ahead to the 1986-90 plans for coordination in energy, metallurgy, engineering, electronics, chemicals and transport. Robots were on the agenda also of the Committee on Material-Technical Supply (meeting in Kiev in March), particularly in storage, warehousing and transhipment.

Only two Comecon bodies seemed to have had direct relations with non-socialist international agencies. The Commission on Foreign Trade (April in Moscow) formulated Comecon's standpoint at UNCTAD VI, and in February the Secretariat signed an agreement with the ECE for cooperation in statistical research (the most useful project being a concordance of industrial classifications). The time was unripe for a resumption of trade negotiations with the European Communities (for the last meetings see AR 1980, pp. 362-3) but Hungary began informal contacts. On 19 April the Minister of Foreign Trade, Peter Veress, saw the EC Vice-President, Wilhelm Haferkamp, to discuss the status of mutual trade relations. A number of expert-level discussions (further raised when the EC President Gaston Thorn visited Budapest in December) led to the arrangement of a mission by Haferkamp to Hungary for January 1984.

Chapter 6

AFRICAN CONFERENCES AND ORGANIZATIONS—SOUTH-EAST ASIAN ORGANIZATIONS—CARIBBEAN ORGANIZATIONS—ORGANIZATION OF AMERICAN STATES

AFRICAN CONFERENCES AND ORGANIZATIONS

AFTER the dramas of 1982, when the Organization of African Unity teetered on the brink of disaster, with two abortive summits in Tripoli, this was the year of healing and reconciliation. In February the organization's Liberation Committee was able to meet in Arusha, Tanzania, but this was because it was only a committee, with a limited number of designated members, so the vexatious issues of the seating of Western Sahara and of which Chad delegation to seat did not arise. Shortly afterwards the OAU received further encouragement from the meeting in Nairobi of the 12-nation contact group which had been set up at the last Tripoli meeting to decide on the arrangements for holding the next summit. At this closed-door meeting it was decided to hold the delayed 19th summit in Addis Ababa, headquarters of the OAU, in May or June, without preconditions.

This decision, although enigmatic, seemed to contain the elements of the compromise which eventually happened. The major development was the decision to change the venue from Tripoli to Addis Ababa. Libya, itself a member of the Group, now seemed reconciled to the idea of not holding the meeting in Tripoli. The change of venue made it much less likely that the Chad question would be raised again seriously, as it had been very much a Libyan preoccupation, which Colonel Qadafi had exploited in his position as host. This left only the diplomatic problem of the Saharwi Arab Democratic Republic, which just over half the member states of the OAU had recognized. Although the only way out seemed to be to persuade the SADR not to attend, this problem had to be left to the very eve of the summit, which it was finally decided to hold in June.

In May there had been, on the one hand, a Moroccan-inspired move to have the meeting further postponed, and on the other hand, at the summit of the Economic Community of West African States (ECOWAS), a concerted move, inspired by Nigeria (which throughout the crisis had always held a centrist conciliatory position) to persuade as many ECOWAS leaders as possible to attend, arguing that the propensity to boycott on all sides was what had brought the OAU to its knees. In fact the formula worked, and the high-level attendance of heads of state, including thirteen of the sixteen ECOWAS leaders, all with their personal prestige engaged, helped to ensure that the old chemistry of African unity prevailed against the fissiparous tendencies.

Even so, the summit was two days late in starting, because of intensive negotiations among the leaders present at which the deep rifts in the organization became dangerously apparent. After one false start, at which a walk-out was narrowly avoided, and the holding of meetings of factions, a bold bid for reconciliation was engineered by the Ethiopian head of state, Mengistu Haile Mariam, and the Presidents of Algeria and Senegal, Chadli Benjedid and Abdou Diouf. This involved making the Ethiopian leader chairman of the OAU for the next year, which although logical enough since Ethiopia was the host country would both offend and therefore isolate the Libyan leader, who had been one of the hardliners supporting the SADR. At the same time the SADR agreed to withdraw 'temporarily and voluntarily' from the summit, thus obviating any boycotts, in return for some unspecified pressure on Morocco from friendly countries (of which Senegal was the most notable example) for the holding of the referendum on independence for the Western Sahara which had been agreed on at the OAU's summit in Nairobi in 1981.

This compromise had the desired effect of causing Libya to withdraw from the meeting, and, after a long debate, a resolution was produced confirming the Nairobi resolution, with an additional section, which the Moroccans were unhappy about, calling for talks between Morocco and the Polisario Front on how to hold the referendum, the holding of which the summit called for before the end of 1983. Passage of this resolution was facilitated by the revelation that there had already been secret contacts between Morocco and Polisario, still not officially admitted by Morocco.

The benign atmosphere of the summit, and its atmosphere of reconciliation, were somewhat tarnished at the end by a prolonged struggle over the election of a new secretary-general for the OAU, because Edem Kodjo, the outgoing secretary-general, was not standing again, having been at the centre of the Sahara controversy when it broke out in 1982. The main candidates were both from French-speaking Africa—Alioune Blondin Beye, Mali's Foreign Minister, and Paul Okoumba d'Okwatsegué, adviser to the President of Gabon—each of whom mustered approximately half the votes. Although it was a secret ballot, the split was said to have been broadly along the lines which had divided the organization on other issues, with 'progressives' supporting Mali and 'moderates' Gabon. An intervention by Botswana's Foreign Minister Archie Mogwe for four rounds failed to break the deadlock, and after more than twenty polls, with a fluctuating margin of not more than five votes, it was eventually decided to recognize the deadlock and appoint one of the assistant secretaries-general, Dr Peter Onu of Nigeria, as acting secretary-general for one year, until the 20th summit, which it was confirmed would be held in Conakry, capital of Guinea (see p. 227).

By the end of the year any euphoria that remained from Addis Ababa was on its way to being dissipated, since not only had a committee meeting in Addis Ababa at the end of September, designed to achieve progress on the Sahara question, broken down on the same issue of Morocco's refusal to meet Polisario, but talks on Chad had also run into serious hot water (see p. 231).

Chad also figured prominently on the somewhat nebulous agenda of the tenth summit of France and African countries, held in the French spa of Vittel in October. This attracted nearly 20 full members (the French-speaking countries less Cameroon and Madagascar) and almost as many observers, including anglophones, but the actual meetings were short and of limited value. Most of those attending said they valued going mainly for the contacts. Even the attempt to find a form of words to accommodate differing views on Chad failed to materialize (perhaps the very informality had led to a lack of preparation) and the communique was of a brevity unequalled even by preceding Franco-African summits. Vittel was followed immediately by the opening in Luxembourg of negotiations between the EEC and 63 countries of Africa, the Caribbean and Pacific (ACP) for a new Lomé Convention.

Africa's own regional groupings struggled along, in spite of the increasing problems the continent was facing, problems like drought and declining food production, graphically detailed at the 25th anniversary celebrations of the UN Economic Commission for Africa. In the west, ECOWAS digested and survived the tensions set up by Nigeria's mass expulsions of illegal immigrants in January (see p. 222). In Central Africa a new ten-nation grouping—the Economic Community of African States—finally saw light of day with a treaty signed in Libreville in October. The Community, stretching from Chad to Zaïre, did not include Angola, which said it was too preoccupied with its current war with South Africa. Angola was, however a member of the Southern African Development Coordination Conference (SADCC), which continued to plan its future in spite of South Africa's violent rearguard action against many of its members.

SOUTH-EAST ASIAN ORGANIZATIONS

Asean again sought to prevent international disapproval of the Vietnamese occupation of Cambodia from diminishing. Malaysia and Indonesia, which had originally believed that Vietnam might be persuaded to reach an accommodation on Cambodian independence, were driven by Vietnamese intransigence towards the Thai and Singaporean view that Hanoi would compromise only under unrelenting pressure. They were agreed that, while any Cambodian Government could properly be expected to be friendly towards Vietnam, it should be equally friendly towards Thailand and other neighbours.

Manoeuvring by Vietnam and Asean was concerned especially with the Non-Aligned conference in March and the UN General Assembly meeting in the autumn. The Vietnamese also wished to shift discussion from their own violation of Cambodian sovereignty to proposals for peaceful co-existence between Asean and the Indochinese countries as a bloc. The Vietnamese, knowing they could not hope to have the Heng Samrin regime accepted as representative of Kampuchea by the Non-Aligned meeting, concentrated on preventing the uneasy coalition of Prince Norodom Sihanouk's supporters, Son Sann's KPNLF and the Khmer Rouge, formed in 1982, from being represented. This they achieved; the meeting remitted the issue to its coordinating committee for report in 1985. The Vietnamese also tried to destroy the credibility of the non-communist components of the coalition. In this they were less successful. The KPNLF in particular emerged as a more effective military force than had been expected, despite its shortages of arms.

At the Non-Aligned meeting the Vietnamese introduced a proposal for private talks between the five Asean countries and Vietnam and Laos, excluding Cambodia. This attracted interest, which waned when Hanoi insisted that the Heng Samrin regime must participate in any negotiations, as opposed to private talks. Thailand and the Philippines were unimpressed by the proposal and the Chinese saw it as a ploy to gain recognition for an Indochina federation. The Vietnamese also again represented their usual rainy-season rotation of troops as a partial withdrawal.

Both Belgium, briefly, and then Australia attempted a mediatory role. An Australian visit to Vietnam in July convinced Canberra that Hanoi had no intention of withdrawing its troops until 'the threat from China' and 'the threat from Thailand' had been removed, the Chinese had carried out various stipulations, including withdrawal from the Paracel Islands, and 'the self-determination of the Cambodian people' had been respected, by which the Vietnamese meant recognition of the regime they had installed. A subsequent meeting of the Vietnamese, Laotian and Heng Samrin Foreign Ministers adopted an unyielding stance, claiming so strong a position that they need make no concessions.

Asean members also made proposals which the Vietnamese rejected. In the spring they suggested that the Thai Foreign Minister should visit Hanoi if the Vietnamese would withdraw their troops 30 km from the Thai border, and in September they proposed a phased, partial Vietnamese withdrawal, starting with areas adjoining the Thai border, a ceasefire guaranteed by an international peace-keeping force in the zones evacuated, Khmer refugees being permitted to return to them, and then an international conference to discuss reconstruction. The Vietnamese and the Heng Samrin regime refused to allow the UN High Commission for Refugees to organize a safe return home of Cambodian refugees; instead, a renewed flow from the villages to the refugee camps started under Vietnamese pressure. A peace-keeping force was also vetoed and the Vietnamese told the Australians that the UN could not participate in a settlement while the coalition held the Cambodian UN seat. On 27 October the General Assembly voted by 105 votes to 23 to continue to accept the credentials of the coalition delegation.

CARIBBEAN ORGANIZATIONS

At the ninth meeting of the Standing Committee of Ministers responsible for foreign affairs in June, it was declared that 'only through genuine respect for, and recognition of, principles of the non-use of force, non-interference and non-intervention in the internal affairs of states, could the peoples of this region hope to achieve their just goals for a better life'.

Problems were created for regional trade by Jamaica's multitiered exchange rates and the floating of the Barbadian currency against the Jamaican dollar in response. Trinidad and Tobago, too, decided accordingly to reduce its imports from Caricom countries which put restrictions on its exports.

At the fourth heads of government meeting of Caricom, held on 4-7 July in Trinidad, it was decided that Barbados would receive at least US$20 million of the US$65 million owing to it under the Caribbean Multilateral Clearing Facility (CMCF) and that the CMCF would be restructured and become a legal entity. Caricom adopted a report on a comprehensive Regional Energy Plan which among other features provided for rationalization of oil refineries and called for an estimated US$16·2 million funding strategy over the period 1984-86. The questions of the 'designation' of one of Caricom's four national airlines as the regional carrier and the rationalization of regional transport were not resolved. Arrangements were made to ensure that the University of the West Indies (UWI) was paid the TT$55 million owed to it, and satisfactory guarantees were offered to the Organization of Eastern Caribbean States (OECS) in the restructuring of the UWI process. The meeting failed to provide solutions to the problems caused by West Indian cricketers' accepting contracts to play in South Africa, and provided unsatisfactory responses to the sensitive issue of location of industries.

On 1 October the OECS established a Central Bank, replacing the 18-year-old Eastern Caribbean Currency Authority. The Caribbean Chamber of Industry and Commerce planned to establish a private sector bank with initial equity of US$2 million, but its launch was delayed by incompleted negotiations with USAID for US$12 million. The

Caribbean Development Bank (CDB) and the International Development Association signed an agreement under which the CDB would provide sub-loans to the Eastern Caribbean states totalling 6·5 million special drawing rights.

Trinidad and Tobago, a significant importer of Caricom goods, caused further consternation in the region's manufacturing sector when it tightened its foreign exchange, licensing and trade regulations, in a move to protect its economy. Many workers were laid off in Caricom countries affected by difficulties in getting orders from and products into Trinidad.

Several Caricom countries received certificates from the USA entitling them to receive benefits under the Caribbean Basin Initiative programme, including duty-free access for most goods in the US market.

THE ORGANIZATION OF AMERICAN STATES

The Organization of American States was effectively excluded from all the major issues of 1984. As a member of the UN Security Council, Nicaragua took direct to that body in March its complaint about United States backing for the FDN guerrillas. Initiative for a peaceful settlement in Central America rested with the so-called Contadora Group (see p. 74), and President Reagan's call for it to be transferred to the OAS (26 July) gained no support. It was not from the OAS but from the hitherto insignificant Organization of Eastern Caribbean States that President Reagan obtained his 'mandate' for the invasion of Grenada on 25 October. This act was in breach of the OAS Charter, yet on 26 October the Special Meeting of Consultation failed to agree. At the opening of the General Assembly, held in Washington on 14-17 November, the Secretary-General, Sr Alejandro Orfila, submitted his resignation. On 17 November the Foreign Ministers adopted by acclamation a resolution sponsored by the Contadora Group calling for a general peace agreement in Central America and urging other nations 'to desist in carrying out acts that will obstruct the peace negotiations', but US Secretary of State Shultz did not attend.

Chapter 7

THE NON-ALIGNED MOVEMENT

THE seventh summit of the Non-Aligned Movement, which had been due in September 1982 in Baghdad but was postponed because of the Iran-Iraq war (see AR 1982, pp. 376-77), eventually took place in New Delhi on 7-12 March, preceded by a Foreign Ministers' meeting.

Bahamas, Barbados, Colombia and Vanuatu were admitted to membership of the Movement at the summit, bringing the total to 101 members, of which only St Lucia and Kampuchea were unrepresented in Delhi. Sixty kings, sheikhs, Presidents and Prime Ministers attended, the rest being represented by deputies or by Foreign Ministers, making it the largest 'summit', in numbers and in status, that the world had ever seen. Along with the 99 full participants, 16 countries, four liberation movements, the Vatican, the International Red Cross and 19 intergovernmental organs sent 'observer' or 'guest' delegations.

The Foreign Ministers disposed of some controversial membership questions before the full summit opened. The explicit threat of expulsion from the Movement which had hung over Egypt, because of the peace treaty with Israel, since the last summit in 1979 was lifted, with President Mubarak coming to Delhi. After an extensive debate the Foreign Ministers reaffirmed the 1979 decision to leave the Kampuchean seat vacant and decided that the question should not be debated again at the summit. Two African questions which had caused a crisis for the OAU in 1982 (see AR 1982, pp. 368-71) were disposed of quietly. Habré's Foreign Minister, Idriss Miskine, was seated for Chad, while no attempt was made to obtain membership for Western Sahara.

In Mrs Gandhi's opening speech, in the debates and in the final documentation the summit gave priority to economic questions. A summary of the deepening crisis as 'a slide into a protracted world-wide depression', which was 'threatening to assume unmanageable proportions and to become irreversible', was contained in a Declaration on Collective Action for Global Prosperity. This went on to urge two responses to the crisis: a short-term programme of immediate measures, 'to be taken on an emergency basis' and a start to a long-term review of the structure of the world economy and its institutions in global negotiations at the UN. The short-term programme contained 40 specific, detailed, practical measures on aid, debts, the IMF's resources, the policies of the World Bank and the IDA, trade, commodities, energy and food. The final item called for an international conference to discuss 'comprehensive reform of the existing inequitable and outdated international monetary and financial system'.

The Non-Aligned also strongly reaffirmed their commitment to mutual cooperation for 'collective self-reliance' among the developing countries. However, a review of the 'Action Programme' showed the failure to make significant practical progress in most areas since the last summit. This was partly due to the decision in 1979 to abolish the annual ministerial meetings of the Coordinating Bureau, which used to review the Action Programme. In May 1981 the Group of 77 had for the first time moved beyond its role as a UN caucus group into promotion of joint cooperation (ECDC) with its Caracas Programme, which included establishing a small secretariat in New York. The Non-Aligned summit, recognising the need to coordinate and avoid duplication between the two programmes, approved a division of the subject areas between them. The Non-Aligned took seventeen subjects and the Group of 77 took six, but these included all the vital ones—commodities, trade, finance, food and energy.

In the summit's Political Declaration, Indian influence was shown by the heightened emphasis on disarmament and concern over the dangers of nuclear weapons. As always Southern Africa and the Middle East were central concerns. The Movement rejected 'the extraneous issue of linkage between Namibia's independence and the withdrawal of Cuban forces from Angola'. On the Middle East the most notable point was the absence of any mention of the Reagan Plan (see AR 1982, pp. 498-9), which, along with endorsement of the Fez Plan, failure to recommend Israel's expulsion from the UN and implicit acceptance of the Israeli-Egyptian Peace Treaty represented willingness by the Non-Aligned to endorse a general peace with Israel, provided it withdrew to its 1967 boundaries.

Other notable new points since the last summit were support for claims by Mauritius to Diego Garcia (see p. 273); an 'urgent call for withdrawal of foreign troops from Afghanistan'; a special appeal, issued separately, to Iran and Iraq to bring an immediate end to their war; support for the moves to form a new Latin American regional organization without the United States, to replace the OAS; support for 'Argentina's right to have its sovereignty over the Malvinas', but also recognizing Britain's desire 'to take due account of the interests of the population' of the Falklands; strong support for Guyana against Venezuela's claim to its territory; a threat to take counter-action against countries not respecting the Law of the Sea Convention; and extension of the 'common heritage of mankind' principle to both outer space and Antarctica.

Concern at the increased conflict in Central America had led the Non-Aligned to convene the fifth, special, ministerial meeting of the Coordinating Bureau in Managua in January, and alarm over United States actions was evident at the summit. When the US-Caribbean intervention in Grenada occurred the Coordinating Bureau in New York immediately met, issuing a sharp condemnation and calling for withdrawal.

Five countries, Iraq, Syria, Libya, North Korea and Nigeria, had offered to be the host to the next Non-Aligned summit due in 1986. The majority of the members favoured going to Baghdad, provided that the Iran-Iraq war had ended by then. All the existing members of the Coordinating Bureau, except Lesotho, were re-elected and new members were endorsed, bringing its size up to 74 countries. At the start of the Delhi summit, Mrs Gandhi took over from President Castro as chairman of the Movement until 1986. Using this position she called upon all heads of governments in the world to attend the UN General Assembly session and 38 leaders or their deputies, along with 60 Foreign Ministers, did so.

XII RELIGION

CHURCH AND BOMB. Continuing anxiety by the churches about nuclear weapons was revealed throughout the year. On 10 February the General Synod of the Church of England rejected by 338 votes to 100 the unilateral nuclear disarmament line advocated by its policy committee the previous October (see AR 1982, p. 381). The Archbishop of Canterbury, Dr Robert Runcie, claimed a 'moral seriousness in the multilateral approach', fearing that unilateral action would 'actually undermine the negotiations now in progress in Geneva', negotiations which broke down before the end of the year. To a general motion for reduction of nuclear arsenals Bishop Hugh Montefiore of Birmingham proposed an amendment to repudiate the first use of nuclear weapons in any circumstances, since a first strike would be 'not defence but naked aggression in the form of pre-emptive action'. 'The nature of the act', he said, 'is evil. It is deliberately to loose hell on earth.' The Synod approved this amendment by 275 votes to 222, referring it to discussion in the dioceses.

In May the Scottish Episcopal Church urged the policy of no-first-nuclear-strike and the rejection of Cruise and Trident missiles. The general assembly of the Presbyterian Church of Scotland demanded a freeze on the development and deployment of nuclear arms, declaring them to be morally wrong. The Methodist Conference in June received, without commending, a unilateralist report, but voted with little opposition against Cruise missiles and for a nuclear freeze. The United Reformed Church, on 25 May, was the first English denomination to adopt unilateralism, voting by 381 votes to 180 for the removal of nuclear bases from Britain. American Roman Catholic bishops (see AR 1982, p. 381) called in May for a halt in expansion of nuclear arsenals, but Catholic bishops in West Germany upheld the right to use the threat of nuclear retaliation as a deterrent to war, and French bishops supported this view as 'morally acceptable for the time being', though Protestant and Jewish leaders in France were strongly critical. The World Council of Churches, at its governing assembly at Vancouver in August, declared the production and deployment of nuclear weapons to be crimes against humanity, opposing Cruise and Pershing together with Soviet intermediate range missiles. An estimated two million people demonstrated against new missiles in Western Europe, Christian organizations uniting with others.

In Britain, both criticism and support came for Mgr Bruce Kent, general secretary of the Campaign for Nuclear Disarmament (CND). In

May a letter circulated by Archbishop Bruno Heim, apostolic pro-nuncio in London, described Mgr Kent and unilateralists as 'blinkered idealists' or 'useful idiots' for the Russians. This attack was condemned as 'unbelievable' and 'offensive' by the Roman Catholic auxiliary bishop of Westminister, and Cardinal Hume indicated his respect for Bruce Kent's integrity. In November Mgr Kent appeared at a conference of the British Communist Party, praising it and the Society of Friends for supporting CND during slack years; this brought an outraged accusation from the Defence Secretary, Michael Heseltine, of 'carrying naivety to the point of recklessness'. In an article in *The Times* on 17 November (see DOCUMENTS) Cardinal Hume, Archbishop of Westminster, declared his belief that possession of nuclear missiles need not conflict with Christian ethics. Its moral acceptability, however, rested 'solely on condition that it constitutes a stage towards disarmament'. Mgr Kent commented: 'in practical terms I don't think we're very far apart, except that CND believes British nuclear weapons serve no purpose and should be removed unilaterally.'

DOMESTIC ISSUES. Modifying its traditional attempt to operate the strictest marital discipline in Christendom, the Anglican General Synod in November approved procedures for the remarriage of divorced persons in church, practised already in ten overseas Anglican provinces. Anglo-Catholic opponents of the scheme recognized remarriage only in the Roman Catholic sense of annulment of the first union as technically invalid. Eastern Orthodox churches had long permitted divorce for incompatibility and by mutual consent, and the Free Churches gave similar options, remarrying more than 16,000 persons annually in Britain. The Anglican procedures now required a dispensation from the bishop, following investigation into the culpability of either partner in a previous marriage, sincerity of 'repentance', care of former wife and children, and acceptance of the permanence of church marriage. Since the Church's Synod in 1981 had approved remarriage in principle, the Archbishop supported the new scheme, saying that the church could not explain to couples how it accepted 'something in principle which it is either unwilling or unable to do in practice'.

An opinion survey showed that most people in Britain wanted to get married and make the marriage work. The divorce rate had become stable at about one marriage in three, compared to 50 per cent in America. There were fewer teenage marriages and pre-marital conceptions. Cohabitation had increased but was considerably lower than in many European states.

In a national referendum on 7 September voters in the Irish Republic approved by a two to one majority a draft amendment, strongly supported by the Roman Catholic Church, but opposed by Protestant and Jewish organizations, to enshrine in the constitution the country's already legal ban on abortion (see p. 147).

In Northern Ireland sectarian tensions increased on 21 November when gunmen from a new Catholic Reaction Force entered a Pentecostal church at Darkley in South Armagh and sprayed the congregation with bullets, killing three and injuring seven others. Cardinal Tomas O'Fiaich went to visit bereaved families with Protestant clergy and declared: 'Don't dare to claim the name Catholic for your band of evildoers.'

On 12 July, the eve of a parliamentary debate on the restoration of capital punishment (see p. 28). the Anglican General Synod voted by 407 votes to 36 against the proposal. It was argued that execution was 'to take upon ourselves the right that belongs to God alone.' Roman Catholic, Methodist, Reformed and Baptist churches and the Society of Friends also strongly opposed the death penalty.

PAPAL CONCERNS. Pope John Paul II visited Central America from 2-9 March with several aims: regulating the involvement of the Church, especially priests, in politics; urging non-violent solutions to social problems; and promoting unity among all Christians, most urgently between the established Church and so-called 'popular churches' with a 'liberation theology'.

In Nicaragua the Pope had previously asked five priests in government office to resign but they had disregarded his request. Welcoming him a government official stated that 'our experience shows that one can be a believer and a consistent revolutionary', but an open-air Mass at Managua was interrupted by cries of 'people's power' and 'a church on the side of the poor'.

In Guatemala the Pope was received by the 'born again' Protestant General Ríos Montt, overthrown in August, who asked the pontiff to call on Catholic clergy to refrain from politics. In reply His Holiness said that the Church 'continues to raise its voice to condemn injustice and to denounce abuses'. In a later sermon he advised peasants to 'organize associations for the defence of your rights'. The Pope described Haiti as a country full of 'division, injustice, excessive inequality, misery, hunger and fear', and called for the freedom of the press.

In February the Polish Primate, Josef Glemp, was made a cardinal, and from 16 June the Pope began his deferred visit to Poland (see p. 110), during which he met the Prime Minister General Jaruzelski and the Solidarity leader Lech Walesa, urging reconciliation of government and people.

In the Philippines in February Roman Catholic bishops issued a pastoral letter critical of official corruption, militarization and violation of human rights, warning that 'insurgency is the response of a segment of Philippines society that despairs of righting such wrongs'. In South Africa Roman Catholic, Methodist and other English-speaking churches criticized the Government's proposed new constitution (see DOCUMENTS), which excluded blacks from the vote, declaring 'it is an affront to the people concerned and ensures that racial discrimination will continue'.

For the 500th anniversary of the birth of Martin Luther there were celebrations throughout Germany and in many other lands, and he was hailed by the Communist Government of East Germany as a people's hero and leader of 'the first revolution of the bourgeoisie'. The Pope praised Luther for his 'deep religious sense' and on 12 December visited and preached in the Lutheran church in Rome, addressing the congregation in German as 'distinguished brothers and sisters in Christ'. In May, speaking to scientists in Rome, the Pope declared that the Church had erred in condemning the astronomer Galileo Galilei 350 years ago.

JEWISH TENSIONS. Only 1,300 Jews were allowed to emigrate from the Soviet Union, the lowest total in 20 years, contrasting with 51,000 in 1979, the year before the Olympic Games.

In Israel a new political party, Matzah, 'Rally of Religious Zionism', was established in February by Rabbi Haim Druckman, formerly of the National Religious Party. Matzah had support among the Shvut Yisrael, 'Whole Land of Israel', which was opposed to any territorial concessions by Israel. Jewish zealots harassed Christian and Muslim neighbours in Jerusalem, daubing swastikas on holy places. A Russian Orthodox convent at Ein Karem, traditional birthplace of John the Baptist near Jerusalem, was attacked by fire, and in May two Russian nuns were murdered there. In April Muslim Arabs were beaten near a Yeshiva (religious school) in Jerusalem, and by December harassment became so intense that the civil authorities asked the army to take over the Yeshiva, saying 'this particular school is populated by students of such violence that they have even antagonized other ultra-orthodox Jews in the Old City'. Liberal Jews deplored the 'inevitable expansion of the Zionist universe'.

SIKH STRUGGLES. After opposition from evangelicals and Anglo-Catholics, the Church Commissioners on 23 February allowed the sale of a redundant church, St Luke's, Southampton, for use as a Sikh temple. On 24 March the House of Lords ruled that the Sikhs were an ethnic group entitled to protection by the 1976 Race Relations Act, holding that Sikhs were more than a religious sect, indeed 'almost a nation', with long history, cultural tradition and social customs 'often but not necessarily associated with religious observance' (see also Pt. XIV, Ch. 2).

In India militant Sikhs, agitating for Sikh political autonomy in the Punjab, attacked Hindus and their temples.

ISLAMIC FUNDAMENTALISM. In August Ayatollah Khomeini of Iran declared that Islam was the 'religion of the sword' which could 'survive only through war', and he sent armed pilgrims to Mecca to spread the Shia cause. Sunni Muslims retorted that Islam was the 'religion of reason', and that Allah was merciful and compassionate as well as avenger and enforcer. In Iran pressures grew on Sunnis to be converted to Shi'ism, and in June ten Baha'i women were executed for their faith. In Iraq six leading Shia clergy were executed in August.

In Yugoslavia accusations of trying to establish the first fundamentalist Islamic state in Europe in Bosnia-Herçegovina brought long terms of imprisonment to 12 Muslims. Sunni Islamic law was imposed in the Sudan, and in December received public demonstration in Khartoum when two thieves had their right hands amputated. Advertisements in British papers from a Muslim Solidarity Campaign congratulated the Sudanese President for 'decolonizing the country's socio-legal system' and giving a 'living example of the Divine mercy'. In the British House of Lords a Bill sought to prohibit operations for female circumcision (clitoridectomy), common in some Islamic and African countries and sometimes performed elsewhere. Lord Chancellor Hailsham regarded this practice as 'grievous bodily harm' which could lead to charges of manslaughter or murder.

CHINA. The Archbishop of Canterbury visited churches in China in December and urged Christian teachers to respect local customs. Estimates of the numbers of Christians in China varied, Roman Catholics at between three and six million, Protestants at around three million (see AR 1981, p. 380). It was officially stated that 120 Catholic and 40 Protestant churches were in use, and some that had been closed or damaged had been opened and restored. There was tension between churches in communion with Rome and the Patriotic Catholic Association, despite appeals from the Pope for opening talks. Priests with whom Rome still had contact, mostly Jesuits, opposed the Patriotic church, going underground if necessary. In March two priests of the 'loyal church' were imprisoned, accused of endangering the sovereignty and security of the country. 'Patriotic' Catholic seminaries were opened near Peking and Shanghai.

An Institute of Islamic Theology was reopened in Peking with 40 students. 160,000 copies of the Koran had been printed in the last two years.

BOOKS

A New Dictionary of Christian Theology, edited by Alan Richardson and John Bowden, and *A Dictionary of Christian Spirituality*, edited by Gordon Wakefield, were hailed as major events in English religious publishing and covered many subjects with readable scholarly exposition. Barnabas Lindars, in *Jesus Son of Man*, examined this enigmatic title from the Gospels, and Owen Chadwick in *Hensley Henson* related the story of a modern turbulent bishop. *The Reader's Bible*, from Reader's Digest Publications, condensed the full scripture by 'smoothing away' parts regarded as dull, repetitive or irrelevant from the Revised Standard Version.

Unholy Warfare, edited by David Martin and Peter Mullen, brought together powerful articles on the church and the bomb, and in *Walking on Water* Jo Garcia and Sara Maitland presented women talking about spirituality. In *Apartheid is a Heresy* John de Grouchy presented essays by nine of South Africa's leading theologians condemning the doctrine. Alan Race in *Christians and Religious Pluralism* discussed problems in the encounter of faiths, distinguishing Exclusivism, Inclusivism and the Pluralism which he favoured. Martin Lings wrote a biography of *Muhammad*, based on the earliest sources but without critical apparatus, and Louis Massignon's *The Passion of al-Hallaj, Mystic and Martyr of Islam*, in four volumes translated by Herbert Mason, was hailed as a very great book but based on the mistaken thesis that Hallaj deliberately suffered and died as a 'substitute saint' for the Muslim community. Christoph von Fürer-Haimendorf's *Tribes of India* crowned this scholar's forty years of industrious ethnography and concern for the survival of India's tribal peoples.

XIII THE SCIENCES

Chapter 1

SCIENCE, MEDICINE AND TECHNOLOGY

PARTICLE PHYSICS. In January an international team of physicists working in the European Nuclear Physics Centre, CERN, near Geneva, announced their discovery of a fundamental particle new to science. Its existence had been predicted by theorists and the finding of it was a major step towards the vindication of Grand Unification Theory, which attempts to unify the four forces of nature—gravity, electromagnetism, the weak and the strong nuclear forces—into a single mathematical framework. Several years earlier Abdus Salam, Steven Weinberg and Sheldon Glashow had constructed a theory which united the weak nuclear force and the electromagnetic force. The discovery of the so-called W boson, announced in January 1983, was experimental confirmation of this theoretical unification.

The W boson and another particle also discovered at CERN later in the year, the Z boson, had been predicted to exist and to carry the weak nuclear force between other particles in the same way as photons, particles of light, were known to carry electromagnetic force. But because the W and Z particles were many times heavier than photons—for which reason they were nicknamed 'heavy light'—it required enormous energies to produce them in a detectable form. This was done at CERN by colliding beams of particles of matter and anti-matter, each travelling at nearly the speed of light, with each other head-on.

On 13 September the Presidents of France and Switzerland formally inaugurated the construction of the largest piece of scientific equipment in the world, the Large Electron Positron Ring, LEP. When completed, this would be used to collide forms of matter and anti-matter other than those already being collided at CERN.

ENERGY. The public inquiry into the application of the UK Central Electricity Generating Board to build a power station powered by a pressurised water reactor (PWR), the first of its kind in the UK, at Sizewell in Suffolk opened on 11 January. In PWRs one circulation of water, under high pressure to raise its boiling-point, removed heat from the reactor core and passed this through a heat exchanger to another circulation of water which was turned into steam to drive turbogenerators. This design differed from that used in all previous British nuclear power stations, in which heat was taken away from the core by circulating gas. Opponents of the project included members of the National Union of Mineworkers, engineers favouring the British advanced gas-cooled reactor (AGR) design and objectors who feared a major accident like that which had occured at Three Mile Island in the USA (see AR 1979, p. 57). The supporters of the PWR claimed that worldwide its overall safety record was good, and that a station based on one could be built and operated more cheaply than an AGR station. PWR work would also provide the British nuclear power industry with badly-needed export opportunities. Supporters also claimed that the costs of operating PWR-based power stations were potentially lower than those of any other source of energy in the UK, a claim that was hotly disputed. The inquiry was still in progress at the end of the year.

Important steps towards power from nuclear fusion were taken during the year. In June the experimental fusion reactor, the Joint European Torus (JET), at Culham in Oxfordshire was started up, with a current of 60,000 amps passed through hydrogen gas for one-tenth of a second to ionize the gas. By November the experimenters were using currents of 1,300,000 amps for more than one second, demonstrably rapid progress towards the long-term target of a self-sustaining fusion reaction between the nuclei of hydrogen atoms stripped of their electrons by the ionizing current. At the Massachusetts Institute of Technology scientists announced on 7 November that in experiments using another type of experimental fusion reactor they had demonstrated that it was possible to control a plasma—a gas made entirely of ionized, electrically-charged particles—in such a way that the fusion energy generated would be more than the energy consumed.

On 23 September a small wind-driven power station was ceremonially inaugurated on the Isle of Orkney, as a pilot plant designed to prepare the way for a large wind-power plant on the same site in the future. This cautious endorsement of wind as an alternative source of energy was at least matched by the decision, announced in mid-June, to provide a further £12·5 million for further development of the 'hot dry rocks' project at Camborne in Cornwall. This had reached a crucial stage in experiments in pumping water down and up holes drilled deep into granite rocks, gathering heat along the way.

TECHNOLOGY. A marriage between the two fastest-advancing technologies, microelectronics and biotechnology, was symbolized during the year by the development and testing of biosensors by Cambridge Life Sciences and other companies. In biosensors, enzymes extracted from living bacteria, used to detect and measure small quantities of various compounds for diagnostic and other purposes, were teamed with 'silicon chips' which would either display the data gathered digitally or use it in feed-back systems for such purposes as controlling the rate of administration of insulin to diabetic patients.

The state of the art reached by contemporary 'chips' was illustrated by the launch of the Inmos Transputer project, to make a computer with processor, memory and all connections crammed into a wafer the size of a fingernail but with the power of a hundred home computers, its circuitry being as complex as a complete street plan of London with gas, electricity and sewer services superimposed.

Superconductor materials of the near future were demonstrated at a seminar held at Malvern, England, in September when leading experts in optoelectronics presented their futuristic ideas to a group of young researchers. The use of gallium arsenide rather than silicon as a semiconductor made it possible to miniaturize components much further and so to speed up computing by shortening the distances over which electric currents had to travel, and also to replace current with light for some computing purposes, with still greater advantages in operating speed.

'The Compassionate Face of Technology' was the title given by Britain's enthusiastic Minister for Information Technology, Mr Kenneth Baker, in a widely-reported speech at the annual meeting of the British Association for the Advancement of Science held in September, in which he summed up several developments which together demonstrated how IT, as his field was becoming known, could raise the quality of life for the handicapped. Educational aids of several kinds using microprocessors, the development of which was being government funded, were quoted, as was the development of equipment used to help deaf children to speak properly and to allow blind children to hear the letters they had keyed into Braille machines. Mr Baker also praised Vistel, a device which enabled deaf people to plug into a telephone and send messages down a line, various devices to enable frail, elderly people to summon aid more easily, and the equipment being developed to allow paralysed people to walk again with the aid of electronically programmed stimulation of their muscles.

SPACE AND ASTRONOMY. The second American space shuttle, *Challenger*, made its first four flights during the year, following five missions using its predecessor *Columbia*. The first mission ended successfully for the shuttle itself on 9 April, but a communications satellite which had been launched from *Challenger* as part of the preparations for a later mission went into an irregular orbit. This Tracking and Data Relay satellite, known as Teeders, was to have been one of two to be used to relay data to and from the European Spacelab, due to be carried into orbit later in the year. But NASA decided not to launch the second Teeders at all, fearing it might suffer the same fate as the first one. After an anxious few weeks, however, ground controllers ingeniously managed to lift the satellite into the right orbit by firing its attitude control jets. Meanwhile *Challenger* made its second flight, ending on 24 June, during which Canadian and Indonesian communications satellites were launched, emphasizing the now-routine use of the shuttle system for such commercial launches. Challenger's third flight, starting on 30 August, launched an Indian communications satellite.

A considerable amount of scientific research was carried out on all these missions but the fourth shuttle mission of the year, using the by-then-reserviced *Columbia*, opened what for once it was true to call a new era in space. This ninth shuttle mission carried the first Spacelab, a sophisticated laboratory built by the nations of the European Space Agency (ESA). West Germany bore more than half the overall cost and a West German scientist, Ulf Merbold, flew with the mission, which began on 28 October and lasted ten days, one longer than originally planned because of two computer failures which had to be investigated before landing. The Spacelab consisted of two main units fitting closely into the long cargo bay of *Columbia*—an enclosed air-pressurized pod where scientists were able to work in shirt sleeves and an outer pallet exposed to space, a miniature open terrace where telescopes and other instruments were deployed. Even on this first Spacelab flight, when much time had to be devoted to testing the laboratory's systems, more scientific work was done than in all the three, much longer missions of the previous most sophisticated space laboratory, the American Skylab.

The 70-odd experiments on board were equally divided between ESA and NASA. About half were concerned with materials processing in weightless conditions, but the most important single group of experiments consisted of those attempting to establish the cause of space sickness, the nausea and vomiting which had affected about half of all the astronauts and cosmonauts and which threatened the whole future of work in weightlessness for ordinary scientists. Other research included ultraviolet astronomy studying the birth and death of stars and investigations of the composition of the upper atmosphere.

Even the occasional equipment failures on the mission were hailed as an argument for the value of man in space, because the crew—led by veteran flight commander astronaut John Young—were able to do repairs. Overall the mission was rated a great success, with most of the research targets achieved. The first Spacelab was capable of forty-nine more flights and a second Spacelab was planned.

On 16 June the sixth attempt was made to launch the big European space rocket *Ariane*, a three-stage vehicle designed to put large satellites into orbit for ESA as a commercial rival to the shuttle. *Ariane* had suffered two complete failures out of the first five launches of the system and was coming to be regarded as unreliable. Its sixth flight, however, was flawless, successfully placing in orbit a European communications satellite and another satellite for amateur radio enthusiasts and establishing *Ariane* as a genuine rival to the shuttle for the expected growing numbers of launchings of communications, Earth resources survey and other satellites.

On 23 January the main part of a Russian satellite powered by a nuclear reactor, *Cosmos 1402*, fell out of orbit. Fortunately the satellite's radioactive fuel caused no ill effects, though it led to renewed concern about the likelihood of other such dangerous descents, amplified by the American decision, made during the course of the year, to follow Russia in developing nuclear reactors for use in space.

Two Russian space probes, *Venera 15* and *16*, arrived in orbit around Venus in mid-October. Unlike some earlier Russian probes they did not send down landing modules but instead mapped from orbit the surface of Venus, hidden by cloud, using radar. Their pictures revealed intense geological activity on the planet's surface. American radar astronomers, using radio waves transmitted from the huge radio aerial in Puerto Rico, also mapped parts of the surface of Venus by radar and published pictures showing a volcano which had clearly recently poured lava into a canyon, and also providing evidence of violent geological activity in the shape of mountain building.

An international infra-red astronomy satellite, *IRAS*, was built in the Netherlands, launched on 26 January by NASA from California and tracked by the UK Rutherford-Appleton laboratory, where its data were received and first analysed. It gave a view of stars too cool to emit visible light which were previously unknown. *IRAS* had a highly successful career before it stopped transmitting on 22 November. The satellite observed many stars being formed, plotted more than two million infra-red sources in all, identified a likely system of planets around a star, Vega, 26 light years from Earth, revealed rings of dust around the entire solar system and located an asteroid which some calculations suggested might collide with Earth in AD 2115.

In December, NASA, which had launched the first satellite to be built by engineers at Surrey University, *UOSAT 1*, confirmed that it would launch a second *UOSAT* for the university, but gave the Surrey team the tightest-ever schedule: their second satellite had to be ready for launch in March 1984. Like *UOSAT 1*, *UOSAT 2* was to be used for educational purposes by schools and colleges as well as for transmitting messages for radio amateurs and for some research purposes. Both satellites were unusual in that they relayed some data by voice, using synthetic speech with a vocabulary of about 120 words on *UOSAT 1* and rather more planned for *UOSAT 2*.

In June work began on the construction of a new 'millimetre telescope' on the Mauna Kea mountain in Hawaii. This was to be the world's largest radio telescope, designed to operate at very short wavelengths, shorter than one millimetre, the wavelengths at which clouds of dust and gas between stars mainly emit radiation. The new telescope, planned to be complete in 1986, was paid for 80 per cent by the

British and 20 per cent by the Dutch governments. Its main purpose was to study the processes of star and galaxy formation from clouds of dust and gas.

Astronomers used telescopes in Chile and Australia to take pictures of a strange object which appeared to be an elliptical galaxy producing violent outpourings of energy. Some astrophysicists conjectured that this energy was produced by dust falling into a 'black hole' at the galaxy's centre. Most exciting was the fact that the object was relatively near at hand; similar objects had been seen before, but only at very great distances.

In a surprise announcement on 23 March, President Reagan declared that the USA was to embark on a vast scientific programme, intended to devise a defensive system against Soviet ballistic missiles. In September 1982 the US Defense Department had awarded contracts to three aerospace companies to develop technology for short wavelength lasers, which seemed likely to be the principal anti-missile weapons, the contracts being part of a general endorsement by the US Defense Secretary, Caspar Weinberger, of the overall development of technology for defence against intercontinental ballistic missiles. During the year American prototype laser weapons were tested against both missiles and unmanned aircraft. Opinions differed widely as to their probable effect on the balance of nuclear deterrence.

WEATHER AND CLIMATE. Two reports published during the year by American organizations, the Environment Protection Agency and the National Academy of Sciences, predicted likely serious problems due to the warming-up of the Earth through the so-called 'greenhouse effect', caused, it was feared, by a build-up of carbon dioxide through the burning of fossil fuels. This acted as a suntrap like glass in a greenhouse, letting in the sun's heat but not allowing it to be re-radiated. This, both reports said, would eventually cause temperature rises of up to five degrees Centigrade, with consequent melting of polar ice, flooding of coastal areas and inland drought. Research by the UK Antarctic Survey and the UK Climatic Research Unit, published in December in *Nature*, confirmed that a noticeable global warming had already taken place over the past twenty years and attributed this to increased carbon dioxide from fossil fuel burning. Increased monitoring to give early warning of any serious consequences of the 'greenhouse effect' was recommended by both authorities.

PALAEONTOLOGY AND BIOLOGY. Half a skull, some bits of lower jaw and an assortment of teeth found in Pakistan were reconstructed into a creature which, it was believed, represented the important missing link between whales and the land. Whales, in their evolution from land-living mammals, had gone through an intermediate stage, represented by these fossil remains of a creature which had short stubby legs and toes that had not yet fully evolved into fins. Pakicetus, as the creature was named, had probably been encouraged to evolve towards the water by the presence of rich marine life in shallow, salty ocean basins, the remains of the drying-up Tethys ocean, fifty million years ago. The find was reported in *Science* for 22 April.

The world's first man-made chromosome was assembled at Harvard University. It was proved to be an accurate copy of a real yeast chromosome by the fact that, when inserted into yeast cells, it was duplicated and passed on to successive generations of yeast cells along with their natural chromosomes. A long-term aim of such work was to build artificial mammalian and, eventually, human chromosomes to use in genetic engineering for the treatment of diseases caused by complex genetic defects. But researchers agreed that, because of the much greater complexity of human chromosomes, that achievement was still many years away.

AGRICULTURAL RESEARCH. Genetic engineering techniques made rapid strides in agricultural applications. Scientists working for Monsanto, the multinational chemical concern, used a bacterium, Agrobacterium, which naturally infected plant cells, as a vector to introduce new genes into plant cells. They showed, for the first time ever, that the new genes were expressed—that is, products were made according to their instructions—in the infected plant cells. This important achievement opened up the prospect of using Agrobacterium as a means of introducing genes into crop plants, for such purposes as higher yield or disease resistance or herbicide resistance, taking the genes from other species. Another group, at Michigan State University, identified the precise gene which conferred resistance to herbicides in certain weeds, and began work to clone the gene—to multiply it many times over in bacteria, with the aim of implanting the gene in crop plants to make them impervious to herbicides sprayed around them.

MEDICINE AND MEDICAL RESEARCH. Important discoveries were made in cancer research. Studies published in *The Lancet* for 22 October revealed links between the use by young girls of contraceptive pills containing high levels of the hormone progestogen and a higher-than-normal risk of breast cancer, and between the use of any form of contraceptive pill and a slightly higher-than-normal risk of cervical cancer. The details of these findings, especially those concerning cervical cancer, were disputed. But the general conclusions, that it was wise for young girls to use pills with the lowest possible progestogen content and that all women using oral contraceptives for four years or more should have regular cervical smear tests to give early warning of cancer, were undisputed.

More oncogenes—genes which, while normally forming vital parts of cells' genetic make-up could help to transform the cells into malignant cells when misplaced—were discovered. Their mode of action became increasingly clear. The pattern emerging was one in which oncogenes became displaced, 'translocated' as geneticists say, to the wrong site on a chromosome. As a result the product of the oncogene, the protein for which it carried the genetic code, was made in the wrong place, with the wrong timing and perhaps in excessive quantities. Such misplaced and mistimed activity, together with some environmental stimulus, was thought to take a cell half-way to malignancy, to transform it into an immortal cell like an embryonic, continually-dividing cell. But a further influence, a second translocated oncogene, was thought to be required to complete the second stage of the process and to transform the immortalized cell into a truly malignant cell.

Another important discovery in cancer research, reported virtually simultaneously by Dr Russell Doolittle in the US and Dr Mike Waterfield in the UK, was that the gene for the chemical growth factor, which normally had the function of encouraging wound healing, by stimulating cells to divide rapidly, could transform cells into malignant cells, if the gene produced the growth factor in the wrong place and at the wrong time. This was also shown to be due to translocation, in this case by the gene's being picked up and moved about by a virus.

Genetic research took a step forward in a different direction with the demonstration, by virologists in the Salk Institute in the US, that it was possible to insert normal genes into cells with defective genes in laboratory cultures, and thus to restore the abnormal cells to normal functioning. In this way the cell cultures were 'cured' of an abnormality which, when it affected a whole human body, caused an incurable disease known as the Lesch-Nyhan syndrome. Doing this in cell culture was still a long way from doing it in the human body.

Profound ethical problems were foreshadowed by the development, by researchers in the Massachusetts General Hospital and the Welsh National School of Medicine, of a test which made it possible, virtually infallibly, to identify people who were going to develop Huntington's chorea, an incurable and progressive disease which caused irreversible mental and physical deterioration in middle and old age. While the test promised to allow the steady elimination of the genetic defect responsible for the condition, by counselling and therapeutic abortion, it also posed great problems for doctors who might use the test in the future. Should doctors, for example, convey the results of such tests to insurance companies and employers?

A similar test for another common condition caused by genetic defects, phenyl ketonuria, pku for short, was also announced during the year and others had been or were being developed for forms of muscular dystrophy and cystic fibrosis. Doctors agreed that the implications of these tests, and many more like them to come, the products of new genetic manipulation techniques, needed publicizing, so that proper guidelines could be decided upon for their use.

The first commercial, synthetic versions of prostacyclin, the human body's natural anti-blood-clotting agent, were marketed simultaneously by British and American drug companies. They were for use, in the first place, in patients undergoing dialysis or treatment involving heart-lung machines, in which blood was shunted outside the body through tubing, since this rendered blood specially liable to clot. The world's first artificial heart patient, Barney Clark, died in America in March. But the 112 days for which he had lived with his artificial heart gave doctors much valuable data to help in the design of future improved versions for other patients. The first British recipient of a combined heart and lung transplant died after a few days, but the overall record for the new operation remained encouraging, mainly because of the use of the relatively new immuno-suppressive drug Cyclosporin A. Out of 16 patients who had received heart-lung transplants over the past three years at Stanford University in California, where nearly all the world's such operations had been performed, only five had died and all the rest were past the stage at which rejection usually occured.

A new technique reported by Japanese doctors in *The Lancet* in November promised to raise the success rate for kidney and other transplant operations considerably. It involved selectively blocking the immune reaction against foreign grafted organs by using agents called monoclonal antibodies. These were products of a new form of biotechnology, which reacted selectively with and killed only those white cells in a patient receiving a graft which reacted against the graft, without damaging other white cells. Seventeen out of nineteen patients who had begun to reject their grafted kidneys, when so treated with monoclonal antibodies, stopped rejecting them and showed no further evidence of rejection.

By November the mysterious Acquired Immune Deficiency Syndrome, AIDS, had affected over 2,000 people in the US and had appeared in several European cities. Up to sixty new cases of the syndrome, in which patients lost all natural resistance and were at the mercy of any form of cancer or any infection which came along, were being reported each month. The best theory which had been produced was that AIDS was the product of many repeated infections, the result of an exceptionally promiscuous lifestyle, causing a continued lowering of immune defences against infection.

The first antigen specific to the leprosy bacillus to be found was identified by workers in the UK National Institute for Medical Research and in Colorado State University. This provided a new and more sensitive and reliable means of early diagnosis of the disease, which was already being used in 1983. Australian doctors achieved two pregnancies by external fertilization of eggs donated by women other than those who

received the eggs after fertilization—the so-called 'donor egg' technique—foreshadowing many ethical problems for the future.
A drug used for hypertension, Minoxidil, gave some promise of effectiveness in treating baldness. Viruses which prey naturally on bacteria, phages, were used experimentally at the UK Houghton Poultry Research Station to treat bacterial diseases of poultry, with such good results that those involved foresaw the technique being used for humans, with effects which might be comparable to the introduction of antibiotics.

THE NOBEL PRIZES. The prize for medicine or physiology was awarded to Dr Barbara McClintock of the Cold Harbour Spring Laboratory near New York, for her work on mobile genetic elements which, thirty years earlier, had laid the foundations for the work on gene translocations described above, by revealing the significance of translocated genes in plant genetics and thus, by implication, in human genetics.

The prize for physics went to Professor William Fowler of the California Institute of Technology and Indian-born Professor Subramanyan Chandrasekhar of Chicago University for their work on the nuclear 'burning' in stars and on processes which take place when stars burn out and collapse into white dwarfs.

The prize for chemistry went to Canadian-born Professor Henry Taube of Stanford University in the US, for his work in inorganic chemistry on reactions such as those involved in nitrogen fixation, whereby some bacteria living symbiotically with plants are able to absorb and make use of nitrogen from the air.

Chapter 2

ENVIRONMENT

RAIN in various forms was the dominant environmental concern of 1983. In the northern industrialized nations it continued to come down acidic—destroying life in lakes, corroding metal and killing trees. In the developing nations of the South, either too little or too much fell; and these natural weather aberrations proved how fragile, and how dangerous, growing populations had made their environments.

The year 1983 marked a key change in attitudes toward acid rain. The US Government had maintained that the sulphur and nitrogen dioxide pollution from power stations was not necessarily the cause of the sulphuric and nitric acid affecting trees and lakes in Canada, New York and New England. But in June a federal task force on acid precipitation announced that man-made pollutants were 'probably the major contributors' to acid rain in the north-eastern United States. Later that month a panel of the President's science office recommended 'meaningful reductions' in sulphur emissions, and at the end of June the National Research Council announced that the occurrence of acid rain in the eastern US was roughly proportional to the annual emission of suphur dioxide in the region.

In Europe, the West German Government—which until recently also denied the pollution/acid rain connections—ordered that all new power stations be equipped with 'gas scrubbers' to cut smokestack emissions, and announced a policy of having new cars equipped with catalytic converters for the same purpose (although this required European Community agreement). Critics said this would not halt the loss of forests in the nation, where according to some reports one-fourth of all trees had already been damaged by acid rain. There were even exemptions on clean-up standards for West German power plants where anti-pollution investment would threaten the utility's profitability. In all, 205 of the nation's 216 coal-fired power stations would be exempt until between 1987 and 1993. Even the Eastern European countries, which rarely discussed industrial pollution, were admitting to serious damage. Forests were dying in Czechoslovakia and East Germany; and the Polish Academy of Sciences predicted that the nation's forests could disappear by the end of the century.

Britain, which produced considerable sulphur pollution but had soil and lakes less prone to acid damage, continued to call for more research before limiting emissions. But there was growing evidence of acid rain damage to British crops. The only result of a Royal Society symposium on acid rain was the announcement of a five-year, £5 million research programme on the subject, to be paid for by the National Coal Board and the Central Electricity Generating Board. This angered environmental organizations in Scandinavia, as well as scientists at the International Union for Conservation of Nature. The newsletter, *Acid News*, of the Swedish and Norwegian non-governmental Secretariats on Acid Rain alleged that Britain was merely 'buying time' by going over ground already covered some time ago by Scandinavian scientists. There was, however, great uncertainty as to the role of soil elements in 'buffering' for some years the effects of acid rain.

The British press carried more revelations about escapes of radioactive materials containing dangerous levels of plutonium from the British Nuclear Fuels' Sellafield (formerly Windscale) plant on the north-west coast to beaches and into the Irish Sea. Charges that cancer rates in the area were higher than elsewhere led to a government inquiry, which was getting under way at the end of the year.

Drought and floods—in some cases both—affected over 40 Third World countries in 1983. These disasters were 'natural' in that weather triggered them, but scientists had been warning for at least a decade that the over-grazing, over-cultivation and deforestation of the world's arid and semi-arid lands would make droughts more devasting. They had warned that the rapid clearing of tropical forests would greatly exacerbate any flood damage. In 1983 these warnings bore fruit.

In November the UN Food and Agriculture Organization (FAO) reported that the 150 million people who lived in 22 western, eastern and southern African countries were 'on the brink of starvation' and that 'famine has already caused deaths in some countries'. Ethiopia was suffering its worst famine for a decade and refugees were once again moving into the Sudan. Harvests also failed in several countries on the southern fringes of the Sahara.

The last major drought in the Sahelian region (1968-73) had ended ten years ago. Studies published in 1983 showed that $7,500 million in aid had poured into that region over 1975-80—a period in which all aid givers and receivers had agreed that agriculture was the main priority. But only 8 per cent of this money went to the sort of agriculture which grows the region's main foodcrops, and only 1·4 per cent went to ecology/forestry programmes. Most of it went to build such things as roads, buildings and dams, and in the form of food aid to feed city dwellers. Meanwhile the Sahel's population was growing at a rate of 2·5 per cent a year while its cereal production increased at only 1 per cent a year. New irrigation projects were being so badly handled in the Sahel that for every new acre of land brought into production by new works an acre was lost through badly built or managed irrigation projects.

Throughout Africa, agricultural land was suffering a similar lack of care and attention; erosion was devasting once productive farmland in countries as far afield as Ethiopia, Kenya and Zimbabwe.

Bolivia suffered massive droughts and record floods, while Peru faced floods in the north and drought in the south. Floods struck in Ecuador; and the city of Guayaqil was ravaged by mudslides from slopes cleared of trees for land development. Floods also afflicted land around the common border of southern Brazil and north-eastern Argentina. In Brazil's Parana state, forests had diminished from 85 per cent coverage in 1930 to 8 per cent in 1980. Typhoon 'Georgia' savaged Vietnam, Kampuchea and Thailand in October, affecting 1·5 million Vietnamese and the vital rice-growing area of Kampuchea. Here too, damage was increased by deforestation and general mismanagement of watersheds.

In the early spring, newspapers carried stories of a massive 500-mile-long oilspill from damaged Iranian wells at the head of the Arabian/Persian Gulf, but reports of damage varied. The World Wildlife Fund said the oil took a heavy toll of wildlife, especially the threatened dugong (a large aquatic, herbivorous 'sea cow'), while some press reports said the slick was never more than a thin, harmless film. The eight Gulf nations, which signed a treaty in 1978 to cooperate in the event of an oil emergency, appeared at present incapable of such cooperation.

In late March, 13 of 27 nations around the Caribbean signed treaties to combat marine pollution and to prevent and clean up oil spills in the region. States with widely differing politics—from the US to Cuba and Nicaragua—took part in the negotiations, and other states were expected to add their names eventually. But the high debts of the bigger states (Mexico and Venezuela, especially) and the refusal of the US to contribute meant that the Caribbean nations had little money to follow up their ambitious joint plans.

The year saw the resignations of the two US government officials most loathed by American environmentalists. Environmental Protection Agency (EPA) chief Anne Burford went first, stepping down after charges of mismanagement and questionable agreements with polluting industries. She was replaced with former EPA head William Ruckelshaus, who managed quickly to improve both the image and the budget of the EPA without running foul of the free-enterprise ideology of the Reagan Administration. Interior Secretary James Watt, whose plans to 'develop' national parks, wilderness areas and coastlines had swelled the memberships of the environmental activist groups, resigned in October, not because of his policies but because of a questionable joke he made during a speech. He was replaced by National Security Adviser William Clark, a former California supreme court judge with no experience in resource management. A 1980 study of that court's rulings described Clark as 'markedly development-oriented', while the environmentalist Sierra Club found he had dissented on 11 of 12 pro-environment court rulings.

Environmental crusaders in Britain won a victory when a Royal Commission report recommended in April the introduction of unleaded petrol, and within an hour of its publication the Government announced its intention to introduce 92-octane unleaded petrol by 1990 at the latest. As recently as March 1983 a Government spokesman had insisted that such a move would be impossible because of the difficulties of redesigning engines for leadless petrol.

Britain, West Germany, the Netherlands, Denmark and Greece now all favoured European Community (EC) legislation controlling lead in petrol. Britain was concerned over public health implications, West Germany because leaded petrol fouled catalytic converters meant to decrease acid precipitation, and Greece because of smog which was harming the Acropolis. France and Italy opposed such controls, partly because they feared increased petrol consumption.

Following an EC directive, Britain and other EC countries put into operation in 1983 programmes controlling the marketing of new chemicals. The mysterious appearance in a French barn of 41 drums of highly toxic dioxin from the clean-up of a plant in Seveso, Italy, not only made headlines but pushed the EC closer to legislation on the trans-frontier shipment of hazardous wastes.

Finally, the ultimate environmental doomsday story emerged from

Washington, DC, when a meeting of 500 scientists from 15 nations found that a large-scale nuclear war could spread a cloud over the entire planet, triggering a global 'nuclear winter'. The biological results would be more profound than anything that had happened in the past 65 million years, according to Stanford University president Donald Kennedy. Temperatures would be below freezing for months in the North and there would be localized sub-freezing temperatures in the South. Northern crops and Southern rainforests would be wiped out. When the cloud cleared a damaged ozone layer would let in more than usual ultra-violent rays, with resulting cancers, blindness, lowered disease resistance and genetic mutations. Civilization as humans had built it would be destroyed. Cold, darkness, fire, toxic smog, radiation, violent coastal storms and disease would usher in a new civilization based on misery.

XIV THE LAW

Chapter 1

INTERNATIONAL LAW—EUROPEAN COMMUNITY LAW

INTERNATIONAL LAW

INTERNATIONAL law was intimately involved in a number of international incidents in 1983, such as the invasion of Grenada, events in the Lebanon and the shooting-down of a South Korean airliner (see pp. 91-93, 186-9 and 60); there were, however, no developments of first-rank importance in the technical aspects of the law.

The dissension caused by the refusal of the United States and some of its Western allies to accept the 1982 Convention on the Law of the Sea (see AR 1982, pp. 400-1) continued to rumble on, both at the initial meetings of the Preparatory Commission for the International Sea-Bed Authority and the International Tribunal for the Law of the Sea, and elsewhere. In March President Reagan proclaimed a 200-mile Exclusive Economic Zone for the United States; this proclamation was expected to accelerate the acceptance of such zones as part of customary international law.

Another controversial (though less important) treaty to be adopted was the Vienna Convention on Succession of States in respect of State Property, Archives and Debts. The Convention, intended to complement the Vienna Convention on the Succession of States in respect of Treaties (see AR 1978, p. 385), was based on a draft produced by the UN International Law Commission. The question was what legal situation should obtain with regard to state property, archives and debts when sovereignty over a territory changes through secession, unification, independence or other events. The provisions adopted at the international codification conference called by the UN were thought by many Western states to be excessively burdensome to predecessor states and unduly favourable to successor states, particularly newly-independent ones; consequently, 11 voted against the text and another 11 abstained, while 54 states voted in favour of its adoption.

The International Court of Justice continued its consideration of the dispute between the United States and Canada concerning delimitation of the maritime boundary in the Gulf of Maine (see AR 1981, p. 398) and of the continental shelf delimitation dispute between Libya and Malta (see AR 1982, p. 398). In October Italy applied to the Court for permission to intervene in the latter case; hearings were scheduled for early 1984. Also in October, Upper Volta and Mali agreed to submit to a chamber of the Court the question of delimitation of part of their land frontier. July saw the establishment of a new regional international court, the Andean Court of Justice. This was set up by Bolivia, Colombia, Ecuador, Peru and Venezuela in order to deal with disputes arising out of the Cartegena Agreement on Subregional Integration.

The European Court of Human Rights had an increasingly large case-load, partly due to the new policy of the European Commission of Human Rights of referring to the Court even some cases where the Commission had itself come to the conclusion that no breach of the European Convention of Human Rights had occurred. One judgment of particular interest concerned *Silver and Others* v. *United Kingdom*, where the Court unanimously ruled that the censorship of prisoners' letters to solicitors, MPs, relatives and journalists in relation to such matters as prison conditions or legal proceedings, in many instances on the basis of somewhat imprecise internal directives, violated the Convention. Another interesting development was the revision of the Court's rules of procedure to allow intervention by third parties and separate representation of individual petitioners in proceedings before it. When the Convention was originally drafted it was provided that only the Commission would have the conduct of the case against a government before the Court, although in recent years there had been some *de facto* relaxation in favour of applicants. In a related development the Council of Europe adopted a new (Sixth) Protocol to the European Convention on Human Rights. This would oblige the states which adopted it to abolish the death penalty, except in time of war or imminent threat of war. The death penalty had already been abolished in about a half of the member countries of the Council of Europe; however, in the other half (including the UK), the penalty had so far been retained for a small number of specific offences, such as treason.

EUROPEAN COMMUNITY LAW

Nationalism was the Community's *leitmotiv* during 1983. This was due partly to economic developments and partly to legal pigeons coming home to roost.

Economic and financial considerations culminated in a variety of constitutional issues being raised in an acute fashion—but not solved. Of these, the most straightforward was the question of enlargement. In the inconclusive talks for the eventual accession of Spain and Portugal, the strictly constitutional issues posed by the resultant enlargement of the Community's working organs and thus of its decision-making process were raised but more as an arguing point than as a real objection.

More serious and immensely complicated was the problem of the Community budget. Community revenue consisted of the whole of the income from customs duties and levies on all goods entering the Community plus up to one per cent of VAT rate levied on nearly all goods and services sold within that area. The combination of inflation and relatively undisciplined increases of agricultural prices led to a near-exhaustion of Community revenue and the likelihood that in the following year the one per cent VAT would no longer be sufficient. That ceiling being entrenched in the Rome Treaty (art. 201, together with art. 4 of the 'Own Resources' decision of 21 April 1970), a 'constitutional amendment' would be necessary to raise it, which would require parliamentary approval by all the existing member states.

The Athens summit, which it was hoped would settle a new budgetary pattern solving both the 'British problem' and the revenue ceiling difficulty, failed utterly. At the same time, the urge for a federalist reform of the Communities, which had surfaced every few years, was given added impetus by the Stuttgart mandate during the German presidency, and this led not only to continuing rumbles of discussion throughout the year but also to a detailed proposal for an amending treaty to establish a European Union. This was drafted for the Institutional Committee of the European Parliament by a group of rapporteurs led by Sr Altiero Spinelli and assisted by a quadrumvirate of lawyers, including ex-Advocate-General Francesco Capotorti.

While a certain amount of national self-interest is justifiable in political and constitutional questions it is not so acceptable when compliance with the law is involved. Signs of restiveness in recent years on the part of several member states grew stronger during 1983. The European Commission itself, which had always shown forbearance when states had failed to comply with Community law, began to display a tougher attitude. The Commissioner for Competition, Mr Andriessen, adopted a conscious policy of enforcing the state aids provisions of the EEC Treaty, and not only were many more decisions issued forbidding proposed or actual aids but proceedings were also more frequently taken in the European Court for violation of the procedural rules in arts. 92-94 of the Treaty.

The Commission also took a much stronger view of failure to implement directives. During the year a steady stream of cases were initiated before the Court of Justice and a considerable number of judgments delivered. These covered not only failure to implement directives at all but also disagreement as to whether the national law purporting to do so did in fact comply with the specific rules in the directive. Thus the action against the United Kingdom in *Re Equal Treatment* (165/82)[1] successfully complained that the UK implementing

[1] [1984] 1 CMLR 44.

law, in the Sex Discrimination Act 1975, did not properly apply the Sex Discrimination Directive 1976 because it gave blanket exemption to small enterprises with fewer than six employees and also to employment in private households and did not apply at all to non-binding collective agreements between employers and trade unions.

Another series of cases and actions related not to genuine disagreement on interpretation of the law but to disingenuous attempts to defend overt protectionist acts. Among these were the French insistence on the use of the French language in import documents (which was softened, at Commission urging, as regards imports from other member states) and a revival of the infamous 'Poitiers' device from the previous year (see AR 1982, p. 404) by restricting the number of customs posts which could clear imports of meat, this latter ploy being aimed specifically at imports from EEC states. These did not go to the Court. The wine and milk cases did. In *Re Italian Table Wines* (42/82)[2] the attempt by France to justify its procedural restrictions on the import into France of Italian wine by arguing that the accompanying documentation was defective and that compliance with oenological standards was unreliable, thus necessitating delays while the documents were rectified and the wine was submitted to laboratory analyses, failed. Likewise, in *Re Ultra Heat Treated Milk* (124/81)[3] the Court held that the UK ban on import of UHT milk was unjustified. After a six-month delay in drafting appropriate department regulations the first French consignment was landed, tested and rejected for excessive water content (the argument before the European Court had been based on danger to health linked to adequate sterilization techniques, not on traditional consumer protection); the second consignment passed the test, however, and was admitted to the English market.

The Court delivered a judgment of Solomon in *Re Excise Duties on Wine (No. 2)* (170/78)[4]. This marked the end of part of a long-standing saga involving national protection of domestic alcoholic drinks through discriminatory taxation throughout Europe, each country classifying such drinks in a way that favoured those produced locally. In Britain's case the tax difference was between wine and beer, the former (not produced in significant quantities in Britain) being taxed higher than the latter. The UK argued that there was no real discrimination since in practice each bore the same tax burden if the amount contained in a normal container (wine glass or beer mug) was taken as the unit. The Court accepted neither this criterion nor the Commission's alternative of the respective alcoholic content; it did, however, give credence to an Italian suggestion that as beer was drunk as a thirst-quencher it should be compared with

---

[2] [1984] 1 CMLR 160.
[3] [1983] 2 CMLR 1.
[4] [1983] 3 CMLR 512.

those wines which performed the same function, e.g. Italian light wines; and as the latter were more highly taxed than beer the UK was held to be at fault—in that respect only.

After the changes of the previous year, the Court of Justice itself continued quietly on its way. There were rumours that the President was about to retire, but they were not confirmed. The German Advocate-General, Gerhard Reischl, retired after ten years' service. The relatively recent French Advocate-General, Mme Simone Rozès, also left the Court at the year end on being appointed President of the French Supreme Court (Cour de Cassation)—a reminder that a large number of ex-Judges, ex-Advocates-General and ex-Commissioners were active in European legal and political life at various degrees of prominence ranging downwards from the last President of Ireland, who left the Court in order to take up that office. One such, Professor Andreas Donner, who was a Judge of the Court for some twenty years and served a term as its President, and who now occupied a Dutch university chair, himself initiated an interesting VAT case, *Donner* v. *Netherlands* (39/82)[5], in which he queried not that he was charged VAT on books sent to him by booksellers in other member states but that he was charged an additional fee by the Dutch post office for clearing them through customs for him. The Court held that probably that was wrong, depending on facts which had not been established.

The year was notable for the first case after Greek accession on the right of Greek nationals to enter other member states, *Peskeloglou* v. *Bundesamt für Arbeit* (77/82)[6], and for an unsuccessful attempt by Luxembourg to prevent the European Parliament from moving most of its meetings to Strasbourg and Brussels, *Luxembourg* v. *European Parliament* (280/81)[7]. The Parliament not only won that case but also brought one of its own against the Council (judgment not yet delivered) complaining that the latter had failed to legislate for a common transport policy as required by art. 75 of the EEC Treaty.

In the field of anti-trust law the year saw a number of important judgments, mostly upholding decisions of the Commission, e.g. in 'Pioneer': *Musique Diffusion Française SA* v. *E.C. Commission* (100-103/80)[8], *Michelin* v. *E.C. Commission* (322/81) and *AEG-Telefunken AG* v. *E.C. Commission* (107/82). The *GVL* case (7/82)[9] condemned a German copyright collecting society for discriminating against non-German artistes, and the Commission in *AKZO*[10] ordered a

[5] [1983] 1 CMLR 711.
[6] [1983] 2 CMLR 381.
[7] [1983] 2 CMLR 726.
[8] [1983] 3 CMLR 221.
[9] [1983] 3 CMLR 645.
[10] [1983] 3 CMLR 694.

dominant firm to cease predatory pricing aimed at driving a competitor out of the market.

The Community's legislative machine seemed to be moving once again, and important directives were enacted on motor car insurance, banking and company group accounts. The Commission issued two very important regulations on exclusive distribution and exclusive purchasing (together replacing the much-used Regulation 67/67) after a long delay caused by criticism of their detailed rules. The second regulation contained major concessions to the tied system endemic in the brewery and oil industries for public houses and petrol stations respectively. A draft regulation on research and development agreements was finalized at the end of the year and far-reaching proposals for copyright harmonization were brought to an advanced stage of preparation. The draft directive and regulation on trade marks were reported out of the European Parliament and the draft 5th company law directive, after further amendment by the Commission, was sent to the Council working party for final consideration.

Chapter 2

LAW IN THE UNITED KINGDOM

VERY little important legislation reached the statute book, mainly because the general election automatically terminated many Bills. The Representation of the People Act consolidated a number of measures on the franchise. The Marriage Act enabled marriages of housebound and detained persons and the Matrimonial Homes Act dealt with the rights of spouses to occupy a dwelling house that had been a matrimonial home. The Mobile Homes Act strengthened the position of owner-occupiers of mobile homes; there was a new Merchant Shipping Act and a British Nationality (Falklands Islands) measure. Considerable excitement was caused at the end of the year by a House Buyer's Bill introduced by Mr Austin Mitchell, MP, which survived its second reading despite Government opposition. The Bill, which threatened to remove solicitors' conveyancing monopoly, was greeted with alarm by that profession.

The Government's industrial legislation came under severe attack during the year. In April the House of Lords held that a shipowner's cause of action at common law in respect of interference with contractual rights by unlawful secondary action had been restored by the Employment Act 1980.[1] In November the Court of Appeal found that, although there had

---

[1] *Merkur Island Shipping Corp.* v. *Laughton* [1983] 2 All E.R. 189

been a dispute between British Telecom and the Post Office Engineering Union, it was not a trade dispute entitled to immunity.[2] Sir John Donaldson MR was at pains to establish that under the 1982 Act the courts had an independent role akin to that of a referee. Parliament made the law and was solely responsible for what the law was. The *cause célèbre*, however, was undoubtedly the National Graphical Association's attempt to impose a closed shop on Mr Selim (Eddie) Shah's small chain of newspapers (see pp. 32-34). The mass picketing and the ugly scenes that resulted were clearly illegal under existing law, as was the proposed national printing strike. The courts imposed severe fines on the union for contempt and ordered sequestration of assets. Several newspapers won court injunctions forbidding their employees to strike over matters which had nothing to do with conditions in their own work-places. An injunction against the National Union of Journalists was obtained by another newspaper company in December.[3] The case brought about the 'curious result' (per Griffiths LJ) that an employer could 'illegalize' industrial action by operating through a subsidiary company, but on the construction of the 1980 Act there was no escape from the conclusion that the union's instruction to journalists to withdraw their labour was unlawful secondary action.

Contempt of court issues were also to the fore in other areas. The Press Council report on the 'Yorkshire Ripper' case (see AR 1981, p. 39) castigated the West Yorkshire police for revealing information which created the possibility of 'a substantial risk of serious prejudice' to the proceedings against the accused. The Divisional Court made similar findings in relation to press discussion of the proceedings against Michael Fagan (see AR 1982, p. 32) following his two incursions into Buckingham Palace in 1982,[4] and newspaper revelations in respect of the *Nilsen and Waldorf* cases (see p. 42) also gave rise to considerable concern. In December it was held that s.10 of the Contempt of Court Act 1981 (which was intended to protect editors from having to disclose their sources) did not apply when the editor of the *Guardian* was sued for the return of an embarrassing political document leaked by a civil service 'mole'. Moreover, the 'national security' exception in s.10 would still have allowed the plaintiffs (the Attorney-General and the Secretary of State for Defence) to succeed even though the document involved was not vital to security.[5] Not surprisingly this curious outcome was widely criticized in the press.

The House of Lords disapproved of its earlier view (in *Zamir*, 1980) that immigrants owed a 'positive duty of candour' to disclose all material circumstances to immigration officers, and also strengthened the *habeas*

[2] *Mercury Communications Ltd.* v. *Stanley* 'The Times' 10 November 1983
[3] *Dimbleby & Sons Ltd.* v. *N.U.J.* 'The Times' 7 December 1983
[4] *A.-G* v. *Times Newspaper Ltd.* 'The Times' 12 February 1983
[5] *Secretary of State for Defence* v. *Guardian Newspaper Ltd.* 'The Times' 16 December 1983

corpus remedy.[6] In *Mandla* v. *Lee* the House, reversing the Court of Appeal, held that Sikhs were an ethnic group under the Race Relations Act 1976 and that a headmaster's 'no turban' rule was discriminatory.[7] In *Sullivan* their Lordships reluctantly attached the label of insanity to a sufferer from psychomotor epilepsy who temporarily did not know what he was doing, but invited Parliament to legislate on the matter.[8] *Richards* v. *Richards* was an important family law decision which established that, although the needs of the children were an important consideration, they did not justify the eviction of an innocent husband from the matrimonial home.[9] Lord Scarman called for a comprehensive and coherent statute to replace the existing hotchpotch of enactments in this field. By 3 to 2 the House held that courts should not automatically inspect documents for which 'public interest' immunity was claimed; they should not 'take a peep on the off-chance' but should inspect documents only where there were definite grounds for expecting to find material of real importance to the party seeking disclosure.[12]

The lady barrister who had persuaded the lower courts to allow her tax deductions for clothes worn in court failed to convince the House of Lords, which decided that her wardrobe also kept her warm and decent and was thus nondeductible.[11] A company operating in the North Sea outside UK waters was still liable for PAYE tax,[12] but employees were not taxable in respect of scholarships awarded to their children by their employers.[13] Shell Oil was unable to recover over $56 million from insurers for the misappropriation of oil by the owners of a ship which later mysteriously sank.[14] In *Miller*, a defendant who failed to take any steps to extinguish a fire he had accidentally started was found guilty of arson,[15] while in *Morris* a switcher of price labels in a supermarket was guilty of 'appropriating' the goods under the Theft Act 1968.[16] Lord Roskill commented that ingenious arguments about the meaning of the legislation had bedevilled this branch of the criminal law without contributing to the efficient administration of justice, rather the reverse. 'The law to be applied to simple cases should be equally simple'.

In a case with considerable political overtones the Court of Appeal refused to prevent recommendations of the Boundary Commission from going to the Home Secretary. The Leader of the Opposition had argued

---

[6] *Khawaja* v. *Secretary of State* [1983] 1 All E.R. 765
[7] [1983] 1 All E.R. 1062
[8] [1983] 2 All E.R. 673
[9] [1983] 2 All E.R. 807
[10] *Air Canada* v. *Secretary of State for Trade* [1983] 1 All E.R. 910
[22] *Mallalieu* v. *Drummond* [1983] 2 All E.R. 1095
[12] *Clark* v. *Oceanic Contractors Inc.* [1983] 1 All E.R. 133
[13] *Wicks* v. *Firth* [1983] 1 All E.R. 151
[14] *The Salem* [1983] 1 All E.R. 745
[15] [1983] 1 All E.R. 978
[16] [1983] 3 All E.R. 288

that insufficient emphasis had been given to the objective of equalizing numbers in electorates, but Sir John Donaldson MR said that the distinctive nature of the Commission's functions would make the court slow to intervene. It was not its function to review any matter which pertained to Parliament itself.[17] Lord Lane CJ criticized the convoluted system of penalty points and disqualification provisions in offences involving motor vehicles,[18] and expressed the hope that Parliament would enable the courts to suspend youth custody sentences in whole or in part.[19] He also commented that, in many cases, juries were required to perform difficult feats of intellectual acrobatics when told that they could use evidence of previous convictions to test credibility but could not infer guilt.[20]

The Court of Appeal also dismissed an appeal by a deserted mistress for a share in a house where she had lived for 19 years and brought up children. The court thought it unfair that a mistress had no rights against the man in a situation where no trust in her favour could be demonstrated but (*pace* Lord Denning's views) this was a matter which could be remedied only by Parliament.[21] It was also held that a person born male remained biologically and legally a man even though, after a sex-change operation, he had become 'philosophically or psychologically' female.[22] A man who had been committed to prison for failing to comply with a court order to hand over a valuable cross found on the plaintiff's land was released after a year in prison on the grounds that he showed no inclination to purge his contempt and further punishment would have no coercive effect.[23] It was also decided that manslaughter could be established even though the unlawful and dangerous act was not directed at the person killed,[24] and that a person in total control of a limited company could still steal from it.[25] A father, however, could not be guilty of kidnapping his own child.[26]

Because of the spiritual nature of his calling, a minister of religion was held not to be an employee and an industrial tribunal had no jurisdiction to entertain his complaint of unfair dismissal.[27] In a case involving a London wine bar, Griffiths LJ said that the question of whether or not a woman was being treated less favourably under the Sex Discrimination

---

[17] *R* v. *Boundary Commission for England, ex p.Foot* [1983] 2 W.L.R. 458
[18] *R* v. *Kent* [1983] 3 All E.R. 1
[19] *R* v. *Dobbs* 'The Times' 8 November 1983
[20] *R* v. *Watts* [1983] 3 All E.R. 101
[21] *Burns* v. *Burns* 'The Times' 2 August 1983
[22] *R* v. *Tan* 'The Times' 15 February 1983
[23] *Enfield L.B.C.* v. *Mahoney* [1983] 2 All E.R. 901
[24] *R* v. *Mitchell* [1983] 2 All E.R. 427
[25] *Attorney-General's Reference (no.2 of 1982)* 'The Times' 25 November 1983
[26] *R* v. *D* 'The Times' 1 November 1983
[27] *President of the Methodist Conference* v. *Parfitt* 'The Times' 29 October 1983

Act by being forbidden to drink and converse at the bar admitted of only one answer, 'of course she is'.[28]

The Queen's Bench Division allowed the Greater London Council to restructure its fares, services and expenditure under a 'balanced plan'. Unlike the 'Fares Fair' policy struck down in the *Bromley* case in 1982, the new scheme was within statutory limits and a justifiable exercise of the Council's discretion.[29] The decision reaffirmed the separation of powers and marked a retreat from the more interventionist approach of Lord Denning. A wife-swapping agreement whereby each husband would have assumed financial responsibility for the other's former wife was held to be unenforceable and not to be encouraged.[30]

Woolf J refused to declare that the supply of a booklet entitled 'A Guide to Self-Deliverance' was an offence under the Suicide Act 1961 since that would be to usurp the functions of a jury,[31] but he would not deny to doctors their discretion to prescribe contraceptive advice and treatment for children under 16 without parental knowledge or consent. Contraception in itself did not directly assist with the commission of the crime of unlawful sexual intercourse, and the fact that the child was under 16 did not automatically mean that she could not give consent to the treatment.[32] Jupp J held that it was contrary to public policy to award damages to a mother whose child had been conceived after the mother had undergone a negligently performed sterilization operation, since the birth of a healthy, normal baby was a beneficial and not a detrimental event. Damages could, however, be awarded for suffering, inconvenience, anxiety and disruption to finances caused by the unexpected pregnancy.[33] Hirst J extended the law on breach of confidence when three young musicians successfully sued Thames TV for breach of contract. An option on their idea for a series had been taken by the defendant for £500 and a promise not to use the idea without employing the plaintiffs: Thames then produced the highly successful 'Rock Follies' without the plaintiffs, who were nevertheless protected even though their ideas were oral and inchoate.[34]. The Divisional Court overturned a decision of the Basingstoke justices who had refused to accept as a 'statement' a print-out from the breath-testing machine (the Lion Intoximeter 3000). The court held that the magistrates should have taken into account the certificate explaining the print-out figures as this made the document (taken as a whole) plainly intelligible.[35]

[28] *Gill* v. *El Vino Co. Ltd.* [1983] 1 All E.R. 398
[29] *R* v. *London Transport Executive, ex.p.G.L.C.* [1983] 2 All E.R. 262
[30] *H* v. *H* 'The Times' 28 April 1983
[31] *A.-G.* v. *Able* 'The Times' 29 April 1983
[32] *Gillick* v. *West Norfolk A.H.A.* 'The Times' 27 July 1983
[33] *Udale* v. *Bloomsbury A.H.A.* [1983] 2 All E.R. 522
[34] *Fraser* v. *Thames T.V.* [1983] 2 All E.R. 101
[35] *Gaimster* v. *Marlow* 'The Times' 9 December 1983

The Attorney-General clashed with the Charity Commissioners after the latter failed to set up an inquiry into the charitable status of the Unification Church (Moonies). The Commissioners' reluctance seemed well-founded, since approval of the practices of a religious sect is not a prerequisite for registration as a charity and no evidence had yet been produced to a court to show that its doctrines were adverse to the foundations of all religion and subversive of all morality. In March the Lord Chief Justice issued guidelines to judges to be followed in summing-up to juries in criminal trials, following an increasing number of cases going to appeal and consequently costly and unnecessary delays. The particular *casus belli* was a rape trial where the judge omitted to direct the jury on the standard of proof and defence counsel felt no duty to draw the matter to his attention. In October the Master of the Rolls reported on the effect of the Scarman Committee reforms in court procedure and announced that outstanding civil appeals had fallen from 1,100 to 930 and the average waiting period in two-judge cases had been reduced from 9 or 10 months to 6 or 7.

The use of 'supergrass' evidence in terrorist trials in Northern Ireland gave rise to considerable disquiet during the year and *The Times* (13 September) stated that 'the Courts are now themselves on trial'. The nature of the evidence of informers, *agents provocateurs* and accomplices, the powers of arrest and detention, the absence of juries and the test for admissibility of evidence were considered by many to be in drastic need of reform if the law was to retain the respect of all the people of Northern Ireland.

XV THE ARTS

Chapter 1

OPERA—BALLET—THEATRE—MUSIC—CINEMA—TELEVISION
AND RADIO

OPERA

EVEN more than most years, 1983 was dominated by Wagner, the centenary of whose death was marked in a number of ways. At Bayreuth a new production of *Der Ring des Nibelungen* was mounted (25-30 July), the so-called 'English Ring' conducted by Sir Georg Solti, produced by Sir Peter Hall, and designed by William Dudley. The team aimed at a romantic, naturalistic staging, which drew withering scorn from many continental critics—especially the French—accustomed to the highly politicized, socio-critical productions following in the wake of Patrice Chéreau's version of 1976. Technical problems and vocal crises meant that this was not the happiest of occasions.

In Munich there was a complete Wagner cycle conducted by Wolfgang Sawallisch, including a lavish production of the early *Das Liebesverbot,* based on *Measure for Measure* (6 February). For the English National Opera, Nicholas Hytner not inappropriately set *Rienzi* in a 20th-century fascist state (29 September), and the same company launched a new *Ring* cycle with David Pountney's grandly pictorial *Die Walküre* (22 October). Many other companies started new *Rings,* among them the San Francisco Opera, whose spectacular decor was based on Schinkel, and the Welsh National Opera, with a gently didactic staging of *Das Rheingold* by Göran Järvefelt. The Welsh also had a success with their *Parsifal,* despite the fact that the original conductor and producer were forced to withdraw at a late stage.

Rameau's tercentenary was marked by a lavish version of *Les Indes galantes* at the Théâtre du Châtelet, Paris (later seen in Venice), and a witty production of his comedy *Platée* mounted by the English Bach Festival (later seen in France). A complete Rameau edition was announced under the auspices of the Bibliothèque Nationale.

There was a distinctly 'sacred and profane' feel to the year's new operas. Messiaen's first work for the stage, *Saint François d'Assise,* an uncompromisingly meditative (and long) study of the saint who preached to the birds—grist to Messiaen's mill—was received with respect at the Paris Opéra (28 November). In Brussels Philippe Boesmans's *La Passion de Gilles* (18 October) was made of sterner stuff, dealing with Gilles de Rais and his relationship with Joan of Arc. Charles Chaynes's *Erzsebet* (Paris Opéra, 28 March) was a monodrama about the infamous Countess Bathory written for the soprano Christiane Eda-Pierre. A rediscovered Delius opera, the *verismo* melodrama *Margot la Rouge* (1901), was belatedly premiered at St Louis (8 June).

Less heated but highly successful were Henze's *The English Cat*, a social satire to a libretto by Edward Bond based on Balzac (Schwetzingen, 2 June) and *Rebecca*, a straightforward setting of Daphne du Maurier's novel by Wilfred Josephs (Opera North, Leeds, 15 October). Leonard Bernstein's second opera, a family drama entitled *A Quiet Place*, was premiered in Houston on 17 June.

In Britain, the Royal Opera had a quiet year with only three new productions, including an excellent *Boris Godunov* produced by the Russian film director Andrei Tarkovsky, but maintained artistic momentum with major revivals of Poulenc's *Dialogues des Carmélites*, *Don Carlos* (sung in the original French) and Maxwell Davies's *Taverner*. A government financial scrutiny led by Clive Priestley concluded that the Royal Opera House was severely underfunded.

At the English National Opera the new director of productions, David Pountney, set his seal on the company's work with—apart from *Die Walküre*—a highly controversial *Queen of Spades* and excellent stagings of Dvořák's *Rusalka* and Prokofiev's *The Gambler*. Scottish Opera, in a year marked by a series of gruesome financial crises, managed to mount a most satisfying version of *Die Zauberflöte* by Jonathan Miller. Also worthy of note were Opera North's *Il trovatore*, updated by Andrei Serban to the time of the Spanish civil war, and the Welsh National's *Carmen*, played as street theatre in the aftermath of a Central American revolution. Glyndebourne opened their festival with a generally admired *Idomeneo*, Trevor Nunn's first opera production.

Abroad, the Hamburg State Opera continued their investigation of Zemlinsky's operas with *Der Kreidekreis*, and brought his Wilde-based double-bill of *Der Zwerg* and *Eine Florentinische Tragödie* to the Edinburgh Festival. As already indicated, production-sharing continued to be the favoured method of cost-cutting: for instance, in the course of the year the Geneva Opera borrowed *Lucia di Lammermoor* from La Scala, *Le nozze di Figaro* from Glyndebourne, and *Giulio Cesare* from the Coliseum, and lent their *Death in Venice* to Scottish Opera. In the USA the Metropolitan Opera celebrated their centenary with an eight-hour gala (in two parts), and a new aid to audience appreciation, 'surtitles' (simultaneous translation projected over the proscenium), was tried out in New York and Toronto with some success.

The year had its fair share of agreeable 'scandals'. Ken Russell set *Madame Butterfly* in a brothel (Spoleto) and projected pornographic films on huge model breasts in *Die Soldaten* (Lyons). Joan Sutherland

and the conductor Richard Bonynge walked out of a performance of *La traviata* in Genoa because of the audience's disapproval of the Australian tenor (the performance eventually continued without the *diva* but with the unfortunate tenor).

The year's obituary list included the composers William Walton (see OBITUARY), Werner Egk and Alberto Ginastera; the conductors Adrian Boult (see OBITUARY), Anthony Lewis and Jaroslav Krombholc; the singers Vin Bovy, Edith Coates, Donald Gramm and David Ward; and the noted Viennese author and critic Joseph Wechsberg.

BALLET

In the world of ballet 1983 was a year of dissolution and change; for although the established companies like the Royal and Festival Ballets continued on their courses some of the best of their dancers drifted temporarily away into musical shows, such as *Song and Dance, Cats, Dash* and the like—new forms of entertainment requiring highly-trained ballet dancers yet using different disciplines and a superabundance of energy. After a spell in the commercial theatre most of them returned, considerably richer, to their ballet companies. But the arts of 'ballet' and 'the dance' are not the same, and this record attempts to cover neither the latter nor the new 'aerobic dancing'.

At the beginning of the Royal Ballet's season Nureyev choreographed *The Tempest* to Tchaikovsky music—an obscure version of the play with overpoweringly heavy costumes by Georgiadis. It had little of the magic of Shakespeare's island. The return of Antoinette Sibley from retirement and of Anthony Dowell from America enabled Ashton's *A Month in the Country* to be seen at its best. Most of the ballerina rôles of the season were shared by Lesley Collier and Marguerite Porter, while Natalia Makarova also appeared as guest-artist—returning from New York where she was dancing the leading rôle in the old musical *On Your Toes*. A major creation of the year was MacMillan's *Valley of Shadows*, telling of the terrible sufferings of an Italian-Jewish family persecuted by the Nazis and their death in a concentration camp. To music by Tchaikovsky and Martinu, and with realistic decors and costumes by Yolande Sonnabend, it chilled the spine and provided an outstanding rôle for Alessandra Ferri, the Royal's newest discovery, who was voted 'Dancer of the Year' by the public.

David Bintley's undoubted talents as a choreographer were demonstrated by his creation of *The Swan of Tuonela* (music by Sibelius) for the Sadlers Wells Royal Ballet and his *Winter Play* (music Dudley Simpson) and *Consort Lessons* (music Stravinsky) for the Royal Ballet. Both companies made extensive tours abroad—the Royal to New York, China and the Far East, and the Sadlers Wells company to Australia, New

Zealand, Canada, Singapore and Bangkok. Evelyn Hart, the ballerina of the Royal Winnipeg ballet and former prize-winner at Varna, joined them in London as a guest.

London Festival Ballet had severe financial problems but remained in operation and toured to Venezuela. A notable 'coup' was to secure for their repertoire Cranko's *Eugene Onegin*. The world laughed at their vain efforts to dismiss one of their male dancers on account of 'effeminacy and inability to lift the ballerinas'.

After many years in charge of the Canadian National Ballet, Alexander Grant retired and was succeeded by the Dane Erik Bruhn. The Australian Ballet, which for years had been suffering from internal strife, appointed the English ballerina Maina Gielgud as its director, a move which immediately restored it to a state of equanimity.

In the United States events were overshadowed by the death in April of George Balanchine at the age of 84, after a long illness (see OBITUARY). His company, the New York City Ballet, performed in London at the Royal Opera House during the summer as scheduled, but led by Peter Martins and Jerome Robbins who had been appointed to succeed their founder. Their success was enormous, as predicted, but it would be idle to pretend that Balanchine's athletic, *depouillé* style of choreography was universally admired in Britain, where ballets of sentiment (such as Ashton's) were preferred by the general public. America's other great company, American Ballet Theatre, had a troublesome year financially but survived under its director, the Russian Mikhail Baryshnikov, who continued to dance incomparably.

In Russia, the director of the Bolshoi Ballet, Yuri Grigorovich, made a new version of *The Age of Gold* (music of Shostakovich) first produced in 1930 with a story about Soviet footballers playing in a fascist city but using an even more bizarre propaganda plot. Many groups of Russian dancers were sent out—notably to Paris and to Italy—and in Rome was mounted an important exhibition 'Russian Ballet from the origins to the present day', most of the exhibits being drawn from Moscow's Bakhrushin Museum. Although it contained Nijinski's *Spectre* costume and the famous Serov poster, Diaghilev's name was never mentioned—the expression used was 'Les Saisons Russes'.

In September Nureyev took up his direction of the Paris Opéra Ballet, announced more new productions than had been held in a season before, and opened with his reconstruction of the great full-length classic *Raymonda*.

The Hungarian National Ballet from Budapest appeared at the Edinburgh Festival with a single work, *Proba,* choreographed by Antal Fodor to rock-type music by Gabor Presser. It was a superb spectacle on the theme of the Crucifixion much in the style of *Jesus Christ Superstar*. It was enormously successful in Hungary but appeared a trifle old-hat in Scotland.

On her 85th Birthday Dame Ninette de Valois was honoured by a gala at Sadlers Wells. The Royal Ballet School acquired a new director, Merle Park, who continued to dance. The deaths were exceptionally numerous and sad—the dancers Sir Anton Dolin (see OBITUARY), John Gilpin, Mona Vangsaa, Igor Schwezoff and Errol Addison, the teacher Audrey de Vos, the composer and conductor Leighton Lucas, the writers Caryl Brahms and Edwin Denby, and Alan Hooper, director of the Royal Academy of Dancing. Finally, a hint of things to come, students and dancers from Japan and Hong Kong came flooding over to Britain to study, join companies and above all to carry off prizes in competitions, including the prestigious Adeline Genée gold medal of the Royal Academy of Dancing.

THEATRE

The fact that more than a dozen musicals were playing in London's theatres at the end of 1983, plus more pantomimes than had been seen in the West End for years, might have suggested that British theatre was in a more parlous state than it was. Certainly the 'musical' is a bastard form—neither straight play nor opera; it hedges its bets, tries to be all things to all audiences—and it has to be said that the year was more memorable for acting, staging and production than for new plays. The fact is that, whereas in the autumn of 1982 no fewer than 16 of the West End's 40 or more theatres were dark, 12 months later none was.

Arguably the most salutary theatrical event of the year was Ed Mirvish's purchasing that most famous of theatres, the Old Vic, and then spending £2·5 million on refurbishing it to recreate its nineteenth-century glory. The first production was Tim Rice's new musical *Blondel*, about the minstrel who rescued Richard I from an Austrian prison. Sadly, Mr Rice's collaborator this time was not Andrew Lloyd Webber but Stephen Oliver, and the show was an empty if pretty bauble. Mr Lloyd Webber himself had failed to buy the Vic. To compensate, he acquired the Palace Theatre, where his *Song and Dance* continued to run.

The best of the musicals was probably *Poppy*, Peter Nichols's account, couched as pantomime, with music by Monty Norman, of the background to the Chinese opium wars; the Royal Shakespeare Company (RSC) had revamped and revived it with a little help from their American friends, the production being destined for Broadway. The lesson of the National Theatre's much-heralded musical about the life and death of *Jean Seberg*—St Joan into St Jean—was less that Marvin Hamlisch had not created hummable tunes, or that Christopher Adler's 'original idea' should have been discarded on the drawing-board, than that Britain's National Theatre should not act as a tryout for Broadway.

Sir Peter Hall, whose indiscreet, essential *Diaries*, the most important theatrical prompt-book in ages, were published during the year should have known better than to justify mounting such a limp show at the British taxpayer's expense by asserting that if *Jean Seberg* were a success the National would benefit from the Broadway receipts: the National should have resisted playing commercial impresario. That *Guys and Dolls* and *The Beggar's Opera* continued to play to packed houses during 1983 misses the point: each is a proven masterpiece in a genre with desperately few.

The only other musical worth mentioning is Willy Russell's *Blood Brothers*, which the Liverpool Playhouse brought to Shaftesbury Avenue, about twins separated from their parents at birth and coming together in death. It was an old-fashioned, tuneful, ballad opera; and such are the vagaries of the West End that its closure was announced weeks before it came off and as soon as its imminent demise was known it played thereafter to full houses.

The lack of new plays at the National and, to a lesser extent, the RSC was a serious cause for complaint. At the Olivier (National), David Hare's *A Map of the World*, set at a Unesco conference on world poverty in Bombay, implied that the liberal conscience was dead in England. The ambition and scope of the play were to be applauded but the characters were more embodiments of political attitudinizing than flesh-and-blood creations. Christopher Hampton's *Tales from Hollywood* (Olivier) explored what happened to certain writers, including Brecht, Thomas and Heinrich Mann, who left Germany for California immediately before World War II. This stylish, literate play was fastidiously directed by Peter Gill. Athol Fugard's *Master Harold . . . And The Boys*, in which the South African dramatist tried to exorcise a childhood incident, was brought to the Cottesloe (National) by its Johannesburg company. And in the same theatre Chicago playwright David Mamet's *Glengarry Glen Ross*, about useless real estate being aggressively sold to gullible buyers, received its world premiere in Bill Bryden's production and was much admired because of the authenticity of the dialogue. To others, there was too much of the Studs Terkel tape-recorder about it.

Mr Bryden's Cottesloe company took over the larger Lyttelton Theatre to stage the National's first pantomime, *Cinderella*, with delicious sets by William Dudley which seemed derived from a spectacular Pollock's toy theatre: Mr Dudley also designed Peter Hall's Bayreuth *Ring*. Stage design was one of 1983's glories, including distinguished work, mostly for the two national companies, by John Bury, John Napier, Hayden Griffin, Alison Chitty, Maria Björnson, Grant Hicks, John Gunter, Deirdre Clancy, Bob Crowley, Chris Dyer, John Byrne, Carl Toms, Geoff Rose, Ralph Koltai, Voytek, Paul Dart, Peter Rice, Ultz and Christopher Morley.

David Edgar's *Maydays*, the first new play to be put on in the RSC's main Barbican auditorium, did not dispel the feeling that only epic or mock epic justified itself there. Mr Edgar's report of how the political left in Britain had gone right since Hungary 1956 was wordy and intelligent but, as with other ambitious new plays, seemed in production concerned more with discussing politics than with creating characters and justifying itself dramatically. Nevertheless, Bob Peck gave an extraordinary performance as a Russian soldier in Hungary, later interned, then emigrating to the West and becoming the embodiment of Cold War suffering.

The wittiest play the RSC mounted was Nicholas Wright's elegant *The Custom of the Country*, set in the Zambesi valley and Johannesburg in the 1890s. Mr Wright is almost alone among serious contemporary British playwrights in being fundamentally concerned with narrative. His version of *The Crimes of Vautrin* for Joint Stock, directed by William Gaskill, was underrated.

The Priestley report, commissioned by the Government, declared that the RSC was seriously underfunded, and performed miracles within its budget. But at Stratford-upon-Avon, with the exception of Adrian Noble's production of *Measure for Measure* with Juliet Stevenson luminous as Isabella, the five Shakespeare productions in the main house were routine or worse—the season opened with the eponymous *Julius Caesar's* murder shown simultaneously on vast closed-circuit television screen above the stage as well as being enacted thereon. No one liked to ask whether this was connected with the fact that the production was sponsored by Link Electronics.

On the other hand, the studio theatre at Stratford, The Other Place, housed a number of fine productions, culminating in John Barton and Adrian Mitchell's romantic, elegaic version of Calderon's *Life's a Dream*. Richard Griffiths played *Volpone*; and there was immaculate ensemble acting in William Saroyan's *The Time of Your Life*. A play derived from the life of a Stratford man earlier in the century, *The Dillen*, involved cast and audience traversing the town during performances. Emrys James had the time of his life as Sir Giles Overreach in Massinger's now little-performed Jacobean drama about the rising mercantile class, *A New Way to Pay Old Debts*.

Stratford's 1983 productions all went to London. In addition, Middleton and Decker's *The Roaring Girl*, with Helen Mirren, was given a disappointing new production. The production of the year, by the RSC or anyone else, was by Terry Hands—Anthony Burgess's version of *Cyrano de Bergerac* with Derek Jacobi (who also, in the year, essayed Benedick, Prospero and Peer Gynt). At the Barbican studio theatre, The Pit, Antony Sher glittered as *Tartuffe*, and as that play's creator in Bulgakov's *Molière*. The RSC's year ended with a revival of their last year's *Peter Pan* which, freshly excavated, revealed Barrie's hackneyed Christmas piece as a brooding, flawed masterwork.

The National, too, presented a number of well-cast revivals, notably Sheridan's *The Rivals* (Olivier). John Gunter's set recreated majestically eighteenth-century Bath, and Sir Michael Hordern and Geraldine McEwan were Sir Anthony Absolute and Mrs Malaprop absolutely. *The Fawn* (Cottesloe) by John Marston suggested that the National could, with advantage, revive more lesser-known Jacobean plays. Alfred de Musset's *Lorenzaccio* (Olivier), translated by John Fowles, seemed ridiculously overblown, and Giraudoux's *The Trojan War Will Not Take Place* (Lyttelton) in Christopher Fry's cloying translation was unredeemed by Harold Pinter's direction. Eduardo de Filippo's *Inner Voices* (Lyttelton) was notable for, sadly, presenting Sir Ralph Richardson (see OBITUARY) in his last stage role, as a bemused citizen of Naples to whom everybody, at the end of World War II, confessed their secrets. Sir Ralph's memorial service at Westminster Abbey was one of the year's grandest theatrical occasions.

The Royal Court had an unexceptional year, but staged new plays by Howard Barker (*Victory*, about the restoration of the monarchy to Britain after the Commonwealth) and by Howard Brenton (*The Genius*, about an American scientist who, having discovered a formula for blowing up the world, retreats to England). The Royal Court Theatre Upstairs showed two biting, anti-male plays by Sarah Daniels, *The Devil's Gateway*, about the road to Greenham Common, and *Masterpieces* (Foco Novo), about how pornography corrupts. At the same theatre Tony Marchant's *Welcome Home* was an indictment both of army discipline and of the Falklands war.

Riverside Studios mounted a superlative production of O'Neill's *Moon for the Misbegotten*, with Frances de la Tour and Ian Bannen, and Chichester a magnificently rich revival, with Alan Bates, of John Osborne's possibly most lasting play, *A Patriot for Me*. Glasgow Citizens, ambitiously and triumphantly, took their production of Karl Kraus's *The Last Days of Mankind* (translated and directed by Robert David MacDonald) to the Edinburgh Festival, and Michael Elliott at The Exchange Theatre, Manchester, achieved the previously unthinkable, a stageworthy version of *Moby Dick*, whales and all.

The London West End originated little of much worth—even Botho Strauss's *Great and Small* with Glenda Jackson began elsewhere. Charles Dyer's weird foursome, *Lovers Dancing*, was intriguing, though most critics found it tawdry, and Hugh Whitemore's *Pack of Lies*, starring Judi Dench at her most morally convincing, about the 1960 Portland spy case was the commercial theatre at its best.

Much of the most consistent, intelligent new work and revivals occurred on the Fringe, at such theatres as the Bush (Snoo Wilson's *Loving Reno*; Brian Thompson's *Turning Over*), Tricycle, New End (Arnold Wesker's *Annie Wobbler*), Hampstead (Hanif Kureishi's *Birds of Passage*), Lyric Hammersmith (two productions of Marivaux by

Shared Experience; Yuri Lyubimov's *Crime and Punishment* with British actors via three interpreters), the Almeida (Caryl Churchill's *Fen*, about depressing, flat lives in East Anglia), King's Head, Stratford East (Ultz's *Pericles*; 7:84 Theatre Company Scotland's *Men Should Weep*) and, not least, the Donmar Warehouse, to which John Retallack's Actors' Touring Company brought five imaginative and stimulating productions, classics mainly, which touched down in London for the first time after travelling the world representing the possibilities of British theatre at its best.

New York Theatre

The most significant event of the year was Peter Brook's 80-minute-long production, from Paris, of *La Tragédie de Carmen*. Great pains were taken to make clear that it was not the Bizet opera, and, considering that, the evening was a triumph. Merimée's text as well as Bizet's music had been rearranged, creating a thrilling melodrama staged in the nearly defunct Vivian Beaumont theatre, on a semi-circular floor strewn with sand representing a bullring. Against walls and two wings of simple wood partially concealing the small orchestra, furniture was artfully carried on and off by the actor/singers with no perceptible break in action for scene changes. The paramount achievement was the utter truthful simplicity of the acting without clichés, which not only surpassed virtually anything seen on opera stages in the past generation, but challenged much non-musical acting. The performance was literally breathtaking, eliciting gasps from the audience.

Billed as a 'new' Gershwin musical, *My One and Only* had an irrepressible collage of a score, a fragile derivative book, the wan charm of Twiggy, and supple gentle choreography by her co-star, Tommy Tune. *La Cage aux Folles*, based on the popular film, had a thumping old-fashioned score by Jerry Herman and two glittering performances by its stars, Gene Barry and George Hearn, as the homosexual lovers, owner and star of the transvestite cabaret. The book seemed sanitized of the sexuality and acerbic wit which its characters and subject needed. Despite an unlikely subject, *Baby*, a realistic musical about three couples anticipating or dreading imminent offspring births, surmounted the frequently symbolic characters to achieve an airy, affecting, unsentimental work, through David Shire's score and Richard Maltby Jr's lyrics and direction. Too long neglected, William Saroyan had his film script, *The Human Comedy*, revamped as a musical. This view of a small-town California family during World War II, wistfully nostalgic if not rhapsodic, had an eclectic score by Galt MacDermot based on US folk and art songs. Two pinnacles of US musicals came to New York from the Houston Grand Opera Company, Kern and Hammerstein's *Showboat* and Gershwin's *Porgy and Bess* (the latter in a staging of seven years earlier using the nearly complete original score). Both had impressive scores, and particularly superior voices, although *Porgy* suffered from the vastness of Radio City Music Hall, and *Showboat* from pedestrian staging. The musical *Zorba* was revived with Anthony Quinn recreating his film role for the first time in a musical; elemental and powerful, his work was balanced by the enchanting Lila Kedrova recreating the dying French courtesan.

Numerous off-Broadway companies continued their struggle to foster new playwrights. This year alone the 12-year-old Ensemble Studio Theatre presented 240 projects—readings, partially or fully staged works. Among them was Michael Brady's play *To Gillian on Her 37th Birthday*, about a man, aet. 35, who wishes his dead wife alive again, and their battle when, indeed, she briefly returns. The writing of this promising playwright was both mature and thoughtful. Christopher Durang's new play, fostered and presented by a similar group, Playwright's Horizons, *Baby with the Bathwater*, written in his customary, unique absurdist style, revealed the horrors of over-anxious parental authority, which predictably created a psychopathic adult of their child. From this estimable company also came an improved working by Wendy Wasserstein of her *Isn't it Romantic*, in which two girls, friends, battling with careers and romance, are guarded and guided by mothers over-ambitious for them.

From Second Stage came Tina Howe's *Painting Churches*, a study of the disintegration of an aged father afflicted with arteriosclerosis, and his wife, packing to leave their elegant ancestral Boston home for a compact cottage in which to finish their days. Their daughter returns after a long absence, to paint their portrait, and in the process they reveal their mutual misunderstandings and conflicting truths. It was moving and hilarious, with Marian Seldes giving a beautifully orchestrated portrait of the mother. Although Charles Ludlam had for years been delineating females, like Garbo as Camille, this year, with his Ridiculous Theatrical Company, he presented a spoof of Molière called *Le Bourgeois Avant-Garde*, and *Galas*, indisputably based on the phenomenon, if not the truth, of Maria Callas. His writing and production were more professional than previously, and he had developed from mere caricature to genuine satire. Sam Shepard had three plays running in 1983. His newest, *Fool for Love* which he also directed, was perplexing, affecting, vigorous and sexual, set in a motel room near the Mojave desert—familiar territory for this highly original writer, who frequently celebrates the American West.

The 1983 Pulitzer Prize for drama was awarded to Marsha Mason's *'Night Mother* in the Cambridge (Massachusetts) production. In it a mother who has lived her vacuous life through her daughter's failures tries unsuccessfully to dissuade her daughter from committing suicide. The evening was harrowing in its depiction of two lives with no firm values. Neil Simon continued his recent exploration of an autobiographical lode in *Brighton Beach Memoirs*, about his adolescence in Jewish

Coney Island. Although it struck close to home, it was not so deep as it promised, yet won the Drama Critic's Award.

One tribute to Tennessee Williams, who died in February (see OBITUARY), was a revival, alas! feebly mounted, of *The Glass Menagerie,* starring Jessica Tandy as the mother, in yet another of her stunning, heart-rending performances.

The annual ration of stimulation from overseas included Simon Gray's *Quartermaine's Terms*, a metaphor of Britain's decline set in the masters' common-room of a school where foreign students are taught English, a wry, humorous and tender work. Trevor Nunn's production, for the Royal Shakespeare Company, of Shakespeare's *All's Well That Ends Well* was set in Edwardian England, filled with shimmering, silvery visual delights, which did not quite meet the challenges of the play. Michael Frayn's forced, hysterical farce, *Noises Off*, succeeded by dint of its meticulously choreographed physical mayhem. However, Shaw's *Heartbreak House*, which was splendidly cast, including Rex Harrison in the lead, was mechanically staged with little depth or perception for one of Shaw's major statements about civilization.

MUSIC

In both theatre and concert-hall, 1983 was a year of revivals. Perhaps the most successful, certainly the most ambitious, took the form of an attempt to revive an entire period, that of Vienna at the beginning of the twentieth century. This was the brainchild of John Drummond, artistic director of the Edinburgh Festival, and his last achievement before retiring from that position. Music, theatre, the visual arts, the spoken and written word were all encompassed by this grand retrospective concept; and the result was not only a broad historical survey, but also an illustration of the stark contrast between the cultural explosion that took place in the Vienna of 1900 and the diffuse results of that explosion in the Europe of 1983.

As for the revival of single works, some were notably successful, such as the brilliant production by Götz Friedrich of Berg's *Lulu*—first seen at Covent Garden in 1981—with Karen Armstrong in the title role; others were notably unsuccessful, such as Maxwell Davies's *Taverner* and Alexander Goehr's *Babylon the great is fallen*. Goehr's oratorio had been a failure when the BBC first performed it at the Festival Hall in 1979; included in a Promenade Concert four years later, its results fulfilled expectations. Both these revivals served to underline one of the inherent weaknesses of British musical society in the 1980s (see AR 1980, pp. 419-20), namely, the absence of an informed aesthetic valuation of contemporary music. Performances were often given for other than artistic reasons, which could only lead to public apathy; for faced with performances such as these, which were musically unsatisfying, it was only to be expected that the public, who might be initially well-disposed, should turn aside in favour of the familiar classics.

One well-known figure to whom they might turn from the familiar classical period—Brahms—enjoyed even more worldwide performances than usual in 1983, the 150th anniversary of his birth. Composers whose centenaries fell in the year were Varèse and Bax; others of a less venerable age were Berkeley (80), Messiaen (75), Lutoslawski (70), Ligeti and Ned Rorem (60). If none of these was quite the same household name as Brahms, they were all recognized with some notable performances, largely in their own countries. One of the most remarkable works to be so unveiled in 1983 was Messiaen's much-heralded new opera *St Francis of Assisi*, whose vast score, extreme length and extravagant resources caused many raised eyebrows when it was performed at the Paris Opéra (see also p. 399).

If advance publicity is any criterion, whose trumpet-blasts turn out to be in inverse proportion to the results achieved, one of the biggest disappointments of the year was the series of events entitled 'Britain salutes New York'. As far as the musical events were concerned it should more aptly have been called 'The British Arts Council salutes New York', since the programme highlighted, with unconscious irony, another of the chief weaknesses of official British musical life: the concentration of public funds, and attention, on a handful of organizations to the exclusion of everyone else. What was vital and progressive in British music was not on offer in this official salute. Poor management led to cancelled performances, and the most successful concerts were three given by the group founded and directed by Maxwell Davies for the performance of his own works, *The Fires of London*. New Yorkers heard a representative cross-section of his music, as well a new commissioned piece by the leading American composer Elliott Carter, called *Triple Duo*.

Carter at the age of 75 was one more example of a living composer being accorded the interest customarily shown to those who reach an age divisible by five. He enjoyed many performances in 1983 as a result of this fortuitous circumstance, particularly in Britain and the United States. A study of his music was published, written by a former pupil at the Juilliard School, David Schiff, and published by an English admirer and advocate, William Glock.

If a review of musical achievement in any particular year tends to focus on what is new or contemporary, this must in no way be taken to imply that what is familiar or old has disappeared from the repertory. Quite the contrary. In London, on the South Bank alone more than 1,200 concerts were given in 1983, making it by far the busiest concert complex in the world in terms of quantity. And in all this activity it was, as usual, the repertory of the past that formed far the greater part of the works performed. This indeed is equally the case in all countries. Perhaps it could hardly be otherwise in a musical culture, such as that of Europe and America, that has become so performer-orientated. Moreover, among the enormous number of repetitive performances of familiar pieces only very occasionally does there appear the exceptional, the adventurous, the original. So it was with considerable surprise and excitement that one noticed in 1983, in both New York and London, the first stirrings of what might one day develop into a significant movement. Concerts were presented in both cities that were intended for the mass public, yet consisted entirely of contemporary works.

American composers, less inhibited than their British counterparts, openly, directly and effectively challenged the stagnation of the *status quo*, with the result that in 1983 the New York Philharmonic presented a series of new music concerts, 'Horizons 83', directed by the American composer Jacob Druckman. As well as being Professor of Music at Yale University, he was 'in residence' with the Philharmonic. He recognized the need for a simple label, or theme, if this new idea was to be projected successfully to a broad public. 'The New Romanticism' was his theme for a two-week festival of seven concerts. His starting-point was Berio's *Sinfonia* (1968), and the term New Romanticism was understood as referring to music written since that year, and conceived in terms of the modern orchestra. 27 works were played by as many composers, three-quarters of them American. That was the strength, as well as the purpose, of the series. Nothing was included of purely experimental, electronic, computer, conceptual or so-called 'minimal' music—though John Adams's *Grand Pianola Music* was perhaps on the borderline. Interestingly, this work was one of the few to be poorly received. Composers included Wuorinen, Schuller, Foss, Rzewski, Del Tredici, Rochberg, Druckman and others. The concerts represented a serious, intelligent attempt to bridge the gap between the living composer and the broad concert public. They were concerned with the present state of American music.

The equivalent series in London was 'Music of Eight Decades'; but the differences between the two approaches were significant and instructive. The London concerts, following the normal British custom, were arranged by a committee (London Orchestral Concert Board/BBC), and were not under the unified direction of a composer; they attempted to cover the entire twentieth century, like an academic course of study, and to include all countries as well as Britain, which was scantily, and questionably, represented with six works out of the total 30; instead of being concentrated into a fortnight, the eight concerts were spread over as many months; they lacked Druckman's artistic commitment, and were more concerned with the past of European music as a whole than with the present of any one country; finally, and most important, they did not involve the four London orchestras. This arose because the first such attempt at a twentieth-century series in 1981 had led to such problems among the self-governing orchestras that for the 1983 series the concerts were divided equally between the BBC Symphony and a chamber ensemble, the London Sinfonietta. The concerts as a whole were concerned not so much with the restoration of communication between the composer and the public as with a demonstration of some of the directions music had taken since 1909, the year of Webern's *Six Pieces, Op.6*, the earliest work included.

As a somewhat frosty response, and not to be outdone, the four London orchestras mounted their own series, 'The Great British Music Festival', built round certain music written by British composers between 1925 and 1975. Unfortunately this was parochial music of the sort best forgotten; and of the series as a whole the less said the better. The title proved an embarrassment; the music even more so. It was true that, in the words of the publicity, 'for the first time ever' the four London orchestras were acknowledging British composers; this only served to explain their total unawareness of the range of British composers' work over recent years.

While it would be premature, in the light of these developments, to proclaim a rebirth of Western musical culture, nevertheless a certain concern for the composer, and the composer-listener relationship, was undoubtedly apparent in 1983, and it emanated from America. Terms like 'accessibility', 'romanticism', 'tonality' began to be freely used in connection with new music; and composers made their existence more directly felt.

As for specific achievements in 1983, two strong contenders for the most successful new work by a British composer—in a year weighed down with premieres—might be, in the choral category, Paul Patterson's *Mass of the Sea (Missa Maris)*, which was heard at the Gloucester meeting of the annual Three Choirs Festival; and in the instrumental category Patric Standford's *Taikyoku*, for two pianos and six percussion, first played by a percussion ensemble formed at the Royal College of Music—another important new development in Britain where hitherto no such ensemble existed.

In the complementary field of musicology, two of the most important new books published in the year—notable for their breaking fresh ground, and challenging accepted ideas— were, first, the masterly initial volume of a projected three-volume study of *Franz Liszt* by Alan Walker; and, next, a scholarly translation (the first ever) by Thomas Mathieson of the third-century treatise *On Music* by Aristides Quintilianus, which opened up the whole unexploited field of early Greek music theory.

Finally, one of the greatest surprises of the year came with the performances, some of them premieres, of early works by Benjamin Britten. They served to show that the composer greatly over-wrote at an early age (the earliest work was written when he was just eleven), developing facility at the expense of deeper invention. These juvenilia proved to be numerous in quantity, very slight in musical worth.

Among the musicians who died in 1983 were the composers William Walton, Herbert Howells, Bernard Stevens and Elisabeth Lutyens and the veteran conductor Adrian Boult (for Walton, Boult and Howells, see OBITUARY).

THE CINEMA

An outstanding event in 1983 was the success of a British production, Sir Richard Attenborough's *Gandhi*, in winning the major American Oscar award, as *Chariots of Fire* had done the previous year. *Gandhi* in fact won eight important Oscars. This boost to British film production, however, was not reflected in any corresponding increase in British cinema attendance, which in 1982 had dropped to a total of only 60 million, a fall of no less than 26 per cent in face of the developing competition of video-cassette home viewing. Some fillip came with the universal box-office success of *E.T., Return of the Jedi* (the box-office phenomenon of the year in both the US and Britain) and the British Bond film, *Octopussy*.

While the Irish Republic's well-equipped National Studios had to face closure through bankruptcy in the spring, Britain's studios, led by Pinewood, were busy, mainly engaged on the production of such American 'blockbusters' as *Supergirl* and *The Last Days of Pompeii*. Nevertheless, there remained a distinct revival of interest in indigenous, low-budget British production represented by such films as *Gregory's Girl, The Draughtsman's Contract, Local Hero* and *The Ploughman's Lunch*, an interest much encouraged by the success of such films in the US. A new factor in British production appeared in the form of patronage by Britain's new television Channel Four, which invested in subjects intended for theatrical release prior to television airing; titles included *The Draughtsman's Contract, Angel, Another Time, Another Place,* and *Giro City*, in which Channel Four was prepared to invest up to some $300,000 per film in return for three television screenings.

A new British organization, the Directors Guild of Great Britain (established in 1982) had by April 1983 a membership of some 200 directors of theatre, radio, television and film. Its aim was to lobby for the rights of directors in areas such as copyright, censorship and government legislation affecting the film industry.

The popularity of *Gandhi* in India increased audience-interest in English-language films (usually shown on only some 600 of the nation's 12,000 screens). While the average budget for an American film rose to $11·3 million, that for an Indian film in the most popular genres stood at a maximum of $2·3 million. India's National Film Development

Corporation aided the production of more realistic, indigenous films with budgets as low as $50,000.

The year saw the continued struggle by production organizations to suppress the wholesale pirating of current feature films by the manufacturers of video-cassettes, who had enjoyed a trade turnover in 1982 of some $100 million. There were estimated to be 3·6 million home video-owners in Britain, 5 million in the US, and 31 million world-wide. Prints of new films had been stolen or otherwise illegally obtained, copied on tape, and rushed on the market; among the most sought-after titles had been *E.T., Return of the Jedi* and the like. Renting such cassettes amounted to handling stolen property. In America, security methods to protect prints of new products were greatly improved in studios, laboratories and cinemas—where projectionists were frequently offered a 'standard' bribe of $500 to supply prints for a few hours for copying. Titles had normally been withheld from the legal cassette market for some six months after initial release, and the loss to the industry from pirated prints anticipating legal release was estimated at $700 million. Pursued by the FBI, some 300 pirates had so far faced prosecution, while in London, which had become the headquarters for such international piracy, a court award in June against a major pirate won Universal Pictures some $7 million in damages.

Turning to the films themselves, comedy after a lean period reasserted itself in a number of American and British titles, including Norman Jewison's *Best Friends*, in which a romantic couple of Hollywood screenwriters (Goldie Hawn and Burt Reynolds) experience temporary disillusionment in marriage after a long, extra-marital relationship; an attempt by George Roy Hill to match the fatalistic absurdism of John Irving's novel, *The World according to Garp;* Sydney Pollack's *Tootsie*, with a brilliant performance by Dustin Hoffman as a needy actor who only too successfully poses as a woman; Woody Allen's delightful parody, *Zelig*, about a multi-personality hero (with remarkable reconstructions of old newsreels); and three British absurdist comedies, *The Missionary* (Richard Loncraine), with a fine cast led by the film's scriptwriter and star, Michael Palin, *Privates on Parade* (Michael Blakemore) and *The Meaning of Life*, a feature-length assembly of somewhat variable sketches by the Monty Python team, who also had a hand in the two other films. Perhaps *Octopussy* (John Glen, with Roger Moore) should also be classed as comedy, along with *Never Say Never Again* (Irving Kershner), with its welcome return of Sean Connery as Bond.

Martin Scorsese's *The King of Comedy* (Robert de Niro, Jerry Lewis) concerned the desperate, least funny aspect of obsessive show-business humour. Indeed, films about show business and film-making became a marked genre of the year, with the German director Wim Wenders's American-Portuguese *The State of Things*, a fatalistic study of the problems involved in making an under-financed Hollywood film in

Portugal, and *Carny* (Robert Kaylor), set in the stylized world of a travelling carnival show, to say nothing of one of Fassbinder's last films, *Veronika Voss*, Antonioni's *Identification of a Woman* and a study of the yearning of ordinary people to become entertainers in Coppola's highly stylized *One from the Heart*. The biographical film, *Frances* (Graeme Clifford), with its fine performance by Jessica Lange as the ill-fated, mentally afflicted star of the 1930s, Frances Farmer, came more into the category of a psychological story than a portrayal of the theatre and film 'industries' of the period. In *Come Back to the 5 and Dime Jimmy Dean, Jimmy Dean*, Robert Altman handled the strange obsessions of James Dean fans.

War formed the background to an important group of films. An outstanding success in America, *An Officer and a Gentleman* (Taylor Hackford with Richard Gere), offered an old-fashioned, highly emotional and reactionary view of exaggerated army discipline in the training of officer-cadets, with a parallel exploitation of sexual politics in their attitude to women. *The Lords of Discipline* involved intrigue in a military institute in Carolina, significant only as another in the series of current American military service films (*Stripes, Private Benjamin, Taps*, etc.). *War Games* (John Badham) was a frightening film about a computer-obsessed teenager's accidental involvement in real computer-controlled 'war games', the outcome being the computer itself declaring 'The only winning move is not to play'. Two films that faced the ethical problems of journalists covering distant, Third World wars with complex political issues in which they can become personally involved were the Australian Peter Weir's impressive *The Year of Living Dangerously* (set in Indonesia 1965) and Roger Spottiswoode's *Under Fire* (Nick Nolte, Gene Hackman), set in Nicaragua, but filmed in Mexico. The British film, *The Ploughman's Lunch* (Richard Eyre), posed ethical problems in the behaviour of an ambitious journalist.

Meryl Streep won a well-deserved Academy award for her sensitive performance in Pakula's study (*Sophie's Choice*) of an ultimately fatal love affair between a refugee from Auschwitz and her schizoid lover; she followed this with another extraordinary performance in Mike Nichols's *Silkwood*, a true-life story of a woman worker supposedly murdered when in the process of exposing a defective plutonium plant in 1974. Coppola's *The Outsider* was a period piece about disaffected youth in the 1960s. Nicholas Roeg produced a dauntingly complex Anglo-American film in *Eureka* (with Gene Hackman), while the Japanese director Nagisa Oshima offered an equally complex study of East-West relations in his British film, *Merry Christmas, Mr Lawrence* (David Bowie), with its background of a Japanese prisoner-of-war camp in Java in World War II. James Toback's subtle film *Exposed* (with Nastassia Kinski, Rudolf Nureyev) projected the fatal outcome of a Svengali-like reshaping and subsequent exploitation of a fashion model. In *Terms of Endearment*

(James L. Brooks, with Shirley MacLaine, Debra Winger, Jack Nicholson) America produced a study of a complex mother-daughter relationship of unusual sensitivity.

1983 was a year, too, for unpretentious but realistic studies of youth in Britain—*Bloody Kids* (Stephen Frears, made 1979), *Runners* (Charles Sturridge) and *Looks and Smiles* (Ken Loach)—and for further low-budget, realistic films such as the Scottish *Local Hero* (Bill Forsyth, with Burt Lancaster). A surprising success in America was *Educating Rita* (Lewis Gilbert, with Michael Caine, Julie Walters), about a persistent girl-student in the Open University. Another success was David Jones's meticulous version of Pinter's play *Betrayal* (Jeremy Irons, Patricia Hodge, Ben Kingsley).

Among the outstanding foreign-language films were Bergman's reputedly final film, *Fanny and Alexander*, Wajda's French-based production *Danton*, Syberberg's *Parsifal*, Antonioni's *Identification of a Woman* and Gianni Amelio's *Blow to the Heart* (both from Italy), Fassbinder's last two films, *Veronika Voss* and *Querelle*, Godard's *Passion*, Rohmer's highly-sophisticated comedy *Pauline*, and Margarethe von Trotta's *Friends and Husbands*, a successor to her highly acclaimed film, *The German Sisters* (1981).

Among the film personalities who died during the year were the directors Luis Buñuel, George Cukor and Robert Aldrich, the British producer Sydney Box, the film composer Georges Auric, the stars Pat O'Brien, Walter Slezak, Dolores del Rio, Louis de Funes, Norma Shearer, Gloria Swanson, Raymond Massey and David Niven, the much-filmed dramatist Tennessee Williams, and Otto Messmer, the creator in 1919 of the star cartoon character, Felix the Cat. (For Buñuel, Cukor, Shearer, Swanson, Niven and Williams, see OBITUARY.)

TELEVISION AND RADIO

Following America but ahead of the rest of Europe, Britain in 1983 entered the breakfast televison era. Two programmes, the BBC's *Breakfast Time* and ITV's *Good Morning Britain*, competed for the available pre-9 am audience. The BBC enjoyed the advantage, on 17 January, of going first. Their complex 2½-hour live programme, backed by a new computerized newsroom and the resources of the world's largest broadcasting organization, won immediate audience approval for brightness, informality and professional expertise.

Most observers predicted that the ultimate advantage would lie with the rival TV-am, a City-backed ITV consortium fielding an impressive line-up of star presenters: David Frost, Michael Parkinson, Angela Rippon, Anna Ford and Robert Kee. Their chairman, Peter Jay, who had spent £10 million equipping and embellishing the company's extravagantly designed headquarters in North London, promised enlightened early-morning fare based on a 'mission to explain'. He dismissed the BBC's lighter-weight format of chat, keep-fit sessions and popular astrology as 'all stage directions and no substance'.

The viewing public decided otherwise. Within weeks, TV-am's daily peak audience had sunk to only 300,000, against the BBC's regular 1·7 million. Jay was replaced by Timothy Aitken, a grandson of Lord Beaverbrook, who quickly set about reducing the company's inflated expenditure, engaging new on-screen and production staff, and introducing a more popular programme style. Gradually the new regime of cartoons, contests and pop videos, coupled with the appeal of younger presenters and a brisker pace, won viewers from the BBC. By the year's end both programmes were attracting more than one million viewers each; TV-am faced an accumulated loss of £4 million.

The breakfast company's near-disaster was blamed on initial misjudgment of what the early-morning audience wanted. Too many famous faces, too little attention to behind-screen organization, and too much earnestness, could not prevail against the BBC's expertly-judged mix of shirt-sleeved informality and superior news presentation. Between them, *Breakfast Time* and *Good Morning Britain* had proved that more than two million people in the UK were ready to watch television before they went to work, provided it was not too serious.

The well-publicized tribulations of TV-am served as a welcome diversion from the continuing problems of Channel 4. At the beginning of the year the two-month-old channel's audience share had dropped to 3 per cent, or half the number of viewers it had initially attracted in November 1982. A continuing cause of concern was the long-running dispute (still unresolved at the year's end) between the Institute of Practitioners in Advertising and Equity, the actors' union, over the level of repeat fees to be paid to actors appearing in Channel 4 commercials. This was estimated to be costing the ITV companies, effectively Channel 4's paymasters, as much as £10 million per month.

In August Jeremy Isaacs, Channel 4's chief executive, revealed that he was actively seeking more 'right-wing' programme-makers. This was a response to regularly-voiced criticism that the channel tended to be 'too left-wing' in its general approach. It followed the withdrawal of *The Friday Alternative*, a controversial weekly programme which offered a platform for dissentient views. Journalists involved with the programme complained that the IBA's requirement of 'due impartiality' amounted to a mandate to 'reinforce an Establishment consensus that is at odds with popular opinion in politically fragmented Britain'.

Throughout 1983 broadcasters continued to be preoccupied with the impending technologies of cable and satellite transmission and their implications for established television. In April the Government published its expected White Paper proposing a seven-member Cable Authority which would award 12-year franchises (for operators of localized cable systems) and licences (for providers of the physical network). All franchise-holders would be required to relay the existing BBC, ITV and Independent Radio services, plus five projected satellite TV channels. Their own additional services would be paid for by subscription, from advertising, or on a pay-per-view basis, and would be subject only to general retrospective supervision by the Authority.

Government plans were criticized in Parliament for being 'rushed' and by the broadcasting unions and broadcasters for offering no safeguards against a flood of cheap American programmes. The Home Secretary, Leon Brittan, told MPs that, while the Cable Authority would be expected to exercise 'a light touch', 'it will have real teeth to prevent undesirable material appearing on cable'.

The proliferation of 'video nasties', and their availability to younger viewers, gave rise to increasing concern. In November the House of Commons gave an unopposed second reading to a private member's Bill requiring all videos to be certificated and imposing fines of up to £10,000 for selling uncertificated cassettes. Mr Graham Bright, Conservative MP for Luton South, who introduced the Bill, arranged a showing of 'video nasties' at the House. Their scenes of violence, sexual abuse, mutilation and even cannibalism were so disturbing that many MPs walked out.

A related cause of anxiety was the booming trade in 'pirated' video cassettes. Another Parliamentary Bill, to deal with what the Trade Under-Secretary, Ian Sproat, described as 'a cancer eating at the heart of the British film industry', provided for unlimited fines and two-year prison sentences.

A Consumers' Association survey revealed that, although daily average viewing in Britain had dropped from 3 hours 40 minutes in 1981 to 3 hours in 1983, viewers generally were more satisfied with what they saw. More than half thought that breakfast television should be scrapped and the money saved applied to improving programmes at other times of the day.

The American concept of the 'mini-series', or multipart popular drama designed for screening on successive evenings, seemed to weigh rather heavily on British television during 1983. Most ambitious among many imported examples was *The Winds of War*, a 16-hour personalized history of the 1939-45 conflict whose hero, played by Robert Mitchum, contrived to meet and advise the leaders on both sides. Britain responded with *Kennedy*, a three-part series from Central ITV which followed the career of America's youngest President from inauguration to assassination. Praised for its accuracy of detail and the title performance of Martin Sheen, the programme was screened simultaneously in 27 countries, including the United States, to coincide with the 20th anniversary of Kennedy's death.

In contrast, the most widely-acclaimed drama production of the year, Alan Bennett's *An Englishman Abroad*, ran for a mere hour. This was tragi-comedy in Bennett's most brilliant vein, based on a personal memoir of the defector Guy Burgess by the actress Coral Browne. Other major BBC drama ventures were less felicitous. *The Cleopatras*, intended as an Egyptian successor to the celebrated *I Claudius*, proved little better than low farce spiced with nude orgies. *The Old Men At The Zoo* put Britain's most recently-knighted author, Sir Angus Wilson, on the TV screen for the first time, but coarsened the novel's tentative prophecy of right-wing military takeover.

In general, 1983 was not a distinguished year for series drama. Thames TV's *Reilly, Ace of Spies*, supposedly based on the exploits of a real-life James Bond figure, was handsomely filmed but lacked dramatic conviction. The BBC's *Reith* presented a somewhat cardboard image of the Corporation's first director-general, despite the sterling central performance of Tom Fleming. Yorkshire TV's *Number 10*, a series of portraits of British Prime Ministers, concentrated on sexual peccadilloes rather than political achievements.

In its first full year of transmission Channel 4 scored a number of critical successes in both the drama and the documentary fields. *The Nation's Health* by G. F. Newman mounted a trenchant if rather obsessive four-part attack on the National Health Service and orthodox medicine in general. Three major documentary series, *The Spanish Civil War*, *The Arabs* and *Vietnam*, all won praise for their consistency, the depth of their research, and their overall objectivity in dealing with controversial and often sensitive subjects.

Two less controversial BBC series, *Aristocrats* and *The Great Palace*, looked absorbingly at flourishing survivors among the great European landed families and the workings of the Mother of Parliaments. *Timewatch*, a new monthly BBC-2 historical magazine, ranged from Prince Albert to the Black Death. Outstanding among the year's crop of single documentaries, *Solzhenitsyn* gave the Russian sage full rein in his own language, while another genius, a crippled Cambridge mathematics don, fascinated viewers in *Professor Hawking's Universe* in the Horizon series.

Radio 4's daily *Election Call*, transmitted simultaneously on television, allowed BBC viewers to see as well as hear leading politicians being quizzed by Sir Robin Day and the electorate. Almost no one had a good word for *Sixty Minutes*, the autumn replacement for the early-evening *Nationwide*.

Americans in 1983 were watching less network television than for many years, according to an independent survey sponsored by the National Association of Broadcasters. The three major networks were reported to be attracting 78 per cent of the total potential audience, compared with 92 per cent in 1975. Counter-attractions such as television games, home computers and cable TV were blamed for the decline. At the same time the American audience had become more reliant on the medium as a prime source of news: another survey showed that 67 per cent of the audience watched news on TV every day, against fewer than 40 per cent in 1971.

Despite recruitment of new subscribers at an estimated rate of 400,000 a month, cable entrepreneurs faced their own problems. Many cable channels were expected to show heavy losses by the end of the year, while others contrived to stay in business only through mergers with rivals. The author of one survey concluded: 'Cable services are not going to be the goldmine that many anticipated, and for some it may be no business at all.'

A major television event was the screening by the ABC network on 20 November of *The Day After*, a 2¼-hour 'documentary drama' showing the aftermath of a nuclear attack on Kansas City. An audience estimated at between 70 and 100 million reacted with varying degrees of shock to the scenes of mass destruction and human suffering, though many experts claimed that the true effect of a thermonuclear strike had been played down (see p. 57).

After years of heated debate about the merits of commercial television, West Germany prepared to launch its first privately-owned TV channel in the Rhineland town of Ludwigshafen. The experimental cable service, the first of four, planned to relay 19 channels, including German and French state TV and a private British satellite channel, to some 1,200 homes at an annual cost of £25 million.

Plans for France's fourth television channel, expected to be in operation by May 1984, were announced by the Communications Minister, Georges Fillioud. It would be the first national TV channel anywhere to be distributed by cable.

Elements of farce attended the resignation at the beginning of the year of Maurice Remy, chairman of Télédiffusion de France, the company providing facilities for the three French TV channels. He took the blame when a privately-hired mobile crane needed to help relay a New Year message from President Mitterrand's home in the Landes failed to arrive. The President's TV chat had to be postponed for 24 hours.

Western monitors of Soviet broadcasting were intrigued to learn in May that a newsreader in the Moscow English language service, Vladimir Danchev, had been suspended for making repeated references to 'invasion' of Afghanistan by 'Soviet bandits'. An official spokesman admitted that 'one or two errors' had been committed. Danchev was confined to a psychiatric hospital in his native Tashkent but later allowed to resume work in Moscow after being 'cured'.

Russian and other Eastern bloc countries secured what appeared to be a bargain in buying the rights to the 1984 Los Angeles Olympics for only $3 million. This compared with $20 million paid by Western Europe, and $225 million bid by American television.

Princess Anne and her husband, Captain Mark Phillips, talked frankly about their private and public lives when they appeared on Australian television in the *Michael Parkinson Show* in October. The Princess dismissed rumours of a rift in their marriage and accused newspapers of 'sex discrimination' when they criticized her 'aloofness' on some public occasions: 'It's difficult to take an intelligent interest and wear a grin. Men are allowed to be serious'.

In Canada women demonstrators protested against the proposal of one of the country's new pay-TV channels, First Choice, to screen soft porn films specially produced by the American *Playboy* organization. First Choice won its franchise after undertaking to help promote the Canadian feature film industry.

In India it was reported that cinema box office receipts had fallen by 30 per cent because of the booming popularity of pirated video cassettes. One estimate put the number of video recorders in use at 300,000, with a growth rate of 20,000 per month. The Indian film industry, with 350,000 employees and an annual turnover of more than £500 million, pressed the Government to introduce enforceable copyright laws.

In South Africa some white viewers reacted angrily to the appearance on their screens of a coloured (mixed race) announcer, Vivian Solomon, in the Afrikaans service, followed by an Indian, Julie Ally, in the English-speaking schedules. The SABC (South African Broadcasting Corporation) said that the number of objections received had been relatively few and that more non-whites would be employed in future.

The Japanese announced plans to spend £95 million over four years in remodelling their overseas broadcasting. The extended service would broadly follow the lines of the BBC External Services, whose Japanese language broadcasts celebrated their 40th anniversary during 1983.

Chapter 2

ART—ARCHITECTURE—FASHION

ART

IN BRITAIN, the word 'crisis' was used again and again to describe the potentially disastrous situation in public funding for the arts: the new Minister for the Arts, the Earl of Gowrie, temporarily stopped the new building for the Theatre Museum in Covent Garden (reactivated with the help of a substantial, anonymous private donation) and the Arts Council suffered a retrospective one per cent cut in central funding. However, by the year's end the Arts Council as a whole had been given a rise, even though it was described as a small cut in real terms. The talk of crisis in terms of the nation's heritage was a continuing concern: the fate of both Calke Abbey and Kedleston Hall remained undecided, and the destiny of the top-quality Duccio painting of the Crucifixion was also uncertain as the year ended. Purchased in 1983 for a price thought to be £1·7 million by the richest museum in the world, the Getty Museum at Malibu, California, the Duccio's export licence was withheld while British museums tried to find the funds to keep permanently in the UK what after all had been a nineteenth-century purchase of an early fourteenth-century Sienese painting.

Thus, while the Getty Museum's endowment increased apace, and plans were announced for a new Getty Museum, and a huge Getty-Museum-financed complex in Los Angeles which would support art history, a computer record of all known works of art and an institute of conservation, Lord Montagu, President of the Museums Association, was among the prominent lobbyists campaigning for further changes in the British tax system to protect works of art still in the country.

Meanwhile, London hung on to its supremacy as the leading art market—but only just. Dealers and auction houses alike benefited from the continuing expansion of museums and private and public collections around the world, but for many months it looked as though Sotheby's, the art auctioneers, might actually go under (see AR 1982, p. 433). A take-over battle ensued. In December 1982, two Americans, Stephen Swid and Marshall Cogan, became serious bidders, provoking distinctly huffy reactions from the company—based, thought some, on social considerations; but by mid-autumn 1983 Sotheby's was indeed taken over, the rescuing 'white knight' being the Chicago-based multi-millionaire Alfred Taubman, who paid £83 million for Sotheby's. Since the United States remained the biggest buyer of art in the world, it seemed fitting that an American now owned the world's biggest auction house. The rejuvenated Sotheby's scored the world record price for any art object: the Saxon illuminated manuscript (c. 1175 AD) bought at Sotheby's London on 6 December by a West German consortium for £8,140,000. Other world record auction prices at Sotheby's in 1983 were: for an item of decorative art, £1,925,000 paid for the suit of Milanese armour made for Henri II, from the Astor collection, Hever Castle; and, for furniture, £990,00 for a Louis XVI secretaire.

London's market success owed as much to the skill of the art galleries and commercial dealers—demonstrated by the exceptional quality of the Burlington House Antiques Fair in the autumn—as to the auction houses, among which Phillips reported its biggest year yet. Christie's had a remarkably successful season: among world record prices were, for an abstract painting, a Mondrian at £1,512,000, and, for Victorian art, a group portrait by James Joseph Tissot at £561,000.

In spite of Sir Roy Strong's declaration that the age of the great exhibition, and of the exhibition as spectacle, was coming to an end, among the public museum fever was unabated. The French continued to pour money into the arts, and continued their fruitful official collaboration with America. A record-breaker was the great centenary exhibition of the art of Manet (who died in 1883) held at the Grand Palais, Paris, and subsequently at the Metropolitan Museum, New York. Britain could muster only a small but telling show, 'Manet at Work', at the National Gallery, but even that, one room big, was visited by nearly 300,000 people, contributing to another record, for attendance overall at the National Gallery, 2,896,676 in 1983.

In Britain, museum fever was confirmed by three major openings. The Burrell Collection in Pollock Park, Glasgow, displayed the unusually wide interests of Sir William Burrell, who when he died in 1944 left his collections to his beloved Glasgow. The building itself, designed by Barry Gasson and associates, was universally praised. In March the six-floor Henry Cole wing opened at the Victoria and Albert, housing the nation's first permanent galleries devoted to photography-as-art, as well as galleries for prints, drawings, water colours, works on paper, painting and the V and A's world-famous Constable collection. Opening in phases from June 1983 on, Bradford's National Museum of Photography, Film and Television proved an amazing popular success. It became the first museum anywhere to be devoted exclusively to the visual revolution of the past 150 years that followed the use of a camera and chemical treatment to fix an image, presenting the subject in terms of history, technique and aesthetics. A branch of the National Science Museum, it is housed in a brilliantly-converted former municipal theatre and office block in Bradford's centre. It is altogether an exceptionally exciting venture, employing vivid presentation techniques, which aim successfully both to entertain and to inform, using light, sound, colour and movement for explanatory tableaux and demonstrations.

In America, the proposed Los Angeles Museum of Contemporary Art (MOCA) opened in the autumn in temporary premises, with the witty exhibition of modern art from nine private collections entitled 'The Temporary Contemporary'. At the turn of the year, the Los Angeles County Museum announced the start of construction of a new gallery for twentieth-century art. The St Louis Art Museum received from the estate of Morton D. May bequests which further strengthened its holdings of twentieth-century German painting—mostly expressionism—and the arts of Africa, Oceania and the Americas, making both collections among the finest anywhere in the world. The St Louis Museum also held, under the title 'Expressions', one of the first extensive showings in America of neo-expressionism from five contemporary painters, chosen as representative of the 'phenomenonal current art activity in Germany', and confirming the trend among artists of the 1980s.

In London, the show of contemporary British sculpture at the Serpentine and Hayward received ample coverage for its shock value—including the sad episode when a protester, setting fire to David Mach's out-of-doors sculpture of Polaris, made out of rubber tyres, burnt himself to death. While the British press declared itself appalled by the art-as-rubbish, rubbish-as-art of which they claimed to find evidence in the exhibitions, many a young British sculptor, such as Bill Woodrow, Kate Blacker, Edward Allington, Julian Opie, Jean-Luc Vilmouth, to name a few, was being exhibited extensively in important group shows in Europe. In Rotterdam, in a survey of the best contemporary sculpture from America and Western Europe, over a third of the artists selected were British. There did seem to be a genuine new vitality in British sculpture—and British painting. The former received a further boost from the installation of much contemporary sculpture at Margam Country Park, Port Talbot, Wales, while the Portland Stone Quarries at Portland Bill, Dorset, hosted a summer-long exhibition of artists actually at work in the quarries, and their products.

Artists also began to design more and more for the theatre: Bridget Riley designed *Colour Move* for the Ballet Rambert, John Hubbard designed *Midsummer* for the Royal Ballet, and Patrick Procktor, Deanna Petherbridge, Helen Frankenthaler and Victor Pasmore were among those slated to design 1984 productions for Covent Garden. Two of David Hockney's stage designs for the Metropolitan, New York (for the Stravinsky *Le Rossignol* and Ravel's *L'Enfant et les Sortilèges*), were premiered at Covent Garden in the autumn. 'Hockney Paints the Stage!' opened at the Walker Art Center, Minneapolis, at the start of a three-year world tour.

In Paris, the largest Turner exhibition ever seen outside Britain proved a great success; Balthus's retrospective drew crowds; more public sculpture was commissioned, and the fantastic fountain at the Beaubourg, designed by Tinguely and Niki de Saint Phalle, proved an instant classic, delighting the public with its scores of witty, brightly-coloured sculptures, in as much motion as the flowing water.

Spain, under its new socialist Government, began what some thought to be a cultural renaissance. Certainly, the Madrid Art Fair of Contemporary Art (ARCO) had its third successful edition; the Prado continued to remodel itself and to hold temporary exhibitions (Murillo, Turner); and contemporary Spanish artists began again to make an impact abroad. A major exhibition of the life and work of Salvador Dali at the Spanish Museum of Contemporary Art was opened by King Juan Carlos on 15 April.

West Germany continued to have major exhibitions, perhaps the most spectacular being the most complete exhibition of Picasso's sculpture yet held; while Max Beckmann (1884-1950) was honoured with two exhibitions in Frankfurt. Italy, particularly Milan, with exhibitions devoted to Boccioni and to kinetic art, continued to be exceptionally lively in the contemporary field; and plans were announced at the end of the year for major expansion of Milan's Brera, while major conservation programmes devoted to Leonardo's *Last Supper* and to Botticelli and Piero de Francesca proceeded in Florence and Milan. A spectacular exhibition of Alexander Calder sculpture was held in Turin. Europe contributed, as did America, to two major Council of Europe exhibitions held in the same year. In May a five-part exhibition, 'Portugese Discoveries and Renaissance Europe', opened in Lisbon; in the same month, an enormous show, calling on over fifty museum collections from all over Turkey, and examining Anatolian civilizations, opened in Istanbul.

For those devoted to modern art, though, perhaps the most purely beautiful—and informative—exhibition anywhere was 'The Essential Cubism', a one-off show at the Tate in London, devised by Douglas Cooper and the young art historian Gary Tinterow. London had another scoop with the biggest exhibition ever held on the art of Dufy—including applied art, such as his textile designs— which rehabilitated the quality of a great artist whose very popularity had injured his critical reputation. The Costakis collection of Russian avant-garde art was shown at the Royal Academy in the autumn.

Another one-off show, and an exhilarating success, was the scholarly, yet intensely enjoyable 'The Genius of Venice' exhibition at the Royal Academy, which examined in depth the art of Venice's Golden Age, the sixteenth century; the love affair of the English with Italian art was brilliantly confirmed. Raphael's quincentenary (1483-1520) was celebrated at the British Museum, with the largest show of Raphael drawings ever held. Paris held no less than three exhibitions devoted to Raphael, of which the most surprising mixed kitsch and high art in a survey called 'Raphael and French Art', showing not only his influence, but his cult, in numerous bathetic paintings based on supposed episodes in his life which were a favourite theme of ninteenth-century French artists.

An interesting trend was confirmed as trade and university publishers collaborated more and more with museums to produce catalogues, where much of the new impetus of art publishing was emerging. In art publishing, numbers of titles seemed very gradually to be giving way to a search for quality. Professor Lorenz Eitner's *Géricault* (Orbis/Cornell) was awarded the 1983 Mitchell prize for the history of art.

ART BOOKS OF THE YEAR: *Géricault*, by Lorenz Eitner (Orbis); *Grant Wood: The Regionalist Vision*, by Wanda M. Corn (Yale); *The New Sculpture*, by Susan Beattie (Yale); *John Singer Sargent*, by Carter Ratcliff (Phaidon); *The Drawings of Raphael*, by Paul Joannides (Phaidon); *The Art of Describing: Dutch Art in the 17th Century*, by

Svetlana Alpsers (John Murray); *Constable: The Painter and the Landscape*, by Michael Rosenthal (Yale); *Raphael*, by Roger Jones and Nicholas Penny (Yale); *Caravaggio*, by Howard Hibbard (Thames and Hudson).

ARCHITECTURE

There was excitement in the British press in early January over two competition results decided by the Secretary of State for the Environment at the end of 1982. First, an amended scheme by architects Ahrends Burton & Koralek, linked with Trafalgar House Developments, was chosen winner of the limited competition for extending the National Gallery in Trafalgar Square. The second decision was to grant planning permission for the Coin-street redevelopment (see AR 1981, p. 439, and 1982, p. 437) to both the scheme by architect Richard Rogers with Greycoat Estates, and that of the Association of Waterloo Groups. Whoever acquired the land first—and Greycoat Estates already owned most of it—could take up its permission.

In the City of London the last had not been heard of Chamberlin Powell & Bon's Barbican scheme. A vast conservatory linking the theatre fly-tower with the sculpture court was completed and open to the public, who could now promenade amidst exotic growths whilst gazing out on the various Barbican courts below.

One of the most important commercial architectural conceptions of the past few years in Britain came to completion. This was the final phase of IBM (UK)'s national headquarters at North Harbour near Portsmouth by architects Arup Associates, the master plan for which was conceived in 1972. Four office blocks, each three storeys high, were stepped back at each floor, to produce terraces. In the last phase the separate offices were linked together at first-floor level with a single-storey arched-roof glazed 'way'. The main entrance to the complex was a glazed pavilion containing entrance hall, exhibition space and assembly room.

In the autumn interest shifted north to Scotland for the opening of the Burrell Museum in Glasgow's Pollock Park (see p. 423). The completed building had scarcely changed in design from that of the original competition won by the architects Barry Gasson and John Meunier with Brit Andreson in 1972. During the year Barry Gasson received the Royal Scottish Academy gold medal for architecture in commendation of the museum's design.

In France, a Danish architect, Johan Otto von Sprekelsen, won the international competition for redevelopment of the Tête de la Défense site in Paris. The competition attracted 424 projects. A vast open cube-shaped building, slightly offset from the axis of the Arc de Triomphe, was the high point of the Sprekelsen scheme. The project included an international centre for communications, offices for ministries, shops and services. Another important competition result was the choice from nine finalists of Bernard Tschumi's designs for the Parc de la Villette, Paris, in the international competition held in 1982, which attracted 470 entries. Tschumi's scheme for the 30-acre site included conversion of a nineteenth-century Grande Halle into an exhibition hall, and a never-used abattoir into a museum of science and industry. A circuitous path was to link all areas of the park, and was to pass through gardens laid out in various schemes. Large open spaces defined by groups of trees would provide areas for recreation and sports. At intervals would be sited restaurants, bars, kiosks and so on.

Similar to the outcry over the UK's National Gallery competition, a row broke out in Paris in the autumn when no outright winner was announced in the Bastille Opéra international competition: three shortlisted architects from the 750 entrants were to go on to a second stage, namely, Carlos Ott of Canada, Sen Kee Rocco Yim of Hong Kong and Dan Munteanu, a Romanian architect. President Mitterrand himself was to select the winner from the second-stage designs, and ultimately chose Carlos Ott in November.

In contrast with British architects' preference for low-rise development, interest in the Netherlands was centred on the 39-storey high-rise sky-scraper in Rotterdam by the Dutch architect Henk Klunder. Nicknamed the 'punch card' because of the distinctive pattern of the fenestration, the building, due to start on site in 1984, was to provide 247 apartments for families and students.

In West Germany, the second stage took place in the limited competition for an Energy Centre in Essen. The scheme was to accommodate a natural science and technological museum with demonstration areas, a forum for interchange of ideas and an interdisciplinary research institute. All five architects, Hans Hollein of Vienna, Harald Deilmann of Munster, Planungsgruppe Me di um of Hamburg, Bernd Faskel and Vladimir Nikolic of Kassel, and Erich Schneider-Wessling of Cologne, were asked to proceed with the second stage.

In Portugal, the Gulbenkian Foundation's Centre for Modern Art, Lisbon, designed by British architect Sir Leslie Martin and built in association with the foundation's technical staff, was formally opened in July. The new building, containing galleries, research centre, workshop and stores, faced the foundation's administrative building across a landscaped park.

The British 1983 Royal Gold Medal for Architecture was awarded to Norman Foster for drawing the advanced technology of the aerospace and electronic worlds into architecture and building. The American Institute of Architects' gold medal for 1983 was awarded to Nathaniel Alexander Owings, co-founder of the American architectural firm of

Skidmore Owings & Merrill (SOM). I.M. Pei, principal of the New York firm of architects, I. M. Pei & Partners, was awarded the 1983 Pritzker Prize.

In America, architecture reflected a concern for history and the arts. The 70-year-old, 54-storey Woolworth building, New York City, was given Landmark status, so that it could not be demolished or altered without official sanction. In Buffalo, the famous Guaranty building, by Sullivan and Adler (1894-95), was undergoing renovation and cleaning to preserve both its external and internal features.

Numerous museum and art centre schemes were either completed or planned. The Indiana University Art Museum, Bloomington, by architect I. M. Pei, was dedicated in October. The mainly teaching facility, built in reinforced concrete, contained four galleries, a fine arts library, conservation laboratories and offices. The museum's two interlocking wings were connected by an atrium, 110 feet high. A large new centre for the arts, occupying a 60-acre site, was moving towards completion in Dallas. The Dallas Arts District consisted of the nearly-completed Dallas Museum of Art (architect Edward Larrabee Barnes), a proposal for an elegant new concert hall by I. M. Pei & Partners, and a 50-storey office building by SOM Houston. The overall landscape plan was by Sasaki Associates of Watertown, Mass.

The Santa Barbara Art Museum two-stage competition was won by Michael Dennis and Jeffrey Clark of Newton, Mass., with Greg Conyngham and Gary Lapara. The architects' single-storey solution included a welcoming forecourt and an enclosed courtyard for outdoor exhibitions. The main programme included a large museum, a 100-seat lecture hall and other accommodation. Another arts project was the proposed $16 million Visual Arts Center at Ohio State University in Columbus, Ohio, the subject of a competition won by architects Trott and Bean and Eiseman/Robertson Association. Among other projects completed or nearly so were Vassar College's Art Department and Museum, Poughkeepsy, N.Y., Emory University's Art Department Museum by Michael Graves; and in New York the Metropolitan Museum of Art's big building programme by Kevin Roche/John Dinkerloo Associates.

In Canada, a revised scheme for Canada Place, Vancouver, B.C., was released to and accepted by the public during the year. The earlier scheme's architects, Down/Archambault and Musson Cattell and Partners, had been joined by Zeidler/Roberts Partnership of Toronto to produce the new design for the site on an existing pier thrusting out into the Burrard inlet. The main building-block, containing a tent-like structure with sails, reminiscent of Sydney Opera House, covering the Canada Pavilion for Expo '86, the world transportation fair, was stretched out in front of the bulky main building containing an hotel and trade centre offices.

The Aga Khan 1983 awards for architecture in the Muslim tradition, given every three years, were announced in September, 1983 being the second occasion of the award. Eleven schemes were chosen for their strong continuity with Muslim traditions, revitalization of traditional crafts and appropriate building techniques. Among the varied premiated schemes were the mud-brick art centre at Hurrania, Egypt, by architect Ramses Wissa Wassef; the white mosque, by architect Zlatko Ugljen, serving a mainly Muslim population of 30,000 in Visoko, a red-roofed Bosnian town in Yugoslavia; and Skidmore Owings and Merrill's structure of the Hajj Terminal, Jeddah airport, Saudi Arabia, to provide shade and cool for the pilgrims travelling by air to Mecca (see AR 1982, p. 440).

José Luis Sert, born in Barcelona, Spain, one of the modern movement's supporters along with Walter Gropius and Le Corbusier, died in March, aged 80. The American designer R. Buckminster Fuller, renowned for his geodesic structures, died in July, aged 88. Sir Nicholas Pevsner, author of the 47 volumes of *The Buildings of England*, died in August. (For all three, see OBITUARY).

FASHION

In the middle of 1983 a new fashion was born that came directly from the current craze for keeping fit, a two-piece outfit with loose trousers closed in at the ankles. Starting as workwear for jogging and dance enthusiasts, it consolidated its place as a favourite form of dress for leisure and party wear and proved to have a strong appeal for contemporary thought. Nothing like this had happened for years—the coming of a really new and different line of fashion that, by the end of 1983, was available at all price ranges, made in both inexpensive and luxury materials.

In general, day and evening clothes tended to get a straighter, slimmer silhouette, with skirt lengths variable from short above the knee to mid-calf. The most popular style of trouser was cropped a few inches above the ankle. The T-shirt, which had started life some time back as a sporty, short-sleeved cotton-knit vest, became established as a classic garment and was made in silk or linen for wear on formal occasions. This was one of the clearest indications of the simplicity in dress that during the year was heavily promoted by the rising number of important Japanese designers showing their collections internationally. Led by Japanese designer Issey Myake, who had a shop in London, the influence of a loose, wrap shape, often layered and made in sombre colours, made a big impact on the more traditional style of most European clothes.

That hardy perennial, the safari look, came back again, bringing with it bush jackets, safari shirts and tropical shorts. Made in khaki or white cotton, these summer clothes were worn by all sections of society for informal day wear and, to a large extent, replaced the still strong-running denim jeans.

In May, Mr Frank Russell, chairman and founder of Mansfield-Cache d'Or, a well-known British fashion manufacturing company, established a trust fund of £25,000 for the fashion school of the Royal College of Art—the first time such an award had been made to a fashion school. The annual income from this trust would be used to fund specific projects.

During the summer the famous Paris couture house of Chanel appointed Karl Lagerfeld as chief designer. He also assumed responsibility for their ready-to-wear collections. This talented man proved his gift for designing beautiful clothes for women when he showed his first couture collection for Chanel in July to a standing ovation. Formerly he was designer for Chloe, the successful ready-to-wear Paris house.

In Scotland, the Shetland Knitwear Trade Association launched, with the help of £450,000 from the Shetland Islands Council, its own trademark to identify specifically Shetland-made knitwear, in order to secure traditional occupations. The islands had given the name to a whole type of knitting—the famous Fair Isle patterns in particular—and also to a grade of wool.

Chapter 3

LITERATURE

For the first time in 30 years the Nobel prize for literature was in 1983 awarded to a British writer, the novelist William Golding. There was some surprise at the choice; many thought that, if a British writer was to be chosen, a more likely candidate would have been Graham Greene, whose international reputation stood higher than Golding's. This surprise was underlined by the fact that, for the first time in the history of the prize, one of the judges made public his dissent from the majority view. He declared that Golding was 'a little English phenomenon'. This again was a slightly surprising statement since, though it might be agreed that Golding was undoubtedly English in his attitudes and was something of a phenomenon, his boldness of choice of theme, usually one of the great moral predicaments, could hardly qualify for the adjective 'little'.

The actual title named by the Nobel committee was Golding's *Rites of Passage*, which won the 1980 Booker prize and was, in fact, the earliest book to benefit in terms of sales from the fact that a literary prize had become, for the first time in Britain, a national institution, the subject not only of television programmes but even of interest to the bookies, who laid odds against the novels mentioned on the short list. The winner of the

1983 prize was *The Life and Times of Michael K* by the South African novelist J. M. Coetzee, a complex work which owed something, as the inclusion of the letter K in the title acknowledged, to the work of Franz Kafka. In a rather dreamlike way it told of the struggles of the simple-minded Michael to live in peace and quiet self-sufficiency in a hostile state, unnamed but clearly based on South Africa.

Although the publishers were able to demonstrate that this novel, which had been only a modest success before it was included on the Booker short list, sold some 40,000 copies in the immediate aftermath of the announcement of the prize and continued to sell reasonably well, its nature prevented its becoming as much a best-seller as several of its predecessors, notably Salman Rushdie's 1981 winner, *Midnight's Children*. Rushdie's 1983 novel, *Shame*, was the close runner-up for the Booker prize. This time he turned from his native India to Pakistan for his theme, demonstrating in his fiction the authoritarian nature of the regime. This novel was not quite such a critical success as his earlier one because some found the constant direct address to the reader by the author somewhat mannered and intrusive.

The Whitbread award for fiction went to *Fools of Fortune*. This work, surprisingly omitted from the Booker short list, made its author William Trevor the first man to win the Whitbread for a second time. It showed yet again Trevor's skill at character-drawing as he used a background of 60 years of Anglo-Irish history. A new award, the Triple First, sponsored by a hardback publisher, a paperback one and a book club, provided a winner that raised little interest. This was a foggy allegory, *The Viaduct*, by David Wheldon. Far more excitement was provided by the first novel by the poet John Fuller, *Flying to Nowhere*, which not only made the Booker short list but also won the Whitbread first-novel award. This short book described life in a medieval Welsh monastery in a vivid yet surreal way. Other first novels which received critical praise were Patricia Roberts's psychological study of a New York murderer, *Tender Prey*, M. S. Power's delicate Irish novel, *Hunt for the Autumn Clowns*, and the surprise inclusion on the Booker short list, Anita Mason's *The Illusionist*.

Of the established novelists most praise went to Malcolm Bradbury for *Rates of Exchange*, which combined a lively story of the adventures of an English academic travelling behind the Iron Curtain with fairly complicated linguistic speculations turning on the creation of an entirely imaginary European language. Both Lawrence Durrell's latest instalment of his pentalogy, *Sebastian, or Special Tastes*, and Iris Murdoch's vastly overlong *The Philospher's Pupil,* were not particularly well received, though in a much more kindly way than Norman Mailer's rambling chronicle of Egypt in the time of the Pharaohs, *Ancient Evenings*. John Masters, who died during the year, did live to see more enthusiastic reviews for his last book, *Man of War*, than he had received for some years. The praise was not just obituary magnanimity; it represented acknowledgement of a much better novel. Anthony Powell produced his first piece of fiction since the completion of *The Dance to the Music of Time* sequence. It was barely more than a long short story, a funny, rather bitchy account of the rivalry between a smug, successful author and a less eminent rival who posthumously had a small revenge. Only the title was unwieldy, *O, How the Wheel Becomes You*.

Eva Figes's account of a day in the life of the impressionist painter Manet, *Light*, was a clever piece of imaginative reconstruction. In *Londoners; an Elegy*, Maureen Duffy painted, mostly in dialogue form, a lively picture of low life in West London. Three women novelists chose various aspects of grief for their theme and produced notable results—Anita Brookner in *Look at Me*, Penelope Lively in *Perfect Happiness* and Nina Bawden in *The Ice House*. Both Brian Aldiss and Doris Lessing produced further volumes in their science fiction sequences, he with *Helliconia Summer* and she with *Sentimental Agents in the Volyen Empire*. Both were solid achievements and, in particular, the Lessing novel showed that, after a slightly uncertain start, her multi-volume work would be a notable contribution. The two thrillers that attracted the most attention were John le Carré's *The Little Drummer Girl* and Len Deighton's *Berlin Game*. Although its sales were vast, the latest le Carré caused some critical disappointment. Its unlikely plot about an English actress trained to be an Israeli agent seemed to be too directly aimed at the making of a large-scale international film.

The novel from outside Britain that became a best-seller there was a slightly unlikely work, *The Name of the Rose* by Umberto Eco. It had already been an immense success on the Continent. This well-written combination of thriller and historical romance proved successful. Of far more literary importance were the novel by the Czech dissident writer, Milan Kundera, *The Joke*, and a vast, complicated and subtle South American novel, *Aunt Julia and the Scriptwriter* by Mario Vargas Llosa.

Undoubtedly the outstanding biography of the year was the third and final volume of Alan Bullock's life of the great trade union leader and Labour politician, *Ernest Bevin, Foreign Secretary, 1945-51*. This was by general assent regarded as the most important political biography of recent years. Nicholas Mosley also completed his life of his father in *Beyond the Pale: Sir Oswald Mosley, 1933-80*. This was a delicate task well done; for the author, while never for a moment ceasing to be a devoted son, managed to express his distaste for his father's friendship with dictators and his fascist policies. Another difficult man to write about, *F.E. Smith, First Earl of Birkenhead*, was dealt with most competently by John Campbell, who managed to convey the contradictions in the brilliant though arrogant barrister and the sometimes uncertain politician. Both a share of the Whitbread award for biography and one of the Wolfson prizes went to Kenneth Rose for his life of *George V*, which was able to be more objective and understanding than the original one, written some 30 years earlier by Harold Nicolson. The first volume of Robert Skidelsky's *John Maynard Keynes*, which bore the subtitle *The Foundations*, gave promise of being an important work, while the fact that Nigel Hamilton had found it necessary to take his biography of Field Marshal Lord Montgomery into a third volume, covering as he did less than two years, in *Monty: Master of the Battlefield, 1942-44*, was regretted. The rather forgotten figure of Auberon Herbert, amateur secret agent and rebellious MP, was competently revived by Margaret FitzHerbert in *The Man Who Was Greenmantle*, and a strangely neglected figure among World War I generals was done full justice to by Jeffrey Williams in *Byng of Vimy: General and Governor-General*.

It was a good year for literary biography. The most interesting was the life of the American poet *Robert Lowell* by the British poet Ian Hamilton, which managed to combine intelligent criticism of the subject's work with a revealing account of Lowell's life, punctuated as it was by bouts of insanity. The Whitbread biographical award's joint winner with *George V* was *Vita: the Life of Victoria Sackville-West* by Victoria Glendinning. Vita's ambivalent life, including her marriage with Harold Nicolson and her affairs with Virginia Woolf and others, had been written about several times before, but this latest work was probably the last word that need be said. Two minor turn-of-the-century figures both of whom taught at Eton and later at Cambridge were revived in workmanlike biographies. Michael Cox reintroduced *M.R. James*, whose enduring reputation was as a writer of accomplished ghost stories but who was Provost both of Eton and of King's College, Cambridge. James was a rather grey figure; far more highly-coloured was *Oscar Browning*, whose up-and-down career involving several scandals was chronicled by Ian Anstruther. Maurice Cranston provided a good first volume, in *Jean-Jacques: the Early Life of Jean-Jacques Rousseau*, of what obviously would be an important biography, and Ronald Hingley provided an informative life of the Russian poet and novelist, *Pasternak*.

Two more recent writers who could certainly not be included in the first rank were dignified with biographies. Violet Powell explained the problems of a novelist who had a best-seller with an early book and never achieved the same fame again in *The Constant Novelist: a Study of Margaret Kennedy, 1896-1967*, and Tony Gould with some success unravelled the enigma of an eccentric writer in *The Outsider: the Life and Times of Colin MacInnes*.

Some virtual autobiographies were quarried out of their subjects' writings by other hands. Examples of this were *Cyril Connolly: Journal and Memoir*, where the shaping was done by David Pryce-Jones, and *Julia: a Portrait of Julia Strachey*, which was unusually described as being 'By Herself and Frances Partridge'. Much of the same could be said about *Peter Hall's Diaries*, John Goodwin's abridgement of the daily tape-recordings made by the director of the National Theatre telling of his daily struggles with his governing body and his actors. This was a book that caused more discussion than almost any other during the year. The general opinion was that much of the material produced was unfair.

It was not a great year for historical writing. Indeed perhaps the most important work of the kind did not on the face of it appear to be a history. It was the last two volumes of the massive complete text of *The Diary of Samuel Pepys*. They comprised an index highly praised for its precision and, more importantly, a volume of historical commentary which put Pepys's sometimes cryptic remarks into context. Probably the most interesting original work was Keith Thomas's *Man and the Natural World*, which studied in great detail the change of attitude during the three centuries from 1500 towards wild and domestic animals. This proved to be a metaphor for discussing moral standards more generally. John Ehrmann produced a second volume of his monumental life of *The Younger Pitt* and Muriel Chamberlain managed to make interesting the rather grey figure of the Victorian Prime Minister, *Lord Aberdeen*.

The year saw the death of a number of notable writers. Among them were the novelist, journalist and critic Dame Rebecca West, the novelist and philosopher Arthur Koestler, and the French communist poet Louis Aragon. The historians who died included Sir Roger Fulford, Professor Leonard Schapiro and the French political writer Raymond Aron. Among the novelists were the historical writer Mary Renault, the detective story expert Gladys Mitchell, Richard Llewellyn and Constantine FitzGibbon. The travel writer and journalist Alan Moorehead and the popular journalist Beverley Nichols also died during the year. (For Dame Rebecca, Koestler, Aragon, Schapiro and Aron, see OBITUARY.)

Once again the number of books produced during the year rose. For the first time the total of new books and new editions passed the 50,000 mark. The figure was 51,071 of which new titles comprised 38,980. The biggest increases were shown in children's books, works on literary topics and religious books of all kinds.

Among the interesting new books published during the year were:

FICTION: *The Last Testament of Oscar Wilde* by Peter Ackroyd (Hamish Hamilton); *Helliconia Summer* by Brian Aldiss (Faber); *The Ice House* by Nina Bawden (Macmillan); *Holy Pictures* by Clare Boylan (Hamish Hamilton); *Rates of Exchange* by Malcolm Bradbury (Secker); *Look at Me* by Anita Brookner (Cape); *The Life and Times of Michael K* by J.M.Coetzee (Secker); *Scenes from Later Life* by William Cooper (Macmillan); *Slouching towards Kalamazoo* by Peter de Vries (Gollancz); *Berlin Game* by Len Deighton (Hutchinson); *Leila* by J. P. Donleavy (Allen Lane); *Londoners: an Elegy* by Maureen Duffy (Methuen); *Sebastian, or Special Tastes* by Lawrence Durrell (Faber); *The Name of the Rose* by Umberto Eco (Secker); *Light* by Eva Figes (Hamish Hamilton); *Flying to Nowhere* by John Fuller (Salamander); *Burning Book* by Maggie Gee (Faber); *The Riding Mistress* by Harriett Gilbert (Constable); *The Woman in Black* by Susan Hill (Hamish Hamilton); *Brilliant Creatures* by Clive James (Cape); *Time after Time* by Molly Keane (Deutsch); *The Joke* by Milan Kundera (Faber); *The Little Drummer Girl* by John le Carré

LITERATURE

(Hodder); *The Sentimental Agents in the Volyen Empire* by Doris Lessing (Cape); *Perfect Happiness* by Penelope Lively (Heinemann); *Aunt Julia and the Script Writer* by Mario Vargas Llosa (Faber); *Ancient Evenings* by Norman Mailer (Macmillan); *The Illusionist* by Anita Mason (Hamish Hamilton); *Man of War* by John Masters (Michael Joseph); *Cold Heaven* by Brian Moore (Cape); *The Philosopher's Pupil* by Iris Murdoch (Chatto); *A Hot Country* by Shiva Naipaul (Hamish Hamilton); *O, How the Wheel Becomes You* by Anthony Powell (Heinemann); *Hunt for the Autumn Clowns* by M. S. Power (Chatto); *More Collected Stories* by V. S. Pritchett (Chatto); *Tender Prey* by Patricia Roberts (Chatto); *Shame* by Salman Rushdie (Cape); *The Proprietor* by Ann Schlee (Macmillan); *Waterland* by Graham Swift (Heinemann); *Ararat* by D.M. Thomas (Gollancz); *Fools of Fortune* by William Trevor (Bodley Head); *Bech is Back* by John Updike (Deutsch); *An Innocent Millionaire* by Stephen Vizincey (Secker); *Deadeye Dick* by Kurt Vonnegut (Cape); *Kate's House* by Harriet Waugh (Weidenfeld); *The Viaduct* by David Wheldon (Bodley Head); *A Boy's Own Story* by Edmund White (Picador); *Scandal* by A. N. Wilson (Hamish Hamilton).

POETRY: *Against a Setting Sun* by Ronald Bottrell (Allison & Bishby); *Mirror* by Robert Creeley (Marion Boyars); *Collected Poems* by Donald Davie (Carcanet); *The Mystery of the Charity of Charles Peguy* (Deutsch); *Nights in the Iron Hotel* by Michael Hofmann (Faber); *The River* by Ted Hughes (Faber); *Poem of the Year* by Clive James (Cape); *The Long Darkness* by George MacBeth (Secker); *Now It Can Be Told* by Ian Macmillan (Carcanet); *Quoof* by Paul Muldoon (Faber); *Collected Poems* by Peter Porter (Oxford); *A Quiet Gathering* by David Scott (Bloodaxe); *Later Poems* by R. S. Thomas (Macmillan).

LITERARY CRITICISM: *A Mania for Sentences* by D. J. Enright (Chatto); *New Pelican Guide to English Literature*, Vol. 8 *The Present* edited by Boris Ford (Penguin); *John Galsworthy: A Reassessment* by André Fréchet (Macmillan); *Brecht* by Ronald Hayman (Weidenfeld); *Dostoevsky* by J. Jones (Oxford); *Collected Essays I: the Englishness of the English Novel* by Q.D. Leavis (Cambridge); *Africa and the Novel* by Neil McEwan (Macmillan); *The Religious Life of Samuel Johnson* by Charles E. Pierce (Athlone); *Dickens and Women* by Michael Slater (Dent); *The Canterbury Tales: a Reading* by Derek Traversi (Bodley Head); *The Life of John Milton* by A. N. Wilson (Oxford); *The Borders of Vision: William Wordsworth* by Jonathan Wordsworth (Oxford).

BIOGRAPHY: *Oscar Browning, a Biography* by Ian Anstruther (Murray); *Pierre Loti: Portrait of an Escapist* by Lesley Blanch (Collins); *Ernest Bevin: Foreign Secretary 1945-51* by Alan Bullock (Heinemann); *F. E. Smith, First Earl of Birkenhead* by John Campbell (Cape); *M. R. James* by Michael Cox (Oxford); *Jean-Jacques: the Early Life of Jean-Jacques Rousseau* by Maurice Cranston (Allen Lane); *Runcie: the Making of an Archbishop* by Margaret Duggan (Hodder); *The Man Who Was Greenmantle* by Margaret FitzHerbert (Murray); *Vita: the Life of Vita Sackville-West* by Victoria Glendinning (Weidenfeld); *The Outsider: the Life and Times of Colin MacInnes* by Tony Gould (Chatto); *Robert Lowell, a Biography* by Ian Hamilton (Faber); *Monty: Master of the Battlefield, 1942-44* by Nigel Hamilton (Hamish Hamilton); *Pasternak* by Ronald Hingley (Weidenfeld); *Edwina, Countess of Mountbatten* by Richard Hough (Weidenfeld); *Elizabeth R.* by Elizabeth Longford (Weidenfeld); *Beyond the Pale: Sir Oswald Mosley, 1933-80* by Nicholas Mosley (Secker); *Difficult Women: a Memoir of Three* by David Plante (Gollancz); *The Constant Novelist: a Study of Margaret Kennedy, 1896-1967* by Violet Powell (Heinemann); *John Singer Sargent* by Carter Ratcliff (Phaidon); *King George V* by Kenneth Rose (Weidenfeld); *Ranji: King of Cricketers* by Alan Ross (Collins); *John Maynard Keynes: I. the Foundations* by Robert Skidelsky (Macmillan); *Vanessa Bell* by Frances Spalding (Weidenfeld); *The Tolstoys: Twenty-Four Generations in Russian History* by Nikolai Tolstoy (Hamish Hamilton); *Mr George Eliot: a Biography of George Henry Lewes* by David Williams (Hodder); *Byng of Vimy: General and Governor-General* by Jeffrey Williams (Leo Cooper).

AUTOBIOGRAPHY AND LETTERS: *Donkey Work* by Edward Blishen (Hamish Hamilton); *Still Life: Sketches from a Tunbridge Wells Childhood* by Richard Cobb (Chatto); *Cyril Connolly: Journal and Memoir* by David Pryce-Jones (Collins); *Collected Letters of Joseph Conrad. Vol. I: 1861-1897* edited by Frederick R. Karl and Laurence Davies (Cambridge); *By Safe Hand: the Letters of Sybil and David Eccles* by David Eccles (Bodley Head); *Back from the Brink* by Michael Edwardes (Collins); *Good Times, Bad Times* by Harold Evans (Weidenfeld); *Selected Letters of E. M. Forster,* Vol I: 1879-1920, edited by Mary Lago and P. N. Furbank (Collins); *Peter Hall's Diaries: the Story of a Dramatic Battle, 1972-80* edited by John Goodwin (Hamish Hamilton); *Journey Home* by John Hillaby (Constable); *O Beloved Kids: Rudyard Kipling's Letters to his Children,* selected and edited by Elliot L. Gilbert (Weidenfeld); *Caves of Ice: Diaries, 1967-7* by James Lees-Milne (Chatto); *The Truth that Killed* by George Markov (Weidenfeld); *Eight Feet in the Andes* by Dervla Murphy (Murray); *At the Jazz Band Ball* by Philip Oakes (Deutsch); *A World Apart* by Daphne Rae (Lutterworth); *Siegfried Sassoon's Diaries, 1915-18* edited by Rupert Hart-Davis (Faber); *Julia: a Portrait of Julia Strachey* by Herself and Frances Partridge (Gollancz); *Blue Remembered Hills* by Rosemary Sutcliff (Bodley Head); *A Personal History* by A. J. P. Taylor (Hamish Hamilton); *The Kingdom by the Sea* by Paul Theroux (Hamish Hamilton); *Among the Russians* by Colin Thubron (Heinemann); *The Diaries of Beatrice Webb. Vol II, 1892-1905: All the Good Things of Life* edited by Norman and Jeanne Mackenzie (Virago).

HISTORY: *A Social History of England* by Asa Briggs (Weidenfeld); *The Lisle Letters: an Abridgement* edited by M. St Clare Byrne, selected and edited by Bridget Boland (Secker); *Lord Aberdeen* by Muriel E. Chamberlain (Longman); *French and Germans: Germans and French: a Personal Interpretation of France under Two Occupations* by Richard Cobb (New England); *The Religion of the Protestants* by Patrick Collinson (Oxford); *SOE in the Far East* by Charles Cruickshank (Oxford); *The Younger Pitt: the Reluctant Transition* by John Ehrman (Constable); *Finest Hour: Winston S. Churchill, 1939-41* by Martin Gilbert (Heinemann); *The Battle for the Falklands* by Max Hastings and Simon Jenkins (Michael Joseph); *The Invention of Tradition* edited by Eric Hobsbawn and Terence Ranger (Cambridge); *The History Men* by John Kenyon (Weidenfeld); *The Diary of Samuel Pepys,* Vols. X & XI, compiled and edited by Robert Latham and William Matthews (Bell & Hyman); *India Britannica* by Geoffrey Moorhouse (Harvill); *The People of Providence: a Housing Estate and its Inhabitants* by Tony Parker (Hutchinson); *Man and the Natural World: Changing Attitudes in England, 1500-1800* by Keith Thomas (Allen Lane); *The Squandered Peace* by John Vaizey (Hodder).

XVI SPORT

ASSOCIATION FOOTBALL: Qualification for the European championship finals (to be held in France in June 1984) proved to be difficult for some of the more powerful of the Continental teams who had appeared in the World Cup finals in Spain only a year earlier. The most notable absentee would be the world champions themselves, Italy, who, in an astounding reversal of form, failed to win any of their first seven matches, were beaten at home by Sweden 3-0 and held 1-1 away by Cyprus. England were also knocked out following a 1-0 defeat by Denmark and a 0-0 draw against Greece, both at Wembley. The USSR fell to Portugal in the last match in their group and Scotland had a disastrous tournament, winning only one match in its group with Belgium, East Germany and Switzerland to finish last. The World Cup runners-up, West Germany, were beaten twice by Northern Ireland, including a 1-0 victory in Hamburg which was the Germans' first defeat at home in a competitive match for more than 10 years, and they eventually had to struggle to beat Albania 2-1 at home to win their group on goal-difference. But the most astonishing result of all came in the last match of Group 7 when Spain faced Malta in Seville needing at least a double-figure score to oust their nearest rivals, the Netherlands, on goal-difference. The Spaniards won 12-1, scoring nine of their goals in the second half: in their last three matches in the group—all away—Malta conceded 25 goals and scored only one.

Two historic decisions were made on the British domestic front. England and Scotland decided to withdraw from the Home International Championship after the 1983-84 season, thus effectively ending the tournament after 100 years. Except for the annual England-Scotland matches, the tournament had steadily declined in popularity (only 24,000, the lowest attendance in Wembley's history for a full international, saw England beat Wales in February), although both the Wales and Northern Ireland associations protested that the decision would place them in serious economic difficulties. The English Football League, first established in 1888 and the oldest of its type in the world, changed its title and became the Canon League as a result of accepting sponsorship from the UK branch of the Japanese camera and copying company worth £496,000 a year.

This deal, which was entirely dependent upon television coverage, brought to an end protracted negotiations between the League and the ITV-BBC consortium which resulted in two other innovations. The television companies agreed to allow teams appearing on the screens to carry shirt-advertising, and in exchange obtained the rights to screen a number of First Division matches and Cup ties live and in full on days when other games were not being played. These decisions were not accepted without a great deal of controversy within the professional game over its future, particularly as they followed rejection by the League of nearly all the proposals for restructuring the competition made by a committee which the League itself had set up under the chairmanship of Sir Norman Chester—the second such investigation he had conducted in the past 15 years and with virtually the same results.

English domination of the European Champion Clubs' Cup came to an end after six successive seasons when West Germany's Hamburg FC won the trophy. But the outstanding team in Scotland, Aberdeen, won the European Cup-Winners' Cup and went on to become the first Scots to take the European Super Cup by beating Hamburg. Aberdeen followed their European triumphs by becoming the first club outside Glasgow to win the Scottish FA Cup in successive seasons, beating Rangers 1-0 in the final. The English FA Cup final also nearly produced a sensation when Brighton & Hove Albion, already doomed to relegation to the Second Division, beat League champions Liverpool in the semi-finals and held runners-up Manchester United to a draw at the Wembley climax before losing the replay 4-0. Liverpool retained the League championship, to provide a fitting climax for their manager Bob Paisley, who retired after 44 years with the club and who in nine years in charge of the team had won the League title six times, the European Cup and the League Cup each three times, the UEFA Cup and the European Super Cup once each and the FA Charity Shield six times, a record which, said *The Times*, 'will surely never be equalled, let alone surpassed.'

ATHLETICS: The high-light of the year was the first official world championships staged by the International Amateur Athletic Federation (IAAF) in Helsinki from 7 to 14 August, bringing together 1,572 competitors (1,037 men and 535 women) from 157 countries before a total of 422,402 spectators and over one billion TV viewers each day. Although the IAAF had been criticized for its tardiness in setting up this event, athletics being the last of the major sports to organize world championships in addition to the Olympic Games, it could, in the event, rightly claim to have launched the most successful operation of its kind—not least because it was completely free from political interference or charges of bias of any kind. It was also a financial success, realising an income of over £2 million, although all accommodation and travel expenses for the competitors and over 800 officials were paid for by the IAAF and the TV signal was provided free to all small countries unable to pay a fee.

The only disappointment for the aficionados was that the vast collection of talent—'the largest global representation in sports history' according to the IAAF—produced only two world records. The first came in the 400 m relay, which the US team won in 37·86 sec. anchored by Carl Lewis, who broke off from winning a gold medal in the long jump to take part. Lewis also won the 100 m title. The second world record fell to a remarkable Czech athlete, Jarmila Kratochvilova, who won the women's 400 m in 48·99 sec to add to her 800 m title earlier in the championship. But many considered greater the achievements of the 25-year-old American Mary Decker in winning both the women's 1500 m and 3000 m titles—events dominated by Europeans in the past. Sebastian Coe, holder of the Olympic 1500 m title, was forced to withdraw from these championships through illness, but another Briton, Steve Cram, took the world title at that distance, while his compatriot Daley Thompson added the world decathlon gold-medal to those he already held for European, Olympic and Commonwealth championships. The astonishing American 400 m hurdler Ed Moses also claimed his expected world title, but saved his best effort for a few weeks later when at a meeting in Koblenz he broke the world record for the fourth time in 47.02 sec and registered his 85th successive victory in the event.

CRICKET: The third World Cup, held in England in June, was won by India against all the odds, beating the holders West Indies in the final at Lord's by 43 runs after being put out themselves for only 183. In the past, India had appeared to be singularly unadapted to one-day World Cup cricket, having won only one match—against East Africa—in previous tournaments. But this time they beat both West Indies and Australia in their group matches and followed up with an outstanding six-wickets win over England in the semi-finals. There was also a fine performance by Zimbabwe, the only non-Test-playing side in the tournament, in beating Australia by 13 runs; and Sri Lanka beat New Zealand besides creating high-scoring records with Pakistan when the two made an aggregate total of 626 runs at a cost of only 14 wickets in their match.

Earlier in the year there had been some prolific scoring in a three-Test series between Pakistan and India, in which four batsmen of the unbeaten Pakistani side ended with averages of over 100 runs each and the four leading Indian batsmen had averages of over 50. The latter did not include Sunil Gavaskar, who at the end of the year was to make his own individual mark on cricket history in a series against West Indies. In October, Gavaskar equalled the 35-year-old world record of Australia's Sir Donald Bradman of 29 Test centuries; in November he passed the Englishman Geoff Boycott's record Test aggregate of 8,114 runs; and on 28 December, in Madras, the little 34-year-old batsman finally eclipsed Bradman's record with his 30th century in the sixth Test—his 99th appearance for his country.

All New Zealand celebrated victory over England by five wickets in the third Test at Headingley, Leeds, on 1 August. It was the country's first Test win after 29 matches in nine tours starting in 1931. Wright, Edgar and Hadlee made the major contributions with the bat towards victory but the man-of-the-match was bowler Lance Cairns, who destroyed England's first innings with a New Zealand record of seven wickets for 74 runs and added 3 for 70 in the second innings. In the other major international series of the year, Australia regained the Ashes in January with a 2-1 home Test series win over England.

There were two record shocks in the English county championship. Surrey were dismissed for 14 by Essex, their lowest-ever total and only two above the all-time record shared by Oxford University (1877) and Northamptonshire (1907). It was not until the ninth pair were batting that Surrey's total runs scored moved ahead of the wickets they had lost, and two Essex fast bowlers, Phillip and Foster, finished with six wickets for four runs and four for 10 respectively, both in under eight overs.

Troubled Yorkshire, previously winners of the county title 33 times, finished bottom of the championship table for the first time in their long history—a performance only partly redeemed by their winning the John Player Sunday League, their first trophy win of any kind for 14 years. However, the county's subsequent decision not to offer its leading player, Geoff Boycott, a contract for the 1984 season, his benefit year, caused more controversy within the club and a demand from the player's supporters for a vote to be held among all the membership, numbering several thousands, on Boycott's future.

GOLF: Although Tom Watson, of the United States, created a record in winning the British Open Championship for the fifth time in eight years by a comfortable three strokes from two other Americans at Royal Birkdale, European golfers were far from dominated in other tournaments. Severiano Ballesteros, of Spain, already only the second non-American to win the US Masters, repeated his victory of 1980 in holding off the challenges of three American former Masters in the last round for a four-stroke margin. He also shattered an international field to collect one of the richest prizes of the season—$300,000 in the Sun City million-dollar classic in Bophuthatswana, in Southern Africa.

Ballesteros was also a leading figure in the European challenge for the Ryder Cup at Palm Beach, Florida, where the United States retained the trophy $14\frac{1}{2}$-$13\frac{1}{2}$ after three days of fascinating golf during which there was never more than one point between the two sides. Under the new captaincy of Tony Jacklin, the Europeans, all British except three, displayed a tenacity not usually a feature of challenges in the US in the past, and the outcome was not decided until Watson beat Bernard Gallagher 2 and 1 in the very last singles.

The young Englishman Paul Way—later to receive the British Sports Writers' Association award as the International Newcomer of the Year—made a particularly impressive Ryder Cup debut, losing only one of four matches in partnership with Ballesteros and winning his singles;

but it was his compatriot, Nick Faldo, who went on to set records on the European circuit after an equally impressive Ryder Cup record. Faldo became the first in European golf to win over £100,000, the first to win five tournaments and the first to win three in succession. He also reached the final of the world match-play tournament, won by Greg Norman of Australia, to create a record second only to Jacklin's in 1969.

The top American golfers were also upstaged by South Africa's Nick Price, who took the world series in Akron, Ohio, leading from start to finish with a four-stoke margin over Jack Nicklaus and Johnny Miller. Another US Classic, the Hawaiian Open, fell to Isao Aoki, the first Japanese to win an American tournament—an achievement he followed up by beating Ballesteros and Faldo by two strokes in the European Open.

MOTOR SPORT: Changes in the regulations for Formula I cars, particularly the ban on side skirts and limitations on the dimensions of chassis and tyres, made the world drivers' championship and the constructors' championship an intriguing affair for designers and the expectation of more exciting racing for the spectators. The competition over 15 Grands Prix was indeed close right until the end, with Brazil's Nelson Piquet winning the drivers' title by only two points from the Frenchman Alain Proust and Ferrari taking the constructors' championship from Renault by 10 points.

The world championship title was the climax to a somewhat unusual career for Piquet, whose real surname is Soutomaier. He changed it to avoid opposition from his wealthy parents when he gave up a career in tennis to follow the first Brazilian world champion driver, Emerson Fittipaldi, on the race-track in 1972. He was so successful as a beginner that he was able to by-pass Formula II class and graduate into full Grand Prix status in 1978. He won his first world title two years later and now, at 31, became the first double champion since Niki Lauda. But for being forced to retire in five races through mechanical trouble, Piquet might well have had a more emphatic championship victory; for he was never lower than fourth in any event he completed, was always in the top three in the points table and played the major part in Brabham-BMW's climb to third place in the constructors' championship.

However, the outstanding single drive of the season was made by Britain's John Watson in the US Grand Prix at Long Beach, California, when he took his Marlboro McLaren-Ford from 22nd place on the starting grid into the lead after 45 of the race's 75 laps and held on to win by 28 seconds from his team-mate Lauda, who had started in 23rd place. Watson had overtaken more rivals to win than anyone else had done in the whole history of Formula I racing.

After ten years of planning, 37-year-old London businessman Richard Noble regained the world land speed record for Britain, covering a measured mile in 633·468 mph at Black Rock Desert, Nevada, in October, beating the previous best, set 13 years ago by the American Garry Gabelich, by 11 mph. Noble, driving a jet car Thrust 2, became the first Briton since Donald Campbell in 1964 to hold the record.

RUGBY FOOTBALL: A result likely to have a far-reaching effect on the future of international rugby union came from Bucharest on 12 November when Romania beat Wales by 24 pts to 6, their biggest ever win over an International Board country. The victory enhanced Romania's claim—first established against the 1977 French Grand Slam team and encouraged by a successful tour of Wales two years later—to join the present Five Nations championship. Like the French at their best, the Romanians play an open, fast-running and handling game, and against Wales their backs had plenty of scope for scoring their four tries, thanks to the domination of the lines-out and the scrums by a big and powerful pack. Although Wales fielded a comparatively inexperienced side, the Romanian victory was 'as merited as it was emphatic', according to the authoritative magazine *Rugby World*, which added that the result 'will send a shiver through the world's top half-dozen rugby-playing nations'.

The British Lions also suffered more than their usual share of shocks in New Zealand, where they were not only soundly beaten in all four Tests, conceding 78 points against 26 scored, but also lost to a provincial side, Auckland, for the first time since 1966. Their defeat 28–6 in the final Test was the heaviest ever suffered by a British team and was the occasion for Stuart Wilson to set a New Zealand record of 19 tries in internationals when he crossed the Lions' line three times.

The England players in the Lions' party gained some revenge on 19 November at Twickenham, under new captain Peter Wheeler, when New Zealand were beaten at headquarters 15-9 for the first time since the famous 'Obolensky's Match' of 1936. This time the hero was veteran full-back Dusty Hare, who kicked three penalties and a conversion for 11 of England's points. In another outstanding result in April, the Welsh champion club Swansea gave the touring Barbarians their heaviest defeat in history, scoring six goals, two penalties and four tries in a 58-6 victory.

The sudden death from a heart-attack at the age of 53 of Carwyn James in January came as a shock to the British game as a whole and Welsh rugby in particular. Although he gained only two international caps, James proved to be an outstanding coach for his club, Llanelli, his country and the British Lions, whom he led to their first-ever international series win in New Zealand in 1971. His understanding of the tactics of the game and the psychology of extracting the best from players either as individuals or as a team was unmatched. In August a veteran England player and administrator, Lord Wakefield of Kendal (W. W. Wakefield), died aged 85. At the height of his playing career in the 1920s he gained 31 caps, a record which stood for more than 40 years, and captained every team for which he played from school through Cambridge and the Army to international level. In later years he became president of several sports organizations, including the Rugby Union, the Ski Club of Great Britain, the British Sub-Aqua Club and the British Water-Ski Federation.

TENNIS: The retirement from competition of Bjorn Borg, who played his last match in April after winning 62 titles in ten years, including five successive Wimbledon championships, left a gap at the top of the men's game not completely filled by either of the major contenders, John McEnroe and Jimmy Connors of the United States, or the latest challenger from Czechoslovakia, Ivan Lendl. It was significant that Bjorg's absence from the French championships, the first of the European season's major events, which he had won six times, resulted in a Frenchman, Yannick Noah, winning the men's singles for the first time since 1946.

McEnroe regained the Wimbledon title from Connors, but not in the final, where he beat a young New Zealander, Chris Lewis, ranked 91st in the world and the first unseeded man to reach the final since 1967, in just 85 minutes, losing only six games. In fact, the best match of the tournament was provided by Lewis and another comparative unknown, Kevin Curren of South Africa, whose superb service had taken Connors out of the tournament in the fourth round, leaving the American without a place in the quarter-finals for the first time in 12 Wimbledons. Curren, partnered by Stan Denton, was beaten in the men's doubles semi-finals by the American pair Tom and Tim Gullikson, who became the first twins this century to reach a Wimbledon final, where they were predictably overwhelmed by McEnroe and Peter Fleming. But there was an unusual triumph in the mixed doubles for John Lloyd who, partnered by Wendy Turnbull of Australia, became the first British man to win at Wimbledon since Fred Perry in 1936.

This match saw yet another Wimbledon Centre Court appearance for the apparently ageless veteran Mrs Billie Jean King, at 39 overcoming persistent injury as well as personal problems to maintain a record second to none. However, a record she did not want fell to her in her 110th Wimbledon singles match and 14th semi-final appearance when she was thrashed 6-1, 6-1 by her 18-year-old fellow-American Andrea Jaeger. It was Mrs King's heaviest defeat in all her long Wimbledon career.

Whatever the doubts about the succession to Borg, however, there was no question that 26-year-old Martina Navratilova remained Queen of the Courts. She again stormed through the year almost unbeaten, disposing of the upstart Miss Jaeger 6-0, 6-3 in 54 minutes at Wimbledon for her fourth successive singles title and adding the women's doubles for the third consecutive time. Two months later, she at last added the only crown so far to elude her, the United States Open, beating six-times winner Chris Lloyd in equally crushing fashion, 6-1, 6-3. An added mark of Miss Navratilova's superiority was that she won both the Wimbledon and US titles without dropping a set. The rewards were immense: in New York she won a total of £413,000, or over £1,131 for every minute she was on court—an earning power which outstripped any of the men, Borg included—and at the end of the season her total prize-money from the game had risen to well over £4 million.

THE TURF: The event which astounded the world and seemed more appropriate to one of former jockey Dick Francis's successful thriller novels about the Turf than real life was the kidnapping of English and Irish Derby winner Shergar from the Aga Khan's Irish stud farm at Newbridge, Co. Kildare, on the night of 8 February. Five armed men took the bay stallion from his stable in a horse-box and told the head groom that a ransom of £2 million would have to be paid for the return of the horse alive. Investigations by the police and, indeed, any thoughts the owners may have entertained of coming to terms with the kidnappers were thwarted by a succession of hoaxes and false leads which followed. A reward of about £200,000 said to have been offered by the Irish Thoroughbred Breeders Association for the safe return of the horse 'with no questions asked' also brought no response. At the year's end, Shergar had still not been found, and the insurers faced the tricky problem of deciding on compensation for the 40 people who had shares in his stud value, estimated at £10 million. Some of them were not insured at all, it was reported, and others were covered only for death and would possibly not be paid until, and if, a body were found. In the meantime, the value of Shergar at stud was revealed when the first of the 36 foals he sired before the kidnap, a six-month-old bay colt, was sold at the Irish November auctions for a record 260,000 guineas. Another shock to breeders was the sudden death, at the age of 7, of the 1979 Irish and English Derby winner Troy, who was retired to stud after only one defeat that season and was subsequently valued at £7·2 million.

Otherwise, 1983 was the year in which women fully made their mark on the Turf. Mrs Jenny Pitman became the first of her sex to saddle a Grand National winner in Corbiere, ridden by the 23-year-old Ben de Haan and owned by 22-year-old London stockbroker Brian Burrough. Two weeks earlier, Caroline Biche, aged 25, became the first woman jockey to win at the Cheltenham National Hunt Festival and Mrs Mercy Rimell the first to saddle a winner of the prestigious Champion Hurdle. Aintree also saw the first woman bookmaker, Angela Marlow, to set up on its rails. On the flat, Criquette Head was the first woman to train an English Classic winner when Ma Biche, ridden by her brother Freddie, won the 1,000 Guineas. In Sweden, there was an extraordinary climax to a history-making event when 20-year-old Sofia Nordgren became the first woman to become champion jockey. She was level with the leading male jockey, Gunnar Nordling, on 60 winners each at the last race of the season, which Nordling won with Sofia second. But she was awarded the race and the title when a dope test on Nordling's horse proved positive—the first case of its kind in the history of Swedish flat racing. A final 'feminine' touch of triumph was added in Britain when Sun Princess became the first maiden to win the Oaks this century—and that by a record 12 lengths.

Among the men, the outstanding achievement of the year came from 33-year-old National Hunt trainer Michael Dickinson, whose horses, led by Bregawn, filled the first five places in the Cheltenham Gold Cup, putting him well on the way to finishing as the season's leading trainer with a record 120 winners. On the flat, the outstanding figures were Lester Piggott again with his ninth Derby winner, Teenoso, and the combination of Walter Swinburn (Shergar's regular jockey) and the French filly All Along, who together won nearly £1·5 million in four races in five weeks, starting with the Prix de l'Arc de Triomphe and ending with the Washington International.

YACHTING: 'Australians conquer last great pinnacle of sport' headlined the London *Daily Telegraph*, as if some super Everest had been found and conquered. In fact, the most momentous sports event of the century had been achieved at sea level when the 12-metre yacht *Australia II* at last took the America's Cup away from the New York Yacht Club, where it had resided for most of the previous 132 years since the schooner *America* won it in a challenge race against British yachts around the Isle of Wight. It had resisted competition from all over the world 25 times and the latest defender, *Liberty*, looked like maintaining the series of victories when it took a 2-0 lead, stretched to 3-1, in the best of seven races off Newport, Rhode Island, the traditional defending ground, against *Australia II*, which had beaten Britain's *Victory 2* for the right to challenge after a long series of elimination races involving other challengers from Italy, Canada and France. But *Australia II*, helped by a revolutionary winged keel, recovered to force the final into a seventh deciding race for the first time, and it won by 41 seconds after being 52 seconds down at one stage. When the ornate silver jug was at last unbolted from its display plinth at the NYYC and transported to the Royal Perth Yacht Club by Mr Alan Bond, the millionaire owner of *Australia II* who had spent several fortunes in three attempts to win the trophy, he remarked: 'We are going to put it under a steam-roller and call it the "Australia Plate".'

ICE SKATING: Britain's Christopher Dean and Jayne Torville made history in ice-dancing when they won their third successive world title in Helsinki with nine maximum scores of six for their free-skating, following the first complete series of 5·9s for a compulsory dance the previous day. They were also awarded seven maximum marks of six—more than ever given before—in the original set-pattern dance.

XVII ECONOMIC AND SOCIAL AFFAIRS

Chapter 1

A WORLD OF DEBT

THE debt problems of the non-oil developing countries remained a serious threat to the stability of the international financial system throughout 1983, even though the immediate danger of widespread defaults receded somewhat. Several countries, especially in Latin America, faced difficulties in refinancing their debts and were vulnerable to fluctuations in interest rates and in the price of oil.

The origin of the problem lay in the big expansion in lending by commercial banks to non-oil developing countries during the 1970s. Many of these loans were short-term and were willingly granted by the banks, including most of the big international names, in an environment of intense competition. This policy was backed by expectations that Western governments and international financial institutions would never permit a default. The borrowing countries—more those with apparently good prospects like Mexico and Brazil than the obviously very poor ones in Africa and elsewhere—increased their debts on the view that, while interest rates might increase when the world economy expanded, so too would their ability to pay as a result of rising export income.

However, these calculations were all upset by the second oil price shock, the world recession and the financial squeeze from 1979 onwards—especially when interest rates rose and remained high. The sharp rise in the oil price is estimated to have cost the non-oil developing countries $260,000 million in total between 1974 and 1982, while real interest rates in excess of historical averages, together with losses of export income as a result of the world recession, cost a further $140,000 million. The result was a $500,000 million rise in the debt of the non-oil developing countries between 1973 and 1982.

At the same time, the banks began to realise that their lending could not continue indefinitely at the previous rate in face of the increasing inability of the countries to repay their loans. By 1983 the nine largest US banks had the equivalent of 280 per cent of their equity capital out in loans to developing and East European countries; two banks had the equivalent of 75 per cent of their equity capital lent to Brazil alone.

The impact was not the same on all borrowing countries. Even some of the newly industrializing countries in Asia which had borrowed most, such as South Korea, had succeeded in ensuring that their foreign debt never got too far out of line within their export earnings. Consequently, Asian countries were in a better shape to withstand the financial strains of the early 1980s. Moreover, their economies continued to grow, albeit at slower rates than in the 1970s.

In contrast, the major Latin American countries had borrowed too much in relation to their exports, so that the decline in world trade left them exposed, with large burdens of capital debt and of interest payments. Their total output actually fell in 1981 and 1982. These were also the countries to which the big US banks had lent most.

The resulting crunch led, on the one hand, to a desire by the banks to cut back on their new loans and, on the other, to requests by some of the most affected countries to postpone both interest and debt repayments. The trigger for the debt crisis was the expiry of various loans and the realization by both borrowers and lenders that these sums could not be repaid. Mexico's near-default in August 1982 (see AR 1982, p. 96, and p. 87 above) led to shock waves throughout the international financial community.

The leading banks involved immediately organized a series of emergency meetings—in effect clubs of creditors concerned with protecting their own capital. Those with most to lose from a default tried to persuade the smaller banks that nothing would be gained from foreclosures which might lead to an uncontrollable series of collapses, as in the 1929-31 period, which could engulf major Western banks as well as borrowing countries. This process proved to be extremely difficult, involving as it did a combination of the rescheduling of debts and policy adjustments by the borrowers to improve their financial positions and ability to repay. This in turn led to the involvement of the Bank for International Settlements, the Basle-based club of central bankers, and the US Treasury in providing emergency loans. There was also an increased role for the international financial organizations, notably the International Monetary Fund, both as an additional lender and as a guarantor of policy adjustment programmes. The IMF's lending increased substantially, requiring in turn an expansion in its resources, with a 47·5 per cent rise in the quotas supplied by member countries. The IMF also urged reforms in domestic policies—cutting back on public spending and shifting resources into exports.

The result was the postponement of an immediate collapse—though only a postponement, in the view of some central bankers. Problems remained—partly because some of the countries failed to achieve the performance targets set by the IMF as a condition for its loans. In Brazil, for instance, consumer prices rose by 211 per cent during the course of 1983 compared with the original objective of 87 per cent predicated in the IMF's austerity programme. Admittedly, the target improvement in Brazil's trade balance was achieved, but only at the cost of a squeeze on imports and living standards.

Moreover, there was no once-and-for-all solution to the debt problems: talks continued throughout 1983 on a series of major loan packages to cover continuing large financing needs. It took lengthy negotiations for Citibank to arrange a $6,500 million loan for Brazil which combined the rescheduling of short-term loans and trade finance. Similar problems were faced in the raising of a $3,800 million credit for Mexico.

By the end of 1983 large-scale defaults looked unlikely but there were clearly continuing risks—not least because of domestic political resistance in both Mexico and Brazil to the adjustment programmes—as well as uncertainties over the scale of further IMF support in view of the doubts of the US Congress.

Chapter 2

THE INTERNATIONAL ECONOMY

THE major industrialized countries, especially the USA, enjoyed a year of unexpected economic improvement in 1983, at least by comparison with the disappointments of the previous three years of recession. Output rose in all the major economies so that unemployment started to level-off. Nevertheless, there remained serious problems as a result of high real (inflation-adjusted) interest rates, the continuing debt difficulties of developing countries (see Ch. 1) and international arguments over protectionism in farm products and steel.

OUTPUT AND EMPLOYMENT. The key development of 1983 was the expansion of output, as measured by real Gross National Product, by roughly 2½ per cent in the 24 industrialized countries covered by the Organization for Economic Cooperation and Development. This was somewhat more than had been expected in the early months of the year and compared with a decline of roughly ½ per cent in GNP in 1982. The engine of recovery was the USA (see pp. 451-3), where output rose rapidly throughout the year, but there was also an increasingly marked upturn during the period in Japan and Canada, whereas the performance in parts of Western Europe, particularly France and Italy, remained more muted.

The main stimulus to the revival came from a sharp rise in consumer spending. This accounted for four-fifths of the rise in GNP in the seven major industrialized countries, the balance coming from an upturn in private housebuilding and from a start in rebuilding stock levels. The expansion of consumer demand was in turn generally explained by the impact on household behaviour of the falling rate of inflation and by the partly-associated improvement in consumer confidence. This was reflected in falling levels of personal savings. Corporate profits also improved significantly, in part reflecting unexpectedly large increases in productivity and low rates of increase in unit labour costs.

There were still big contrasts between countries. Total output rose by nearly 3½ per cent in the USA in 1983 compared with the previous year, but at less than that rate in the rest of the big seven economies (Japan, West Germany, France, UK, Italy and Canada). Nevertheless, in each of the latter, apart from Italy, the growth performance was substantially better than in 1982. These differences were reflected in the labour market, where the sharp rise in employment in the USA—and to a lesser extent in Japan—overshadowed continued declines in the size of work-forces in some European countries. Total unemployment in the OECD area rose by nearly 1 million to 32¼ million between the second halves of 1982 and 1983. A big drop in the USA—and in the second half of the year in Canada—was offset by further rises in most of the European economies, though at a slower rate than in the previous three years. There was also evidence of sizeable increases in unemployment rates in the smaller European economies, notably Spain, Turkey and the Benelux countries. Rates of unemployment among young people, aged up to 24, again increased, averaging 17½ per cent in 1983 in the big seven economies.

INFLATION. The 1982 slowdown in inflation continued during 1983. After peaking at nearly 13 per cent in 1980 in the OECD area as a whole, the annual rate of consumer price inflation had slackened to just under 8 per cent on average in 1982 and fell to around 5 per cent by late 1983. There was an even lower rate of increase in some of the big seven economies, the average rate being roughly 3 per cent or less in the USA, West Germany and Japan and at its lowest level for more than a decade in Canada and the UK, while only France and Italy still experienced double digit rates of increase.

Price increases were generally less than had been expected earlier in the year. A rise in non-oil commodity prices (partly reflecting a fall in the value of many currencies against the dollar, in which many commodities were priced) was more than offset by a slower rate of growth of domestic costs. In particular, there were above-average rates of increase in productivity in many countries, while wage increases remained moderate. The rate of increase in unit labour costs in manufacturing slowed from 8½ per cent in 1982 to roughly 1½ per cent in 1983, according to OECD estimates for the big seven economies. These changes in turn reflected alterations in the structure of collective bargaining as a result of a weakening in the power of trade unions and a widespread de-indexing of wage increases from past inflation rates. However, the overall slowdown in inflation rates seemed to have come to a halt by the end of 1983.

WORLD TRADE AND CAPITAL MARKETS. The sharp expansion in activity in the USA stimulated a revival in world trade, with a particularly beneficial effect on the exports of Canada, Japan and some developing countries. This ended the falling trend of import volume in the OECD area since 1980. Trade within the 24 member countries grew at an annual rate of 9 per cent in the first half of 1983 and at 8 per cent in the second half. This partly reflected a rebuilding of stock levels. National export performance varied considerably, depending on changes in competitiveness. Oil prices remained very weak, in both nominal and real terms, through the year, while the prices of other commodities rose faster than expected, partly in response to the turn-round in the stock cycle.

The result of these relative price and volume movements was a fall in the aggregate current account deficit of the OECD countries from around $30,000 million in 1982 to $24,000 million in 1983, while the improvement in the terms of trade of the non-oil developing countries led to a $20,000 million drop in their deficit to $45,000 million. These changes were matched by a doubling in the deficit of the oil-producing countries to over $30,000 million, compared with a surplus of more than $50,000 million in 1981. Within this overall pattern, there was a deterioration of over $30,000 million in the USA's current account position, partly matched by a rise of over $12,000 million in Japan's surplus and by a $12,000 million turn-round in the current accounts of the EEC countries towards a small overall surplus.

In capital markets, the main feature was again the further strengthening of the dollar, particularly against the main European currencies. This was widely attributed to high US interest rates produced by the big federal budget deficits. As the year ended there was increasing speculation as to how far this position was sustainable, especially in view of the rising US current account deficit, and much talk about what were seen as the over-valuation of the dollar and the under-valuation of the Japanese yen.

MONETARY AND FISCAL POLICIES. Economic recovery was combined with continued tight fiscal and monetary policies, with the important exception of the USA. In most major industrialized economies the aim was to dampen inflation and to continue to cut public sector deficits, in the hope that this would still allow room for higher economic growth.

In the USA, however, fiscal policy was expansionary, though no less so than previously, while elsewhere budgetary measures were generally contractionary, as a result of policies to cut the underlying level of borrowing in Western Europe and Japan. However, the differences in 1983 were less than in 1982, and overall there was a slight move towards a more restrictive stance in the big seven economies in 1983.

On the monetary side, the rate of growth of the main aggregates decelerated during the course of 1983 in most of the big seven economies.

However, real interest rates generally stayed high—in the range of 3 to 7 per cent. There was, however, an intensive debate about how far such rates were dampening recovery.

NOBEL PRIZE. Professor Gerard Debreu of the University of California at Berkeley was awarded the Nobel prize for economics in 1983. French-born though a citizen of the USA since 1975, he received the award for his work in proving the existence of equilibrium-creating prices.

Chapter 3

THE ECONOMY OF THE UNITED STATES

THE economy of the USA recovered sufficiently strongly from recession in 1983 to produce both a sharp rise in employment and a significant reduction in unemployment. At the same time, the annual rate of consumer price inflation remained low and rates of pay increase were moderate. The OECD's *Economic Outlook* for December 1983 commented that the year 'brought one of the most impressive combinations of strong growth and low inflation seen in recent decades.' However, there were renewed worries about whether the recovery could be sustained in face of an easy fiscal policy and a relatively tight monetary policy.

OUTPUT AND EMPLOYMENT. The growth of economic activity started to accelerate during the spring of 1983. This was partly in response to the end of the rundown in stocks and the beginning of stockbuilding. Over the year as a whole this accounted for about two-fifths of the total rise in real Gross National Product; a sharp increase in private housebuilding and buoyant consumer spending were the other main positive features. Overall, the annual rate of growth of real GNP accelerated from 2½ per cent in the first quarter of 1983 to nearly 10 and 8 per cent in the second and third quarters respectively, before slipping back to a more normal 4½ per cent rate in the fourth quarter of the year.

Consequently, real GNP rose by over 6 per cent during the course of the year and by nearly 3½ per cent in 1983 as a whole compared with the previous year. This performance compared well with past recoveries, as measured by the rises in industrial production, in the composite index of leading indicators, in manufacturing employment, in business investment and in capacity utilization, while consumer confidence was at its highest level for more than a decade. This was reflected in a decline in the level of personal savings and a sharp rise in household borrowing, which led to a

60 per cent rise in private housing starts in 1983 compared with the previous year, and a 15 per cent increase in new car sales.

One result was a sharp rise in the number of people with jobs—up by more than 4 million during the year—so that the percentage unemployment rate declined from 10·7 per cent in December 1982 to 8·2 per cent by the end of 1983. This was a record decline for a single year. Moreover, productivity, which had been flat between 1977 and 1981, rose by 3·7 per cent between the third quarters of 1982 and 1983.

INFLATION. The level of pay rises, in both nominal and real terms, remained low by historic standards as the rate of growth of hourly earnings in manufacturing slackened from $6\frac{1}{2}$ per cent in 1982 to an average of 4 per cent in 1983. Indeed, a number of union contracts included cuts in pay and in fringe benefits. And, with a big expansion in output, unit labour costs dropped during the year, following a rise of over 10 per cent in 1982. This turn-round, coupled with a strong dollar in foreign exchange markets, offset some firming of food and commodity prices in the second half of 1983. Consequently, the 12-month rate of increase of consumer prices slackened from roughly 5 per cent at the end of 1982 to only just over 3 per cent by the end of 1983, slightly up from a low point of about $2\frac{1}{2}$ per cent in the summer.

EXTERNAL TRADE. The combination of the strong economic recovery and the appreciation of the dollar led to a further major deterioration in the competitive position of the USA. The volume of exports dropped by around $6\frac{1}{2}$ per cent during the year, while imports rose by over 10 per cent in real terms. This resulted in a near doubling in the visible trade deficit to $70,000 million, while the current account deficit rose by nearly $30,000 million to over $40,000 million. This in turn led to big changes in the net external financial position of the USA, as the current account deficit was financed by a large build-up of short-term financial assets by overseas residents, mainly financial institutions and central banks attracted by relatively high US interest rates.

MONETARY AND FISCAL POLICY. The favourable output and inflation trends in the USA were combined with an intense and growing debate about the Reagan Administration's fiscal and monetary policies. The main issue was the size of the federal budget deficit, which rose as a percentage of GNP from just over 2 per cent in 1981 to $5\frac{1}{2}$ per cent in 1983. There was much discussion during the year about possible measures to limit the size of the deficit, and Congress agreed measures to improve the financing of the social security system. Otherwise, there was no agreement either on limiting the sharp rise in defence expenditure initiated by the Administration itself or on trimming back other programmes.

President Reagan refused to agree to any substantial tax increases in order to limit the size of the deficit. The short-term impact of the massive government borrowing was limited by the easing of monetary policy in mid-1982. This lasted into the first half of 1983. But from May 1983 onwards, as the evidence of the recovery of output mounted, a decision was taken to tighten monetary policy. Interpretation of monetary action was complicated, however, by institutional changes in banking structure which altered the make-up of certain monetary aggregates.

Nevertheless, by the end of the year, there were worries about the fiscal-monetary mix in view of the record real (inflation-adjusted) interest rates and the tight liquidity position of some companies. Mr Paul Volcker, the chairman of the Federal Reserve Board, became increasingly outspoken as the year ended in arguing that the budget deficit must be reduced and that monetary policy alone could not be expected to bear the brunt of efforts to restrain inflation. Similarly, Mr Martin Feldstein, the chairman of the Council of Economic Advisers, warned that the prospect of annual $200,000 million federal deficits for the rest of the decade (after a deficit of $194,500 million in the 1982-83 fiscal year) would make the expansion 'fragile and more inflationary'. But at the end of the year there was no sign of any political willingness to take action when a presidential election was due in November 1984.

Chapter 4

THE ECONOMY OF THE UNITED KINGDOM

THE long-awaited recovery of the UK economy was at last confirmed in 1983. After three years of recession, output growth outstripped most economists' expectations, consumer spending rose sharply, inflation remained at a relatively low rate and unemployment showed some signs of levelling off. As the Bank of England pointed out in its December *Quarterly Bulletin*, 'the UK economy, having suffered a deeper recession than most, is now among the leaders, and from having been amongst the most inflationary industrial countries it is now among the low inflation ones'.

GOVERNMENT POLICY. The Thatcher Administration's policy goals remained unchanged in theory throughout 1983—containing inflation through monetary and fiscal means being given overriding priority as a prerequisite for sustained expansion. These objectives were restated with firmness when Mr Nigel Lawson took over as Chancellor of the Exchequer from Sir Geoffrey Howe on 11 June. Yet in practice the year was marked by variations in the implementation of policy in anticipation of the general election on 9 June and in the aftermath of the Conservative Party's big victory (see p. 19).

In retrospect it was clear that fiscal policy had been eased from mid-1982 onwards. This may in part have been unintended, as a result of forecasting errors, but the result, nonetheless, was to stimulate consumer spending. In particular, the abolition of the remaining hire-purchase controls in July 1982 could be seen to have boosted personal borrowing.

Moreover, government spending was rising faster than expected. In late 1982, the fear had been that public spending and borrowing would undershoot, so that in November 1982 there was a further reduction in the employers' national insurance surcharge and encouragement was given to short-term publicly-financed capital investment projects such as house improvement. In the event, there was a surge in public expenditure from late 1982 onwards, though this was not apparent by the time of the March 1983 Budget. The more optimistic assessment made when Sir Geoffrey Howe was reaching his Budget decisions led to sizeable cuts in personal taxation, aimed at lower income groups. This was within the framework of holding public sector borrowing in 1983-84 to £8,000 million. The starting-point for paying income tax, the personal allowance, was raised by 14 per cent, compared with the 5½ per cent rise needed to match inflation, thus taking a large number of people out of the income tax net completely. There were similar changes in higher rate thresholds, and concessions were introduced to encourage both small businesses and North Sea oil exploration. At the same time, the Budget statement set out objectives consistent with the medium-term financial strategy for a continued reduction in inflation; in particular, the target range for the growth of the monetary aggregates was set at 7 to 11 per cent in 1983-84, compared with 8 to 12 per cent for the previous year.

By midsummer, after the general election, it became clear that public spending and borrowing, as well as the monetary aggregates, had been growing faster than the published targets. For instance, the Treasury was forced to admit that its March Budget estimate of public sector borrowing for the 1982-83 financial year (which ended a fortnight later) was £1,500 million less than the final figure of just over £9,000 million.

The public expenditure figures for the first few months of 1983-84 led to emergency action by Mr Lawson. On 7 July he announced an all-round squeeze on expenditure amounting to £500 million, together with the sale of an additional £500 million of state assets (achieved through the disposal of a further tranche of the government's holding of British Petroleum shares). Nevertheless, despite these measures and buoyant tax revenue, the autumn economic statement in November indicated that public sector borrowing was likely to be about £2,000 million higher than the original estimate. To reinforce its fiscal aims the Government announced that public spending was to be held roughly constant in real (inflation-adjusted) terms from 1984-85 onwards, with an implied tightening in overall budgetary policy after the earlier relaxation. For instance, tight limits were set for public sector pay rises.

The rate of monetary growth slowed during the late summer of 1983

THE ECONOMY OF THE UNITED KINGDOM 455

after the earlier overshoot, allowing cuts in short-term interest rates in the summer and early autumn.

THE RECOVERY. Domestic demand rose sharply from late 1982 onwards. Since real living standards remained largely unchanged after 1981, the main stimulus came from a sharp increase in personal borrowing, mainly via mortgage lending from building societies and banks. Household borrowing rose by 40 per cent in real terms in the three years to 1983. This resulted in a sharp rise in consumer spending—up nearly 4 per cent in real terms in 1983 compared with 1982, while on the same basis spending on consumer durables increased by about 15 per cent. Much of this was reflected in a surge in imports but there was also at last some impact on manufacturing production, which increased by around $1\frac{1}{2}$ per cent in 1983.

After the big rundown in stock levels in 1980-81, and the levelling-out towards the end of 1982, there was a rebuilding of stocks in 1983. Fixed investment also recovered, notably private housebuilding, though there was also a pick-up in industrial investment, in part reflecting a sharp rise in corporate profits. North Sea oil production increased as well, so that, despite a jump in imports, total national income, as measured by real Gross Domestic Product, rose by around $2\frac{3}{4}$ per cent. At the end of the year there was no sign of an immediate slowdown, as was underlined by a series of optimistic Confederation of British Industry quarterly trends surveys. But there was concern about whether exports and investment would provide a sustained boost as the growth in consumption slackened.

The upturn in activity led to the end of the four-year-long decline in the numbers employed; the total started to rise, even in manufacturing, during the autumn of 1983. And there was also some impact on the unemployment total, which fell slightly during the summer and early autumn, though without any clear evidence of a sustained down-turn. Over 1983 as a whole, the total number of adults out of work rose by 152,000 to 3·1 million after adjusting for the effect from April 1983 onwards of the change whereby some men aged 60 or over no longer had to sign on at an unemployment benefit office. Voluntary registration at Job Centres also rose during the year.

One of the main positive influences on the economy remained the inflation rate, which stayed at around the lowest level since 1970. Productivity growth was about 3 to 4 per cent a year and unit labour costs grew only slowly, so that the 12-month rate of retail price inflation declined from 5·4 per cent in December 1982 to a low of 3·7 per cent in May 1983 before rising again to 5·3 per cent by the end of the year. Despite a sharp rise in import prices during 1983, as a result of the decline in sterling against the dollar, there was no sign of any significant acceleration in inflation by the end of the year.

FOREIGN TRADE. The upsurge in consumer spending, coupled with the earlier deterioration in Britain's competitive position, led to an inflow of imports, particularly of manufactured goods, which rose by more than a tenth in volume in 1983 compared with the previous year. At a time when export volume was sluggish, at least until towards the end of the year, the result was a sharp adverse swing in the trade balance. The deficit on non-oil visible items rose by £5,400 million in 1983 to £7,900 million. This was partially offset by a £2,300 million rise in the surplus on oil trade to £6,900 million. With a small drop in the surplus on invisible items such as services and transfers, the current account surplus fell from £5,400 million in 1982 to just over £2,000 million in 1983—though admittedly this was substantially better than had been expected in the early part of the year.

Chapter 5

ECONOMIC AND SOCIAL DATA

The statistical data on the following pages record developments from 1978 to the latest year, usually 1983, for which reasonably stable figures were available at the time of going to press. Year headings 1978 to 1983 are printed only at the head of each page and are not repeated over individual tables unless the sequence is broken by the insertion of series of figures recording developments over a longer period than is shown on the remainder of the page.

Pages to which the point is relevant include a comparative price index, allowing the current-price figures to be reassessed against the background of inflation.

Unless figures are stated as indicating the position at the *end* of years, they should be taken as annual *totals* or *averages*, according to context.

Tables 2, 3, 4 and 5. Statistics which are normally reported or collected separately in the three UK home jurisdictions (England and Wales, Scotland, and Northern Ireland) have been consolidated into UK series only to show general trends. As the component returns were made at varying times of year and in accordance with differing definitions and regulatory requirements, the series thus consolidated may therefore be subject to error, may not be strictly comparable from year to year, and may be less reliable than the remainder of the data.

Symbols. — = Nil or not applicable .. = not available at time of compilation.

Sources

A. THE UNITED KINGDOM
   Government Sources
   Annual Abstract of Statistics: Tables 1, 2, 3, 4, 5, 15, 16, 21, 22, 27.
   Monthly Digest of Statistics: Tables 1, 10, 11, 12, 13, 14, 18, 19, 20, 21, 22, 23, 24, 26, 27, 28.
   Financial Statistics: Tables 9, 10, 12, 13, 17, 29.
   Economic Trends: 6, 7, 8, 9, 10, 29.
   Social Trends: Tables 2, 3, 4, 5.
   Department of Employment Gazette: Tables 23, 24, 25, 26.
   Housing and Construction Statistics: Tables 5, 15.
   Additional Sources
   National Institute of Economic and Social Research, *National Institute Economic Review:* Tables 6, 7, 8.
   Bank of England Quarterly Bulletin: Tables 11, 12.
   Midland Bank: Tables 13, 14.
   United Nations, *Monthly Bulletin of Statistics:* Table 1.
   The Financial Times: Tables 12, 14.
   British Insurance Association: Table 16.

B. THE UNITED STATES
   Government and other Public Sources
   Department of Commerce, *Survey of Current Business:* Tables 30, 31, 32, 33, 34, 35, 40, 41, 43.
   Council of Economic Advisers, Joint Economic Committee, *Economic Indicators:* Tables 33, 39.
   Federal Reserve Bulletin: Tables 36, 37, 38.
   Additional Sources
   A. M. Best Co.: Table 38.
   Insurance Information Institute, New York: Table 38.
   Bureau of Economic Statistics, *Basic Economic Statistics:* Tables 41, 42.

C. INTERNATIONAL COMPARISONS
   United Nations, *Annual Abstract of Statistics:* Tables 44, 45.
   UN *Monthly Bulletin of Statistics:* Tables 44, 45, 47.
   IMF, *International Financial Statistics:* Tables 44, 46, 48, 49, 50, 51, 52.
   OECD, *Main Economic Indicators:* Table 45.
   Institute of Strategic Studies, *The Military Balance:* Table 53.
   OECD, *Labour Force Statistics*, Table 54.

ECONOMIC AND SOCIAL DATA
A. THE UNITED KINGDOM

SOCIAL

1. Population

	1978	1979	1980	1981	1982	1983
Population, mid-year est. ('000)	55,835	55,881	55,945	56,010	56,341	..
Live births registered ('000)	687·2	735	754	731	719	..
Crude birth rate (per 1,000 pop.)	12·3	13·1	13·5	13·0	12·8	..
Deaths registered ('000)	667·2	675·6	661·5	658	663	..
Crude death rate (per 1,000 pop.)	11·9	12·1	11·8	11·8	11·8	..

2. Health

	1978	1979	1980	1981	1982	1983
Public expenditure on National Health Service (£ million)(1)	7,689	8,858	11,483	13,087	14,014	..
Hospitals:						
staffed beds, end-year ('000)	470·9	463·4	457·9	445·0	..	..
ave. daily bed occupancy ('000)	380·0	373·4	369·0	366	..	..
waiting list, end-yr. ('000)	801·0	809	767	745	..	..
Certifications of death ('000)(2) by:						
ischaemic heart disease	180·1	174·1	172·3	173·7	173·2	..
malignant neoplasm, lungs and bronchus	38·4	38·9	39·1	38·8	38·9	..
road fatality	7·6	6·7	6·6	6·3	6·1	..
accidents at work (number)	751	711	700	700	660	..

(1) Central government and local authority, capital and current. (2) Great Britain.

3. Education

	1978	1979	1980	1981	1982	1983
Public expenditure (£ million)(1)	8,544	9,652	11,923	13,359	14,292	..
Schools ('000)	38·5	38·4	38·2	38·9	34·5	..
Pupils enrolled ('000) in schools	11,221	11,091	10,891	10,632	10,367	..
maintained primary(2)	5,751	5,594	5,398	5,171	4,961	..
maintained and aided secondary(3)(4)	4,617	4,643	4,636	4,607	4,559	..
assisted and independent	614	615	620	619	612	..
Pupils per full-time teacher at:						
maintained primary schools	23·4	23·0	22·4	22·3	22·3	..
maintained secondary schools	16·7	16·7	16·4	16·4	16·4	..
independent schools(4)	–	..	13·0	13·2	12·5	..
Further education: institutions(5)	7,184	6,121	5,734	5,434	5,105	..
full-time students ('000)	499	498	495	510	564	..
Universities	46	46	46	46	46	..
University students ('000)	288	296	301	307	277	..
First degrees awarded (number)	63,657	65,982	68,151	70,542	..	..
Open University graduates ('000)	6·5	6·9	7·2	..	..	..

(1) Central government and local authority, capital and current. Figures are for financial year: 1975=year ending March 1976, etc. (2) Including nursery schools. (3) Including special schools. (4) England and Wales. (5) Great Britain.

Overall price index (1980=100)	74·3	84·0	100·0	110·2	117·2	124·6

UNITED KINGDOM STATISTICS

4. Law and Order

	1978	1979	1980	1981	1982	1983
Public expenditure (£ million)(1)	2,233	2,828	3,286	3,948	4,471	4,681
Police	1,397	1,691	2,100	2,551	2,934	..
Prisons	315	342	470	545	554	..
Administration of justice(2)	430	497	714	852	983	..
Police establishment ('000)(3)	130·8	131·5	132·1	133·2	133·5	..
Full-time strength(3)	119·8	124·8	129·1	132·6	132·6	..
Ulster, full-time strength	6·1	6·6	6·9	7·3	7·7	..
Serious offences known to police(4)	2,943	2,934	3,105	3,431	3,708	..
Persons convicted, all offences ('000)(4)	2,086	2,154	2,499	2,359	2,287	...
Burglary or robbery(5)	74	64	74	83	83	..
Handling stolen goods/receiving, theft	228	223	236	225	242	..
Violence against person	43	49	53	58	52	..
Traffic offences	1,118	1,108	1,323	1,261	1,181	..
All summary offences(4)	1,667	1,730	1,797	1,670	1,587	..
Prisons: average population ('000)	49·7	49·5	49·6	50·3	51·1	..

(1) Gross expenditure, capital and current, by central government (direct and by grant to local authorities) and by local police authorities. Figures are for financial year: 1975 = year ending March 1976, etc. (2) Includes expenditure on parliament and courts. (3) Police establishment and full-time strength: Great Britain only. (4) Because of differences in juridical and penal systems in the three UK jurisdictions, totals of offences are not strictly comparable from year to year: they should be read only as indicating broad trends. (5) Specific offences: England, Wales and N. Ireland.

5. Housing

	1978	1979	1980	1981	1982	1983
Public expenditure (£ million)(1)	5,260	6,275	7,289	5,603	5,484	..
Dwellings completed ('000)						
by and for public sector(2)	136	108	110	88	53	54
by private sector	152	142	130	117	124	141
Housing land, private sector, weighted ave. price (£/hectare)	54,334	77,637	101,991	105,765	115,072	..
Dwelling prices, average (£)(3)	16,297	21,047	24,307	24,810	25,553	28,593

(1) Capital and current, net of rents, etc., received, and adjusted to eliminate double counting of grants and subsidies paid by central government and expended by local authorities. Figures are for financial year: 1976 = year ending March 1977. (2) Including government departments (police houses, military married quarters, etc.) and approved housing associations and trusts. (3) Of properties newly mortgaged by building societies.

Overall price index (1980 = 100)	74·3	84·0	100·0	110·2	117·2	124·6

PRICES, INCOME AND EXPENDITURE

6. National Income and Expenditure
(£ million, 1980 prices)

	1978	1979	1980	1981	1982	1983
GDP(1), expenditure basis	198,000	201,456	196,642	195,213	199,301	206,277
income basis(2)	147·0	170·2	198·5	215·1	233·6	257·0
output basis (1980 = 100)	100·4	103·3	100·0	98·0	99·3	101·4
average estimate (1980 = 100)	100·3	102·6	100·0	98·5	100·4	103·5
Components of gross domestic product:						
Consumers' expenditure	131,485	138,004	137,324	137,559	139,552	144,800
General government consumption	46,728	47,612	48,419	48,329	48,942	50,141
Gross fixed investment	41,210	41,411	39,241	35,557	37,646	39,262
Total final expenditure	282,537	292,785	284,950	280,727	287,952	292,057
Stockbuilding	2,090	2,490	−3,236	−2,655	−1,000	372
Adjustment to factor cost	30,270	31,492	30,854	30,023	30,927	32,065

(1) At factor cost. (2) Current prices, £ 000 million.

7. Fixed Investment
(£ million, 1980 prices, seasonally adjusted)

	1978	1979	1980	1981	1982	1983
Total, all fixed investment(1)	41,210	41,411	39,241	35,557	37,646	39,262
Dwellings	7,734	7,134	6,342	4,828	5,375	6,047
public	3,144	2,876	2,522	1,674	1,991	1,971
private	4,590	4,258	3,820	3,154	3,384	4,076
Private sectors	27,620	28,225	27,062	25,273	27,554	28,092
manufacturing	7,866	8,172	7,274	5,763	5,472	5,191
other	19,754	20,053	19,788	19,510	22,082	22,901
Government public corporations	13,590	13,186	12,179	10,284	10,092	11,170

8. Personal Income and Expenditure
(£ million, seasonally adjusted, current prices unless otherwise stated)

Wages and salaries	83,674	98,196	116,004	124,021	132,452	141,493
Current grants	17,905	20,979	25,493	31,276	36,249	39,400
Forces' pay	1,645	2,020	2,435	2,708	2,904	3,105
Other personal income(1)	26,712	33,816	38,902	41,319	46,892	48,648
Personal disposable income	113,404	136,802	160,820	174,491	186,274	200,424
Real personal disposable income(2)	149,602	138,296	160,727	156,903	156,487	158,149
Consumers' expenditure	99,596	118,503	137,324	152,836	167,899	

(1) From rent, self-employment (before depreciation of stock appreciation provisions), dividend and interest receipts and charitable receipts from companies. (2) At 1980 prices.

9. Government Finance
(£ million)

Revenue(1)	63,217	75,618	92,244	106,653	119,689	..
taxes on income	22,449	25,032	30,740	35,789	40,300	..
corporation tax(2)	3,343	3,941	4,646	4,645	4,925	5,564
taxes on expenditure	22,956	29,755	36,157	42,090	47,082	..
value added tax(2)	4,230	4,837	8,186	10,968	11,860	13,840
taxes on capital(3)	940	1,155	1,344	1,636	1,681	..
National Insurance surcharge(2)	1,914	2,987	3,542	3,597	2,831	..
Expenditure(2)(4)	56,261	70,357	82,527	96,448	109,604	121,203
social services(5)	33,945	39,185	48,228	57,512	63,557	..
defence	7,566	8,976	11,428	12,639	14,497	..
net lending(6)	1,690	3,273	3,469	2,552	2,718	..
Deficit(−) or surplus	−7,041	−6,275	−8,144	−6,855	−5,637	..

(1) Total current receipts, taxes on capital and other capital receipts. (2) Financial years ended 5 April of year indicated. (3) Capital gains and estate/death duties. (4) Total governmental expenditure, gross domestic capital formation and grants. (5) Including expenditure by public authorities other than central government. (6) To private sector, local authorities, public corporations, and overseas.

Overall price index (1980=100)	74·3	84·0	100·0	110·2	117·2	124·6

10. Prices and Costs (index 1980=100)

Total home costs per unit of output(1)	74·3	84·0	100·0	110·2	117·2	124·6
Labour costs per unit of output	72·1	82·7	100·0	109·4	113·4	..
Mfg. wages, salaries/unit of output	71·1	81·9	100·0	109·8	115·5	118·7
Import unit values	85·2	90·9	100·0	107·7	116·8	128·1
Wholesale prices, manufactures	79·1	87·7	100·0	109·5	118·0	124·4
Consumer prices	74·7	84·8	100·0	111·9	121·5	124·1
Tax and prices	76·1	85·2	100·0	114·8	126·1	131·2

(1) Used as 'Overall price index' on all pages of UK statistics.

UNITED KINGDOM STATISTICS

FINANCIAL

11. Banking(1)
(£ million, at end of period)

	1978	1979	1980	1981	1982	1983
Current and deposit accounts	204,051	243,038	286,328	398,333	510,858	..
Advances: to						
local authorities	4,688	5,382	7,026	2,319	2,380	..
public corporations	2,880	2,065	1,799	1,317	1,245	..
financial institutions	5,238	6,695	7,155	10,891	15,849	..
companies	29,248	32,892	38,959	45,749	50,025	..
construction	1,707	1,979	2,326	2,603	3,491	..
personal sector	10,860	14,017	17,617	12,871	21,170	..
overseas residents	106,083	128,681	150,838	..	..	..
Eligible liabilities	45,003	51,647	67,462	77,651	93,405	..

(1) Unless otherwise stated, this table covers all banks in the UK observing the common 12·5 per cent reserve ratio introduced on 16 Sept. 1971 and includes the accepting houses (merchant banks), discount houses and, for deposits, the National Giro and the banking department of the Bank of England. Except in the case of overseas advances, inter-bank transactions have been omitted.

12. Interest Rates and Security Yields(1)

(%) per annum, end of year)

Treasury bill yield	11·91	16·49	13·45	15·39	10·20	8·88
London clearing banks base rate	12·50	17·00	14·00	14·50	10·13	9·00
2½% consols, gross flat yield(2)	11·92	11·38	11·86	13·00	11·91	9·90
10-year government securities(2)	12·12	12·93	13·91	14·88	13·09	11·27
Ordinary shares, dividend yield(2)	5·54	5·78	6·32	5·89	5·05	4·58
Interbank 3-month deposits	12·54	17·00	14·81	15·66	10·56	9·38
Clearing bank 7-day deposits	10·00	15·00	11·75	12·38	6·88	5·50

(1) Gross redemption yields, unless stated otherwise. For building society see Table 15 (2) Revised series.

13. Companies
(£ million unless otherwise stated)

Total income	29,477	38,994	40,193	43,918	46,248	..
Gross trading profit in UK	25,093	31,277	32,392	35,504	37,960	..
Total overseas income	2,656	5,273	4,640	5,032	4,578	..
Dividends on ord. and pref. shares	2,591	4,169	4,173	4,582	5,723	..
Net profit	17,393	21,913	17,994	18,248	17,634	..
Companies taken over (number)	567	534	469	452	463	447
Total take-over consideration	1,140	1,656	1,475	1,144	2,206	2,343
Liquidations (number)(1)	5,080	4,537	6,891	8,596	12,067	13,421
Receiverships (number)(1)	3,902	3,500	4,038	5,151	5,700	7,000

(1) England and Wales.

14. The Stock Market
(£ million, unless otherwise stated)

Turnover (£000 mn.)	138·8	168·9	196·3	190·7	260·0	287·6
ordinary shares (£000 mn.)	19·2	24·1	30·8	32·4	37·4	56·1
New issues, less redemptions (value)	819·7	738·4	773·2	1,970	1,556	3,328
Government securities	4,888	10,525	11,245	7,488	5,909	8,183
Local authority issues(1)	48·0	− 170·0	− 166	− 157	− 174	− 66
UK companies (gross)	833·7	932·4	933	1,832	1,167	2,812
FT ordinary share index (1935=100)(2)	479·4	475·5	464·5	517·9	574·7	693·0
FT-Actuaries index (750 shares)(3)	216·68	245·52	271·32	307·7	341·4	434·7
Industrial, 500 shares	237·80	267·31	285·68	322·2	373·3	432·5
Financial, 100 shares	165·99	188·36	218·81	253·2	254·5	323·1

(1) Includes public corporation issues. (2) Average during year. (3) (1962=100).

Overall price index (1980=100)	74·3	84·0	100·0	110·2	117·2	124·6

15. Building Societies

	1978	1979	1980	1981	1982	1983
Interest rates (%):						
Paid on shares, ave. actual	6·46	8·45	10·34	9·19	8·77	..
BSA(1) recommended, end-year	8·00	10·50	9·25	9·75	6·25	7·25
Paid on deposits, ave. actual	5·65	7·67	9·71	8·71	9·08	..
Mortgages, ave. charged	9·55	11·94	14·92	14·00	13·32	
BSA recommended, end-year	11·75	15·00	14·00	15·00	10·00	11·25
Shares and deposits, net (£ min.)	4,822	5,769	7,159	7,196	10,515	10,830
Mortgage advances, net (£ min.)	5,115	5,271	5,722	6,331	8,147	11,401

(1) BSA: Building Societies Association.

16. Insurance(1)
(£ million)

	1978	1979	1980	1981	1982	1983
Life assurance(1)(2), net premiums	6,718	7,158	7,787	9,195	11,053	..
investment income	3,717	4,562	5,428	6,410	7,620	..
benefits paid to policyholders	2,520	2,910	3,605	4,518	5,661	..
life funds, end-year	34,800	39,600	46,700	55,000	67,500	..
Non-life(1)(2), net premiums	5,275	6,182	7,255	8,793	9,465	..
underwriting profit+(—)loss(3)	−27·0	−216·4	−338·8	−610·9	−1,250·0	..

(1) Companies only; excludes Lloyd's. (2) World-wide business of UK companies and authorized UK affiliates of foreign companies. (3) Including net transfers of marine, aviation and transit branch revenues to/from profit and loss accounts.

17. Money and Savings
(£ million, amounts outstanding at end period, unless otherwise stated)

	1978	1979	1980	1981	1982	1983
Money stock M_1(1)	27,535	30,046	31,230	34,301	38,190	42,690
Money stock M_3(2)	56,963	63,996	75,934	94,830	104,580	117,620
Sterling M_3	52,062	58,677	69,591	83,820	91,670	101,540
Notes and coins in circulation	8,904	9,701	10,411	11,027	11,196	12,119
Personal savings ratio (%)(3)	12·1	12·8	14·6	12·3	10·8	8·5
National savings	11,233	10,733	12,102	18,164	21,810	24,740

(1) M_1 = Notes and coins in circulation with the public plus resident private sector sterling current accounts with the banks minus 60 per cent of transit items. (2) M_3 = notes and coins in circulation plus total deposits of the domestic sector. (3) Personal savings as a percentage of personal disposable income.

Overall price index (1980 = 100)	74·3	84·0	100·0	110·2	117·2	124·6

PRODUCTION

18. Industrial products and manufactures, output

	1978	1979	1980	1981	1982	1983
Crude steel (million tonnes)	20·3	21·5	11·3	15·3	13·7	14·9
Man-made fibres (million tonnes)	0·61	0·60	0·50	0·40	0·33	0·38
Cars ('000)	1,223	1,070	924	955	888	1,040
Motor vehicles, cars imported ('000)(1)	807	1,021	858	827	898	..
Commercial vehicles ('000)	384	408	389	230	269	244
Merchant ships(2) completed ('000 gr.t)	1,135	707	431	216	453	540

(1) Including imported chassis. (2) 100 gross tons and over.

19. Industrial Production
(Index, average 1980 = 100, seasonally adjusted)

	1978	1979	1980	1981	1982	1983
All industries	103·0	107·0	100·0	96·3	98·0	100·5
Energy and water	84·9	100·3	100·0	103·8	110·0	115·8
Coal and coke	97·6	97·6	100·0	97·3	93·2	89·5
Manufacturing industries	109·5	109·4	100·0	93·6	93·7	95·0
Food, drink and tobacco	99·4	101·0	100·0	97·7	98·9	100·3
Chemicals	107·5	110·5	100·0	100·2	100·8	106·4
Oil processing	109·6	113·7	100·0	92·8	92·8	95·3
Metal manufacture	126·8	132·1	100·0	107·0	105·2	102·5
Engineering and allied	109·4	107·4	100·0	91·1	92·2	93·1
Textiles	126·2	121·0	100·0	91·5	88·4	89·3
Intermediate goods	99·0	107·6	100·0	99·2	102·7	107·1
Consumer goods	108·5	108·4	100·0	95·9	94·4	96·2
Paper, printing, publishing	103·8	108·0	100·0	94·8	90·7	90·5
Construction	105·0	105·6	100·0	89·9	91·6	..
Gas, electricity & water	97·9	102·2	100·0	99·5	98·6	100·7

20. Productivity
(Index of output per head 1975 = 100)

All production industries(1)	108·2	108·5	104·8	107·0	113·0	..
Manufacturing	108·1	109·5	105·5	109·4	115·3	..
Mining and quarrying(1)	94·3	97·0	98·1	98·3	101·4	..
Metal manufacture	110·0	118·7	92·1	120·1	127·1	..
Engineering	102·4	102·0	101·1	101·7	109·9	..
Textiles	110·0	112·9	105·5	111·8	113·7	..
Gas, electricity, water	113·3	117·7	113·9	114·8	116·9	..

(1) Excluding extraction of mineral oil and natural gas.

21. Agriculture
(Production, '000 tonnes, unless otherwise stated)

Wheat	6,610	7,170	8,470	8,707	10,310	..
Barley	9,850	9,620	10,320	10,227	10,960	..
Sugar, refined from UK beet	984	1,138	1,238	1,061	1,213	1,281
Beef and veal	1,027	1,048	1,102	1,058	965	1,046
Mutton and lamb	228	232	277	263	263	286
Pork	634	696	685	710	730	764
Milk, disposals (million litres)	15,096	15,120	15,180	15,085	15,939	16,439

22. Energy

	1978	1979	1980	1981	1982	1983
Coal, production (mn. tonnes)	123·7	124·4	130·1	127·4	124·7	119·2
Power station consumption (mn. tons)	80·7	88·8	89·5	87·3	80·2	81·6
Power stations' demand for oil (million tonnes coal equivalent)	19·2	18·2	11·4	8·84	10·4	7·8
Electricity generated ('000 mn. kwh.)	266·8	279·8	266·2	259·5	255·3	260·5
by nuclear plant ('000 mn. kwh.)	33·3	34·8	33·3	33·8	40·0	45·8
Natural gas sent out (mn. therms)	15,813	17,295	17,066	17,098	16,713	17,170
Crude oil output ('000 tonnes)(1)	53,376	77,796	80,472	89,388	103,080	114,600
Oil refinery output (mn. tonnes)(2)	89·2	90·6	79·2	72·0	70·8	71·6

(1) Including natural gas liquids. (2) All fuels and other petroleum products.

LABOUR

23. Employment
(millions of persons, in June each year)

	1978	1979	1980	1981	1982	1983
Working population(1)	26·37	26·65	26·87	26·77	26·80	26·77
Employed labour force(2)	24·99	25·37	25·31	24·32	23·96	23·72
Employees: production industries	9·21	9·18	8·82	7·92	7·48	7·10
Manufacturing	7·26	7·19	6·84	6·09	5·76	5·47
Transport and Communications(3)	1·48	1·50	1·51	1·44	1·38	1·35
Distributive Trades	2·78	2·87	2·88	2·77	2·71	2·69
Professional and Scientific	3·70	3·76	3·77	3·76	3·77	3·76
Insurance, Banking, financial	1·20	1·26	1·31	1·32	1·32	1·35
Public service(3)	1·61	1·62	1·59	1·57	1·55	1·55
Total employees	22·78	23·11	22·87	21·72	21·24	20·92
of whom, females	9·39	9·66	9·62	9·26	9·12	9·00

(1) Including registered unemployed and members of the armed services. (2) Including employers and self-employed. (3) Excludes employees of nationalized industries but includes British Rail and Post Office.

24. Demand for Labour

	1978	1979	1980	1981	1982	1983
Average weekly hours worked, manufacturing industry, men over 21(1)	43·5	43·2	41·9	42·0	42·0	42·6
Manufacturing employees:						
Total overtime hours worked ('000)(2)	15,610	15,070	11,760	9,370	9,980	10,300
Short time, total hours lost ('000)(2)	558	781	4,006	4,352	1,769	985
Unemployed, excl. school-leavers, adult students (monthly ave. '000)(3)	1,299	1,227	1,561	2,420	2,793	2,970
Percentage of all employees	5·5	5·1	6·4	10·0	11·7	12·4
Unfilled vacancies, end-year ('000)	235·8	219·4	98·8	107·5	117·6	154·9

(1) October. (2) Great Britain. (3) Seasonally adjusted.

25. Industrial Disputes

	1978	1979	1980	1981	1982	1983
Stoppages (number)(1)(2)	2,471	2,080	1,330	1,338	1,528	1,255
Known official stoppages (number)	90	82	67	..	..	..
Workers involved ('000)(3)	1,001	4,583	830	1,499	2,101	538
in official stoppages ('000)	123	3,648	404	..	..	..
Work days lost ('000), all inds., services	9,405	29,474	11,964	4,266	5,313	3,593

(1) Excluding protest action of a political nature, and stoppages involving fewer than 10 workers and/or lasting less than one day except where the working days lost exceeded 100. (2) Stoppages beginning in year stated. (3) Directly and indirectly, where stoppages occurred; lay-offs elsewhere in consequence are excluded.

26. Wages and Earnings

	1978	1979	1980	1981	1982	1983
Average earnings index (Jan. 1980 = 100).						
Whole economy	79·9	92·3	111·4	125·8	137·6	149·1
Manufacturing	80·1	92·6	109·1	123·6	137·4	149·7
Average weekly earnings(1)(2)						
Men						
Manual	80·7	93·0	111·7	121·9	133·8	143·6
Non-manual	100·7	113·0	141·3	163·1	178·9	194·9
All occupations	89·1	101·4	124·5	140·5	154·5	167·5
Women						
Manual	49·4	55·2	68·0	74·5	80·1	87·9
Non-manual	59·1	66·0	82·7	96·7	104·9	115·1
All occupations	56·4	63·0	78·8	91·4	99·0	108·8
Average hours(3)	41·4	41·5	41·1	40·3	40·2	40·1

(1) In all industries and services, full-time. (2) April. (3) All industries and services, all occupations, men and women over 18 years.

Overall price index (1980=100)	74·3	84·0	100·0	110·2	117·2	124·6

UNITED KINGDOM STATISTICS

TRADE

27. Trade by Areas and Main Trading Partners

(£ million; exports f.o.b.; imports c.i.f.)

	1978	1979	1980	1981	1982	1983
All countries: *exports*	35,380	40,637	47,339	50,698	55,538	60,386
All countries: *imports*	39,533	46,925	49,886	51,169	56,940	66,123
E.E.C.: *exports*	13,621	17,479	20,541	20,940	23,118	26,447
E.E.C.: *imports*	16,547	20,888	20,619	21,718	25,252	30,159
Other Western Europe: *exports*	4,425	5,559	6,750	6,293	6,714	7,603
Other Western Europe: *imports*	5,998	7,192	7,274	7,799	8,347	10,514
North America: *exports*	4,249	4,792	5,310	7,121	8,335	9,267
North America: *imports*	5,314	6,197	7,493	7,587	8,113	9,055
Other developed countries: *exports*	2,323	2,475	2,659	2,928	3,241	3,133
Other developed countries: *imports*	2,998	3,043	3,374	3,677	4,436	5,220
Oil exporting countries: *exports*	4,665	3,648	4,781	5,911	6,447	6,110
Oil exporting countries: *imports*	3,326	3,213	4,270	3,666	3,455	2,830
Other developing countries: *exports*	4,927	5,354	5,847	6,255	6,572	6,671
Other developing countries: *imports*	4,187	5,104	5,686	5,600	5,900	6,761
Centrally planned economies: *exports*	1,070	1,186	1,308	1,124	974	1,116
Centrally planned economies: *imports*	1,100	1,196	1,070	1,015	1,327	1,542

28. Terms of Trade

(index 1980=100)

	1978	1979	1980	1981	1982	1983
Volume of exports(1)	94·4	99·1	100·0	99·3	101·8	103·3
manufactures	100·0	99·0	100·0	94·0	96·0	94·0
Volume of imports(1)	95·5	105·7	100·0	97·3	101·0	108·2
food	106·0	109·0	100·0	103·0	108·0	108·0
fuels	121·0	119·0	100·0	82·0	74·0	68·0
Unit value of exports(1)	79·0	87·5	100·0	108·8	116·5	126·9
manufactures	83·0	91·0	100·0	107·0	115·0	126·0
Unit value of imports(1)	85·0	90·7	100·0	107·7	116·8	128·1
food(2)	95·0	98·0	100·0	104·0	112·0	120·0
fuels(2)	61·0	72·0	100·0	128·0	146·0	154·0
Terms of trade(3)	92·9	96·5	100·0	101·0	99·7	99·1

(1) Seasonally adjusted; Overseas Trade Statistics basis (2) c.i.f. (3) Export unit value index as percentage of import unit value index, expressed as an index on the same base.

29. Balance of Payments

(£ million: current transactions seasonally adjusted; remaining data unadjusted)

	1978	1979	1980	1981	1982	1983
Exports (f.o.b.)	35,063	40,687	47,415	50,997	55,565	60,658
Imports (f.o.b.)	36,605	44,136	46,182	47,325	53,181	61,158
Visible balance	−1,542	−3,449	+7,233	+3,652	+2,384	−500
Current balance	+1,018	−853	+2,929	+7,272	+5,551	+2,049
Capital transfers	−1,777	−2,254	−2,107	−1,967	−2,109	−2,320
Official long-term capital	−336	−401	−91	−336	−347	−562
Overseas investment in						
UK public sector	−97	+902	+589	+188	+320	+693
UK private sector	+2,005	+3,459	+4,654	+3,270	+3,289	+5,712
UK private investment overseas	−4,634	−6,533	−8,204	−10,670	−10,872	−10,895
Current surplus (+)/deficit (−)	+1,158	−653	+3,235	+7,272	+5,551	+2,049
Overall surplus (+)/deficit (−)	−1,573	−3,497	+1,177	−765	−3,577	−821
Official reserves, end of year	7,689	10,129	11,487	12,217	10,508	12,271
Foreign liabilities net, do.	7,765	6,555	5,010	4,381	4,865	5,638
Overall price index (1980=100)	74·3	84·0	100·0	110·2	117·2	124·6

B. THE UNITED STATES

30. Population

	1978	1979	1980	1981	1982	1983
Population, mid-year est. (mn.)	218·72	220·58	227·64	229·81	232·06	..
Crude birth rate (per 1,000 pop.)	15·3	15·8	16·2	15·9	15·8	..
Crude death rate (per 1,000 pop.)	8·8	8·7	8·9	8·7	8·7	..

31. Gross National Product
('000 million current dollars)

	1978	1979	1980	1981	1982	1983
Gross national product	2,164	2,418	2,633	2,954	3,073	3,309
Personal consumption	1,346	1,507	1,667	1,857	1,992	2,159
Gross private domestic investment	387	423	402	475	415	441
Net exports, goods and services	−1·1	13·2	25·2	26·3	17·4	−10·6
Government purchases	431·9	474·4	538·4	595·7	649·2	690

32. Government Finance
('000 million dollars, seasonally adjusted)

	1978	1979	1980	1981	1982	1983
Federal government receipts	431·5	494·4	540·8	628·2	617·4	643·3
from personal taxes(1)	194·9	231·4	257·8	298·1	304·7	295·8
Federal government expenditure	460·7	509·2	601·6	688·3	764·4	826·2
Defence purchases	103·0	115·0	132·8	153·7	179·4	200·3
Grants to state/local govts.	77·3	80·4	88·1	87·7	83·9	86·5
Federal surplus or (−) deficit	−29·2	−14·8	−61·2	−59·9	−147·1	−182·9
State and local govt. receipts	327·7	351·2	384·1	416·8	439·1	483·3
from indirect business tax(1)	150·3	159·0	171·7	192·8	210·0	232·0
State and local govt. expenditure	299·8	324·5	355·0	385·0	407·8	432·3

(1) Includes related non-tax receipts on national income account.

33. Balance of Payments
(millions of dollars)

	1978	1979	1980	1981	1982	1983
Merchandise trade balance	−33,996	−27,555	−25,544	−28,067	−36,389	−60,550
Balance on current account(1)	−15,447	−967	+421	+4,588	−11,219	−40,777
Change in US private assets abroad(2)	−57,202	−59,469	−72,746	−98,982	−118,045	..
Change in foreign private assets in US(2)	30,358	52,157	39,042	73,136	87,866	..

(1) Includes balance on service and remittances and US government grants other than military. (2) Includes reinvested earnings of incorporated affiliates.

34. Merchandise Trade by Main Areas
(million of dollars)

	1978	1979	1980	1981	1982	1983
All countries: *exports* (f.o.b.)	143,662	181,802	220,705	233,740	212,276	..
All countries: *imports* (f.o.b.)	171,978	206,327	241,195	260,982	254,884	..
Western Europe: *exports*	43,608	53,617	66,817	64,724	59,701	..
Western Europe: *imports*	37,985	43,548	46,352	51,430	52,908	..
Canada: *exports*	28,374	33,096	35,395	39,564	39,275	..
Canada: *imports*	33,525	38,099	41,024	45,912	48,473	..
Latin America						
exports	20,185	26,257	36,030	38,950	33,164	..
imports	18,556	24,782	29,916	32,056	38,561	..
Japan: *exports*	12,885	17,579	20,790	21,823	20,694	..
imports	24,458	26,243	30,866	37,655	37,685	..
Dollar purchasing power (1967=100)	*51·2*	*46·0*	*40·6*	*36·7*	*34·6*	*33·5*

35. Merchandise Trade by Main Commodity Groups
(millions of dollars)

	1978	1979	1980	1981	1982	1983
Exports:						
Machinery and trasnport equipt.	59,255	70,040	84,553	95,717	87,128	82,524
Motor vehicles and parts	13,237	16,077	14,590	16,214	13,907	..
Electrical machinery	6,967	8,635	10,485	11,468	12,939	..
Food and live animals	18,311	22,245	27,744	30,291	23,952	24,168
Chemicals and pharmaceuticals	12,618	17,308	20,740	21,187	19,891	19,752
Imports:						
Machinery and transport equipt.	47,590	53,678	60,546	69,627	73,320	86,208
Motor vehicles and parts	20,631	22,074	24,134	26,217	29,361	..
Food and live animals	13,522	15,171	15,763	15,238	14,453	15,408
Petroleum and products	39,104	56,046	73,771	75,577	60,835	..
Iron and steel	7,259	7,466	7,364	7,540	7,269	..

36. Interest Rates
(per cent per annum, annual averages, unless otherwise stated)

Federal Funds rate(1)	7·93	11·19	13·36	16·38	12·26	9·09
Treasury bill rate	7·22	10·04	11·51	14·02	10·61	8·61
Government bond yields: 3-5 years	8·30	9·58	11·51	14·34	12·96	10·63
Long-term (10 years or more)	7·89	8·74	10·81	12·87	12·23	10·84
Banks' prime lending rate(2)	9·06	12·67	15·27	18·87	14·86	10·79

(1) Effective rate. (2) Predominant rate charged by commercial banks on short-term loans to large business borrowers with the highest credit rating.

37. Banking, money and credit
('000 million dollars, outstanding at end of year, seasonally adjusted)

Money supply M1 (1)	363·2	389·0	414·5	440·9	478·5	521·1
Money supply M2 (2)	1,404	1,519	1,656	1,823	1,999	2,185
Money supply M3 (3)	1,629	1,779	1,963	2,188	2,404	2,603
Currency	97·4	106·1	116·2	123·1	132·7	146
Deposits of commercial banks	1,009·9	1,073·2	1,239·9	1,288·4	1,409·7	1,524·8
Advances of commercial banks	747·8	849·9	915·1	975·0	1,059·4	1,149·3
Instalment credit	273·6	312·0	313·5	333·4	344·8	387·9
Motor vehicle contracts	101·6	116·4	116·8	125·3	130·2	146·1
Mortgage debt	1,113	1,276	1,419	1,583	1,654	1,820

(1) Currency plus demand deposits, travellers cheques, other checkable deposits. (2) M1 plus overnight repurchase agreements, eurodollars, money market mutual fund shares, savings and small time deposits. (3) M2 plus large time deposits and term repurchase agreements.

38. Insurance
($ million, unless otherwise stated)

Property-liability, net premiums written	81,690	90,122	95,600	99,276	104,320	..
Automobile(1)	33,218	36,640	39,153	41,143	..	..
Underwriting gain/(−) loss(2)	−1,296	−1,301	−3,334	−6,288	..	..
Net investment income(3)	7,290	9,279	11,064	13,249	..	..
Combined net income(3)	8,586	7,978	7,729	6,961	..	..
Annual rate of return (%) (4)	20·9	14·8	14·5	12·9	..	..
Life insurance, total assets, end-year	389,920	432,280	479·210	525,803	525,803	652,904

(1) Physical damage and liability, private and commercial. (2) After stockholder and policy-holder dividends and premium rebates. (3) Property, casualty. (4) Per cent of net worth.

Dollar purchasing power (1967=100)	51·2	46·0	40·6	36·7	34·6	33·5

ECONOMIC AND SOCIAL DATA

39. Companies(1)
('000 million dollars)

	1978	1979	1980	1981	1982	1983
Net profit after taxes	145·9	165·1	157·8	150·9	115·1	126·5
Cash dividends paid	47·0	52·7	58·1	65·1	68·7	73·3

(1) Manufacturing corporations, all industries.

40. The Stock Market
(millions of dollars, unless otherwise stated)

	1978	1979	1980	1981	1982	1983
Turnover (sales), all exchanges	249,257	299,973	475,934	490,688	596,670	..
New York Stock Exchange	210,426	251,098	397,670	415,913	514,263	..
Securities issued, gross proceeds	120,399	120,808	154,729	156,447	162,738	..
Corporate common stock	7,937	8,709	16,858	23,552	25,449	..
Stock prices (end-year):						
Combined index (500 stocks)(1)	96·11	107·94	135·76	122·55	140·64	164·93
Industrials (30 stocks)(2)	805·01	838·74	963·99	875·00	1,046·54	1,258·64

(1) Standard and Poor Composite 1941-43=10. (2) Dow-Jones Industrial (Oct. 1928=100).

41. Employment
('000 persons)

	1978	1979	1980	1981	1982	1983
Civilian labour force(1)	100,420	102,908	104,719	108,679	110,204	111,550
in non-agricultural industry	91,031	93,648	93,960	97,032	96,129	97,440
in manufacturing industry	20,476	21,062	20,363	20,174	18,850	18,677
in agriculture	3,342	3,297	3,310	3,368	3,692	3,381
unemployed	6,047	5,963	7,448	8,279	10,716	10,690
Industrial stoppages(2) (number)	219	235	187	145	96	..
Workers involved ('000)	1,006	1,021	795	729	656	..

(1) Aged 16 years and over. (2) Beginning in the year. Involving 1,000 workers or more.

42. Earnings and Prices

	1978	1979	1980	1981	1982	1983
Average weekly earnings per worker (current dollars): mining	332·88	365·50	396·1	437·40	472·72	479·0
contract construction	318·69	342·99	367·78	395·60	423·46	441·9
manufacturing	249·27	268·94	288·62	317·60	330·65	354·6
Average weekly hours per worker in manufacturing	40·4	40·2	39·7	39·8	38·9	40·1
Farm prices received (1977=100)	115	132	134	138	133	135
Wholesale prices (1967=100)	195·9	217·7	246·9	269·9	280·6	285·2
Petroleum products	321·0	444·8	674·7	805·8	761·3	..
Consumer prices (1967=100)	195·3	217·4	246·8	272·4	289·1	298·4
Food	211·4	234·5	254·6	274·6	285·7	291·7
Dollar purchasing power (1967=100)(1)	51·2	46·1	40·6	36·7	34·6	33·5

(1) Based on changes in retail price indexes.

43. Production

	1978	1979	1980	1981	1982	1983
Farm production (1977=100)	104	111	103	118	117	..
Industrial production (1967=100)	146·1	152·5	147·0	151·0	138·6	147·7
Manufacturing	146·8	153·6	146·7	150·4	137·6	148·5
Output of main products and manufactures						
Coal (million tons)	671·3	781·1	829·7	823·8	838·1	784·9
Oil, indigenous (000 barrels/day)	8,707	8,552	8,597	8,572	8,649	8,656
Oil refinery throughput (000 barrels/day)	14,739	14,648	13,481	12,470	11,774	11,672
Natural gas (000 barrels/day)	1,567	1,584	1,573	1,609	1,550	1,564
Electricity generated ('000 mn. kwh)	2,204	2,247	2,286	2,293	2,241	2,287
Steel, crude (million tonnes)	137·0	136·0	111·8	120·8	74·6	82·6
Aluminium ('000 tonnes)	4,804	5,023	5,130	4,948	3,609	..
Cotton yarn (000 running bales)	10,549	14,262	10,826	15,150	11,526	..
Man-made fibres (million lbs.)	9,526	9,029	9,493	9,743	7,892	..
Plastics/resins (million lbs)	37,605	41,577	37,347	39,867	..	..
Motor cars, factory sales ('000)	9,165	8,419	6,400	6,225	5,049	..

C. INTERNATIONAL COMPARISONS

	Area '000	Population (millions), mid-year estimate		Gross Domestic Product (1) US$ mns (2)	
44. Population and GDP, Selected Countries	sq. km.	1981	1982	1982	1983
Argentina	2,777	28·09	28·43	123,864	..
Australia (3)	7,695	14·93	15·17	158,430	..
Belgium	31	9·86	9·85	86,230	..
Canada	9,976	24·34	24·63	289,049	..
China	9,561	1,007·8	..	834,233	..
Denmark	34	5·12	5·12	56,380	..
France	552	53·96	54·22	540,716	..
Germany, Western (incl. W. Berlin)	248	61·67	61·64	660,389	654,565
India (incl. India-admin. Kashmir)	3,268	676·22	711·66	..	..
Irish Republic	69	3·44	3·48	17,686	..
Israel (excl. occupied areas)	21	3·95	4·02	23,069	..
Italy	301	57·20	56·28	347,355	..
Japan	370	117·65	118·45	1,062,867	1,156,277
Kuwait (4)	18	1·460	1·560	..	..
Netherlands	34	14·25	14·31	137,589	129,831
New Zealand (4)	104	3·13	3·16	23,870	..
Norway	324	4·10	4·11	56,176	..
Portugal	92	9·97	10·03	..	..
Saudi Arabia	2,150	9·32	9·68	153,100	120,320
South Africa (incl. S.W. Africa)	1,221	30·13	31·01	73,580	..
Spain	505	37·65	37·93	179,656	..
Sweden	450	8·32	8·33	99,158	..
Switzerland	41	6·43	6·48	96,537	..
Turkey	781	45·37	46·31	52,772	..
USSR	22,402	267·70	269·99	669,600	..
UK	244	55·83	55·78	474,333	456,036
USA	9,363	229·85	232·06	3,025·7	3,263·4

(1) Expenditure basis. (2) Converted from national currencies at average exchange rates. (3) Years beginning 1 July. (4) Years beginning 1 April.

45. World Production (index 1975=100)	1978	1979	1980	1981	1982	1983
Food(1)	109	110	110	114	116	..
Industrial production (2)	118·7	124·2	124·0	125	124	..
OECD	117·7	123	123	124	119	..
EEC(3)	111·4	118	117	115	113	..
France	113	118	118	117	118·0	..
Germany, West	112	117	117	116	112·5	..
Italy	114	121	128	125	121·7	..
UK	111	115	108	103	104·9	..
Japan	123	133	142·0	146	146·6	..
Sweden	92	98	98·0	94	93	..
USSR	116	120	124	129	133	..

(1) Excluding China. (2) Excluding China, USSR, Eastern Europe. (3) Community of ten.

46. World Trade(1)
(millions of US dollars. Exports f.o.b.; imports c.i.f.)

	1978	1979	1980	1981	1982	1983
World(1): *exports*	1,200,000	1,523,700	1,868,500	1,836,300	1,708,900	..
World(1): *imports*	1,238,000	1,559,700	1,923,200	1,910,600	1,779,800	..
Industrial Countries: *exports*	813,871	1,056,900	1,243·9	1,218,800	1,155,500	1,142,400
Industrial Countries: *imports*	839,224	1,141,900	1,369·1	1,297,100	1,219,900	1,198,100
USA: *exports*	143,659	181,802	220,706	233,739	212,276	200,538
USA: *imports*	183,137	218,927	252,997	273,352	254,884	269,878
Germany, West: *exports*	142,295	171,887	192,861	176,091	176,435	169,440
Germany, West: *imports*	121,820	159,711	188,002	163,912	155,370	152,940
Japan: *exports*	98,415	102,299	130,435	151,495	138,403	146,963
Japan: *imports*	79,900	109,831	141,291	142,866	131,516	126,518
France: *exports*	79,205	100,691	116,016	106,425	96,688	94,943
France: *imports*	80,909	107,008	134,874	120,953	115,708	105,416
UK: *exports*	67,887	86,397	110,095	103,164	96,982	91,430
UK: *imports*	75,813	99,600	115,808	101,879	99,646	100,183
Other Europe: *exports*	29,000	34,800	43,640	46,570	45,590	..
Other Europe: *imports*	46,800	56,800	68,790	68,360	63,920	..
Australia, NZ, S. Afr: *exports*	30,946	41,769	53,132	48,241	45,232	..
Australia, NZ, S. Afr: *imports*	26,828	31,723	47,200	54,573	50,992	..
Less Developed Areas: *exports*	330,400	341,506	346,640	324,230	315,170	..
Less Developed Areas: *imports*	243,900	357,031	377,069	429,930	386,030	..
Oil exporters: *exports*	141,400	207,740	293,530	271,870	216,030	..
Oil exporters: *imports*	37,834	101,620	133,380	160,980	154,130	..
Saudi Arabia: *exports*	37,935	57,616	102,503	133,328	75,838	54,898
Saudi Arabia: *imports*	19,068	24,021	30,171	35,268	40,653	..
Other W. Hemisphere: *exports*	49,550	64,370	85,720	89,550	86,360	..
Other W. Hemisphere: *imports*	59,270	79,270	107,680	109,040	83,260	..
Other Middle East(2): *exports*	9,877	11,930	15,980	17,840	16,040	..
Other Middle East(2): *imports*	23,990	24,780	29,520	39,240	35,420	..
Other Asia: *exports*	76,240	96,900	120,320	129,740	127,100	..
Other Asia: *imports*	87,907	117,460	150,420	164,080	152,330	..
Other Africa: *exports*	28,473	41,500	52,460	46,950	39,980	..
Other Africa: *imports*	32,205	37,080	54,990	58,997	49,370	..

(1) Excluding trade of centrally planned countries (see Table 47). (2) Including Egypt.
(3) Unweighted average of IMF series for US$ import and export prices in developed countries.

World trade prices (1980=100)(3)	72·9	85·3	100·0	97·2	92·6	88·8

47. World Trade of Centrally Planned Countries
(millions of US dollars)

European(1): *exports*	113,500	136,153	157,338	159,115	163,445	..
European(1): *imports*	118,372	134,361	154,354	155,579	155,448	..
USSR: *exports*	52,219	64,762	76,450	78,999	86,949	..
USSR: *imports*	50,546	57,744	68,523	72,960	77,793	..
China: *exports*	10,120	13,657	18,255	21,561	20,719	..
China: *imports*	10,316	15,674	19,530	21,565	19,493	..
Total: *exports*	122,569	151,548	176,873	182,776	186,185	..
Total: *imports*	128,747	152,792	176,914	180,297	179,031	..

(1) Except Yugoslavia and Albania.

INTERNATIONAL COMPARISONS

48. Prices of Selected Commodities
(index 1980=100)

	1978	1979	1980	1981	1982	1983
Aluminium, (Canada)	70·3	82·2	100·0	87·4	75·4	76·1
Beef, Irish (London)	70·2	85·8	100·0	99·1	96·4	82·0
Copper, wirebars (London)	62·3	90·6	100·0	79·4	67·6	72·7
Cotton, Egyptian (L'pool)	90·3	99·6	100·0	99·0	81·4	91·2
Gold (London)	31·8	50·4	100·0	75·6	61·8	69·2
Newsprint, S. Quebec	76·1	83·7	100·0	117·2	122·1	113·6
Petroleum, Ras Tanura	44·3	60·2	100·0	113·4	116·8	102·2
Rice, Thai (Bangkok)	84·7	77·1	100·0	111·3	67·6	63·8
Rubber, Malay (Singapore)	68·0	87·3	100·0	77·6	61·6	74·2
Steel bars (W. Germany)	92·7	92·7	100·0	99·8	115·1	98·8
Soya beans, US (R'dam)	90·2	100·0	100·0	97·0	82·4	95·1
Sugar, f.o.b. (Caribbean)	27·4	33·8	100·0	59·1	29·4	29·5
Tin, spot (London)	76·3	91·8	100·0	84·5	76·1	77·3
Wheat, (Canada No. 2 CW)	61·1	83·9	100·0	105·5	95·8	..
Wool, greasy (Sydney)	77·7	84·2	100·0	108·6	101·2	90·3

49. Consumer Prices, Selected Countries
(index 1980=100)

	1978	1979	1980	1981	1982	1983
Argentina	19·19	49·81	100·0	204·5	541·4	1320·0
Australia	83·3	90·8	100·0	100·3	111·1	..
France	79·7	88·2	100·0	113·3	127·1	138·9
Germany, West	91·0	94·8	100·0	105·9	111·5	114·8
India	84·4	89·7	100·0	113·0	121·9	136·5
Japan	89·4	92·6	100·0	104·9	107·7	109·6
South Africa	77·7	87·9	100·0	115·2	132·1	148·3
Sweden	82·0	88·0	100·0	112·1	121·7	132·5
UK	74·7	84·8	100·0	111·9	121·5	127·1
US	79·2	88·1	100·0	110·4	117·1	120·8
World trade prices (1980=100)	72·9	85·3	100·0	97·2	92·6	88·8

50. Industrial Ordinary Share Prices
(Index 1980 = 100)

	1978	1979	1980	1981	1982	1983
Amsterdam	108	107	100	106	107	154
Australia, all exchanges	54	66	100·0	104	79	100
Canada, all exchanges	50·6	73	100	97	78	110
Germany, West, all exchanges	109	106	100	101	99	133
Hong Kong (31 July 1968=100)(1)	496	879	1,580	1,406	784	867
Johannesburg	51	68	100	99	86	109
New York	79	85	100	107	99	134
Paris	68	87	100	88	85	115
Tokyo	88	95	100	116	116	136
UK	82	94	100	113	131	170

(1) Hang Seng index for Hong Kong Stock Exchange only: last trading day of year.

51. Central Bank Discount Rates
(per cent per annum, end of year)

	1978	1979	1980	1981	1982	1983
Canada	10·75	14·00	17·26	14·66	10·05	9·96
France	9·50	9·50	9·50	9·50	9·50	9·50
Germany, West	3·00	6·00	7·50	7·50	5·00	4·00
Italy	10·50	15·00	16·50	19·00	18·00	17·00
Japan	3·50	6·25	7·25	5·50	5·50	5·00
Sweden	6·50	9·00	10·00	11·00	10·00	8·50
Switzerland	1·00	2·00	3·00	6·00	4·50	4·00
UK	12·50	17·00	14·00	14·50	10·13	9·00
USA (Federal Reserve Bank of N.Y.)	9·50	12·00	13·00	12·00	8·50	8·50

ECONOMIC AND SOCIAL DATA

52. Exchange Rates
(middle rates at end of year)

	Currency units per US dollar					per £
	1979	1980	1981	1982	1983	1983
Australia (Australian dollar)	0·9046	0·8469	0·8866	1·0198	1·1142	1·6145
Belgium-Luxembourg (franc)	28·05	31·52	38·46	46·92	56·15	80·70
Canada (Canadian dollar)	1·1681	1·1947	1·1859	1·2294	1·243	1·8055
China (yuan)(1)	1·50	1·53	1·75	1·92	1·9889	2·8784
France (franc)	4·020	4·516	5·748	6·725	8·422	12·07
Germany W. (Deutschmark)	1·732	1·959	2·255	2·419	2·753	3·955
Italy (lire)	804·0	930·5	1,200	1,370	1,670	2,401
Japan (yen)	239·70	203·0	219·90	235·0	233·7	336·5
Netherlands (guilder)	1·906	2·130	2·469	2·625	3·091	4·445
Portugal (escudo)	49·78	53·04	65·25	89·06	132·85	192·65
South Africa (rand)	0·8268	0·7461	0·9566	1·0737	1·2191	1·7745
Spain (peseta)	66·15	79·25	97·45	125·6	157·8	227·45
Sweden (krona)	4·147	4·373	5·571	7·295	8·051	11·615
Switzerland (franc)	1·580	1·761	1·796	1·995	2·188	3·165
USSR (rouble)(1)	0·654	0·667	0·753	0·717	0·7926	1·1270
UK (£)(2)	2·224	2·385	1·908	1·615	1·434	–

(1) Official fixed or basic parity rate. (2) US dollars per £.

53. Defence Expenditure

	Expenditure or budget (US $ mn.)				$ per capita	% of GNP
	1979	1980	1981	1982	1982	1982
France	18,776	26,067	23,545	21,969	408	4·1
Germany, East	4,762	4,790	6,960	6,163	368	3·7-6·6
Germany, West (incl. W. Berlin)	24,391	33,611	29,047	28,453	461	4·3
Greece	..	2,275	2,273	2,574	265	6·7
Iran	3,974	4,461	4,402	7-13,000(1)	329	31·8
Israel	4,932	4,834	6,056	8,242	2,060	37·9
Japan	10,083	12,637	10,453	10,361	87	1·1
Saudi Arabia	14,184	20,766	24,417	27,022	2,780	..
South Africa	2,118	2,556	2,760	2,769	94	3·9
Sweden	3,328	3,834	3,431	3,042	365	3·1
Turkey	2,591	2,306	2,632	2,755	59	5·2
USSR	17·20	17·10	17·10	17·10	..	..
UK	17,572	25,921	24,223	24,200	432	5·1
USA	114,503	142,700	176,100	215,900	938	7·2

(1) Last two columns based on upper estimate.

54. Employment and Unemployment

Civilian Employment (000)	1978	1979	1980	1981	1982	1983
USA	96,048	98,824	99,303	100,397	99,525	100,169
Japan	54,080	54,790	55,360	55,810	56,380	57,294
W. Germany	24,700	25,507	25,745	25,548	25,066	24,592
France	21,113	21,118	21,127	20,959	20,946	..
U.K.	24,625	24,775	24,865	23,819	23,233	..
EEC, Employment by Sectors (%)						
Agriculture	8·4	8·1	7·8	7·7	7·5	..
Industry	38·0	37·7	37·2	36·2	35·5	..
Services	53·6	54·3	55·0	56·1	57·0	..
Unemployment (%)						
OECD	5·1	5·1	5·7	6·7	8·2	8·7
EEC	5·5	5·5	5·9	7·8	9·1	10·1
USA	5·9	5·7	7·0	7·5	9·5	9·4
Japan	2·2	2·1	2·0	2·2	2·4	2·7
U.K.	6·2	5·5	6·9	11·0	12·4	13·2

XVIII DOCUMENTS AND REFERENCE

POLITICAL DECLARATION OF THE WARSAW TREATY MEMBER-STATES

Issued on 5 January 1983 at the end of a two-day summit meeting of the Warsaw Pact political consultative committee in Prague: text by courtesy of Soviet News.

The introductory paragraphs have been omitted; together with certain other passages, indicated by . . ., mainly of a polemical or repetitious character. Words not appearing in the original text are in italics. Some crossheads have been altered from the text supplied.

I

The states represented at the present meeting draw the attention of all countries and peoples to the fact that the Moscow (1978) and Warsaw (1980) declarations of the political consultative committee had pointed to the enhanced threat to peace and to the need to counter the aggravation of the international situation. Today, they point out with concern that, as a consequence of the further activisation of the aggressive forces, world developments are acquiring an even more dangerous character. . . . *They* are convinced that however complex the world situation may be, there exist possibilities for overcoming the dangerous state of international relations. The present course of developments must and can be stopped and redirected in accordance with the aspirations of the peoples. . . .

Relying on an analysis of the international situation, the states represented at the meeting of the political consultative committee propose an alternative to nuclear catastrophe and call for large-scale international cooperation to preserve civilisation and life on Earth.

II

The task of curbing the arms race and going over to disarmament, particularly nuclear disarmament, is central to the struggle for averting war.

The American programmes for the development and production of nuclear weapons . . . and also the development of weapons based on the latest scientific achievements and discoveries, including systems and means for waging war in and from space, are called upon to multiply manifold the deadly power of the US military arsenal, including in Europe. This policy of an arms build-up pursued by the United States and some of its allies to achieve military superiority is leading to the frustration of international stability.

Their drawing up of new programmes for building up arms is inseparable from the escalation of the strategic concepts and doctrines, such as those of the 'first disarming nuclear strike', 'limited nuclear war', 'protracted nuclear conflict' and others. All these aggressive doctrines, which jeopardise peace, are based on the assumption that it is possible to win a nuclear war through the first use of nuclear weapons.

The states represented at the meeting stress most forcefully that any hope of unleashing a nuclear war and winning it is nonsensical. There can be no winners in a nuclear war once it breaks out. It is bound to lead to the annihilation of whole peoples, to colossal destruction and to catastrophic consequences for civilisation and for life on Earth as a whole.

Military policy based on such hopes insuperably entails other very dangerous consequences.

Firstly, the development and deployment of newer and newer systems of nuclear weapons and other means of mass destruction will even further undermine the stability of the military-strategic situation, escalate international tension and complicate relations among states.

Secondly, fresh escalation of the arms race contravenes the aim of maintaining military-strategic parity at increasingly lower levels—a goal of the Warsaw Treaty member-states, which are opposed to military rivalry. The implementation of the above-mentioned arms build-up programmes will lead to higher levels of military confrontation. Peace will become less stable and more fragile.

And thirdly, another round of the arms race will make nuclear weapons and other means of mass destruction even more sophisticated. In this way the difficulties involved in drafting international agreements to limit and reduce them will grow considerably.

For this reason the states represented at the meeting believe that it is necessary to act without delay, while it is still possible to curb the arms race and to go over to disarmament. They proceed from the assumption that all states, if they care for the future, their peoples and mankind at large, should have an objective interest in preventing a slide to war.

It is necessary first and foremost that the states, particularly nuclear powers, should display the political will and readiness for cooperation. It is necessary that their military policies should proceed exclusively from defensive purposes and reckon with the legitimate security interests of all the states. They should not make it more difficult to reach agreements leading to effective reductions in the armed forces and armaments in strict observance of the principle of equality and equal security.

LIMITATION OF ARMAMENTS

In this connection the participants in the meeting expect that after the Soviet Union unilaterally adopted the commitment not to be the first to use nuclear weapons, all the nuclear powers which have not yet done so will do the same.

In the present complex international situation it is particularly necessary to break the deadlock over the real limitation and reduction of armed forces and armaments. In this connection the participants in the meeting call for the resolute activisation of the ongoing talks and for the resumption of the interrupted talks on the entire range of questions of ending the arms race, for persevering and patient work to reach agreements on the reduction and elimination of weapons, particularly nuclear weapons. They support and welcome the proposals of the Soviet Union on ending the arms race and promoting disarmament.

The states represented at the meeting attach much importance to the achievement of success at the Soviet-American talks on the limitation and reduction of strategic arms. . . . They note with satisfaction that the overwhelming majority of states and ever broader sections of the world public are advocating a freeze on nuclear arsenals today. A mutual quantitative freeze on the strategic arms of the USSR and the USA and the maximum possible restrictions on their modernisation could become one of the more tangible embodiments of this idea.

The states represented at the meeting resolutely advocate, furthermore, the drafting of a programme of stage-by-stage nuclear disarmament and, within its framework, of agreements to end the development and production of new systems of nuclear weapons, the production of fissionable materials to develop different types of these weapons, and the production of the means of delivery of nuclear weapons. . . .

They also believe it necessary to speed up the reaching of agreements on a number of concrete questions and in this connection they call upon all states to give a fresh impetus to talks, including those within the framework of the Geneva Disarmament Committee, with a view to:

—drafting in the shortest possible time a treaty on the complete and universal prohibition of nuclear weapons tests;

—speeding up the drafting of an international convention on the prohibition and elimination of chemical weapons;

—going over to the drafting of a convention to ban neutron weapons;

—beginning talks without delay on prohibiting the deployment of weapons of any type in outer space;

—finalising as soon as possible an international convention on the prohibition of radiological weapons;

—and speeding up the solution of the question of strengthening security guarantees to non-nuclear states.

. . . The participants in the meeting welcome the recent increase of the number of states which are parties to the Treaty on the Non-Proliferation of Nuclear Weapons and express the hope that those countries which have not yet joined it will do so in the near future. They favour the reaching of an international agreement on the non-deployment of nuclear weapons in those countries which do not have them at the moment and on the non-build-up of these weapons in those countries in which they have already been deployed.

They believe that the drafting of measures to ensure the safe development of nuclear power engineering and to prevent attacks on civilian nuclear projects with the use of any means would help to strengthen universal security and to extend international co-operation in the peaceful use of nuclear power.

CONVENTIONAL FORCES

In view of the continuous improvement of conventional weapons, which are becoming increasingly formidable, it is necessary to make fresh efforts to substantially lower the present levels of conventional arms and armed forces both on a global scale and in individual regions and to conduct relevant talks for this purpose. It is also useful to resume talks on limiting the sale and supply of conventional weapons.

In view of the growing role of navies, the participants in the meeting are in favour of beginning talks on limiting naval activities and limiting and reducing naval armaments, and also on extending confidence-building measures to the areas of seas and oceans. They advocate the withdrawal of ships carrying nuclear weapons from the Mediterranean and the renunciation of the deployment of nuclear weapons in the territories of the non-nuclear Mediterranean countries.

The participants in the meeting also reiterate their invariable position in favour of fresh efforts on an international scale for the dismantling of foreign military bases and the withdrawal of troops from foreign territories.

The states represented at the meeting proceed from the assumption that any agreements on reducing armaments and on disarmament should provide for proper meaures to verify their implementation, including, when necessary, international procedures.

... *They* urge the Nato countries to reach practical agreement on not escalating military spending and on its subsequent reduction both in percentage and in absolute terms. Agreement on this problem should, of course, embrace all the states having major military potentials. The resources released as a result of cutbacks in military spending should be used to promote economic and social development, in particular, to assist the developing countries in this field.

The participants in the meeting ... suggest that direct talks between the states participating in the Warsaw Treaty Organisation and the Nato member-states begin without delay ....

III

The strengthening of security in Europe is a major component of the task of removing the threat of war and strengthening universal peace. This is so first and foremost because vast quantities of arms, both nuclear and conventional, are concentrated on the European continent and because the armed forces of the two military alliances are in direct contact there.

At the same time a foundation has been created in Europe by the joint efforts of states for the consistent development of relations of good-neighbourliness and co-operation among them, based on mutual respect and trust. All the European states have learned from their own experience the benefits offered by detente. There are among them no states whose interests would not be promoted by the preservation and advancement of the achievements of detente.

In this context the participants in the meeting issue a reminder of the significance attached to the strict observance of the treaties and agreements determining the territorial-political realities of present-day Europe. They particularly stress the importance of the jointly formulated and thoroughly agreed principles and clauses of the Helsinki Final Act, which should be strictly respected and consistently translated into reality.

Analysing the situation taking shape in Europe at present, the participants in the meeting have drawn attention to the most serious threat posed to the European nations by the intention of the Nato bloc to implement its decision, reiterated in December 1982, to deploy new American medium-range missiles in a number of West European countries. The implementation of this decision is bound to diminish trust and worsen the situation on the European continent. ...

The Warsaw Treaty member countries believe that the best solution would be to completely rid Europe of nuclear weapons, both medium-range and tactical ones. They proceed from the assumption that if this truly 'zero' decision cannot be reached at the moment, it is feasible to proceed to the radical reduction of medium-range nuclear systems in Europe on the basis of the principle of equality and equal security. In this respect the importance of the Soviet-American talks on the limitation of nuclear weapons in Europe is very great. ...

The participants in the meeting advocate ridding Europe of another type of weapon of mass destruction, chemical weapons. Their states are prepared to examine together with other interested states all the possible ways and means leading to the solution of this problem, and to enter into appropriate negotiations. ... They speak anew in favour of the reduction of the armed forces and armaments in Central Europe and believe it particularly necessary to advance the Vienna talks, which have lasted for many years now. It is the belief of the participants in the meeting that there is every condition for working out agreement at the Vienna talks as soon as possible, within not more than one or two years, and it is important that this should be done. They, for their part, will facilitate this in every way.

In this context the participants in the meeting advocate a practical step in reducing armed forces and armaments by the Soviet Union and the United States in Central Europe on the basis of reciprocity. Verification of the implementation of this step by representatives of both sides could be organised. Upon its completion the levels of the armed forces and armaments of the direct participants in the Vienna talks on both sides could be frozen until agreement is reached at the talks. ...

The states represented at the meeting declare themselves in favour of proposals to establish nuclear-free zones in the north of Europe, in the Balkans and in other parts of the continent, and to turn the Mediterranean into a zone of peace and co-operation. They advocate appropriate talks on these questions.

MADRID MEETING OF ECSC

The situation existing in Europe demands more than ever before the pooling of the efforts of states to pursue consistently a policy of detente, peace and disarmament. That is why the continuation and extension of the multilateral process initiated by the European Conference on Security and Co-operation is acquiring particular significance....

They attach particular importance to the achievement by the Madrid meeting of an agreement on convening a conference on confidence-building measures, security and disarmament in Europe....

The states represented at the meeting are prepared to develop mutually beneficial contacts with all European states. In accordance with this, they advocate:

—the continuation and extension of political dialogue and consultations at all levels and the broadest possible political intercourse. What is meant here also is the development of contacts on a bilateral and multilateral basis between parliaments, political parties, trade unions, youth, women's and other organisations to promote peace and security in Europe;

—the extension in every way of business co-operation in the trade, industrial, agricultural, scientific and technological fields without any discrimination, and confidence-building measures in economic relations....

—and the extension of the mutual spiritual enrichment of the European peoples, cultural exchanges, propagation of truthful and honest information, and cultivation of sentiments of mutual friendliness and respect.

The states represented at the meeting share the position of the Polish People's Republic that any attempt at outside interference in questions lying solely within its competence runs counter to the commonly recognised norms of international relations and will continue to be firmly rebuffed. They strongly denounce the 'sanctions' introduced by the United States and certain other Western countries against Poland. Polish internal affairs will continue, as before, to be decided solely by Poland. Socialist Poland can always count on the moral, political and economic support of the fraternal socialist countries.

In Europe, where states with different social systems have been coexisting for many decades now, only a policy of peaceful coexistence can be viable.

IV

In exchanging opinions on other international issues, the delegations ... noted that the improvement of the world situation depended to a considerable extent on the elimination of the existing seats of armed conflicts and the prevention of the emergence of new ones in Asia, Africa, Latin America and other regions.

There are no problems, worldwide or regional, which could not be resolved fairly by peaceful means. The main thing is that everyone should recognise in practice the legitimate right of the people of every country to decide themselves, without outside interference, their internal affairs and to participate on the basis of equality in international affairs; that everyone should respect the independence and territorial integrity of states and the inviolability of their borders and respect the principle of the renunciation of the threat or use of force; that no power should try to pursue a policy of hegemony and establish 'spheres of interest' or 'spheres of influence'....

The danger of local conflicts erupting into armed confrontation on a worldwide scale is connected to a large extent with attempts to directly or indirectly involve states in Asia, Africa, Latin American and Oceania in military-political alliances and the spread of the sphere of activities of blocs to those countries. Reiterating that the Warsaw Treaty member-states have no intention to extend the sphere of activity of their alliance, the participants in the meeting call upon the Nato member countries to renounce the extension of the zone of action of their bloc to any part of the world, particularly the Persian Gulf.

NON-ALIGNED

A major contribution towards the elimination and prevention of crisis situations is being made by the non-aligned movement, whose practical steps towards these goals deserve recognition and support from all states. Such regional associations of states as the Organisation of African Unity and the Arab League are also called upon to play a positive role in this respect....

The proposal to turn the Indian Ocean into a zone of peace is particularly important. The resumption and successful completion of the Soviet-American talks on the limitation and subsequent reduction of military activity in the Indian Ocean would also play an important role. It is necessary to use political means to achieve solutions to problems existing in the Caribbean and South-East Asia, and to contribute towards stronger peace in Asia and the Pacific.

The participants in the meeting attach special importance to the task of resolving the most protracted and dangerous conflict, that in the Middle East. They strongly denounce the invasion of Lebanon by

Israel, the Israeli aggression against the Palestinian and Lebanese peoples, and the barbarous massacre of the civilian population of West Beirut. Here, Israel was encouraged to carry out its aggressive actions by those who were giving outside assistance and support.

The participants in the meeting demand an immediate and complete withdrawal of Israeli troops from Lebanon and the ensuring of the independence, sovereignty, unity and territorial integrity of that country.

They view positively the principles of the solution of the problem of settlement in the Middle East put forward by the conference of the Arab heads of state and government in Fez (*see AR 1982, p. 499*) and express their conviction that a comprehensive settlement in the Middle East should provide: for the complete withdrawal of Israeli troops from all the Arab territories occupied since 1967, including the eastern part of Jerusalem; for recognition of the legitimate rights of the Arab people of Palestine, including their right to establish their own independent state; for ensuring the right of all the states in the region to a secure and independent existence and development; for termination of the state of war and establishment of peace between the Arab states and Israel; and for the drafting and adoption of international guarantees for a peaceful settlement.

The accomplishment of these tasks calls for the convocation of an international conference with the participation of all the parties concerned, including the Palestine Liberation Organisation as the only legitimate representative of the Arab people of Palestine. The United Nations can and must play an important role here.

The states represented at the meeting advocate the cessation of the war between Iran and Iraq and the settlement of contentious problems between them through negotiations; the peaceful solution of the conflict between the countries of the Horn of Africa and other disputes in Africa on the basis of mutual respect for each other's independence and territorial integrity; and the solution of conflict situations in Central and South America by political means.

OUTSIDE INTERFERENCE

An end should be put to the policy of continuous threats and provocations against Cuba and Nicaragua and to any attempts at outside interference in their internal affairs.

The participants in the meeting positively appraise the initiation of talks between Afghanistan and Pakistan through a personal envoy of the UN secretary-general.... *They* reiterate their position in favour of restructuring international economic relations on a fair and democratic basis, establishing a new international economic order, and ensuring the complete sovereignty of the countries of Asia, Africa, Latin America and Oceania over their natural resources. They declare themselves in favour of the soonest possible beginning of global talks on major economic problems in accordance with UN resolutions.

The states participating in the meeting advocate a greater role for the United Nations in international affairs as an important forum for pooling the efforts of states to promote peace and international security and to contribute to the solution of urgent world problems....

V

The lessening of the threat of war is impossible without the creation of trust in relations between states. This requires, in addition to the development of political dialogue and the adoption of appropriate measures in the economic and military spheres, the propagation of truthful information, renunciation of claims to a great-power status and renunciation of the propagation of racism, chauvinism and national exclusiveness, of attempts to teach other peoples how to arrange their lives, and of the professing of violence and incitement of war psychosis.

... The lessons of history are a reminder that anti-communism has always been a component of the onslaught on the democratic freedoms and rights of the peoples, and of the policy of aggression and war. The attempts to organise another anti-communist crusade result in the escalation of international tension, threatening the interests of all countries.

No one will succeed in subverting the socialist system with the help of misinformation and slander. ...One of the major achievements of socialism was the formation of a new type of international relations based on voluntary and equal co-operation and internationalist solidarity between sovereign socialist states. The participants in the meeting, expressing the will of their communist parties and peoples, reiterate their resolve to continue to strengthen the cohesion of the socialist countries, to develop and extend political, economic and cultural co-operation and to pool their efforts in the struggle for the cause of peace and progress....

The states particpating in the meeting stress that every people has the sovereign right to decide freely, without any outside interference, how to live and what social system to establish, just as it has the legimate right to defend its choice. . . . The socialist countries strictly separate in their policies ideological issues from problems of state-to-state relations, they build their relations with capitalist states on the basis of peaceful co-existence, and consistently advocate large-scale co-operation with the developing countries. Co-operation among states regardless of their social systems meets the interests of all the peoples and the vital demand for stronger universal peace.

VI

Given the entire multifaceted character of present-day international problems, the prospects for the development of the situation in Europe and in the world at large depend to a very large extent on whether mistrust is removed and the level of confrontation lowered between the two largest military and political alliances, the Warsaw Treaty Organisation and Nato. . . .

The Warsaw Treaty member-states have long been advocating the dissolution of both alliances and, as the first step, the dismantling of their military organisations. This proposal remains in force. The tense situation of the present day, however, makes it impossible to wait any longer. There is a need for urgent and effective measures which can lessen mistrust immediately between the Warsaw Treaty member-states and the Nato member-states and diminish their fears of possible aggression.

The Warsaw Treaty member-states do not seek military superiority over the Nato member-states and nor do they have any intention to attack them or any other country in Europe or elsewhere. The Nato member-states also declare that they have no aggressive intentions. In this situation there should be no reason preventing the adoption by the states comprising the two alliances of appropriate mutual commitments of an international legal character. In the context of the present situation this would have a particular beneficial effect on the whole subsequent development of international events.

Proceeding from these considerations, the Warsaw Treaty member-states, in the person of their highest representatives, address the member-states of the North Atlantic Treaty Organisation with the proposal to conclude a treaty on the mutual non-use of military force and on the maintenance of relations of peace.

The core of the treaty could be the mutual commitment of the member-states of both alliances not to be the first to use either nuclear or conventional weapons against each other and therefore not to be the first to use against each other any military force at all. This commitment could apply to the territories of all the other states joining the treaty, and also to their military and civilian personnel, to sea-going, air and space craft and other objects belonging to them wherever they may be.

It seems proper to provide in the treaty for a similar commitment on the non-use of force by the member-states of both alliances against third countries, whether those having bilateral relations of alliance with them, or non-aligned or neutral countries.

Another substantial component of the treaty could be the commitment of the member-states of both alliances not to jeopardise the safety of international sea, air and space communications passing through areas outside any national jurisdiction.

It seems desirable to complement in the treaty the commitment not to use military force by the commitment to conduct in the spirit of goodwill talks on effective measures to end the arms race, to limit and reduce armaments and to promote disarmament or to contribute by other possible means to the success of such talks with a view to achieving practical results at them.

The same goal could be promoted by the commitment to examine jointly practical measures to avert the threat of a surprise attack and also to contribute to the development of mutual exchanges of military delegations and visits of naval ships and air force units.

COLLECTIVE SECURITY

It is important to combine the commitment not to use military force in the treaty also with provisions on strengthening the United Nations as a universal instrument of collective security. . . .

The treaty would not, of course, limit the legitimate right of the participants in it to individual and collective self-defence in accordance with Article 51 of the UN Charter. At the same time it would relieve the members of both alliances of the fears that the commitments of alliance within each of them can be used for aggressive purposes against the member-states of the other alliance and that these commitments therefore pose a threat to their security.

Although the treaty . . . is proposed to be concluded between the member-states of the two military and political alliances, other interested European countries would have the right to participate in drafting it and to sign it. The treaty would also be open from the outset for other willing states of the world to join as equal parties.

The participants in the meeting of the political consultative committee are convinced that the conclusion of this treaty could help to overcome the division of Europe into confronting military groupings and would meet the desire of the peoples to live in peace and security. They call upon the member-states of the North Atlantic alliance to consider with the utmost attention this new initiative and to respond to it in a constructive manner.

Having stated in the present political declaration their ideas on the ways and means of strengthening peace and preserving and extending the relaxation of international tension in the conditions of the present day, the states participating in the Warsaw Treaty declare their readiness for dialogue and cooperation with all those who seek to achieve this great goal.

Todor Zhivkov, *Bulgaria*
Janos Kadar, *Hungary*
Erich Honecker, *The German Democratic Republic*
Wojciech Jaruzelski, *Poland*
Nicolae Ceauşescu, *Romania*
Yury Andropov, *USSR*
Gustav Husak, *Czechoslavakia*
Prague, 5 January 1983

NUCLEAR ARMS: A ROMAN CATHOLIC VIEW

An article in The Times *(London) of 17 November 1983 by Cardinal Basil Hume, Roman Catholic Archbishop of Westminster: reproduced by courtesy of the Editor of* The Times.

In recent days the debate about nuclear armaments and possible nuclear conflict has been brought home to people much more sharply than before. It is not an easy task to see clearly the way forward and to come to terms with these complex and threatening issues.

Tension has undoubtedly increased because of the public protests and mass demonstrations of the recent past. In a free society, the peace movements play an important role. They bring before us the terrible questions we might otherwise ignore but which must be answered. They rightly alert us to the dangers of nuclear escalation and proliferation. They compel us to question whether new weapons are intended to deter or whether they serve an aggressive purpose.

Inevitably, though, the peace movements bring pressure to bear primarily on the governments of the West and not on those of the East. In communist regimes movements critical of official policy are rarely tolerated. There are different perceptions in East and West about the threat to peace.

No one can deny the moral dilemma which faces us today. On the one hand we have a grave obligation to prevent nuclear war from ever occurring. On the other hand, the state has the right and duty of legitimate self-defence, thus ensuring for its citizens justice, freedom and independence. Although nothing could ever justify the use of nuclear arms as weapons of massive and indiscriminate slaughter, yet to abandon them without adequate safeguards may help to destabilize the existing situation and may dramatically increase the risk of nuclear blackmail.

There is a tension, then, between the moral imperative not to use such inhuman weapons and a policy of nuclear deterrence with its declared willingness to use them if attacked. To condemn all use and yet to accept deterrence places us in a seemingly contradictory position.

It is then perhaps surprising, and puzzling to some Christians, that Pope John Paul II could say to the United Nations on 11 June, 1982:

'In current conditions "deterrence" based on balance, certainly not as an end in itself, but as a stage on the way towards a progressive disarmament, can still be judged morally acceptable. None the less, in order to preserve peace, it is indispensable not to be satisfied with this minimum which is always susceptible to the real danger of explosion.'

It is noteworthy that every Catholic bishops' conference pronouncing subsequently on these issues has followed this judgement. As an authoritative pronouncement of the Holy Father, it is an important contribution to Catholic thinking.

In the first place, this view recognizes that, because of the world situation, deterrence may be accepted as the lesser of two evils, without in any way regarding it as good in itself. Furthermore this view can be held even by those who reject the morality of nuclear deterrence. It constitutes an acknowledgment that even a morally flawed defence policy cannot simply be dismantled immediately and without reference to the response of potential enemies.

To retain moral credibility, however, there must be a firm and effective intention to extricate ourselves from the present feaful situation as quickly as possible. We must work towards our declared objective of de-escalation and disarmament. But mutual and verifiable disarmament can be achieved only in stages, and so gradually. This approach is both realistic and morally acceptable.

The acceptance of deterrence on strict conditions and as a temporary expedient leading to progressive disarmament is emerging as the most widely accepted view of the Roman Catholic Church.

It may in some respects be an untidy view, risky and provisional, yet it is at the same time important. It has immediate consequences.

First, the Church hereby gives a strictly qualified assent to the policy of deterrence but solely on condition that it constitutes a stage towards disarmament. This is a crucial condition. If any government, in the East or West, does not take steps to reduce its nuclear weapons and limit their deployment, it must expect its citizens in increasing numbers to be doubtful of its sincerity and alienated from its defence policies.

Second, it would be wrong to apply to the policy of nuclear deterrence the same moral condemnation that would be given to the actual use of nuclear weapons against civilian targets.

Third, since the purpose and intention of deterrence is to avoid war and keep the peace, service personnel can be rightly commended as custodians of the security and freedom of their fellow countrymen and as contributors to the maintenance of peace. None the less they, too, face grave moral issues which they themselves do not ignore.

Fourth, deterrence has to be seen clearly as a means of preventing war and not of waging it. If it fails and the missiles are launched, then we shall have moved into a new situation. And those concerned will have to bear a heavy responsibility.

Disarmament is hindered by mutual fear and hostility between the superpowers. They already have the capacity to destroy each other many times over. There is urgent need to halt the spiral of armaments. Our vast expenditure on national defence is out of balance and should be cut back. It necessarily diverts resources from other needs, both those of the Third World and our own at home. People everywhere have a right to know in what ways their governments are pursuing policies that will lead to disarmament. Without such policies, deterrence has to be condemned.

We are all faced with an agonizing and unclear situation, further complicated by state secrecy on security matters. Christians must themselves recognize that there is room for differences of opinion in the present situation. All of us must retain the right to our conscientious beliefs. And I would judge that this does not give us the right seriously to defy the law in the present situation. We must have due regard for democratic processes and for the institutions of a free society.

Within the framework of our democratic system, the Christian can find scope enough to work with wholehearted enthusiasm and commitment for the cause of peace and for the making of a world where both sides in our present confrontation will be encouraged to enter with greater determination the path of negotiation and effective disarmament.

It seems to me that we often approach the problem from the wrong angle. Our representatives have spent many hours of negotiation over the contents of successive disarmament proposals. But disarmament will follow the lowering of tension and the building of confidence and not vice versa. We have to stress rather the need for political will on both sides to achieve 'detente'.

It is possible, if leaders and people want it, to overcome fears and insecurity in international relationships. History abounds in examples. If the confidence to live and let live is built up on both sides then it should not prove impossible to reflect a newly found security by means of progressive disarmament proposals. Here is a task for all of us, but especially for our political parties and leaders.

The present situation is grave. Those with political power must have the will to discover a better way to achieve peace than through amassing nuclear weapons. The future of humanity depends on it.

COMMONWEALTH HEADS OF GOVERNMENT MEETING IN NEW DELHI

At the end of its meeting from 23 to 29 November 1983 the CHOGM issued four documents: The Goa Declaration on International Security, The New Delhi Statement on Economic Action, a Communique and a statement on Commonwealth functional cooperation.

Reproduced here are the first of these and extracts from the Communique concerning certain urgent international situations.

THE GOA DECLARATION ON INTERNATIONAL SECURITY

As we meet together in India at the end of 1983, representing a quarter of the world's people from every continent and many regions, we have shared both our concerns and our hopes for international security. Despite differences of approach which affect the way we analyse and judge events, it is our perception that relationships between the world's major military alliances are in danger of becoming more confrontational. In the context of heightened tensions and a continuing build-up of nuclear arsenals, the future of civilisation as we know it could be threatened. None of our countries or peoples would be insulated from that fate.

We are alarmed by increasing disregard for the moral and legal principles which should govern the conduct of states; by the degree to which the ethic of peaceful settlement of disputes is being eroded and by the readiness of nations to resort to the illegal use of force.

At this time of crisis, we believe it to be imperative that the Soviet Union and the United States should summon up the political vision of a world in which their nations can live in peace. Their first objective must be to work for the resumption of a genuine political dialogue between themselves leading to a relaxation of tensions. We believe that Commonwealth governments can make a practical contribution in encouraging them to do so and in promoting a larger measure of international understanding than now exists.

Essential to that enlargement of understanding is the need to increase contacts at a variety of levels between the governments and peoples of East and West. A concerted effort is required to restore constructive dialogue to the conduct of East-West relations. Only thus can a climate of confidence be rebuilt in place of the prevailing one of fear and mistrust.

In all these pursuits we emphasise the supreme importance of political will. We therefore welcome Prime Minister Pierre Trudeau's call for a new political dimension in the quest for international security. We support his efforts to restore active political contact and communication among all the nuclear weapon powers, and are willing to help these and other such efforts in all appropriate ways.

As Prime Minister Indira Gandhi has so consistently emphasised, the central issue in securing wider progress on disarmament is the stopping of the nuclear arms race. These are essential steps for progress in working towards a world released from the menace of nuclear weapons and their wider spread. If the resources released by disarmament were ploughed back in some measure into world development, the needs of the developing countries which are in the forefront of our concern could be significantly met.

We are concerned also over the diminishing capacity of international institutions to play an effective role in world affairs. Rejecting this negative trend, we pledge our renewed support for the principles enshrined in the United Nations Charter. There is, in our view, an urgent need to consider what practical steps can be taken to strengthen the United Nations system and to improve its capacity to fulfil the objectives of the Charter.

We are particularly concerned at the vulnerability of small states to external attack and interference in their affairs. These countries are members of the international community which must respect their independence and, at the very least, has a moral obligation to provide effectively for their territorial integrity. We have separately agreed on an urgent study of these issues. Additionally, however, we will play our part in helping the international community to make an appropriate response to the UN Secretary-General's call for a strengthening of collective security in keeping with the Charter.

Meeting here in India, we cannot emphasise too strongly our belief that an ethic of non-violence must be at the heart of all efforts to ensure peace and harmony in the world. That ethic requires close adherence to the principle of peaceful settlement. Only by such commitment on all sides will the world's people enjoy an environment of true international security.

Finally, we retain faith in human capacity to overcome the dangers and difficulties that threaten the world and to secure for all its people the prospect of a more peaceful international environment. We shall work together to fulfil that faith.

Fort Aguada, Goa, 27 November 1983.

COMMUNIQUE
(Extracts)

Cyprus

5. Heads of Government condemned the declaration by the Turkish Cypriot authorities issued on 15 November 1983 to create a secessionist state in Northern Cyprus, in the area under foreign occupation. Fully endorsing Security Council Resolution 541, they denounced the declaration as legally invalid and reiterated the call for its non-recognition and immediate withdrawal. They further called upon all states not to facilitate or in any way assist the illegal secessionist entity. They regarded this illegal act as a challenge to the international community and demanded the implementation of the relevant UN Resolutions on Cyprus.

6. At this critical moment for a member country of the Commonwealth, Heads of Government, reaffirming their Lusaka and Melbourne communiqués and recalling the relevant Security Council resolutions, pledged their renewed support for the independence, sovereignty, territorial integrity, unity and non-alignment of the Republic of Cyprus; and in this respect, they expressed their solidarity with their colleague the President of Cyprus.

7. They agreed to establish a special Commonwealth Action Group on Cyprus at high level to assist in securing compliance with Security Council Resolution 541. The Group would consist of the following five countries, together with the Secretary-General: Australia, Guyana, India, Nigeria and Zambia.

8. Finally, they urged all states and the two communities in Cyprus to refrain from any action which might further exacerbate the situation.

Grenada

9. Commonwealth leaders discussed recent events in Grenada which have caused such deep disquiet among them and in the wider international community, and on which most of them had already expressed their views at the United Nations. They reaffirmed their commitment to the principles of independence, sovereignty and territorial integrity and called for the strict observance of these principles. They recorded their profound regret over the tragic loss of life in Grenada.

10. Heads of Government agreed, however, that the emphasis should now be on reconstruction, not recrimination. They welcomed the establishment of an interim civilian administration in Grenada. They looked forward to its functioning free of external interference, pressure, or the presence of foreign military forces and noted its intention to hold, as early as possible, elections which would be seen by the international community to be free and fair. On this basis, and given the readiness of the countries of the Caribbean Community to assist in the maintenance of law and order in Grenada if so requested by the Interim Administration, Commonwealth leaders confirmed their readiness to give sympathetic consideration to requests for asistance from the island state. In doing so, they stressed the importance they attached to an early return of Commonwealth countries of the Caribbean to the spirit of fraternity and co-operation that had been so characteristic of the region.

11. Time and again in their discussion, Commonwealth leaders were recalled to the special needs of small states, not only in the Caribbean but elsewhere in the Commonwealth. They recognised that the Commonwealth itself had given some attention to these needs in the context of economic development but felt that the matter deserved consideration on a wider basis, including that of national security. Recalling the particular dangers faced in the past by small Commonwealth countries, they requested the Secretary-General to undertake a study, drawing as necessary on the resources and experience of Commonwealth countries, of the special needs of such states consonant with the right to sovereignty and territorial integrity that they shared with all nations.

Central America

28. Heads of Government noted with great concern the escalation of tensions in Central America which posed a threat to the peace and stability of the region, with potentially dangerous consequences for international security. They stressed the urgent need to reduce these tensions and to achieve a lasting peace through dialogue and negotiations. In this connection, they welcomed the efforts of the Contadora Group of states to seek a negotiated settlement to the region's problems. They noted that these problems were rooted not in East-West ideological rivalry but in deep-seated social and economic ills. They urged all the states to refrain from aggression, from the use of force or the threat of the use of force, and from intervention and interference in the internal affairs of other states.

Other sections of the Communique concerned Southern Africa (especially Namibia), the Middle East, South-East Asia (including the refugee problem), Afghanistan, Guyana, Belize, an Indian Ocean zone of peace, the South Pacific, the Mediterranean, the Law of the Sea, International Economic Cooperation, Food and Agriculture, Population and the next CHOGM, to be held in the Bahamas in 1985.

REPUBLIC OF SOUTH AFRICA CONSTITUTION ACT

Adopted by the South African Parliament on 9 September 1983 and approved by a referendum of existing (white) voters on 2 November 1983. (Abbreviated as indicated by italics)

IN HUMBLE SUBMISSION to Almighty God, Who controls the destinies of peoples and nations,
Who gathered our forebears together from many lands and gave them this their own,
Who has guided them from generation to generation,
Who has wondrously delivered them from the dangers that beset them,
WE DECLARE that we
ARE CONSCIOUS of our responsibility towards God and man;
ARE CONVINCED of the necessity of standing united and of pursuing the following national goals:

To uphold Christian values and civilized norms, with recognition and protection of freedom of faith and worship,
To safeguard the integrity and freedom of our country,
To uphold the independence of the judiciary and the equality of all under the law,
To secure the maintenance of law and order,
To further the contentment and the spiritual and material welfare of all,
To respect and to protect the human dignity, life, liberty and property of all in our midst,
To respect, to further and to protect the self-determination of population groups and peoples,
To further private initiative and effective competition;
ARE PREPARED TO ACCEPT our duty to seek world peace in association with all peace-loving peoples and nations; and
ARE DESIROUS OF GIVING THE REPUBLIC OF SOUTH AFRICA A CONSTITUTION which provides for elected and responsible forms of government and which is best suited to the traditions, history and circumstances of our land:
BE IT THEREFORE ENACTED by the State President and the House of Assembly of the Republic of South Africa, as follows:-

PART I
THE REPUBLIC

1. The Republic of South Africa, consisting of the provinces of the Cape of Good Hope, Natal, the Transvaal and the Orange Free State, shall continue to exist as a republic under that name.
2. The people of the Republic of South Africa acknowledge the sovereignty and guidance of Almighty God.

PART II
NATIONAL FLAG AND ANTHEM

3 and 4. *National Flag*
5. *National Anthem*

PART III
THE STATE PRESIDENT

6. (1) The head of the Republic shall be the State President.
(2) The command-in-chief of the South African Defence Force is vested in the State President.
(3) The State President shall, subject to the provisions of this Act, have power—
(a) to address any House, or the Houses at a joint sitting;
(b) to confer honours;
(c) to appoint and to accredit, to receive and to recognize ambassadors, plenipotentiaries, diplomatic representatives and other diplomatic officers, consuls and consular officers;
(d) to pardon or reprieve offenders, either unconditionally or subject to such conditions as he may deem fit, and to remit any fines, penalties or forfeitures;
(e) to enter into and ratify international conventions, treaties and agreements;
(f) to proclaim or terminate martial law;
(g) to declare war and make peace;
(h) to make such appointments as he may deem fit under powers conferred upon him by any law, and to exercise such powers and perform such functions as may be conferred upon or assigned to him in terms of this Act or any other law.
(4) The State President shall in addition as head of the State have such powers and functions as were immediately before the commencement of this Act possessed by the State President by way of prerogative.

7. (1) (a) The State President shall be elected by the members of an electoral college present at a meeting called in accordance with the provisions of this section and presided over by the Chief Justice or a judge of appeal designated by him.
(b) An electoral college referred to in paragraph (a) shall be constituted whenever necessary in terms of this Act, and shall consist of—
(i) 50 members of the House of Assembly designated by it by resolution;
(ii) 25 members of the House of Representatives designated by it by resolution;
(iii) 13 members of the House of Delegates designated by it by resolution, or, in the case of a particular House, such smaller number of members thereof, if any, as may be so designated by it.

(c) *excludes nominated and indirectly elected members of Houses from those proceedings.*

(d) A House shall designate the relevant members of a particular electoral college as often as it may deem necessary.

(e) An electoral college shall dissolve after disposing of the matters for which it is constituted in terms of this Act.

(2) The election of a State President shall be held, subject to the provisions of subsection (4), at a time and place fixed by the Chief Justice and made known by notice in the *Gazette* not less than 14 days before the election.

(3) The date so fixed shall—

(a) in the case of the first such election, be a date not more than seven days after the commencement of the first session of Parliament after the commencement of this Act;

(b) whenever a general election of members of the Houses has been held after a dissolution of Parliament, be a date not more than seven days after the commencement of the first session of Parliament after the general election;

(c) if the State President dies or for any other reason vacates his office *provision is made*.

(4) If any electoral college removes the State President from office in terms of section 9, it shall forthwith proceed to elect a State President.

(5) No person may be elected or serve as State President unless he is qualified to be nominated or elected and take his seat as a member of a House.

(6) Any person who holds a public office in respect of which he receives any remuneration or allowance out of public funds, and who is elected as State President, shall vacate such office with effect from the date on which he is elected.

8. (1), (2), (3) and (4). *Procedure for nominations of candidates for the State Presidency, and for uncontested elections.*

(5) Where more than one candidate is nominated for election, a vote shall be taken by secret ballot.

(6) and (7) provide for eliminating ballots if necessary, and for the event of a tie.

9. (1) The State President shall hold office, subject to the other provisions of his section—

(a) during the continuance of the Parliament from which the electoral college that elected him was constituted; and

(b) after the dissolution of that Parliament . . . until a State President has . . . been elected . . . but shall be eligible for re-election.

(2) The State President shall vacate his office—

(a) if in terms of section 7 (5) he becomes disqualified from serving as State President; or

(b) if he is removed from office under subsection (3).

(3) *The State President may be removed, on the ground of misconduct or inability to perform the duties of his office, by majority at a meeting of the electoral college convened at the request of each of the three Houses, each of which must have considered a report from a committee of Parliament set up on petition of not less than half the members of each House.*

(4) *The State President may resign by lodging his resignation in writing with the Chief Justice.*

10. (1) *Whenever the State President is for any reason unable to perform the duties of his office, a member of the Cabinet nominated by the State President shall serve as Acting State President.*

(2) *Provides for an Acting State President when the above procedure is inoperative.*

(3) and (4) *Further provision as to a vacancy.*

11. Oath of office by State President and Acting State President.

12. *The State President's salary and allowances to be determined by Parliament.*

13. Pension payable to State President and State President's widow or widower.

PART IV
OWN AFFAIRS AND GENERAL AFFAIRS

14. (1) Matters which specially or differentially affect a population group in relation to the maintenance of its identity and the upholding and furtherance of its way of life, culture, traditions and customs, are, subject to the provisions of section 16, own affairs in relation to such population group.

(2) Matters coming within the classes of subjects described in Schedule 1 are, subject to the provisions of section 16, own affairs in relation to each population group.

15. Matters which are not own affairs of a population group in terms of section 14 are general affairs.

16. (1) (a) Any question arising in the application of this Act as to whether any particular matters are own affairs of a population group shall be decided by the State President, who shall do so in such manner that the governmental institutions serving the interests of such population group are not by the decision enabled to affect the interests of any other population group, irrespective of whether or not it is defined as a population group in this Act.

(b) All such questions shall be general affairs.

(2) *How the State President may proclaim such a decision.*

(3) When the State President assigns the administration of a law to a Minister of a department of State for own affairs of a population group under section 26 or 98 he shall do so in pursuance of a decision under this section that the law, in so far as its administration is so assigned, deals with own affairs of the population group in question.

17. (1) The State President may refer any question which is being considered by him in terms of section 16 to the President's Council for advice.

(2) (a) Before the State President issues a certificate under section 31 in respect of a bill or an amendment or a proposed amendment thereof, he shall consult the Speaker of Parliament and the Chairmen of the respective Houses in such manner as he deems fit.

(b) Paragraph (a) does not apply to the issue of a certificate in respect of a bill or an amendment thereof which has been altered as a result of the consultation in terms of that paragraph.

18. (1) Any division of the Supreme Court of South Africa shall be competent to inquire into and pronounce upon the question as to whether the provisions of section 17 (2) were complied with in connection with a decision of the State President contemplated in those provisions.

(2) Save as provided in subsection (1), no court of law shall be competent to inquire into or pronounce upon the validity of a decision of the State President that matters mentioned in the decision are own affairs of a population group, or are not own affairs of a population group, as the case may be.

(3) For the purposes of subsection (2), the matters dealt with in any bill which, when introduced in a House, is not endorsed with or accompanied by a certificate contemplated in section 31, shall be deemed to be matters which are not own affairs of any population group by virtue of a decision of the State President.

PART V
THE EXECUTIVE AUTHORITY

19. (1) The executive authority of the Republic—

(a) in regard to matters which are own affairs of any population group is vested in the State President acting on the advice of the Ministers' Council in question;

(b) in regard to general affairs is vested in the State President acting in consultation with the Ministers who are members of the Cabinet.

(2) Except in sections 20 (c) and (d), 21 (2), 24, 25, 26, 27, 33, 39 (3), 66 and 98 (3) (b), or where otherwise expressly stated or necessarily implied, any reference in this Act to the State President is a reference to the State President acting as provided in subsection (1).

20. The Cabinet shall consist of—

(a) the State President, who shall preside at its meetings;

(b) the Ministers appointed to administer departments of State for general affairs;

(c) any Minister appointed to perform functions other than the administration of a department of State and designated by the State President as a member of the Cabinet; and

(d) any member of a Ministers' Council designated by the State President as a member of the Cabinet whether for a definite or for an indefinite period or for a particular purpose.

21. (1) A Ministers' Council shall consist of—

(a) the Ministers appointed to administer departments of State for own affairs of one and the same population group;

(b) any Minister who is a member of the population group in question and who has been appointed as a member of the Ministers' Council to perform functions other than the administration of a department of State;

(c) any Deputy Minister appointed to exercise or perform powers, functions and duties on behalf of any of the Ministers referred to in paragraph (a); and

(d) any Minister of the Cabinet who is a member of the population group in question and who has been co-opted by the Ministers' Council as a member thereof, whether for a definite or for an indefinite period or for a particular purpose.

(2) The State President shall designate a Minister who is a member of a Ministers' Council and who, at the time of the designation, in the opinion of the State President has the support of the majority in the House consisting of members of the population group in question, as the Chairman of such Ministers' Council.

22. *Seal of Republic.*

23. *Confirmation of executive acts of State President in writing under his signature and, where appropriate, ministerial counter-signature.*

24. (1) The State President may appoint as many persons as he may from time to time deem

necessary to administer such departments of State of the Republic as the State President may establish, or to perform such other functions as the State President may determine.

(2) Persons appointed under subsection (1) shall hold office during the State President's pleasure and shall be the Ministers of the Republic.

(3) (a) No Minister shall hold office for a longer period than 12 months unless he is or becomes a member of a House.

(b) A Minister of any department of State for own affairs of a population group shall—

(i) be a member of the population group in question; and

(ii) at the time of his appointment as such Minister, in the opinion of the State President have the support of the majority in the House consisting of members of that population group.

(4) *Ministers' oath of office.*

25. *Temporary performance of Minister's functions of office by another Minister.*

26. *Assignment of powers, duties and functions of one Minister to another.*

27. *Appointment and functions of Deputy Ministers.*

28. The appointment and removal of persons in the service of the Republic shall be vested in the State President, unless the appointment or removal is delegated by the State President to any other authority or is in terms of this Act or any other law vested in any other authority.

29. Save as is otherwise provided in section 36, Pretoria shall be the seat of the Government of the Republic.

PART VI
THE LEGISLATURE

The Legislature and its Powers

30. The legislative power of the Republic is vested in the State President and the Parliament of the Republic, which, as the sovereign legislative authority in and over the Republic, shall have full power to make laws for the peace, order and good government of the Republic: Provided that the powers of Parliament in respect of any bill contemplated in section 31 shall be exercised as provided by that section.

31. (1) A bill which, when introduced in a House, is endorsed with or accompanied by the certificate of the State President that the bill deals with matters which are own affairs of the population group in question, shall be disposed of by that House, and shall not be required to be, or be, introduced in or dealt with by any other House.

(2) and (3) *Invalidity of amendments certified by the State President to deal with matters which are not 'own affairs' of the population group in question.*

32. (1) *In the event of disagreement among the Houses on a bill* the State President may during that session refer the bill or the different versions thereof which have been passed, as the case may be, to the President's Council for its decision: Provided that the State President may withdraw the reference at any time before the President's Council gives its decision.

(2) *The State Parliament may set a time-limit on consideration by a House of a bill passed by another House.*

(3), (4) and (5) *Further procedure concerning bills on which Houses disagree.*

33. (1) When a bill which—

(a) has been passed by Parliament; or

(b) in terms of section 32 (4) is deemed to have been passed by Parliament; or

(c) has been passed by a House in accordance with section 31,

is presented to the State President for his assent, he shall declare that he assents thereto or that he withholds assent, but he shall not declare that he withholds assent unless he is satisfied that the bill has not been dealt with as provided in this Act.

(2) *Subsection (1) does not apply to invalid amendments under section 31(2).*

34. (1) A bill referred to in section 33(1) to which the State President has assented shall be an Act of Parliament.

(2) (a) Any division of the Supreme Court of South Africa shall, subject to the provisions of section 18, be competent to inquire into and pronounce upon the question as to whether the provisions of this Act were complied with in connection with any law which is expressed to be enacted by the State President and Parliament or by the State President and any House.

(b) *Excludes rules and orders of the Houses.*

(3) Save as provided in subsection (2), no court of law shall be competent to inquire into or pronounce upon the validity of an Act of Parliament.

35. *Signature and enrolment of Acts.*

36. Cape Town shall be the seat of the Legislature of the Republic.

Parliament

37. (1) Parliament shall consist of three Houses, namely, a House of Assembly, a House of Representatives and a House of Delegates.

(2) If and for as long as any House is unable, during a session of Parliament, to meet for the performance of its functions or to perform its functions because of the resignation or absence of members—

Parliament shall consist of the Houses that are or, according to the circumstances, the House that is able to perform their or its functions, and the provisions of this Act and any other law shall be construed accordingly.

38. (1) The State President may appoint such times for the sessions of Parliament as he thinks fit, and may also from time to time, by proclamation in the *Gazette* or otherwise, prorogue Parliament.

(2) There shall be a session of Parliament at least once in every year. . . .

(3) The first session of Parliament after the general election of members of the Houses held in pursuance of a dissolution of Parliament, shall commence within 30 days after the polling day of the election.

39. (1) Every Parliament shall continue for five years from the day on which its first session commences.

(2) The State President—

(a) may dissolve Parliament by proclamation in the *Gazette* at any time; and

(b) shall so dissolve Parliament, unless he resigns from office, if each House, during one and the same ordinary session of Parliament—

(i) passes a motion of no confidence in the Cabinet within any period of 14 days; or

(ii) rejects any bill which appropriates revenue or moneys for the ordinary annual requirements or services of the departments of State controlled by members of the Cabinet.

(3) *The State President may or shall dissolve any House in circumstances similar to the above.*

40. *Members of Houses remain members, and Parliament or any House may be recalled for business, between dissolution and polling day.*

The Houses

41. (1) The House of Assembly shall consist of—

(a) 166 members, each of whom shall be directly elected by the persons entitled to vote at an election of such a member in an electoral division delimited as provided in section 49;

(b) four members nominated by the State President, of whom one shall be nominated from each province;

(c) eight members elected by the members contemplated in paragraph (a) according to the principle of proportional representation, each voter having one transferable vote.

(2) The number of members of the House of Assembly to be elected as provided in subsection (1) (a) in each province, shall be as follows:— Cape of Good Hope, 56; Natal, 20; Orange Free State, 14; Transvaal, 76.

42. (1) The House of Representatives shall consist of—

(a) 80 members, each of whom shall be directly elected by the persons entitled to vote at an election of such a member in an electoral division delimited as provided in section 49;

(b) two members nominated by the State President;

(c) three members elected by the members contemplated in paragraph (a) according to the principle of proportional representation, each voter having one transferable vote.

(2) The number of members of the House of Representatives to be elected as provided in subsection (1) (a) in each province, shall be as follows:—Cape of Good Hope, 60; Natal, 5; Orange Free State, 5; Transvaal, 10.

43. (1) The House of Delegates shall consist of—

(a) 40 members, each of whom shall be directly elected by the persons entitled to vote at an election of such a member in an electoral division delimited as provided in section 49;

(b) two members nominated by the State President;

(c) three members elected by the members contemplated in paragraph (a) according to the principle of proportional representation, each voter having one transferable vote.

(2) The number of members of the House of Delegates to be elected as provided in subsection (1) (a) in a province, shall be as follows:—Cape of Good Hope, 3; Natal, 29; Transvaal, 8.

44. Any reference in this Part to a directly elected member, a nominated member and an indirectly elected member of a House, shall be construed as a reference to a member of such House who, as the case may be and as the context may require, has been elected or nominated or is to be elected or nominated as

provided in section 41 (1) (a), (b) and (c), respectively, or section 42 (1) (a), (b) and (c), respectively, or section 43 (1) (a), (b) and (c), respectively.

45. Notwithstanding any provision to the contrary contained in this Act, the number of members of any House to be elected in the various provinces as provided in section 41 (2), 42 (2) or 43 (2), as the case may be, shall not be altered until—

(a) in the case of the House of Assembly, a period of five years has elapsed from the last delimitation of its electoral divisions in terms of the previous Constitution; and

(b) in the case of the House of Representatives and the House of Delegates, a period of 10 years has elapsed from the first delimitation of the electoral divisions of the House in question in terms of this Act.

46. (1) The State President may make regulations in regard to the election of indirectly elected members of a House....

(2) A casual vacancy in the seat of a nominated or an indirectly elected member of a House shall be filled by the nomination or election of a member for the unexpired portion of the term of office of the member in whose stead he is nominated or elected...

(3) *Further provision as to nominated and indirectly elected members.*

47. (1) At any general election of members of the Houses held in pursuance of a dissolution of Parliament, all polls shall be taken on one and the same day in all the electoral divisions of all three Houses throughout the Republic, such day to be appointed by the State President.

(2) At any general election of members of a House held in pursuance of its dissolution otherwise than at a dissolution of Parliament, all polls shall be taken on one and the same day in all the electoral divisions of that House throughout the Republic, such day to be appointed by the State President.

(3) the day appointed by the State President in terms of subsection (1) and (2), shall be a day not more than 180 days after the dissolution of Parliament or the House in question, as the case may be.

48, 49, 50 and 41. *Delimitation of electoral divisions by a judicial commission at intervals of not less than five nor more than ten years.*

52. Every White person, Coloured person and Indian who—

(a) is a South African citizen in terms of the South African Citizenship Act, 1949; and

(b) is of or over the age of 18 years; and

(c) is not subject to any of the disqualifications mentioned in section 4(1) or (2) of the Electoral Act, 1979,

shall, on compliance with and subject to the provisions of the Electoral Act, 1979, be entitled to vote at any election of a member of the House of Assembly, the House of Representatives and the House of Delegates, respectively, in the electoral division of the House in question determined in accordance with the last-mentioned Act.

53. No person shall be qualified to be a member of a House under this Act unless he—

(a) is qualified to be included as a voter in any list of voters of the House in question in an electoral division thereof; and

(b) has resided for five years within the limits of the Republic.

54. No person shall be capable of being elected or nominated or of sitting as a member of a House if he—

(a) has at any time been convicted of any offence for which he has been sentenced to imprisonment without the option of a fine for a period of not less than twelve months, unless he has received a grant of amnesty or a free pardon, or unless the period of such imprisonment expired at least five years before the date of his election or nomination; or

(b) is an unrehabilitated insolvent; or

(c) is of unsound mind, and has been so declared by a competent court; or

(d) is an officer or other employee in the service of any institution, council or body contemplated in section 84 (1) (f) of the previous Constitution; or

(e) holds any office or profit under the Republic *(exemption of Ministers, pensioners, JPs, councillors paid only expenses, and certain others.)*

55. (1) A member of a House shall vacate his seat if he—

(a) becomes subject to any disability mentioned in section 54; or

(b) ceases to be qualified as required by law; or

(c) fails for a whole ordinary session of Parliament or of the House of which he is a member to attend without the special leave of that House, unless his absence is due to his serving, while the Republic is at war, with the South African Defence Force or any other force or service established by or under the Defence Act, 1957.

(2) A member of a House who—

(a) is designated or appointed as a member of the President's Council...*or*

(b) is elected as a member of a provincial council, shall vacate his seat as a member of such House....

56. *Penalty for sitting or voting when disqualified.*

57. *Oath to be taken by every member of a House.*

58. (1) An electoral college referred to in subsection (1) of section 7 shall, after having elected a State President... proceed to elect a Speaker of Parliament, who shall be a member of a House.

(2), (3) and (4) *Further provision as to Speaker and Deputy Speakers.*

59. (1) The Speaker of Parliament shall be the Speaker of each of the respective Houses and shall preside at a meeting of a House whenever he deems it necessary or desirable.

(2) The Speaker shall, when presiding at a meeting of a House, be vested with all the powers, duties and functions of the Chairman of the House in question, in so far as they are consistent with any functions assigned to the Speaker by rules and orders approved by all three Houses: Provided that the Speaker may only vote in the House of which he is a member.

60. (1) Every House shall at its first meeting, before proceeding to the dispatch of any other business, elect a member to be the Chairman of the House, and, as often as the office becomes vacant, the House shall again elect a member to be the Chairman.

(2) and (3) *Further provision as to Chairman of Houses.*

61. To constitute a meeting of a House for the exercise of its powers, the presence shall be necessary of—

(a) in the case of the House of Assembly, at least 50 members;

(b) in the case of the House of Representatives, at least 25 members;

(c) in the case of the House of Delegates, at least 13 members.

62. All questions in a House shall be determined by a majority of votes of members present other than the Chairman or the presiding member, who shall, however, have and exercise a casting vote in the case of an equality of votes.

63. A House may make rules and orders in connection with the order and conduct of its business and proceedings.

64. *Regulations for joint committees, consisting of members of each of the Houses, and for joint rules and orders.*

65. (1) A Minister who is a member of the Cabinet, and any deputy to such a Minister, has the right to sit and to speak in any House, but may only vote if he is a member of a House and only in the House of which he is a member.

(2) A member of a Ministers' Council who is not a member of any House or of the Cabinet has the right to sit and to speak in the House of which the members are of the same population group as the members of the Ministers' Council in question, but may not vote therein.

66. The State President may by proclamation in the *Gazette* summon any House for the dispatch of business in connection with own affairs when Parliament is not in session, and may prorogue the House in like manner before the commencement of the next ensuing session of Parliament.

67. (1) A joint sitting of the Houses shall be called by the State President by message to the Houses.

(2) The State President may call such a joint sitting whenever he deems it desirable, and shall call such a joint sitting if requested to do so by all three Houses.

(3) The Speaker of Parliament shall preside at such a joint sitting.

(4) The Speaker shall determine the rules and orders for the order and conduct of the proceedings of such a joint sitting.

(5) No resolution shall be adopted at any such joint sitting.

PART VII
ADMINISTRATION OF JUSTICE

68. (1) The judicial authority of the Republic is vested in a Supreme Court to be known as the Supreme Court of South Africa and consisting of an Appellate Division and such provincial and local divisions as may be prescribed by law.

(2) The Supreme Court of South Africa shall, subject to the provisions of sections 18 and 34, have jurisdiction as provided in the Supreme Court Act, 1959.

(3) Save as otherwise provided in the Supreme Court Act, 1959, Bloemfontein shall be the seat of the Appellate Division of the Supreme Court of South Africa.

69. All administrative powers, duties and functions affecting the administration of justice shall be under the control of the Minister of Justice.

PART VIII
PRESIDENT'S COUNCIL

70. (1) There shall be a President's Council consisting of—

(a) 20 members designated by resolution of the House of Assembly;

(b) 10 members designated by resolution of the House of Representatives;
(c) 5 members designated by resolution of the House of Delegates; and
(d) 25 members appointed by the State President,

or, in the case of members contemplated in paragraph (a), (b) or (c), such smaller numbers of members, if any, as may have been so designated by the House in question.

(2) *Provides that the 25 members appointed by the State President shall include ten supporters of opposition parties, nominated by such members of the House of Assembly (6), the House of Representatives (3) and the House of Delegates (1).*

71. (1) No person shall be qualified to be designated or appointed as a member of the President's Council—
(a) unless he is of or over the age of 30 years;
(b) in the case of a member designated by a House, unless he is a member of such House or is qualified to be elected or nominated and take his seat as a member of such House;
(c) in the case of a member appointed by the State President, unless he is a member of a House or is qualified to be elected or nominated and take his seat as a member of a House:

Provided that the provisions of section 54 (e) shall not apply with reference to the qualification of a person to be designated or appointed as a member of the President's Council or to be such a member.

(2) A member of the President's Council shall hold office until the next ensuing dissolution of that Council in terms of section 77, but shall be eligible for redesignation or reappointment.

(3) A member of the President's Council shall vacate his office—
(a) on the dissolution of that Council;
(b) subject to the proviso to subsection (1), if he becomes disqualified to be elected or nominated and take his seat as a member of any House;
(c) if he becomes a member of a House or of a provincial council;
(d), (e) and (f) *upon other contingencies.*

(4) A member of the President's Council may resign as such member by lodging his resignation in writing with the State President, who shall, in the case of a member designated by a House, forthwith notify the Chairman of the House in question of the resignation.

(5) *When the designation or redesignation of a person as a member of the President's Council by a House takes effect.*

72. (1) The President's Council shall elect a Chairman from among its members at its first meeting after its constitution, at which a person designated by the State President shall preside until a Chairman is elected.

(2) The Chairman of the President's Council shall hold office until the dissolution of that Council in terms of section 77 unless he—
(a) ceases earlier to be a member of that Council; or
(b) resigns as Chairman by lodging his resignation in writing with the State President; or
(c) is removed from office as Chairman by resolution of that Council.

(3) The President's Council shall at its first meeting elect one of its members as Deputy Chairman, who shall act in the stead of the Chairman when the Chairman is unable to perform the functions of his office.

(4) When neither the Chairman nor the Deputy Chairman is able to act, the President's Council shall elect one of its members to act in the stead of the Chairman.

73. (1) *The members of the President's Council shall receive such remuneration, allowances and other benefits as the State President may determine, and these may differ between members.*

74. The presence of at least 30 members of the President's Council shall be necessary to constitute a meeting of the President's Council for the exercise of its powers.

75. All questions at a meeting of the President's Council shall be determined by a majority of votes of the members present other than the presiding member, who shall have and exercise a casting vote in the case of an equality of votes.

76. (1) Subject to the provisions of this Act, the President's Council may make rules and orders in connection with the order and conduct of its business and proceedings, the establishment, constitution and powers of committees of the Council and the order and conduct of their business and proceedings.

(2) Any Minister or Deputy Minister has the right to sit and to speak in the President's Council, but shall not vote therein.

77. The President's Council shall be dissolved by the first dissolution of Parliament following the constitution of that Council, but the dissolution of the President's Council shall take effect on the day on which the State President elected after such dissolution of Parliament assumes office.

78. (1) The President's Council shall at the request of the State President advise him on any matter referred to it by the State President for its advice, and may, in its discretion, advise him on any matter (excluding draft legislation) which, in its opinion, is of public interest.

(2) Whenever a matter is referred to the President's Council for its advice or when that Council is of the opinion that a matter is of public interest, it may refer such matter to a committee . . . for advice . . . .

(3) The President's Council may transmit any advice received by it in terms of subsection (2) to the State President as the advice of the Council, whether with or without its comments thereon.

(4) (a) *Bills referred to the President's Council under section 32 may be referred to a committee of the Council.*

(b) The President's Council may from time to time advise the State President that any bill or bills so referred to it, be amended or otherwise dealt with in the manner recommended by the President's Council.

(5) Unless the State President withdraws the reference, the President's Council shall decide—

(a) in the case of a bill referred to in section 32(1) (a), either that the bill is to be presented to the State President for assent or that it shall not be so presented;

(b) in the case of a bill referred to in section 32 (1) (b), either which one of the different versions of such bill that were passed is to be presented to the State President for assent, or that none of those versions shall be so presented;

(c) in the case of a bill referred to in section 32 (1) (c) or (d), which one of the different versions of such bill that were passed is to be presented to the State President for assent.

(6) The President's Council or a committee thereof may, for the purposes of the performance of its functions and in its discretion, consult with any person or State institution on any matter, and may for such purpose establish consultative committees . . . .

(7) Advice received by the State President in terms of subsection (1) shall be laid upon the Table in every House that has an interest in it within 14 days after its receipt, if Parliament is then in session, or, if Parliament is not then in session, within 14 days after the commencement of its next ensuing session.

(8) Advice received by the State President in terms of subsection (4) (b) and accepted by him, and any decision of the President's Council in terms of subsection (5), shall be laid upon the Table of every House within 14 days after its receipt by the State President.

PART IX
FINANCE

(s. 79 to s. 86 omitted.)

PART X
GENERAL

87. Subject to the provisions of this Act, all laws which were in force in any part of the Republic or in any territory in respect of which Parliament is competent to legislate, immediately before the commencement of this Act, shall continue in force until repealed or amended by the competent authority.

88. The constitutional and parliamentary conventions which existed immediately before the commencement of this Act shall continue to exist, except in so far as they are inconsistent with the provisions of this Act.

89. (1) English and Afrikaans shall be the official languages of the Republic, and shall be treated on a footing of equality, and possess and enjoy equal freedom, rights and privileges.

(2) All records, journals and proceedings of Parliament shall be kept in both the official languages and all bills, laws and notices of general public importance or interest issued by the Government of the Republic shall be in both the official languages.

(3) Notwithstanding the provisions of subsection (1) an Act of Parliament or a proclamation of the State President, issued under an Act of Parliament, whereby a Black area is declared to be a self-governing territory in the Republic, or a later Act of Parliament or a later proclamation of the State President (which in the absence of any other empowering provision may be issued under this subsection) may—

(a) provide for the recognition of one or more Black languages for any or all of the following purposes, namely—

(i) as an additional official language or as additional official languages of that territory; or

(ii) for use in that territory for official purposes prescribed by or under that Act or later Act or by any such proclamation; and

(b) contain provisions authorizing the use of any such Black language outside the said territory for such purposes connected with the affairs of that territory and subject to such conditions as may be prescribed by or under that Act or later Act or any such proclamation.

90. *Applies equality of use of official languages to provincial councils and local authorities.*

91. *Applies equality in use of official languages to official notices published in newspapers.*

92. (1) Any person who—

(a) maliciously destroys or spoils the National Flag of the Republic as described in section 4; or

(b) commits any other act which is calculated to hold the National Flag of the Republic in contempt; or

(c) without being authorized thereto (the burden of proof of which shall be upon him), removes the National Flag of the Republic as so described from any place where it is displayed in terms of instructions or directions issued by any State authority,

shall be guilty of an offence and liable on conviction to a fine not exceeding R10,000 or imprisonment for a period not exceeding five years.

(2) *Onus on the defence to prove that the offended flag was not the National Flag.*

93. The control and administration of Black affairs shall vest in the State President, who shall exercise all those special powers in regard to Black administration which immediately before the commencement of this Act were vested in him, and any lands which immediately before such commencement vested in him for the occupation of Blacks in terms of any law shall continue to vest in him with all such powers as he may have in connection therewith, and no lands which were set aside for the occupation of Blacks and which could not at the establishment of the Union of South Africa have been alienated except by an Act of the Legislature of a Colony which became part of the Union of South Africa in terms of the South Africa Act, 1909, shall be alienated or in any way diverted from the purposes for which they were set aside, except under the authority of an Act of Parliament.

94. All rights and obligations under conventions, treaties or agreements which were binding on any of the Colonies incorporated in the Union of South Africa at its establishment, and were still binding on the Republic immediately before the commencement of this Act, shall be rights and obligations of the Republic, just as all other rights and obligations under conventions, treaties or agreements which immediately before the commencement of this Act were binding on the Republic.

95. All powers, authorities and functions which immediately before the commencement of the previous Constitution were in any of the provinces vested in the Governor-General or in the Governor-General-in-Council or in any authority of the province, shall as far as they continue in existence and are capable of being exercised after the commencement of this Act, be vested in the State President, or in the authority exercising similar powers under the Republic, as the case may be, except such powers, authorities and functions as are by this Act or any other law vested in some other authority.

96. Any person who is in terms of any provision of this Act required to make and subscribe an oath may in lieu of such oath make and subscribe a solemn affirmation in corresponding form.

97. *Construction of certain references.*

98. (1) Any Act of Parliament or other law which at the commencement of this Act is administered by a Minister of the Republic or in a department of State controlled by such a Minister and which relates to a matter referred to in section 14 shall, notwithstanding the fact that it relates to such matter, be regarded as a general law for the purposes of this Act until, and except in so far as, its administration is assigned under section 26 to a Minister of a department of State for own affairs of a population group.

(2) Any ordinance of a province or other law which entrusts any power, duty or function to the executive committee or other executive authority of such province established by the previous Constitution and which relates to a matter referred to in section 14 shall, notwithstanding the fact that it relates to such matter, be administered according to its provisions unless, and except in so far as, its administration is assigned to a Minister under sub-section (3) (b).

(3) The State President may by proclamation in the *Gazette*—

(a) after consultation with the executive committee of the province concerned, declare that the provisions of Part IV apply to a law referred to in subsection (2) to the extent stated in the declaration;

(b) when he so declares or at any time thereafter, assign the administration of such law to a Minister;

(c) *when he so assigns, amend or adapt such law in order to regulate its application or interpretation; repeal and re-enact those of its provisions to which the assignment relates; regulate any other matter necessary, in his opinion, as a result of the assignment.*

(4) Section 26 shall apply *mutatis mutandis* to an assignment under subsection (3) (b) . . . .

99. (1) Subject to the provisions of subsections (2) and (3), Parliament may by law repeal or amend any provision of this Act.

(2) No repeal or amendment of the provisions of section 89 or of this subsection or of any corresponding provisions of any law substituted for them, shall be valid unless the bill embodying such repeal or amendment has been agreed to in every House by not less than two-thirds of the total number of its members.

(3) No repeal or amendment of s. 7 (1) (b), (5) or (6), s. 8 (5), s. 9 (1) or (3) (a), s. 14 or 15, s. 16 (1), s. 19, 20 or 21, s. 23 (2), s. 30, s. 31 (1) or (2), s. 32 (1), (2), (3) or (4), s. 33, s. 34 (2) (a), s. 37 (1), s. 38 (2), 39 (1) or (2), s. 41 (1), 42 (1), s. 43 (1), s. 52, 53 or 54, s. 64 (3), s. 70 (1), s. 71 (1) or (3) (b) or (c), s. 77,

s. 78 (5), this subsection, subsection (4) of this section or Schedule 1 shall be valid unless the bill embodying such repeal or amendment has been agreed to in every House by a majority of the total number of its members.

(4) A bill embodying the repeal or amendment of any provision mentioned in subsection (2) or (3) of this section shall not be referred to the President's Council for its decision under the circumstances contemplated in section 32 (1).

(5) *Construction of references in sub-section (3).*

100. (1) In this Act, unless the context indicates otherwise—

(i) 'Chief Justice' means the Chief Justice of South Africa;

(ii) 'Coloured person' means a person classified as a member of the Cape Coloured, Malay of Griqua group or the group Other Coloureds in terms of the Population Registration Act, 1950;

(iii) to (vi) *Construction of 'department of State', 'general affairs', 'general law' and 'House'.*

(vii) 'Indian' means a person classifed as a member of the Indian group in terms of the Population Registration Act, 1950;

(viii) 'own affairs' means matters referred to in section 14 . . . .

(ix) 'population group' means the White persons, the Coloured persons or the Indians . . . .

(x) 'previous Constitution' means the Republic of South Africa Constitution Act, 1961, and, in so far as it is not repealed by section 101, the Provincial Government Act, 1961;

(xi) 'Republic' means the Republic of South Africa;

(xii) 'the Coloured persons', 'the Indians' or 'the White persons' includes persons who would be classified as Coloured persons, Indians or White persons, respectively, in terms of the Population Registration Act, 1950, had the provisions of that Act applied to them;

(xiii) 'White person' means a person classified as a White person in terms of the Population Registration Act, 1950.

(2) In this Act and in any other law, except where it is inconsistent with the context or clearly inappropriate, any reference to a resolution or the approval of, or any other act of or with reference to, Parliament (except any act consitituting a law of Parliament), or to a member or a committee or the Tables of Parliament, or to any other matter in relation to Parliament (except any law of Parliament), shall be construed as a reference to a resolution or the approval or other act of, or with reference to, each of the different Houses, a member of a House, a joint committee contemplated in section 64, the Tables of the different Houses or such other matter related to the different Houses, as the case may be.

101. *Repeal and amendment of laws listed in Schedule 2.*

101. *Transitional provisions.*

103. (1) This Act shall . . . come into operation on a date fixed by the State President . . ...

(2) Different dates may be so fixed in respect of different provisions of this Act . . . .

(3) A reference in this Act to its commencement shall be construed as a reference to the applicable date so fixed.

(4) The State President referred to in subsection (1) may exercise any power vesting in the State President in terms of any provision of this Act, in so far as it is necessary in order to give effect to such provision or any other provision of this Act as contemplated in subsection (1) or, as the case may be, if the relevant provision has been put into operation as contemplated in subsection (2).

Schedule 1
SUBJECTS REFERRED TO IN SECTION 14

1. Social welfare, but subject to any general law in relation to—

(a) norms and standards for the provision or financing of welfare services;

(b) the control of the collection of money and other contributions from members of the public for welfare services or charity; and

(c) the registration of social workers, and control over their profession.

2. Education at all levels . . .

but subject to any general law in relation to—

(a) norms and standards for the financing of running and capital costs of education;

(b) salaries and conditions of employment of staff and professional registration of teachers; and

(c) norms and standards for syllabuses and examination and for certification of qualifications.

3. Art, culture and recreation (with the exception of competitive sport) which affect mainly the population group in question.

4. Health matters, comprising the following, namely—(1) hospitals, clinics and similar or related institutions; (2) medical services at schools and for indigent persons; (3) health and nutritional guidance; and (4) the registration of and control over private hospitals, but subject to any general law in relation to such matters.

5. Community development, comprising the following, namely—
(1) housing;
(2) development of the community in any area declared by or under any general law as an area for the use of the population group in question, including the establishment, development and renovation of towns and the control over and disposal of land (whether by alienation or otherwise) acquired or made available for that purpose; and
(3) rent control and control over and clearance of squatting, in such an area in terms of any general law,
but subject to—
(a) any general law in relation to norms, standards and income groups for the financing of housing;
(b) the provisions of the general law referred to in paragraph (2).

6. Local government within any area declared by or under any general law as a local government area for the population group in question, but subject to any general law in relation to matters to be administered on local government level on a joint basis, and excluding—
(a) any matter assigned to local authorities by or under any general law; and
(b) the exercise by any local authority, otherwise than in accordance with general policy determined by the State President acting as provided in section 19 (1) (b), of any power to raise loans.

7. Agriculture, comprising the following, namely—(1) agricultural development services, which include research, advisory services and extension; (2) training at agricultural colleges; and (3) financial and other assistance to farmers or prospective farmers, or for the promotion of agriculture.

8. Water supply, comprising the following, namely—(1) irrigation schemes; (2) drilling for water for agricultural and local government purposes; (3) subsidizing of drilling work and water works for agricultural or local government purposes; and (4) financial assistance in relation to water works damaged by flood.

9. Appointment of marriage officers under any general law.

10. Elections of members of the House of Parliament in question, excluding matters prescribed or to be prescribed by or under any general law.

11. Finance in relation to own affairs of the population group in question, including—
(1) estimates of revenue and expenditure, but excluding the form in which such estimates shall be prepared;
(2) the appropriation of moneys for the purposes of such estimates, but excluding such appropriation of moneys for any purpose other than that for which they are by or under any general law made available for appropriation;
(3) levies authorized by or under any general law, on services rendered over and above payments for such services;
(4) the receipt of donations;
(5) the making of donations not amounting to a supplementation of appropriations contemplated in paragraph (2); and
(6) the control over the collection and utilization of revenue, subject to the provisions of the Exchequer and Audit Act, 1975,
but excluding the levying of taxes and the raising of loans.

12. Staff administration in terms of the provisions of any general law in relation to staff in the employment of the State.

13. Auxiliary services necessary for the administration of own affairs of the population group in question . . . general law in relation to such matters.

14. The rendering of services, either with the approval of the State President acting as provided in section 19 (1) (b) or in terms of arrangements made between Ministers with such approval, to persons who are not members of the population group in question.

Schedule 2
ACTS REPEALED OR AMENDED
(Omitted)

DOCUMENTS AND REFERENCE

THE UNITED KINGDOM CONSERVATIVE ADMINISTRATION

(as at 6 January 1983)

THE CABINET

Prime Minister, First Lord of the Treasury and
  Minister for the Civil Service — Rt. Hon. Margaret Thatcher, MP
Secretary of State for the Home Department — Rt. Hon. William Whitelaw, CH, MC, MP
Lord Chancellor — Rt. Hon. The Lord Hailsham of Saint Marylebone, CH, FRS
Chancellor of the Exchequer — Rt. Hon. Sir Geoffrey Howe, QC, MP
Secretary of State for Foreign and Commonwealth
  Affairs and Minister of Overseas Development — Rt. Hon. Francis Pym, MC, MP
Secretary of State for Education and Science — Rt. Hon. Sir Keith Joseph, Bt, MP
Secretary of State for Northern Ireland — Rt. Hon. James Prior, MP
Secretary of State for Defence — Rt. Hon. Michael Heseltine, MP
Minister of Agriculture, Fisheries and Food — Rt. Hon. Peter Walker, MBE, MP
Secretary of State for Scotland — Rt. Hon. George Younger, TD, MP
Secretary of State for Wales — Rt. Hon. Nicholas Edwards, MP
Secretary of State for Industry — Rt. Hon. Patrick Jenkin, MP
Lord President of the Council and Leader of the
  House of Commons — Rt. Hon. John Biffen, MP
Secretary of State for Transport — Rt. Hon. David Howell, MP
Secretary of State for Social Services — Rt. Hon. Norman Fowler, MP
Chief Secretary to the Treasury — Rt. Hon. Leon Brittan, QC, MP
Lord Privy Seal and Leader of the House of Lords — Rt. Hon. The Baroness Young
Secretary of State for Energy — Rt. Hon. Nigel Lawson, MP
Secretary of State for Employment — Rt. Hon. Norman Tebbit, MP
Chancellor of the Duchy of Lancaster and
  Paymaster General — Rt. Hon. Cecil Parkinson, MP
Secretary of State for Trade — Rt. Hon. The Lord Cockfield
Secretary of State for the Environment — Rt. Hon. Tom King, MP

(as at 31 December, following changes on 11 June and 16 October; office-holders between June and October in brackets)

THE CABINET

Prime Minister, First Lord of the Treasury
  and Minister for the Civil Service — Rt. Hon. Margaret Thatcher, FRS, MP
Lord President of the Council and Leader
  of the House of Lords — Rt. Hon. The Viscount Whitelaw, CH, MC
Lord Chancellor — Rt. Hon. The Lord Hailsham of Saint Marylebone, CH, FRS
Secretary of State for Foreign and Commonwealth
  Affairs and Minister of Overseas Development — Rt. Hon. Sir Geoffrey Howe, QC, MP
Secretary of State for the Home Department — Rt. Hon. Leon Brittan, QC, MP
Chancellor of the Exchequer — Rt. Hon. Nigel Lawson, MP
Secretary of State for Education and Science — Rt. Hon. Sir Keith Joseph, Bt, MP
Secretary of State for Northern Ireland — Rt. Hon. James Prior, MP
Secretary of State for Energy — Rt. Hon. Peter Walker, MBE, MP
Secretary of State for Defence — Rt. Hon. Michael Heseltine, MP
Secretary of State for Scotland — Rt. Hon. George Younger, TD, MP
Secretary of State for Wales — Rt. Hon Nicholas Edwards, MP
Secretary of State for the Environment — Rt. Hon Patrick Jenkin, MP
Lord Privy Seal and Leader of the House of
  Commons — Rt. Hon. John Biffen, MP
Secretary of State for Social Services — Rt. Hon. Norman Fowler, MP

Secretary of State for Trade and Industry	Rt. Hon. Norman Tebbit, MP
	(Rt. Hon. Cecil Parkinson, MP)
Chancellor of the Duchy of Lancaster	Rt. Hon. The Lord Cockfield
Secretary of State for Employment	Rt. Hon. Tom King, MP
	(Rt. Hon. Norman Tebbit, MP)
Minister of Agriculture, Fisheries and Food	Rt. Hon. Michael Jopling, MP
Chief Secretary to the Treasury	Rt. Hon. Peter Rees, QC, MP
Secretary of State for Transport	Rt. Hon. Nicholas Ridley, MP
	(Rt. Hon. Tom King, MP)

MINISTERS NOT IN THE CABINET

Ministers of State, Ministry of Agriculture, Fisheries and Food	Rt. Hon. The Lord Belstead
	John MacGregor, OBE, MP
Minister for the Arts	The Earl of Gowrie
Ministers of State, Ministry of Defence:	
Minister for the Armed Forces	John Stanley, MP
Minister for Defence Procurement	Geoffrey Pattie, MP
Ministers of State, Department of Employment	Hon. Peter Morrison, MP
	John Selwyn Gummer, MP
Minister of State, Department of Energy	Rt. Hon. Alick Buchanan-Smith, MP
Ministers of State, Department of the Environment:	
Minister for Housing and Construction	Ian Gow, TD, MP
Minister for Local Government	The Lord Bellwin
Ministers of State, Foreign and Commonwealth Office	Richard Luce, MP
	Malcolm Rifkind, MP
	Rt. Hon. The Baroness Young
Minister for Overseas Development	Rt. Hon. Timothy Raison, MP
Ministers of State, Department of Health and Social Security:	
Minister for Health	Kenneth Clarke, QC, MP
Minister for Social Security	Dr. Rhodes Boyson, MP
Ministers of State, Home Office	Rt. Hon. Douglas Hurd, CBE, MP
	David Waddington, QC, MP
Ministers of State, Northern Ireland Office	Hon. Adam Butler, MP
	The Earl of Mansfield
Minister of State, Scottish Office	Rt. Hon. The Lord Gray of Contin
Ministers of State, Department of Trade and Industry:	
Minister for Industry	Norman Lamont, MP
Minister for Industry and Information Technology	Kenneth Baker, MP
Minister for Trade	Rt. Hon. Paul Channon, MP
Minister of State, Department of Transport	Lynda Chalker, MP
Financial Secretary, Treasury	John Moore, MP
	(Rt. Hon. Nicholas Ridley, MP)
Economic Secretary, Treasury	Ian Stewart, MP
	(John Moore, MP)
Minister of State, Treasury	Barney Hayhoe, MP
Parliamentary Secretary, Treasury	Rt. Hon. John Wakeham, MP
Minister of State, Welsh Office	John Stradling Thomas, MP

LAW OFFICERS

Attorney-General	Rt. Hon. Sir Michael Havers, QC, MP
Solicitor-General	Sir Patrick Mayhew, QC, MP
Lord Advocate	Rt. Hon. The Lord Mckay of Clashfern, QC
Solicitor-General for Scotland	Peter Fraser, QC, MP

OBITUARY

Abboud, General Ibrahim, Hon. GCB (b. 1901), was Prime Minister of Sudan 1958-64 after leading a military coup, and was ousted by another. He was simultaneously President of the Supreme Council of the Armed Forces and their commander-in-chief, having been army commander 1955-58. Died 8 September

Aleman, Miguel (b. 1905), was President of Mexico 1946-52, after serving as a senator, Governor of Veracruz and Minister of the Interior. Though hated by the left for his strong anti-socialism, and accused of lining his own pocket lavishly in office, he was acknowledged to have given his country a dynamic economic impulse. From 1961 he was head of the national tourist office. Died 14 May

Aquino, Benigno (b. 1932), Philippine politician, was a fierce opponent of President Marcos from the 1960s, when he was governor of his native province. In 1967 he was elected to the national Senate as a Nationalist Party member and later became leader of the opposition People's Power Movement. In 1972, after the imposition of martial law, he was imprisoned on capital charges and sentenced to death, but Marcos, unwilling to make him a martyr both for the Filippinos and for sympathisers in America, ordered a new trial and eventually released him in 1980 to go to the US for heart surgery. There he became a Fellow of Harvard and also worked at MIT. Although a military court had confirmed his death sentence and he was warned of danger to his life, he decided in 1983 to go home, only to be immediately murdered, 21 August

Aron, Raymond (b. 1905), French political philosopher, was rivalled in national and international influence among his intellectual peers in France only by his contempoary and critical friend Jean-Paul Sartre, largely because of his brilliance as an expositor and teacher as well as thinker, and the moderation and pragmatic cast of his ideas. Already advanced in a distinguished academic career before World War II, after the fall of France he joined de Gaulle in England, for whom he edited *La France Libre* 1940-44. He returned to academic life (Institut d'Etudes Politiques 1945-72, the Sorbonne 1956-68, Ecole Pratique des Hautes Etudes from 1960) but combined teaching and research with prolific writing both in books and in the press, especially *le Figaro*. His major works included *Introduction à la philosophie de l'histoire* (1938), *L'Opium des Intellectuels* (1954), *Paix et Guerre entre les nations* (1962), *La République imperiale* (1973), *Histoire et Dialectique de la violence* (1973) and his *Mémoires* (1983). Died 17 October

Balanchine, George (b. Georgi Melitonovitch Balanchivadeze, 1904), ballet-master and choreographer, contributed more to the ballet repertory than any other choreographer of the 20th century. He began creating his own ballets while still a young dancer in the Russian Imperial Theatres, from which he defected in 1924. Diaghilev, who abbreviated his name, recruited him for his Russian Ballet, and in 1925 made Balanchine his ballet master and choreographer. Among the dances Balanchine created for Diaghilev were *Apollo* and *The Prodigal Son*. After Diaghilev's death in 1929 Balanchine staged new dances for the Royal Danish Ballet, London impresarios, the Ballets Russes de Monte Carlo and his own short-lived company *Les Ballets* (1933). In 1934 he was invited to the USA, where he spent the rest of his life, to found the School of American Ballet, for whose pupils he created, among other ballets, *Serenade* and *Orpheus* (Gluck). When American Ballet foundered in 1939, the School continued under Balanchine, whose output in the 1940s included *Ballet Imperial*, *Danses concertantes*, *Night Shadow* and *Theme and Variations*. For the Ballet Society, of which he was joint founder in 1946, he made, among other creations, *The Four Temperaments* and another *Orpheus* ballet (Stravinsky). In 1948 the company became the New York City Ballet, with whose performance, teaching and provision of countless new ballets Balanchine's name and fame became indissolubly connected. In his choreography, Balanchine showed an unsurpassed versatility both in style and in the use of an immense range of music, from Mozart to Hindemith and contemporary vaudeville composers. Died 30 April

Bidault, Georges (b. 1899), Prime Minister of the French Provisional Government 1946 and Prime Minister of France 1949-50, fled his native country in 1963 to avoid arrest for plotting the armed overthrow of de Gaulle's Government, and spent five years in exile in Brazil until the charges were lifted and he returned to a private retirement in France. After conscript service in World War I, Bidault became a professor of history at the universities of Valenciennes, Rheims and Paris, then political adviser and leader-writer for the Catholic daily *L'Aube*. After 1940, released from imprisonment by the Germans, he joined the Resistance and was its acknowledged representative upon the return of General de Gaulle, who made him Minister of Foreign Affairs. In that role he pursued an Atlantic and European policy. After the fall of his own short-lived Government he served as Deputy Prime Minister, Minister of National Defence or Foreign Minister in a succession of Governments 1951-54. He supported de Gaulle's return to power in 1958, but clashed with him over Algeria, on which his policy was that of the extreme right. Died 26 January

Birla, Ghanshyan Das (b. 1894), Indian (Marwari) business magnate, was best known to the world as the friend of Mahatma Gandhi, who was assassinated in the grounds of his New Delhi house, and as a munificient supporter of the Indian National Congress. With his younger brother he had founded the great Calcutta firm of Birla Brothers, whose interests spread into sugar, cotton, engineering, steel, automobiles, insurance, banking and newspapers. He had been a member of the Bengal Legislative Council and of the Indian Legislative Assembly and an adviser to governments in the 1920s and '30s. Despite his strong and acquisitive belief in private enterprise, he promoted business with Soviet Russia; he was also a generous benefactor of education. Died 11 June

Bishop, Maurice (b. 1944), was Prime Minister of Grenada from 1979 until his death in the military coup of October 1983. He entered politics at the age of 26 in opposition to the right-wing regime of Eric Gairy and in 1976 became leader of the socialist New Jewel Movement, mustering six seats in a parliament of 15, which seized power in 1979 by an army-backed coup as the People's Revolutionary Government. His marxist principles and close relations with Cuba were mitigated by defence of private business and an aim to develop tourism—pluralist policies which split his party and led to his overthrow and murder. Died 19 October

Blunt, Anthony (b. 1907), British art historian, earned a more sinister fame when in 1979 it was revealed that he had become a Russian agent in the 1930s, recruiting young men at Cambridge into the Soviet spy network; that he had secretly served the Soviet Union while he worked for British intelligence in World War II, had been the 'fourth man' who engineered the escape of the spies Burgess and Maclean (*q.v.*) in 1951, and, having confessed his treachery in 1965, after the defection of the 'third man', Philby, had been granted immunity from prosecution in return for his cooperation in further investigations. His knighthood was annulled and his brilliant professional career was tainted with dishonour. A Fellow of Trinity College, Cambridge, 1932-36, in 1937 Blunt joined the staff of the Warburg Institute, and two years later that of the Courtauld Institute, of which he became the greatly admired director 1947-74. He was Surveyor of the King's (Queen's) Pictures 1945-72, and thereafter adviser on the Queen's collections of pictures and drawings. Among a large output of learned material his most important books were *Art and Architecture in France 1500-1700* (1953) and *Nicholas Poussin (1966-67)*. Died 26 March

Boult, Sir Adrian, CH (b. 1889), British conductor, as director of music at the BBC 1930-50 founded and nursed to musical distinction the BBC Symphony Orchestra. From 1924 he had been permanent conductor of the City of Birmingham Orchestra, and from 1927 conductor of the London Bach Choir. Before World War I he had studied conducting under Nikisch in Leipzig. Retiring from the BBC under the age-limit, he became chief conductor of the London Philharmonic Orchestra 1950-57, and continued conducting, both on the concert platform and for recording, well into his 80s. While his range was catholic, he was specially admired for his interpretations of the 20th-century English school (Elgar, Holst, Vaughan Williams), where his own warmest affection lay. Died 23 February

Boyd of Merton, Viscount, PC, CH (b. 1904), as Alan Lennox-Boyd was Secretary of State for the Colonies 1954-59, a crucial period for the advance of British colonial territories to independence. His policy was one of cautious moderation, lightened by happy and hospitable relations with the African and Caribbean leaders who were demanding a swifter pace. His more conservative approach than that of the Prime Minister, Mr Macmillan, was one reason, the other being ill-health, for his leaving the Cabinet after the general election of 1959. He had earlier been Minister of State at the Colonial Office 1951-52 and Minister of Transport 1952-54. In political retirement he became managing director and vice-chairman of the Guinness brewing firm. Died 8 March

Buñuel, Luis (b. in Spain, 1900), Mexican film director, was the acknowledged master of surrealist cinema. His devotion to anarchist-surrealism went back to his friendship with Salvador Dali while he was a student at Madrid University. Dali scripted the first film Buñuel made on his own, *Un Chien Andalou* (1929) and helped him with his highly creative *L'Age d'Or* (1930). After the fall of the Republic in Spain Buñuel went to the United States and for 15 years worked on humbler cinematic tasks, until he made, in Mexico, *Los Olividados* (1950), which won the Grand Prix at the Cannes film festival. Thereafter he was respected throughout the cinema world as the unrivalled exponent not only of surrealist techniques but also of a pattern of social ideas, unpalatable and even blasphemous to many, anti-clerical and anti-bourgeois. Among his best-known creations were *Nazarin* (1958, made in France), *Viridiana* (1961, made and suppressed in Spain), *Belle de Jour* (1967, Golden Lion award in Venice), *Le Charme Discret de la Bourgeoisie* (1972, Oscar for best foreign-language film) and *That Obscure Object of Desire* (1977). Died in Mexico 29 July

Buttigieg, Dr Anton (b. 1912) was President of Malta 1976-81. A journalist by profession (editor of the Labour newspaper *Voice of Malta* from 1959), he was president of the Malta Labour Party 1959-61, deputy leader 1962-76, Deputy Prime Minister 1971-74 and

Minister of Justice 1971-76; he also published books of lyrical and light verse. Died 5 May

Charlton, Evan, CBE (b. 1912), who contributed the Commonwealth chapter to the Annual Register, was editor of *The Statesman* (Calcutta) 1964-67—the last British editor of a leading Indian newspaper—and of *The Round Table* 1977-81. Although imprisonment in a Japanese p.o.w. camp during the war had undermined his health, from 1967 he worked for the BBC's overseas services. Died 25 June

Citrine, Lord (Walter Citrine), PC, GBE (b. 1887), British trade unionist, was general secretary of the TUC 1926-46. In 1928 he was president of the International Federation of Trade Unions, and in 1945 was one of the founders of the World Federation to which both the Soviet unions and the American CIO originally belonged. In 1946 he left the TUC to become a member of the National Coal Board, and was chairman of the Central Electricity Authority 1947-57. Died 22 January

Clark, Lord (Kenneth Clark), OM, CH, KCB (b. 1903), British art historian and administrator, achieved his widest international fame with the BBC's television series *Civilization*, first shown in 1969, in which he took the viewer on a personal tour of the seminal sites and works of European art. A pupil and devotee of Bernard Berenson, he became Keeper of Fine Art at the Ashmolean Museum 1931-33, Director of the National Gallery 1934-45, Surveyor of the King's Pictures 1934-55, chairman of the Arts Council 1953-60, Slade Professor of Fine Art at Oxford 1946-50 and 1961-62, and chairman of the Independent Broadcasting Authority 1954-57. Meanwhile a flow of books had established him as an elegant and sensitive writer on the history and understanding of art in the Ruskin tradition; they included *The Gothic Revival* (1928), *Landscape into Art* (1949), *Piero della Francesca* (1951), *The Nude* (1955), *Rembrandt and the Italian Renaissance* (1966). Two self-deprecatory volumes of autobiography were entitled *Another Part of the Wood* (1974) and *The Other Half* (1977). Died 21 May

Cooke, H. E. Cardinal Terence (b. 1921), was Archbishop of New York from 1968; in 1969 he had become the youngest Cardinal in the Church. Ordained in 1945, he was appointed personal secretary to his predecessor in the see, Cardinal Spellman, in 1957, and became chancellor and vicar-general of the diocese. Though generally conservative, he joined his fellow Catholic bishops in the US in denouncing nuclear war as immoral. Died 6 October

Cukor, George (b. 1899), American film director, went to Hollywood in 1929 as a successful Broadway stage producer. After David Selznick had given him the direction of *Dinner at Eight* (1933) he became a leading director for MGM. His films included *David Copperfield* (1934), *Camille* (with Greta Garbo, 1936), *The Women* (1939), *A Star is Born* (1954), *My Fair Lady* (1964), *Travels with My Aunt* (1972) and *Rich and Famous* (1981). Died 24 January

de la Guardia, Ernesto (b. 1904), was President of Panama 1956-60, a period of violent agitation against the United States presence in the Canal Zone which he had difficulty in quelling. Died 2 May

Dempsey, Jack (b. 1895), American boxer, was world heavyweight champion 1919-26. He won the title by hammering Jess Willard in three rounds, and successfully defended it against Billy Miske, Bill Brennan, Georges Carpentier and Luis Firpo, then after seven years was outpointed by Gene Tunney, whom he also failed to defeat in a return bout in 1927 marked by the notorious Long Count against the floored challenger. He remained a national sporting hero long after his retirement from the ring to a prosperous career as exhibition fighter, television performer and host of a New York restaurant. Died 31 May

Dike, Professor Kenneth Onwuka (b. 1917), Nigerian academic, was outstanding both as a historian and as a university administrator. He was lecturer in history at the University College of Ibadan 1950-56, professor 1956-60, principal of the college 1958-60, and, when it achieved university status, vice-chancellor 1960-66. He moved to Harvard University as professor of history 1971-73 and of African history 1973-82. He had been founder-director of the Nigerian National Archives 1951-64, president of the Historical Society of Nigeria 1955-69, and chairman of the Association of Commonwealth Universities 1965-66. Died 25 November

Dolin, Sir Anton (b. Sydney Healey-Kay 1904), British ballet dancer, studied under Astafieva, danced in Daighilev's corps de ballet in 1921, and became a Diaghilev soloist in 1923 under the stage name by which he was known thereafter. His superb skill and grace as a male partner were immediately recognized, and flourished especially in his partnership with Alicia Markova; from 1935 to 1938 they had their own ballet company in London. Dolin, who left the Diaghilev Ballet in 1926 but rejoined it for the 1929 season, danced for his own company, for the Camargo Society, for the Vic-Wells Ballet and elsewhere before settling during World War II in America, where he helped to found and raise to distinction the American Ballet Theatre. After returning to England to dance at Covent Garden with Markova in 1948, he did the same for London's Festival Ballet, with which he remained until 1961. While still occasionally dancing he then devoted himself mainly to direction, teaching and choreography. Died 25 November

Dortico, Torrado Osvaldo (b. 1919) was President of Cuba 1959-76 until Fidel Castro took over the presidency. A distinguished lawyer, he had backed the Castro revolution and was exiled 1958-59. After 1976 he became Minister of Justice and a deputy Prime Minister. Reported 25 June to have committed suicide.

Fitzgibbon, Constantine (b. 1919), American author, was known most widely for his novel *When the Kissing had to Stop* (1960), an attack on the marxism which he had previously embraced, and to a narrower public for *The Selected Letters of Dylan Thomas* (1966), his friend of the 1940s, which he edited. But his output included a number of other novels, histories, autobiographical books and translations from French, German and Italian. Died 23 March

Fontanne, Lynn (b. 1893), British-born American actress, was most famous for her stage partnerships with her husband Alfred Lunt, whom she married in 1922 and who died in 1977. Together they appeared in the New York Theatre Guild's productions of classical comedies in the 1920s, and under the same auspices in London in *Elizabeth and Essex* (1934). This English debut was followed by Coward's *Design for Living*, Sherwood's *Reunion in Vienna*, Giraudoux's *Amphitryon 38* and other successful London productions during World War II. Among their post-war appearances on both sides of the Atlantic the most memorable was in Dürrenmatt's *The Visit*. Before her marriage Lynn Fontanne had made her own name on Broadway with the title parts in O'Neill's *Anna Christie* and Connelly and Kaufman's *Dulcy*. Died 30 July

Fuller, Dr R. Buckminster (b. 1895), American inventor, architect and philosopher, was most famous for his invention of the geodesic dome, of which thousands were erected, though his dream of their becoming a cheap and universal form of architecture was not fulfilled. Among many provocative books his *Operating Manual for Spaceship Earth* (1969) conveyed his belief in man's ability to overcome the ecological challenges of the future. He was a professor of design science at Southern Illinois University 1959-75, Professor of Poetry at Harvard 1961-62 and a gold medallist both of the American Institute of Architects and of the RIBA. Died 1 July

Gershwin, Ira (b. 1896), American song-writer, partnered his still more famous brother George, the composer, in some of the most triumphant musicals of their time, including *Lady Be Good*, *Of Thee I Sing*, *Porgy and Bess*, *Funny Face*, *Girl Crazy* and *The Man I Love*. They also collaborated in two Astaire films, *Shall We Dance* and *A Damsel in Distress*, and together wrote countless songs which became classics. After George's death Ira worked with other composers, but never to the same brilliant effect. His book on the musical theatre, *Lyrics on Several Occasions*, was another much-praised achievement. Died 17 August

Gilpin, John (b. 1930), British ballet dancer, was a young prodigy when he danced leading roles for the Ballet Rambert 1945-49. At the age of 13 he had won the gold medal of the Royal Academy of Dancing. After dancing for the Ballets de Paris and the Grand Ballet du Marquis de Cuevas, he joined Dolin's Festival Ballet in 1950, and succeeded Dolin (*q.v.*) in major classical and modern roles, and for a while as artistic director. Festival Ballet's tours made him internationally famous, and he was a guest star with the Royal Ballet at Covent Garden and the American Ballet Theatre; but he stayed with Festival Ballet for twenty years. He was a dancer of elegant style, simplicity and beauty. Died 6 September

Gruenther, General Alfred M. (b. 1899), American soldier, was Supreme Allied Commander in Europe (Saceur) 1953-56, after serving for three years as chief of staff to his predecessors Generals Eisenhower and Ridgway. In those capacities he did more than any other man to build the strength of Nato in a period which saw the integration of the German armed forces and the emergence of a nuclear strategy. In World War II he had been chief of staff 5th Army and 15th Army Group and deputy commander in Austria. At the Pentagon he became director of the joint staff 1944-49 and deputy chief of staff for plans 1949-50. Known as 'the brains of the Army', Gruenther was also an expert bridge player and wrote two classic books on the game. Died 30 May

Headley, George (b. 1909), West Indian cricketer, scored 176 in the first Test played against England in the West Indies in 1929, and his record as a Test batsman, with an average of 60.83 including ten centuries, ranked third in the history of cricket; he scored 270 not out against England in 1935. He was also a brilliant fielder and competent spin-bowler. Died 30 November

Hinton of Bankside, Lord (Christopher Hinton), OM, KBE, FRS (b. 1901), British scientist and administrator, after service in the Ministry of Supply in World War II became a leading figure in the development of the atomic energy industry, as deputy controller of atomic energy production 1946-54, as technical member (with Cockroft and Penney) of the new Atomic Energy Authority from 1954, and as chairman of the Central Electricity Generating Board 1957-64. He was largely responsible for the choice of US water-cooled reactors for the expansion of the CEGB's atomic energy programme. Died 22 June

Holyoake, Rt. Hon. Sir Keith Jacka, KG, GCMG, CH (b. 1904), was Prime Minister of New Zealand briefly in 1957 and from 1960 to 1962, and Governor-General 1977-80. Elected to Parliament in 1931, he helped to found the National Party in 1936 and became its deputy leader in 1931. He was Minister of Agriculture and Deputy Prime Minsiter in the Holland Government 1950-57. The National Party, which he now led, was defeated in the 1957 election but returned to power three years later and won four consecutive elections. A working farmer from his early youth, Holyoake succeeded in obtaining special terms for New Zealand when Britain entered the EEC and in his efforts to diversify the country's primary production and markets. His general policy was pragmatic and moderate, emphasizing national development and maintenance of the welfare state, and relying on astute consensus politics. Died 7 December

Howells, Dr Herbert, CH, CBE (b. 1892), British composer, made a major contribution to contemporary music, especially that of the Church, combining the English tradition with a more French romanticism and modern harmonies. His finest works included the *Missa Aedis Christi* (1962), the oratorio *Hymnus Paradisi* (1950) and much delightful chamber music and songs. Educated at the Royal College of Music, he taught theory and composition there for 50 years; he was director of music at St Paul's Girls School (in succession to Gustav Holst) 1936-62 and King Edward Professor of Music, London University, 1952-63. Died 23 February

Idris I (Muhammad Idris al Mahdi al Sanusi), King (b. 1899), was monarch of Libya from the inception of the federal state in 1951 until his intended abdication was anticipated by a coup in 1969, whereafter he lived in passive exile in Egypt. During his reign Libya had risen from poverty to riches through the exploitation of oil, and the spirit of the people had become anti-Western and pro-Egyptian, especially after the Suez crisis of 1956, neither development pleasing the austere and pro-British King. As hereditary head of the Sanusi, he had resisted the Italian colonial suzerainty and in 1940 had offered the services of his people to the British cause in North Africa. His efforts secured the independence of a federal Libya in 1951, but in 1963 he inspired a more unitary constitutional reform. Died 25 May

Illia, Dr Arturo (b. 1900), President of Argentina 1963-66, entered politics in Cordoba in 1936 as a Radical, was elected to the national Chamber of Deputies and then, though not a well-known figure, to the presidency. Overthrown by a military coup, he remained an ardent democrat and constitutionalist. Died 18 January

Jackson, Senator Henry Martin (b. 1912), American Democratic politician, vainly sought nomination for the Presidency in 1972 and 1976, but continued to be a powerful voice in Washington. Known to all as 'Scoop' Jackson, he was a liberal in domestic affairs but a 'hawk' in foreign and military affairs, vigorous in support of the Vietnam war, constant in denunciation of communist expansionism and hostile to any concessions to the USSR in arms limitation agreements. He was elected to the US Senate for Washington state in 1952 and became chairman of its sub-committee on arms control. Died 1 September

Kahn, Herman (b. 1922), American political writer, founded the Hudson Institute, a prestigious 'think tank' on international issues, in 1961, after achieving wide fame for his book *On Thermonuclear War* (1961), the theme of which was that nuclear war was not only possible but probable and nevertheless could be contained. His later book, *The Year 2000* (with Anthony Wiener, 1967), took an optimistic view of an affluent post-industrial world. Died 7 July

Koestler, Arthur (b. in Hungary 1905), British author, won instant worldwide fame for his *Darkness at Noon*, published in English translation in 1940 (till then his books had been written in German), the story of an old Bolshevik arrested under Stalin and induced to confess to offences of which he is not guilty. The London *Times* obituarist described *Darkness at Noon* as 'by far and away the greatest novel of its kind in this century'. Other works of distinction included *Spanish Testament*, based on his experiences as a newspaper correspondent in the Spanish civil war, when he was captured and condemned to death as a spy; *The Gladiators* (1939), a piece of ancient Roman history written as an allegory on contemporary Russia; *Promise and Fulfilment* (1949), a history of Palestine after 1917; *Arrival and Departure* (1943), a novel which exposed the horrors of totalitarian police methods; *The Yogi and the Commissar* (1945); and *Arrow from the Blue* (1952), an autobiography. Educated in Vienna, as a journalist he travelled widely in Europe, the Middle East, Central Asia and Russia. He joined the Communist Party in 1933 but left it in 1938 in reaction to the notorious Moscow trials; and during World War II (after imprisonment in France as an enemy alien) he joined the Foreign Legion and then the British army, and thereafter worked for the British Ministry of Information. From 1945 to 1949 he was special correspondent for *The Times* in Palestine. In later life he became deeply concerned with voluntary euthanasia and with parapsychology, for the study of which he bequeathed his fortune. Committed suicide, with his wife, 3 March

Knox, H. E. Cardinal Robert James (b. 1914), was Archbishop of Melbourne 1967-74, and thereafter served in the Vatican (President of the Pontifical Council for the Family from 1981). Died 26 June

Leopold III, H.M. King of the Belgians (b. 1901), succeeded his father, King Albert, in 1934. A year later he lost his dearly-loved wife Queen Astrid in a motor accident. In 1941 he married a commoner, who was given the title of Princesse de Rethy. When the German armies invaded Belgium in May 1940, his Ministers begged him to leave, but he thought it his duty to stay with his troops. His surrender on 28 May was bitterly and unjustly criticized, both by Belgians and in Allied quarters, and his return to the throne, after imprisonment by the Germans for the rest of the war, was strongly opposed, especially by the left. In a referendum in 1950 he won nearly 58 per cent of the votes, but a wave of strikes and violence that followed caused him to abdicate in 1951 in favour of his son Prince Baudouin. Died 25 September

Maclean, Donald (b. 1913), British diplomatist and defector to the USSR, the son of an austere Liberal Cabinet Minister, entered the Foreign Office with a first-class degree after a conventional public-school and Cambridge education. Despite bouts of drinking and a homosexual aberration his brains and industry led to rapid advancement—as first secretary and later head of chancery in Washington 1944-48, counsellor of embassy in Cairo 1948-49, head of the American department of the Foreign Office from 1950. In the following year, warned by a 'third man' (Kim Philby) of their impending exposure, Maclean and his friend Guy Burgess fled to Moscow. It then emerged that from Cambridge days he had been not only an avowed communist sympathiser but also a source of information to the Russians on the atomic bomb, Nato plans and other important secret matters. Died in Moscow 6 March

Masters, Lieut.-Col. John, DSO (b. 1914), British soldier and author, was known throughout the English-speaking world chiefly for his novel of Anglo-India, *Bhowani Juction*, which was made into a successful film; of his other novels the critically most acclaimed were *Nightrunners of Bengal* (1951) and *The Deceivers* (1952). His family had served India for generations, and he joined the Indian Army from Sandhurst, rising in World War II to become chief of staff, 19th Indian Division, victors in Burma. Died 7 May

Micombero, Lieut.-General Michel (b. 1940), was President of Burundi 1966-76. Previously Minister of National Defence and Chief Secretary of State, he led the 1966 coup which overthrew the monarchy. While President he also served as Prime Minister (with a break in 1972-73) and for short periods Minister of Foreign Affairs and of the Interior. Died in exile 16 July

Miró, Joan (b. 1893) Spanish painter, sculptor, printmaker and theatre designer, was one of the most prolific and original artists of modern times. Born in Barcelona, Miró's art studies included exercises in drawing by touch; by his mid-twenties he was working in Paris as well as Catalonia; he was friendly with Picasso, influenced by Cubism, and soon made contact with the Dadaists in Paris, and subsequently the Surrealists, with whom he exhibited throughout the 1930s. Miró contributed to the Spanish Pavilion at the Paris World Fair in 1937, and stayed in France through the Spanish civil war; but, unlike Picasso, he returned to Spain after the fall of France in 1940. Visiting America after the war, he was received enthusiastically. In 1950 he executed a ceramic mural for Harvard University. He collaborated on ceramic work with the artist-potter Joseph Artigas; major public works using ceramic by Miró include several in Madrid, two murals for the Unesco building in Paris and ceramic sculpture at the Maeght Foundation in the South of France. In 1975 the Miró Foundation, designed by Sert (*q.v.*), opened in Barcelona, housing an important collection of the artist's work. Miró's art was almost always abstract, or fanciful, the scenes he depicted coming from the inner recesses of the mind. He invented strange creatures, often recalling birds or mythical beasts; in his paintings he set black forms, suggesting life, into fields of colour with no suggestion of depth or horizon. He created a world of his own, with elements from Spanish folklore and personal dreams, lively yet serene, and usually free of the menace common to most surrealists. In his 80s he even designed outrageously witty costumes for La Claca, a Catalan experimental theatre group. He was once described as a 'surrealist with his feet on the ground'. Died 25 December
M.V.

Mozzoni, H. E. Cardinal Umberto (b. 1904), was Papal Nuncio to Bolivia 1954-58, to Argentina 1958-69 and to Brazil 1969-73. He devoted himself particularly to the protection and support of foreign missionaries in Latin America. Died 7 November

Niven, David (b. 1910), British film actor, began his working life as an officer in the army, and returned to military service in World War II, rising to the rank of colonel. His army experience was useful in many of the roles he played, invariably as the clean-cut English gentleman, in such films as *The Charge of the Light Brigade* (1936), *The First of the Few* (1941), *The Guns of Navarone* (1961). Starting in Hollywood as an extra, he soon won major roles, but found it difficult to re-establish himself on his return in 1946. Better parts came in the 1950s, and in 1958 Niven won an Oscar for best actor in *Separate Tables*. His last great cinema success was as the Rafflesian thief offsetting Peter Sellers' Inspector Clouseau in *The Pink Panther* (1964). His witty, anecdotal autobiographies *The Moon's a Balloon* (1971) and *Bring on the Empty Horses* (1975) sold between them more than 10 million copies, adding much to the large fortune he had made from films and television. Died 29 July

Pevsner, Sir Nikolaus (b. in Germany 1902), British art historian, was famed above all for the monumental series of books, *The Buildings of England*, which he edited and largely wrote between 1949 and 1970, recording with discriminating and eclectic comment every notable building of whatever age in the country. He had been assistant keeper of the Dresden Gallery 1924-28 and lecturer in the history of art and architecture at Göttingen 1929-33 before he fled from Nazi Germany to England. There he held a research post at Birmingham University, edited the *Architectural Review* 1942-45, and lectured at Birkbeck College, London, 1942-59, where he became professor of the history of art 1959-69. He was also Slade Professor of Fine Art at Cambridge 1949-55 and at Oxford 1968-69, and a gold medallist of the RIBA. His books included *Italian Painting from the End of Rococo* (1927-30), *Pioneers of the Modern Movement from Morris to Gropius* (1936), *An Enquiry into Industrial Art in England* (1937) and the widely popular *Outline of European Architecture* (1942). Died 18 August

Pinheiro de Azevedo, Admiral José Baptista (b. 1917), Portuguese naval officer and politician, was a member of the coordinating committee of the Armed Forces Movement which staged the revolution in 1974, and thereafter of the Junta of National Salvation and naval chief of staff. For nine months he was Prime Minister of Portugal 1975-76, but his Government's retreat from the revolutionary socialism that he had previously espoused cost him the support of the far left, and in June 1976, standing for election as President, he failed dismally, remaining an outspoken critic of the winner, President Eanes. Died 10 August

Podgorny, Nikolai Viktorovich (b. 1903), as chairman of the Praesidium of the Supreme Soviet was titular head of state of the USSR from 1965 to 1977, when he was abruptly displaced by Leonid Brezhnev, the Party's general secretary, and removed from the Politburo. Most of Podgorny's early Party service was rendered in the Ukraine, his birth-place. A Khrushchev protégé, he became a candidate member of the Politburo in 1958 and a full member in 1960, and in 1963 a secretary of the Central Committee, a post from which he was 'pushed upstairs' in 1965 after the defeat of Khrushchev. Died 11 January

Pridi Phanomyong, Dr (b. 1901), was briefly Prime Minister of Thailand in 1947; thereafter he remained, though in exile, a formidable force in Thai politics. When a professor of law he had largely inspired the radical revolution of 1932. Exiled for a while by a royalist counter-revolution, he returned to become Minister successively of the Interior, Foreign Affairs and Finance. During the Japanese occupation he was a member of the Regency Council and also leader of the underground 'Free Thais', in which capacity he negotiated the peace settlement with the Allies. Died 2 May

Rey, Jean (b. 1920), Belgian politician, was President of the Commission of the European Community 1967-70. He had been a Commissioner of the EEC, responsible for external relations, from its foundation in 1958, after holding ministerial office in Brussels 1949-50 and 1954-58. In 1974, now prominent in Belgian business, he became president of the European Movement. Though as hostile to de Gaulle's European stance as had been his predecessor at the head of the Commission, he avoided Hallstein's open confrontations with the French President. Died 19 May

Richardson, Sir Ralph (b. 1902), British actor, played in his time an immense range of parts, both in Shakespeare (of which his Falstaff, Old Vic 1945-46, was one of the most memorable) and other classics (notably his Peer Gynt and Cyrano de Bergerac) and in modern plays. While working as an office boy in Brighton at the age of 18 he got his first job in the theatre as a premium-paid apprentice in a half-amateur local company. After playing in a Shakespearean touring company and in a provincial tour of

Outward Bound he joined Birmingham Rep under Barry Jackson, and in 1930 moved to the Old Vic, when a life-long association with John Gielgud began. Richardson acted with him or under his direction in many productions, from *Henry IV* in 1930 to Pinter's *No Man's Land* in 1976. Among other roles, they played together in *A Day by the Sea* (1953), in Gielgud's production of *The School for Scandal* (1962), in *Oh What a Lovely War* (1968) and in Lindsay Anderson's production of *Home* (1970). Another close association, with Laurence Olivier, began in 1937 when they both joined the Old Vic company, which they co-directed from 1944 after both had served in the Fleet Air Arm. Richardson continued acting, to great acclaim, right up to his last short illness. Television was not his best medium, but he appeared in some 40 films, including *Richard III* and *Long Day's Journey into Night*. Died 10 October

Robinson, The Right Rev. John (b. 1919), was suffragan Bishop of Woolwich 1959-69. A brilliant academic theologian, he was Dean of Clare College, Cambridge, 1951-59, and when he resigned his bishopric he returned to Cambridge as Fellow and Dean of Chapel at Trinity College. Meanwhile his output of distinguished theological studies had included a paperback book which made him a highly controversial figure throughout the Christian world, *Honest to God* (1963), in which the Almighty was stripped of myth and anthropomorphism. His Christian radicalism extended from theology to politics. Died 5 December

Samoré, H. E. Cardinal Antonio (b. 1905), was made an archbishop in 1950 and a cardinal in 1967. Most of his career was spent as a Vatican diplomat, and after serving as Papal Nuncio in Colombia he became secretary and from 1967 president of the Pontifical Commission for Latin America. In 1978 he was sent to effect the Pope's mediation in the Beagle Channel dispute between Argentina and Chile (see AR 1978, pp. 70-2), in which after four years he had still not succeeded. From 1974 he was also librarian and archivist to the Holy Roman Church. Died 3 February

Schapiro, Professor Leonard, CBE (b. 1908), British scholar, was one of the Western world's most respected analysts of Soviet politics. A lawyer by profession, he practised at the Bar before World War II and, after war service in military intelligence, until 1955. Then he accepted a teaching post at the London School of Economics and Political Science, where in 1963 he became professor of political science with special reference to Russia until his nominal retirement in 1975. His major books included *The Origin of Autocracy* (1955), *The Communist Party of the Soviet Union* (1960, revised edition 1970) and *Turgenev: His Life and Times* (1979). Among other honours he was an honorary member of the American Academy of Arts and Sciences. Died 2 November

Sert, Professor José Luis (b. in Spain 1902), adoptive American architect, migrated first to France and then, in 1939, to the United States after the Spanish civil war, being an ardent republican. He had designed the Spanish pavilion for the 1937 Paris exhibition, which housed Picasso's famous mural *Guernica*. His American buildings included the Holyoke Center at Harvard and the Boston University Tower. After democracy was restored in Spain he returned to design in 1976 the Miró Foundation art gallery in Barcelona, considered by some to be his finest work, dedicated to his lifelong friend Joan Miró (*q.v.*). He had been professor of architecture 1953-58 and dean of the graduate school of design at Harvard 1958-69. Died 15 March

Shearer, Norma (b. 1900), Canadian film actress, owed much to her marriage in 1927 to Irving Thalberg of MGM, then the most brilliant young producer in Hollywood. Under him she starred in such films as *The Last of Mrs Cheyney*, O'Neill's *Strange Interlude* (1932) and *The Barretts of Wimpole Street* (1934). After Thalberg's death in 1936 she lost her way, acting in unsuccessful pictures and turning down the part of Scarlett O'Hara in *Gone with the Wind*. Died 12 June

Swanson, Gloria (b. 1899?), American film actress, began her career in Hollywood in 1915 with parts in Mack Sennett comedies. Four years later she joined Paramount, and quickly rose to stardom under the direction of Cecil B. de Mille. In 1926 she set up her own company, in which she triumphed in the title-role of *Sadie Thompson* and sang in her first sound film, *The Trespasser*. After a long interval of disputes, failures, poor films and obscurity she resurfaced with the greatest success of her life as the superannuated star in Wilder's *Sunset Boulevard* (1950). In old age she remained a famous figure of the cinema, as flamboyant in private character as in any of her lush parts: she married six times. Died 4 April

Thoroddsen, Gunnar (b. 1910), Prime Minister of Iceland 1980–83, a lawyer by profession, had been Minister of Finance 1959–65 and of Industry, Energy and Social Affairs 1974–78, also ambassador to Denmark 1965–69. Died 25 September

Umberto II, King of Italy (b. 1904), succeeded to the throne when his father Vittorio Emmanuele abdicated in May 1946, but reigned for only 34 days, departing for exile after a referendum had shown a 6 to 5 majority for replacing the Italian monarchy with a republic. Died, never having again seen his native country, 18 March

Vorster, B. John (b. 1915), was Prime Minister of South Africa 1966-78 and President 1978-79. By profession a lawyer, he joined the intensely nationalist and authoritarian *Ossewabrandwag* in the late 1930s, and was interned during World War II for subversive activity. After the war his extremist past delayed his admission to the National Party, but he was elected to Parliament on its ticket in 1953. In 1961 he became Minister of Justice in the Government of Dr Verwoerd, whom he succeeded in 1966 after the Prime Minister's assassination. Notwithstanding his earlier opinions and his stern reputation, he loyally supported parliamentary democracy and pursued a relatively liberal external policy, publicly meeting President Banda of Malawi and clandestinely Presidents Houphouet-Boigny of Ivory Coast and Senghor of Senegal, and in 1975, on the Malawi border, President Kaunda of Zambia, in an attempt to mediate a settlement in Rhodesia (Zimbabwe); refusing, against pressure from his right, to intervene in Mozambique after the revolution; and eventually agreeing in principle to the independence of Namibia, though he declined to treat with Swapo and ordered repeated South African incursions into Angola. At home he implacably supported apartheid, the stern maintenance of law and order, and Verwoerd's policy of quasi-independent bantustans. His regime saw the Soweto riots of 1976, the outcry that followed the death of Steve Biko in prison in 1977, the creation of the Bureau of State Security (BOSS) and the exclusion of South Africa from the Olympic Games. After eight months in presidential office, he was forced to resign by exposure of his implication in the 'Muldergate' scandal (see AR 1979, p. 260-1). Died 10 September

Walton, Sir William, OM (b. 1902), more than any other contemporary English composer, was successful in appealing to the broad mass of the musical public. In this, as in other respects, he was Elgar's successor. Faced with the artistic choice, after *Façade* (1923), of pursuing an experimental path, or of staying with the musical mainstream, he opted—like Strauss—for the latter. The qualities that drove many 20th-century composers to forge a new musical language were the very qualities that separated them from their audiences; and it was with these that Walton established his affinity. So, starting with the *Viola Concerto* (1928) the series of masterworks began on which his reputation was built. His output resembled Elgar's—overtures, concertos, orchestral variations; two symphonies; a small amount of chamber music and songs, which served to highlight Waltonian romanticism—largeness of scale, boldness of concept, intensity, rhythmical and physical urgency. Another side of Walton's work resembled Elgar's: the provision of music for state celebrations. The Coronation marches *Crown Imperial* and *Orb and Sceptre* and his ceremonial choral works *Te Deum* and *Gloria* reflect all the pomp and splendour of a grand public occasion. Like Elgar, Walton was virtually self-taught. His time at Christ Church, Oxford, where he had been educated at the cathedral school, resulted not in a musical degree but in a fruitful friendship with the Sitwell family—the passport to *Façade*. Died 8 March

F.R.

West, Dame Rebecca, DBE (b. Cicely Isobel Fairfield 1892), British author and critic, adopted the name by which she was thereafter universally known when she embarked on writing as a career at the age of 19. While working as a political and literary journalist, devoted to women's rights, she fell in love with H. G. Wells, and became his mistress and bore him a son. In 1930 she married Harry Andrews, a banker of wide taste, who died in 1968. Her first novel, *The Return of the Soldier*, was published in 1918, her last, *The Birds Fall Down*, in 1966. Other novels included *The Thinking Reed* (1936) and *The Fountain Overflows* (1956). But her fame rested rather on her non-fictional work, especially the massive *Black Lamb and Grey Falcon*, in effect a biographical study of Yugoslavia, her studies of spy trials like *The Meaning of Treason* (1949) and *The Vassall Affair* (1963), and her brilliant writing for the newspaper and periodical press, on such varied themes as the Nuremberg trials and apartheid in South Africa. To a keen intellect she added vivid imagination, deep emotion and a refreshing literary style. Died 15 March

Williams, Tennesee (b. Thomas Lanier in Mississippi 1911), American playwright, turned to writing as relief from a monotonous job in the St Louis firm for which his businessman father worked. Returning to university in 1935, he wrote a stream of plays, of which some gained more than local success, before *The Glass Menagerie* (1944), which directly reflected his love for his sister during an unhappy boyhood. Among the most acclaimed of his later plays were *A Streetcar Named Desire* (1947), *The Rose Tattoo* (1951), *Camino Real* (1953), *Cat on a Hot Tin Roof* (1955), *Orpheus Descending* (1957), *Suddenly Last Summer* (1958) and *The Milk Train Doesn't Stop Here Any More* (1962), but he continued writing for the stage into the 1980s. He wrote *Baby Doll* for the screen, and six of his plays were turned into films. Altogether he wrote over 70 plays, seven collections of short stories and three of poems, two novels (the better known was *The Roman Spring of Mrs Stone*) and an autobiography. Died 25 February

CHRONICLE OF PRINCIPAL EVENTS IN 1983

JANUARY

4 Two-day summit conference of Warsaw Pact leaders opened in Prague; a 'new grand peace proposal' was launched (see DOCUMENTS).
6 In UK Cabinet reshuffle Mr Michael Heseltine became Secretary of State for Defence and was succeeded at Environment by Mr Tom King.
7 Captain Kent Kirk, Danish fisherman and member of European Parliament, fined £30,000 for fishing within British 12-mile limit in North Sea; 18 Jan. Denmark ended fishing dispute with EEC.
8 Mrs Margaret Thatcher in the Falkland Islands for four-day visit.
16 Soviet Foreign Minister Gromyko on 3-day visit to West Germany for discussion on progress of Geneva arms limitation talks.
In Turkey, 47 died in air crash at Ankara.
17 Nigeria ordered immediate expulsion of estimated 2 million illegal immigrants; 30 Jan. Ghana reopened border with Nigeria (closed since Sept. 1982) to speed exodus of refugees.
18 In UK, publication of the Franks Report; maintained that the Argentine invasion of the Falklands could not have been foreseen and cleared Thatcher Government of blame.
19 In Namibia, direct rule from Pretoria was reimposed after 5 years of semi-autonomous government.
20 In UK, publication of Serpell Report on future of railways: suggested greatly reduced network and higher commuter fares.
21 Chancellor Kohl of W. Germany in Paris for 20th anniversary of Franco-German treaty.
24 In UK, water and sewerage workers began strike; ended 22 Feb.
In Italy, 32 Red Brigade terrorists gaoled for kidnapping and murder of Aldo Moro in 1978 and other acts of terrorism.
25 In China, death sentence on Jiang Quing commuted to life imprisonment.
27 USSR proposed nuclear-free zone in Central Europe.
31 In UK, wearing of seat-belts by front-seat car passengers became compulsory.
President Reagan proposed summit meeting with President Andropov but offer rejected; Vice-President Bush began 12-day tour of W. Europe.

FEBRUARY

2 Strategic arms limitation talks resumed in Geneva (see 23 Nov.).
President Mubarak of Egypt on official visit to London.
3 In New Zealand, Mr David Lange succeeded Mr Wallace Rowling as leader of Parliamentary Labour Party.
5 Klaus Barbie (alias Altmann), Nazi war criminal, imprisoned in Lyons following deportation from Bolivia.
In Lebanon, 22 died in bomb explosion at PLO research centre in W. Beirut.
6 In presidential election in Paraguay, General Stroessner returned for seventh five-year term of office.
8 In Israel, report of Kahane Commission on massacres in Sabra and Chatila in Sept. 1982 condemned role of Israeli Government and recommended dismissal of Defence Minister Sharon; 11 Feb. Mr Sharon resigned as Defence Minister but remained in Cabinet; 14 Feb. Prof. Moshe Arens named Defence Minister.

CHRONICLE OF PRINCIPAL EVENTS 511

9 In Ireland, 1981 Derby winner Shergar stolen from stables in Co. Kildare; £2 million ransom demanded but horse had not been recovered at year's end.
 In UK, Oxford Union defeated motion that 'this house would not fight for Queen and country' on 50th anniversary of historic debate.
10 In UK, Church of England General Synod voted overwhelmingly against unilateral nuclear disarmament.
11 Brandt Commission published further report: *Common Crisis, North-South* took a pessimistic view of future prospects because of global uncertainties and reduced expectations of economic growth.
13 In elections in Cyprus, President Kyprianou was returned for a five-year term.
 In Italy, 10 died in cable car accident and 64 died in cinema fire in Turin.
 HM Queen Elizabeth II and Prince Philip began month-long tour of Jamaica, Cayman Islands, Mexico and west coast of America.
16 69 died in severe bush fires in southern Australia.
24 In India, some 1,500 people reported to have died in violence surrounding local elections in Assam, including 1,000 in massacre of Bengali immigrants in Nowong (see 23 March).
25 Italian PM Fanfani in London for talks with Mrs Thatcher.

MARCH

2 Pope John Paul II began 8-day visit to Central America and Haiti.
5 In Australian general election, Labour Party led by Mr Bob Hawke defeated ruling coalition of Mr Malcolm Fraser.
6 In W. Germany, Christian Democrats led by Chancellor Kohl gained resounding victory in general election; Green Party gained 24 seats in new Bundestag.
7 Seventh Non-Aligned summit conference opened in Delhi.
 Australian dollar devalued by 10 per cent.
 In Turkey, 96 miners died in explosion at colliery on Black Sea.
9 Mr Joshua Nkomo fled from Zimbabwe following raid on his home; 15 Aug. returned to Zimbabwe after exile in London.
11 In Australia, Mr Andrew Peacock succeeded Mr Malcolm Fraser as leader of the Parliamentary Liberal Party.
15 In UK, Budget day; tax allowances raised by 14 per cent, exempting 1·75 million people from tax; mortgage relief limit raised; excise duties up in line with inflation; PSBR projected at £8,000 million.
18 Arab League delegation led by King Husain in London for discussions with PM and Foreign Secretary on Middle East peace plan.
19 In Swaziland, PM Prince Mabandala Dlamini reported dismissed by Queen Dzeliwe and replaced by Prince Bhekimpi Dlamini (see 10 Aug.).
20 The Prince and Princess of Wales began 6-week tour of Australia and New Zealand.
 Following Finnish general election, Government of Mr Kalevi Sorsa remained as caretaker pending formation of new coalition; 6 May, new 4-party coalition under Mr Sorsa sworn in.
21 Two-day summit conference of EEC heads of government opened in Brussels.
 Large areas of Ethiopia reported in grip of worst drought since 1973, bringing famine to one million.
22 Mr Chaim Herzog elected President of Israel.
 President Kaunda of Zambia on four-day state visit to Britain.
 President Mitterrand reappointed M Mauroy as PM of new 15-man Cabinet.
23 In India, death toll after 7 weeks of violence in Assam reported as 5,000.
 In UK, TUC and Labour Party issued statement, *Partners in Rebuilding Britain*.
24 In USSR, Foreign Minister Gromyko named Deputy PM.
25 In France, Cabinet approved tough package of economic measures including severe restrictions on private spending abroad (see 5 May).

26 In UK, Oxford won Boat Race by 4½ lengths.
29 In UK, Labour Party launched election campaign document, *New Hope for Britain*: massive progamme for expansion and increased public spending.
30 President Reagan announced compromise proposals for reducing medium-range land-based missiles in Europe, a shift of policy from the 'zero option'.
31 500 died in earthquake at Popayan, Colombia.

APRIL

1 In UK, thousands of CND supporters took part in anti-nuclear demonstrations in Berkshire.
2 In UK, armed raiders escaped with £7 million in cash from Security Express in London, largest theft of money in British history.
US space shuttle *Challenger* launched from Cape Canaveral on 5-day maiden flight.
5 France expelled 47 Soviet diplomats for alleged spying.
9 In UK, Corbiere won Grand National at 13-1.
10 President Reagan's Middle East plan collapsed when King Husain of Jordan failed to reach agreement with PLO.
541 relatives of British servicemen attended ceremonies on Falkland Islands to commemorate those who died in 1982 campaign.
12 Sir Richard Attenborough's film *Gandhi* awarded 8 Oscars.
13 A fleet of 12 Royal Navy ships began visit to Gibraltar despite Spanish protests.
Mr Harold Washington elected first black mayor of Chicago after racially divisive campaign.
In W. Germany, cities of Bonn, Cologne and Koblenz swamped in worst flooding of Rhine since 1926; 12 died in severe flooding in northern France.
15 King Juan Carlos of Spain opened largest-ever exhibition of work of Salvador Dali in Madrid.
18 In Lebanon 39 died in bomb explosion at US embassy in Beirut.
In UK, Environment Secretary announced proposals for all new cars to run on lead-free petrol by 1990.
19 In Thailand no party achieved majority in general election; 7 May PM Gen. Tinsulanond named new Cabinet including 10 retired military officers.
20 Four British relief workers among party kidnapped by guerrillas in Ethiopia; released 8 June.
21 In UK, £1 coin came into circulation.
W. German Chancellor Kohl in London for talks with Mrs Thatcher.
22 W. German magazine *Stern* announced discovery of 60 volumes of Adolf Hitler's diaries which were later found to be forgeries.
23 No party achieved majority elections in Iceland; 26 May, Mr Steingrimur Hermansson became PM of new coalition of Progressive and Independent parties.
24 Chancellor Kreisky resigned after 13 years in office when Socialist Party failed to win overall majority in Austrian general election; 11 May, coalition Government formed under Dr Fred Sinowatz.
25 General election in Portugal; Socialist Party (PSP) gained 100 seats in Nat. Assembly; 4 June, coalition Government of PSP and PSD formed under Mario Soares (see 9 June).
US Secretary of State George Shultz began tour of Middle East in renewed peace effort (see 13 May).
27 In address to Congress, President Reagan declared that US did not seek to overthrow left-wing Sandinista Government in Nicaragua, denied planning to send US combat troops to Central America but sought further military assistance for El Salvador.
29 In Italy, Government of Signor Fanfani resigned (see 26 June).
Argentine junta banned planned visit to Falklands war graves by relatives, Britain having refused consent.

CHRONICAL OF PRINCIPAL EVENTS

MAY

1 In Poland police broke up massive demonstrations by Solidarity supporters in Warsaw and other cities.
3 Spanish PM González in Bonn for talks with Chancellor Kohl.
President Mitterrand of France began official visit to China.
5 In France, riot police were involved in serious clashes with protesters demonstrating against austerity measures (see 25 March).
7 In Turkey, 42 died in hotel fire in Istanbul.
13 In UK, Parliament was dissolved pending general election on 9 June.
President Asad of Syria refused to accept terms of Israeli-Lebanese troop withdrawal proposals negotiated during Shultz peace shuttle (see 25 April, 17 May).
15 Government forces put down military rebellion in southern Sudan.
16 In UK, Labour Party published manifesto promising to spend its way out of recession and create 2·5 million new jobs in 5 years.
17 Israel and Lebanon signed agreement on withdrawal of Israeli troops from Lebanon within three months despite Syrian rejection of agreement.
18 In UK, Conservative manifesto promised further trade union reforms and changes in local government and nationalized industries.
20 In S. Africa, 18 died in car bomb explosion in Pretoria.
22 In W. Germany, 5 people died when plane crashed during Frankfurt air show.
24 General Nimairi sworn in for 3rd term as President of Sudan.
25 In Egypt, some 300 died when ferry caught fire and sank on Upper Nile
HM Queen Elizabeth II and Prince Philip began 3-day state visit to Sweden.
US Senate voted to release funds for controversial MX missile project.
27 People's Express airline began operating between London and New York for £99.
28 Summit conference of Western leaders opened at Williamsburg, USA, ending 30 May.
30 A sixty-day state of emergency was declared in Peru because of political crisis and increasing terrorism.
31 In Uganda, 200 refugees reported massacred by armed guerrillas.

JUNE

1 In UK, the Derby was won by Teenoso ridden by Lester Piggott at 9-2.
2 23 passengers died but 23 survived when Air Canada pilot landed blazing plane at Cincinnati airport.
5 In USSR, more than 100 believed dead in passenger ship accident on R. Volga.
6 Australian PM Bob Hawke began official visit to UK.
USSR and Finland signed documents renewing 35-year friendship pact during first official visit to Moscow by President Koivisto.
8 OAU summit conference opened in Addis Ababa, ending 14 June.
In Norway, three-party non-socialist coalition led by PM Willoch succeeded minority Conservative Government.
9 General election in UK; Conservatives won overall majority of 144; Labour won 209 seats, smallest representation in any Parliament since World War II.
In S. Africa, three African National Congress guerrillas hanged for armed attacks on police stations.
In Portugal, new centre-left coalition led by Mario Soares sworn in.
11 In UK, Cabinet reshuffle; Mr Nigel Lawson succeeded Sir Geoffrey Howe, transferred to Foreign Office, as Chancellor and Mr Leon Brittan became Home Secretary.
In Canada, Mr Brian Mulroney elected leader of Progressive Conservative Party in succession to Mr Joe Clark.
The Prince and Princess of Wales began 17-day visit to Canada.
14 In UK, Mr Roy Jenkins resigned as leader of Social Democratic Party and was succeeded by Dr David Owen (21 June).

16 Pope John Paul II began 8-day visit to Poland during which he held talks with General Jaruzelski and Mr Lech Walesa.
Yuri Andropov elected Chairman of Presidium of Supreme Soviet of USSR.
European rocket *Ariane* launched two satellites into space from base in French Guiana.
17 Two-day summit conference of EEC heads of government opened in Stuttgart.
In UK, annual rate of inflation fell 3·7 per cent, lowest for 15 years.
19 Li Xiannian elected President of China.
20 In UK, £6 million worth of diamonds stolen in raid on Mayfair jewellers.
Queen Elizabeth the Queen Mother paid official visit to N. Ireland.
22 In UK, state opening of parliament; Queen's Speech emphasized continuation of Government's existing policies and outlined some 16 new Bills.
In Israel, hunger strike by 2,000 doctors in pursuit of pay claim brought medical system almost to collapse; 26 June, Government agreed to independent arbitration.
24 PLO leader Arafat ordered out of Syria while Syrian tanks laid siege to his guerrilla bases in Lebanon (see 15 Nov.).
Leaders of 20 Western Conservative parties attended launch in London of International Democrat Union.
26 General election in Italy resulted in major setback for Christian Democrats; 4 Aug. Sr Bettino Craxi became Italy's first Socialist PM at head of coalition Government.
In elections in Japan, ruling Liberal Democratic Party increased majority in Upper House of Diet.
In India, 1,000 reported dead in severe flooding in Gujarat.
In UK, a second inquest returned an open verdict on Signor Roberto Calvi, found hanging from Blackfriars bridge in 1982.
27 Two Britons, Adrian and Richard Crane, completed record 2,100-mile run along entire length of Himalayas in aid of charity.
In UK, Defence Secretary announced plan for building £215 million airport in Falkland Islands.
28 Warsaw Pact leaders, meeting in Moscow, failed to agree on policy of retaliation against Nato over medium-range missiles.
29 In Malawi, two days of elections for new Parliament; several MPs lost seats; 7 July, Dr Banda appointed new Cabinet.

JULY

1 In Australia, High Court ruled that federal Government's stopping of the controversial planned dam in Tasmania was constitutional.
4 Chancellor Kohl of W. Germany began 3-day official visit to Moscow.
Summit meeting of Caribbean Community (Caricom) opened in Port-of-Spain.
6 In UK, publication of White Paper: *Statement on the Defence Estimates* (Cmnd. 8951); repeated Government's intention to deploy Cruise missiles at Greenham Common and Molesworth in absence of agreement with USSR (see 14 Nov.).
7 In UK, Chancellor of Exchequer announced emergency package of £500 million expenditure cuts in current year.
10 In Western Sahara, 7-year war flared up again (after 18-month lull) when Polisario guerrillas attacked Moroccan defensive positions.
12 In UK, Employment Secretary Tebbit announced further proposals for trade union reforms, including compulsory ballots before strikes.
OECD report forecast 20 million unemployed in Europe by end 1984.
13 In UK, House of Commons, in free vote, rejected reintroduction of capital punishment.
14 In UK, General Synod of Church of England approved in principle scheme for remarriage of divorced people in Church.
15 European Security Conference in Madrid ended with new agreement on cooperation between East and West.

CHRONICLE OF PRINCIPAL EVENTS   515

    In France, 5 died in Armenian terrorist attack at Orly airport.
16 In UK, 20 people died in helicopter crash off Scilly Isles.
18 Presidents of Mexico, Colombia, Venezuela and Panama (Contadora Group), meeting in Cancún, issued declaration listing peace proposals for Central America.
    President Reagan named Dr Henry Kissinger to head advisory commission on Central America.
19 Seven Greenpeace anti-whaling protesters detained in Siberia, their ship *Rainbow Warrior* having been chased by Soviet gunboat.
20 Israeli Cabinet voted unanimously for partial withdrawal of occupying troops in Lebanon (see 4 Sept.).
21 Polish Government declared an end to martial law and amnesty for political prisoners.
22 President Gemayel of Lebanon held talks in Washington with President Reagan on withdrawal of foreign forces from his country.
25 Sri Lankan Government imposed curfew as mobs went on rampage, attacking minority Tamil homes and businesses (see 1 Aug.).
27 In Portugal, 5 Armenian terrorists died in raid on Turkish embassy in Lisbon.
28 President Jayawardene of Sri Lanka announced ban on political parties advocating partition (notably the Tamil United Liberation Front).
31 World Council of Churches, meeting at Vancouver, reached new accord covering central aspects of faith and worship and held historic inter-denominational Eucharist.

AUGUST

1 Death toll in violence against Tamil community in Sri Lanka rose to 179; eventual death toll put at 350.
2 President Habré of Chad accused Libya of genocide after four days of bombing raids on Faya-Largeau by Libyan aeroplanes (see 11 April).
4 In Upper Volta, Major Ouedrago overthrown in military coup led by former PM Capt. Thomas Sankara; 25 Aug. new Government (mostly civilian) formed.
6 In Nigerian election, President Shagari won landslide victory (see 31 Dec.).
8 Military coup in Guatemala; General Oscar Humberto Meija Victores sworn in as President.
10 In Swaziland, Queen Dzeliwe (The Great She-Elephant) removed from office, Queen Ntombi to assume title of Indlovukazi and act as Queen Regent until 21st birthday of 15-year-old Prince Mokhosetive, named to succeed late King Sobuzha (see 19 March).
11 In Chad, northern town of Faya-Largeau fell to Libyan troops and rebels: 12 Aug., President called for help by US and French forces.
12 President Zia of Pakistan announced that elections would be held in March 1985 and martial law lifted.
14 President Reagan and President Madrid of Mexico held talks in La Paz on Central America.
    Pope John Paul II on two-day visit to Lourdes.
    In Pakistan, campaign of civil disobedience launched in Sind province; 29 Sept., at least 30 died when troops opened fire on demonstrators.
19 3,500 French troops left for Chad to reinforce some 3,000 already supporting Government of President Habré.
21 In general elections in Mauritius 3-party alliance led by PM Jugnauth defeated opposition MMM by 41 seats to 19.
    In the Philippines, opposition leader Benigno Aquino assassinated at Manila airport upon return from 3-year exile in USA (see 21 Sept., 10 Oct.).
26 President Andropov offered to destroy 'a considerable number' of SS-20s in return for US not deploying new missiles in Europe.
28 37 died in severe flooding in Basque region of Spain and S.W. France.

31 Lebanese army fought its way back in Beirut, driving back Muslim militias.
  In Zimbabwe, 6 white air-force officers acquitted on sabotage charges were immediately rearrested; all deported to Britain by year's end.

SEPTEMBER

 1 South Korean Boeing 747 airliner carrying 29 passengers shot down by Soviet fighter planes after straying into Soviet air-space (see 8 Sept.).
 4 In Lebanon, civil warfare broke out in Chouf mountains following Israeli withdrawal to new front line along Awali River.
 5 Canada suspended landing rights of Soviet airline Aeroflot in protest against shooting-down of South Korean jet; most West European nations subsequently imposed 14-day ban on Aeroflot flights.
 6 Final document of European Conference on Security and Cooperation adopted by all 35 delegates at Madrid conference: it committed Governments to continuation of the Helsinki process.
 8 US Secretary of State Shultz, after talks with Soviet Foreign Minister Gromyko in Madrid, said Soviet response over jumbo jet disaster was totally unsatisfactory and that US would continue to press for justice.
10 Pope John Paul II on 4-day visit to Austria.
11 In Chile, 40 people reported dead in several days of violent protests marking 10th anniversary of coup.
12 Lebanese Government appealed to UN Security Council to call again for withdrawal of foreign forces.
15 Mr Menachem Begin resigned as PM of Israel (see 10 Oct.).
18 A Briton, Mr George Meegan, ended a 19,000 mile walk from Tierra del Fuego to Northern Alaska, believed to be the longest walk in recorded history.
19 Caribbean islands of St Kitts-Nevis became independent of Britain after 360 years.
  In Lebanon, US warships began bombardment of Druze areas in mountains around Beirut.
  Mrs Thatcher began three-day visit to Netherlands and W. Germany.
21 In the Philippines, 11 died in violent demonstrations demanding the resignation of President Marcos.
23 112 died in air crash near Abu Dhabi.
25 In N. Ireland, 38 Republican prisoners escaped in mass breakout from Maze prison; 17 recaptured.
26 In general elections in Kenya, 5 Ministers lost seats and 40 per cent of MPs replaced; 1 Oct., President Moi reshuffled Cabinet naming 8 new Ministers.
  Mrs Thatcher began official visit to Canada and Washington.
26 A ceasefire came into effect in Lebanon, following three weeks of fighting, when Government agreed to conference of national reconciliation (see 31 Oct.);
Government resigned to make way for government of national unity.
  Australia II won America's Cup, defeating US yacht *Liberty* and ending America's 132-year hold on trophy.
29 In UK, Lady (later Dame Mary) Donaldson became first woman to be elected Lord Mayor of London in 800 years of the mayoralty.

OCTOBER

 2 In UK, Mr Neil Kinnock elected leader of Labour Party, Mr Roy Hattersley deputy leader.
 3 Tenth annual Franco-African summit conference opened in Vital, Lorraine.
 5 The Nobel peace prize was awarded to Lech Walesa (Poland).
  Hong Kong dollar dropped sharply, having lost 30 per cent of its exchange value during year because of uncertainty over political future.

CHRONICLE OF PRINCIPAL EVENTS 517

Richard Noble (UK) captured world land speed record, reaching 633·6 m.p.h. in jet-powered car in Nevada.
7 In UK, White Paper published on eliminating Greater London Council and metropolitan counties (Cmnd. 9063).
8 In Burma, four S. Korean Ministers and at least 15 others killed in bomb blast in Rangoon; 9 Dec. two N. Korean army officers sentenced to death for complicity in bombing.
10 Mr Yitzhak Shamir took office as PM of Israel; new Government immediately announced 23 per cent devaluation of shekel and introduced austerity measures.
In the Philippines, commission (appointed by President Marcos) investigating murder of Aquino resigned (see 21 Aug.).
12 In Japan, former PM Kakuei Tanaka convicted of accepting bribes from Lockheed Corporation in early 1970s.
Chinese Communist Party launched biggest purge of membership since Cultural Revolution.
14 In UK, Trade and Industry Secretary Cecil Parkinson resigned following revelations about his affair with Miss Sara Keays, now expecting his child.
Chin Lee Chong succeeded Kim Sang Hyup as PM of S. Korea.
16 In UK Government reshuffle, Mr Norman Tebbit became Secretary for Trade and Industry and was succeeded at Employment by Mr Tom King.
19 In Grenada, PM Maurice Bishop killed in left-wing military coup (see 25 Oct.).
20 President Mitterrand of France in London for two-days of talks with Mrs Thatcher.
23 In Lebanon, 242 US and 62 French troops of peacekeeping force died in bomb attacks on military compound.
General election in Switzerland led to little change in balance of power.
25 US Marines invaded Grenada despite efforts by Mrs Thatcher to dissuade President Reagan; 27 Oct. organized resistance by Cubans and Grenadian rebels ended; 8 US servicemen and 100 Cubans reported dead in fighting; 600 Cubans captured; 28 Oct. US vetoed UN Security Council Resolution declaring invasion illegal; UK abstained; 31 Oct. Governor of Grenada confirmed he had requested assistance from E. Caribbean forces and indirectly from US.
27 Presidential and parliamentary elections in Zambia; 3 Nov. President Kaunda named new Cabinet.
30 In elections in Argentina, Radical Party led by Sr Raul Alfonsín gained absolute majority (see 10 Dec.).
1,200 died in earthquake in eastern Turkey.
31 National reconciliation conference on Lebanon opened in Geneva; attended by leaders of principal Lebanese militias and political parties, Syrian delegates and Israeli observers.
Former PM Bishop Abel Muzorewa arrested in Zimbabwe.

NOVEMBER

1 In UK, Defence Secretary warned that demonstrators who got near Cruise missile bunkers at Greenham Common could be shot.
2 In South Africa, an all-white referendum approved new constitution giving limited political rights to Coloureds and Asians (see DOCUMENTS).
US began withdrawal of troops from Grenada; wounded Cubans airlifted home by International Red Cross.
3 In northern Lebanon fighting broke out around refugee camps in Tripoli between PLO loyalists and dissidents demanding overthrow of Yassir Arafat (see 5 Nov., 20 Dec.).
4 60 died when suicide bombers attacked Israeli military hq in Tyre, Lebanon.
In UK, Dennis Nilsen gaoled for 25 years on six counts of murder (he had admitted 15).

6 In elections in Turkey, Mr Turgut Özal's Motherland Party won nearly 45 per cent of vote (see 6 Dec.).
7 In UK, Mrs Thatcher held talks with Irish PM FitzGerald at Chequers.
9 President Reagan began official visit to Japan and Korea.
   HM Queen Elizabeth II and Prince Philip left UK for visits to Kenya, Bangladesh and India (for Commonwealth conference).
   Mrs Thatcher in Bonn for two days of talks with Chancellor Kohl.
14 In UK, Defence Secretary announced arrival of first Cruise missiles at Greenham Common; 15 Nov. 141 arrested during violent demonstrations outside base.
15 Turkish Cypriot Legislative Assembly issued unilateral proclamation of independence of Turkish section of island: immediately recognised by Ankara Government. 18 Nov. UN Security Council Resolution 541 declared action legally invalid.
   Syrian forces and Palestinian dissidents launched final assault on last refuge of PLO leader Arafat in Tripoli, northern Lebanon.
18 In Grenada, Governor-General Sir Paul Scoon signed proclamation handing power to 9-member advisory council.
21 Official Unionist Party withdrew from N. Ireland Assembly following sectarian murders of 3 church elders in Armagh.
22 Bundestag voted for deployment of Pershing missiles in W. Germany.
23 Conference of Commonwealth heads of government opened in New Delhi; 'The Goa Declaration' issued 27 Nov.; conference ended 29 Nov. (see DOCUMENTS).
   USSR walked out of arms limitation talks in Geneva and refused to set date for resumption.
24 Mother Teresa of Calcutta received insignia of honorary Order of Merit from HM The Queen in Delhi.
25 In UK, thieves stole £26 million worth of gold bullion and diamonds from warehouse near Heathrow—Britain's largest-ever robbery.
26 183 died when Colombian Boeing 747 crashed at Madrid, Spain; 7 Dec. 90 died when two planes collided on runway at Madrid airport.
28 65 died in aircrash in Enugu, Nigeria.
30 In UK, Court of Appeal ordered seizure of £10m assets of National Graphical Association, following union's failure to comply with previous court orders to end picketing of Stockport Messenger Group (see 9 Dec.).

DECEMBER

4 In elections in Venezuela, the Democratic Action Party won comfortable victory over ruling Christian Democrats; 12 Dec., Dr Jaime Lusinchi formally proclaimed President (to take office in Feb. 1984).
  Eight US marines died when Syrians shot down two US Navy jets during first US air strike against Syrian positions in Lebanon.
5 In Lebanon, 14 died when car bomb exploded in Muslim area of Beirut.
  Two-day summit conference of EEC leaders opened in Athens; ended in failure, leaders being unable to agree measures to resolve Community's financial crisis.
6 In Turkey, National Security Council formally dissolved, ending 3 years of military rule.
  Four died when PLO bomb exploded in bus in Jerusalem.
  In UK, a record of £8,140,000 was paid at Sotheby's by W. German bidder for a 12th-century manuscript.
8 In UK, House of Lords voted in favour of experimental period of televising its proceedings.
  In USA, Administration ended 5-year ban on arms sales to Argentina.
9 Lord Carrington appointed to succeed Dr Joseph Luns as Secretary-General of Nato in 1984.
  W. Germany Minister of Economics, Otto Graf Lambsdorff, charged with corruption.

CHRONICLE OF PRINCIPAL EVENTS

In UK, National Graphical Association fined £525,000 for contempt (the largest fine ever imposed by a British court) in addition to two earlier fines totalling £150,000.
10 Sr Raul Alfonsín inaugurated as President of Argentina after 8 years of military rule.
11 General Ershad named himself President of Bangladesh.
12 In UK, High Court ordered National Graphical Association to call off planned nationwide newspaper strike; 14 Dec. TUC General Council refused to support NGA and strike was called off.
Four died in bomb attacks by Shia Muslim extremists in Kuwait.
13 President Gemayel of Lebanon on 2-day visit to London for talks with Mrs Thatcher. Mr Turgut Özal took office as PM of Turkey.
In Lebanon, US and Israeli navies launched bombardment of Palestinian and Syrian army positions near Lebanese coast.
15 In general elections in Jamaica, ruling Jamaica Labour Party gained control of 60 seats in Parliament.
European Parliament voted to block rebates due to UK and W. Germany while passing £15,500 million budget for Community in 1984.
16 In Irish Republic, two members of security forces killed during operation to rescue Mr Don Tidey, kidnapped by IRA on 24 Nov.
17 In UK, 6 people died, 90 injured when IRA car bomb exploded outside Harrods store in London.
In Spain, 80 died in discotheque fire in Madrid.
18 General election in Japan: Liberal Democratic Party led by PM Nakasone captured only 250 seats in 511-man Lower House, losing previous overall majority; 26 Dec., Mr Nakasone re-elected PM and named new Cabinet.
20 PLO leader Yassir Arafat and 4,000 loyal guerrillas evacuated from Lebanon by Greek ships; 22 Dec. Arafat held talks in Cairo with President Mubarak.
21 In Lebanon, 8 died in bomb attack on French troops of peacekeeping force.
28 270 people reported to have died after 10 days of record low temperatures throughout the USA.
29 In S. Africa, former commanding officer of Simonstown naval dockyard, Commodore Dieter Gerhardt, and his wife convicted of spying for USSR; both sentenced to life imprisonment (31 Dec.).
US formally announced intention to withdraw from Unesco at end of 1984.
30 In Argentina, former President Galtieri indicted for murder, torture and treason.
31 President Shagari of Nigeria overthrown in bloodless coup led by Maj.-Gen. Mohammed Buhari.

INDEX

ABBOUD, General Ibrahim, obit., 497
ABDERAMANE, Ahmed Abdallah, President of Comoro State, 275
ABDULLAH, HRH Crown Prince, of Saudi Arabia, 192
ABDULLAH, Dr Farooq, 261
ABE, Shintaro, 299
ABU DHABI, see under United Arab Emirates
ADAMI, Dr Fenech, 165
ADAMOU, Oumarou (alias Bonkano), 229
ADAMS, Gerry, MP, 48
ADAMS, John, 411
ADAMS, John M. G., Prime Minister of Barbados, 92, 93
ADDISON, Errol, death, 403
ADELMAN, Kenneth, 55
ADLER, Christopher, 403
AFGHANISTAN, 103, 131, 259-60; and non-aligned nations, 259-60; UN and, 260, 264, 317; USSR and, 259
AFRICAN CONFERENCES AND INSTITUTIONS, 360-2; Franco-African summit, 362; see also Organization of African Unity
AFRICAN NATIONAL CONGRESS (ANC), 238, 250-1, 252, 253-4, 294, 306
AHIDJO, Ahmadou, 230
AHRENDS BURTON & KORALEK, 426
AIKEN, Frank, death, 148
AIKINS, Addo, 219
AITKEN, Timothy, 417
ALBANIA, 123-4; and China, 124, 294; and Yugoslavia, 122, 123; economy, 124; religious persecution, 124
ALDISS, Brian, 432
ALDRICH, Robert, death, 416
ALEMAN, Miguel, obit., 497
ALFONSÍN, Raul, President of Argentina, 38, 76
ALGABID, Hamid, Prime Minister of Niger, 230
ALGERIA, 190, 205, 206, 207-8, 227; foreign policy, 207; Greater Maghreb concept, 207
ALIA, Ramiz, 123
ALIBUX, Errol, Prime Minister of Suriname, 98
ALIER, Abel, 202
ALIEV, G. A., 106
ALLENDE GOSSENS, Salvador, 79
ALLINGTON, Edward, 424
ALLY, Julie, 421
ALPSERS, Svetlana, 426
ALTMAN, Robert, 415
ALTMANN (Barbie), Klaus, 76
ALVAREZ, General Gregorio, President of Uruguay, 82
ALVAREZ, General Gustavo, 86
AMADOU, Lieut. Idrissa, 229

AMARAL, Freitas do, 163
AMELIO, Gianni, 416
AMERY, Julian, MP, 40
AMES, Robert, death, 66
AMIN, Idi, 218
AMIRTHALINGAM, Appapillai, 268, 269
AMNESTY INTERNATIONAL, 234, 235, 237
AMPFIELD, Pierre, 243
AN SUNG HAK, 301
ANDEAN PACT, 343
ANDREOTTI, Giulio, 139
ANDRESON, Brit, 426
ANDRIESSEN, Franciscus H. J. J., 390
ANDROPOV, Yuri Vladimirovich, President of USSR, 58, 59, 62, 73, 104, 108, 113, 124, 317; and agriculture, 105; and nuclear arms limitation, 102-3, 335-7; Comecon and, 356, 357; speculation about health, 100-1; talks with Herr Vogel, 102, 136; Warsaw Pact summit, Prague, 112, 357
ANDROSCH, Dr Hannes, 157
ANGOLA, 103, 239-42; and China, 294; and South Africa, 240, 241, 249; ceasefire proposal, 241; Cuban soldiers, 241-2, 249; diamond smuggling, 240; Unita activities, 240-1, 249
ANNE, HRH Princess, Mrs Mark Phillips, 421
ANSTRUTHER, Ian, 433
ANTARCTICA, 263; Antarctic Treaty, 263, 310, 320
ANTIGUA AND BARBUDA, 93-4; and China, 294
ANTONIONI, Michelangelo, 415, 416
ANWAR IBRAHIM, 280
AOKI, Isao, 441
AQUINO, Benigno, assassination, 68, 284; obit., 497
ARAB WORLD, 179-81; Arab League, 184, 185, 193, 306; Euro-Arab dialogue, 343; see also Islam; Palestine Liberation Organization; and individual countries
ARAFAT, Yassir, 67, 104, 168, 176, 177, 179-81, 182, 191, 203; and King Husain, 183-4; and Syria, 179-80, 184; leaves Lebanon, 180; sets up in S. Yemen, 195
ARAGON, Louis, death, 434
ARCHITECTURE, 426-9; Muslim, 429
ARENS, Moshe, 176
ARGENTINA, 74, 75-6; Beagle Channel dispute, 76; 'disappeared' persons, 75; economy, 75; political reform, 75-6, 82, 349; rearmament, 75; relations with: UK, 26, 37, 38, 65, 76; USA, 65
ARGOV, Shlomo, 178
ARIDOR, Yoram, 175
ARMADA COMYN, General Alfonso, 161
ARMS CONTROL, see Defence Organizations and Nuclear Arms

INDEX

ARMSTRONG, Karen, 409
ARON, Raymond, death, 434; obit., 497
ART, 421–6; books, 425–6
ARTHIT KAMLANG-EK, General, 278
ARUP ASSOCIATES, 426
ASAD, Hafiz al-, President of Syria, 184, 186
ASAD, Rifa'at, 186
ASHTON, Sir Frederick, 401
ASIAN DEVELOPMENT BANK, 312
ASKEW, Reubin, 56
ASSOCIATION OF SOUTH-EAST ASIAN NATIONS (ASEAN), 282, 306, 362–3
ATHANASSIADIS, George, assassination, 168
ATTENBOROUGH, Sir Richard, 413
AURIC, Georges, death, 416
AUSTIN, General Hudson, 92, 93
AUSTRALIA, 302–6; aid to PNG, 306–7; and British monarchy, 305; and Indonesia, 282; and Kampuchea, 363–4; Anzus treaty, 306, 310; Budget, 304; citizenship, 305; economic relations with New Zealand, 310; economy, 304; foreign affairs 306; Labour win election, 302–3; oil, 304; Tasmanian dams issue, 305; unemployment, 304; uranium mining, 305; yacht race triumph, 445
AUSTRIA, 155–7; economy, 156–7; general election, 155–6; Pope's visit, 156
AVNER, Yehuda, 178
AWOLOWO, Chief Obafemi, 222
AYANG, Luc, Prime Minister of Cameroon, 230

BABANGIDA, Maj.-Gen. Ibrahim, 221
BADHAM, John, 415
BAGAZA, Jean-Baptiste, President of Burundi, 236
BAHAMAS, THE, 92, 97–8, 366
BAHR, Egon, 134
BAHREIN, 199; finance, 198; oil, 196, 197
BAKALLI, Mahmut, 122
BAKARÍC, Vladimir, 122
BAKER, Kenneth, 376
BAKO, Brigadier I., 220
BALANCHINE, George, death, 402; obit., 497–8
BALDRIDGE, Malcolm, 293
BALLESTEROS, Severiano, 440
BALLET, 401–3
BALSEMÃO, Francisco Pinto, 163
BANDA, Dr H. Kamuzu, 244–5
BANDARANAIKE, Anura, 269
BANDARANAIKE, Sirimavo, 268
BANGLADESH, 262, 266–8; economy, 267; foreign relations, 267; riots, 266
BANK FOR INTERNATIONAL SETTLEMENTS, 78, 447
BANNEN, Ian, 406

BARBADOS, 92, 93, 96–7, 366
BARBIE, Klaus, see Altmann
BARKER, Howard, 406
BARNACHEA, Alfredo, 82
BARNES, Edward Larrabee, 428
BARRANTES, Alfonso, 82
BARRIENTOS, Zenon, 77
BARRY, Gene, 407
BARTON, John, 405
BARYSHNIKOV, Mikhail, 402
BATEMAN, Jaime, death, 79
BATES, Alan, 406
BATLLE, Jorge, 82
BAUM, Gerhart, 135
BAWDEN, Nina, 432
BEATTIE, Susan, 425
BEGIN, Menachem, Prime Minister of Israel, 176; resignation, 175, 177
BELAÚNDE TERRY, Fernando, President of Peru, 81
BELGIUM, 141–3; economy, 141–3; King Leopold III, obit., 504; language problem, 142; Prime Minister's special powers extended, 141
BELIZE, 92, 97; Guatemala and, 86, 97; UK and, 86, 97; USA and, 63
BEN BELLA, Ahmad, 208
BENIN, 228
BENN, Tony, MP, 11, 18, 19, 24
BENNETT, Alan, 419
BENNETT, William, 70
BÉRENGER, Paul, 273
BERGE, Gunnar, 355
BERGMAN, Ingmar, 416
BERIO, Luciano, 411
BERLINGUER, Enrico, 138
BERNSTEIN, Leonard, 400
BETANCUR, Belisario, President of Colombia, 80
BEYE, Alioune Blondin, 361
BHUTAN, 262, 267
BICHE, Caroline, 444
BIDAULT, Georges, obit., 498
BIERMANN, Wolf, 109
BIFFEN, John, MP, 27
BIKO, Steve, 252
BINTLEY, David, 401
BIRCH, Bishop Peter, death, 148
BIRENDRA, HM King, of Nepal, 270–1
BIRLA, Ghanshyan Das, death, 263; obit., 498
BISHOP, Maurice, Prime Minister of Grenada, 84, 91–2; murder, 39, 62, 84, 92; obit., 498
BISSIOUNI, Mary, 202
BITTEL, Deolindo, 76
BIYA, Paul, President of Cameroon, 230
BJÖRNSON, Maria, 404
BLACKER, Kate, 424
BLAKEMORE, Michael, 414
BLECHA, Karl, 156

BLUFORD, Lieut.-Col. Guion S., 56
BLUNT, Anthony, obit., 498–9
BO NI, 276
BOESAK, Dr Allan, 252
BOESMANS, Philippe, 399–400
BOKASSA, Jean-Bedel, former Emperor (Central African Empire), 232
BOLIVIA, 76–7; economy, 76; poverty, 77
BOND, Alan, 445
BOND, Edward, 400
BONGO, Omar, President of Gabon, 232
BONKANO, see Adamou, Oumarou
BONNICI, Dr Mifsud, 165
BONYNGE, Richard, 401
BOOTH, Albert, MP, 19
BORG, Bjorn, 443
BOSSANO, Joe, 166
BOTCHWAY, Kwesi, 220
BOTHA, Piet W., Prime Minister of South Africa, 252, 254
BOTSWANA, 248, 250
BOUABID, Abderrahim, 208
BOUABID, Maati, Prime Minister of Morocco, 208
BOULT, Sir Adrian, death, 401, 413; obit., 499
BOUMÉDIENNE, Houari, 207
BOURGUIBA, Habib, President of Tunisia, 205, 207
BOURGUIBA, Wasifa, 205
BOUTERSE, Desi, 98
BOVY, Vin, death, 401
BOWIE, David, 415
BOX, Sydney, death, 416
BOYCOTT, Geoffrey, 440
BOYD OF MERTON, Viscount, obit., 499
BRADBURY, Malcolm, 431
BRADY, Michael, 408
BRAHMS, Caryl, death, 403
BRANDT, Willy, 134, 136
BRAZIL, 74, 77–8; and Paraguay, 80; and Uruguay, 82; economy, 74, 77–8; political unrest, 77–8
BRENTON, Howard, 406
BRIGHT, Graham, 418
BRITISH INDIAN OCEAN TERRITORY, 273–4
BRITTAN, Leon, MP, 27, 29, 34, 418
BRITTEN, Benjamin, 412
BROOK, Peter, 407
BROOKNER, Anita, 432
BROOKS, James L., 416
BROWNE, Coral, 419
BRUHN, Erik, 402
BRÜLL, Maria, 359
BRUNEI, 280–1
BRYDEN, Bill, 404
BUHARI, Maj.-Gen. Muhammed, seizes power in Nigeria, 220–1
BUJAK, Zbigniew, 109–10
BULGARIA, 119–20; and assassination attempt on Pope, 120; and Comecon, 120; foreign affairs, 120; proposed nuclear-free zone, 120; social and economic issues, 120
BULLOCK, Lord (Alan), 432
BUÑUEL, Luis, death, 416; obit., 499
BURFORD, Anne, 55, 386
BURGER, Chief Justice Warren, 53–4
BURGESS, Anthony, 405
BURMA, 267, 276–7; and North Korea, 276; oil and gas, 277; Rangoon bombing, 276, 300, 301
BURNHAM, Forbes, Executive President of Guyana, 96
BURRELL, Sir William, 423
BURROUGH, Brian, 444
BURUNDI, 236
BURT, Richard, 168
BURY, John, 404
BUSH, George, 59; visits Europe, 116, 119, 137; visits North Africa, 207
BUTHELEZI, Chief Gatsha, 253
BUTTIGIEG, Dr Anton, obit., 499–500
BYRNE, John, 404

CACERES, Carlos, 78
CAINE, Michael, 416
CAIRNS, Lance, 440
CALDEIRA, Dr Winston, 98–9
CALDERA, Rafael, 83
CALLAGHAN, L. James, MP, 18, 24, 36
CALLEJA, Mgr Philip, 165
CALP, Necdet, 172–3
CALVI, Roberto, 42, 140
CAMBODIA, see Kampuchea
CAMEROON, 230
CAMPBELL, John, 432
CANADA, 69–73; and EEC, 347; architecture, 427; British Columbian election, 70; Cabinet shuffle, 70; constitutional measures, 71; economy, 71; foreign affairs, 71–3; legislation, 70–1; political parties, 69–70; relations with USA; 71–2television, 421
CAPE VERDE, 236
ČAPKA, Miroslav, 114
CAPOTORTI, Francesco, 390
CARIBBEAN, 88–99; map, 90
CARIBBEAN COMMUNITY (CARICOM), 91, 92, 364–5; Regional Energy Plan, 364; summit, Trinidad, 364
CARIBBEAN ORGANIZATIONS, 364–5
CARRINGTON, Lord, 39; becomes Secretary-General of Nato, 39, 332
CARTAGENA CONVENTION, 321
CARTER, Elliott, 410
CARTER, James E., 55, 86
CASTRO RUZ, Fidel, President of Cuba, 84, 367

CEAUŞESCU, Nicolae, President of Romania, 118, 119, 334
CELAURO, Dr Fulvio, 80
CENTRAL AFRICAN REPUBLIC, 232
CENTRAL AMERICA, 53, 62–5, 74, 85–7; map, 90; UN and, 318
CENTRAL AMERICAN DEFENCE COUNCIL (CONDECA), 86, 330
CHAD, 67, 131, 231–2, 235, 360, 362; civil war, 203, 231–2; reconciliation hopes, 232; UN and, 319
CHADHA, Jagdish, 54
CHADLI, Benjedid, President of Algeria, 131, 205, 206, 207, 208, 361
CHADLI, Mme, 207
CHAE HUI CHONG, 301
CHAMBERLAIN, Muriel, 434
CHAMBERLIN POWELL & BON, 426
CHAMBERS, George, Prime Minister of Trinidad and Tobago, 95
CHAMORRO, Edgar, 86
CHAN, Sir Julius, 307
CHAND, Lokendra Bahadur, Prime Minister of Nepal, 270
CHANDRASEKAR, Prof. Subramanyan, 383
CHARLES, Eugenia, Prime Minister of Barbados, 92
CHARLTON, Evan, obit., 500
CHAVES DE MENDONÇA, Aureliano, 77
CHAYNES, Charles, 400
CHEBRIKOV, V. M., 101
CHEN MUHUA, 272, 294
CHÉREAU, Patrice, 399
CHERNENKO, Konstantin, 100
CHERVENKOV, Valko, 120
CHESTER, Sir Norman, 438
CHEVALLAZ, George-André, 157
CHÉVÈNEMENT, Jean-Pierre, 127, 128
CHEYSSON, Claude, 131, 132, 311, 350
CHIDZERO, Dr Bernard, 247
CHILE, 74, 78–9; economy, 78; political unrest, 78–9
CHIN-A-SEN, Henck, 98
CHIN PENG, 280
CHINA, PEOPLE'S REPUBLIC OF, 38, 282, 289–94; agriculture, 289–90; economy, 289–91; foreign policy and visitors, 293–4; foreign trade, 291; ideological campaign, 291–2; oil, 291; population, 290, 292; Sino-British talks on Hong Kong, 288, 293, 296; RELATIONS WITH: Albania, 124, 294; Angola, 294; Antigua and Barbuda, 294; EEC, 291; India, 262, 294; Ivory Coast, 294; Japan, 291, 293, 299; Lesotho, 294; Mongolia, 125; Pakistan, 265; South Korea, 294; Taiwan, 293, 294, 295–6; Thailand, 277; USA, 67–8, 291, 293; USSR, 103, 293; Yugoslavia, 121; Zaïre, 235; Zimbabwe, 248
CHINA, REPUBLIC OF, see Taiwan

CHIRAC, Jacques, 127
CHIRWA, Orton, 245
CHIRWA, Vera, 245
CHITTY, Alison, 404
CHOWDHURY, Mahabbat Jan, 266
CHUN DOO HWAN, President of South Korea, 276, 300, 301
CHURCHILL, Caryl, 407
CINEMA, 413–16
CITRINE, Lord, obit., 500
CLANCY, Deirdre, 404
CLARK, Barney, 382
CLARK, Jeffrey, 428
CLARK, Joe, 70
CLARK, Lord (Kenneth Clark), obit., 500
CLARK, William, 55, 386
CLAUDE, Marie-France, 85
CLAUDE, Sylvio, 85
CLERIDES, Glafkos, 170
CLIFFORD, Graeme, 415
CLUSKEY, Frank, 146
COARD, Bernard, 84, 91, 93
COATES, Edith, death, 401
COE, Sebastian, 439
COETZEE, J. M., 431
COGAN, Marshall, 422
COGHLAN, Eamon, 148
COHEN-ORGAD, Yigal, 175
COLLEY, George, death, 148
COLLIER, Lesley, 401
COLOMBIA, 74, 79–80, 366; domestic violence, 79
COLOMBO, Emilio, 139
COLVILLE OF CULROSS, Viscount, 323
COMECON, 356–9; and EEC, 359; and IMF, 358–9; balance of payments, 358; Bulgaria and, 120; Ethiopia and, 211; International Bank for Economic Cooperation, 359; political statement, 357; programmes approved, 358; railway system improvements, 356–7; science and technology, 359; Soviet policy, 357–8
COMMONWEALTH, 324–6; Commonwealth Day stamps, 326; Commonwealth Foundation, 326; heads of government meeting, New Delhi, see Commonwealth Conference; Queen's visits within, 214, 326; specialist and regional meetings, 326
COMMONWEALTH CONFERENCE, 262, 267, 310, 324–6; communique, (extracts) 481–2; Diego Garcia issue, 273–4; economic issues, 325; Goa Declaration, 325, (text) 480–1; New Delhi Statement, 325; political issues, 324–5; pro-Arab declaration blocked, 178; small-nation security, 271, 482
COMORO STATE, 275
COMPTON, J. G. M., Prime Minister of St Lucia, 202

524 INDEX

CONGO, PEOPLE'S REPUBLIC OF, 232
CONNERY, Sean, 414
CONNORS, Jimmy, 443
CONTADORA GROUP, 64–5, 74, 80, 86, 318, 365
CONYNGHAM, Greg, 428
COOK, Robin, MP, 43
COOK ISLANDS, 312, 313
COOKE, Cardinal Terence, obit., 500
COOPER, Douglas, 425
COPPOLA, Francis Ford, 415
CORDOVEZ, Diego, 317
CORN, Wanda M., 425
COSTA RICA, 87; economy, 74, 87; US and, 63, 64, 65
COUNCIL OF EUROPE, 349–50; and Argentina, 349; and Middle East, 349; and Turkey, 349; conference on parliamentary democracy, 349–50; European unity, 350
COUNCIL OF THE ENTENTE, 228
COX, Michael, 433
CRABBE, Mr Justice Azu, 220
CRAM, Steve, 439
CRANKO, John, 402
CRANSTON, Senator Alan, 56
CRANSTON, Maurice, 433
CRAXI, Bettino, Prime Minister of Italy, 138, 139, 141, 341
CRESPO, Prof. Vitor Pereira, 163
CRISTINA, Orlando, assassination, 238
CROSS, Mr Justice Ulric, 326
CROWLEY, Bob, 404
CUBA, 74, 83–4, 312; and Angola, 241; and Suriname, 98; and US/Grenada, 84, 91, 93; defence, 84; economy, 83–4
CUKOR, George, death, 416; obit., 500
CURREN, Kevin, 443
CYPRUS, 169–71; and Middle East, 171; economy, 171; presidential election, 169–70; Turkish-Cypriot declaration of independence, 40, 168, 171, 174; UN and, 169–71, 314, 318–19
CZECHOSLOVAKIA, 112–14; and USSR, 113, 114; Charter 77 movement, 113; Communist Party developments, 113–14; economy, 114; Soviet missiles, 112–13; suppression of dissent, 113

DABENGWA, Dumiso, 246
DALYELL, Tam, MP, 37
DANCHEV, Vladimir, 420
DANKERT, Piet, President of European Parliament, 344
DANIELS, Sarah, 406
DART, Paul, 404
DASCALESCU, Constantin, Prime Minister of Romania, 358
D'AUBUISSON, Maj. Robert, 85

DAVIES, Denzil, MP, 23
DAVIES, Maxwell, 409, 410
DAVIGNON, Viscount Etienne, 342, 347
DAVIS, Sir Thomas, Premier of Cook Islands, 313
DAY, Sir Robin, 419
DEAN, Christopher, 445
DEBREU, Prof. Gerard, 451
DEBT PROBLEMS, 74, 314, 321, 446–8; Antigua, 94; Argentina, 75; Bolivia, 76; Brazil, 74, 77–8, 446–8; Chile, 78; Costa Rica, 87; Cuba, 84; Dominica, 94; Ecuador, 80; Guyana, 96; Hungary, 115; Israel, 175; Jamaica, 88–9; Kenya, 215; Liberia, 224; Mauritius, 273; Mexico, 74, 87, 446–8; Morocco, 209; New Zealand, 308; Nigeria, 221; Peru, 81; Philippines, 284; Poland, 111; Portugal, 163, 164; St Kitts-Nevis, 94; Sudan, 202; Tanzania, 216; Trinidad and Tobago, 95; Venezuela, 83; Vietnam, 285; Yugoslavia, 121; Zaïre, 235; Zambia, 243
DECKER, Mary, 439
DEFENCE ORGANIZATIONS AND DEVELOPMENTS, 327–40; arms control negotiations, 335–8; Conference on Disarmament in Europe (CDE), proposed, 338, 340; Conference on Security and Cooperation in Europe, Madrid, 119, 123, 165, 338–40; conventional forces reduction talks, Vienna, 335; expenditure, 472; INF (intermediate nuclear forces) talks, Geneva, 331, 332, 333, 335–8; mutual and balanced force reductions, 335; START talks, Geneva, 58–9, 61–2, 103, 118, 131, 152, 332, 335–8; US-Japanese cooperation, 327; *see also* Nato; Nuclear Arms; Warsaw Treaty Organization;
PERSONAL INITIATIVES: Mr Andropov, 102–3; President Castro, 84; President Ceauşescu, 118; President Reagan, 61, 102; Mr Trudeau, 72–3;
REGIONAL INITIATIVES: Balkan nuclear-free zone proposal, 120, 123, 168; Caribbean Joint Defence Force, 93; Central American Defence Council, 86, 330; Contadora Group, 64–5, 75, 80, 86, 318, 365; Gulf Cooperation Council, 198–9; Indian Ocean peace zone proposals, 270–1, 273; Nordic nuclear-free zone proposal, 356; North Atlantic Assembly, 351–2; South Pacific nuclear weapon-free zone proposal, 311–12; Warsaw Pact, 102; Western European Union, 350–1
DE FUNES, Louis, death, 416
DE HAAN, Ben, 444
DEIGHTON, Len, 432
DEILMANN, Harald, 427
DEJID, Bugyn, 125

DE LA ESPRIELLA, Ricardo, President of Panama, 87
DE LA GUARDIA, Ernesto, obit., 500
DELAMURAZ, Jean-Pascal, 157–8
DE LA TOUR, Frances, 406
DE L'ESTRAC, Jean Claude, 272
DELFIM NETTO, Prof. Antônio, 77
DELORS, Jacques, 127
DEL RIO, Dolores, death, 416
DEMIREL, Süleyman, 172, 173
DE MITA, Ciriaco, 138
DEMPSEY, Jack, obit., 500–1
DENBY, Edwin, death, 403
DENCH, Judi, 406
DENG YINGCHAO, 293
DENG XIAOPING, 291–2, 293, 296
DE NIRO Robert, 414
DENKTASH, Rauf, 168, 170–1, 319
DENMARK, 148–9; and EEC fisheries policy, 38, 149; economy, 148; foreign affairs, 149; Greenland, 149, 346; resignation of Government, 149
DENNIS, Lieut.-Col. Ekow, 219
DENNIS, Michael, 428
DENTON, Steve, 443
DE POI, Alfredo, President of WEU Assembly, 351
DE SAINT PHALLE, Niki, 424
DE SAINT PHALLE, Tinguely, 424
DE VALOIS, Dame Ninette, 403
DE VOS, Audrey, death, 403
DHLAKAMA, Afonso, 238
DÍAZ BRUZUAL, Leopoldo, 83
DÍAZ SERRANO, Jorge, 88
DICKINSON, Michael, 445
DIKE, Prof. Kenneth Onwuka, death, 222; obit., 501
DIKEBIE, Pascal N'guessan, 227
DINKERLOO, John, 428
DIOP, Cheikh Anta, 226
DIOUF, Abdou, President of Senegal, 225–6, 227, 361
DIRO, Ted, 307
DISARMAMENT, *see* Defence Organizations *and* Nuclear Arms
DJIBOUTI, 213
DLAMINI, James, 251
DLIMI, General Ahmad, death, 208
DOE, General Samuel, head of state of Liberia, 223, 224
DOHERTY, Sean, 146
D'OKWATSEGUÉ, Paul Okoumba, 361
DOLDAN, Senator Enzo, 80
DOLE, Elizabeth, 55
DOLIN, Sir Anton, death, 403; obit., 501
DOMINICA, 93, 94
DOMINICAN REPUBLIC, 84
DONALDSON, Sir John, MR, 394, 396, 398
DONNER, Prof. Andreas, 392
DOOLITTLE, Dr Russell, 381
DORTICO, Torrado Osvaldo, obit., 501

DOS SANTOS, Eduardo, President of Angola, 240
DOWELL, Anthony, 401
DOWN/ARCHAMBAULT, 428
DRUCKMAN, Rabbi Haim, 371
DRUCKMANN, Jacob, 411
DRUMMOND, John, 44, 409
DUBAI, *see under* United Arab Emirates
DUCLERVILLE, Gerard, 85
DUDLEY, William, 399, 404
DUFF, Sir Antony, 36
DUFFY, Maureen, 432
DUGERSUREN, Mangalyn, 125
DUKES, Alan, 145
DU MAURIER, Daphne, 400
DUMBUTSHENA, Mr Justice Enoch, 247
DUNWOODY, Gwyneth, MP, 23
DURANG, Christopher, 408
DURRELL, Lawrence, 431
DUVALIER, Jean-Claude, President of Haiti, 85
DYER, Charles, 406
DYER, Chris, 404
DZANDU, Johnny, 220
DZELIWE, ex-Queen Regent of Swaziland, 251

EEC, *see* European Economic Community
EANES, Antonio, President of Portugal, 163
ECEVIT, Bülent, 172
ECO, Umberto, 432
ECONOMIC COMMUNITY OF AFRICAN STATES 362
ECONOMIC COMMUNITY OF WEST AFRICAN STATES, 227, 360, 362
ECONOMIC AND SOCIAL AFFAIRS, 322–4, 446–56 (*see alo under* country headings *and* Debt Problems); alcoholism, 243, 324; capital markets, 450, 472; cocoa prices, 220; copper prices, 243; drug problems, 97–8, 147, 276, 277, 301, 322; famine and relief works, 210–11, 217, 229, 237, 255, 286, 323–4, 385; financial market crises, 175–6, 197–8, 288; gold price, 77; human rights, 322–3, 389; inflation, 449, 471; monetary and fiscal policies, 450–1, 471; oil prices, 80, 83, 87–8, 193, 196, 208, 221, 446, 450; output, 448–9, 469; protectionism, 391–2, 448; racism, 323; refugees, 324; statistical data, 457–72; third-world poverty, 77, 229, 233, 314, 324; UK economy, 453–6, 458–65; US economy, 451–3, 466–8; unemployment, 449, 472; world trade, 450, 470
ECUADOR, 80
EDA-PIERRE, Christiane, 400
EDGAR, Bruce, 439
EDGAR, David, 404–5
EDWARDS, Nicholas, MP, 45
EGK, Werner, death, 401

EGYPT, 181–3, 201, 202; economy, 182–3; Egyptian-Sudanese assembly, 182; internal politics, 182; relations with: Israel, 178, 181; Non-Aligned Movement, 366; other Arab states, 181–2, 184; Soviet bloc, 182; USA, 181
EHRMANN, John, 434
EISEMAN/ROBERTSON ASSOCIATION, 428
EITAN, Raphael, 176
EITNER, Prof. Lorenz, 425
EL SALVADOR, 85–6; Dr Kissinger visits, 65; US and, 53, 63–4, 74, 84
ELIZABETH II, HM Queen: Christmas Day broadcast, 324, 326; Commonwealth Day broadcast, 326; Commonwealth visits, 214, 326; visit to Mexico, 87
ELLIOTT, Michael, 406
ENDERS, Thomas, 64, 85
ENNALS, David, MP, 19
ENVIRONMENT, 320–1, 383–7; acid rain, 383–4; drought and floods, 384–5; greenhouse effect, 379; lead in petrol, 10, 386; marine oil pollution, 385–6; 'nuclear winter', 387; radioactive pollution, 384
EPTON, Bernard, 56
EQUATORIAL GUINEA, 233
ERSHAD, General H.M., Chief Martial Law Administrator of Bangladesh, 266–8
ETHIOPIA, 201, 210–12; and Soviet bloc, 211–12; economy, 211–12; famine, 210–11
EUROPEAN COMMUNITY LAW, 348, 389–93; alcoholic drinks, 391–2; antitrust law, 392–3; Community Budget, 390; Court of Justice decisions, 390; implications of enlargement of Community, 389; regulations enacted, 393; rights of Greek nationals, 392
EUROPEAN ECONOMIC COMMUNITY (EEC), 340–8;
EXTERNAL AFFAIRS, 342–4; ACP countries, 343; Andean Pact, 343; Canada, 347; Efta, 343, 352; Ethiopia, 210–11; Euro-Arab dialogue, 343; Hungary, 359; Israel, 178, 299, 342; the Maghreb, 205; Norway, 347; Portugal, 341, 346; South Pacific Forum, 311; Spain, 162, 166, 341, 346; Suriname, 99; USA, 342–3; USSR, 343; Yugoslavia, 121;
INTERNAL AFFAIRS: Athens summit, 137, 147, 167, 341; Budget, 38–9, 341, 344–5; Common Agricultural Policy, 38, 341, 345, 346–7; Councils, 342; dairy products surplus, 346; Denmark, 38, 149; economic and monetary policy, 348; economic performance, 341–2; European Strategic Programme for Research and Information Technology (ESPRIT), 347; fisheries, 38, 347; Foreign Ministers' conference, 167; Greece, 167, 345; Greenland, 346; investment instrument, 348; Northern Ireland, 48–9; steel, 347–8; UK, 38–9, 341; UK Labour Party, 12, 18; unemployment, 348; VAT, 344, 345, 390, 392
EUROPEAN FREE TRADE ASSOCIATION (Efta), 352–3; and EEC, 343, 352; and Yugoslavia, 353; Finland, 352; Portugal, 352; unemployment, 353
EUROPEAN MONETARY SYSTEM (EMS), 142, 348
EUROPEAN PARLIAMENT: accuses Malta of infringement of civil liberties, 165; and famine relief for Ethiopia, 211; blocks Budget relief to UK and West Germany, 342; 344; location of meetings, 392; resolution on missile deployment, 345; role and powers, 345–6
EUROPEAN SPACE AGENCY, 57, 377
EVANS, Daniel, 56
EVREN, Kenan, President of Turkey, 173
EYANG, Lieut. Pablo Obama, 233
EYRE, Richard, 415

FADDEEV, Nikolai, 357
FAGAN, Michael, 394
FAHD, HM King, of Saudi Arabia, 192
FAHNBULLEH, Henry, 225
FALDO, Nick, 441
FALKLAND ISLANDS: defence, 37–8; rehabilitation and development, 37; sovereignty, 38, 319
FANFANI, Amintore, 138
FASHION, 429–30
FASKEL, Bernd, 427
FASSBINDER, Rainer Werner, 415, 416
FELDSTEIN, Martin, 453
FELDT, Kjell-Olof, 355
FELEKE GEDLE-GIYORGIS, 210
FERNÁNDEZ MARMOL, Manuel, death, 84
FERRI, Alessandra, 401
FIGES, Eva, 432
FIGUEIREDO, João Batista, President of Brazil, 77–8
FIJI, 312
FIKRE-SELASSIE WOGDERESS, Captain, 210
FILLIOUD, Georges, 420
FINLAND, 154–5; and Efta, 352; and USSR, 155; Budget, 155; election, 154
FISHLOCK, Trevor, 266
FITT, Gerry, MP (*later* Lord Fitt), 19, 22, 48
FITZGERALD, Dr Garret, Prime Minister of Republic of Ireland, 41, 145–7
FITZGIBBON, Constantine, death, 434; obit., 501
FITZHERBERT, Margaret, 433
FLEMING, Peter, 443
FLEMING, Tom, 419
FLORIJANČIČ, Jože, 122

FODOR, Antal, 402
FONTANNE, Lynn, obit., 501
FOOT, Michael, MP, 8-9, 11, 14, 17, 18, 20, 22, 24, 28; resigns as Labour leader, 22
FORD, Anna, 416
FORSYTH, Bill, 416
FOSTER, Neil, 440
FOSTER, Norman, 427
FOWLER, Prof. William, 383
FOWLES, John, 406
FRANCE, 127-33; ARTS: architecture, 426-7; art, 424; television, 130, 420; DEFENCE AND FOREIGN AFFAIRS: Africa, 131, 229, 231-2, 233, 249; expulsion of Soviet diplomats, 131; Iran/Iraq war, 190, 256-7; Lebanon, 131-2; military programme, 132; Nato, 130, 131; New Caledonia, 312; nuclear policy, 131, 132, 350; nuclear testing in Pacific, 310-11; relations with: USA, 130-1; USSR, 131; West Germany, 130; HOME AFFAIRS: administrative reform, 129-30; austerity programme, 127-8, 129; Budget, 129; devaluation, 128; immigration, as issue, 129, 131; inflation, 127; municipal elections, 127; political and industrial unrest, 128, 129; terrorist activity, 128-9, 132; unemployment, 129; OVERSEAS DEPARTMENTS AND TERRITORIES: decentralization policy, 132; violence, 132-3
FRANCO-AFRICAN SUMMIT, 229
FRANKENTHALER, Helen, 424
FRANKS, Lord, 35
FRASER, Malcolm, Prime Minister of Australia, electoral defeat, 302-3
FRAYN, Michael, 409
FREARS, Stephen, 416
FRIEDRICH, Götz, 409
FRISCHENSCHLÄGER, Friedhelm, 156
FROST, David, 416
FRY, Christopher, 406
FUGARD, Athol, 404
FUKUDA, Takeo, 297
FULFORD, Sir Roger, death, 434
FULLER, John, 431
FULLER, Dr R. Buckminster, death, 429; obit., 501-2
FURGLER, Kurt, 158

GABON, 232
GADAFI, see Qadafi
GALEA, Louis, 165
GALLAGHER, Bernard, 440
GALLINARI, Prospero, 140
GALMAN, Rolando, 284
GAMBIA, THE, 223-4; by elections, 224; economy, 223-4
GANDHI, Indira, Prime Minister of India, 260-1, 262, 264, 268, 314, 324, 366, 367
GANDHI, Maneka, 262

GANDHI, Rajiv, 261, 262
GANDHI, Sanjay, 262
GANTT, Harvey, 56
GARCIA, General José Guillermo, 85
GARCIA MEZA TESADA, Luis, 76
GASKILL, William, 405
GÁSPÁR, Sándor, 117
GASSON, Barry, 423, 426
GAVASKAR, Sunil, 439
GEMAYEL, Amin, President of Lebanon, 39, 67, 188, 203; visits to Washington, 189
GENERAL AGREEMENT ON TARIFFS AND TRADE (GATT), see under United Nations
GENSCHER, Hans-Dietrich, 135, 137, 344
GEORGIADIS, Nicholas, 401
GERE, Richard, 415
GERHARDT, Commodore Dieter, 255
GERHARDT, Ruth, 255
GERMAN DEMOCRATIC REPUBLIC, 107-9; and West Germany, 107-8; economy, 107; politics, 108; Martin Luther celebrations, 109
GERMANY, FEDERAL REPUBLIC OF, 133-8; DEFENCE AND FOREIGN AFFAIRS: acceptance of US nuclear missiles, 103, 107, 108, 134; relations with: East Germany, 107-8; France, 130; USA, 136-7; USSR, 136-7; SPD opposition to nuclear missile deployment, 136; HOME AFFAIRS: architecture, 427; art, 424-5; Budget, 136; Cabinet posts, 134-5; economy, 135-6; general election, 102, 133-4; Green Party wins Bundestag seats, 133-4; law and order, 135; new identity cards, 135; reunification question, 137; television, 420; unemployment, 136
GERSHWIN, Ira, obit., 502
GHANA, 219-20, 225; attempted coup, 219; coup-related judgments, 219-20; economy, 220
GHANI, Abdul Aziz Abdul, 194
GHAZALIE SHAFIE, Tan Sri, 280
GIBRALTAR, 38, 162, 166
GIELGUD, Maina, 402
GILBERT, Lewis, 416
GILL, Peter, 404
GILPIN, John, death, 403; obit., 502
GINASTERA, Alberto, death, 401
GLEMP, HE Cardinal Josef, 110, 112, 370
GLEN, John, 414
GLENDINNING, Victoria, 433
GLENN, Senator John, 56
GLISTRUP, Mogens, 149
GLOCK, William, 410
GODARD, Jean-Luc, 416
GOEHR, Alexander, 409
GOH KENG-SWEE, Dr, 281
GOLDING, William, 430

GONZÁLEZ, Felipe, Prime Minister of Spain, 159, 162, 209, 338
GOODE, Wilson, 56
GOODWIN, John, 433
GOONEWARDENA, Leslie, death, 269
GORBACHEV, M. S., 101, 105
GOSHU WOLDE, Colonel, 210
GOULD, Tony, 433
GOWON, General Yakubu, 223
GOWRIE, Earl of, 421
GRADOS BERTORINI, Alfonso, 81, 82
GRAHAM, Alastair, 33
GRAMM, Donald, death, 401
GRANT, Alexander, 402
GRAVES, Michael, 428
GRAY, Hamish, MP, 43
GRAY, Simon, 409
GREECE, 167–9; and EEC, 167, 345; and Middle East, 168; and Turkey, 167–8, 174; economy, 168–9; relations with Eastern Europe, 119, 120, 168; requests return of Elgin Marbles, 169; US bases, 167, 332
GRENADA, 91–3; American invasion, 1–2, 39–40, 51, 62–3, 72, 74, 84, 87, 91, 92–3, 103, 130–1, 137, 162, 310, 365; Cuba and, 84, 91, 93; economy, 91; map, 90; political unrest, 91–2; UN and, 63, 318
GREY, Robert, 55
GRIFFIN, Hayden, 404
GRIFFITHS, Richard, 405
GRIGOROVICH, Yuri, 402
GRIMOND, Jo, MP (*later* Lord Grimond), 15, 22
GROMYKO, Andrei, 61, 102, 131, 136
GROVE, Brandon, 200
GRUENTHER, General Alfred M., obit., 502
GUATEMALA, 65, 86
GUINEA, 226–7
GUINEA-BISSAU, 236
GULF COOPERATION COUNCIL (GCC), 198–9
GULF STATES, ARAB, 186, 195–200; *see also individual countries and* Oil
GULLIKSON, Tom and Tim, 443
GUMMER, John Selwyn, MP, 26
GUNTER, John, 404, 406
GUYANA, 92, 96

HAAGERUP, Niels, 48
HABBASH, George, 180
HABIB, Philip, 66, 187
HABRÉ, Hissène, President of Chad, 67, 231–2, 319
HABYALIMANA, Juvenal, President of Rwanda, 236
HACKFORD, Taylor, 415
HACKMAN, Gene, 415
HADLEE, Richard, 440
HAFERKAMP, Wilhelm, 342, 359
HAIDALLAH, Ould, 207
HAILSHAM, Lord, 21, 372
HAITI, 84–5
HALEFOGLU, Vahit, 173
HALL, Sir Peter, 404, 433–4
HALLGRÍMSSON, Geir, 150
HAMAD, A.Y. al-, 197
HAMILTON, Ian, 433
HAMILTON, Nigel, 433
HAMLISCH, Marvin, 403
HAMPTON, Christopher, 404
HANDS, Terry, 405
HARALAMBOPOULOS, Yannis, 167, 168
HARE, David, 404
HARE, W. H. (Dusty), 442
HARRIMAN, Averell, 102
HARRISON, Rex, 409
HART, Evelyn, 402
HART, Senator Gary, 56
HASBIU, Kadri, 123
HASSAN, HM King, of Morocco, 203, 206, 207, 208–9
HASSAN, Sir Joshua, 166
HASSAN AL SHAER, General Ali, 193
HATTERSLEY, Roy, MP, 22–4, 31
HAUGHEY, Charles, 146
HAVASI, Ferenc, 115
HAWATMEH, Naif, 180
HAWKE, R. G. (Bob), Prime Minister of Australia, 178, 302–5, 306
HAWN, Goldie, 414
HAYDEN, Bill, 303, 306
HEAD, Criquette, 444
HEAD, Freddie, 444
HEADLEY, George, obit., 502
HEALEY, Denis, MP, 17, 18, 23, 24, 37, 39, 40
HEARN, George, 407
HECKLER, Margaret, 55
HEFFER, Eric, MP, 23
HEIM, Archbishop Bruno, 369
HELLEINER, Prof. Gerald K., 325
HENDERSON, Sir Nicholas, 37
HENRY, Geoffrey, 313
HENZE, Hans Werner, 400
HERAT, Sirisena B., death, 269
HERMAN, Jerry, 407
HERMANNSSON, Steingrímur, 150
HERNU, Charles, 130
HERRERA CAMPINS, Luis, President of Venezuela, 83
HERSANT, Robert, 130
HERZOG, Chaim, President of Israel, 177
HESELTINE, Michael, MP, 10, 14, 18, 21, 41, 369
HIBBARD, Howard, 426
HICKS, Grant, 404
HILL, George Roy, 414
HILLERY, Patrick, President of Republic of Ireland, 148
HINGLEY, Ronald, 433

INDEX 529

HINTON OF BANKSIDE, Lord, obit., 502
HOCKNEY, David, 424
HODGE, Patricia, 416
HOFFMAN, Dustin, 414
HOLLEIN, Hans, 427
HOLLINGS, Senator Fritz, 56
HOLYOAKE, Sir Keith J., death, 311; obit., 502–3
HON SUI-SEN, death, 281
HONDURAS, 86; USA and, 63, 64, 65, 74, 84, 86
HONECKER, Erich, 107, 108, 109
HONG KONG, 38, 287–9; and China, 287–8; economy, 38, 288; property and industry, 289; Sino-British talks, 288, 293, 296
HOOPER, Alan, death, 403
HORB, Major Roy, 98
HORDERN, Sir Michael, 406
HOŘENÍ, Zdeněk, 114
HOUPHOUET-BOIGNY, Félix, President of Ivory Coast, 220, 227–8
HOWE, Sir Geoffrey, MP, 7, 21, 40, 453, 454
HOWE, Tina, 408
HOWELL, David, MP, 10, 21
HOWELLS, Dr Herbert, death, 413; obit., 503
HOXHA, Enver, 123, 124
HU NA, 68, 293
HU YAOBANG, 121, 293, 294, 299
HUBACHER, Helmut, 157
HUBBARD, John, 424
HŮLA, Václav, 113
HUME, HE Cardinal Basil, 13, 369; article on nuclear arms in *The Times*, (text) 479–80
HUME, John, 48
HUNGARY, 115–17; economy, 115, 358; electoral reform, 116; National Ballet, 402; politics, 115–16; relations with: EEC, 359; Romania, 116, 119; USA, 116; USSR, 116
HURTADO LARREA, Oswaldo, President of Ecuador, 80
HUSAIN, HM King, of Jordan, 66, 179, 182, 185; and Yassir Arafat, 183–4; and President Reagan, 183; visit to China, 294; visit to London, 184
HUSAIN, Saddam, President of Iraq, 190, 191
HUSSEIN, Hamzah Abbas, 197
HYTNER, Nicholas, 399

ICELAND, 150–1; economy, 150–1; election and electoral reform, 150
IDRIS I, former King of Libya, obit., 503
ILLIA, Dr Arturo, obit., 503
ILLUECA, Jorge, 314
INDIA, 120, 260–3, 267; Aid-India Consortium, 263; cinema, 413–14; economy, 263; elections, 260–1; ethnic conflict, 261–2; foreign relations and trade, 262, 263; oil, 263; relations with: China, 262, 294; Pakistan, 262, 263–4; Sri Lanka, 268; television, 421; World Cup (cricket) won, 439
INDONESIA, 68, 282–3; and Australia, 282; and PNG, 307; East Timor, 282; economy, 282–3; oil, 283; presidential election, 282
İNÖNÜ, Prof. Erdal, 172
INTERNATIONAL ENERGY AGENCY, 354
INTERNATIONAL LAW, 388–93; Andean Court of Justice established, 389; European Community Law (*q.v.*), 348, 389–93; European Court of Human Rights, 389; International Court of Justice, 388–9; land and sea frontier disputes, 388–9; Law of the Sea Convention, 321, 351, 367, 388; Vienna Convention on Succession of States, 389
INTERNATIONAL MONETARY FUND (IMF), 37, 53, 76, 83, 93, 96, 182, 202, 216, 218, 220, 221, 266, 310, 321, 358–9, 447–8; BORROWERS: Argentina, 75; Barbados, 97; Brazil, 78; Chile, 78; Ecuador, 80; Grenada, 91; India, 263; Jamaica, 89; Mauritius, 272; Morocco, 209; Peru, 81; Philippines, 284; Portugal, 163, 164; Sierra Leone, 223; South Korea, 301; Western Samoa, 312; Yugoslavia, 121; Zaïre, 235; Zambia, 243; Zimbabwe, 247
INTERNATIONAL RED CROSS, 217, 366
IRAN, 185, 186, 223, 256–8; and Lebanon, 186; and PDRY, 195; economy, 257–8; foreign relations, 257; Kurds, 257; oil, 258; UN and, 317–18; war with Iraq, 190–1, 192, 198–9, 256–7
IRAQ, 174, 181, 184, 186, 190–1; economy, 191; Kurds, 191; oil, 191; UN and, 317–18; war with Iran, 190–1, 192, 198–9, 256–7
IRELAND, REPUBLIC OF, 145–8; abortion amendment, 147, 369; and UK, 41–2, 146–7; cinema studios closure, 413; drug problem, 147; economy, 145, 147–8; New Ireland Forum, 48, 147; oil, 148; telephone-tapping scandal, 146; theft of racehorse Shergar, 147, 444; violence, 147
IRONS, Jeremy, 416
IRYANI, Abdul Karim al-, 194
ISAACS, Jeremy, 417
ISKANDER, Ahmad, death, 186
ISLAM AND ISLAMIC MOVEMENTS: Algeria, 207–8; architecture, 429; China, 372; fundamentalism, 371; Indonesia, 282; Iran, 257, 372; Iraq, 257; Islamic Conference, 257, 267; Lebanon, 187; Mecca and Medina pilgrimage, 194;

Pakistan, 265; Sudan, 201, 372; Syria, 185–6; Tunisia, 204; UK, 372; Yugoslavia, 372
ISRAEL, 168, 175–8, 225; Beirut massacre enquiry, 176; finance and economy, 175–6; Israeli-Lebanese security pact, 176, 187, 189; Jerusalem disturbances, 178; Lebanon incursion, 176–7, 186; peace movement, 177; relations with: Egypt, 178, 181; Kenya, 215; UK, 178; UN, 315; USA, 1, 65, 67, 103, 178; West Bank settlements, 177–8, 315
ITALY, 138–41; austerity programme, 138, 139; Banco Ambrosiano, 140; corruption scandals, 139; economy, 139, 140; foreign aid, 213; general election, 138–9; law and order, 139–40; terrorist trials, 140; US nuclear missiles, 141
IVORY COAST, 219, 220, 227–8, 229; and China, 294
IZAGUIRRE, Maritza, 83

JACKLIN, Tony, 440
JACKSON, Glenda, 406
JACKSON, Senator H. M., obit., 503
JACKSON, Rev Jesse, 56
JACOBI, Derek, 405
JAEGER, Andrea, 443
JAKOBSEN, J. J., 151
JALAN-AAJAV, Sampiliyn, 125
JAMAICA, 88–9, 92
JAMAL, Amir, 215
JAMES, Carwyn, death, 442
JAMES, Emrys, 405
JAPAN, 258, 265, 296–300; election, 298; economy, 299–300; influence of Mr Tanaka, 296–8; overseas broadcasting, 421; relations with: China, 291, 293, 299; EEC, 299, 342; USA, 68, 297, 299
JARUZELSKI, General Wojciech, 103, 109–12, 370
JÄRVEFELT, Göran, 399
JAWARA, Sir Dawda, President of The Gambia, 223
JAY, Peter, 416–7
JAYAWARDENE, J. R., President of Sri Lanka, 268
JELLICOE, Earl, 265
JENKIN, Patrick, MP, 30
JENKINS, Roy, MP, 14, 18–19; resigns as SDP leader, 22
JEWISON, Norman, 414
JEYARATNAM, J. B., 281
JIANG QING, 293
JOANA, Monja, 274
JOANNIDES, Paul, 425
JOHN PAUL II, HH Pope, 124; attempt to assassinate, 120; Soviet attacks on, 334; visits to Austria, 156; Central America, 85, 86; Poland, 110–11
JOHNSON, Dr de Graft, 220

JOHNSON, Frank, death, 66
JONATHAN, Chief Leabua, Prime Minister of Lesotho, 250
JONES, Barry, MP, 45
JONES, Bob, 310
JONES, Colin, 46
JONES, David, 416
JONES, Roger, 426
JOPLING, Michael, MP, 22
JORDAN, 182, 183–4, 203; half-Palestinian Parliament, 184
JORGE BLANCO, Dr Salvador, President of Dominican Republic, 84
JØRGENSEN, Anker, 355
JOSEPH, Sir Keith, MP, 21
JOSEPHS, Wilfred, 400
JUAN CARLOS I, HM King, of Spain, 207, 424
JUGNAUTH, Aneerood, Prime Minister of Mauritius, 273–4
JUMBE, Aboud, President of Zanzibar, 217
JUMBLATT, Walid, 187
JUSU-SHERIFF, Salia, 223

KÁDÁR, János, 115, 116
KADZAMIRE, Cecilia, 244
KAHN, Herman, obit., 503
KAMPUCHEA, 286, 362–4; Khmer Rouge, 286; resistance to Vietnam, 277, 286; UN and, 277, 319–20
KANG NING-HSIANG, 295
KANG YANG UK, death, 301
KANO, Alhaji Aminu, death, 222
KARADUMAN, Necmettin, 173
KARAMANLIS, Constantine, President of Greece, 167, 168
KARJALAINEN, Ahti, 155
KARMAL, Babrak, President of Afghanistan, 259–60
KAUFMAN, Gerald, MP, 10, 41
KAUNDA, Kenneth, President of Zambia, 242
KAYLOR, Robert, 415
KEAYS, Sarah, 26–7
KEDROVA, Lila, 408
KEE, Robert, 416
KEITA, Dr Balla, 227
KENNEDY, Donald, 387
KENT, Mgr Bruce, 13, 368–9
KENYA, 213–15; and Israel, 215; assets of East African Community, 214; economy, 215; relations with: Tanzania and Uganda, 214–15; UK, 213–14; security, 213
KÉRÉKOU, Mathieu, President of Benin, 228
KERSCHNER, Irving, 414
KHALIFA, Shaikh Ali, 196
KHALIFAH, Shaikh Isa bin Sulman al-, 199
KHAN, Yaqub, 265

INDEX 531

KHOMEINI, Ayatollah Ruhollah, 203, 257, 371
KIBAKI, Mwai, 214
KILFEDDER, Jim, 48
KILLEK, Teddy, 178
KIM CHONG IL, 301
KIM DAE JUNG, 300
KIM HWAN, 301
KIM IL SUNG, President of North Korea, 301
KIM YOUNG SAM, 301
KIMCHE, David, 168
KING, Billie Jean, 443
KING, Tom, MP, 10
KINGSLEY, Ben, 416
KINNOCK, Neil, MP, 18, 37, 45; and NGA dispute, 34; becomes Labour leader, 23-4
KINSKI, Nastassia, 415
KIRCHSCHLÄGER, Dr Rudolf, President of Austria, 156
KIRIBATI, 312
KIRK, Norman J., 310
KISELEV, T. Ya., 100
KISSINGER, Dr Henry, Central America commission, 64-5
KITSON, Alex, MP, 18
KLEPPE, Per, Secretary-General of Efta, 352
KLUNDER, Henk, 427
KNOX, HE Cardinal Robert James, obit., 504
KOBBEKADUWA, Hector, death, 269
KODJO, Edem, 361
KOESTLER, Arthur, suicide, 434; obit., 503-4
KOHL, Dr Helmut, Chancellor of West Germany, 13, 102, 108, 299; and EEC, 137-8; and reunification, 137; election victory, 133-4, 341; visit to Moscow, 137
KOIVISTO, Mauno, President of Finland, 101, 155
KOLTAI, Ralph, 404
KORAH, Lieut. Kenneth, 219, 220
KOUNTCHÉ, Colonel Seyni, President of Niger, 229
KRATOCHVILOVA, Jarmila, 439
KRAUS, Karl, 406
KREISKY, Dr Bruno, Chancellor of Austria, stands down, 156
KROMBHOLC, Jaroslav, death, 401
KULIKOV, Marshal Viktor Georgiyevich, 333
KULLBERG, Rolf, 155
KUNDERA, Milan, 432
KUREISHI, Hanif, 406
KUWAIT, 186, 191; and Iran/Iraq war, 198-9; and US, 199-200; bomb attacks, 192, 199; expatriate labour, 200; oil, 196, 197; stock-market crash, 197-8
KWASHIGAH, Captain Courage, 219

KWEI, Joshua Amartey, 220
KYESMIRA, Yoweri, 218
KYPRIANOU, Spyros, President of Cyprus, 168, 170-1, 319

LAGERFELD, Karl, 430
LAKING, George R., 311
LALONDE, Marc, 71
LAMRANI, Karim, 208
LANC, Erwin, 156
LANCASTER, Burt, 416
LANE, Lord, LCJ, 396, 398
LANGE, David, 310
LANGE, Jessica, 415
LAOS, 259, 287
LAPARA, Gary, 428
LATIN AMERICA, 74-83
LAUDA, Niki, 441
LAW OF THE SEA CONVENTION, 321, 351, 367
LAWSON, Nigel, MP, 21, 30, 31, 453, 454
LÁZÁR, György, 358
LEAKEY, Philip, 214
LEBANON, 179-81, 186-9, 192-3, 203; Beirut escalation, 66, 131, 187-8; economic effects of the war, 189; Israeli-Lebanese security pact, 176, 187, 189; Israeli partial withdrawal, 176, 186; national reconciliation conference, 188; siege of Deir al Qamar, 188-9; Syrian refusal to withdraw, 176, 184-5, 186; UN and, 315; Western military involvement, 1, 39, 50, 65-7, 103-4, 131, 141, 184-5, 186-9, 349
LE CARRÉ, John, 432
LEE SAN-CHOON, Datuk, 279
LEE KUAN-YEW, Prime Minister of Singapore, 281
LEMOINE, Georges, 312
LENDL, Ivan, 443
LEOPOLD III, HM King, of the Belgians, obit., 504
LE PEN, Jean-Marie, 129
LESOTHO, 250-1, 254-5; and China, 294; UN and, 320
LESSING, Doris, 432
LEVITAN, Yurii, death, 106
LEWIS, Anthony, death, 401
LEWIS, Carl, 439
LEWIS, Chris, 443
LEWIS, Drew, 54
LEWIS, Jerry, 414
LI JUQING, 125
LI XIANIAN, 292
LIAO CHUNGZHI, death, 293
LIBERIA, 203, 224-5
LIBYA, 182, 186, 202-4, 220, 227; and other Arab/Muslim states, 201, 203, 205, 207, 209, 257; and USA, 67, 202-3; economy, 204; European hostages, 203; UN and, 319

LIGACHEV, E. K., 101
LIGONDE, Archbishop François, 85
LILOV, Alexander, 119
LIM CHEE-ONN, 281
LIMANN, Dr Hilla, 220
LING YUN, 293
LINI, Fr Walter, Prime Minister of Vanuatu, 312
LITERATURE, 430–6; biography, 432–4; books of the year, 434–6; fiction, 430–2
LIU FUZHI, 293
LIVELY, Penelope, 432
LIVINGSTONE, Ken, 9
LLEWELLYN, Richard, death, 434
LLOYD, Chris, 444
LLOYD, John, 443
LLOYD WEBBER, Andrew, 403
LOACH, Ken, 416
LOMÉ CONVENTION, 239, 343, 362
LONCRAINE, Richard, 414
LOPES, Ernani, 164
LOURENS, Johanna, 254
LOWRY, Mike, 56
LUBBERS, Ruud, Prime Minister of the Netherlands, 143
LUCAS, Leighton, death, 403
LUCE, Richard, MP, 22
LUDER, Dr Italo, 76
LUDERS, Rolf, 78
LUDLAM, Charles, 408
LUDWIG, Siegfried, 157
LUNS, Dr Joseph, Secretary-General of Nato, 333, 351
LUSINCHI, Jaime, 83
LUTHER, Martin, 500th anniversary celebrations, 109, 371
LUTYENS, Elisabeth, death, 413
LUXEMBOURG, 144, 392
LYSSARIDES, Dr Vassos, 170
LYUBIMOV, Yurii, 106, 407

MABANDLA, Prince, of Swaziland, 251
McCLINTOCK, Dr Barbara, 383
McCORY, Milton, 46
MacDERMOT, Galt, 407
McDONALD, Congressman Lawrence, death, 60
MacDONALD, Robert David, 406
MacDONNELL, Brian P., 310
McENROE, John, 443
McEWAN, Geraldine, 406
McFARLANE, Robert, 55, 66
McGOVERN, George, 56
MACH, David, 424
MACHEL, Samora, President of Mozambique, 237–9
MACLAINE, Shirley, 416
MACLEAN, Donald, obit., 504
MACMILLAN, Kenneth, 401
MADRID HURTADO, Miguel de la, President of Mexico, 65, 88
MAGAÑA, Dr Alvaro Alfredo, President of El Salvador, 65
MAGHREB, see under Algeria
MAHATHIR MOHAMAD, Dr, Prime Minister of Malaysia, 279, 280
MAIGARI, Bello Bouba, Prime Minister of Cameroon, 230
MAILER, Norman, 431
MAKAROVA, Natalia, 401
MAKHOSETIVE, Prince, heir-apparent of Swaziland, 251
MALAGASY, 274
MALAWI, 244–5
MALAYSIA, 279–80; Brunei independence, 280–1; constitutional reform, 279
MALAYSIA, King of, see Pahang, Sultan of
MALDIVES, 262, 267
MALI, 207, 220, 227
MALIK, Sgt. Abdul, 219
MALTA, 165; and European Security Conference, 339, 340
MALTBY, Richard, Jr, 407
MAMET, David, 404
MAMULA, Admiral, 122
MAO ZEDONG, 291–2; 90th anniversary celebration, 291
MARCHANT, Tony, 406
MARCOS, Ferdinand, President of Philippines, 283–4
MARCOS, Imelda, 284
MARKOVIĆ, Dragoslav, 122
MARLOW, Angela, 444
MARTENS, Wilfried, Prime Minister of Belgium, 141–2
MARTIN, Sir Leslie, 427
MARTÍNEZ, Victor, 76
MARTINS, Peter, 402
MASIRE, Quett, President of Botswana, 248
MASON, Anita, 431
MASON, Marsha, 408
MASSEY, Raymond, death, 416
MASTERS, Lieut.-Col. John, death, 431; obit., 504–5
MASUKU, Lieut.-General Lookout, 246
MATENJE, Dick, death, 245
MATHIESON, Thomas, 412
MATTHEWS, Baccus, 225
MAURITANIA, 207, 227
MAURITIUS, 272–3
MAUROY, Pierre, Prime Minister of France, 127, 128
MEACHER, Michael, MP, 23–4
MEDEIROS, General Otavio, 78
MÉHES, Lajos, 117
MEJÍA VICTORES, General Oscar Humberto, President of Guatemala, 86, 97
MELCHIOR, Arne, 356
MENGISTU HAILE-MARYAM, Colonel, 210–12, 361
MERBOLD, Ulf, 377
MERCIECE, Archbishop Joseph, 165

MERTES, Alois, 134
MESSIAEN, Olivier, 399, 410
MESSMER, Otto, death, 416
MEUNIER, John, 426
MEXICO, 74, 87-8; relations with USA, 64-5
MICOMBERO, Lieut.-General Michel, death, 236; obit., 505
MILANS DEL BOSCH, General Jaime, 161
MILLER, Johnny, 441
MILLER, Dr Jonathan, 400
MILLS, Michael, 148
MILUNGO, Mgr Emmanuel, 244
MINOGUE, Michael J., 309
MINTOFF, Dominic, Prime Minister of Malta, 165
MIRÓ, Joan, obit., 505
MIRREN, Helen, 405
MIRVISH, Ed, 403
MISKINE, Idriss, 231, 366
MITCHELL, Adrian, 405
MITCHELL, Austin, MP, 32
MITCHELL, Gladys, death, 434
MITCHELL, J. F., 94
MITCHUM, Robert, 418
MITTERRAND, François, President of France, 127, 129, 131, 162, 207, 231, 270, 275, 311, 341, 427; and decentralization of territories, 132; and US invasion of Grenada, 130-1; speech to Bundestag, 130; visits to Africa, 205, 206, 209, 232
MOALLA, Mansur, 205
MOBUTU SESE SOKO, President of Zaïre, 231, 234-5
MOCK, Dr Alois, 157
MOGOERANE, Thelle, 254
MOGWE, Archie, 250, 361
MOHAMMED, Maj.-General Mahmoud, 214
MOI, Daniel Arap, President of Kenya, 213-14, 215
MOKHTAR HASHIM, Datuk, 279
MOLYNEAUX, James, 48
MONDALE, Senator Walter, 56
MONGOLIA, 124-6, 260
MONTAGU, Lord, 422
MONTEFIORE, Bishop Hugh, 368
MONTSERRAT, 95
MOORE, Roger, 414
MOOREHEAD, Alan, death, 434
MORÁN, Fernando, 166
MORETTI, Mario, 140
MORLEY, Christopher, 404
MOROCCO, 203, 206, 208-9, 227, 361
MORSE, Sir Jeremy, 325
MOSES, Ed, 439
MOSLEY, Nicholas, 432
MOSOLOLI, Jerry, 254
MOTAUNG, Marcus, 254
MOTLEY, Langhorne, 64
MOTZFELD, Jonathan, 149

MOZAMBIQUE, 237-9; ANC, 238; and South Africa, 237, 238-9, 254, 255; drought, 237; Frelimo congress, 239; Mozambique National Resistance (MNR), 237-8
MOZZONI, HE Cardinal Umberto, obit., 505
MPAKATI, Dr Attati, assassination, 245
MPETHA, Oscar, 254
MSUYA, Cleopa, 215-16
MUBARAK, Husni, President of Egypt, 67, 180, 181-2, 201, 366
MUGABE, Robert, Prime Minister of Zimbabwe, 243, 246, 248, 250
MUHAMMAD, Ali Nasser, President of People's Democratic Republic of Yemen, 195
MULDOON, Robert, Prime Minister of New Zealand, 308, 310, 311
MULRONEY, Brian, 70
MUNANGAGWA, Emmerson, 248
MUNIM, Maj.-General Mohammed Abdul, 267
MUNTEANU, Dan, 427
MURDANI, General Benny, 282
MURDOCH, Iris, 431
MURRAY, Len, 25, 33
MUSAKANYA, Valentine, 243
MUSEVENI, Yoweri, 217
MUSIC, 409-13; books, 420-1; twentieth-century music, 411-12
MUSSOLINI, Benito, centenary, 141
MUSSON CATTELL & PARTNERS, 428
MUZOREWA, Bishop Abel, 178, 248
MYAKE, Issey, 429
MZALI, Muhammad, Prime Minister of Tunisia, 204-5

NATO (North Atlantic Treaty Organization), 41, 330-3; Declaration of Brussels, 332; East-West relations, 332-3; exercises, 331; expenditure, 330-1; France and, 130, 331; Greece and, 332; Lord Carrington named Secretary-General, 39, 332; nuclear debate, 331-2; Spain and, 162, 166, 331, 332; US bases, 332; Warsaw Pact members propose non-aggression treaty, 58, 334
NAKASONE, Yasuhiro, Prime Minister of Japan, 73, 277, 297-301
NAMIBIA, 131, 241, 242, 249-50; South Africa and, 249; UN and, 241, 249, 315-17
NAMSRAY, Tserendashiyn, 125
NAPIER, John, 404
NASIR, Datuk Mohammad, 280
NAVRATILOVA, Martina, 443-4
NE WIN, General, 276
NEGRI, Prof. Antonio, 140
NEO YEE-PAN, Datuk, 280
NEPAL, 262, 267, 269-71

NETHERLANDS, 143–4; architecture, 427; economy, 143–4; nuclear missile deployment, 144
NEW CALEDONIA, 311, 312
NEW ZEALAND, 308–11; anti-nuclear protest, 310–11; Anzus treaty, 306, 310; economy, 308–9, 310; foreign relations, 310; industrial relations, 309; Taranaki coast pollution, 311
NEWMAN, G. F., 419
NGUEMA, Francisco Macias, 233
NGUEMA, Teodoro Obiang, President of Equatorial Guinea, 233
NGWENYA, Simon, 251
NICARAGUA, 86–7, 202, 259; Cuba and, 84; UN and, 318; USA and, 53, 64, 65, 74, 87
NICHOLS, Beverley, death, 434
NICHOLS, Mike, 415
NICHOLS, Peter, 403
NICHOLSON, Jack, 416
NICKLAUS, Jack, 441
NIDAL, Abu, 179, 184, 191
NIEHAUS, Carl, 254
NIGER, 207, 229–30
NIGERIA, 220–3; expulsion of Ghanaians, 220, 222, 228; military coup, 220–1
NIKOLIC, Vladimir, 427
NILSEN, Denis, 42
NIMAIRI, Jaafar, President of Sudan, 200–2, 212
NITZE, Paul, 352
NIVEN, David, death, 416; obit., 505
NJONJO, Charles, 214
NKETIA, Capt. William Ampomah, 219
NKOMO, Joshua, 243, 246
NOAH, Yannick, 443
NOBEL PRIZES: chemistry, 383; economics, 451; literature, 430; medicine, 383; peace, 112; physics, 383
NOBLE, Adrian, 405
NOBLE, Richard, 441–2
NOLTE, Nicke, 415
NON-ALIGNED MOVEMENT, 261, 267, 312, 365–7; and Central America, 367; and European Security Conference, 338; and Middle East, 257, 366, 367; and Southern Africa, 367; China and, 294; economic issues, 366; membership, 366; political declaration, 367; summit, New Delhi, 190, 259–60, 261, 262, 270, 271, 273, 363, 365–7
NORDGREN, Sofia, 444–5
NORDIC COUNCIL, 355–6; membership, 355; Nordic nuclear-free zone proposal, 356
NORDLING, Gunnar, 445
NORMAN, Greg, 441
NORMAN, Monty, 403
NORTH ATLANTIC ASSEMBLY, 351–2; Special Committee on Nuclear Weapons in Europe, 352
NORTH ATLANTIC COUNCIL, 130, 132, 351
NORTH KOREA, 271, 301; and Burma, 276; and death of South Koreans in Rangoon, 276, 300, 301
NORTHERN IRELAND, see under United Kingdom
NORWAY, 151–2; and EEC, 347
NOTT, Sir John, 10
NOVOMBI, Princess, Queen Regent of Swaziland, 251
NUCLEAR ARMS:
ANTI-NUCLEAR PROTESTS: Canada, 72; Czechoslovakia, 112–13; East Germany, 108; France, 132; Italy, 141; Netherlands, 144; New Zealand, 310–11; UK, 12–13; West Germany, 135, 136;
Cardinal Hume's article in *The Times*, (text) 479–80; health hazards, 324; Churches and, 368–9; limitation negotiations, 58–9, 61–2, 131, 335–8; Nato and, 331–2; nuclear-free zones, 6, 120, 123, 168, 311, 356; public support weakened, 2, 57–8, 59; UN and, 320; weapons deployment and reactions to, 62, 102, 107, 108, 112–13, 118, 130, 136, 141, 144, 149, 152, (map), 328; 331–2, 333, 345; weapons testing, 72, 310–11, 320, 333; zero-option proposal, 58–9, 136, 331
NUNN, Trevor, 400, 409
NUREYEV, Rudolf, 401, 402, 415
NYERERE, Julius K., President of Tanzania, 214, 215; planned assassination, 215

OBOTE, Milton, President of Uganda, 214, 217–18
O'BRIEN, Pat, death, 416
OBZINA, Jaromír, 114
OCHOA PÉREZ, Lieut.-Col. Sigifredo, 85
ODINGA, Oginga, 213
ODINGA, Raila, 213
ODURO, William, 219
O'FIAICH, HE Cardinal Tomas, 370
OFNER, Harald, 156
OIL (*see also* Economic and Social Affairs *and* OPEC): Algeria, 208; Antigua, 94; Australia, 304; Barbados, 96–7; Burma, 277; China, 291; Ecuador, 80; Egypt, 181, 182; Guinea-Bissau, 236; Gulf States, 196–7; India, 263; Indonesia, 283; Iran, 190, 258; Iraq, 191; Ireland, 148; Libya, 204; Mexico, 87–8; Nigeria, 221; Saudi Arabia, 193; South Africa, 216; Sudan, 202; Thailand, 279; Trinidad and Tobago, 95; UK North Sea, 43; Venezuela, 83
OKUK, Iambakey, 306–7
OLIVER, Stephen, 403
OLSZOWSKI, Stefan, 111
OMAN, 199; oil, 196–7

ONOFRE JARPA, Sergio, 79
ONU, Dr Peter, 361
OPERA, 399–401; Wagner death centenary, 399
OPIE, Julian, 424
ORFILA, Alejandro, Secretary-General of OAS, resignation, 365
ORGANIZATION OF AFRICAN UNITY (OAU), 227; Addis Ababa summit, 203, 206, 212, 231, 360; and Colonel Qadafi, 203, 231, 361; Colonel Mengistu becomes Chairman, 212, 361
ORGANIZATION OF AMERICAN STATES, 365
ORGANIZATION OF EASTERN CARIBBEAN STATES (OECS), 91, 92, 364, 365
ORGANIZATION FOR ECONOMIC COOPERATION AND DEVELOPMENT (OECD), 35, 258, 353–4, 448–51; development aid, 354; economic and monetary policy, 353; energy policy, 354; unemployment, 353–4
ORGANIZATION OF PETROLEUM EXPORTING COUNTRIES (OPEC), 88, 193, 196, 258
OSBORNE, John, Chief Minister of Montserrat, 95
OSBORNE, John, playwright, 406
OSHIMA, Nagisa, 415
OSPINA, Ivan Marino, 79
OTAIBA, Shaikh Mana Saeed al-, 196
OTT, Carlos, 427
OUEDDEYE, Goukouny, 231–2, 319
OUÉDRAOGO, Commandant Jean-Baptiste, head of state of Upper Volta, 228–9
OUMAROU, Mamane, Prime Minister of Niger, 230
OVIE-WHISKEY, Judge Victor, 222
OWEN, Dr David, MP, 17–19, 25–6, 36–7; becomes SDP leader, 22
OWINGS, Nathaniel Alexander, 427
OYITE-OJOK, Maj.-General David, death, 218
ÖZAL, Turgut, Prime Minister of Turkey, 173

PAHANG, HH Sultan of (Sir Abu Bakar Riayatuddin), 279, 280
PAISLEY, Bob, 439
PAISLEY, Rev Ian, 48
PAKISTAN, 263–6, 269; Afghan refugees, 264–5; economy and trade, 265–6; political reform, 265; relations with India, 262, 263–4
PAKULA, Alan J., 415
PALESTINE LIBERATION ORGANIZATION (PLO), 66, 67, 104, 168, 176–7, 178, 179–80, 183–4, 199, 205, 306; internal split and withdrawal from Lebanon, 176, 179–80, 186; UN and, 315
PALIN, Michael, 414
PALME, Olof, Prime Minister of Sweden, 152, 154, 317, 352, 356

PALMER, Geoffrey, 310
PANAMA, 65, 74, 87
PAPANDREOU, Andreas, Prime Minister of Greece, 119, 167–9
PAPUA NEW GUINEA, 306–7; Australian aid, 306–7
PARAGUAY, 74, 80; and Brazil, 80
PARATHASARATHY, Gopal, 268
PAREDES, General Rubén Dario, 87
PARK, Merle, 403
PARKINSON, Cecil, MP, 21, 26–7
PARKINSON, Michael, 416, 421
PARTRIDGE, Frances, 433
PASMORE, Victor, 424
PATEL, Dr I. G., 325
PATTERSON, Paul, 412
PAVLOV, Aleksandr, 357
PAVLOV, Sergey, 124
PEACE MOVEMENTS, see Defence Organizations and Nuclear Arms
PECK, Bob, 405
PEI, I. M., 428
PEL'SHE, Arvid, 100
PENG ZHEN, 293
PENNY, Nicholas, 426
PEREIRA, Aristide, President of Cape Verde, 236
PÉREZ, Humberto, 83
PEREZ DE CUELLAR, Javier, UN Secretary-General, 170, 314–20, 322
PERÓN, María Estela Martínez (Isabel) de, 75
PERTINI, Alessandro, President of Italy, 138, 139
PERU, 81–2
PETHERBRIDGE, Deanna, 424
PEVSNER, Sir Nikolaus, death, 429; obit., 505–6
PHILLIPPINES, 68, 283–4; Presidential Commitment Orders, 283; murder of Benigno Aquino, 284
PHILLIP, Norbert, 440
PHILLIPS, Capt. Mark, 421
PIANIM, Andrew Kwame, 219–20
PIGGOTT, Lester, 445
PILE, Air Commodore Philip, 247
PINDLING, Sir Lynden, Prime Minister of the Bahamas, 97–8
PINHEIRO DE AZEVEDO, Admiral José Baptista, obit., 506
PINOCHET, Augusto, President of Chile, 74, 78–9
PINTER, Harold, 406
PINTO, Carlos Mota, 164
PIQUET, Nelson, 441
PIRES, Francisco Lucas, 163
PITMAN, Jenny, 444
PLANINĆ, Milka, Prime Minister of Yugoslavia, 121, 168
PLANUNGSGRUPPE MEDIUM, 427
PODGORNY, Nikolai Viktorovich, obit., 506

INDEX

POL POT, 286
POLAND, 109–12, 131; economy, 111–12; martial law lifted, 111; Pope's visit, 110–11; relations with USSR, 334; Solidarity activities, 109–10; UN and, 323
POLLACK, Sydney, 414
POPE, The, see John Paul II
POPESCU, Dumitru, 118
PORTER, Marguerite, 401
PORTUGAL, 163–4; and EEC, 341, 346; and Efta, 352; and Southern Africa, 255; architecture, 427
POUNTNEY, David, 399, 400
POWELL, Anthony, 432
POWELL, J. Enoch, MP, 1, 40
POWELL, Violet, 433
POWER, M. S., 431
PREM TINSULANOND, General, Prime Minister of Thailand, 278
PRESSER, Gabor, 402
PRICE, Anthony, 165
PRICE, George, Prime Minister of Belize, 97
PRICE, Nick, 441
PRIDI PHANOMYONG, Dr, obit., 506
PRIESTLEY, Clive, 400, 405
PRIOR, James, MP, 21, 27, 40, 42, 49
PROCKTOR, Patrick, 424
PROST, Alain, 441
PRYCE-JONES, David, 433
PUJA, Frigyes, 116
PYM, Francis, MP, 18, 21, 32, 166, 193

QABOUS BIN SAID, Sultan of Oman, 199
QADAFI, Colonel Muammar, President of Libya, 67, 186, 202–4, 205, 206, 207, 209, 228, 231–2; 'most dangerous man in the world', 202
QATAR, 199; oil, 196, 197
QIAN QICHEN, 294
QIAO GUANHUA, death, 293
QUINN, Anthony, 408
QUIWONKPA, General Thomas, 225

RAINER, Ove, 154
RAKOWSKI, Mieczyslaw, 111
RALLIS, George, 167
RAMGOOLAM, Sir Seewoosagur, 273
RAMPHAL, Shridath, 326
RANKOVIĆ, Aleksandar, 122
RAO, N. T. Rama, 260
RAO, P. V. Narashima, 268
RASHIDOV, Sh. R., 101
RATCLIFF, Carter, 425
RATSIRAKA, Didier, President of Malagasy, 274
RAWLINGS, Flight-Lieut. Jerry, 219, 220
REAGAN, Ronald, President of USA, 2, 55, 73, 102, 284, 293, 379; and Africa, 238, 248; and Central America, 63–4, 84, 85, 365; and economy, 50–2, 452; and invasion of Grenada, 62–3, 91, 92; and Middle East, 65–6, 179, 183, 185, 189, 202; and Mr Nakasone, 299; and Mrs Thatcher, 40, 63, 65; and nuclear arms limitation, 58–9, 61, 102, 335–6; and shooting-down of South Korean airliner, 60–1; State of the Union address, 51; visit to Asia, 68, 300
REGAN, Donald, 52
REISCHL, Gerhard, 392
RELIGION, 368–73 (see also Islam); Albania, 124; appropriation of Church property, Malta, 165; books, 373–4; capital punishment, 370; Catholic Church and Philippines regime, 283, 370; Christianity in China, 372; Churches and nuclear arms, 368–9; Irish abortion amendment, 147, 369; Jewish affairs, 371; marriage and divorce, 369; Martin Luther 500th anniversary, 109, 371; Pope's visits to Central America, Poland, Austria, 85, 86, 110–11, 156, 370; racial discrimination in South Africa, 370–1; sectarian tension, Northern Ireland, 46–7, 370; Sikh affairs, 371; Soviet attacks on Pope, 334
REMY, Maurice, 420
RENAULT, Mary, death, 434
RENÉ, Albert, President of the Seychelles, 271
RETALLACK, John, 407
REY, Jean, obit., 506
REYNOLDS, Burt, 414
RIBIČIČ, Mitja, 122
RICE, Peter, 404
RICE, Tim, 403
RICHARD, Ivor, 346
RICHARDSON, Sir Ralph, death, 406; obit., 506–7
RIDE, Sally, 56
RIFKIND, Malcolm, 218
RILEY, Bridget, 424
RIMELL, Mercy, 444
RÍOS MONTT, Efraín, President of Guatemala, 86, 97, 370
RIPPON, Angela, 416
RIPPON, Sir Geoffrey, 30
RITSCHARD, Willy, death, 157
ROBBINS, Jerome, 402
ROBERTS, Patricia, 431
ROBINSON, Rt Rev John, obit., 507
ROCHE, Kevin, 428
RODGERS, William, MP, 19
RODRÍGUEZ, Rafael, 87
RODRÍGUEZ PASTOR, Carlos, 81
ROEG, Nicholas, 415
ROGERS, General Bernard W., 330, 350–1
ROGERS, Richard, 426
ROHMER, Eric, 416
ROLANDIS, Nicos, 170
ROMAIN, Colonel Franck, 85

ROMANIA, 117–19; and Geneva disarmament talks, 118; economy, 117; relations with USSR, 118, 334
ROMANOV, G. V., 101
ROMERO, Archbishop Oscar, 85
ROSE, Geoff, 404
ROSE, Kenneth, 432
ROSENTHAL, Michael, 426
ROSTOW, Eugene, 55
ROWLING, Sir Wallace, 310
ROZÈS, Simone, 392
RUCKELSHAUS, William, 55, 386
RUMSFELD, Donald, 191
RUNCIE, Dr Robert, Archbishop of Canterbury, 368, 372
RUSHDIE, Salman, 431
RUSSELL, Frank, 430
RUSSELL, Ken, 400
RUSSELL, Willy, 404
RWANDA, 236

SADAT, Ismet, 182
SADIQ AL-MAHDI, al-, 201
SAHRAWI ARAB DEMOCRATIC REPUBLIC, 360–1
ST KITTS-NEVIS, 93, 94; admitted to UN, 314; Commonwealth membership, 326; independence, 94
ST LUCIA, 94, 202
ST VINCENT AND THE GRENADINES, 93, 94
SALCHER, Herbert, 156
SALEH, Ali Abdullah, President of Yemen Arab Republic, 194, 195
SALIBA, Evarist, 165
SALVATERRA, Angelo, 237
SAMORÉ, HE Cardinal Antonio, obit., 507
SÁNCHEZ, Lieut.-Col. Arturo, 86
SANKARA, Capt. Thomas, Prime Minister of Upper Volta, 228–9
SÃO TOMÉ AND PRINCIPE, 237
SARMIENTO, Sonia, kidnapping, 79
SARTAWI, Isam, 179
SASAKI ASSOCIATES, 428
SASSOU-NGUESSO, Denis, President of People's Republic of the Congo, 232
SAUD, HRH Prince, of Saudi Arabia, 192
SAUDI ARABIA, 191, 192–4, 203
SAVARY, Alain, 130
SAVIMBI, Dr Jonas, 249
SAWALLISCH, Wolfgang, 399
SAWICKI, General Felicjan, 111
SAYAH, Muhammad, 205
SCHAPIRO, Prof. Leonard, death, 434; obit., 507
SCHIFF, David, 410
SCHLUMPF, Leon, President of Switzerland (1984), 158
SCHLÜTER, Poul, Prime Minister of Denmark, 148–9, 356; resignation, 149
SCHMIDT, Helmut, 133

SCHNEIDER-WESSLING, Erich, 427
SCHWEIKER, Richard, 54
SCHWEZOFF, Igor, 403
SCIENCE, MEDICINE AND TECHNOLOGY, 374–8; AGRICULTURE: genetic engineering, 380; nitrogen fixation, 383; BIOTECHNOLOGY: biosensors, 375; monoclonal antibodies, 382; ELECTRONICS AND INFORMATION TECHNOLOGY: aids for the disabled, 376; biosensors, 375; communications/educational satellites, 377–8; Inmos Transputer, 376; superconductors, 376; ENERGY: fusion energy, 375; geothermal energy, 375; Joint European Torus project, 375; pressurized water reactors (PWRs), 374–5; wind power, 375; MEDICINE: Acquired Immune Deficiency Syndrome (AIDS), 382; artificial heart, 382; carcinogenesis, 380–1; contraceptive pill and cancer risk, 380; 'donor egg' pregnancies, 382–3; genetics and genetic disorders, 381–2, 383; leprosy antigen, 382; phages, 383; synthetic prostacyclin, 382; transplants, 382; NOBEL PRIZES: 383; PALAEONTOLOGY AND BIOLOGY: man-made chromosome, 380; Pakistan 'missing link' discovery, 379–80; PARTICLE PHYSICS: Large Electron Positron Ring (LEP), 374; W and Z bosons, 374; SPACE AND ASTRONOMY: *Challenger* space shuttle, 376–7; communications/ educational satellites, 377–8; European rocket *Ariane*, 377–8; infra-red astronomy satellite, 378; laser defence systems, 379; millimetre telescope, 378–9; nuclear reactor satellites, 378; Pope exonerates Galileo, 371; problems with Tracking and Data Relay satellite, 376; Russian Venus probes, 378; Spacelab, 377; stellar collapse, 383; WEATHER AND CLIMATE: greenhouse effect, 379
SCOON, Sir Paul, Governor-General of Grenada, 92, 93
SCORSESE, Martin, 414
SCOTLAND, *see under* United Kingdom
SEAGA, Edward, Prime Minister of Jamaica, 89
SEGUEL, Rodolfo, 79
SELDES, Marian, 408
SEN KEE ROCCO YIM, 427
SENEGAL, 224, 225–6
SENGHOR, Abbé Diamacoune, 226
SENGHOR, Léopold Sédar, 225
SENYA, Michael, 220
SERBAN, Andrei, 400
SEREGNI, General Liber, 82
SERPELL, Sir David, 9
SERRA, Narcis, 161
SERT, Prof. José Luis, death, 429; obit., 507
SETTER, Ib, 355

SEYCHELLES, 271–2; and foreign navies, 272
SEYDOU, Major Amadou, 228
SHAGARI, Shehu, President of Nigeria, 221–2, 242; overthrown by military coup, 220–1
SHAGDARSUREN, Puntsagiyn, 125
SHAH, Selim (Eddie), 32–3, 394
SHAMIR, Yitzhak, Prime Minister of Israel, 67, 175, 177, 178
SHAMWANA, Edward, 243
SHARON, Ariel, 176, 235
SHCHELOKOV, General Nicolay, 104
SHEARER, Norma, death, 416; obit., 507–8
SHEEN, Martin, 418
SHEHU, Feçor, 123
SHEHU, Mehmet, 123
SHENOUDA II, Pope, 182
SHEPARD, Sam, 408
SHER, Antony, 405
SHIMELIS AGDUNA, 211
SHIRE, David, 407
SHORE, Peter, MP, 8, 23
SHULTZ, George, US Secretary of State, 1, 55, 58, 60, 61, 67, 241, 264, 293, 365; and Middle East, 66, 202, 205
SIBLEY, Antoinette, 401
SIERRA LEONE, 223
SIHANOUK, HRH Prince Norodom, of Kampuchea, 294, 363
SILES ZUAZO, Hernán, President of Bolivia, 76
SILVA SIMMA, Enrique, 79
SIMON, Neil, 408
SIMPSON, Dudley, 401
SIN, HE Cardinal Jaime L., 283
SINCLAIR, Sir Clive, 43
SINGAPORE, 281
SINOWATZ, Dr Fred, Chancellor of Austria, 156
SITAL, Sgt.-Major, 98
SITKOV, Vyacheslav, Executive Secretary of Comecon, 357
SIYAD BARRE, General Mohamed, President of Somalia, 212
SKIDELSKY, Robert, 433
SLATTER, Air Vice-Marshal Hugh, 247
SLEZAK, Walter, death, 416
SLYUNKOV, N. N., 100
SMIRNOV, Aleksandr, 124
SMITH, Cyril, MP, 26
SMITH, Ian, 248
SMOLE, Janko, 121
SOARES, Mario, Prime Minister of Portugal, 163–4
SOBHUZA II, former King of Swaziland, 251
SOBUKWE, Robert, 252
SOKOINE, Edward, Prime Minister of Tanzania, 215
SOLOMENTSEV, M. S., 101
SOLOMON, Vivian, 421

SOLOMON ISLANDS, 311
SOLTI, Sir Georg, 399
SOMALIA, 212–13
SOMARE, Michael, Prime Minister of Papua New Guinea, 306
SOMÉ, General Gabriel, 229
SONNABEND, Yolande, 401
SORSA, Kalevi, Prime Minister of Finland, 154–5
SOSA, Arturo, 83
SOUTH AFRICA, 252–5; ANC activity, 253–4; and Angola, 240, 241, 249; and Lesotho, 250–1, 254–5; and Mozambique, 237, 238–9, 254, 255; and Namibia, 249; and Seychelles, 271; and USSR, 103; and Zimbabwe, 248, 255; Constitution Act, 252–3, 370–1, (abbreviated text) 482–94; defence, 255; economy, 255; television, 421; UN and, 316–17, 323
SOUTH ASIAN REGIONAL COOPERATION FORUM, 262, 267
SOUTH-EAST ASIAN ORGANIZATIONS, 362–4; see also Asean
SOUTH KOREA, 300–1; airliner shot down by USSR, 1, 39, 50, 60–1, 71–2, 103, 300, 319; and China, 294; deaths in Rangoon bombing, 276, 300, 301; economy, 301; political liberalization, 300–1; President Reagan's visit, 68, 300
SOUTH PACIFIC, 311–13; Forum, 311–12; proposed nuclear weapon-free zone, 311; US and, 312
SOUTHERN AFRICAN DEVELOPMENT COORDINATION CONFERENCE (SADCC), 362
SPADOLINI, Giovanni, 138, 139
SPAIN, 159–62; abortion law, 162; administrative reform, 159; and Africa, 206, 207, 233; and EEC, 162, 166, 341, 346; and European Security Conference, 338–9; and Gibraltar, 166; and Nato, 162, 166, 331, 332; art, 424; Basque separatist activity, 161–2; Civil Guard, police and army, 160–1; coup trials, 161; defence spending, 161; expropriation of Rumasa, 159–60; foreign affairs, 162; industrial reform, 160; religious aspects of education, 162
SPILJAK, Mika, 122
SPINELLI, Altiero, 390
SPORT, 437–45; association football, 437–8; athletics, 148, 438–9; boxing, 46; cricket, 263, 439–40; golf, 440–1; ice skating, 445; motor sport, 441–2; rugby football, 442–3; television rights for 1984 Olympics, 420–1; tennis, 443–4; the turf, 444–5; yachting, 445
SPOTTISWOODE, Roger, 415
SPREKELSEN, Johan Otto von, 426
SPRING, Dick, 145, 146
SPROAT, Iain, MP, 43, 418
SRI LANKA, 262, 267, 268–9; Tamil

militancy, 268–9
STANDFORD, Patric, 412
STEEL, David, MP, 14, 18, 22, 25–6, 39, 213
STEGER, Norbert, 156
STEVENS, Bernard, death, 413
STEVENS, Siaka, President of Sierra Leone, 223
STEVENSON, Juliet, 405
STICH, Otto, 158
STOLTENBERG, Gerhard, 135
STONE, Richard, 64, 85
STRACHEY, Julia, 433
STRAUSS, Botho, 406
STRAUSS, Franz-Josef, 107–8, 134–5
STREEP, Meryl, 415
STROESSNER, General Alfredo, President of Paraguay, 74, 80
STRONG, Sir Roy, 423
ŠTROUGAL, Lubomír, Prime Minister of Czechoslovakia, 114
STURRIDGE, Charles, 416
SUDAN, 200–2, 212; moves towards integration with Egypt, 182, 201
SUDOMO, Admiral, 282
SUHARTO, General T. N. J., President of Indonesia, 282
SUN YEFANG, death, 293
SUNALP, General Turgut, 172–3
SURINAME, 98–9
SUTHERLAND, Joan, 400–1
SUZUKI, Zenko, 297
ŠVESTKA, Oldřich, 114
SWANSON, Gloria, death, 416; obit., 508
SWAZILAND, 251
SWEDEN, 152–4; economy, 152–3; wage-earner funds legislation, 153
SWID, Stephen, 422
SWINBURN, Walter, 445
SWITZERLAND, 157–9; citizenship, 158–9; political upheaval, 157–8
SYBERBERG, Hans-Jurgen, 416
SYRIA, 182, 184–6; and Yassir Arafat, 179–80; defence spending, 186; economy, 186; refusal to withdraw from Lebanon, 176, 184–5, 186; relations with: Gulf States, 186; Iran, 257; USA, 66–7, 184–5, 186; USSR, 2, 104, 185, 196
SYSOEV, Vyacheslav, 106
SZŰRÖS, Mátyás, 116–17

TABAI, Iremia, President of Kiribati, 312
TAGAWA, Seiichi, 298
TAHA TALIK, Datuk, 279
TAIWAN, 68, 288, 294–6; and China, 293, 294, 295–6; and USA, 295, 297; bombings, 295; economy, 294–5
TAKESHITA, Noboru, 299
TAN, Anthony, 281
TAN ZHENLIN, death, 293
TANAKA, Kakuei, 296–8

TANDY, Jessica, 409
TANZANIA, 215–17, 271; agriculture, 216; and Kenya, 214; and Lonrho, 216; oil import scandal, 216–17; planned coup, 215; Zanzibar, 217
TARKOVSKY, Andrei, 400
TATCHELL, Peter, 11
TAUBE, Prof. Henry, 383
TAUBMAN, Alfred, 422
TEBBIT, Norman, MP, 21
TEJERO, Lieut.-Col. José Antonio, 161
TELEVISION AND RADIO, 416–21; breakfast television, 416–17; cable broadcasting, 28, 130, 417–18; investment in cinema, 413, 421; 'video nasties', 428
TEMBO, John, 244
THAILAND, 68, 277–9, 287; economy, 278–9; oil and gas, 279; frontier security, 277
THANI, Shaikh Abdel-Aziz bin Khalifah al-, 196
THAPA, Surya Bahadur, Prime Minister of Nepal, 269–70
THATCHER, Margaret, MP, Prime Minister of United Kingdom, 7, 9, 13, 14, 16–18, 21, 29, 39, 41, 49, 76, 166, 178, 341; and EEC, 39, 341, 345; and inflation, 28; and NHS, 27–8; and Cecil Parkinson, 26–7; and James Prior, 40; and Francis Pym, 21; and President Reagan, 40, 63, 65; and unemployment, 17; 'megaphone diplomacy', 39; visit to Canada and USA, 39, 72; visit to Falkland Islands, 37
THEATRE, 403–9; New York, 407–9
THOMAS, George, MP (later Viscount Tonypandy), 15
THOMAS, Keith, 434
THOMPSON, Brian, 406
THOMPSON, Daley, 439
THORN, Gaston, President of European Commission, 342, 345, 349
THORODDSEN, Gùnnar, Prime Minister of Iceland, stands down, 150; death, 150; obit., 508
TIKHONOV, N. A., 121, 357–8
TIN OO, 276
TINTEROW, Gary, 425
TITO, Epel, 307
TOBACK, James, 415
TOGO, 219, 228
TOKELAU, 312
TOMÁŠEK, HE Cardinal František, 113
TOMS, Carl, 404
TORRES ROJAS, General Luis, 161
TORVILL, Jayne, 445
TOURÉ, Sekou, President of Guinea, 226–7
TREVOR, William, 431
TRINIDAD AND TOBAGO, 92, 95–6; Tobagan end-of-union resolution, 95
TROTT & BEAN, 428

TROTTA, Margarethe von, 416
TRUDEAU, Pierre, Prime Minister of Canada, 69; peace proposals, 72-3
TSANTES, Capt. George, assassination, 168
TSCHUMI, Bernard, 427
TSEDENBAL, Yamjaagiyn, President of Mongolia, 124, 125
TSERETELI, Z., 106
TSIKATA, Kojo, 219
TUGENDHAT, Christopher, 346
TUNE, Tommy, 407
TUNISIA, 203, 204-5
TURABI, Dr Hassan al-, 201
TÜRKEŞ, Alpaslan, 174
TURKEY, 120, 172-4, 349; and Cyprus, 171, 174; and Greece, 167-8, 174; application of martial law, 172, 174; earthquake, 174; economy, 174; university purge, 173
TURKMEN, Ilter, 168
TURNBULL, Wendy, 443
TUVALU, 312
TWIGGY, 407

UCHTENHAGEN, Lilian, 157-8
UGANDA, 217-18; and Kenya, 214; Asian compensation, 218; overseas aid, 218
UGLJEN, Zlatko, 429
ULANHU, General, 293
ULLSTEN, Ola, 356
ULTZ (David), 404
ULUSU, Admiral Bülent, 172, 173
UMAR WIRAHADIKUSUMAH, General, 282
UMBERTO II, HM King, of Italy, death, 141; obit., 508
UMBRICHT, Dr Viktor, 214
UNION DOUANIÈRE ET ECONOMIQUE D'AFRIQUE CENTRALE (UDEAC), 233
UNION OF SOVIET SOCIALIST REPUBLICS (USSR), 100-6;
ARTS: art, 425; ballet, 402; broadcasting, 420; national war museum, 106; theatre, 106;
DOMESTIC AND POLITICAL AFFAIRS: agriculture, 105; Comecon, 357-8; corruption and inefficiency problems, 104, 105; economy, 100, 104; food shortages, 105; imports of US grain, 60; natural gas, 105; Novosibirsk document, 104; political appointments, 100-2; winter weather, 106;
FOREIGN AFFAIRS AND DEFENCE: Afghanistan, 259; Africa, 103, 206, 207, 238, 255; Central America/Caribbean, 103; Middle East, 2, 103-4, 182, 196, 257; nuclear weapons deployment, 112-13, (map) 328; political world view, 4; relations with: China, 103, 293; Czechoslovakia, 113, 114; EEC, 343; Finland, 155; France, 131; Hungary, 116; India, 262; Liberia, 225; Mongolia, 125; Poland, 103; Romania, 118; USA, 50, 58-61, 100, 102-3; Vietnam, 285; West Germany, 102, 136-7; shooting-down of South Korean airliner, 1, 39, 50, 60-1, 71-2, 103, 300, 319
UNITED ARAB EMIRATES, 196-200; Abu Dhabi, 196; defence, 199; Dubai, 196; economy and finance, 197, 198; expatriate labour, 200; oil, 196
UNITED KINGDOM, 7-49;
ARTS: architecture, 426; art, 421-5; ballet, 401-2; cinema, 413, 416; Edinburgh International Festival, 44, 402, 406, 409; literature, 430-6; music, 409-12; musicals, 403-4; opera, 399-400; sculpture, 424; television, 416-19; theatre, 404-7; theatre design, 404, 424;
CRIME AND VIOLENCE, 42; death penalty debate, 28-9; Heathrow bullion raid, 42; IRA Christmas bombings in London, 41-2; law and order as issue, 27; Northern Ireland, 46-7;
DEFENCE: aftermath of Falklands conflict, 7, 36-8; as election issue, 16-18; Campaign for Nuclear Disarmament, 13; Government public relations, 13, 17; Greenham Common women, 12-13; Joint Intelligence Organization, 36; Scottish submarine base 'peace camps', 44; US bases, 12-14;
ECONOMIC AND SOCIAL AFFAIRS: balance of trade, 455-6; Budget, 7-8, 15, 454; civil service salaries, 31; consumer spending, 454, 455; election issues, 15-18, 453; Government's economic and fiscal policies, 7-8, 16-17, 29-32, 453-5; industrial output, 7, 35, 455; inflation, 7, 17, 28, 453, 455; interest rates, 7, 455; local government finance, 8-9, 30, 45-6; MPs' salaries, 29; National Graphical Association dispute, 32-4; National Health Service, 12, 18, 28, 31; nationalization of private industry, 18; North Sea oil, 43, 454; privatization of state-controlled industry, 10, 16; public expenditure problems, 29-32, 35, 454; racism, 28; railways study, 9-10; recovery, 453, 455; relations with EEC, 38-9, 341, 345; social security benefits, 8; statistical data, 458-65; taxation, 7-8, 16, 27, 454; unemployment, 7, 15-17, 28, 32, 35, 43, 49, 455; water and sewerage strike, 10;
FOREIGN AND COMMONWEALTH AFFAIRS: aftermath of Falklands conflict, 35-8; Belize, 86, 97; Cyprus, 40, 168; Franks Report, 35-6; Gibraltar, 38, 166; Guyana, 96; Hong Kong, 38, 288, 293, 296; Malaysia and Brunei, 280-1;

INDEX 541

Mexico, 87; relations with: Argentina, 26, 37, 38, 65, 76; China, 38; Irish Republic, 41–2, 146–7; Kenya, 213–14; Lebanon, 39; Saudi Arabia, 193; Southern Africa, 247, 255; Spain, 38, 166; USA, 39–40, 62–3; USSR, 39; Uganda, 218; Zimbabwe, 247;
GENERAL ELECTION: dissolution of Parliament, 14; effects of Boundary Commission, 15; issues, 17–18; loss of prominent MPs, 19, 43; manifestos, 15–17; resignations, 15; results, 19–20;
GOVERNMENT AND POLITICS: aftermath of Falklands conflict, 15, 17; by-elections, 9, 11, 24; Cabinet reshuffles, 21–22; dissolution honours list, 22; general election (*q.v. above*), 14–21; Greater London Council, 8–9, 16; local government elections, 15; new Parliament, 28–35; New Year honours list, 22; post-election Cabinet, 21–2, 495; Queen's speech, 28; trade union relations, 9–10, 16–17, 34;
LAW, 393–8; anti-terrorist legislation review, 47; British Nationality (Falklands) enactment, 393; British Telecom sale enabling Bill, 10, 15; cable broadcasting proposals, 28; computer security proposals, 28; contempt of court, 394; conveyancing proposals, 32, 393; Court of Appeal decisions, 395–6; employment and trade union law, 9, 393–4; House of Lords decisions, 394–5; Housing Bill, 9; independent prosecution service proposals, 28; lead-free petrol proposals, 10; Marriage Act, 393; Matrimonial Homes Act, 393; Merchant Shipping Act, 393; Mobile Homes Act, 393; opticians and spectacles proposals, 32; Police and Criminal Evidence Bill, 9, 15; Rates Bill, 30; Representation of the People Act, 393; seat-belt enforcement, 10; Sunday opening Bill, 10;
NORTHERN IRELAND: anti-terrorist legislation review, 47; boycott of Northern Ireland Assembly, 48; deaths by terrorism, 46–7; EEC and, 48–9; general election results, 47–8; industrial condition, 49; Maze prison break-out, 40, 47; political balance within, 47–8; political disagreement over, 40–1, 46; relations with Republic (New Ireland Forum), 48; US support for IRA, 42; use of 'supergrass' evidence, 398;
POLITICAL PARTIES: Alliance, (*see also* Liberal Party *and* Social Democratic Party): election campaign, 18–19; leadership, 14; manifesto, 15–16. Conservative Party: conference, 26–8; election campaign, 17–18; election manifesto, 16–17; wet vs dry, 21, 40. Labour Party:

and EEC membership, 12, 18; and GLC, 9, 25; and Militant Tendency, 11, 24; and Northern Ireland, 40–1; and nuclear disarmament, 23–4; conference, 24–5; election campaign, 18; election manifesto, 16; internal conflict, 11, 17–18, 20, 32–4; leadership, 11, 22–4; loss of popular support, 19–20; policy statements, 12, 16, 20, 23; trade union relations, 11–12, 25, 32–4. Liberal Party (*see also* Alliance *above*): and Northern Ireland, 40; conference, 25–6; leadership, 22; conference, 25–6. National Front, 28. Plaid Cymru, 19, 46. Scottish National Party, 19. Social Democratic Party (SDP) (*see also* Alliance *above*): conference, 25; leadership, 22; policy statements, 26;
SCOTLAND: development projects, 42–3, 44; Edinburgh International Festival, 44, 402, 406, 409; educational systems review, 43; election swing, 19, 43; electronics and semiconductors, 42–3; industrial conditions, 42, 44; North Sea oil, 43;
WALES: development projects, 45; election swing, 45; local government finance, 45–6; Severn Bridge, 46; television, 46; unemployment, 45
UNITED NATIONS, 314–24; Afghanistan, 260, 264, 317; Central America, 318; China and, 294; Cyprus, 169–71, 314, 318–19; debt problems, 314, 321; development, 322; disarmament, 314, 320; East Africa, 214; East Timor, 282; environment, 320–1; Falkland Islands, 162, 319; invasion of Grenada, 63, 318; Iran/Iraq war, 190, 257, 317–18; Israel, 178, 181; Kampuchea, 277, 319–20; Malta, 165; membership, 314; Middle East, 1, 190, 257, 314–15; New Zealand and, 310; North Africa, 319; Poland, 323; sea, 321; social problems, 322–4; South Korean airliner, 319; Southern Africa, 241, 249, 315–17, 320, 323;
AGENCIES: Economic Commission for Africa, 362; Economic Commission for Europe, 358, 359; Economic and Social Council (Ecosoc), 322; Food and Agriculture Organization (FAO), 69, 323–4, 385; General Agreement on Tariffs and Trade (GATT), 299, 310; International Atomic Energy Agency, 69, 178, 294; International Civil Aviation Organization, 319; International Labour Organization, 178, 323; International Marine Organization, 321; International Telecommunications Union, 69; UN Conference on Trade and Development (UNCTAD), 310, 322, 359; UN Development Programme, 322;

UN Environment Programme, 69, 321; UN High Commissioner for Refugees, 212, 213, 317, 324, 363–4; UN Interim Force in Lebanon (Unifil), 315; UNRWA, 315; Unesco, US withdrawal, 69; World Health Organization (WHO), 324
UNITED STATES OF AMERICA, 50–69;
ARTS: architecture, 427–8; art, 423; ballet, 402; cinema, 414–16; music, 410, 411; opera, 400; television, 419–20; theatre, 407–9;
DEFENCE: expenditure, 52, 53, 452; invasion of Grenada, 1–2, 39–40, 51, 62–3, 72, 74, 84, 87, 91, 92–3, 103, 130–1, 137, 162, 310, 318, 365; nuclear missiles arrive in Europe, 62, 103, 141, 332; nuclear policy, 58–9; overseas military bases, 167, 273–4, 332; political world view, 5, 74; weapons-testing over Canada, 72; zero option proposal, 58–9, 136, 331;
ECONOMIC AND SOCIAL AFFAIRS: Budget, 52; budget deficit, 50, 51–3, 452; economic revival, 50, 53, 451; exports of grain to USSR, 60; four-point economic plan, 51–2; inflation, 50, 452; monetary and fiscal policy, 452–3; output, 451; public spending cuts, 51–2; recession, 51; 'standby' tax proposals, 52; statistical data, 466–8; trade deficit, 452; trade with China, 68; trade with EEC, 342–3; unemployment, 50, 51, 452;
FOREIGN AFFAIRS: Africa, 231, 234, 239, 241, 248, 249, 255; Central America, 53, 62–5, 74, 84, 85–7; destruction of South Korean airliner, 60–1, 300; Middle East, 1–2, 50, 65–7, 103–4, 179, 180, 181, 183, 184–5, 187, 189, 191, 199–200, 201, 202–3, 257; private citizens' support for IRA, 42; relations with: Argentina, 65; China, 67–8, 291, 293; Cuba, 84; France, 130–1; Hungary, 116; Mexico, 64–5; Pakistan, 264; Philippines, 284; Romania, 118–19; Somalia, 212; South Pacific, 312; Taiwan, 296, 297; UK, 39–40, 62–3; USSR, 50, 58–61, 100, 102–3; West Germany, 136–7; USAID, 86, 96, 97; withdrawal from Unesco, 69;
HOME AFFAIRS: alleged electoral irregularity, 55; black electoral successes, 55–6; changes in Administration, 54–5; Congressional activities, 52–4; Democratic presidential candidates, 56; heatwave, 57; legislative veto, ruling on, 54; space shuttle programme, 56, 376–7; Times Beach contamination, 57; War Powers Act, constitutionality, 53; winter weather, 51, 57
UPPER VOLTA, 228–9

URUG, General Necdet, 173
URUGUAY, 82
URZUA IBÁÑEZ, General Carol, 79
USMANKHODZHAEV, I. B., 101
USTINOV, Marshal Dmitri F., 100, 333

VALDÉS, Gabriel, 79
VALK, Colonel Hans, 98
VANGSAA, Mona, death, 403
VANUATU, 312, 366
VARGAS LLOSA, Mario, 432
VÁRKONYI, Péter, 116
VATICAN STATE, 366
VELAYATI, Ali Akbar, 195
VENEZUELA, 83
VENTURINI, General Danilo, 98
VER, General Fabian, 284
VERESS, Peter, 359
VIAL, Roberto, 78
VIEIRA, João Bernardo, President of Guinea-Bissau, 236
VIETNAM, 125, 282, 285–6, 362–3; economy, 285–6; Kampuchean resistance, 277, 286; plan for Joint Economic Commission, 287
VILMOUTH, Jean-Luc, 424
VISENTINI, Bruno, 139
VOGEL, Hans-Jochen, 102, 133
VOLCKER, Paul, 453
VOROTNIKOV, V. I., 101
VORSTER, B. John, obit., 508
VOYTEK, 404
VOZNESSENSKY, Andrei, 106

WADE, Maître Abdoulaye, 226
WADE, Joe, 33
WAJDA, Andrzej, 416
WAKEFIELD OF KENDAL, Lord, death, 442–3
WALDORF, Stephen, 42
WALES, see under United Kingdom
WALES, HRH Prince of, visit to Australia and New Zealand, 305, 311
WALES, HRH Princess of, 305, 311
WALESA, Lech, 110, 370; wins Nobel peace prize, 112
WALKER, Alan, 412
WALKER, Peter, MP, 30, 32, 38
WALTERS, Julie, 416
WALTERS, General Vernon, 212
WALTON, Sir William, death, 401, 413; obit., 508–9
WANG BINGQIAN, 293
WARD, David, death, 401
WARDHANA, Ali, 282
WARE, Lance-Corp. Nkrabea Poku, 219
WARING, Marilyn, 309
WARSAW TREATY ORGANIZATION (Warsaw Pact), 333–5; and Poland, 334; exercises, 333; Political Declaration, 5, 102, 334, (text) 473–9; Prague summit,

112, 334, 357; proposed non-aggression agreement with Nato, 58, 334; Romania and, 118, 334; Soviet concern about cohesion, 334; weapons-testing and deployment, 333
WASHINGTON, Harold, 56
WASSEF, Ramses Wissa, 429
WASSERSTEIN, Wendy, 408
WATERFIELD, Dr Mike, 381
WATERSTONE, David, 45
WATSON, John, 441
WATSON, Tom, 440
WATT, James, 55, 386
WAY, Paul, 440
WEATHERILL, Bernard, Mr Speaker, 22
WECHSBERG, Joseph, death, 401
WEINBERGER, Caspar, 68, 264, 293, 331, 379
WEIR, Peter, 415
WENDERS, Wim, 414
WESKER, Arnold, 406
WEST, Dame Rebecca, death, 434; obit., 509
WEST INDIES, see Caribbean
WESTERN EUROPEAN UNION, 350–1
WESTERN SAHARA, 206, 227, 360, 361; Polisario, 206, 361
WESTERN SAMOA, 312
WHEELER, Peter, 442
WHELDON, David, 431
WHITE, Byron, 54
WHITE, Judge J., 312
WHITELAW, William, MP (*later* Viscount Whitelaw of Penrith), 9, 21
WHITEMORE, Hugh, 406
WIJEWARDENE, Upali, disappearance, 269
WILLIAMS, Jeffrey, 433
WILLIAMS, Shirley, MP, 14, 19
WILLIAMS, Tennessee, death, 409, 416; obit., 509
WILLIAMSBURG SUMMIT, 130, 299, 322, 342; 29 May statement, 72
WILLOCH, Kåre, Prime Minister of Norway, 151, 355
WILMARS, Josse Martens de, President of European Court of Justice, 392
WILSON, Sir Angus, 419
WILSON, Sir Harold, MP (*later* Baron Wilson of Rievaulx), 15, 22
WILSON, Snoo, 406
WILSON, Stuart, 442
WINDELEN, Heinrich, 137
WINGER, Debra, 416
WOLF, Jiří, 113
WONG HONG-TOY, 281

WOODROW, Bill, 424
WORLD BANK (IBRD), 94, 95, 96, 97, 121, 213, 214, 215, 216, 218, 220, 236, 263, 266, 272, 273, 291, 312, 321
WORLOCK, Archbishop Derek, 13
WÖRNER, Dr Manfred, 352
WRIGHT, John, 439
WRIGHT, Nicholas, 405
WU XUEQUAN, 67, 293, 294

YAHYAWI, Muhammed Sali, 207
YAMANI, Abdo, 193
YAO, Paul Akoto, 227
YAO YILIN, 293
YE JIANYING, 293
YEMEN, PEOPLE'S DEMOCRATIC REPUBLIC OF, 195
YEMEN ARAB REPUBLIC, 194–5; arrival of Yassir Arafat, 195
YIM CHUN CHU, 301
YONDON, Col.-General Jamsrangiyn, 125
YOUNG, Baroness, 21
YOUNG, John, 377
YOUNG, M., 305–6
YUGOSLAVIA, 121–3; and EEC, 121; and Efta, 353; economy, 121–2; nationalist disturbances, 122; non-aligned status, 121, 122–3; relations with: Albania, 122, 123; Bulgaria, 120; China, 121; Greece, 168; USSR, 121
YUN KI POK, 301

ZAÏRE, 231, 234–5; economy, 235; political prisoners, 234, 235
ZAMBIA, 242–4; economy, 243; treason trial, 243
ZANZIBAR, see under Tanzania
ZEIDLER/ROBERTS PARTNERSHIP, 428
ZEMLINSKY, Alexander, 400
ZHANG CHUNQIAO, 293
ZHAO CANGBI, 293
ZHAO ZIYANG, Prime Minister of China, 68, 73, 235, 248, 293, 294, 311
ZHIVKOV, Todor, head of state of Bulgaria, 119–20
ZHIVKOVA, Lyudmila, 119
ZIA-UL-HAQ, General Mohammad, President of Pakistan, 263–5, 269
ZIMBABWE, 243, 246–8; and South Africa, 248; and UK, 247; arrest of Bishop Muzorewa, 178, 248; economy, 247; foreign relations, 248; internal violence, 246; trial of Air Force officers, 246–7
ZIMMERMANN, Friedrich, 135, 137